Adaption-Innovation

Adaption-Innovation theory (A-I theory) is a model of problem solving and creativity, which aims to increase collaboration and reduce conflict within groups. A-I theory and the associated Kirton Adaption-Innovation Inventory (KAI) have been extensively researched and are increasingly used as tools for teambuilding and personnel management. In *Adaption-Innovation: In the context of diversity and change*, Dr Kirton outlines the central concepts of the theory, including the processes of problem solving, decision making, and creativity. In addition, Dr Kirton focuses on how wide diversity within a team affects problem solving, creativity, and effective management of change, as well as offering practical information for those helping diverse teams succeed in today's demanding climate.

This timely and comprehensive text is written for anyone who wants to know more about problem solving, thinking style, and creativity. As such it will appeal to a broad range of people, from human resource managers, business consultants, and group trainers to students of psychology, business, management, sociology, education, and politics.

Dr M. J. Kirton is the director and founder of the Occupational Research Centre, with many years' experience in academia and management. He originated the Adaption-Innovation Theory and its measure KAI. He was awarded a DSc by the Council for National Academic Awards in 1991 for his work on Adaption-Innovation.

Adaption-Innovation
In the Context of Diversity and Change

M. J. Kirton

Routledge
Taylor & Francis Group

LONDON AND NEW YORK

First published 2003 by Routledge
27 Church Road, Hove, East Sussex BN3 2FA

Simultaneously published in the USA and Canada
by Routledge
29 West 35th Street, New York, NY 10001

Routledge is an imprint of the Taylor & Francis Group

Copyright © 2003 M. J. Kirton

Typeset in 10/12pt Time NR by Graphicraft Limited, Hong Kong
Printed and bound in Great Britain by TJ International Ltd, Padstow,
Cornwall
Paperback cover design by Terry Foley, Anú Design

This publication has been produced with paper manufactured to strict
environmental standards and with pulp derived from sustainable forests.

British Library Cataloguing in Publication Data
A catalogue record for this book is available from the British Library

Library of Congress Cataloging-in-Publication Data
Kirton, M. J.
  Adaption-innovation: in the context of diversity and change/M. J. Kirton.
    p. cm.
  Includes bibliographical references and index.
  ISBN 0-415-29850-4 (alk. paper) — ISBN 0-415-29851–2 (pbk.: alk. paper)
  1. Problem solving. 2. Cognitive styles. 3. Change (Psychology)
  4. Diversity in the workplace. I. Title.
BF449 .K57 2003
153.4—dc21
                                                          2002015743

ISBN 0-415-29850-4 (hbk)
ISBN 0-415-29851-2 (pbk)

To Veronica

Contents

List of tables

List of figures

List of boxes

List of appendices

Acknowledgements

I am indebted to a number of people who have kindly read parts of early drafts or have given permissions to use quotations from their books or to refer to private correspondence. The latter are listed below. I have benefited from the many discussions I have had with the experienced members of the KAI network, in private correspondence, on courses, and in advanced workshops, as well as from their published works, many of which are quoted to support arguments in this text. In addition, four scholars, Dr Ray Clapp, Dr Jeremy Foster, Dr Gordon Foxall, and Dr Peter Herriot, helped me with editing different drafts. I am very grateful for their meticulous and learned assistance as I am also for the secretarial help of Ms Rosanna Tompkins and Mrs Tracey Beaney.

M. J. Kirton

Unpublished references

Thanks are due to those listed below (giving their title and address when the help was given) for the use of their unpublished data:

Mr Maurice Dubras, Atomic Energy of Canada, Ltd
Mr David Flegg, Industrial Training Research Unit, Cambridge, UK
Dr Sean Hammond, S. Sussex University, UK
Mr Alan Iliffe, Civil Service Commission, UK
Dr Marian Kubes, Maxman, Bratislava, Republic of Slovakia
Col Ed Parks, National Defense University, Washington, DC, USA
Dr Linda Philamore, British Airways
Dr Leo Peeters, Jensen Pharmaceutica, Ghent, Belgium
Prof Chris Pottas, University of Pretoria, South Africa
Dr Julia Pounds, Federal Aviation Authority, USA
Dr Guido Prato Previde, Decathlon Consulting, Milan, Italy
Dr Bob Rosenfeld, Eastman Kodak Company, USA
Dr Alesandra Saggin, Independent Consultant, Milan, Italy
Mr R. Shillcox, Occupational Research Centre, UK

Text acknowledgements

Extract from 'Almost like a Whale: The Origin of the Species Updated', by J. S. Jones, 1999, published by Doubleday. Used by permission of Transworld Publishers, a division of The Random House Group Limited.

Approximately 150 words from 'How the Mind Works', by Steven Pinker (Allen Lane The Penguin Press, 1998). Copyright © Steven Pinker, 1998. Reproduced by permission of Penguin Books Ltd.

Approximately 125 words from 'The Prince', by Niccolò Machiavellie, translated by George Bull (Penguin Classics 1961, third revised edition, 1981). Copyright © George Bull, 1961, 1975, 1981. Reproduced by permission of Penguin Books Ltd.

Extract from 'Big Bangs', by Howard Goodall, 2000, published by Chatto and Windus. Used by permission of The Random Group Limited.

Extracts from 'Guns, Germs and Steel', by Jared Diamond, 1997, published by Jonathan Cape. Used by permission of The Random House Group Limited.

Extract from 'The Curse of Progress', by Julian Halsby, 1999, published by The Artists' Publishing Company Limited. Used with permission.

Extract from 'Great Battlefields of the World', by J. MacDonald, 1984, published by Marshall Editions. Copyright © 1984 Marshall Editions, a member of The Quarto Publishing Group.

1 Introduction

A GUIDING OUTLINE

This book offers new insights and understanding for both managers and academics into people's preferred thinking styles and how they affect ways of doing things, their outcomes, and other people, both in organisations and elsewhere. In most organisations individuals are still mostly considered as technically knowledgeable process boxes, where given the right inputs, training, and environmental conditions the required outputs are expected to appear, working well, smoothly, and on time. There is still little consideration of the match between the different ways in which all people think, problem solve, and create and the demands and constraints of efficient management, the organisational environment, and others with whom they work. These different ways of problem solving encompass a range between bringing about change by working with and within the prevailing paradigm and by first altering this structure in order to bring about desired change.

Thinking style is explored, amply supported by research, and located in problem solving as a whole. Then problem solving is set in the wider, entirely practical, context of the management of diversity (including the diversity of styles) and of change. In this wider setting, problem-solving leadership depends less on the technical expertise of a select few and more upon the selection of appropriate groups that can *collectively solve* critical, complex problems, in challenging environments, *aided* by problem-solving leaders. To meet the demands made of managers in today's climate, these leaders require not only the technical expertise to hold the respect of their teams but also knowledge of the problem-solving process and of problem solvers. This notion is currently becoming better considered, as when Khurana (2002) warns against over-reliance on the charismatic superstar: 'When a company is struggling [its directors] will not be satisfied with an executive who is merely talented and experienced. Companies now want leaders.'

This section gives a resume of the ground to be covered. The rest of the chapter reviews a study that became one seminal influence in the development of Adaption-Innovation Theory and its wider setting. It is based on down-to-earth experience and so acts as an introduction, first to the theoretical aspects, and then to the practical considerations, to which we return later in this book.

Adaption-Innovation Theory (A-I theory) relates to thinking style – usually referred to in the literature as cognitive style. This theory explores and describes preferred individual differences in the way humans solve problems; its related psychometric inventory locates individuals on a continuum ranging from high adaption to high innovation.

Thinking is the means by which we solve problems and are creative (whatever the distinctions between these two terms may be). Every living thing has to manage the changing world about it and acquire those things that it needs to survive. If enough individuals of a species survive long enough to reproduce successfully, that species continues to survive. This is not easy: The species that exist today are reckoned to be but 1% of all that have ever lived; we are among the few survivors over the billions of years that life has existed. Mankind, one of the latest arrivals, must also manage change and diversity or perish. In one form or another, whether understood by the individual or not, problem solving is the key to life. Every species does this differently.

This book examines thinking style in the context of problem solving, the key to survival, of which it is an element. In doing so, some elements of problem solving – level (capacity), motive, and perceived opportunity – are dealt with in depth and others more lightly, such as learning, attitude, belief, and group dynamics. Style within problem solving is then set into the wider context of the management of change and diversity. The examples that illustrate the relationships of these elements are drawn mainly from biology, psychology, sociology, politics, management, military history, science, and the arts. This range shows how the brain, unaltered for a hundred millennia, solves a vast diversity of problems in much the same general way. However, every individual is also unique, as each brain operates with small, but vital, characteristic variations. This diversity of problem solver is at once an advantage and an added problem: How to combine to solve those problems that cannot be solved alone, yet how to manage people unlike us. This and a number of other themes are threaded through this book. The paradox of structure, from personal experience to social paradigm, is another; without it we cannot think, but although enabling, it is also limiting. We each solve this paradox, as we solve every other problem, differently.

The breadth of the setting underlines how such seemingly small differences in thinking between people (mankind contains no subspecies) have been exploited so successfully. In fact, so successfully has the human brain worked that most of the trickiest problems it now faces are as a result of its success and our growing expectation of further success. The standards required of today's problem solvers would surely have left mediaeval monarchs amazed – the nature of progress is truly catalytic, feeding with increasing rapidity on its own success. Not surprisingly, perhaps, the theme of the next chapter is that problem solving is the key to all life. The more we understand problem solving and the problem solver the better off we might be; such added knowledge can be put to good advantage, particularly in problem-solving leadership.

The foundations must first be understood. All forms of life, mankind included, have evolved a structure that fits all their survival needs, e.g., finding and absorbing appropriate nutrients. This structure is also limiting, e.g., the eyes that are good in daylight are poor in half-light. Mankind has become expert in overcoming many limitations, but the underlying structure remains the same. The astronaut may get to the moon but still walks to the space vehicle; the image that is enhanced by the telescope passes through the eye developed many millions of years ago to the same model of brain that made our tools in the stone age. So problem solving needs to exploit but not ignore these limits; mankind has developed the greatest facility of working round natural limits that the world has yet experienced.

The more advanced life forms have developed instincts. Instincts are so complex (like building a nest) that they transcend the more primitive built-in biomechanical responses and yet are so rigid that each one is immediately recognisable by experts as belonging to a particular species. Each represents a whole problem-solving process: problem identification, solution selection, and implementation. The survival value of instincts is immense, for they can all operate without learning; indeed, without ever having been seen used by another. Yet they operate almost perfectly on the first occasion they are used, even if learning can be added on to them to enhance the base response they provide. Their weakness is that they are hard wired: Once triggered, every individual must operate in the same way and changes to instincts can only come about by breeding, not by thinking. Using this precise biological definition, mankind is unique in having no instincts. When we perceive a danger ahead while driving, we do not 'brake by instinct'. We have learned to do so – perhaps so well that it is now a conditioned reflex – but all complex problem-solving response is, nevertheless, learned. What mankind needs to know must be taught.

Learned problem solving, well developed in all higher-order species, offers the widest potential range of responses and the greatest problem-solving flexibility. The advantages of problem solving are obvious, for mankind's achievements are huge compared to any other organism (indeed, most of the problems we currently face are of our own making), but the expense is high. Everything we do, except for those inbuilt structures, has to be learned through experience and a great deal of chatter: who our enemies are, what to eat, how to get it, how to mate, how to give birth, or how to nurture our young. As learning takes time and practice, our young are more vulnerable, for longer, than those of any other species. In order to survive we need continually to learn. A-I theory emphasises two key issues: (a) when we problem solve we are limited by the way we are built (e.g., our intelligence; no one has endless capacity or flexibility) but we have no instinct to help or hinder us; (b) all of us are intelligent and creative, at different levels and with different styles, and, therefore, all of us are capable of problem solving, as long as there is both motive and opportunity.

We are indebted to the ancient Greeks for usefully dividing knowledge into that of physics and metaphysics, thereby allowing us to study and reveal understanding of nature's laws in each area with better precision. From physics and chemistry comes the discipline of biology, from which, in turn, emerges the discipline that studies behaviour – psychology. From the study of the problem solving of the human mind emerges most of the other disciplines. A-I theory, therefore, relates to many very different topics, each closely interlinked with the others, stretching from biology across psychology into sociology and on into every area of human problem solving – from anthropology and the progress of science, business, and government, warfare and conflict, to the writing of music and the teaching of art. The same brain, using the same functions, tackles the many kinds of problem it has to solve from whichever discipline they emerge. The distinctions may only be how familiar the problem is, the amount of effort needed to master it, and the degree of satisfaction derived from its resolution. In understanding problem solvers it is useful, then, to view the applicability of any hypothesis, finding, or derived theoretical notion over a wide range of human activity. If they illuminate widely over incident, time, and culture then they are likely to be revealing of problem solvers generally.

It is an added complication that there are many other theories and fields of study that relate to problem solving, including popular but untested beliefs, practices, and plain muddles, particularly those involving such trendy terms as 'creativity and innovation' or 'instinct'. Terms like these, that are notoriously hard to define and harder to measure reliably, either need to be better defined or avoided. Instinct, for example, is defined here so that it is not mistaken either for the way the *structure* of the brain works or for learning. This is rather like the distinction between the hard wiring of the computer (what it is designed to do), the software (built-in problem-solving programs), and the operator's own programs. The value of these distinctions is that we can understand better the limits of the brain's function and learn better to allow for them whilst learning to work round them. Creativity, to take a second example, is treated as a subset of problem solving: useful in general discussion but not much use, at present at any rate, in measurement. Only one term is needed (the brain does not appear to distinguish between them) for serious matters, such as management, counselling, or research. We can, for these purposes, just rely on the term problem solving; this should help us to obtain clearer hypotheses to test and, possibly, clearer answers to our questions.

The core of the theory

Understanding Adaption-Innovation

The Adaption-Innovation Theory is founded on the assumption that all people solve problems and are creative. This theory is directly concerned only with style; with *how* people solve problems. Both potential capacity (intelligence or talent) and learned levels (such as management competence) are completely independent characteristics and assessed by other measures. This means that innovators and adaptors can each be found at every kind of these levels – from the highest to the lowest. In addition, the terms 'more adaptive' or 'more innovative' are more precise than 'adaptors' and 'innovators', for the theory describes a normally distributed continuous range and not just two types. The more adaptive prefer their problems to be associated with more structure, and with more of this structure consensually agreed, than those who are more innovative. The more innovative are more tolerant, at least while in the pursuit of a solution, of a looser guiding structure. However, all brains need such structure or they cannot operate. Indeed, at the very core of the brain's success is the amount of structure it can accumulate and use well in solving the problems it perceives as needing to be solved. Just one example of structure is language – no other organism could have written this text or be able to read it.

Many other structures are required, e.g., the preferred style with which we solve problems, the content of our memory, and our array of skills. Other vital guidelines that are built up by learning are our attitudes and beliefs, which allow us to access information into understood patterns. One of the key notions of the book is the paradox of structure: that it is, at one and the same time, both enabling and limiting. We endeavour constantly to exploit structure and manipulate its limits. Adaptors and innovators do so differently. One way of summing up these differences is to say that the more adaptive prefer to solve problems by the use of rules and the more innovative do so despite the rules. Here, 'rules' are used to represent all cognitive structures. Examples of other terms are theories, policies, precedents, terms of reference, and paradigms. The argument also advanced, supported by research, is that these differences in preferred style are stable but that we nudge the limits they impose by coping behaviour.

Another key element in the theory is that only individuals think. Brains cannot be linked together like computers. Whenever I ask you for help, and you agree, we are each instantly faced with two problems. Problem A is the reason we have formed the group – the reason for the formation of any group of living creatures – for mutual self-help. But we have also acquired Problem B; how to manage each other – all without aid from instinct, as is explored fully in a following chapter. The main thought that emerges is that unsuccessful problem-solving teams spend more energy on Problem B than Problem A. Yet we need each other; there are too many limits on individuals working alone for them to solve most large, complex problems. Another thought explored is that such diversity of problems require, for their resolution, a diversity of resources, *including* a diversity of problem solvers (which brings us back to Problem B). Adaption-Innovation is just such a diversity of resource. The more diversity of resources at a team's disposal, the greater is its potential to resolve an array of problems. But stockpiling diversity is an added burden, for diverse teams are more difficult to manage. In the case of style, this is because each individual's preference can also be seen to have disadvantages and to be a potential source of cost, friction, and distraction. Each individual is a unique diversity (or, strictly, a complex of diversities) and, within a group, has to face this problem in two ways: How to present one's own diversity as more useful than expensive and, for the same reason, to be tolerant of another's similar presentation. The whole range of diversity needs to be managed well for the common good. If not, then although such management of change may be efficient, it will be narrow. It will be argued that the adherents of competing narrow views are liable to produce a pendulum of vacillation instead of a progression of change. Such narrow-ranging views are likely to create resistors to change.

Defining cognitive style

The first time anyone becomes aware of cognitive style is when a predictable difference is noticed between the ways (manner, style) in which any two people appear to go about solving similar problems. A person behaving persistently differently from oneself may be just an intriguing fact, or turn out to be useful or even irritating. These are marked tendencies, within a single continuum, which are so stable that they are liable to persist even in circumstances in which it appears, at least to others, to be a disadvantage. A curiosity is that most such disadvantages that emerge are less noticeable in oneself than in others.

One difference is in the individual's preferred direction of focus. Adaptors more readily anticipate challenges and threats from within the system (often devising, in good time, plans to economise, downsize, etc.), whereas innovators are more ready to anticipate events that might beckon or threaten from outside, such as the earlier signs of changing taste and markets or significant advances in technology that have not yet been fully exploited. In research, it was noted that every manager tended not only to miss some cues that were picked up by others, but also found others' warnings irritating and distracting 'to the real issues' (i.e., the ones *they* could see clearly). Often the cues missed or noted fell into a pattern that suggested the influence of differences in style rather than in skill.

However, there is a marked tendency for people to attribute differences in style (indeed, any differences between them and others) as level differences. The principal reason may be that such judgements rarely take enough of the relevant data into account. It is not clear to any observer making the judgements whether the characteristic is inbuilt or learnt, whether it can be readily varied to accord with circumstance, whether we are all liable to the same kind of tendency (erring by no lesser degree but in different ways, on different occasions), or whether there is an unsuspected advantage to the group for having within it people who have such different attributes. These are rarely serious topics of conversation for managers; yet this knowledge is at the core of problem-solving leadership. Despite the fact that such differences are often erroneously seen as a deficiency of level (ability or capacity), the early work in A-I stated simply that managers' capacities do not account for these differences in approaching problems; they seem to be differences of style. It seems a simple issue, but it has become more and more obvious that this sharp distinction between style and capacity is not wholly understood, much less wholly accepted. The confusion between level and style seems to contribute significantly to difficulties that have above been dubbed as Problem B, so this confusion is well worth untangling. The confusion spreads when such terms as 'creativity and innovation' or 'change agent' are used to imply that innovation alone will solve all problems and only a few of us can bring about change. Such terms are divisive, creating 'resistors to change' among those who think differently but just as clearly and among those who are simply made to feel excluded.

Description of Adaption-Innovation

So far, this description has been in wide terms and in the context of general problem solving – the way the problem solver relates to and manages cognitive structure, although any structure perceived by the brain has to be converted into cognitive structure if it is to be used to problem solve. The A-I characteristic is one such structure, which with other influences on behaviour, like attitudes, plus those behaviours, make up the domain of personality. The rest of this chapter is devoted to this link, listing, in theory supported by research, the many different traits relating to cognitive style such as: risk-taking, dogmatism, tolerance of ambiguity, extraversion, conservatism, flexibility, etc., but excluding such traits as anxiety, neuroticism, or any other element of cognitive affect. This interrelationship with so large an array suggests a continuum at the level of a dimension of personality.

To assist the reader a schema has been devised offering an overview of these terms in the context of brain function. As with all schemata, this is a simplification of a complex reality, which one hopes, nevertheless, may give a useful overview of the brain's interrelated functions. Within this embracing structure, the key elements of the brain's function have been entered as if they were departments of a business enterprise, devoted to its own survival. Style appears in the 'planning' department, taking instruction from the boardroom – the department of cognitive affect that decides what problem is to be tackled and what kind of solution will satisfy. A third 'backroom' department of cognitive resource processes (through learning) and then stores all experience upon which the other two rely for past reliable information. These elements of cognitive function are stable, characteristic influences on behaviour, which together with stable characteristics of behaviour make up an individual's personality.

The wider implications

Finally, it can be salutary to reflect that only by the use of this one same, unaltered brain have all the problems of human survival been solved. Like modern boardrooms and governments, whole populations in the Fertile Crescent, the West, China, America, and Australia have had periods of technological advance, stagnation, and even retreat – variations that often have been attributed to the high or low capacity of the entire population. In the past, the fate of defeated populations attracted little sympathy among the victors. In many quarters today, an alternative extreme view is that the winning groups of the past are tinged with evil and the losers have never done wrong. However, these phenomena need to be seen in a cooler perspective, or the righting of perceived ancient wrongs may cause yet more damage. The indubitable backdrop fact is that all organisms (alone or in groups) succeed at the expense of others – all change, however much it might be deemed as good by the cognoscenti, destroys something. How can we ensure the values of competition yet avoid the disasters of aggression? A brief anthropological review suggests that basic opportunities for social advancement (the natural local occurrence of useful plants, animals, or materials) were available in very different amounts in different environments – with the Fertile Crescent and China being heavily favoured. The argument advanced is that opportunity, or lack of it, must be a prime factor in differences of advancement of whole populations. This is also true within any group or culture. But there is another factor: Some changes that are on offer (or when first on offer) may appear more as threats than chances not to be missed. As with individuals, so with cultures (which are the reflections of their members' shared structures): Different environments offer varying opportunities at differently perceived cost. People, alone or in groups, among hunter-gatherers or in boardrooms, are constantly faced with choices and more of us need, in today's increasingly complex world and with increasing individual expectation, better understanding of the principles by which they are made. This is core knowledge for problem-solving leadership at every stage of opportunity exploitation – whenever revealed, whenever sought or whenever it needs to be made.

The winners among groups of people may start off with only a small advantage over others, but change is catalytic in its nature – one change leading to an advantage is the base for another change that leads to greater advantage. Gradually, this spiral of change becomes irresistible, giving overwhelming power to those in the lead. All organisms succeed at the expense of others. The winners take over space and re-sources for their own ends; others, even subsets of their own kind (unless protected by an instinct mankind does not possess) can be killed, eaten, enslaved, absorbed (lose identity) or brushed aside into unfashionable addresses. Mankind has tried all this with other organisms and within its own barely defined subsets. The process of col-laborative problem solving needs to be better understood so that it can be applied more insightfully. We all need to understand better how to manage diversity so that we can manage change more effectively. To manage diversity one must first accept that it exists; every individual is unique and so is a minority of one. Each person needs to consider the balance of the costs against the advantages of uniqueness to a group's survival; that every right an individual claims needs to be offset by obligation, for rights without obligations are accorded only as charity, not as a part of an equal mutual exchange. These are not just matters of ethics but of mutual survival, because:

- a diversity of problem solvers is required to solve a diversity of problems;
- style is a diversity in the very core of each individual's problem-solving process;
- managing diversity is a key to achieving required change efficiently.

Summary of key points

- Problem solving is the key to life.
- All people problem solve (creativity is a subset of problem solving).
- Problem solving creates change – every individual is a 'change agent'.
- All individuals evaluate each change opportunity against their cost and advantage.
- Adaption-Innovation is the stable, preferred style within which an individual solves problems; it relates to the way people manage (cognitive) structure.
- Coping behaviour permits departure from preferred style, at a cost.
- Style is not correlated with any form of level.
- A diversity of problem solvers, deploying a diversity of resources, is needed to solve life's diversity of problems, many an outcome of mankind's success.
- Difference in style is one of the many kinds of diversities that problem solvers need to manage well; all our diversities and the ways they are managed make up our personalities.
- Individual diversity is at the start point of creating the specialist.
- If one cannot manage diversity well, one cannot manage change both widely and well.
- Managing change narrowly and well is efficient, until the problem range being tackled widens, then past success may make us slow to change (accept the cost to widen).
- How much diversity is needed in a team is dependent on the range of problems it is solving. Too little diversity leads to failure; too much is costly to keep; the problem is in defining the term 'too'.
- If an in-group mismanages the diversities within the wider group, it may 'create' resistors to (all of the in-group's proposed) change.
- All people are unique – therefore, every person is in a minority of one. To collaborate, individuals need to offer their diversity as a resource without destabilising the group.
- Every time a person shares a problem with another, each acquires two problems – Problem A, the prime problem for which they formed the team, and Problem B, managing each other's diversity.
- Problem A should take up more of the collective energy than Problem B – diversity training should not aim to correct the past but to increase future mutual benefit.
- Paradox of structure: No cognitive structure – no thought, no problem solving. Too much structure and problem solving becomes inelastic and inefficient.
- In nature, failure is the norm. Very few of all the species that once lived still do – a warning we do well to keep in mind.

Problems have become so complex, and the penalty for not solving many of them so high, that every individual needs to study the problem solver as one more problem needing to be solved. Experts alone cannot be concerned with this problem; their task is to help others to understand it also. The core lesson is that today the problems of survival directly concern us all, hence the notion of problem-solving leadership.

A BACKGROUND STUDY

Aim

The rest of this chapter is a synopsis of a study, Management Initiative, which had a formative influence in starting the work on Adaption-Innovation and its measure. This study, through the accumulation of experience in completing it and through the analysis of its results and residual problems, both at the time and over many following years, helped define the Adaption-Innovation concept and keep it oriented to practical use. Additionally, it helped provide items that eventually gave rise to the measure, which has provided the many instances of support of the theory's assumptions. There is a third reason for it being reported here in some detail: Its lessons were not only instructive, but they also proved to be applicable to many fields of thought and endeavour, both past and present; because of this they form one of a small number of themes that hold together the many issues explored in this book. The study helped show that that the brain operates in all humans in much the same overall way, over event and time, given only that there are within this common frame individual variations that separate any one human from any other. These variations, albeit small, are highly significant when used in collaboration.

After the study and its findings are outlined, its stimulating residual puzzles are revealed. At the end of this case study there is a review of the information learnt and an indication of its link with A-I theory. There is additional information, particularly for managers, in Appendix 1. The study's prime aim was to reveal a process of corporate initiative so as to understand group dynamics.

Method

The methods for the original collection of data study were as follows.

- Select a number of willing companies. Those chosen were medium–small (less than 1000 employees) or semiautonomous divisions of larger companies, of about the same size.
- Select and study a number of significant examples of recent corporate initiative. These had to be of 'large group' size, i.e., involve the whole of a large department or parts of several departments, involving several key people from start to finish.
- Read all the relevant papers on each of the examples selected. The companies selected were very open – it is successful companies who tend to allow in researchers because they are anxious to learn; unsuccessful companies tend to keep them out.
- Interview everyone who had taken a managerial role in each one at least once.
- Feed back the notes recording this input to key managers for their comment. As a result of the feedback interviews, more was learnt but many managers also greatly improved their own knowledge of what had happened!

These mini-histories of change were then sifted through until it was possible to produce an 'idealised template' or schema of how, in general, management initiative seemed to work. Box 1 shows this dynamic schema, or what later will be described as

Box 1 Management Initiative process

Perception of the Problem
Analysis of the Problem
Analysis of the Solution
Agreement for Change
Acceptance for Change
Implementation

a 'process'. A process is defined as a schematic map of how, ideally, some sequence of behaviour runs its course. In real life the process is not so smooth or clear cut. No schema, such as a road map, tells you all: what is one's means of transport, how good it might be; if the roads are in good repair, what are the weather conditions; how often one stops for a meal or loses one's way! Stripped of cognitive deviations, errors, and iterations an idealised map emerges; in this case, a schema of how a class of problem solving emerges.

Box 1 shows the elements of the management initiative process as it emerged from the analysis of the large amount of collated information collected in the study[1]. Below is a summary of what each of these stages covers. This summary is of interest in its own right as well as being a formative influence on the thinking that led to the Adaption-Innovation notion. It shows that however theoretical and abstract the A-I theory appears to be now, it emerged from the analyses of problems that had just been faced, and for the most part resolved, by people at work. More revealing as an influence on A-I theory are the details of the problems (outlined in Residual Problems) that were not solved at the time. Understanding them better later was what helped shape the theory.

Perception of the problem

The initial brief was to ignore what sort of person perceived the problem or how the problem emerged in the mind of an individual. The main concern was to be with the process as a group phenomenon, so the study of each problem began when its existence was made public, was noted, and became a group concern.

The person who perceived the problem had to persuade the group that it existed and was worthy of resolution, winning over others, sometimes at a stroke, sometimes gradually, until assent was achieved. In short, the problem needed to be 'established' before the group would start to solve it. For the perceiver this could be a problem in itself. Although not invariable, it was not infrequent that the perceiver was, to use a biblical turn of phrase, a 'voice crying in the wilderness.' However, the terms under which the study was undertaken were to 'concentrate on the social process' so that it could be better understood and not to concentrate on the individual. It seemed to be a vogue of the time that sociology could be studied without much regard to the

1 For summaries of some examples see Appendix 1.

individual. As a consequence, this stage was not given the attention it deserved in the study. When the study was later used as a base for further, wider work and study, the originally observed sociological phenomena yielded more understanding, especially by using the emerging A-I concepts.

Analysis of the problem

An early observation that emerged in the study was that all the companies were weakest in the analysis of the problem stage. They tended to skimp what Wallas (1926; see Figure 6) would call an incubation stage, between perceiving the problem and settling on a solution. The pattern became a special interest in reanalysis of the early work because new thinking suggested that this might be a typical pattern of mankind in general, not just a fault of management or these managers. The clue may lie in the origins of the word 'problem' – it comes from the ancient Greek and means 'something that is cast before [one].' Imagine going down the road to the forum having something cast in front of you; you might step to one side, or step over it, but anyway, just deal with it as quickly and as easily as possible. This is what we tend to do with problems; deal with them as neatly and swiftly as possible, hence the wisdom in the adage: do not make a mountain out of a molehill! However, the philosophers Quine and Ullian (1970) opine that, in order to understand anything in the universe, one has to understand the whole of the universe. Of course, this is impossible and any attempt to wait for such mass of information would paralyse action. Judgements are made on the nature of problems to be solved. Extra effort and time is given to the sort of problem that experience warns is the more dangerous and difficult; treating most problems as simply as we can is an intuitive economy of effort. This works very well most of the time, although memorable penalties can be paid when these judgements underestimate critical problems. In this respect, the managers in this study were no different from the rest of mankind, past or present! This stage ends with a proposed solution, however it is obtained.

Analysis of the solution

Although the analyses of problems were often treated casually, this was not true for the analyses of solutions. This stage was where all the companies and all the people involved expended a great deal of effort, often associated with a rise in anxiety. It seemed that the managers, in putting forward a solution, rightly felt that they were putting forward a part of their own reputation. Implementing an agreed solution means engaging others – their time, effort, and resources – in the (our) solution. If a solution we champion goes wrong, do we not fear that people will say: 'Who thought of this, then? Who pushed it?' The analysis of the solution was the bit on which everyone worked hard.

Very often, when a solution is thrown up it throws up a side-problem with it. To take one of the examples in the original study, the directors of a company concluded that a solution to a particular problem was to diversify their product base. They selected a new product that was very different from their present lines but which, if adopted, would solve the problem of an underused sales force at a certain time of the year. They were offered a windfall buy-out of another company and additionally thought there was useful overlapping expertise in its production. When being interviewed in this example of management initiative, the managers talked almost exclusively about their *current* competitors. They knew a good deal about them, including what their main problems were, who their key managers were, and how much it cost them to do this and that. But in the case of the new product, these same managers did not even seem to be sure who their new competitors were. With their eyes still fixed on solving the original problem, the possibility of the solution throwing up a spin-off problem was not something they had thought much about. In other words, concentrating on the analysis of the (new) solution to the (original) problem, they seemed to deal lightly with the analysis of the (spin-off) problem their new solution had just made for them. So this new problem was also treated in the same way as the original problem – as lightly as possible. It was only when outcomes began to become all too apparent, e.g., the new competitors reacted sharply and effectively, that they had to go back to planning and treat them as a serious problem. Only then did the analysis of how to deal with the spin-off problems become a collective issue.

Criticising managers for failing to see all the spin-off problems thrown up by their main thinking is easier than avoiding these oneself – Quine and Ullian's (1970) 'cannot know it all' notion applies again, for one cannot pause to consider every possible effect. However, the criticism is that a search for the more likely of the more dangerous side outcomes was not usually undertaken as a standard procedure. This research showed that it was individuals who usually did such thinking, independently and ad hoc, without it being a specific part of group planning.

Agreement for change

Some people are autocrats who tend to make their decisions quite unilaterally. But most managers, even the most powerful, work more collaboratively. It is rare, in most organisations, to find people in a position of making big, critical decisions without consulting others; outwardly, at least, most want, or have to get, agreement for change. Even strong Managing Directors like to carry their board along with them. Others, less senior, have no option but to seek authority.

One observation made at this stage of the process was that it could take a long time to get agreement for change from a group. Sometimes it took a very long time, and yet many of those who had been involved had not seemed to remember this. When managers were asked some such question as: 'Why do you think it took 3 years to get this decision?' a frequent response was: 'Three years! Really! As much as that?' One story told was of a soap product that floated in water. Apparently the standard myth is that some top R&D experts cooked up a promising formula. They switched on a high-powered mixer and then went off early for a really good and splendid business lunch, coming back very late and somewhat hazy. In place of the mixture still whizzing about, there floated the now famous soap. They cut off a piece and (still with a headache) gave it to the Chairman next morning; it was at once a great success. The real facts turned out to be much less dramatic or amusing. The chemists concerned had worked out how to get a very white soap that floated on water. They had thought these two features a great idea, and set out to produce them. Once they had a suitable sample, they took it to the board (they were both very senior), which turned it down. It then remained around for quite a while, until somebody remembered it again and thought: 'Ah! We'll try this,' but it got turned down, again and again. It was accepted for a major market trial several years after the chemists had first thought of it. This was at the time when more than one main line product suffered from falling sales and some radically new one seemed to be needed at once. This old, radical (an interesting combination of adjectives) product was remembered and at this point the idea broke through. The fate of other products had changed the climate and acted as the conditions for a precipitating event. Two lessons learnt here are that not only can agreement for change sometimes take a very long time, but it may still require unusual conditions (memorable precipitating events[2]) to get it, even among groups that pride themselves on their willingness to change. Yet other changes, somtimes just as large and expensive (e.g., major extensions to existing plant), can slide through easily; sometimes too easily for their own good.

Another repeated observation made was that those who gave agreement and those who received it had different impressions of how much agreement had actually been given. It seemed that the more successful the idea was turning out to be, the smaller the gap between these two views. Conversely, if snags had appeared, the bigger the gap began to appear. When a plan got into trouble, the givers of authority were prone to say: 'Well, I never gave you authority to go that far.' However, if the project appeared to be succeeding, they said something more like: 'You were given all the authority you needed.' Somehow, in the memory of those giving agreement for change, how much they had given tended to open and shut like a concertina depending on prevailing circumstance.

Acceptance for change

Another observation, relating to the agreement for change stage in the process of management initiative, was that organisations tend to keep potential change information confidential or even secret. While a group is trying to make up their minds, they try to prevent other people outside the 'magic circle' from knowing what is going on. They feel that in this way they can exercise some control over time (others cannot forestall them, say). They also believe that they can switch off all leaks of information. Unfortunately, not only did leakage occur but also the information that did leak was distorted. Whilst many people knew something about what was being discussed, often rumour added up to a picture that was both incomplete and incorrect. Yet, these were the people who, if the idea was to be implemented, were vital to be won over as part of the next stage in this management initiative process, that of acceptance for change.

Once agreement for change was obtained, the initiators were set for implementation and for this they needed the full collaboration of many others; subordinates and even peers and superiors who were not originally involved or part of the decision-making stage that had just passed. Some or even most of those about to take part had yet to be won over and be formed into an operating team. Although it could have taken a year or two to get agreement for a change, once it was given the timescale almost invariably altered drastically; the prevailing climate becoming: 'We don't want it perfect, we need it Wednesday.' The champions of the proposed change, having got the agreement they had sought, perhaps after frustrating months of argument as to whether to go ahead or not, now expected *immediate* acceptance for the change from others who were now concerned, so that they could press on without further delay.

---

2 For more on precipitating events, see the last section in Appendix 1.

Those who were being asked for their immediate acceptance for change often had, as has already been observed, inadequate information plus some misinformation as a start. They were expected to take in and consent to a plan it had taken others so much longer to accept, on so much more information, all checked out in searching discussion. However, when the initiators did not get immediate acceptance for change, they turned impatient and often fell back on another term, called 'resistance to change', with which to label anyone slow to agree. In practice, this term seems based on the notion that there are just a few people in any company (of which the informant is always one) on whom all its members are entirely dependant to bring about 'change'. Once these few have made up their minds, anyone who does not agree is classified into that large but inferior group of colleagues who are 'resistant to change'. It seems so unlikely that mankind has progressed in a mere few thousand years from caves to offices packed with technology (spectacular caves, indeed!), with no more than just a few per cent of the population promoting beneficial change, dragging all the others along by their hair. It may be the methods of the 'change agents' that help create their resistors of change. Adaption-Innovation theory is more precise: There are no people who like all changes, and there are no people who like no change. Everyone likes some changes but the question is, which changes? Consider this scenario: Suppose you have just been asked for your support for a (usually complex) change, which may well concern you greatly:

- in a flash you see that you like it;
- you don't know enough about it so you hold off the proposer while you ponder;
- you have thought about it and conclude that it doesn't suit you.

In two of these three cases, you are classified as 'resistant to change', but in reality you are, in those instances, not accepting the particular suggested change. The difference between the general statement, leaving you classified as against all change, and the particular, that you are against *this* suggestion, you will feel is highly significant.

The notion that can be safely advanced here is that mankind is indeed *Homo sapiens*, and selects with deliberate care which change to accept and which to reject, calculating this problem like any other. The users of the term 'resisters to change' may themselves have spent a long time arriving at a decision (constantly modifying it as more is learnt) but then expect others to accept it simply because it has (now) been accepted by them. It is easy to overlook that others have similar brains with similar needs for information and the time to cogitate. Every critical response should not be classed as resistance to change in general rather than resistance to this (or some part of this) change. This is another example of the human tendency to denigrate others with whom they disagree: 'You are different from me, most probably because you cannot be like me, and therefore you are inferior.' We must consider whether we might not be more accurate if we said: 'I haven't given you enough information and enough time to absorb the idea,' or perhaps: 'This idea may be good for the company but it may not be good for you.' Of course, in theory people say: 'We must bring everybody into the decision-making process; we must make sure they understand what it's all about,' but deep down there is another tendency to classify people into an in-group or an out-group. The assumption is that the in-group is select and knows best about this problem. The in-group may be the people who lead and the out-groups are the people who are led, or whatever it is that distinguishes 'them' from 'us'. We are all, at times, the 'we' and at other times the 'them'. Forming in-groups is a characteristic of mankind and the basis of it is called discrimination. We discriminate, on selected cues, between those who are in the in-group and those who are not. It follows, if we are to find comfort and security in the chosen herd, that we deem it better than another herd, that we will fight to preserve our herd against any other, in mutual self-interest. In evolution this outcome of discrimination is a protective device, built into every herd animal so each individual can tell who is in the herd and who is outside it – friend or foe, hunter or hunted, interesting or uninteresting.

Discrimination has become a pejorative term but it is not the process of discrimination that causes problems; it is its use or misuse. For instance, a quite acceptable term in the realm of discrimination is loyalty to our family, company, department, or any other group to which we may belong. All of these structures are vital to us but adherence has its dangers, just as having and adhering to any other form of classification does. Every structure that is enabling is always, at the same time, limiting. This paradox must be resolved to best mutual advantage in society. We need group identity, collaboration, and cohesion from diverse people to get success from a group. But this often requires rapid flexibility in confronting a wide range of problems that the group will need to solve. The management of change and diversity is at the core of A-I theory. The very way in which the problem is perceived, as well as the way that it is tackled, places the problem solver in an in-group or an out-group. Yet the problem solver must manage well in each position and help others to do the same if the group is to be effective.

Implementation

The last stage, unless we envisage a spiral in which an end is the start of the process anew, is that of implementation. Once here, we appear to have progessed through this schema in a neat, simple, straight line, albeit, in places, with some difficulty. Of course, as with all dynamic schemata depicting processes, if things don't go well at any stage then every succeeding stage, and especially the final stage of implementation, will not go well. With all the problems that we have at every stage, it's amazing that we manage to implement anything. Fortunately, mankind is very clever and, despite all the problems, manages to implement a great deal. Nevertheless, few complex problems go though the stages without looping back and digression, pauses for related subprocesses to catch up, rethinks as a result of experience with new data, and feedback at every stage. The movement through this cognitive process is to be envisaged more like a plate of spaghetti than a straight line of uncomplicated progression. One important persistent weakness shown in this stage of the process of most of the cases examined in this management initiative study was that there was little overall analysis in retrospect. Unexpected success was gratefully received but rarely dissected so that, in understanding it better, more useful knowledge could be learnt; this and other similar observations are made by Drucker (1985). Some failures were also written off as 'bad luck' or 'inevitable in retrospect' and little was learnt from these either. This latter observation is picked up again later as this research is itself re-examined to see what else could be learnt from the more puzzling aspects that were not at first understood.

Summary

The study involved first, collecting information on the process of management initiative from all the key people concerned, in over 30 very detailed examples of corporate initiative deemed significant to the senior management in a number of companies. Second, analysing these data to uncover the 'ideal' pattern of steps or stages through which the process went. By 'ideal' is meant the most simplified pattern, ignoring error, day-to-day confusions and uncertainties, changes of mind, and all the other human affairs and failings that would have prevented an 'ideal execution'. This is presented as a schema, which helps us get a better understanding of the way in which individual minds, alone or in concert, solve problems. The number of stages selected to represent the progress implicit in this dynamic process, the boundaries that divide them, and their titles are the subjective choice of their author. This caution is needed, as any problem-solving process is continuous, so the stages are abstractions designed to help understanding. The whole idealised, dynamic (progressive) schema, which an author thinks adequately represents a mental process made manifest by the actions of a person or group, is to be used only if it seems to be accurate and useful to its user.

All the elements or stages in the management initiative process are themselves a process (or subprocess). All the numerous other elements, in their full or partial form or in their positive or negative form, are later embedded in A-I theory. Some key examples of there are examined below.

- The problems in obtaining agreement and authorisation for the proposed change; the problems of getting acceptance for the change as agreed and authorised.
- The failure to anticipate impending precipitating events, despite the fact that some people, but not always the same people, perceived each one. This suggests we all have 'blind spots' which we tend to overlook whilst readily seeing those of others.
- The problems of the proposed change that goes through too easily (and uncritically) for its own good; the problem that looks familiar and readily understood, but isn't.
- The problems that arise from the solution of another problem that is treated too casually.
- The curious unwillingness not only to analyse past (generally unexpected) successes but even many failures that cost dear. In general, a reluctance to treat as a problem an observation that what happened in a significant event and what was intended to happen did not coincide.

Many of the implications of the lessons from this study emerged from an analysis of the problems that seemed left over and unresolved at the study's formal end. This was done in the years that followed the completion of the original study, and what was learnt from these analyses (and added data from further work) also throws more light on the individual problem solver. The lessons are outlined below as the residual puzzles of the study. These were the stimulus for the work on A-I theory and helped in its formation. They also helped in ensuring that the emerging principles of theory remained close to practice. At the end of the analysis of the residual puzzles for which there seemed to be additional answers, there is a summary that will link this study to A-I theory.

ITS RESIDUAL PROBLEMS

The Management Initiative study, plus later experience and further study, threw up key problems (see Box 2). Understanding more about the study's residual problems helped form A-I theory, in and outside the realm of management.

Box 2 Key residual problems

Timescale of Acceptance	– Why do some take so long?
Objections to a Change	– Why is there sometimes a veritable barrage, often including mutually exclusive elements?
Precipitating Events	– Why do some come as bombshells?
Unwillingness to Analyse Past Events	– Who does, who does not?
Status of the Originator	– Can this be a clue?
Types of Change Proposed	– Can this be an answer?

Timescale of acceptance

This was related to the variation in the time taken by individuals and groups both to accept a problem perceived by another and to accept the solutions. These timescales ranged from their being accepted 'on the nod' – to use an English expression meaning 'accepted virtually without debate' – to prolonged and sometimes acrimonious debate lasting months and even years. On occasion, the initiator of the idea was surprised by the ease of its acceptance. It was as if they wanted their pet idea to be thoroughly tested before it became wholeheartedly accepted. On other occasions, some matter involving the expenditure of comparatively little resource ran into real and serious opposition. Of course, obvious factors were playing a part, such as the size and cost of a venture, the number of plausible alternatives available or when most agreed that too little information was available to be able to make a choice, to say nothing of the intrusion of company 'politics'. These and other obvious vectors, however, did not seem to account for all the principal variance. There still seemed to be a missing factor that was playing a significant role in at least some of the decisions being made.

In the early research, it had appeared that the 'on the nod' events and the protracted events were distributed almost bimodally. It turned out, on reflection, that this was an outcome of the way the examples had been selected for study. These had been the ones found by the manager interviewed as interesting or significant, etc., so the selection was certainly not random. Further studies showed these timescales of acceptance to be more normally distributed. As expected, there were a number of examples, especially those occurring in times of crisis, or when different departments lined up as rival protagonists, that were more likely to have a long and difficult passage. However, this reappraisal did not account for all the examples lying on the extremes of this time-lag continuum. It seemed as if a variable was missing, which if known and taken into account would help in understanding why some proposals took such an age to be accepted whilst others, just as large, expensive and complicated, went through much more easily. In Box 2, there is first an outline of all the residual problems in this cluster that later were given a general explanation. Second, there follows an explanation of what seems to be the missing variable. Third, a brief review of the problems is given, using the probable missing variable to make more sense of the observations.

The timescale of acceptance was one residual puzzle; another was related to behaviour that everyone recognises only too well from their personal experience: The array of objections that are put up by people who do not want to accept the idea, but do not appear to have a clear, brief, cogent case. The objectors appear to the proposer not to be sure why, or will not say why, they object, for the objections stated are not only many but often weak and mutually contradictory. Many managers have a list hung up in their office of the 6 best ways of killing off an idea, the 13 best ways of putting someone off, or other such grim wit. The list in Box 3 was recorded during one interview with one manager on a single issue. It includes exclusive statements and looks very much like defensive behaviour. It seems now, as at the time, that this manager might have said almost anything in order to stop an idea going through. But why did this happen? How could some managers, intelligent and experienced people, as was this manager, on occasion be so stupid as to be unable to see that they are saying things that are incompatible? This was a finding for which there was no good understanding at the time, except for an inclination to treat with caution such hypotheses as stupidity, resistance to change, or bloody-mindedness, all of which explanations were routinely advanced by other managers whenever this reaction was encountered in other people. This is a problem that needs to be further explored in the search for plausible explanations.

Box 3 The seemingly illogical objection barrage

> Do Not Need It
> There Is No Problem
> We Have No Resources
> Too Difficult to Do
> No Sale for It
> There Are Other Priorities
> It's Been Tried and Failed
> It's Being Done Now
> It's Not Suitable Here
> We're Doing Well, Why Risk?

Precipitating event

The third of the residual puzzles is a notion founded on that core element of learning theory: the precipitating event. For nearly a century psychologists have used the concept of stimulus–response as a very basic learning mechanism. If, for any response

to happen, there has to be a stimulus (or stimuli), was the precipitating event, sometimes dramatically observed in this study, simply a special subset of this start to a
cognitive process?

In many of the examples studied, the continued progress of an initiative depended
on a precipitating event that acted as a veritable bombshell. They were characterised
as appearing as sudden surprises, their resolution needing to be achieved quickly and
their nature threatening; in short, their revealed existence was associated with crises.
Yet, on every occasion that this happened, there was someone in the company who
had foreseen the event, but those taken aback by its appearance had ignored the
warnings. It was a puzzle as to why groups of high-level people could be taken so
much by surprise from time to time, even when at least one of them had already
predicted and warned of the impending danger. The usual explanations given, such as
stupidity, short-sightedness, inexperience, or complacency, although occasionally valid
as contributing factors, were not adequate to understand many of these phenomena.
One reason for this is that these same able people were found, at the same time, to
be aware of other (potential) precipitating events and be anticipating them in their
decision making. The difference seemed to be that these other precipitating events
appeared as triggers for action within such constructs as 'forward planning' or
'contingency planning'. So some stimuli for action were foreseen and built, relatively
safely, into projected action and some, often despite warnings, sneaked up and created havoc. Although various obvious factors were always present, some additional
explanation seemed missing. It was also puzzling that few of the outstanding successes
or failures were subjected to subsequent detailed analyses for the purpose of revealing
and understanding any underlying general management principles.

Status of the originator

Further study after the successful publication and reception of the Management Initiative study concentrated on the problems it threw up, particularly those relating to the
individual problem solver. At first, looking back through the original notes before
embarking on the collection of new material, it seemed possible that one could crudely
divide people into two groups: those who were in what we might call the Establishment (the inner-group, the inner-core), and those who were on its periphery or in out-
groups. The 'establishment group' is an imprecise notion of a power in-group, often
located within another wider in-group, that typifies more than any other subgroup the
wider group's climate, core of beliefs, rationale, and raison d'être. The members of
this inner core are not wholly identifiable as similar in rank or have any other obvious
feature that is always present, other than membership of the wider group. However,
they do seem to agree on some underlying principles of their problem solving in that
they appear as the interpreters and arbiters on matters of the culture and climate of
the wider group. The group's culture and climate forms a shared cognitive structure
relating to the group's reason for being and its overall aims and approved methods of
operating (problem solving). Its members, therefore, readily and almost intuitively
share the group's notions of key cognitive boundaries and their general content, which
are the ones that are dominant in the (wider) group. Within this climate, any idea that
emerged from the (establishment) core was much more likely to be accepted quickly –
sometimes too quickly for the long-term prospects of its own success. If it came
from outside this group, even from its peripheral (nonestablishment) members, often

irrespective of seniority, it was more likely to be perceived as suspect. Consideration of the importance of these observations and interrelated terms will lead us on later to consider the work of Kelly (1955), Kuhn (1970), and Berger & Luckmann (1967) as support for the A-I theory's assumptions on the notion of structure.

There were some curious tales associated with this residual puzzle that were related by managers in the Management Initiative project. One of these related to the fate of some initiators. There were cases quoted in which the people who put up ideas got them readily accepted and then got promoted, even if the ideas failed. The reason, leaving aside phenomenal luck or capacity for intrigue, was that: 'In this Company we do not penalise risk,' or: 'Well, he learned so much by this mistake, we don't want to lose him,' or even more simply: 'In this Company we do not witch-hunt.'

But this strategy was certainly not universally applied. There were other cases that had occurred in the same company, involving a nonestablishment person, who got an idea through 'the system' with the usual difficulty but which turned out to be spectacularly successful. However, managers often reported that the very next idea from the same person was still suspect! Nor was that all, for another puzzling observation was that should the latter person fail, he (all these managers involved happened to be males) was much more likely to leave the company, taking with him the entire blame for the failed project. In short, the person becomes a 'scapegoat'. What were the differences between these so very different circumstances and people, often located in the same company and treated so differently by the same people? Thinking about the next puzzle helped.

Type of change proposed

Finally came a breakthrough notion in the follow-up research to the original study. It concerned the differing nature of ideas that featured in the examples used to build the schema of the process of Management Initiative. It was that they ranged between the paradigm-consistent ideas to the paradigm-cracking ones (Box 4), and it became clear that the fate of the initiative and that of their originators (and their opponents) differed in a rational pattern. Going back over the array of residual puzzles, one can see what these new thoughts can help reveal. If an idea that has been perceived and advanced is paradigm consistent, it means, by definition, that it presents face validity to the establishment as it is in accord with the prevailing climate.

Paradigms[3] are consensually held (most critically by the relevant establishment) and collectively understood, since they are the set of beliefs of how all key matters work and relate to each other; they are in place because of their power and problem-solving

---

Box 4 Type of change

Paradigm Consistent
Paradigm Cracking

---

3 A term meaning a super cognitive guiding structure – wider, e.g., than theory or rule. Made popular by the work of Kuhn.

guidelines. An idea that emerges from the paradigm is going to be much better understood by, and more acceptable to, those who are a part of its consensus.

The time it takes to accept that a particular problem exists or that a particular solution is both appropriate and viable will depend, in the first instance, on how well it is understood in the context of the circumstances within which it is advanced. An idea that can be shown as 'paradigm consistent[4]' is more likely to be expected to work. In contrast, it is a much greater task having to explain and 'sell' what amounts to a package of change: (a) a new paradigm (or a significant change to an accepted one), (b) changes to the view of the old problem in the new light of the changed paradigm, and (c) the suggested solution as relevant and viable. The idea within the paradigm is so obviously simpler to sell and, later, to implement confidently and safely. The proposal that challenges the paradigm has more 'unknown' elements, making its assessment, in terms of its likely success and the extent of the possible penalty, a much more difficult and hazardous operation. This may be why even the more modest proposals that were seen to be on the periphery of the paradigm often took months to win acceptance. Conversely some quite major and costly proposals, visibly quite in accord with the prevailing paradigm and therefore quite expected and with their underlying principles understood, got through more easily. Indeed, some got through so easily that they came to grief for lack of sufficient analysis of some critical aspect. It also became clear that the more innovative managers were more likely to analyse an innovative past event than the adaptors were (who might have been quite relieved to see the back of it). But the more adaptive learned more from events that were adaptive in nature – whether they succeeded or whether they failed – whereas the more innovative had long since been bored by these proposals.

A-I theory contends that *Homo sapiens* is no way resistant to change in general: Indeed, no species can afford to be; the fossil record beckons the persistent failure! Humans, lacking instinct to guide them, are most discriminating in what changes to accept or reject. Where the proposal, idea, or plan can readily be fitted into consensually agreed, expected structure, it can be assessed more quickly and more certainly than if this is not the case. Not only acceptance but also rejection may not take long, since it can be both probed and defended more coolly, more rationally, and with more consensually agreed knowledge and experience. The reverse is true if the very structure (paradigm, context, theory, policy) has yet to be located, grasped, and evaluated. Hence, whilst playing for time, the defensive barrage of objections noted in Box 3 is liable to be thrown up. Not a case of a stupid person or one pathologically fearful of novelty, but a member of *Homo sapiens*, being sapient enough to try to win time to finish calculating whether the proposal is a pay-off or not! Of course, when the calculation is over the result may still be rejection. For the ordinary person this does not represent a generalised resistance to change, just a calculated rejection of a particular change. The fact that people differ in the outcomes of their calculation is no excuse for them, as a matter of course, to be rude about another's considered conclusions.

---

4 Meaning consensually agreed understanding by a large group of the nature of their operations, their aims, and the appropriate methods of achieving them. The equivalent, for a large group, of the cognitive structures of attitudes, beliefs, and experience needed by individuals to provide an understanding of perceived reality.

ITS CONCLUSIONS

The main conclusion from Management Initiative (Box 1) and the following experience is that analysis of its process helps understand, and even helps predict, the fate of ideas in an organisation. To summarise: When any idea, at any point within the process, put forward by anyone, is outside the prevailing paradigm, an additional problem for the recipients arises. Before they can evaluate the idea (perception, solution) they need to be able to understand and accept the perceived substantial change of structure implied in the shift from the prevailing mode. This constitutes increased processing of a wider or otherwise altered cognitive domain, possibly involving elements hitherto seen as irrelevant. Crossing over into this altered domain involves a reappraisal of knowledge that has hitherto been regarded as securely known, involving an unfamiliar perspective of the problem. These new perspectives may also throw up possible solutions about which little is known and, with them, the attendant risks of not-previously-considered alternative courses of action. The more unfamiliar the variables now appear, the greater seems the risk; so the needful reappraisal takes more time, with all the implications that has for the manager making the proposal. Conversely, if the problem is understood within the paradigm, less information needs to be processed and the attendant risks are better understood. The stimulus for moving forward such a paradigm-consistent proposal hardly needs a dramatic 'precipitating event', more a trigger within an existing forward plan. It is true that *any* change within a paradigm will necessarily modify the enveloping and guiding cognitive structure, but in adaptive mode this will happen as an outcome of its improvement rather than threatening its replacement. There seems more obvious risk in altering the paradigm first, in order to find a solution. Note that the paradigm held by the group can be orientated towards either adaption or innovation, making it just as difficult for innovators to see proposed adaptive change as worthy as it is for adaptors to evaluate favourably the more innovatively orientated notions.

This more complex relationship between cognitive style and change brings into question the oft-repeated supposition that large organisations crush initiative, innovation, or even all change. In the first place the historical evidence is against this notion. The largest, most global organisations – particularly of government and business – have grown up this last century, the very period that has seen the greatest advances mankind has ever achieved. What has been overlooked is that adaptive change can be both creative and far-reaching yet remain within generally accepted structures, getting relatively ready acceptance and support; whilst innovative change, *by its nature*, is more difficult to implement successfully anywhere, at any time.

The management implication of these conclusions is that members of a management team may disagree strongly on the kind of solution needed, but may fail to see that their differing perception of the problem itself may be the cause of the difficulty. Even if this is seen, there is no guarantee that all members of the team will avoid the intuitive feeling that some of their colleagues must be fundamentally (even stupidly) wrong in their approach. Crudely dichotomising these complexities, one group appears to the other as being over reliant, yet again, on 'the way we do things' in finding the answers; that, at least on this occasion, there may be greater risk in reworking the paradigm than in revising it. The other group is quite sure that a radical revision of 'the way we do things' is necessary this time and the risk of doing it is, therefore, worth taking. This kind of disagreement can be difficult enough to resolve, but there is an added complication. It is hard, in such a situation, not to suppose that the other person's views are flawed because of a capacity or moral deficiency (lack of knowledge and experience, courage or prudence) or, worse, an outcome of sheer perversity. Subsequent work and research suggests, for instance, that teams of homogeneous cognitive style have closely held and shared cognitive structure. It is easier to recruit new members who 'fit' (both parties find each other congenial and easy to evaluate). Such teams cohere and collaborate easily, are easier to manage (its members understand or trust what's going on) and are likely to be more successful along a narrower front than heterogeneous groups. Heterogeneous (style) groups[5], in sharp contrast, are more difficult to recruit and form into a cohesive team and are more difficult to manage, because of communication problems, but are more efficient, over a wider range of problems, than homogeneous teams. The pay-off point is hard to calculate.

The difficulty of managing heterogeneous teams has some interesting spin-offs, some of which were detected both during the collection of these case histories (see Appendix 1) and their subsequent analyses. One of these, mentioned earlier, is the general unwillingness to analyse the past so as to squeeze out more learning that can be applied in the future. Managers seemed then, and continue to seem now, obsessed with 'getting things done', personally supervising the ongoing process that could just as readily be undertaken as (or more) competently by more junior staff. To be caught undertaking deep, long-term thinking about the very process they are managing seemed to be an unwarranted indulgence. Of course they did do this from time to time, but almost as an optional extra. Often they chose to go on some training course in the search for solutions or even, occasionally, to seek better definitions of vaguely perceived problems. The indulgence factor entered yet again. The courses frequently chosen were those deemed to be billed as training (immediately practical) rather than theoretical (underlying understanding); as short as possible (so as not to lose time 'doing'); user friendly (not too intellectually demanding, permitting some course members to bring outstanding work with them to finish on the course); and using 'hands-on' methods (small input, gradually presented with spoon-fed integration and frequent, undemanding practice sessions, i.e., no 'heavy' lectures). The suspicion is that managers feared to be seen stockpiling information that might cause fissures in a fragile team. The avoidance of analysing some past failures and nearly all successes, even when these were unexpected, seemed in part to rest on the same need to be seen as safely doing and not digging up potentially divisive analyses[6]. What seemed missing was an understanding of the management of heterogeneous teams (having understanding and respect for differences) wherein argument is seen as a promising route to sound progress rather than conflict. Such understanding of the management of diversity might have helped release a team's members from an intellectual straitjacket of the prevailing mode – adaptive or innovative – brought about by a fear of being seen to create dissent.

The intention of reviewing those intriguing residual puzzles was to show how their review (together with additional information) helped lay some foundations of A-I theory. Also that there is no state that is either ideal or permanent – changes are

---

5 Possibly all heterogeneous groups, whatever the nature of the differences, and not just style.
6 Serendipity is often taken as a rightful reward from Fortune to the successful manager – examining it might seem to be rudely inspecting the teeth of a gift horse.

constantly needed to get a good balance for the moment. A group possessing too little shared structure is inefficient in an adaptive sense and so will find it increasingly difficult to maintain and improve the vital existing operations. Every organisation needs a strong element of adaption for its continued existence; how much depends on the nature of its main problems. Too much structure and adaptive efficiency boomerangs; although continuing to become more efficient, it can be trapped within an inappropriate paradigm or one in dire need of reform. In such cases, it is time for the innovator to come to the rescue, for the innovator is more inclined to solve problems as much despite rules as by their use – an inconvenience when the paradigm seems to rule supremely well. A difficulty in getting an agreed view on the needs of the situation is the definition of the term 'success' in relation to an aim or goal. The term always has some subjective component for each individual concerned because it is itself contingent on the evaluation of many variables. To problem solve successfully, whatever that may mean in any particular situation, we need to view problems and conceive solutions in terms of what is needed – another subjective operation. Most times we need to understand how each person in our problem-solving team works, so as to get the best out of everyone as the nature of each problem changes. This is the essential problem of the heterogeneous team. The aim of the problem-solving leader *and* each team member is to make use of the available pool within the team of individual differences, including thinking style, which can be made useful. Below is a summary of the findings from Management Initiative:

- Analysis of the problem is the stage most likely to be skimped. Often, the assumption is that the problem is better understood than it is and that past solutions will still work. This is not all bad; constantly making more of a problem than is needed will cripple progress. Knowledge, insight, and experience are expected to indicate the level of difficulty of a problem and the value of getting an early, acceptable solution. However, the danger is in underestimating the problem, and those best placed to do so (often those doing the job) need positive encouragement to raise the alarm.
- Analysis of the problem is likely to overlook the spin-off problem that is generated by the solution of the original problem, because the spin-off problem is treated as lightly (when we can) as any other problem.
- The more the accepted consensus of current practice (the paradigm) is challenged, so getting agreement (authority) for a change will be harder. A proposed change of paradigm has to be 'sold' before seeking agreement for the suggested solution. Being seen to understand this helps set up more trust and better rational discussion.
- Getting acceptance of the change from those who have to implement it, once it is agreed, takes time – if such implementation requires enthusiastic and intelligent action (delegation). In any complex task, people of different preferred style, level, experience, and position are often needed. If their diversity is to be well deployed they need to be won over and to work effectively together. Setting this up takes time, effort, and other resources; the pay-off is success. This is hard to do in crises; management's job is to anticipate crises.
- Implementation will get into difficulty if any part of the foregoing process is not adequately carried out. (Any stage that goes wrong will affect every following stage.)

This introduction has covered a summary of content followed by a synopsis of the study in problem solving in management that was a formative influence in developing a theory of cognitive style. A misunderstanding of others' different style, often mistaken for inferior level, played a significant part in the difficulties met in groups solving problems. The Management Initiative study, as a part of the introduction, also helps underline that the theory in this book initially derived from practice and, it is hoped, will not throughout deviate far from practical use. The next chapter takes up the problem of unravelling style but now sets it into the context of problem solving in general. It consists of an exploration, in personal management terms, of how the individual problem solves and where style plays its part among the many other elements. This next chapter completes the general foundations of this work; after that the chapters generally move from personal problem solving to solving problems in groups and so collective management of diversity within oneself, of the problems to be solved and of other involved problem solvers.

2   Organisation of cognitive function

PROBLEM SOLVING IS THE KEY TO LIFE

This chapter deals with the foundation of problem solving, in which thinking style is an element. It defines and interrelates key terms and processes that are part of the function of the brain. This is essential as a foundation of the knowledge of any problem-solving leader – much like expecting an expert in motor cars to know something of the critical elements and process that lie under the hood or bonnet. This difficult territory is covered so that the general reader can obtain a ready grasp of the importance of the terms and functions described without need for detailed technical knowledge – an overall understanding is sufficient to back up practical use of the knowledge arrayed. For instance, a definition of instinct is given because it is part of the problem-solving facility available to animals but not to humans. The use of this sharp distinction is that the leader may make no assumptions that anyone knows anything instinctively – if some knowledge is needed then all need to have learnt it or need to do so now. On the other hand it is no disgrace in not knowing some key matter – we are all learning all the time and can correct any deficiency given insight and time. Such precision of language is critical in having clear, effective, and fair policy that makes best use of individual diversity rather than assumes innate superiority of the current elite.

Adaption-Innovation cognitive (problem-solving) style lies within the discipline of psychology, more specifically as an element within cognitive effect, which is itself within the field of cognitive function. In other words, Adaption-Innovation is the style or manner in which problem solving is undertaken. Problem solving, under one term or another, is the means by which life survives, that is, successfully manages the ever-constant change engendered by itself and its environment. Being successful, in a biological sense, involves living long enough to reproduce viable clones or progeny, so that if enough individuals are successful the species survives. Adaption-Innovation Theory (A-I theory) rests on the assumption that problem solving is the key to life in an ever-changing universe. The coming of each individual into existence is a change and its changing needs engender further change, as do its endeavours to resolve them. Because problem solving and its product, knowledge, are so vital, it is not surprising that an abiding interest in them has generated many terms and a library of literature.

Mankind may be unique in the universe in a number of ways, of which one is being able, consciously, to think about thinking. However, every other organism must solve its problems, but success in doing so is not the norm; biologists such as Richard Dawkins (1995) estimate that the species currently extant on earth (some 30 million of them) represent less than 1% of all species that have ever lived. This is a grim reminder to readers of the very good reason for reading about this subject! Jones (1999, p. 99) reminds us that: 'The creative force of evolution has a dark side, for life today was earned at the cost of the death of almost all that went before.' In the argument of this book, all change has an inevitable consequence of destruction, adaptive change being more conservative. This 'dark side' of creativity (especially innovation) is overlooked or casually dismissed by the protagonists – more easily done when the proposer is not part of the structure that is to be 'reformed', such as being part of the group in charge of it[7]. However, before the argument moves too far from basic structures, which are the main concern at this point in discussion, it may be useful to review the main strategies that organisms have evolved for their survival. The first need is to have the biological means of detecting change (consciously or not) and successfully responding to it – that is, surviving a change (resolving a 'perceived' novelty[8]) by bringing about another (engendering novelty) that leaves the organism ready to meet the next challenge. Means are also required to meet all other basic needs and drives, such as acquiring nutriment (personal need) and reproduction (species need). Such 'problem-solving' means are possessed even by such primitive single-cell organisms as prokaryotes and eukaryotes.

All organisms, mankind included, need these basic survival elements. Even very primitive organisms have problem-solving resources, however basic, which must include the detection of unfavourable conditions and some means of avoiding their full effects – all these means being 'wired-in' to their basic structure. Biological structures have become, through evolutionary development, more complicated and so more able to 'perceive' more novelty and resolve it by being able to generate a wider, more complex repertoire of solutions. Among those available to the highest order of organisms, mankind included, are reactions and reflexes (that operate without need of a cerebral cortex) that are not in the conscious cognitive problem-solving class of response.

There are other biological mechanisms that are at the same level of operation, although of increasing complexity, such as internal biochemical balances and controls, digestion, higher-order sensing (seeing, hearing) and movement (from reflexive eye-blink and knee-jerk to walking and manipulation). These operate 'by construction' but, as they become more complicated, they require practice by the owner to bring their operation closer to maximum potential effect. The need for such practice implies the most primitive form of learning and the possibility of individual differences, even if these cannot be measured (as yet). One of the least sophisticated organisms that are strongly suspected of responding in accord to past events they may have experienced is the lowly roundworm, *Caenorhabditis elegans*. It appears to be able to distinguish between food (the bacterium *E. coli*) presented in a solution containing either sodium or chloride, permitting experiments of classical conditioning in its movement towards a potential food source[9]. It has the first requirement for learning: The ability to

---

7   Even change as extreme as extinction is an inevitable part of evolutionary progress.

8   The term 'perception' does not here necessarily imply awareness.

9   So, even in a very simple organism, 'evolution and learning can [develop] simultaneously, with innate structure evolving in an animal that is also learning' (Pinker, 1998, p. 177). In every organism 'there is a genetic foundation for the development of *all* behavior' (Alcock, 1993, p. 34), or, as Pinker (2002) states it: 'Something in the mind must be innate, if it is only the mechanisims that do the learning' (p. 34). Mankind is the only higher organism that can exploit its mechanisms so successfully so as not to need the programmed problem solving of instinct.

discriminate, for it can sense five different odours (Wes & Bargmann, 2001). Quite an achievement – its 'problem-solving' equipment consists of about 300 nerve cells compared to mankind's 1,000,000,000,000 vastly more elaborate cells!

Conditioned reflexes and operant learning (when a learnt stimulus sets off an existing reflex) are the operations where the collaboration between behaviour that is programmed and behaviour that arises from learning are distinct but clearly linked. Although we may define a trichotomy of strategic responses (as an outcome of structure, as an outcome of instinct, and as an outcome of learning), life strategies are more of a continuum. Nevertheless, these divisions are useful in practice in helping to avoid casual errors of reasoning. So, in this work they retain their identity within a continuum.

Built-in response systems are critical to survival since these simple responses to stimuli, including interally generated needs and drives, are instantly available without the need to expend time or effort learning them; the equipment needed for their operation is modest. The limitation of these systems, which we might call the 'biological machinery' (see Boxes 5a and 5b and Appendix 2), is that they are simple responses to simple changes arising from within the organism or from its environment. Instinct has evolved to meet the need for more complex and compound responses, whilst retaining the prime advantage of the basic responses: Acquisition with less cost in effort and time than is required by learning. Although the terms may overlap at their edges, leading to arguments as to how independent each is from the other, there is an advantage to separating the more primitive response system from instinct and the latter from learning. It seems best to confine instinct to complex pre-set patterns of behaviour that:

- are common to all individuals in a species (there are no individual variations);
- are unlearnt (operating almost perfectly on the first occasion used, even when the operation has never been seen being undertaken by another);
- are activated by a specific trigger (e.g., in some species the mating instinct is triggered by the length of daylight);
- have survival value at least to the species but not necessarily to the individual (a bee dies when it stings; among some spiders, the males are killed and eaten by the females they fertilise); and
- originated (and developed from) the interaction of random mutation and cumulative natural (nonrandom) selection (see, e.g., Dawkins, 1987, 1995).

This definition excludes all the simpler responses that are mostly the operation of basic equipment (e.g., digesting, blinking, walking), for its complexity mirrors much of the higher problem-solving process, from identification of the problem through to the selection of the solution and on to its implementation (see also Appendix 2). The difference is that, like the simpler responses, these elements are genetically wired-in. The advantage of instinct is that it enables greater complexity of task, over long periods of time, it is available to every individual in the species even if there has been no prior contact with an adult of the species – and it works well from the start. The British philosophers of the mid-17th century, Locke, Berkeley, and Hume, all supported Locke's notion of tabula rasa: that the differences between individuals are entirely attributable to learning; experience writes on a blank sheet. They made no reference to instinct, but the early psychologists, often dominated by results of experiments using animals as subjects, were less clear. The elements in their definitions that were built into their experiments were as clearly distinguished as they are in the definition given in Box 5a. This definition has the merit of linking philosopher, psychologist, and biologist by explaining the phenomenon with fewer differences in theoretical assumption.

There are two seeming weaknesses to instinct, as defined above, which are outcomes of the complexity of the tasks undertaken. One is that there are parts of the 'recipe' that need to be practised and some of the activity is left to choice (in building a nest the bird may learn to choose a safer site from among the possibilities on offer that would all 'fit' the instinct model template). Especially for higher-order animals, elements of learning are needed to improve the efficiency of an instinct's operation. Although what is prescribed and what is learnt should be readily distinguishable, leaving separate but collaborating elements, the added requirement of learning shows that the instinct strategy has sharp limits in the complexity of response that can be included. The other disadvantage is the same as for all the more basic systems: its inflexibility of strategy, solution, timing, and method. Variations to instinct must be bred in and cannot be thought out (see Box 5b for added detail).

This distinction between these three separate 'problem-solving' strategies (by construction, by instinct, and by learning) available to organisms permits a more controversial but equally useful theoretical stance. It posits that mankind is unique in having no instinct. This position can be reached by defining all the strategies tightly and by eliminating loose terminology. For instance, no organism has a survival instinct – survival is the outcome of all its behaviour, it is not a unit of behaviour in itself. No organism instinctively recognises the face, sound, or smell of mother, as Conrad Lorenz discovered half a century ago; imprinting can be onto a role model (like a human owner)[10]. Mankind is in no way free, when problem solving, from the evolved and inherited structures of the body, which of course include the brain. All our advances notwithstanding, we still need sleep, still need to ensure that our lungs have oxygen even when we are a mile below sea level, and, once out of the approach vehicles, still use old-style legs to walk to our spaceship and climb up to its ports. It is our fingers on which we depend for most manipulation of even the most advanced tool and it is the eye that carries visual information, even when enhanced by a telescope, to a brain, itself the key organ that has remained essentially unaltered for the last 100,000 years. We are even fooled by the same perceptual illusions (e.g., Carter, 2002, pp. 161, 201). We are still dependent, most of the time, for the smooth working of the body on controls and feedback loops that work without our being aware of them until they falter. But none of this is instinct.

To sum up the distinctions made, as a prelude to deciding whether they are important in the field of problem solving, it can be said that when learning occurs within the confines of structure that the learner cannot alter, except by extension, then that structure is inherited. Inherited structure is of two types that are not exactly defined at their adjoining edges; one is related to how the individual body works (governed by the nature of its construction) and the other is a programmed complex pattern of behaviour, specific to a species. Where learning occurs outside the limits of instinct (inherited structure), changes that the individual wants can be effected, limited only

---

10 Early on, biologists (e.g., Hess, 1964) defined a distinction between imprinting and learning.

Box 5a Definition of instinct

- A complicated pattern of behaviour (e.g., not climbing or being startled by a loud noise but, e.g., building a nest);
- the significance of which the individual is unaware (e.g., Jones, 1999; see also Appendix 2);
- which has survival value to the species but not necessarily (or only incidentally) to the individual;
- is completely unlearnt (e.g., a bird will build a nest despite having been incubated and never having seen another bird);
- is common to the species (e.g., a blackbird only builds blackbird nests); and
- is set off by a specific trigger (e.g., the length of daylight) to which the organism has no option but to respond.

NOTES:
- The above elements include humans.
- In higher organisms (e.g., dog as compared to insect) some parts of instinctive behaviour need to be made more efficient by practice, but the essential elements remain unaltered. Learning supports instinct by allowing more complexity and variation – at the cost of time for learner and parent.

NOTE:
To grasp the core of the difference between instinct and learning, try this example:
It cannot be conceived that:
    a group of blackbirds would ever combine
    to build an eagle's nest,
    for the benefit of aspiring hawks,
    in exchange, thereafter,
    for a regular monthly meal of pigeon.

NOTE:
A computer analogy is the difference between the hardware construction and the software program. Instinct is a software program that has been built as part of the hardware and is bought with the machine. It is the operator who does the learning.

---

by restraints imposed by the organism's structure and its environment, e.g., Mottram, 1952. All life must operate within the limits of its given physical structure. Beyond the simplest organisms, all more complex organisms have evolved the additional resource of instinct, with one exception – man. Humans are therefore unique, being both complex biological entities and free from instinct. As Jones (1999) a leading geneticist,

Box 5b Refinements of the definition

1. The basic 'biological machinery' is not instinct
This term is used for the simpler bodily responses (reactions) to stimuli that are excluded by the definition of instinct given in Box 5a. Damasio (1999, p. 55) refers to this 'biological machinery' as the individual's 'survival kit,' which includes the ways in which the machinery works, drives and mental processes like motivations, together with emotion and feeling. This is the foundation on which reason operates. Concerned only with mankind, he makes no reference in his book to instinct.

2. No instinct in humans – a biologist's definition
Jones (1999) offers this definition of instinct: 'An action, which we ourselves should require experience to enable us to perform, when performed by an animal – more especially a very young animal – and when performed by many individuals in the same way, without their knowing for what purpose it is performed, is usually said to be instinctive' (p. 156). For example: 'If Mozart, instead of playing the pianoforte at three years old with wonderfully little practice, had played a tune with no practice at all, he might truly be said to have done so instinctively' (p. 159). Not that inherited structure plays no part in all learned behaviour – in Mozart's case, the latent ability to discriminate tone and pitch finely was in place at birth, so '. . . his ability to learn the piano came from his ancestors. He played as he did because he was Mozart. Genes set the limits even to genius' (p. 159).

3. Facility with language is not instinct
Ridley (1999), depending heavily on Chomsky, argues strongly that the development of language may be an instinct. The argument in this book is that the equipment, and therefore the facility, is genetically determined but not the development of a specific language, which must be learned. MacNeilage & Davis (2000) suggest that the language facility gives rise to babbling that is similar in babies everywhere because the limitations of the vocal tract make for similar sounds; babbling is the foundation of language. This means that we can learn whatever language we are taught (birds learn only added local variants to an entirely common, unlearnt 'language') but that if we are not taught a language we will not learn one at all (as Ridley also states, p. 95). The similarities of the underlying structures of different languages may be analogous to the underlying similarities of dance (pop, primitive, or ballet), as they all depend on the common structure of the legs and feet, hearing a beat, and coordinating movement and sound. As Alcock (1993) writes, despite there being 4000 different languages, within the brain's facility for learning them: 'there are any number of constraints that structure the way in which language is learned, no matter what the language is' (p. 42). A constraint may limit language but is not a language.

> This disagreement with Ridley lies in the fineness of definition, for he writes that: 'Fear of snakes is an instinct that has to be taught' (p. 103) – a statement that cannot be fitted within the definition of instinct used in this text. The basic equipment (and how it works and how it is limited) is the same for all, but the product needs to be learnt by each individual human, as does every other cognitively engendered behaviour, which is why 'foreign' languages exist and have to be learned as well. Others, like Pinker (1998), agree with Ridley but run into exactly the same problems and contradictions, because they do not separate the basic operation of Damasio's 'biological machinery' from a specific use of it. In any case: 'language is not simply the medium by which we express our idea and experiences to each other. Rather it is fundamental to the thought process itself' (Tattersall, 2000), because it involves categorising, naming and creating symbols. The product of thought process is not instinct. In summary, the biological equipment needed to acquire language is built into the system by the genes, as a facility not an instinct; we use the facility to learn a specific language. We learn differently from others using the same resource, so there are many languages, but just one species. (See Appendix 2 for further explanatory examples of instinct.)

observes: There might be inborn drives for rape and for greed, but *Homo sapiens*, uniquely, need not defer to them (see also: Introduction, Appendix 5).

The question now arises: Is there any practical value in having made these distinctions? The answer is: Yes, if it ensures that we never forget that there are limits to our problem solving, which are ever-present, and which sort they are. Too frequently we make statements about some driver 'braking by instinct' to avoid an accident. But the driver has not evolved an instinct for driving vehicles; all that is available is acquired by training, powerfully reinforced by experience, which leads to insight and facilitates the making of accurate predictions. Some reactions can be so practised that they become conditioned reflexes; but they are all learnt, are amenable to relearning, and are not bred in. To get a competent driver, someone is needed who has to know what to teach, how to teach, and how to design equipment that fits human physical limits. Then the learner needs to learn in the conditions prevailing and to add experience until (relatively) safe. Rather than this being instinct, it is a lengthy cognitive process on the part of all participants (including pedestrians!). Another common error made in casual speech is to attribute to groups the attributes of individuals and to suppose that governments or companies think. Groups cannot think, only individuals can; we are not built in a way that can allow minds to link directly with one another, like computers – each of us has to build up a grasp of reality for ourselves and then act upon it. No two people can experience the same event identically and so cannot think identically. When we collaborate in a group, each member continues to be an individual thinker for whom the others constitute the environment (and, e.g., the culture and the climate). There is no groupthink, in the sense that brains are linked in common processes, but the climate engendered by the interaction of the others in the group (I am part of your environment, you are part of mine) may significantly facilitate or hinder the thinking of each individual. Humans have no instinct to help determine group behaviour under any circumstance; for us *everything* has to be learnt, not just some of it.

By contrast, learnt problem solving, well developed in all higher-order species, offers the widest potential range of responses and the greatest problem-solving flexibility. The advantages of problem solving are obvious, for our achievements are huge compared to any other organism, but the expense is high. Everything we do, except for those inbuilt structures, reactions and reflexes, has to be learnt: who our enemies are, what to eat, how to get it, how to mate, how to give birth, or how to nurture our young. As learning takes time and practice, our young are more vulnerable, for longer, than those of any other species[11]. To survive, we need continually to learn. A-I theory emphasises two key issues:

- When we problem solve we are limited by the way we are built (e.g., our intelligence, as no one has endless capacity or flexibility) but we have no instinct to help or hinder us.
- All of us are intelligent and creative, at different levels and with different styles, and, therefore, all of us are capable of contributing to team problem solving, as long as there is both motive and opportunity.

One other confusion of terms in this field is the use, in common parlance, of intuition. This is sometimes used as synonymous with instinct and sometimes as opposed to reason. A more precise distinction is that intuition is reasoning in which the process is not available to conscious examination. Like reason, it must be based on knowledge acquired by learning and stored in memory, but the steps by which the conclusions are drawn are not readily accessible. The advantage of intuition is that it is a comparatively faster process than reason that can, at a stroke, suggest a solution and, in the process, leap cognitive boundaries that might otherwise take much longer to overcome. Its weakness is that the process cannot be readily modified, as it is not available for inspection[12]. There is value in both means of arriving at a conclusion under different circumstances. Kelly (1955) argued that all people are scientists in that we all use the scientific method, whether we are aware of this or not. But the scientific method is a general formulation, extracted from the problem-solving process. It depends on knowing enough about the environment (having a grasp of reality) from which to anticipate a result (form a hypothesis); then to form a potential solution (formulate a conclusion) that can, in turn, be implemented (tested)[13]. If the result is

---

11 Once past this age of vulnerability, it is humans who are possibly the greatest danger to themselves and every other species. 'Humans have an unfair advantage of attacking, in this life time, organisms that can beef up their defences only in subsequent ones. Many species cannot evolve defences fast enough, even over evolutionary time, to defend themselves against humans. That is why species drop like flies whenever humans first enter a ecosystem' (Pinker, 1998, p. 190).

12 The expertise needed to perform a complex task, for instance, develops well in advance of the ability to articulate, explain, or even to be sure of the patterns of information involved. Reber (1993) states that the brain can operate intuitively before it is able to operate rationally.

13 The word science comes from the Latin scientia, meaning knowledge; scientific method is the explication of the process of acquiring knowledge; a process common to all problem solvers, whether understood by the individual or not.

positive, the conclusion is 'proved'; otherwise it is 'disproved': Whatever the result, the process has resulted in learning. On this definition, much of life uses the scientific method – it is just that people use it consciously and some people use it to such better effect that they are called scientists. In this view of scientific method there is no exclusion of intuition as long as it is applied at an appropriate stage of the process – as a means of setting up a hypothesis as distinct from arriving at a logically derived hypothesis. All hypotheses need to be tested (intuition may be used as a hypothetical conclusion, but this is not proof). Once tested the results can in turn be used as the basis for a further hypothesis, for which intuition could again play a useful part.

In summary: Intuition is clearly not instinct using the definition above. It is a form of problem solving, using all the same process and knowledge available to reason, but the steps by which it arrives at conclusions are not open to examination. The value of intuition is that it operates fast and may even break a structure or two to get to the conclusion, but its disadvantage is that as the steps of operation are not open they cannot readily be tested. In short, intuition can be used with advantage in the setting up of a problem; it cannot be used as proof (test of hypothesis). As Kelly remarked, we all use scientific method, so both reason and intuition can be used in hypothesis formulation (formally derived versus inspired hypothesis) but only reason can be used to test either.

The argument above first posits that problem solving is the key to life on earth, on which problems abound since all its matter, animate and inanimate, is and always has been in a state of constant flux. Second, the human brain is the most formidably efficient problem-solving structure ever to have evolved, even if, inevitably, it is limited by its structure[14]. Its deadly efficiency is not just in its power to solve the problems it encounters but also in being able to perceive them with such depth and clarity in the first instance[15]. One final point is that too many people not only muddle problem solving and instinct, but also exclude from problem solving and its study intuition, emotion, and even play. Problem solving should not be narrowly conceived, for instance, by starting that in its operation reason is invariably opposed to emotion. Brain function does include the notion of pleasure and play, the challenge of self-fulfilment, the appreciation of beauty, and the distinction between right and wrong. In a wide variety of organisms, the young indulge in play as part of their practice for the tasks ahead – only humans use it as an occupation! Self-fulfilment and self-actualisation must originate from some understanding of self – a most useful problem-solving resource – but only man can develop this origin into philosophy, religion, and psychology. Admiring beauty may have begun as no more than a cool appreciation of the environment and others; only humans can turn this into a delight and a study. However far we push away from origins, they remain the base to what we can do and what we actually do. We just take full advantage of our given mental inheritance and

---

14 For a biologist's view: 'Every animal is limited in what it can do by what it started with' (Jones, 1999, p. 139). Although also limited in this way, the human brain is several times: 'too big for a generic monkey or ape of our size' (Pinker, 1998, p. 183) – and hominids are already, in this respect, a select group.

15 This is well explored in Pinker (1998) who emphasises: 'the survival value of information, which brains have been designed to process' (p. 175). The term 'process' is defined widely, so that the brain can be envisaged as more than a mechanical calculating machine – the sort of tool (means of added resource) mankind is supremely expert in devising.

when we enjoy ourselves in the process we continue to learn. To be able to enjoy art we need some understanding of it; to indulge in it we need to solve related problems, e.g., what medium do we want to use, what style, to what effect, on whom? Figures 1a and 1b display organisation charts of the mind[16] as a problem-solving business, showing the elements as functioning departments and outlining the principal task of each and their interrelationships. It includes, as important elements, such terms as motive, attitude, and belief as well as all knowledge. The schema may be useful in setting cognitive style in its problem-solving context.

THE BRAIN'S PROBLEM-SOLVING DEPARTMENTS

The domain of cognitive functioning is very complex and is at the core of the understanding of mankind; within this domain, style forms but a part. What are its other key constituents? How are they related to one another? Can they be measured? A key starting point towards answering these questions is to set up the notion that, even though cognitive function may be multifaceted, its consequence, i.e. behaviour, is a collective result of many operating variables, both internal to the individual and outside, e.g., environment, climate. One consequence of such manifest problem solving and decision making is the creative product itself. If we begin by examining a creative product, be it a technical invention, an idea, an objet d'art, an artefact, etc., we will immediately see that many questions need to be asked when describing it: What is it? How did it get there? What style is it in? Is it of high quality? How was it achieved? and so on. These numerous variables may be divided into two broad groups: (1) those directly related to problem solving and creativity, and (2) those impinging upon them, e.g., environmental factors.

The domain in which cognitive style needs to be located is cognitive function. The schema in Figure 1a aims to represent the fantastically complex operation in a way that is simple but informative, accurate, and useful. Laid out like a company's organisation chart, it shows the main units of operation (as departments) with their titles and subtitles to indicate their scope of operation and a named 'process' that indicates their means of operation. So, the schema endeavours to present a simple plan of the way the human brain goes about its problem-solving business. This is no easy task: 'the human brain . . . comprises a trillion cells, 100 billion of them neurons linked in networks that give rise to intelligence, creativity, emotion, consciousness and memory,' writes Fischbach (1994) in a short, useful description of the brain. An additional value of an 'organisation' map is that it offers some indication of the interrelationship of departments as well as their separate functions and identity. Some of these relationships have been the subject of research in the A-I literature, which is discussed later.

The groups of elements directly comprising the domain of cognition are three: *cognitive effect* (which undertakes the problem-solving operation via the cognitive problem-solving process), *cognitive affect* (which selects the problem to be solved and determines the type of answer needed via another process, that of motive), and *cognitive resource* (which through the process of learning, a by-product of problem solving, amasses the knowledge and skills needed to problem solve, saved by and accessed

---

16 One might describe the mind as the brain's operating process.

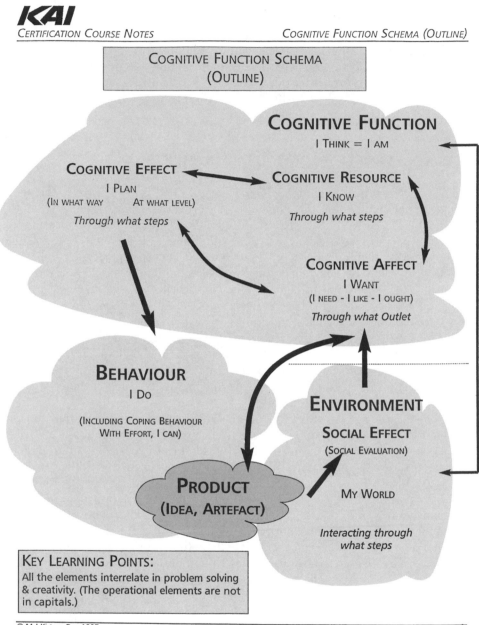

Figure 1a Cognitive function schema (outline)

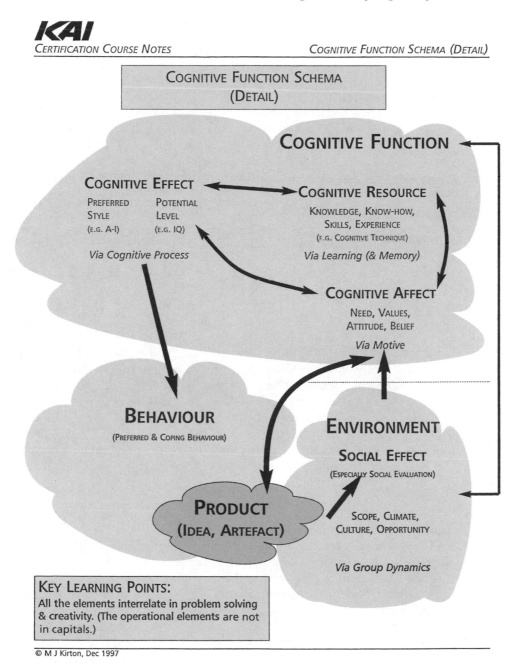

COGNITIVE FUNCTION SCHEMA
(DETAIL)

COGNITIVE FUNCTION

COGNITIVE EFFECT   COGNITIVE RESOURCE

PREFERRED   POTENTIAL   KNOWLEDGE, KNOW-HOW,
STYLE   LEVEL   SKILLS, EXPERIENCE
(E.G. A-I)   (E.G. IQ)   (F.G. COGNITIVE TECHNIQUE)

Via Cognitive Process   *Via Learning (& Memory)*

COGNITIVE AFFECT

NEED, VALUES,
ATTITUDE, BELIEF

Via Motive

BEHAVIOUR   ENVIRONMENT
(PREFERRED & COPING BEHAVIOUR)
                                   SOCIAL EFFECT
                                   (ESPECIALLY SOCIAL EVALUATION)

PRODUCT   SCOPE, CLIMATE,
(IDEA, ARTEFACT)   CULTURE, OPPORTUNITY

                                   Via Group Dynamics

KEY LEARNING POINTS:
All the elements interrelate in problem solving
& creativity. (The operational elements are not
in capitals.)

© M J Kirton, Dec 1997

Figure 1b Cognitive function schema (detail)

through memory). These 'internal departments' of *cognitive function* are also influenced by *social effect*.

The arrows in the schema suggest the flow of interactions between elements. They also underline a first difficulty in describing cognitive function: Where to begin? Where does a thought start and where does it end? – just supposing either question has validity in a continuous flow that starts before birth and continues until death. Arbitrarily, to satisfy human logic, let the description begin at the same point those devising schemata of the thought process do, with (often only the implication of) cognitive function as a whole, then with the identification of a problem, and on to an equally arbitrary end, the feedback from the implementation of some solution; taking in all the many elements they deem relevant on the way. Below are thumbnail sketches of each function; later some aspects that are needed in further detail are taken up in appropriate context.

Cognitive function   This schema suggests that cognitive function is composed of three elements that all lie within the individual and are the influence on behaviour, '*I do.*' Because they are inbuilt or are structures that have been acquired and tested over time, they are at core consistent and predictable over time and event, and therefore they yield characteristic patterns of behaviour. These structures, as Kelly (1955) argued, are constantly altered to retain an adequate grasp of reality. But the thinker is not able to treat these structures lightly lest too rapid change shakes the grasp of reality that is the foundation of the understanding of self and the world. The changes must be made sufficiently prudently so as not to imperil ego integrity; too few changes and our 'reality' will become unreal as the world changes faster than does the perceiver; too many changes (number and time are both involved) and the perceiver's sense of reality will reel. These cognitive structures, featured in this schema, are the bases of personality, which suggests that cognitive function is both '*I think*' and '*I am.*' This is the position that is not far from that taken by the 17th-century philosopher, Decartes, summed up as: '*Cogito ergo sum*,' I think, therefore I am – his proof 'of being', that he existed.

Process   This ('through what steps'; process can be described as 'how I operate') is the operational element of cognitive function: Each of the three cognitive elements of the schema has one process central to its function; for cognitive affect it is motivation (expressed through single or arrays of motives); for cognitive effect there is problem-solving process; for cognitive resource it is the closely related and interacting pair, learning and memory. Social environment, that is, collaborative problem solving, has group dynamics as its process. These processes are part of the genetically constructed mechanism and their basic operation is under way at birth, without learning; they operate whether we are aware of them or not; whether we understand them or not. The outcome of their operation, knowledge, becomes part of cognitive resource when gained. Processes are often presented as dynamic schematic representations: Cognitive process answers questions such as 'where am I?' rather like a road map, by specifying the stages in the progression in the order that they appear, from start to outcome. In this way, unlike level and style, a process is not measured, but rather validated as to its effectiveness in providing useful and truthful information on where we are, between start and finish in problem solving. These are the general terms; below are the sketches for the particular departmental elements taken roughly in the order above.

Cognitive affect This ('I want') comprises needs (some anchored in biology and not learnt), values, attitudes, and beliefs (which are learnt), all associated with motive as the operating process. It is suggested that this element selects the problem to be solved and indicates aspects of (limits the search for) the solution (e.g., plan a marketing campaign whilst abiding by consumer law). This sums up to 'I want' made up of the three elements that Freud suggested: 'I need, I like, I ought.' The differences between these elements of 'I want' are:

I NEED	given need	requiring tension reduction
I LIKE	acquired need	generating incentive
I OUGHT	acquired need	generated by guiding principles, e.g., morals

Cognitive affect is the source of guidance (i.e., cognitive enabling structure that is, therefore, a source of limitation) on the kind of solution to the perceived problem considered acceptable and the means that are deemed appropriate to attain the solution. Within this category, therefore, have been placed those predispositions to action (attitude and belief, as the acquired need structures) that collectively act as a focus (or foci) in directing energy (motivation) towards, and also away from, selected alternatives that the environment currently has on offer.

Motivation This is derived from the Latin verb *movere*, to move (activate) and it is the process ('through what outlet') that concentrates, channels, and directs energy towards the selected target. It therefore determines the priority that an individual will accord a class of perceived problem, and the degree of energy (intensity × persistence) that will be expended to achieve the desired result. In other words, the affect elements, e.g., attitude belief and interest, provide the direction and, through motivation, govern the amount of energy expended over whatever time is deemed appropriate. Motivation can be described as a single motive or a combination of more than one. Each specific motive is measured by the intensity and persistence of the energy needed to attain a goal (implement a solution)[17].

Cognitive effect This ('I plan') comprises cognitive style, cognitive (potential) level (manifest level is part of cognitive resource), and the problem-solving process. The latter is the operation that plans the problem through to implementation. Cognitive effect undertakes detailed problem solving. It is governed by two variables, cognitive style (the preferred manner in which problem solving is undertaken) and

17 The term 'motive' seems to have been first used by Sully (1884) to describe the desire that precedes an act and determines it. Dewey (1886) offers a sharper meaning: A desire, when chosen, becomes a motive. These definitions seem to relate entirely to 'voluntary action' as distinct from 'instinct'. McDougall (1908) muddies this water by his doctrine of instincts, which he considered are the prime movers of all human activity, thereby, incorporating the concept of motivation of voluntary behaviour into a single notion with instinct. Woodworth (1918) does much the same with his word 'drive'. The main problem that underlies these shifts of emphasis was the current preoccupation with the dispute between the (tight) mechanistic or (loose) functionalist philosophic explanations of behaviour. In this text, as is commoner today, 'drive' is reserved only for the stimuli that are associated with the construction of the body, e.g., hunger, and motivation for any decision where there is more obvious choice. However, since this theory is concerned with cognition and since mankind has choices in exactly how drives (but less so for reflexes) are reduced, the term motivation is used exclusively to relate to human problem solving.

cognitive level (the potential cognitive capacity that can be brought to bear). These operate through the *cognitive problem-solving* process. Style and level are *unrelated* (are statistically orthogonal) – that is, knowing a person's level gives no indication of their style; at what stage of the process they are in at a particular point in time; or what technique they might be using. Likewise, knowing someone's style gives no indication of at what level they can operate, where they are in the cognitive process, and so on. One way of perceiving that level and style are separate is to note that they each *imply different questions*. Style implies the question 'what (characteristic) manner or mode of approach?'; level asks 'what capacity, how much, what is the power of the engine?'; process asks 'where am I (are we) in the progression?' The difference between level and style will later be covered in some depth. They both represent individual differences that can be measured psychometrically.

Cognitive affect directs cognitive effect, which in turn is separate from, and is an influence on, behaviour: style determines the 'preferred' mode of behaviour; cognitive level is a limit that influences cognitive resource by limiting manifest level (e.g., management competency – see Cognitive resource), and process is the operational planning for action.

Cognitive resource   This ('I know') comprises knowledge, skills, and other experience of the individual (cognitive technique[18] is a subset of knowledge and skill). Cognitive reource is the outcome of the operation of cognitive function: As problems (novelties) are met, predictions are made and solutions implemented. This information, together with feedback from the environment, is stored for further improved prediction and operation. The learning process, associated with memory, is the operation that converts the outcomes of cognitive affect and cognitive effect into a resource for future problem solving. Hence this department is a backroom powerhouse. Its accumulation and availability of all past knowledge, experience, and skills gives it powerful influence on the scope of the other operations that feed it. All the elements interact, although cognitive affect and cognitive effect (and within this, level and style) have complete independence from each other. However, cognitive resource is not independent, for what it learns, in what style it learns, and the potential limits of its learning are determined elsewhere.

Within cognitive resource is knowledge of technique, the means by which we make the best use of our endowment and learning. One use of technique is learning and enhancing coping behaviour, to simulate a cognitive style unlike one's preferred style – part of cognitive effect.

So far the schema has dealt with the departments operating discretely in the brain. Encased in a bone case, these three departments have no direct contact with the outside world; they make up a representation of that world and then act on it. Hence, it is vital that the representation is both accurate and stable. To achieve both, a balance needs to be struck, especially in comparatively rapidly changing circumstances, between how accurate versus how stable (and, in turn, how understandable) the representation needs to be, in order for the problem solver to remain effective. These departments do not themselves 'behave'; but ideas and yearnings do not serve up supper. Behaviour, which is mostly overt, is the activity that gets the substantive

---

18 Techniques are sometimes aided by 'tools' like run charts and fishbone diagrams.

results. It is influenced by all these cognitive elements within cognitive function, and social effect also impinges on behaviour. An example of the distinction between the moderating elements and behaviour is that preferred style is the way an individual would prefer to behave. Behaviour is also influenced by the other elements (e.g., feedback from the environment) and the individual does not, therefore, always (if ever) behave exactly in accord with preference. The schema shows behaviour as made up of preferred and coping behaviour; both are defined below.

Behaviour   This ('I do') is the sum of the operations that attains the 'product', an idea, or an artefact. Because behaviour is influenced by cognitive function, which covers stable characteristic influences, many patterns of behaviour are themselves carried out in stable, characteristic ways. (Characteristic behaviour, plus all the characteristic influences on behaviour, make up personality.) Behaviour impacts on the environment, from which in turn feedback is gathered and interpreted.

Coping behaviour   This ('with effort, I can') is a learned technique available from cognitive resource; it occurs when behaviour needs to be in a style not in accord with preferred style. Sometimes techniques are learnt to ease the expense and improve the efficiency of coping behaviour. Coping behaviour, like the rest of cognitive resource, is available to cognitive effect when insight (or, better still, foresight) indicates that it is needed; the driving force behind its execution, like all other executions, is motive.

Environment   This is a term that critically includes culture and climate – the social environment that is 'my world' – or 'reality as I have learnt to perceive it'; it is the arena within which the individual functions of the individual's life and fortune are played out. External events play significant moderating roles in an individual's behaviour. Primarily, these events relate to interaction with other people, so others' behaviour (reaction and interaction with self) is each person's environment and each person's behaviour is part of these others' environment. These interactions are represented in the schema by the process of group dynamics; the basic assumption in the schema is that 'I am your environment; you are mine' – hence the use of the term social environment. Where the impact of problem solving is on people (e.g., the individual's input into climate), the (shared) process of group dynamics operates, yielding critical feedback. It is critical in shared problem solving. The feedback – the impact of climate – returns into cognitive affect, modifying both it and cognitive resource and so influencing the future operation of cognitive function in an endless cycle until death.

Social evaluation by others is not an integral part of an individual's cognitive function[19] – it is a part of those that make it! However, the information of others' evaluation is an essential part of an individual's cognitive input and, when integrated into cognitive resource, it has an impact on cognitive process as part of the information on reality that is the setting of any problem. It also affects self-image. Rating some individuals as 'noncreative', however absurd this may be, does not destroy their creative potential but it may undermine their confidence in their problem solving, at least in the field in which the evaluation occurred.

---

19 The creativity literature frequently tries to determine a person's creativity (level, not style) by the creativity's impact on others. Such evaluation may evaluate the judge as much (or more) than the judged.

Social evaluation falls outside the domains of both cognitive affect and effect because it is made of self by others; but when it is noted, it becomes part of the input of cognitive affect and a basis for further operations of the whole of cognitive function. It contributes to the judgement of the outcome of problem solving, as perceived by the problem solver. Evaluation has a long-term importance by leading to the acquisition of sophisticated knowledge and know-how, as well as contributing to the generation of high levels of persistent motivation, particularly if such evaluation takes the form of constructive criticism (e.g., Torrance, 1965).

This ends the sketches of the main elements of the schema. There are some additional matters relating to it that might also be useful to the reader. They may help to round off the picture, but they are also an introduction to more detailed discussions that need to be covered later. The first is the relationship between the elements of the schema and personality.

Personality is not listed in the schema but it pervades the model. Personality is defined, in this theory, as the sum of descriptions of all the stable characteristics of both individual behaviour and the (cognitive function) influences on behaviour. This view of personality distinguishes every individual from any other, as personality descriptions should, but it can also be used to describe differences between mankind and other species (or even between species), at least in terms of problem-solving strategies for survival[20]. The descriptions that relate to all the cognitive processes (e.g., learning, motive) and to cognitive effect (style and potential level) are deeper seated (have genetic origin) and are described as dimensions of personality[21]. The descriptions relating to the rest of cognitive affect are the deep-seated elements of 'pre-dispositions to action' (e.g., attitudes, beliefs). Descriptions that relate to the rest of cognitive resource (being, e.g., a knowledgeable person) can be regarded as characteristic of a person, as can the more stable of the characteristic patterns of behaviour (e.g., traits and habits rather than dimensions of personality). So, for instance, style is thus seen as being also a dimension of personality; behaviour provides information about most of the observed traits and habits.

The schema also suggests relationships between departments that impinge on personality measurement. Measures of elements in cognitive affect should not correlate with those in cognitive effect, unless there are intervening variables that complicate the relationship. So attitudes, beliefs, or anxiety levels are not directly related to (not expected to correlate significantly with) adaption-innovation – unless, e.g., the circumstance in which anxiety is exhibited is more or less suited to a particular style. These suggestions will be further addressed in the chapter on personality.

To move to another matter, the schema deals with problem solving. Creativity is seen as a part of problem solving; some problem solving is called creativity and some not, depending on the opinion of the observer. As the brain seems to make no distinction between these outcomes of cognitive function, no separate place for creativity is allocated in the schema.

'Creativity and innovation' is frequently offered as a single compound term rather than as two discrete ones. The problem, for those wishing to measure these concepts,

---

20 Note that van der Molen (1994) has argued that animals may show traces of adaption-innovation variation among individuals, using mice as an example. If further study sustains this argument then the assumed link of cognitive style with heredity is made stronger.

21 See Chapter 4, Personality and Style.

is what the compound term precisely means. In A-I theory, creativity is treated as a subset of problem solving (some problem solving may be regarded as creativity, some not) or even a synonymous term. Innovation is one pole of a continuum (style) in cognitive effect, which is an element of cognitive function and also, therefore, only a part of an element of creativity. These and other definitions will be reviewed below.

DEFINING STYLE

The key terms and assumptions

More than for any other organism, at the core of the understanding of *Homo sapiens* is the study of the cognitive processes at the command of the species. For a very long time there has been a fascination for probing the variables, real or assumed, that led to successful manifestation of creativity, problem solving, and decision making. Scientific attempts to measure some of these variables, especially the social 'climate' and the individual's potential capacity to learn and solve problems, are comparatively recent. But the fascination has been so strong and the effort so great that, just as with other sciences, more knowledge in this field has been accumulated in the past century than in all the previous millennia of man's existence. Until comparatively recently, concentration has been on the understanding of the basic equipment – the brain and nervous system – and the measurement of its capacity (how well is it done) as well as the environment, such as the organisational climate (in which it is done). Around halfway into the last century attention turned to scientific measurement, as distinct from literary description, of the wide range of different stable characteristic behaviour patterns exhibited by individuals when problem solving or being creative.

One possibility for this later start is that cognitive style (in what manner problem solving is done) is a subtler concept than cognitive capacity; or the difficulty in measuring the many interrelated variables that facilitate or hamper, praise or damn novel thought and action. These variables, however hard to measure they may be, seem simpler in their strategic conception, with one end of any such relevant measure judged 'good' (e.g., high IQ) and the other end less good (e.g., shortage of a necessary resource), almost wholly irrespective of specific context. Cognitive style is not like this, for one style may be more appropriate than another only in a specific set of circumstances, type of problem, strategic aim, or social climate.

Adaption-Innovation, in this theory, assumes that creativity is a part of problem solving on the a priori grounds that the brain seems to make no distinction between problem solving and creativity. The distinction is hard for people to make with any precision; some problem solving could be called creative and some not by one person whereas others may disagree with the first observer and amongst themselves. It may be an entirely linguistic conceit that distinguishes some problem solving as creative and the rest not. In a later chapter on creativity these difficulties will be reviewed; creativity is treated as a part of problem solving, and A-I theory relates equally to both.

In this theory, cognitive style is defined as the strategic, stable characteristic – the preferred way in which people respond to and seek to bring about change. This definition implies the exclusion of some concepts and the inclusion of others that are not necessarily mirrored in other approaches. Each term in the definition is examined below.

The term *preferred* implies a clear distinction between preferred style and behaviour, the former being an influence on the latter. Research shows that cognitive style is set early, if not inherited, and highly resistant to change, whereas behaviour is highly flexible. There may, therefore, be many circumstances, all essentially driven by motive, when one's behaviour may not be in accord with one's preferred style. This 'cognitive gap' between style and behaviour can be partly bridged by 'coping' behaviour.

The term *style* (or *manner*): In this theory there is a sharp distinction between style and the capacity or level of cognition of which a person is capable, whether this is inherent or learned. The latter describes the 'power of the engine' and deals with the question 'how much?'; the former the 'manner in which it is driven', dealing with the question 'in what manner?' This is not a matter that can be taken on trust, especially as this distinction is not always clear in psychology literature and is a good deal more conflated in creativity literature. More discussion and reference to research findings will be made in a later chapter.

The term *stable* (or *characteristic*): The theory assumes that adaption-innovation is a characteristic that is stable, indeed highly impervious to change. There is much evidence in support of this assumption, summarised in the next chapter. It shows that people do not change with age or experience or from culture to culture. This is a finding of surprise to many, especially those who come to the theory mainly from current creativity literature. Mankind is highly flexible, having, as argued above, no instinct. Nevertheless, thinking occurs within the structure of the brain and those of its elements that are inbuilt. There is considerable evidence that adaption-innovation is set early. Studies using hundreds of schoolchildren and students, ranging in age from 13 to 18 years, show that adaption-innovation style is acquired early and is highly resistant to change. It may also be inherited, as was first suggested by van der Molen (1994).

The term *coping behaviour* is behaviour that is not in accord with one's preferred style. It is measured by distance from preferred style and by the duration it is maintained. Coping behaviour is learnt; it is a deliberate response to a particular problem-solving situation that is deemed will not readily be solved unless coping is evoked. The effort required to cope is greater than that required by behaviour in accord with preferred style. It is also used to describe working at the edges of one's ability.

The term *change*: In this theory there is the implicit assumption that change is a constant phenomenon – neither the philosopher nor the scientist supposes a state of 'no change'. Since humans are constantly responding to change and are the world's experts in bringing about intended change, this element in the general definition will buttress the theory's theme that all people are agents of (intended) change.

Problem solving is also taken to embrace the concepts of decision making for the same reason as it does creativity. There are also problems in defining decision making; the most difficult is that it is sometimes used as synonymous with problem solving and sometimes as only the end stages of this process. As has been said, one reason for the intimate link between problem solving and creativity, as well as decision making, is that brain function seems to make no distinction between them. All three terms (creativity, problem solving and decision making) involve the concept of novelty, its generation or its resolution, both interacting and giving rise to each other. All organisms need some means of problem resolution to stay alive. It can be more readily seen from this standpoint that to describe someone with an intact cortex as uncreative is an elitist view; to describe a person as incapable of problem solving is absurd. Problem solving can be measured in terms of its level or its style but no one can be dismissed as not being able to do it.

The implications in this theory are of an ever-changing universe in which all living organisms must respond successfully to change by initiating their own, or perish. The story of life is replete with species that have failed, but although mankind is a relative latecomer compared to almost all other forms of life, our species has shown a remarkable capacity to generate widespread change to its own advantage. To suggest that some people like change and some dislike it must be an inadequate statement. We must all surely like changes that can be perceived to suit us and resist those we judge will not, as is logical for a species that has named itself '*Homo sapiens*'. Naturally, there will be wariness to any suggested change (any perceived opportunity) that cannot, for whatever reason, be readily assessed as to its outcome. One reason may be that the change proposed by another is outside one's preferred style of problem-solving search – hence the hesitation. Cautious or negative judgements, however, do not automatically imply a global, quasi-pathological syndrome of 'resistance to change', though 'resistance to *your* change proposal' is another, more understandable, matter. Equally, it may be quite feasible to understand (even measure) people's calculations of how change affects them (their perceived value of any particular change). Some will be more adventurous and risk-taking (or rash, depending on one's viewpoint) than others, but that is not the same thing as supposing that a large percentage of people dislike all change. If change is a constant and since all living beings must survive (remembering that they came about because of change in the first place), then the specific changes to which different organisms respond and the means by which they do so is the essential difference between them.

Finally, cognitively driven change implies cognitive structure – the guidelines we develop to arrange input and experience into meaningful packages, the better to understand them. Without structure there can be no analysis of the past and no learning, no projection to the future, no prediction, and no theory; no classification of events, no abstraction of principle, no order in the universe, no language, and no thought. This challenges much creativity literature, which supposes that the less structure involved in idea generation the more the idea is creative. A-I theory differs, suggesting that all problem solving requires cognitive structure but that people handle this structure differently. The more adaptive prefer more structure, and more of it consensually agreed, than do the more innovative. The more innovative manage with less structure, and less of it consensually agreed, than do the more adaptive. There are limits in both directions. In any situation, an excess of structure inhibits the generation of new thought, or if not thought, then certainly action. Equally, too little structure and the thought processes have too few frames of reference to be able to operate effectively – equivalent to a state of infancy. The range between too much and too little may be narrower than it appears as we take so much of enabling structure for granted. It is noticeable only when it is found to be particularly useful, and more so when it impedes us. The range does, however, look great when we have to collaborate with another person who has a markedly different style. There is a marked tendency in us to overlook the disadvantages of our own preferred structure, especially when we expect to succeed, but note those of others only too clearly. This ground for potential conflict will be explored again later, but the main point can now be stated succinctly:

Every location on the style continuum has its advantages and disadvantages, depending on the problem-solving context. However, a preference for more or less structure does not imply greater or less capacity.

Summary

Key assumptions underlying A-I theory are that cognitive style:

*   relates to the individual's preferred cognitive strategies involved in change (ideation made manifest) and to strategies of creativity, problem solving, and decision making, themselves overlapping or even synonymous concepts;
*   is related to numerous aspects (traits) of personality that appear early in life – these traits are particularly stable, as is cognitive style;
*   is bipolar and nonpejorative (unlike capacity, to which it is unrelated);
*   is nonevaluative, although more or less appropriate to the specific problem;
*   is not altered by learning or training, whereas behaviour is flexible;
*   is modified by coping behaviour that permits functioning, for limited amounts and limited periods, when the need is perceived;
*   can be simulated by learned cognitive techniques (sometimes supported by tools) that have been developed to enhance effective cognitive performance[22].

22 Other sorts of techniques are designed to tap more cognitive potential, e.g., mnemonics.

3 Describing and measuring Adaption-Innovation

DESCRIPTION

The Adaption-Innovation Theory (A-I theory) is founded on the assumption that all people solve problems and are creative – both are outcomes of the same brain function. The theory sharply distinguishes between level and style of creativity, problem solving, and decision making and is concerned only with style. The theory states that people differ in the cognitive style in which they are creative, solve problems, and make decisions. These style differences, which lie on a normally distributed continuum, range from high adaption to high innovation. Cognitive structure is a vital requirement to marshalling input to the brain and making sense of it and the world it represents, and to any hope of problem solving. We are all dependent on this structure and we must manage vast amounts of it – so much that it may not be possible even to estimate its extent. However, what must be comparatively small, individual, characteristic variations in its management are very noticeable in the identification of individuals and seem to be critical in each person's problem-solving success. It is not surprising that, as it is essential that we collaborate among ourselves, we take great note of these variations.

The key to the adaptive-innovative distinction is the way people prefer to manage cognitive structure. The more adaptive prefer their problems to be associated with more structure, with more of this structure consensually agreed; the more innovative prefer solving problems with looser structure and are less concerned that the structure they use is consensually agreed[23]. That is not to say that those who are more adaptive never break or bend structure and those who are more innovative do nothing but – far from it. Everyone brings about change, including change in the structure they use to do so. Adaptors are likely to do so as an outcome of solving problems with the help of the prevailing structure; innovators are liable to bring about change by first altering the prevailing structure. Adaptors have more regard for agreed structure because they seem more appreciative of its enabling possibilities than are the more innovative. They are less sensitive to the current structure's limiting aspects – but when they become so, they will also be quite willing to alter it, more usually as an outcome to solving problems with its assistance. They are likely to have greater concern to re-establish a tighter, sounder structure sooner than innovators, so as to exploit its enabling

---

23 It is worth using the terms 'more adaptive' or 'more innovative' frequently so as to emphasise that we are dealing with a continuous range, not two distinct types.

advantage. Innovators also need structure (probably more than they ever expect) and so abide by much of the current system much of the time. However, they find it limiting sooner and more often than more adaptive colleagues – this is a break in pattern quickly noticeable to those more adaptive. Innovators are comparatively more tolerant of ambiguity, at least for a time and in the area of current operations. Like adaptors, they are more or less tolerant of ambiguity depending on how critical the matter is to them (for instance, how much it may impinge on strongly held beliefs).

A-I theory, when first formulated, assumed preferred style to be set at an early age and to be highly stable. The evidence currently available supports this assumption. The KAI score was not devised so that individuals could be compared to a general population mean because, as no one associates with an entire population, more meaningful comparisons are between people who interact. Such comparisons mean that a person can be described as more adaptive compared to one person and more innovative compared to another, without any change of personal score. Likewise, one could be seen as noticeably adaptive in a work team, as in the middle at the tennis club, and as clearly innovative at home. Although one's preferred style does not change, different people might perceive the same person differently in regard to themselves than they do when making a more general comparison: 'We are both innovators, but you are more innovative than I.' This does imply that an individual's behaviour may need to vary (using learnt coping behaviour) in order to achieve success in various roles (with different people) and in pursuit of different goals in different contexts.

The foundations have now been laid to develop the adaption-innovation description, provide more detail, and attempt to integrate these elements into a coherent whole. Those who are more adaptive approach problems within consensually accepted, given terms of reference, theories, policies, precedents, and paradigms of the enveloping situation. They are more willing than the more innovative to master the details within these structures and respect them for their potential use. The rationale for this is part of their wider problem-solving strategy, which is to use current cognitive structure deliberately, and as a matter of cognitive strategy, to solve their problems. This strategy permits them to use this selected structure to limit the range of the problem in terms of that structure, producing sharper definition that is aimed at finding a solution that is patently relevant to it. Within the boundary of the definition of the problem the adaptor wants to solve, the area is economically limited to what seems to be necessary for problem solution. The understanding of the elements included within this definition (boundary) is aided by the adaptor strategy of problem solving within the prevailing (outer) paradigm. The paradigm is evaluated by the extent to which it gives guidance on what problem should be its domain, what elements should be relevant, what methodology it is wise to use, and so on. All the elements set by defining the problem (setting the substructure) are, therefore, generally understood. Given this start, and the more adaptive take more pains to establish such a start than do innovators, the more adaptive are more able to limit the breadth of likely solutions to those that appear relevant to the agreed definition of the problem. This limitation encourages them to believe that any solution that may now emerge will be seen as relevant to the problem, more likely to be accepted by others, and more likely to work; all of which is the rationale for the careful definition in the first place. This strategy further leads them to strive to provide solutions aimed more at being 'better' rather than being 'different'. The value of adaptors is obvious; they are the experts in the current system and dedicated to its continuance and efficiency –

no organisation can survive long without adaption, offered either by adaptors or by coping innovators. Adaptors, especially in innovator-orientated settings, report just as much coping behaviour, trying, they claim, to hold the works together and prevent frequently threatened collapse in the teeth of their more innovative colleagues' 'strangely inefficient ways' – as one adaptor phrased it.

By contrast, the more innovative are more liable to detach the problem from the way it is customarily perceived. In doing so they shed varying amounts of the detail that would otherwise help them define it more closely and that would indicate (as well as threaten to confine them to) the more expected avenues of solution. Working from this looser start, they are liable to indulge in wider solution search and so produce solutions that are more readily seen as different. The more they are indeed different (i.e., detached from existing structures that have been developed to understand reality *as generally conceived*) the more difficult it may be, even for the originators, to determine if their notions and solutions will turn out to be better. The more innovative are liable to be more critical of the structure they are likely to shed, including the very organisation within which they operate. Discarding structures hitherto perceived as useful has its obvious problems and involves more risk, but the strategy permits a more ready perception of the radical views and solutions that are likely to rearrange the very structure in which the problem resides. There is logic (reasoned structure) in both these approaches; the respective values depend on the extent to which the current structure offers its users the promise of solution within its boundary. No structures (including paradigms) can be used without altering them, as they were formulated on a base of past experience. The difference in problem solvers is how this structure is to be altered. The more adaptive problem solvers more readily accept modifications to the paradigm (or any structure) *as a result of* the improvements to it that they initiate; the more innovative are likely to see the need to change the paradigm (or any structure) *in order* to solve the problem. The term 'any structure' is inclusive; besides paradigms, it includes such structure as rules, mores, theories, customs, and even language.

The more adaptive are more likely to perceive current structures as worthy of their support not just because they are sanctioned but because they know them to be based on past success and therefore likely to prove useful again. They have already lasted for some time because they have proved their value and have been amenable to modification. Innovators tend not to believe this as readily, and often mistake those more adaptive than themselves to be simple conformers to authority (i.e., more structure!). Kirton (1977) showed that there was no statistically significant difference between adaptors and innovators on their stated likelihood of identifying with superiors. Curiously, in discussion with high innovator bosses, it transpires they both believe adaptors to be conformists and also complain that these same folk can be irritating in that they do not agree with them – their own high innovator bosses. It is just this kind of divisive misconception that prompted such studies to be undertaken, for these bosses have missed a cue; adaptors are not 'conformists' in their over-generalised sense (agreeing with anyone who fancies themselves as a model of authority), but conform, as a matter of cognitive strategy, to generally agreed guidelines that have been formed by many, over test and time, to assist in solving problems. They are not slaves to rules but respect them because, generally, they find them useful. The more adaptive like structure that they believe to be reasonable, and Kubes (1992), and Tullett & Davies (1997), found that using Schultz's Firo-B inventory (Fisher et al., 1995), they have a slightly (but significantly) higher tendency to accept instructions whereas the more innovative have an equally slight significant tendency to hand them out.

The more innovative are more likely to see some of the enveloping structure within which they currently work as more immediately limiting and, so, more of a hindrance to their enabling scope, than are adaptors. Again, misconceptions seem to abound. Innovators tend to believe they can manage with no structure – until, in class exercises, they realise how many they must take for granted; adaptors are often convinced that their innovative colleagues set out to irritate them by challenging all their cherished structures. The truth is that innovators are more likely to 'bend' such cherished structures without deliberate intention, on the way to trying to solve problems. Indeed, they are often not aware of the structures they have molested. What probably worries many adaptors more than the 'bending' is that innovators, when this is pointed out, do not seem to care as much as adaptors think they should. Another source of misunderstanding is that innovators tend to believe that adaptors are 'against change' and adaptors tend to believe that their more innovative colleagues like 'change for the sake of it' and have little interest in ensuring that the changes they propose are relevant to the group's current needs.

It is often difficult, in group discussions and exercises, to convince all parties that all people, irrespective of style, are likely to welcome change but that no one welcomes any and every change; that we are problem-solving organisms, par excellence, and so are carefully selective as to which problems to respond to and which proffered solution to accept. However, we are more comfortable problem solving in our preferred style of change, which implies one view of structure rather than another and a compatible style of solution. Like mankind in general, the majority of members of the groups we work in are successful and, rightly, attribute their individual problem solving as the reason for this success. It is easy, therefore, for those established in a field to lean to the conclusion that 'my way' tends to be superior to 'your way', whenever your way is different from mine. This seems to lead us often to ascribe level (capacity) judgements to differences in style – indeed, to all differences. Sometimes this seems justified, as a style will *on a specific occasion* be more effective than another, which is a far cry from assuming that it is *intrinsically* better, irrespective of circumstance.

Another common misunderstanding, this time in marketing, on the differences between the more innovative and 'others' (however defined), is that the former like and adopt new ideas and new products whereas the 'others' do not. As a consequence there is a search for 'new adopters', as they are described in innovative terms. There are in fact two distinct variables involved, the liking of what is 'new' and early adoption. Foxall and associates have undertaken five studies that show that innovators have only slightly greater taste for new products than do those more adaptive. What distinguished the styles is the nature of the product. Using T. S. Robertson's (1971) distinction between 'continuous' and 'discontinuous' products (all new), Foxall (see review, 1994) found that adaptors were significantly inclined to buy the one sort and innovators the other. Early adoption was not a significant distinguishing factor between adaptors and innovators but the nature of the product was. Another factor is brand loyalty; Foxall's work showed that the adaptors who believed in healthy foods bought new variants of such products more systematically than innovators. Mudd's studies (reviewed, 1990) also supported this distinction in relation to the adoption of new ideas. A-I theory assumes that all people problem solve and all people are, therefore, creative; all people like new ideas and all people like new products. However, it is obvious that no one likes all new ideas or all new products. Style is a variable that influences which new idea or product is preferred.

It comes as a surprise to most of the more innovative that they have what appears to be a marked adaption to defend structures that they have themselves just set up. First, they tend to overlook that they require structure in order to problem solve – as does any other thinking organism – even if they can remain more comfortable with somewhat less, at least for a while. However, the structure they require need not be as consensually agreed as the structure preferred by the more adaptive. At the end of the problem-solving process (if we can suppose an end for the sake of making this point) innovators like to feel they have solved the problem they have tackled and, in doing so, have created new structure. They are surprised if the more adaptive do not accept this new structure because elements of it are not founded on structure that is consensually agreed; the more innovative seem to have fewer doubts about it on these grounds, in such problem-solving circumstances. The shift is where the vital referent point for legitimacy lies; in consensus for the high adaptor and for self in the high innovator. The key to the innovators' dedicated defence of structure is that they believe their perception of the problem is useful, their solution based on it is useful and, therefore, it is consensual agreement that now needs to be changed. For the more adaptive to reach this kind of conclusion they require comparatively more evidence – the more adaptive one is, the more evidence is required. But if the adaptors take up an innovation, the scene becomes reformed. New political thoughts may not rise to being more than meetings in beer cellars, where manifestos are revised nightly, until the more adaptive join. Then adaptive structure helps form a party with an agreed structure and with a manifesto, revised not more often than yearly, aimed at gathering in others to join them.

Rogers (1959) in his elaboration of his 'creative loner', who resembles a person at the innovative pole of adaption-innovation, suggests that: '. . . the source or locus of evaluative judgement is internal . . . [although this] . . . does not mean that the constructively creative man is oblivious to, or unwilling to be aware of, the judgement of others. It is simply that the basis of evaluation lies within himself, in his more organismic reaction to, and appraisal of, his product' (p. 76). The innovator needs personal insight to consolidate a change within, or to, a paradigm; consensus is not enough. The adaptor, on the other hand, needs consensus to achieve the consolidation of a paradigm change; personal insight is not enough. Drawing strength from legitimacy but from different sources, both adaptors and innovators can be fanatical in the defence or promulgation of an idea – how else would some innovations, like jet engines or hovercraft, have become accepted? Indeed, there are often occasions when no amount of argument, no amount of common sense (as Schon, 1967, noted) will shake the innovation-inventor's confidence – any opposing contrary public view is just another structure that needs modifying! However, these statements of observations may have gone too far, in at least one aspect, and need refining. High innovators can produce ideas that others reject and which they protect and promote with fervour. But there are many examples of high-level, high innovators putting forward views that eventually collect (more adaptive) adherents – and they then move on, leaving these adherents to defend their last positions against the current ones the innovator-originator now holds. Freud was noted as a person whose theories moved on, leaving different sets of adherents behind in disagreement.

More confusion occurs over the term 'intuition'. Many high innovators believe they have a virtual monopoly on intuition, which they contrast with logic. As stated earlier, intuition is a thought process that is not consciously retrievable (the steps by which the conclusion is arrived at are not known or remembered). But the process may, nevertheless, be based on sound experience and lead to a conclusion. An advantage of such thinking is the speed at which one reaches a conclusion; the disadvantage is that if events prove it wrong there is no easy way to go back over the process and check for error. So, many innovators use logic well, just as all adaptors must use intuition. There are, however, differences between the more adaptive and the more innovative here also: As has been discussed earlier, adaptors like to check back their conclusions to consensually agreed positions before implementing them. If their intuitively derived solution can be seen as fitting the problem as initially defined (and in accord with agreed view), they are prepared to accept it; if not, they are likely to distrust it and rework their conclusions. Innovators are less likely to have the same need to check an intuition that is in discord with consensus – they may instead rework their original definition of the problem or they may set about consensus. However, those who have been well trained in science are more likely to know that intuition can be very useful as a way of setting up a hypothesis but is unacceptable as 'proof'; those poorly trained in scientific method cannot tell the difference between a hunch and the test of their hypotheses.

Innovators tend to overlook and even dismiss intrastructure change as unimportant, mere tinkering, and the process of getting there boring. Adaptors are wary of 'buying' innovative change that seems to treat essential structure too casually, to be overly risky and, by adaptor standards, to be inefficient or even irrelevant to the current view of a shared problem. We all have the tendency, in most situations with which we are familiar, to fancy our own style preference – seeing its virtues clearly but just as clearly seeing the faults of others' different style preference. It appears somewhat more difficult to see the faults emanating from one's own style and the advantages of a different style. That helps explain the persistence of one's own style preference even when it may not appear to be working effectively in some situations. An aspect of attribution theory also contributes to such stability of style preference. Mostly, people tend to attribute their failures to bad luck or to others; likewise people tend to attribute the success of others not like them to luck or to their own intervention. All these influences can readily lead us into the trap that all people who are different from us are so because they can't be like us or do not want to be like us; if the latter, could they be not only inferior but also hostile?

The scientific method is a template, a schema, of the ideal way (process) that a brain solves problems. A-I theory, like that of Kelly, assumes that all people use the scientific method whether they know it or not – indeed, any problem-solving animal uses the same basic steps – but if we do not know we are using it then we may not be able to apply it so rigorously. In this method, the first need is to understand the problem (Kelly's 'grasp of reality' or the problem-solving creativity field's 'problem identification'). The next stage is the formulation of a hypothesis ('solution search') followed by a test of it. If it works (the psychologist's 'positive reinforcement') or it doesn't ('negative reinforcement'), the information becomes part of the knowledge (science's 'addition to theory') of the individual. Taking the first stage, the perception of the problem, the physicist, according to Krauss (1994), needs to abstract from the problem as presented only the detail that is relevant and set aside all that is irrelevant. In an amusing example, he opines that if a physicist was asked to help with a problem of production in a dairy, he might well begin by drawing a circle on a blackboard and say: 'Assume the cow is a circle. . . .' The principle is that irrelevant detail will delay or prevent the problem being perceived in a form that allows a solution. The converse is just as true, for omitting a detail essential to a practical formulation of the problem will also prevent its solution. The difficulty is to determine what is essential and what is not. In A-I theory, the adaptor inclines to parsimonious inclusion aided by guideline structure and the innovator tends to more generous inclusion by liberal interpretation of the same or modified guidelines. Neither approach can guarantee success on every occasion; success often depends on matching an appropriate approach to what is needed to solve the specific problem, in the light of current knowledge and in prevailing circumstances. Style influences the perception of (and the methods applied to) all stages of the problem-solving process. Hence we always need all the variations in the style continuum, at some time and in some way, to solve complex, compound problems.

In the course of the Management Initiative study it was repeatedly noticed that managers tended not to be very willing to re-examine past failures (or even past successes) for fear of opening up damaging rifts within teams. They seemed to fear that such re-analyses would show up, too often for comfort, that essential detail, which should have been retained as a key element in the resolving of a problem, had been dropped and other detail, which greatly distracted them to no good purpose, should have been dropped but was retained. They were convinced that such an error 'should' have been obvious at the time. This is to use reanalysis with hindsight as a means of attributing blame rather than for learning – not usually a productive process. During a reanalysis that is intended as a learning exercise, a general guideline might be usefully kept in mind. When experience (cognitive resource) can be brought to bear on the problem, which is more obviously possible when the problem and its solution lie within the paradigm, progress is more confident and likely because the dangers can be more surely assessed. However, occasionally such adaptive confidence leads to inadequate critical analysis. Legitimate query may be wrongly taken as an assault on received wisdom and the integrity of the group itself. Hindsight should be used to learn more about when this can happen and arrange better guards against it – such as, in matters of great importance to the group, appointing a devil's advocate.

There are occasions when past knowledge becomes as much a hindrance as a help; when a departure from past patterns of thought and operation is needed. The more a hitherto useful detail needs to be dropped to obtain a quite different perception, the more the adaptor has difficulty – but especially so when such a detail is, at the time, part of the core understanding of the structure in which the problem is embedded. For this is normally the very material to be relied upon to get the solution. The innovator has less of a problem on what to drop but has more trouble deciding what to retain. The danger, then, is that those more adaptive fail to solve the problem because of retaining more than was essential; the more innovative because too much of what is still essential has also been dropped. There are some problems that lead their problem solvers in different directions before being resolved. The ancient Egyptian texts clearly pointed to the Valley of Kings as the most likely site for the tomb of Tutankhamun, yet persistent search had failed to find it. The force of the 'ancient guideline' diminished among all archaeologists and the search widened to many alternative sites without, however, any new clear direction to guide the seekers. Carter, with a distinctly more adaptive approach, returned to accepting the 'detail' of Egyptian text that had been shed, and revised the strategy from 'it's not here, we must look elsewhere' to 'it must be here, we have not looked hard enough.' A lesson derived from Management Initiative was that some perceptions of forthcoming problems could be read relatively easily by the core of a group (both adaptor or innovator) and be anticipated and prepared for by early action, by inclusion into forward planning, or even by contingency planning. Other forthcoming problems were missed by most (but never all) and required the greater stimulus of a precipitating event to restart the process of problem identification and resolution. We are reminded that both capacity and style are always variables in every part of the problem-solving process.

Of course the nature of the problem may outwit all comers, whatever their current capacity or preferred style. Some problems require a detailed grasp of the paradigm in which it is embedded beyond the current knowledge of anyone so far (such as the infilling and extension of the periodic table over years of scientific endeavour), whilst some problems require so innovative a perception that even the highest innovator might currently be too adaptive by comparison to cope (like needing to accept that the Earth is not necessarily at the centre of the universe, which also took many centuries to come about). Krauss (1994) argues that science, by creating systems and making its processes conscious and clear, helps us overcome these difficulties. These systems are not just in the identification of the appropriate style (or method) in which to tackle a problem but also in identifying and acquiring the necessary levels (manifest capacity) for all its appropriate elements. This observation applies widely, not just to science and high-level theory, but also to common problem solving in every team.

These differences in problem solving and creativity style produce distinctive patterns of behaviour of the kind that are usually described as traits, and so associate style with personality theory – see Box 6. As suggested earlier, all the elements of cognitive function, including style, are influences on behaviour. The more they are inbuilt in origin, like cognitive style, cognitive (potential) level, basic needs, and all processes that represent the operating elements of the cognitive departments (Figure 1), the more they have stable and widespread influences on behaviour. All these influences, together with the resulting stable patterns of behaviour, are collectively what describe and differentiate mankind from other organisms and, within mankind, one person uniquely from another; in short, the totality of these descriptions is personality. Various styles, because of the power of their influence on behaviour, can be equated with dimensions of personality. The summary table of A-I descriptions is, then, full of terms that are generally used as personality traits; they interrelate (intercorrelate) in meaningful patterns. The results of many studies show that they do this much as would be expected by the theory-generated hypotheses. They factor analyse into subsets that can find similarities with writings in other literature. These style factor traits relate to idea generation (sufficiency of originality), method of problem solving (efficiency style), and relationship to structure (rule–group conformity – representing, respectively, formal and informal structures). These factors also correlate with each other – they are all part of the same measure of the same theory. Finally, the traits generally relate to each other in an intuitively logical pattern; for example, the more one is innovative, the less one problem solves in ways that respect the paradigm and the more one can be seen as being a risk taker. Risk-taking has also (Jackson, 1976) been found, not unreasonably, to relate to sensation seeking. Goldsmith (1984), in his study, found these two traits not only to be correlated positively and equally highly with each other but also equally highly and positively to adaption-innovation. This is the kind of

Box 6 Trait characteristics of adaptors and innovators

Adaptors	*Innovators*
Perceived behaviour – as viewed by each other:	
Adaptors are seen by Innovators as: sound, conforming, safe, predictable, inflexible, wedded to the system, intolerant of ambiguity.	Innovators are seen by Adaptors as: glamorous, exciting, unsound, impractical, risky, abrasive, threatening the established system, and causing dissonance.
In problem defining:	
Adaptors tend to accept the problems as defined by consensus, accepting generally agreed constraints. Early resolution of problems, limiting disruption, and immediate increased efficiency are their more important considerations.	Innovators tend to reject the generally accepted perception of problems and redefine them. Their view of the problem may be hard to get across. They seem less concerned with immediate efficiency, looking to possible long-term gains.
In solution generating:	
Adaptors prefer to generate a few novel, creative, relevant, and acceptable solutions aimed at 'doing things better'. They have confidence in implementing such solutions effectively, despite size and complexity.	Innovators generally produce numerous ideas, some of which may not appear relevant or be acceptable to others. Such ideas often contain solutions which result in 'doing things differently'.
In policy formation:	
Adaptors prefer more well-established, structured situations. They are best at incorporating new data or events into existing structures or policies, making them more efficient.	Innovators prefer less tightly structured situations. They use new data as opportunities to set new structures or policies, accepting greater risk to the current paradigm.
In organisations:	
Adaptors are essential to managing current systems, but in times of unexpected changes from unexpected directions encounter difficulty regrouping established roles.	Innovators are essential in times of radical change or crisis, but may have trouble applying themselves to managing change within ongoing organisational structures.

pattern that, if predicted and then empirically supported, gives powerful validity both to the theory and its instrument.

The whole range of adaption-innovation (and not just, e.g., high innovation or moderate adaption) is essential for solving the wide diversity of problems that face individuals and groups over time. Of course, narrower elements of the range are more immediately useful in solving those problems that require mostly adaptive or innovative solutions. A diversity of problems requires a diverse team, which is difficult to manage because each individual's preference can also be seen to have disadvantages, especially by people not like them. It is easier (more comfortable, seemingly more safe) to get along with people like us. Yet having within a group a diversity of both capacity and style is an added resource to solving a greater array of problems. The summary of this is already well known in practice: Diversity within a team has great potential as long as its members can manage it. Helping the team's members to manage their diversity to common good, solving Problem A, is a prime task of the problem-solving leader.

The value to be had from the theory is that it reveals more of the problem-solving process, so encouraging better, more conscious, and more deliberate use of others' strengths, whilst remembering that what may appear as a strength or a weakness in one situation may be the exact opposite in another. Further, as members of a group come to appreciate the value of diversity in problem-solving styles, they tend to become more tolerant and even more appreciative of other kinds of diversity. A common mistake is to capitalise on others' weaknesses when it is mutually more profitable to make use of those others' strengths. This happens because we learn to solve problems naturally without the need to understand the process; theory helps to make this process open to inspection and part of conscious knowledge. It is valuable to know that some individual differences are stable – no life experience (becoming more mature, knowledgeable, or senior) will change them. The value of this knowledge is that it can assist us:

- to acquire fresh insight into interperson conflict (people with widely different styles tend to fall out);
- to use this insight to pave the way to more and more fruitful collaboration in teams;
- to assist each person in a team to get on with others while remaining different from them, by valuing the difference between them;
- to appreciate that there are advantages to the fact that preferred style is resistant to change, which makes colleagues more predictable; this stability is the basis of collaboration if the differences can be managed;
- to understand that coping behaviour is often needed but it is also expensive; the balance struck should be of mutual benefit to the members of the group (do not call for more than is needed).

Users of A-I theory generally agree that the more a team is heterogeneous the more difficult it is to recruit (to select appropriate people from among those unlike the selector), the more difficult it is to manage (the further people are away from one's own style, the harder it is to gauge their worth), and so the more effort needs to be expended to ensure effective collaboration. The pay-off is that those who can manage diversity well have added opportunity to manage change *both* widely and well. Conversely, those who cannot manage diversity well may be able to manage change well as long as the problems faced are not widely diverse. This approach may well be very efficient, concentrating on a narrow range of problems without the hassle of having to accommodate too much diversity – but this lasts only as long as the environment stays much the same. If it does not, and the change is not foreseen, then the narrowly diverse team is at a disadvantage, compounded by the very length and magnitude of their past, recent success – fertile ground for the disconcerting appearance of a precipitating event.

This is not new thinking. In exploring the conservative–radical dimension, Butler and Stokes (1969) show that political parties are coalitions, and so there are likely to be radical groups in conservative parties and conservative groups in radical parties. Indeed, in some cases over time the nature of a party can alter, the Communist party in Russia became notoriously conservative without changing its name or, seemingly, its orientation. Its original manifestos had been subject to considerable change but were locked within paradigmatic structures laid down at the beginning of that century. It faced parties to the West, of which even the most conservative had altered more significantly. The problems that institutions face alter as they mature (van der Molen, 1994; Vicere, 1992) and so does the balance of adaption-innovation of their members; it is not surprising, therefore, that an image may alter even if its name does not. All groups need their members to appraise the changing nature of the problems that face them and ensure that the diversity of their members reflect the changes, be they towards more adaption or more innovation. Similar changes are needed to reflect the changes in skills required. These changes need not only to reflect what is to be done now (or it will not survive into tomorrow) but also to prepare for what may need to be done in the future (while there is time to prepare efficiently).

We are not limited by instinct; the disadvantage is that there is so much more to learn and so much more that can go wrong while we learn. The pay-off is that we have added flexibility. In animals, the amount of variation of behaviour that is allowed for herd acceptance is ruled by instinct; even in humans, similarity is easier to accept. We have more freedom, at some cost, in learning wider tolerance to mutual advantage. We cannot, of course, dispose of all interpersonal structure or we would not be able to form teams or families. To form groups we need the facility of discrimination, so we may know who is rightly in-group and who is out-group. However, if we have the insight (and therefore the motive), we have the capacity, far beyond other animals that live in herds, to manipulate our own discrimination, and decide logically who we will or will not accept, although it may take time (and some reassurance) to accommodate the more unusual or unexpected diversity. There is wariness that this unfamiliar diversity might turn out to be a threat. The barriers, once up, may make it more difficult to form a contrary perception; many prophesies are self-fulfilling. Those with the diversity that is suspect may themselves, for exactly the same reasons, have similar wary views. Simple exhortations to be nice to one another may cause whoever makes such suggestions to be perceived as another threat. Fortunately, there is no instinctive bar to these views being relearnt – the value of diversity to mutual benefit can be taught.

Descriptions from factor traits

In addition to the total score, the adaption-innovation measure KAI also yields three subscores, representing three style subscales, relating to:

- idea generation: Sufficiency of Originality versus Proliferation of Originality (SO);
- problem-solving method: Efficiency (E);
- social structures: Rule (impersonal) and Group (personal) Conformity (RG).

These subscores have been obtained by factor analysis. Although they are significantly interrelated (as they must be, as subscores of a single measure of a unitary theory) they are also sufficiently conceptually and statistically separated (and have such high internal reliabilities – circa .8) that they can be used for additional interpretation. The analyses of the different general population samples show that they have the same constructional characteristics across languages. These analyses involve 12 further studies, using populations in several countries ($N = 4770$), with almost all the items in each study falling into the same factors as the original study[24]. Inspection of these factors showed that one pole of each factor showed resemblance to studies already in the literature: SO to Rogers (1959) when describing the creative loner; E to Weber (1970) when describing bureaucrats; R to Merton (1957) in his analysis of managers. These authors, however, envisaged their concepts as *unipolar* and, almost certainly, as *level* measures of *behaviour*. They are, therefore, different from A-I theory in these crucial ways. Further description will be given below after the general description of Adaption-Innovation.

Style of idea generation

The first factor (SO) is labelled Sufficiency–Proliferation of Originality. Adaptive ideation tends to operate within the prevailing paradigm, improving it as a by-product of problem solving. As an outcome, adaptors *prefer* (irrespective of capacity) to produce fewer ideas that are aimed at being seen as sound, useful, and relevant to the situation. They find this production strategy manageable, efficient, and satisfying. Innovators, with looser regard for the prevailing cognitive structures, *prefer* (also irrespective of capacity) to proliferate ideas. Among these ideas may be both paradigm-consistent and paradigm-cracking notions – innovators are less sure where the boundaries of the paradigm structures are. They tend to implement those that they find exciting and satisfying – often selecting one from among the more innovative. This ideation includes a characteristic similar to one that Rogers suggests for his creative loner: compulsively toying with ideas. When the two extreme types view each other pejoratively, as they tend to (see also Myers' notes for her S and N types – 1962, p. 76), the innovator claims that the adaptor originates with a finger on the stop button. The adaptor, in turn, sees the innovator as an idea originator who cannot find such a button.

These preferred styles have corresponding disadvantages. Even when they are needed, the more adaptive tend to produce too few truly radical paradigm-cracking ideas, especially when close in to the heartlands of a paradigm. Innovators are inclined to produce many more ideas, even when this proliferation does not seem to be needed, and they may have difficulty in selecting an appropriate one for implementation. Most high innovators seem well aware that the nature of their problem-solving strategy must lead to much of their idea output being discarded. As a strategy, the rejection of many of their ideas can be accepted as long as one or two pay off. Adaptors tend to

24 For 10 studies the overlap exceeds 80%.

produce fewer ideas as a matter of strategy; similarly, innovators tend to produce more, unless restricted. Under some conditions, for instance by varying the instructions, no differences between adaptors and innovators in the number of ideas that they *can* generate are exhibited (Kirton, 1978a; Casbolt, 1984; Kubes & Spillerova, 1992). However, the limit for *everyone* is the (task-relevant) level of his or her capacity, be that intelligence, knowledge, or experience.

Style of method

The second factor (E), a preference for adaptive efficiency (or intra-paradigm thoroughness), has a parallel with Weber's (1970) analysis of the aims of burcaucratic structure. In contrast to Rogers, Weber concentrates on what is, in A-I theory, the adaptor pole. He describes bureaucrats as being concerned with precision, reliability, and efficiency. Preference for thoroughness, attention to detail, and search in depth are also found in the adaptor description. Innovation involves a greater degree of discontinuity, and can rarely be expected to be adaptively efficient. A newly devised innovative product can only be expected to reach a state of high adaptive efficiency by development, itself more of an adaptive process. An example is the first paddle steamer. The promise of its radical new design principle rendered the sailing ship obsolete when it first appeared, but at that time it was a long way from achieving an efficient state compared with contemporary sailing ships, which embodied centuries of development of their design principle. However, the most efficient way to crack a paradigm is innovator 'efficiency' – rarely called such even by innovators – which entails, at the start of problem perception: shedding detail, treating paradigm boundaries as more permeable, working in less consensually agreed structure, ordering the contents of such structure in less consensual ways, being willing to accept less expected solutions, and being more willing to accept failure. But note the words 'more' and 'less' in this description; A-I theory stresses those more innovative also need structure to be able to think and language (another structure) to talk and write about it. They can feel more comfortable with less structure than the more adaptive and can manage with less of it consensually agreed, but not without it. These A-I differences are of degree, not absolute.

More innovative problem solvers who break, bend, or otherwise manipulate boundaries and their supporting substructures not only achieve a wider overview but tend to take themselves out of the system in which they began. The disadvantage is that they thereby often threaten their 'organisational fit'. Adaptors can work more easily in organisations, can achieve neater argument, and are less likely to get into a muddle or to find they are supporting unworkable solutions. In organisations, particularly those more mature, adaptors and their adaptive ideas are viewed as safe hands and good bets. Adaptive solutions to problems often seem so fitting as to be relatively easily acceptable to most others; indeed, many of these ideas seem to be just what has been needed. There is a danger here that such new ideas can be so readily accepted that they may not be examined with enough care and may then falter or fail for that reason. Fortunately for the more adaptive problem solvers, because their ideation tends to seem plausible (fitting the paradigm) and they tend to have a track record as sound paradigm improvers, they are better protected against their failures than those who are more innovative (particularly high innovators). Innovative ideas, conversely, may be discarded too soon, because they often appear to be irrelevant and half-baked – this is not surprising; they often are. The knack that management as a whole, especially the problem-solving leader, needs to acquire is how to select and run with the innovative idea they badly need whilst holding on to the adaption they also need.

Style of managing structure

The third factor (R), the style preference for relating to (difference in conforming to) structure, is primarily made up of two sorts: the formal, impersonal Rule and the more personal, less formal Group. These two elements within one factor are closely related, in practice as well as in theory, in that the members of a group monitor Rule, whether or not they originate it. If they do not, the rule ceases to operate, at least as far as the members of the group are concerned. Rule covers operating within rules, policies, theories, mores, and consensus (the social structure elements of paradigm). It has marked similarity to Merton's (1957) analysis of bureaucratic structure, which '. . . exerts a constant pressure on officials to be methodical, prudent, disciplined (and to attain) an unusual degree of conformity . . .' (p. 198). These qualities, for those who prefer them and use them well, yield high-quality adaption but markedly less innovation. Innovator preference is less responsive to such pressures, being more liable to disregard some current rule (or elements of it) in the development of ideas. Those who are more adaptive endeavour, whenever possible, to solve problems through relevant rules and groups. Conversely, the more innovative are more willing to solve problems at the expense of rule and group cohesion (or by first rearranging a rule), the integrity of which is less important to their cognitive operation and sense of well-being.

The more adaptive help members of a group work together to effect change. They generate ideas acceptable to the group and within agreed structure, modifying the rules in a more cautious, incremental, even piecemeal fashion, but gradually they achieve great changes for the better at a safer, more manageable pace than do innovators. The creative problem solving of adaptors, which is primarily concerned with continuously improving performance, is vital, long-term, to any organisation. On the other hand, the more innovative are better placed both to meet and to bring about challenging, unexpected changes swiftly at the expense of a current order within the group, which may, at times, need such a shake-up. So all groups also need those who are more innovative, in large or small doses, in one place or another, and at one time or another. Managing this balance profitably, but with minimum intragroup friction, tension or conflict, is a hallmark of successful problem-solving leadership.

PERCEPTION OF CHANGE

The concept of change has, explicitly or implicitly, been a key variable in the discussion so far. It plays an even more critical role from now on. We are all aware of a lot of change occurring around us, some of which we initiate ourselves. Before moving on, there are some aspects of change and the way we habitually handle it that are worth considering here in order to generate some common view that may fit our respective experiences. This may avert some danger of misunderstandings later.

The study of Management Initiative revealed that the perception of the problem stage was the one least likely to be examined with care before the process got fully under way. It seems from this that whereas specific changes, novelties, and challenges in the environment are taken up as problems, setting them into a wider context (e.g., into a whole class of such problems) is less often formally undertaken. This is readily understandable in a sound common-sense way – if the problem can be resolved without going to all this effort, why bother? As was noted in the study, occasionally this simple view backfired; but once set on a line of thinking (that one knows all that is needed in the case in hand) it requires insight and effort to reset the line.

One problem in understanding change is the need to define what is 'no change'. We talk as if there is such a state and, from a general practical point of view, at times and in some conditions this does appear to be the case. However, in strict fact, there is no such state of permanence if all examples are, on examination, not as unchanging as first perceived. Only recently we have become aware that the continents we stand on are not stable; they have been in motion since this planet was formed. Even our position in the galaxy and our galaxy's position in the universe are in constant change. In science all is change, whether we can perceive it or not. Heraclitus, a philosopher in the 5th century BC, wrote that 'no man steps the same river twice.' Carter (1998), two and a half millennia later, offers a modern version of the same view in a text on the operations of the brain: 'Millions of neurons fire in unison to produce the most trifling thought. New neural connections are made with every incoming sensation and old ones disappear as memories fade. In theory, each time a particular inter-connected group of neurons fires together it gives rise to the same fragment of thought, feeling or unconscious brain function, but in fact the brain is too fluid for an identical pattern of activity to arise – what really happens is that similar but subtly mutated firing patterns occur. *We never experience exactly the same thing twice*. . . . Little explosions and waves of new activity, each with a characteristic pattern, are produced, moment-by-moment, as the brain reacts to outside stimuli. This activity in turn creates a constantly changing environment, which the brain then reacts to as well. This creates a feedback loop . . . *that ensures constant change*' (quoted from Carter, 1998, p. 19; our italics). So, a modern parallel to Heraclitus' dictum that 'all is in a state of flux' is that *no one ever thinks the same thought twice*.

As another example, let us take a beautifully crafted flywheel, floating on a thin film of the purest oil. If the flywheel makes a single revolution round a perfectly constructed spindle, has there been any change to wheel or spindle as a consequence of that single revolution? The answer is, of course, nothing that is detectable by the most discerning instrument. However, if the flywheel rotates a thousand or perhaps a hundred thousand times, minute signs of wear may begin to appear. We could argue, however, that wear began with the first revolution. So change, however minute, can be securely assumed to have occurred from the first revolution, without even making reference to the fact that we would have changed the oil long before any detectable change to the wheel or spindle! The unlikelihood of there being any such state as 'no change' might be an interesting question to pose philosophically, but from a practical point of view, we may not be concerned about undetectable changes or, for that matter, changes that are of no consequence to us. We tend to dismiss such changes as 'no change' until such times as the flywheel exhibits a detectable wobble. However, we do not persist with such indifference if this flywheel is part of an aircraft, for then we may, prudently, apply preventative maintenance to replace it even before a detectable wobble is apparent. The loose use of the term 'no change' depends on a subjective evaluation, varying according to its perceived importance to us.

In fact, we must ignore a vast amount of change that goes on about us, and this makes for good sense. We cannot attend to every change; we are subjectively selective in problem identification. Indeed, a primitive part of the brain has a centre, the amygdala, that is heavily implicated in just such a process: 'The amygdala, in its capacity as intermediary between the senses and the emotions, is one structure that could underlie such "selective attention" . . . The amygdala's reciprocal on the cortex may explain why, in both monkeys and humans, emotionally charged events make a disproportionate impression' (Mishkin & Appenzeller, 1987, p. 10)[25]. This latter point was well represented in the theories of Thorndike at around the turn of the last century. He posited 'vividness' as one of the variables that brought about stimulus–response (S–R) bonding in basic trial-and-error learning. Among the changes we acknowledge, we tend to draw our own subjective line somewhere along a scale from a point of magnitude that we dismiss as no change, through to a point where we shrug off it off as 'trivial' change and on to what we consider 'real' change. The latter is further graded from minor change to great change, radical change, or even catastrophic change. Of course, this continuum has no clear internal boundaries and, again, our classifications are based on purely subjective judgements of what we feel is important to us at any particular time in some specific circumstance. Subjective judgement can be shared with others, so that groups can agree which changes that impinge on each one of us are to be addressed and which ignored. As there is so much change that we can detect, selecting which to attend to is a major problem for the brain. We cannot treat every change detected as a problem or every problem perceived as of anything like equal importance. We cannot stop to consider every conceivable aspect of a problem (or subject) before being able to make a decision. Quine & Ullian (1970) remind us, in their philosophical notion, the 'web of belief', that to understand any one thing in the universe, one has to understand every other aspect of the universe. We are also always short of information, making decisions in what, in the field of decision making, is called the condition of operating in a 'bounded rationality' (Simon, 1971), i.e., we can never know every possible outcome and its consequences beforehand. We need to take mental short cuts in order to survive – by dealing only with those problems that are deemed critical. Naturally, then, we have to make decisions before we can understand the universe or all possible outcomes, and here our subjective (often intuitive) interpretation comes into its own. However, these subjective judgements may sometimes lead to disagreement between us on what is change, what is radical change, and whether a change for one person is radical and for another conservative, trivial, or even 'no change at all'. Although disagreements occur, they are only about interpretations that we ourselves have made in the first instance. Yet, we cannot attend to all change but only to change that we deem important. Collaboration between people requires agreement on what change is to be addressed and what ignored. All aspects of brain function are involved: knowledge, experience, and skill; reason, intuition, and emotion; style can play a significant role.

---

25 The amygdala is part of the limbic system, so centrally placed within the brain as to have wide contact and effect elsewhere, see Figure 2, p. 90.

Perception of change moderated by style

Our perception of change is the essential first step in the perception of a problem and both of these are influenced by our thinking style – we perceive change differently from others. There is, for example, a marked tendency for those who are more innovative to dismiss more adaptive change (internal to an ordered system) as trivial or barely a change at all; whereas those who are more adaptive will often dismiss more innovative change (emanating at the edges of consensually agreed system) as being irrelevant and, therefore, useless. Of course, on a great many occasions there can be working agreement; it may be that we are barely aware of how much we tend to agree (not always wisely). The ability to arrive at decisions and evaluation rapidly, based on experience, is clearly a valuable asset in our adjustment to the world and for the most part serves us well. However, from time to time the very same approach turns out to have led us astray or to have led to division and dissent in a group, as we push for different solutions that are not recognised as being based on our different cognitive style. The resulting clash can make collaboration difficult, especially as the differences may develop into divisive generalisations. As has been said, innovators (or, to be more accurate, the more innovative) tend to dismiss adaptive change as mere tinkering with or within the current system. Yet these may be crucial changes that improve the system and keep it going. Similarly, adaptors may dismiss much innovative change as irrelevant or wild. Indeed, adaptors (or, to be more accurate, the more adaptive) may go a step further by saying that very often the innovators do not follow through in implementing their proposed changes, so in the end, after all the ideational froth, no useful change actually occurs! As pejorative views emanating from the contrary viewpoints start to multiply, the likelihood of personal conflict and clash increases, impairing healthy disagreement and debate.

Types of change in organisations

Thinking about the nature of change soon leads us to the concerns of the practitioner engaged in facilitating the implementation of planned change in organisations. Planned change, proposed or achieved, may be characterised as falling along a continuum, ranging from incremental (high adaptive) changes that involve fine-tuning the organisation, to discontinuous (high innovative) changes that entail fundamentally altering how the organisation operates (see, for instance, Nadler, 1988; Meyer et al., 1990). Such terms as 'Continuous Improvement' in TQM[26] and 'Business Process Re-engineering' are examples of current methodologies for organised change that may lie in the middle of the adaption-innovation range. In general, the current techniques commonly favoured in the creativity field simulate different degrees of innovation rather than adaption; others outside this field tend to simulate adaptive approaches. The differences between these techniques in the degree of innovation or adaption simulated are mostly determined by the design of the method; however, the interpretation of the instructions that go with each technique may well reflect the differences in the natural style of the operator (Isaksen et al., 2000). Adaptors tend to modify techniques that were intended to simulate innovation and innovators introduce innovation into essentially adaptive techniques.

26 Total Quality Management.

The different techniques were devised as suitable for encouraging different styles of problem solving. If appropriate to the problems being faced, brainstorming, for example, aiming at 'discontinuous changes', is often successful in assisting a group to concentrate, in one area and for a time, on 'doing things differently' (Drucker, 1969). Conversely, the TQM (total quality management) approach is thought to be better used to encourage problem solving within the context of an organisation's current and existing business strategy, structure, and culture, and so is aimed at 'doing things better' (Drucker, 1969). It seems likely that techniques such as 're-engineering' occupy the middle ranges of the continuum – having a useful spread from mild adaption to mild innovation, although failing to reach the heights of adaption or innovation that the others can. All these methods tend to involve several organisational dimensions, including structure, culture, reward systems, information processes, and work design. They also involve changing multiple levels of organisation, from top-level management through departments and work groups to individual jobs. At the individual level, discontinuous change involves a significant alteration of the mental structure in which the problem was originally perceived, whereas continuous change involves the mastery of the current system and all its detail. In the latter case, the individual has the 'protection of the system' that is to be modified; changes to the system come about as a result of solving the problem in hand. In the former case, as the new structure is as yet untried, all further action, which is now dependent on it, is a riskier operation. Understanding these distinctions is an important element in A-I theory, as are the value of these differences and the problems of collaboration.

Having set up these descriptions, however, a word of caution might be pertinent. The literature on planned change, particularly in the field of organisation development (OD), has an implicit bias (explicit in some writings, e.g., Tom Peters) towards equating 'large-scale' change with innovation and small changes with adaption. Of course, planned change, whether on a large scale or not, may be adaptive or innovative (see, for example, both Miles & Snow, 1978, and Nyström, 1979, on such notions as prospector and defender companies). In short, we are not dealing with *scope* or *magnitude* of change; not even with its effectiveness (these are all level matters); but rather with the *style* in which it is brought about. Level and style touch edges in that a style may be more or less appropriate in any specific situation; their clear distinction is, nevertheless, a critical element in the understanding A-I theory. In Box 7 are two examples of success, one adaptive and one innovative, but both at high levels of professional operation; there are four more contrasting examples, taken from military history, in Appendix 5. In Chapter 7, on Style, level, process and technique, these terms will be explored in detail.

Consultants using A-I theory often suggest that an effective way of putting over these style descriptions of people to others is not initially in personality terms, as this leads all too easily to defensive positioning, because personality descriptions often seem pejorative. Imagine this dialogue between person A and person B:

A: You take risks.
B: Everyone takes risks.
A: You take foolish risks.
B: I take calculated risks.
A: Everyone calculates risk; your calculated risks are foolhardy.
B: When you compare yourself to me, maybe; when I compare myself to you, you're timid.

Box 7 Examples of adaptive and innovative success

Because style and level are so frequently conflated, here are two examples of differing style both at high level and both successful.

Carter, in searching for the undiscovered tomb of Tutankhamun, combined his high intellectual capacity, a detailed knowledge of literary sources, and a search technique not hitherto used by archaeologists, with his preferred personal strategy of methodical, detailed cognitive operations. Relying on early Egyptian sources and eschewing the current intuitive flights of fancy of his colleagues, he settled on the Valley of the Kings as his search area. Then he applied a grid to the map of the area and from a meticulous search of the records eliminated each square known to have been subject to thorough field exploration. His own fieldwork began to cover the remaining areas. He ignored the opinion from site level that none of the areas left looked archaeologically promising. Guessing which of these remaining areas was likely did not much help him find the tomb at once. He was on his last season and an even more unpromising site when the tomb was found. His preferred adaptive cognitive style was not switched off at this success. He used the same mental strategy of operation that found the tomb: an ordered, painstaking, meticulous opening of the tomb, cataloguing and pre-serving the artefacts, which brought a new level of rigorous scientific method into this relatively new science of archeology.

By comparison, the search for a plausible structure for benzene with its six carbon and six hydrogen atoms defied the most persistent systematic reasoning, from its discovery by Faraday in 1825 to its resolution by Kekulé in 1865. The line of his solution, as he related years later, was set up in a reverie while on a bus journey. In his half-sleep, he seemed to see chains of carbon atoms come alive and dance before his eyes, then one chain coiled like a snake taking its tail into its mouth. He awoke with a start with the answer: The benzene molecule is a ring! Although much subsequent work and theorising were built on to this finding, it contained an awkward paradox. To fit the elegant, intuitively satisfy-ing pattern, three double carbon links were needed: Double-bonded compounds had been found to be unstable; but benzene was known to be stable. It was not until 1912 that Debye was able to propose a solution to this paradox (in a ring, negative poles can link with positive poles without a break) and not until 1936 that a Nobel Prize to Debye confirmed Kekulé's innovative intuition and the (meticulous) work subsequently carried out (see also Appendix 5 for more examples – culled from military history).

A way of avoiding this confrontational track is to start the descriptive differences in cognitive terms. Those who are more adaptive prefer tend to use more structure; those who are more innovative tend to solve problems with less of the originally given structure. Those who are more innovative often succeed by dropping some of the structure; the more adaptive often succeed by adding to current structure and refining it. Innovators tend to widen or develop uniquely held definitions; adaptors tend to tighten definitions. The key points are:

1   Adaption-innovation is:
   a   a cognitive style, which is the preferred manner of bringing about change;
   b   characteristic of the individual, i.e., it is stable over time and across situations;
   c   stable as distinguished from actual behaviour, which is flexible.
2   The gap between style and behaviour, when it occurs, is managed by coping behaviour, which is psychologically more costly to the individual than when behaving in one's preferred style.
3   Change is occurring all the time.
4   Judgements as to what is change, what is not change, and to what degree it is important, are all subjective.

MEASURE

Description

It is now necessary to provide information about KAI (Kirton Adaption-Innovation Inventory), the theory's measure. This book is not the manual and what is given here is enough information on KAI so that it can be relied upon and its findings (in the literature) can be placed in meaningful context.

This section is for the reader interested in the technical areas (otherwise, move on to The significance of KAI distributions on p. 71); it covers:

- a general description of the measure, with general population ranges and means;
- basic information on reliability and social desirability;
- normal distribution of general population samples;
- predictability of skewed distribution in selected samples;
- age of onset and stability of A-I preference;
- examination of the 'culture-free' assumption in this theory.

Kirton Adaption-Innovation Inventory (KAI) is a printed single page of items that require a paper-and-pencil response. Respondents are asked to assess themselves against each item presented, by indicating how it relates to them. The measure is untimed, but as the items are relatively few and the responses are relatively easy to give, in practice the measure is completed in about 10 to 15 minutes. Boredom and fatigue are not, therefore, problems in administration. Only a certified user can obtain KAI, which not only gives added protection to respondents but also enhances confidence in published results.

Discussions with selected experts assisted in the initial selection of items, so that they might have face validity, precision, and clarity. Rigorous item analyses followed, aimed at obtaining the high internal reliabilities. This led to obtaining repeated patterns among the items in the subsequent factor analyses, using general population samples, and using different language versions in several countries. Each item needed to survive a series of stringent conditions.

Initial validation is based on six general population samples, specially collected for that specific purpose *and not increased by any casual additional information collected for other purposes*. The samples came from 10 countries and totalled nearly 3000 subjects. The internal reliabilities range from .84 to .89 (mode: .87). The items yield scores that have an effective range of just over 100 points, that is, within the range of 40 to 150. The observed mean hovers around 95 (± 0.5) with a standard deviation of around 17 for all samples. For comparison, the theoretical range is 32 to 160; the theoretical mean is 96. Not one of these general population samples differs more than minutely from the average of the others; see Table A in Appendix 6. The results from each general population sample distribute on an almost perfect normal curve. This is exactly what was expected for any human (and animal) attribute – the normal, bell-shaped, Gaussian curve. This distribution is also the one expected from large, general population samples. The theory expects such a distribution whether the data represent a cognitive style or a dimension of personality – a distinction that is the subject of a later chapter.

There needs to be only a small difference between KAI scores of two people, or between a person and the mode of a group, for a difference to be noticed. Less than 10 points is unlikely to be noticed but 10 points or more is sure to be, over time[27]. When collaborating, people often try to close such gaps, temporarily and with some effort, by behaving differently from the way they prefer (to do) by using coping behaviour. If 10 points difference between individuals is, in psychology terminology, the 'just noticeable difference', 20 points is very clearly noticeable and large enough to require care to avoid breakdowns in communications (e.g., McCarthy, 1988). A gap of 30 or 40 points can cause real problems; such a gap needs constant attention to avoid misunderstanding and friction (Lindsay, 1985; Kubes & Spillerova, 1992; Rickards & Moger, 1994). These gaps are referred to in the A-I literature as the 'cognitive gap': This information will be useful in putting research findings into perspective; people having scores less than 10 apart are regarded as having 'same' score, between 10 and 19 apart as 'similar' scores and 20 or more apart as having 'different' scores.

The distribution of A-I scores in relation to the psychosocial variables of education, occupational status, age, and sex are discussed in appropriate sections below; in brief, the first three are not significantly correlated with KAI but there is a small, significant, and persistent difference between the sexes. Women are, on average, about one third of a standard deviation (6 to 7 points) more adaptive then men; this is so in all general population samples and every large relatively heterogeneous sample in every country for which there is such data. Males' scores generally are normally distributed around a mean of 98 and females' scores around 91, see Table F, Appendix 6. These findings are elaborated below.

KAI scores are always given back to respondents as actual scores and not blocked into 'boxes' such as 'high innovator' or 'moderate adaptor'. Most people object to being put into such 'boxes'; in addition, exact scores are more precise and therefore

27 The standard error of measurement (used for individual comparison) is approximately 6; the just noticeable difference is based (tested in some research and much practice) on this and one half of the standard deviation (of about 9) derived from general population samples. The standard error of the mean (for comparisons between groups of 50+) is less than 1.

more useful. Boxed scores are based on general population data and although most people have a passing interest in where they score generally, more important to them are the comparisons between themselves and some other person they know or between themselves and the mean of a group to which they belong. The mean difference between their group and that of another group is also of significance to them. If general population statistics are mostly more useful for researchers or as general guidelines, in practice an individual is more or less adaptive (or innovative) than others, rather than an adaptor or innovator in absolute terms. If one is a high adaptor then it is likely that most persons in comparison will be more innovative (and vice versa for high innovators). But even a high adaptor or innovator could be close to the mean of some groups he or she currently happens to be in, whilst being close to the extreme in some others. So all comparisons are relative to the chosen benchmark of significance to the person. This is not just a statistical issue – moving from one group to another and moving from being the most adaptive member to the most innovative does not alter one's KAI score but does alter one's role within the group. A person is either an adaptor or innovator to someone else, but if boxed scores are used they might suggest that there is a middle category made up of those who are 'neither adaptors nor innovators'. There are no such people.

Reliability

The measure was designed for the adult with work experience. The six general population samples, totalling over 2500 respondents, yielded internal reliability coefficients of around .87 (ranging from .84 to .89). Twenty-five other studies are listed in Table B, Appendix 6 (all with samples from 70 to more than 800); they show reliabilities of between .83 and .91 and 16 of them range from .86 to .89.

Teenagers

The inventory was intended for the sort of samples listed above – adults with work experience. However, it was not long before studies were attempted using younger subjects with little work experience. These proved successful to an unexpected degree. The first finding was, however, that KAI could not be administered in schools by untrained staff, even if they were teachers – the results were too variable. Teachers who were skilled in administering psychometric measures or other skilled administrators were uniformly more successful in getting reliable results. Skilled administrators, in five countries, carried out five studies involving a total of 800 students and pupils (aged between 14 and 18, with a small proportion of 19-year-olds). These studies yielded internal reliabilities of between .74 and .86. Three further studies, from Britain and the USA, using unskilled staff, did less well. One group of 15-year-olds ($N = 87$) yielded particularly poor results at .34; fortunately they were atypical, although what went wrong never became quite clear, except for one known factor – they were a group acknowledged to be less bright than average. This compared with the two samples of 14-year-olds that were selected as above average in capacity. The remaining seven groups, ranging between 14 and 17 years with a small number of 18-year-olds, totalling over 1700 subjects, yielded reliability coefficients of between .62 and .80. If a coefficient of .70 is accepted as the cut-off point at which confidence in the results can be sustained, then four of the seven groups (comprising a total of nearly

1200) achieved this level (between .76 and .80) even with inexperienced administrators. In addition to the critical need to use skilled administrators, two more lessons were learnt. One was that although younger people than expected could manage this sophisticated instrument, they needed to be of at least average brightness when aged 14–15 years, and above average brightness at 13 years (probably the youngest age limit for the measure's use). The key variable was simple command of English. A second variable was that they were less able to respond consistently to items which asked them to rate themselves, although they did well enough when it involved rating others or situations, which seems to be a matter of maturation rather than ability – see Table C in Appendix 6.

Reliability – other checks

Four test–retest studies have been undertaken in four countries, using 300 subjects, involving gaps between administrations of between 5 and 43 months. These studies yielded correlations of between .82 and .86. Two other studies, in two countries with over 200 subjects, but using *t*-tests of differences between means, yielded insignificant results. In two of these six studies the subjects knew their results from the first administration before they undertook the second administration – see Table D in Appendix 6. Five further studies (Watts, 1985; Goldsmith & Kerr, 1991; Murdock et al., 1993; Blissett & McGrath, 1996; Bobic et al., 1999) were undertaken in which the time between the first administration and the second was filled by a course that the authors assumed would lean the group towards increased innovation. In all four studies each group's results were unaffected by the intervention. To detail, as an example, the results of the most recent of these studies, six groups of managers (group size between 23 and 27; total $N = 149$) were retested after a gap of between 1 and 3 years. The mean difference between tests for these six groups ranged from −1.9 to +2.5, with an insignificant average for all groups combined of +0.15 KAI points.

There is a general expectation that level variables alter with age; some are expected to go up and others down. When style is confused with level, there is a general belief that innovation and 'therefore' creativity will decline. A-I theory assumes no change because no preference is expected to 'deteriorate' – but, if it did, what would constitute deterioration? Would that be a movement from adaption to innovation or a movement from innovation to adaption? Would the hypothesis vary according to the preference of whoever planned the study? If deterioration is ruled out, will it change, not because of age but for reasons of growing experience or the needs of an ongoing situation? The theory is firm that no change is expected – the scores show no significant variation, so such behavioural variation that occurs is usually recognised as temporary coping behaviour. Some evidence is reviewed in this section. These are studies that used adults as their subjects; studies using schoolchildren yielded similar results.

KAI has a number of checks that help indicate whether the respondent is answering as intended. The 'reject' rate is low in ordinary circumstances (less than 2%); but it can rise to unacceptably high levels under special conditions. One is if the administrator has not been clear as to why the instrument is being administered or what will happen to the results (e.g., who has access to them). The other main condition is a hostile environment – like a company that is undergoing downsizing; many in these samples gave what they estimate to be a 'politic' response. In the case of young subjects, the rejection rate is higher than for adults – rising, when using unskilled administrators, up to nearly 20%.

Social desirability

When the variable that an instrument has been designed to measure has one pole that might be regarded as more desirable than the other, a test of its possible inbuilt bias is needed. The procedure is to correlate it against a test of social desirability. The latter measure is deliberately designed to be biased; it is usually made up of items that almost beg the respondent to agree with them, so as to attain a score showing a socially desirable image. If both measures correlate, the newly designed one is suspected of yielding socially desirable results.

The six social desirability studies, using five different measures and nearly 800 subjects, yielded results that average close to zero – see Appendix 6, Table E. Of the six studies, five involved three different measures and, using 650 subjects, yielded insignificant correlations ranging between .13 and –.15. The sixth, by Elder & Johnson (1989), gave mixed results. They used two measures on 104 subjects; one aimed to tap 'conscious presentation' and the other 'unconscious presentation'. The first yielded an expected insignificant result at .15 but the second was just significant at .22. The actual gap is not large (it could be a chance result), but no explanation was offered. The overall result of the studies is that KAI is not, in general, affected by social desirability. However, this does not mean that care must not be taken against contamination. Some consultants and training establishments include the term 'innovation' as part of their titles, titles of their courses, or of the whole organisation. This proclaims their bias as if blazoned on the chest. The effect on those who have dealings with them is to ensure that, given this blatant cue, they 'do well' in their presence by according the bias appropriate reverence. In other places and times, the terms 'sound', 'professional', or 'workmanlike' had just the same effect, almost certainly in the opposite direction. Such bias will have unfortunate effect on the scores of any measure of this kind.

Social desirability arises when respondents have an evaluative view of the different ends of the A-I continuum, a motive for presenting the 'right' image relating to the context they are in, and know how to fake but be undetected. It is not hard for anyone to detect when groups feel under pressure to conform to some 'ideal image' required by management (or, e.g., teachers). When respondents try to present the acceptable image, their responses are often so erratic as to be easily detectable. People find it hard, for instance, to have a deeply seated preference for using structure to solve problems and, at the same time, present themselves as having just as deeply seated a preference for bending those same structures. An early exploration of people's capacity to present what they thought was an ideal was by Skinner (1989). Students were asked to respond as if they were an 'effective manager'; the female students' responses averaged 99 (the same as the general population male mean) whereas the males' responses averaged 91 (almost exactly the female mean). The sex of this 'effective manager' had not been specified: When it was, the male and female students again disagreed; this time the 'effective' male manager was thought to be more innovative than 'effective' female managers at about the male mean; the female students guessed the male manager's mean as more innovative than the general population male mean. These students were also asked to respond as if they were 'typical' males and females.

The female students exaggerated the sex gap, placing typical males on nearly 100 and females at 84; the males made a more accurate guess that lay within this range. Furnham (1990; see also Kirton, 1991) actually asked his students to fake scores as if applying for a job. The results were so unlikely as to fool no researcher or administrator. When respondents were asked to guess the A-I orientation of colleagues they knew, however, they were both highly accurate (correlation of .8 and more) and their estimates were statistically reliable (Kirton & McCarthy, 1985; Clapp & de Ciantis, 1989).

The significance of KAI distributions

The distribution of scores with large populations, when plotted, may also form a normal curve, as general population samples do. These are groups that include a wide range of people within them and in which wide ranges of adaptors and innovators can thrive equally well, e.g., managers in Italy or teachers in the United States. The reason is that these jobs are made up of identifiable subsets that face different sets of problems and can, therefore, have a wide range of different people to solve them. These subsets, when aggregated into larger groups, then yield means close to those of general populations. The breakdown of teachers into subsets by subject shows predictable differences, with, for instance, drama teachers being almost all younger female innovators and maths teachers being mostly older male adaptors (Kirton et al., 1991). From the first validating general population sample, subsets were extracted and their means and standard deviations noted; for instance, in the main general UK population sample ($N = 532$), 88 respondents (mainly males) described themselves as managers. The mean score of this group was found to be 97, with a standard deviation of 17. Since then, four more studies involving managers have been completed in Britain, Italy, and Singapore; all five studies, with 937 managers, yielded a weighted mean of 96 with a standard deviation of about 16. A year's intake of US officers ($N = 388$, mostly males) into a standard course required for future promotion held at the National Defense University, Washington yielded a mean KAI score of 97, *SD* 18 (unpublished correspondence, Parks, 1987). There were many more men than women in all these samples, which may largely account for the small difference between their mean and that of the general population (95), and their being closer to the male mean (of 98). Male managers as a group exhibited a wide age range and are distinguished from other males by an average higher level of education and, of course, socioeconomic status but not style preference. The largest analysis of a single occupation, showing the means of identifiable subsets skewed in predictable directions, is for engineers (Table K, Appendix 6). It must be stressed that although the means of these groups may be significantly different from the population mean, there is little suggestion (if the group is of even modest size, e.g., about 50) that the range is narrow, as these groups tend to be well distributed around their mean. For instance, production and accounting departments usually have mean scores between 80 and 90, with some people in them being as much as 40 points from the average of their group. All the recorded means of marketing and R&D departments lie between 100 and 110, with equally wide ranges.

Smaller samples, however, may not be large enough to mask incidental bias in selection. On the other hand, selected samples may need to have a different distribution in order to be in accord with what they are, mainly, expected to do. These distribution variations, away from normal curves, need to be expected by the theory to which the measure is related. KAI results do skew predictably, as numerous studies show. A-I theory assumes that people form groups in order to solve problems more effectively than individuals can alone (as do all organisms). Some problems, or problem situations, are best tackled by use of the prevailing paradigm, meticulous mastery and use of available detail, and an inductive drilling towards the identification of the key factors in the domain. Others cannot readily, if at all, be solved this way, requiring an initial wider viewpoint obtained through a deductive approach. Nevertheless, the complex of problems generally requiring resolution by specific groups may well contain a preponderance of those that are more readily solved by either more adaption or more innovation. A-I theory assumes that each working group's mean will reflect this inclination. Hence the differences in the means found between production and accounting departments compared with marketing and R&D. However, as these groups cannot hope to have all their problems solved by any one skill or any narrow range of style, the ranges of all these groups are usually also large, almost always reflecting the size of the group, as would be expected statistically. The results of many studies show that they supported their authors' expectations: (a) means in occupations are in accord with the style required to deal with the bulk of the tasks and (b) score ranges remain wide.

Two arguments are being developed to account for these systematic differences in group means. One is that any occupational group, because of the nature of the principal tasks to be solved, has a mean different from that of the general population. The other is that a group's mean may be that of the general population because it contains clearly defined subsets of people who have a different set of tasks from others reflected by a different KAI group. These subset means, when aggregated into the whole group mean, will balance out the variation until the whole group's mean approximates that of the general population – as in the example of engineers. Such groups need to be of large size for this phenomenon to be noticed.

A group's mean will play a large role in setting the group's 'cognitive' climate, which is an important influence on all members of the group as another shared cognitive structure. The group generates a climate that is either more adaptive or innovative than that of the general population, reflecting both its members' style distribution and the style of most of the tasks they perform. In such circumstances it has been found that whether the new intakes are similar to the established members of the group or not, over a period of time they will become so, as a result of turnover (Hayward & Everett, 1983), and the range will narrow somewhat. It has been argued that groups such as bankers, accountants, and those involved in production, all of whom are largely required to work within a single system (however complex its operation) in which the answer to problems can be found, tend to be adaptive (Kirton, 1980; Thomson, 1980; Kirton & Pender, 1982; Gul, 1986; Hayward & Everett, 1983; Holland, 1987; Foxall, 1986a; Gryskiewicz et al., 1987). Conversely, those groups of employees required to work in an environment where more than one main system is involved (such as having to interface between other systems, like the company and the market; the management and the workforce) tend to have more innovative means. Research shows employees in R&D, planning, personnel, and marketing to be on the innovative side of the general population mean (Keller & Holland, 1978a; Kirton, 1980; Thomson, 1980; Kirton & Pender, 1982; Foxall, 1986a; Gryskiewicz et al., 1987; Lowe & Taylor, 1986; McCarthy, 1993).

It has already been noted that ranges of large groups are wide, in whatever direction the mean may be skewed. This provides a degree of diversity and causes some interesting problems as well as advantages to the problem-solving leadership of the group (Kirton, 1987). There is a yet more complicated position to uncover. Not only do individuals survive in groups whose 'climate' mean is far from their own, but there may be whole subsets of such people (see Gul, 1986; Foxall, 1986b; Gryskiewicz et al., 1987; Foxall & Payne, 1989; Foxall et al., 1990; Foxall, Payne & Walters, 1992). For example among accountants (in Gul, ibid), who are generally adaptive, there are subsets who are, on average, more innovative (such as financial advisors; Kirton, 1980); they may be so even compared to the general population and not merely from their colleagues. The danger of stereotyping can readily be seen from the breakdown of those subsamples of engineers (see Appendix 6, Table K).

Thomson (1980) has shown that English-speaking ethnic Chinese managers working in local industry in Singapore had means (98) identical to those of UK, US, and Italian managers in general. They differed in mean score from middle-ranking civil servants in Singapore (89), who are just as mildly adaptive as civil servants in the West (85). The Singapore managers in local industry yielded the generally expected score of just over 95, whereas (Thomson, 1985) those managers who had joined multinational companies (becoming boundary-breakers by shifting into pockets of Western culture) had a significantly more innovative group mean (106).

Male–Female score difference

When A-I theory was conceived, one assumption was that this characteristic style is so deep-seated in cognitive function that no differences would be found between people of different ages, sex, or background of any kind: class, occupational status, country, or culture. All these are found to be correct except for sex differences; as already stated, the difference between males and females is small (between one quarter and one third standard deviation or between 5 and 7 points) but completely consistent for all large groups. No explanation of this difference has yet been published, although discussions with anthropologists suggest that it may have been useful to the species during hunter-gatherer times. However, for small groups there are more variations. As with the (mostly male) Chinese managers above, groups of women who appear in places where the prevailing culture would find that 'unexpected' have a more innovative mean score. It may not only be more innovative when compared to other women but also than comparable male means. This variation does not appear to be a function of gender but is more general, as the Chinese male manager data suggest. So, one source of data for females (McCarthy, 1988, 1993) suggests that it may be a function of how long the fields they occupy have employed women. Means are as expected where the women have had a long history of being in the job but more innovative where they have only recently been employed in it. For personnel managers the difference between males (108) and females (101) was the same as the difference between males and females generally. This suggests that neither the job nor 'culture expectation' played a role. For engineering managers the gap was much larger, with the women having a mean significantly more innovative (102) than the male engineers (98) – as is seen in Table K, Appendix 6. A variant on this is a study on the 'glass ceiling' notion – that women are still less 'expected' in the higher ranks of management. Kaufmann et al. (1996) find that mean scores of junior manager males ($N = 93$)

are more innovative than women ($N = 37$) at the same level; at middle management, males ($N = 282$) averaged the same as the females ($N = 102$); at senior levels males ($N = 30$) scored more adaptively than females ($N = 9$). Despite the small N in the last category, the pattern is persuasively consistent. There are other examples, not related specifically to male–female differences, of group means being more innovative when its members have 'broken boundaries' (that is, have indulged in something that is not usual in the cultural setting). For example, this is true of those in entrepreneurial enterprises (Tandon, 1987; Buttner & Gryskiewicz, 1993) as well as those Singaporean nationals working in a multinational company.

Differences that seem to derive from cultural expectation are likely to change; as the cultural expectation changes so might the mean of the groups. This was shown in the difference between personnel managers (women have held such jobs almost from the beginning of the last century) and engineering jobs (women have only comparatively recently taken these up). To conclude these analyses of sex differences, Foxall et al. (1990, 1992; see Table 1) provide a set of comparisons that helps to give clarity to this discussion: '. . . women whose occupations are not usually followed by female members of their societies tend to score more innovatively than men in those occupations. While it is commonplace for female managers in the USA to undertake MBA programs, this is comparatively rare in Australia where such programs are less well established and even rarer in the UK where MBA programs are a comparatively more recent development. Three relationships may, therefore, be hypothesised. (a) In the UK women MBA students should score more innovatively than the female norm, to the point of exceeding the scores for men. (b) In Australia the women should score more highly than "expected", equalling the scores for men. (c) In the USA the scores of MBA students should follow the pattern for the general population, with men scoring more innovatively than women.' This pattern was the one supported by the results (based on $\Sigma N = 369$) of Foxall's study. Rickards & Puccio (1992), using US data, closely confirm the British results, which met the prediction that women MBAs in the UK, being fewer in number, are on average more innovative (see Table 1).

To place these data into the wider context of the breaking of boundaries: In Western business culture, becoming an entrepreneur is seen as risky and boundary-breaking, and the mean for this group has been found to be more innovative, as expected (Tandon, 1987; Buttner & Gryskiewicz, 1993). Evidence from the MBA studies and others suggest that whereas perceived risk may continue to influence means by selectively attracting or putting off different people, other variables (like sex) can also become involved as different groups may perceive risk differently. They may also have different mean likes and dislikes. Conversely, as the MBA data show, where it becomes customary for women to take up the study, the mean of the enlarged group becomes less innovative.

Table 1 Scores and the breaking of boundaries

N	Country	Mean	SD	Reference
131	US	101.9	15.6	
123	Australia	106.1	13.8	Foxall et al. (1990)
115	UK	110.2	14.4	
120	UK	107.8	15.2	Rickards & Puccio (1992)

Self-select versus other groups

Another example of group differences that yield different KAI means is between those who choose to go on some courses and those who are sent on them. Kirton & Pender (1982) show mean differences related to two selection factors for managers attending courses: the type of course and the degree to which the participating individual chose to come as opposed to being sent. Some courses could be seen as 'unusual', 'different', or 'on the edge of current practice', such as courses in creativity. However, the mean for the successive course members of one such course has been steadily becoming more adaptive over the years (Gryskiewicz et al., 1982). While 'trendy' courses will disproportionately attract innovators, 'specialist' courses that give technical updates will attract a wide range because they are needed, but they may appeal to the more adaptive (e.g., Gul, 1986; Foxall & Bhate, 1991). At the time that the Singapore data were collected there was, and had been for some years, a boom leading to shortages of manpower of all sorts, including managers. Under these conditions managers could easily either opt to work in a multinational (and so cross a 'cultural boundary') or follow a more usual route of employment in local industry. Just as for women breaking into a new area (for them) and for entrepreneurs in general, the more adventurous tend to be the more innovative. The key point to remember in this phenomenon is the relative meaning of 'minority'. Entrepreneurs are a minority in that few people take the risk of failure and the attendant costs of setting up a private venture. Women who gamble on entering an area not traditional for them take similar risks and are a minority among women at work; likewise, most of the young managers in Singapore work in local industry. So, in this context, 'minority' also means a minority in a particular context but not necessarily in the general population; e.g., in general there are as many women as men; Chinese managers are in the majority in Singapore with expatriate managers in the very distinct minority, even within their multinational organisations. The expatriate managers, interestingly, may themselves have, on average and for the same reasons, a more innovative mean than the average for staff in their Head Office! For all individuals, crossing boundaries involves added risk, which is more attractive (or less aversive) to innovators.

To summarise, innovativeness helps a person get to places that are unusual for the group to which the person may belong, but once into the 'unlikely' structure it becomes as enveloping a 'structure' as any other. That means, unfortunately for many who cross these cultural boundaries, that innovation is not the ideal preferred cognitive style for staying comfortably in the 'unexpected' (or just plain riskier) place – adaption may now be more appropriate. The failure rate for newly founded entrepreneurial ventures is high. This suggests that the complex, continuous problem is a moving target, in which an individual may be cognitively ideally suited to some phases but, as a result of *successful* resolution, may not be as well suited to the succeeding phases that emerge later.

No culture differences

There are now available validation data on a number of the different language versions of KAI (Italian, French, Dutch, and Slovak/Czech). All were based on general population samples, totalling nearly 3000 from the UK, USA, Canada, France, Italy, Netherlands, Belgium, Switzerland, and (the then) Czechoslovakia – see Table A in

Appendix 6. What can be noted from this table is that there are no distinguishing differences in distribution among them – nor were any expected in the theoretical formulation of this theory and measure. This is convenient, as scores obtained in one place in one language are closely comparable to scores obtained elsewhere in another language. This required the same rigorous item analysis undertaken in the initial UK general population samples to be repeated in all the others; each required 2 or 3 years work. Even the factor analysis replicated closely. However, this concordance of data could not have been achieved unless the underlying structure was the same. If the concept of A-I and what is being measured by KAI is the inbuilt style preference of individual cognition, it is possible that the basic construction of the brain is involved. If linked to biology (see van der Molen, 1994), this bias would have appeared earlier than culture and, therefore, is likely to have a deeper, wider, and more significant effect on behaviour within the species as a whole. That is not to say that culture does not affect behaviour, but rather that culture does not affect the way the brain operates, as Prato Previde (1991) and Kubes (1998) observe, based on their work that involved the completion of the Italian and Slovak/Czech translations and validations respectively. It should follow, then, that patterns of differences found in one country should be found in others; this is what has been found. For instance, the means reported for teachers in the USA and Britain are identical; as are the means for Italian, British, and Singaporean managers; the teacher mean is around 95 and the manager mean is around 97, suggesting a difference attributable to occupation rather than to culture. The difference between the two occupation groups is that there are more males than females in management than in teaching, in each country.

Tullet (1997, see also Table L, Appendix 6), after assisting in the validations of the KAI French and Dutch language versions, also supported this view. He was able to study not only all the national general population samples then available but also was able to compare data derived from 13 samples (with over 3000 subjects) relating to five occupational groups (with at least two samples from different countries for each occupation) from five countries. The means of the samples from the same occupation groups but from different countries were always away from the mean of the general population in the same direction and by roughly the same amount. This suggests that, as the KAI scores are thought to be highly resistant to change, the nature of the problems met in each occupation affected the selection and self-selection of people who took up the occupation.

The A-I concept, and therefore its measure, is culture-free in theory and so far has been found so in practice. Different groups (such as countries) may seem to have a cultural value for more or less adaption or innovation, but this tends to vary over time. What may be a trendy acceptable value today may not be the one valued in decades past or, probably, in decades ahead. Whatever the trend, A-I is normally distributed.

Stability

In the earlier chapters the theoretical structure of A-I suggested that cognitive style is part of cognition function and that it is deep-seated and its influence pervasive – as are dimensions of personality. Van der Molen (1994) suggested that A-I related behaviour can be observed in animals and that in style, an inherited component is probable. If potential level (like intelligence) also has an inherited component, as seems most likely, then so does all cognitive effect. It was also argued that one's preferred style does not alter but behaviour can be varied, at the cost of coping behaviour, to fit the demands of the problems being solved. (We are also ingenious in finding ways round level limits.) These arguments can be subject to test, such as the stability of individual style preference. The measure of adaption-innovation depends, necessarily, on items that describe behaviour, although in each case the respondent is asked for a response that reflects a general, persistent pattern. The response to each item may, therefore, reflect a mini-survey of behaviour within a narrow sphere; since all the items are individually significantly related to the remainder, the internal reliability of the measure is high. This is the first sign of a general stability of concept, since if the concept were unstable the items would be too, and high reliability would not be achieved and maintained over time.

Cultural pressure does not affect personal preference, as argued above, although it may well alter occasional behaviour. Those that suppose that there is a general, culture-wide pressure to be more adaptive or innovative should expect that the distribution would show skew between large samples drawn from different cultures. This has not been found to be so (see Appendix 6, Table A and particularly Tullett, 1997, Table L). For those old enough to have been schooled before and during the Second World War, there is a memory that although behaviour we might now label 'innovation' was admired by some (when it proved successful and especially if it happened somewhere else, disturbing other people), the prevailing mode in most institutions (e.g., school, government, established industry) was adaptive orientated. Many people living then were included in the population samples. Age differences were not significant; there is no suggestion in A-I research that populations change their mean scores. Also, the popularity nowadays of anything that might be classed as innovative might suggest that KAI results would show high correlations with measures of social desirability. The evidence is overwhelmingly to the contrary.

The stability of KAI scores is one of the measure's validity criteria, as it is expected from most scholars, e.g., McKenna, 1983, that they should be virtually impervious to change. Any operations away from preference can only be achieved by coping behaviour; that costs more effort than behaviour in accord with preference, and is so used economically. Cognitive gap is the discrepancy between what one would prefer to do and what one is expected to do, between self and (a) job requirement, (b) another person, (c) the mean (climate) of a group that one is in or that one is dealing with. Difficulty rises sharply with increasing gap (as reported earlier, starting at about 20 points), though that does not necessarily mean that these disparate people do not get on. They may do so very successfully and admire each other, differences and all; indeed, the most successful accommodation is to admire the difference rather than tolerate it. However, success in no way implies diminished difficulty; it means successfully managed difficulty to mutual benefit. The added effort does not go away, it is seen as a more than acceptable price for the pay-off.

Stability is further observed, not only in the persistence of scores over time and the way that the internal reliabilities are uniformly high, but in the relationship between A-I and personality. In the next chapter, on style and personality, the large array of trait correlates of adaption-innovation tested in the literature will be seen. For a person to appear suddenly to be an innovator, having previously been a marked adaptor, would mean a change of scores on all, or at least most, traits. This is the kind of metamorphosis that gave rise to the story of Dr Jekyll and Mr Hyde – which is a horror story, after all! The next indication of stability is that the numerous validation studies that have tested each theoretical and descriptive element of adaption-innovation interrelate significantly, in the same expected directions. The studies with clear hypotheses and adequate samples report stable correlates of adaption-innovation. Of course the correlations are not perfect; they never are. However, to be generally recognised as more or less adaptive (say) and to score so on the measure, it is not necessary to have each characteristic element of the total personality description to the same level. This is analogous to any 'gene package' responsible, say, for family likeness, in that it may be sufficient only to partake of a critical number of elements, of which some are taken to a critical level, for recognition to be secure. In addition, the elements presumed to be part of the 'gene package' can be shown to be intercorrelated. All the personality measures deemed to represent correlates of A-I (see Table G, Appendix 6) are themselves highly stable, as traits are expected to be. It is generally expected (e.g., Eysenck, 1967, following in the path blazed by Jung) that dimensions of personality, which are composed of related agglomerates of traits, would be even more pervasive and stable. Indeed, Eysenck argues that all true dimensions may be expected to have an inherited component. It should follow, then, that an individual's KAI score should be persistent over time and circumstance, even in the face of difficulty and at cost – and the studies have shown this.

Rickards & Moger (1994) report a successful relationship between two members 80 KAI points apart, when only 10 is estimated as the just noticeable difference and 20 as the start of problems in communications. They are a successful pair, yet it would surely have been more comfortable if the two members of this partnership could have shifted closer in adaptiveness-innovativeness – they did not. One might dismiss this study because it could be the success of this couple that held the difference intact, despite the problems encountered in collaboration. However, success was not the pattern in the other two case studies so far published. In Lindsay's (1985) study the 'odd-man out' in the team eventually lost his job, despite Lindsay's consultant-cum-counselling endeavours. The gap between the variant team member and his boss and deputy boss was 118 vs. 90 and 82 respectively. The 'cognitive style gap' between the employee and the boss was a mere 28 points on a scale with an observed range of just over 100 points. Allowing for a little goodwill, insight on the need for diversity, and a pinch of coping behaviour, these men needed to move (permanently, or even just on the occasions that they met) by a mere 10 points each to have reduced the gap to about half the KAI's standard error of measurement. It could be argued that other factors may have contributed to the conflict. True, but Lindsay reports that it was differences in the style of problem solving that began the rift. This rift was exacerbated by pressures and anxieties generated within the climate in which the team was working. It continued to develop until deteriorating relationships seemed to have reached a 'point of no return' – at about the time Lindsay became involved. In the Kubes case study above, the 'odd man out', a young woman scientist, was saved by intervention in the nick of time to the benefit of the whole team, including herself. But Kubes had to deal with ominous signs of others taking part in the dispute between the protagonists, which would have entrenched the split. The possibility that additional variables could emerge to feed a growing war, even variables that may not originally be a source of problems, suggests that timeliness is as important a factor as patient tactful counselling based on insights into the management of diversity. Certainly, the evidence from these and other studies (which will be examined in the next chapter) is that preferred style changes do not occur despite pressures on participants to change. Indeed, had such change been of relatively little cost to the participants these problems could have been avoided, or at least substantially mitigated. This would have happened even if each of the participants had changed behaviour patterns by a little. The fact that they did not adds credence to the notion that adaption-innovation preference is highly resistant to change. Unfortunately, under provocation, coping behaviour that might help is liable to be switched off by both parties; divisions are then enhanced and entrenched.

Group collaboration is dependent on people being able to make predictions about each other, thereby engendering understanding and trust – another case of 'structure' being enabling. Being able to project a consistent, predictable image of oneself is reassuring and requires having everyone else in the group do so too. The differences must not only be stable, but also presented as friendly – or at least neutral. Any group that spends its time warily watching its own members is unlikely to be effective for very long; being persistently different can be trouble enough. Hence we have endless fascination, and from time to time, difficulty, with differences between men and women, young and old, one culture and another. It takes much learning and high motivation to manage those different significant others we need in close association for successful day-to-day living. To get sudden, fundamental changes within this pattern would be very hard to manage. The easiest changes to accommodate are those that can be readily understood or even predicted. These are ones in which the motives for change 'make sense'. So when an adaptor observes someone determinedly and persistently trying to solve adaptive problems innovatively (or vice versa), this is contrary to what one might anticipate and makes no immediate sense – impatience rather than understanding may be the immediate reaction.

The notion that problem-solving preference may be deeper-seated than the (learnt) manifestations of most motives may not always be readily grasped. Even more difficult to grasp is that we, as well as they, behave this way – but in other circumstances. These problems arise because the preference for a style of problem solving is so stable that it is sometimes pursued in the teeth of circumstance. One study that helps make this point clearly is that of Hayward & Everett (1983). When a UK local government experimental (innovatively orientated) unit was accepted within its (adaptively orientated) establishment, members were offered back-seniority and other advantages of being 'established'; in return they were expected to act as establishment people (i.e., adhere strictly to the rules and customs of the establishment). Table 2 shows that, during a 5-year period, one third of the original group left rather than live with this generous offer. This group initially had had a KAI mean of 107; after losing the departing subset (with its high innovative mean of 121), the remainder averaged 100 – turnover had begun to close the gap between the groups. Although the established group was three times larger, none left over the same period.

Other studies, such as those of Adams (1993, 1994) involving senior US nursing staff, show that large differences between individuals in A-I style at work can lead to such difficulty. Her study was made up of pairs of senior nurses and she found that an increasing cognitive gap between the members of the pairs significantly decreased the chance that the junior of a pair got a renewal of contract. Permanent massive change of style is not an option for any individual.

The data suggest that group means change because of turnover and not because people change their cognitive style preference at work, even if it might be in their

Table 2 An example of cognitive gap

	KAI mean scores[a]		
	Novices *All <5 years service*	*Established* *All >5 years service*	*Total N*
Total sample of local government employees	107.1 (18)	78.3 (49)	(67)
Subset who had left by end of study	121.4 (6)[b]	None	(6)

Notes
a *SD*s are not available. Figures in brackets are *N*s.
b Mean of those <5 years service, still in post, was 99.9.
Printed by kind permission of Dr Hayward; see also Kirton & McCarthy (1988).

immediate interest to do so. Hayward & Everett's study shows this clearly; even organisational rewards will not stop turnover when there has been an uncomfortable change in climate. Thomson (1980, 1985) reported that in her Singaporean sample, the managers most wanting to leave were adaptors who felt they were not in organisational fit. Holland et al., (1991) also noted that when new intakes to a company differed in KAI mean from that of the established group they were entering, subsequent turnover (for whatever given reason) gradually, year by year, left the survivors with average KAI means more like the establishment. The reason is that the differences in climate lead to discomfort and insufficient perceived gain to compensate – those in least fit are the ones to want to leave (e.g., Puccio et al., 1993) or who feel under pressure (Chilton, 2001). In companies where new entrants are moved through a number of different positions for their initial experience, they tend to collaborate with management to prolong stays in 'fitting' units and to shorten their stays in others. McCarthy (1993) found that women who perceived their 'most typical' colleagues as markedly different from themselves (using one KAI to record their score and another to estimate this typical colleague) also reported significantly greater work pressure than other colleagues, exactly confirming Thomson's earlier study.

Of course there are any number of people who offer training in changing others to fit prescriptions. Good sound adaptors with detailed knowledge of how things should be done are sent to suspect departments to dragoon its innovators into line. Then times change and numerous bright refugees from line management and large institutions now offer programmes that will 'make the organisation more innovative'. In each case it is assumed that the target group is second-class and must be wound up to a higher level because their members' style is perceived as of less value than it was once deemed to be (and may be later, when the fashion changes back). Three studies specifically looked at the possibility that prolonged training produced different KAI results in the members of teams (Watts, 1985; Goldsmith & Kerr, 1991; Murdock et al., 1993). Each team was given KAI before and after training and all the results showed that the means of the groups remained insignificantly altered. In the Goldsmith & Kerr study the control group did not change either. It is turnover that changes the group style mean, not threat, exhortation, or training. What is needed is to find a way of managing diversity rather than trying to eliminate it. This would be undesirable, even if it were attainable.

The stability of style preference is not confined to adults. A study by Selby & Treffinger (1993) showed that when schoolchildren tackled a large group task they found the same difficulties of collaborating over wide KAI score ranges as did adults at work. In just the same way these difficulties led to disputes and irritations with specific others and sometimes led to withdrawal from the team. The world of adults may contain more sophisticated problems being tackled by more sophisticated methods, but the basics are no different. There are advantages to this degree of stability of an individual's patterns of behaviour. The first advantage is to the individual, providing an ongoing integrity to the image of self. This ego integrity is built into much personality theory. A critical element of Kelly's theory is that impending changes to an individual's constructs that are perceived as radical are treated as a threat. Such concepts as self-fulfilment and self-actualisation need a stable standard against which to assess the progress of events. Equally, such stability is needed in order to acquire insight into the meaning of the behaviour of others. With such an array of trait concomitants as A-I is known to have, a major change in the way one handles cognitive structures would involve so many other changes in the person's behaviour as to present to others such startling and comprehensive change as to unsettle relationships. As was pointed out earlier, the oscillation between Jekyll and Hyde was not a social success.

Work group means do vary, but they vary predictably and, as has been shown, do so by turnover. Different work group KAI means differ because of selection and self-selection. An early study (Kirton, 1980) tentatively suggested, on pilot data, that although the occupation of accountancy might intuitively be likely to be adaptive orientated, a subset of this occupation, that of finance, was just as likely to be skewed in the other direction. This pilot work found support in later studies, especially a series inspired by Foxall (1986a; Foxall & Payne, 1989; Foxall et al., 1990). He concludes that all occupations contain specialised subsets that reflect their own problem-solving range rather than that of the occupation as a whole. The same can be said for any profession with a wide range of problems – teaching is just another example (see, Kirton et al., 1991) – and the general differences between occupations are the same across cultures, as Tullett (1997) noted.

The lessons to be learned from these studies are that differences between people can be inbuilt or very deeply seated and resistant to change. These differences amount to a diversity that must be managed, since they will not go away. They need to be used to good mutual advantage because they are part of a group's problem-solving resource. In addition, they seem to have been set early in life, a suggestion that is reviewed below.

Early onset of cognitive style

There is no definitive information on how early in life adaption-innovation appears as a stable preferred characteristic in individuals. Some repeated and consistent information is anecdotal. KAI user practitioners often report informally of discussions with parents, other family members, or infant teachers. These reports indicate that quite young children exhibit stable preferred patterns of behaviour that distinguish them from each other on descriptors relating to the A-I continuum. The practitioners themselves also report that their families say that their A-I characteristics have been exhibited from as far back as can be remembered; only the circumstances and how they manifest alter with maturity.

The statistical data derived from schoolchildren have already been given. Although KAI was designed for use with adults it has successfully been used in schools. The samples consisted of hundreds of teenagers (13 to 18 years old) from several schools in the UK and the USA, and a small sample in Europe. There were difficulties with some of the items. Youngsters seem readily able to substitute the word 'bosses' in an item relating to work for those in authority in their lives (such as parents). Most, however, had some work experience. They had more difficulty with items that required self-assessment, e.g., Are you consistent? A few words in the items were on the edges of known vocabulary. Nevertheless, if the scene was set by skilled administrators to obtain a serious response, they returned internal reliabilities that were close to those of adults and well within statistically acceptable standards. If KAI yields such reliable results with teenagers then the likelihood is that A-I characteristics must have been well established for at least some years before early adolescence.

The results from teenage respondents are not just a similarity of the item response of adults to an inventory. Other information collected from them, relating to behaviour, correlates as would be expected from hypotheses derived from adult information, as is clear from published studies containing results and observations as measured and recorded by Taylor (1993), Selby & Treffinger (1993), and Brinkman (1994, 1999). To take some example excerpts from each of these studies: Taylor noted that the more innovative schoolchildren reported more problems with school rules than the more adaptive. Selby noted that parents were slightly better at guessing their children's approximate place on the A-I continuum than the children's teachers, although both guessed well (a correlation of more than .8). Brinkman showed that the style preference of his sample was not related to their capacity (to compose music), just as A-I theory posits and has been found true with adults. For the A-I characteristics to be so well formed and so predictably similar to those of adults indicates that they were formed early, or even determined by a genetic component on which experience has built.

There is also the as yet untested biochemical inference. Van der Molen (1994) has quoted work from Cloninger on the effect of monoamine neuromodulators on personality trait differences. Persons high on dopamine and low on norepinephrine exhibit behaviour similar to exaggerated innovativeness; in the converse condition, behaviour much like exaggerated adaptiveness appears. Van der Molen concludes from this and other arguments that heredity is implicated in adaption-innovation differences. Cloninger's reviewed findings are supported and amplified by a more recent review (Ridley, 1999).

This evidence for stability, fitting as it does with theory, is part of the validity of the A-I concept and its measure. There are many other studies that test validity indirectly. Below are some studies that specifically set out to test validity.

Validity

The studies so far reported, as well as the ones that follow, are part of this validity. The largest closely related group of studies make predictions about other measures with which KAI should (or should not) be related. Many of these are quoted as illustrative examples in the section on the relationship between A-I and personality – see Table G, Appendix 6. A second group of related studies involves prediction of KAI means of different occupational groups – see Table J, Appendix 6.

Face validity is one useful aspect of a measure. One way this can be tested, by experiment, is by showing that people who have been given a good clear description of what is being measured can grasp this notion well enough to make comparative evaluations of others, well known to them, ranking them from high adaptor to high innovator without knowing their scores. Several studies have been carried out, some reviewing others (Kirton & McCarthy, 1985; Masten et al., 1988; Clapp & de Ciantis, 1989; Rickards & Gaston, 1995): These all involved estimates of adults by other adults. Selby (1992; Selby & Treffinger, 1993) used parents and teachers to estimate the same children. The studies yielded correlations (usually rank order) of around .8. When the subjects had only recently met one another (one study was carried out on the second day of a course consisting of people who had not previously met) the estimates fell to about to .4. This suggests that the bulk of the error lies with one's depth of knowledge of the other person rather than not being able to understand and use the concept.

Many of the other studies quoted as testing validity relate to their author's prediction of subjects' behaviour in specified circumstances. Here are some examples. Pershyn (1992) administered KAI to a number of postgraduate students. Then (before receiving any feedback) they were asked to depict, in symbols arranged in patterns, the way in which they think. The patterns they produced showed qualitative differences but were also readily seen, by judges, to be closely related to the owner's KAI score. Foxall & Bhate (1991) showed that the way undergraduates reacted to rules was reflected in their KAI scores, with adaptors being more likely to conform. This confirmed Taylor's (1993) observation in interviews with schoolchildren on the way they related to their school's rules. As expected from theory and adult experience, the more innovative found the rules more limiting than enabling (they complained about them); one group of high adaptors in the same class seemed hardly aware of these same rules. Their view could be summed up by one of them, who remarked, in some surprise: 'If there weren't any rules, Miss, we would have to make them, wouldn't we' – fortunately, for the sake of good future relationships, the higher innovators were not about to listen to that one.

It has been noted that Clapp and Puccio each used KAIs with variant instructions to get respondents to gauge the style nature of the workplace. Bobic et al. (1999), like Pershyn, were interested in testing whether KAI orientation could be predicted by having some specifically collected knowledge about each person. Each of their sample of 24 middle managers was interviewed (for between 20 minutes and 1 hour). They were asked to relate stories about themselves concerning their leadership. The taped version of these interviews was then analysed by independent judges against a list of 14 thematic descriptions culled from A-I literature rated 1 to 14; there was 80% agreement between two judges. Bobic et al. report that the largest number of differences between judges was where scores 'lay close to the midpoint'. The managers were also divided into three equal teams: those most adaptive, those most innovative, and those 'near and on either side of the KAI mean'. They were each given the same complex, high-level task of preparing a plan of action relating to a (US state) Department of Health and Environment. Experts in the field rated the outcome for 'departure from standard practice'. On a 10-point scale the more innovative predictably scored highest (most departure from the norm) at 7 points; the more adaptive scored 3; the middle group scored 5. If it resolves any arguments, the middle group got awarded the highest score for 'best project plan', though what the other two teams thought of this judgement was not recorded.

Hammerschmidt (1996) has carried out the largest study so far on the efficiency of homogeneous (close to same score) A-I groups. A control sample of nearly 500 managers were arbitrarily divided into small competing teams, and given a task that 52% were able to achieve within the time limit. A second sample, of just over 500 managers, was divided into homogeneous teams selected according to A-I scores and asked to solve the same problems. Half this second group were given tasks deemed as incompatible with their A-I orientation (which, it was supposed, would put the team into difficulty). Their achievement level dropped to 42% (despite, one presumes, their coping behaviour); the other groups were given the tasks deemed A-I compatible and had an average achievement level exceeding 80%. Unlike the teams in the control sample, none of the homogeneous teams failed because of internal disputes.

Keller & Holland (1978b) found differences associated with the pattern of communications in an R&D department – the members went to selected adaptors when they wanted information on how things worked inside the company and to selected innovators to get the latest information on what went on outside the company. Palmer (1991) found that adaptive British government scientists tended to go to the library when they were sure they had defined their problem, in order to collect data relating to its resolution. The more innovative went to the library while they were trying to form a clear view of the problem – it is likely that this procedure would redefine the original problem, that is, the one they were given. They would be preparing to alter structure to solve the problem. Gul (1986), in Australia, found that his students on an accountancy course (within a first degree course in economics) were divided along KAI lines as to which parts of the course they liked and disliked and which careers they might or might not pursue thereafter. The more adaptive liked banking, taxation, and auditing but the more innovative liked 'general subjects' and 'extra subjects'. As the adaptors predominated, the classes solemnly and regularly voted, in annual class review, to recommend to authority the dropping of these last two subjects from the curriculum as irrelevant. Authority ignored them.

Some of these studies plus many more, will be referred to again in later chapters – where they will make more impact in the context of group prediction and KAI. It is enough here to state that there are more than another 100 studies and over 50 theses from among the learned literature that have used KAI and have also yielded findings that were deliberately sought to test some aspect of validity; overwhelmingly their hypotheses were supported.

4 Style and personality theory

STYLE AND DIMENSIONS OF PERSONALITY

As the concept of Adaption-Innovation (A-I) formed, it seemed appropriate to place it as a cognitive style, a cognitive strategic operational element that profoundly influences problem solving. As the description of the style unfolded it was apparent that it manifests in distinctive, stable patterns of behaviour, ranging wider than the original observations that revealed its presence. Messick (1976), in the same year that the first article on A-I was published, also applied the term cognitive style to similar patterns of behaviour or personality characteristics. The nature of the patterns, their spread, their presumed stability and, therefore, their amenity to measurement suggested that these patterns could be described as traits. In that original work (Kirton, 1976) these patterns were named as concomitant traits, suggesting that they were generally expected to appear, and associated together, in any description of adaption-innovation as a cognitive style. Later work further suggested that the term 'dimension of personality' would be more appropriate than trait, since these numerous traits were also significantly related to each other. The A-I concept gives an underlying rationale to this pattern of interrelationships. Such thoughts led to a reconsideration of two pairs of terms and their relationships: between problem solving and personality and, within personality, between trait and dimension.

The cognitive function schema (Figure 1) was devised to help in understanding cognitive process, but personality is not included because it is considered to pervade this operational model of the organisation of cognitive function. This is because personality has been defined as the sum of the descriptions of all the stable influences on behaviour and of all the stable patterns of behaviour. Since the central nervous system, with particular reference to the cerebral cortex, evolved for the purpose of solving problems to permit the life of its owner to continue, this view of personality is, fundamentally but not exclusively, a cognitive one. This definition insolubly links personality to problem solving. If problem solving is the key to life, personality is the description of its stable, characteristic patterns of behaviour and the influences that bring them about. The philosopher Descartes' (1637) famous words: *cogito ergo sum* – 'I think, therefore, I am' – were his proof of being. A-I theory's emphasis on the central nature of problem solving in 'my continuing to be' suggests a biopsychological variant: *sum quod cogito* – 'I live because I think.' The theory's definition of personality develops a psychological variant and continuation of these two assumptions: *ita cogito sum* – 'I am as I think,' so distinguishing me from any other individual, as personality description should. However, the nature of this definition of personality has an added, interesting outcome. A personality definition that distinguishes on the basis of problem solving could be used to describe differences between mankind and other species (at least in terms of problem-solving strategies for survival) as well as the more usual task of distinguishing between individuals. The manner in which any organism manages to achieve its 'problem solving' (if one can dignify all such processes by that term) is at the core of its description. Jones (2000), in his review of the nature of the gene, writes: 'Brains and behaviour are what separate humans from any other animal. Since the split with chimps, the brain has added about a thousand cells a year. The human brain is five times bigger[28] than would be expected for a typical primate of the same size. [. . .] Somewhere in that brain, or what it is thinking, is what makes us different. [. . .] Humans, uniquely, are what they think' (p. 171). So, while a biologist could use 'personality' to distinguish one species from another, psychologists use the same kind of description to distinguish individuals within a species. The essential difference is that the biologist compares what is characteristic of all the members of one species with what is characteristic in another; psychologists do the same for groups (e.g., men compared to women) but primarily concentrate on the differences between any one individual and any other. Distinguishing between species is not a usual part of the definition of personality but the second part of the definition used here does. Rejection of the first part does not affect an understanding of A-I theory, which depends upon the second.

The next distinction to make is between trait and dimension of personality, which is best stated by Eysenck (1970). He points out that for decades there had been a sharp division in psychology on the basic definition of personality. The main difference was between those who laid stress on behavioural acts and those who laid stress on dynamic concepts. He quotes two typical authorities (pp. 1–2). First, Watson (1930), for whom personality is 'the sum of activities that can be discovered by actual observation over a long enough period of time to give reliable information.' This definition is essentially that of the trait theorists, where each trait is assumed to have occurred without any necessary connection to any other. It is contrasted with the definition given by those who see more relationships between the elements, leading to Eysenck's championing of the notion of organising and explanatory 'dimensions of personality'. Second, in contrast to Watson, for Prince (1924) personality is 'the sum total of all the biological innate dispositions, impulses, tendencies, appetites and instincts of the individual, and the acquired dispositions and tendencies.' Except for the term 'instincts' we are in agreement with this description also, and the earlier description is a combination of both of these approaches, as Eysenck advocated. His own definition is: 'the more or less stable and enduring organisation of a person's character, temperament, intellect, and physique, which determines his unique adjustment to the environment.' Essentially, the prime difference in A-I theory is the emphasis on problem solving being the driving force in the formation of personality, hence its suggested application at one level to distinguishing between species. There is, however, no definition distinction made in the literature of when a trait can be determined as so wide, deep-seated, and pervasive as to be clearly classified as a dimension. One distinguishing mark adopted by Eysenck is that, besides being seen as underlying and providing cohesion

---

28 Some estimates are that it is three times bigger – the difference is whether the whole brain is compared or the relatively common 'old' brain is excluded.

of meaning to a cluster of traits, dimensions have a hereditary component. These two conditions will be used to suggest that A-I is a dimension rather than a trait.

One further matter that was especially taken up by Eysenck was the notion that personality is a structure. Eysenck (ibid) noted that his definition's inclusion of the notion of structure owes a great deal to Roback (1927), Allport (1937), and MacKinnon (1944), who stress that personality is a concept of system, structure, or organisation. This went counter to the doctrine of specificity of behaviour that is integral to the concept of the independently acquired trait approach. Earlier Eysenck (1965) specifically stated the reason for this notion: Personality was not only a description of a person's behaviour, in term of traits and attitudes, but also a part explanation of them and their stability (p. 53). The core elements of personality, the dimensions of personality, should, therefore, be 'determined by heredity factor and . . . this determination must have some kind of basis in the nervous system' (p. 94). A-I theory stresses the central position of cognitive structure, on the grounds that without it thought is not possible but also stresses that it is, by its very nature, limiting. The paradox applied to personality is that at all its layers (e.g., both traits and dimensions – the one being a superordinate of the other), it, too, is both enabling and limiting. This makes personality not just a description but also part of the understanding of both self and others and, as such, the necessary core for the formation of groups, from the family outwards. The A-I theory endeavours to set structure more firmly into the core of the understanding of not just personality but of problem solving in general; a matter explored further below.

In the discussion between those who place the emphasis on traits in defining personality and those who prefer to stress dimensions, the term trait is sometimes used specifically, sometimes inferred (as in the quotations from Watson and Prince above), and sometimes used with terms such as attitude, which contain overlapping aspects. For us here, it will be useful to concentrate on the similarities between these options and to treat such terms as trait, attitude, belief, etc., as the principal elements, within dimensions of personality that describe the characteristics of individuals. For Allport (1937), trait and attitudes are predispositions to respond, i.e., they lead to predictable patterns of behaviour: 'behind all the confusion of terms, behind the disagreement of judges, and apart from errors and failures of empirical observation, there are none the less *bona fide* mental structures in each personality that account for the consistency of behaviour' (p. 289). So, for Allport, both traits and attitudes initiate and guide behaviour and both are the joint outcome of genetic factors and learning. The essential distinction between them is that an attitude is linked to a specific object or class of objects and a trait is not: 'Between them they cover virtually every type of disposition with which the psychology of personality concerns itself' (p. 295). If structures are enabling they are also limiting, so a balance between stability and flexibility is constantly required if these structures are to be of continuing use. This balance, required by all these mental structures, not only of traits but also of attitudes and beliefs, preoccupied many personality theorists during the middle of the last century. 'Since the mid-1950s, the most active front in the study of attitude change has centred on a group of related theories that seek to come to grips with the dynamics of attitude change via formulations of the interplay between the person's postulated tendency toward consistency in specified aspects of his beliefs and attitudes and the incoming information with which he is confronted' (Smith, 1973, p. 35).

Heider's (1958) theory of balance is primarily concerned with internal cognitive consistency, with specific reference to feeling. Applied with some attempt at precision, a formula, *p–o–x*, is advanced in which the relationship between a person (p) and another (o) is positive; but if the other person does something of which one greatly disapproves (x) a negative relationship exists between o and x, which feeds back as a negative relationship between x and p. This inconsistency needs resolution: either p forgives o on matter x or it negatively affects their relationship. This formula exercised many minds. Newcome (1961) applied it to social situations: People who share the same view of other people will like each other; research already quoted finds that people with similar styles problem solve well together. Rosenberg and Abelson (Rosenberg et al., 1960) argued that in the resolutions of such 'p–o–x' inconsistencies, the individual prefers solutions that maximise his potential hedonic gain. The most noted of these theories was Festinger's (1957) cognitive dissonance theory, which generated much study on the ways in which dissonance is reduced. The problem of understanding the balance between the enabling structure and the need to modify the structure in the light of contrary input from the environment was common to all the theorists, as it is also to A-I theory.

The cognitive function schema and personality

The cognitive function schema (Figure 1) has been constructed to help explain brain function as if it is an organisation, depicting, in briefest detail, its 'departments'. Each department has a main function whilst being in close collaboration with the other departments to achieve the brain's overall raison d'être, the survival of the individual. The schema is intended to cover all aspects of the organisation of cognitive function, and these should now be linked to personality. The view taken is that personality is the sum of descriptions of an individual's stable, characteristic patterns of (observed) behaviour and of the stable, characteristic cognitive influences that bring them about. This includes the individual's stable patterns of interactive association with others within the individual's social environment. This is not greatly different from the general view taken by the principal writers in personality theory, except that it may be more inclusive. Perhaps the closest similarity lies with Allport (see above) and Lewin's (1936) neat formulation that behaviour is a function of a person interacting with the environment, or: B f (P × E). As Denison (1996) comments, in this framework 'the person must, by definition, be analytically separate from the social context. [A] perspective [that] characterises the approach taken in the climate literature.' Of course, this separation is a convenient device to assist the understanding of the closely interacting elements of social climate.

A-I theory takes a further step (from the point of view of the literature on culture and climate) by positing that the extent to which this understanding is achieved is reflected in the predictive accuracy of the description of the person's personality. We base our predictions of the behaviour of others on both their characteristic behaviour and inferences about the stable influences that cause behaviour to be sufficiently stable for it to be perceived as predictable. We can readily divide, in theory at least, the notion of personality into that part that constitutes the influences and that part that constitutes the (behavioural) outcome – in reverse order, what it is and how it gets there. We check our understanding of others (that is, our inferred information on the stable influences that allow us to predict such behaviour) against the feedback derived from observation of those persons' overt action in an understood context[29]. The observed and the observer are both in, and interacting with, their personal and their shared environment. From this interaction there comes understanding not just of an individual's behaviour (as Lewin states) but also of the two conscious selves of observed and observer (or, in introspection, the individual's notion of self and the feedback from the environment against which it is tested). It is this notion of self that Damasio (1999) rightly sees as at the core of individual being, as did Kelly (1955) and others before them. Understanding self and understanding the environment are the two keys to human problem solving. Kelly argues that people need to defend their understanding of self and of 'reality' (as they perceive it) so that they can continue to problem solve. A-I suggests that the differences between people in the way they protect their understanding of self and reality are part of cognitive style and of the definition of personality, since such understanding acts as cognitive structure.

The role of cognitive affect

In explaining the part played by the three elements of cognitive function and their interrelationships, the first problem is where sensibly to begin, since all the parts interreact. A lead can be taken from schemata relating to the problem-solving process (e.g., Figures 5 and 6); they begin with a perception of a problem detached from among the stimuli being received. This entails recognising the stimulus as a problem to be tackled, understanding it, mobilising the energy needed to tackle it, and getting some idea of the desired goal. In the cognitive function schema, cognitive affect has this function, aided by cognitive resource in the understanding of the problem and predicting what constitutes an acceptable solution within acceptable and available means. If the outcome (as behaviour) is successful, then a pattern of such behaviour may emerge that deals with other stimuli which are perceived as sufficiently similar to warrant a similar solution pattern. Once such a pattern is stable and predictable by self and others, then it enters the realm of personality. It is necessary, before proceeding, to decide what lies within the realm being defined and what does not.

The built-in responses such as reflexes (knee jerks and eye blinks) are excluded from the cognitive function schema because they do not involve the problem-solving cortex and are mostly dealt with at the level of the spinal cord. For much more complicated responses, such as digesting or walking, the control has been delegated, except when managing damage, to a very low level of the nervous system's organisational hierarchy, and rarely needs higher-order intervention. This is not to say that these operations are not complicated[30] but, in general, the control of the mechanics of the body is primitive and is regulated to a low level, mostly around its stem – see Figure 2.

29 In attribution theory, advanced by Kelly (1967), it is proposed that much attitude formation and motivation may be outcomes of the individual's attempt to discover the causes of the effects observed. However, he noted that the individual often attributes erroneous causes to these observed effects – it seems more comforting to have a doubtful theory than none at all. These estimates, and errors, are critical elements in problem solving.

30 Six muscles are required to control each eye of a player in a game, so that the flight of a ball can be followed while the player is in swift movement on a different course. Yet it is only the decision to catch the ball (and doing so!) that is perceived as a problem at cognitive level.

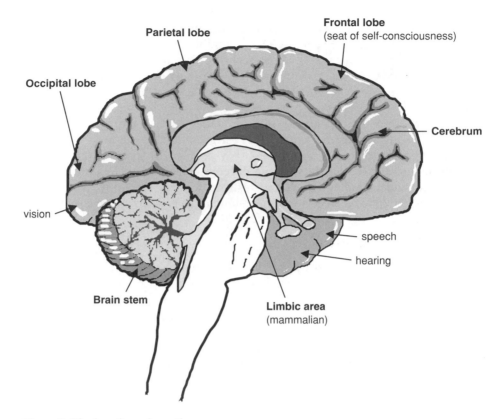

Figure 2 The location of emotion

Although nearly as primitive, the limbic system is more important to problem solving. Buried deeply just above the old brain, it is the seat of emotion. What is its function in problem solving? Whatever the adherents of emotional intelligence might suppose, emotion is not an integral element of the potential power of problem solving, which is how intelligence is defined. It is a mental response mechanism that alerts us to significant stimuli and orientates the general response. Lazarus (1991) describes emotion as an 'affect' programme. So, what we feel may be a programme but how we behave as a result is dependent on learning (Pinker, 2002, p. 39). It must, however, have a significant survival role and, therefore, is important in this exploration of problem solving, Every individual's cognitive affect must accommodate emotion within its function; as must done by every leader of every team. Emotion is located primarily in the limbic system, which is: 'known as the mammalian brain because it is thought to have first emerged in mammals . . . it has a profound effect on our experience because it is densely connected to the conscious cortex above it and constantly feeds information upwards. [. . .] Emotions . . . direct us to behave in a way that (usually) helps us to survive' (Carter, 1998, p. 16). A critical link is an area of the limbic system, the amygdala: a structure to which run all the sensory impulses started from anywhere within the body. It is now thought likely that the amygdala has an intermediary role between the area relating to the senses (the very means of cognitive input from the environment) and the emotions. One's grasp of reality is – at the least – tinged with emotion. The amygdala, then, may be one structure that assists in 'selective attention' and so may help in that part of the decision process that selects which stimuli to respond to from a vast and constant input. It seems it acts as a filtering function that affects higher cortical sensory processing by tending to limit attention to stimuli with emotional significance – the 'vividness' principle of the behaviourists (see, e.g., Mishkin et al., 1984; Mishkin & Appenzeller, 1987). Certainly, emotion readily affects the cortical processing through the nearby centres, registering its presence by, for instance, alteration to heartbeat, breathing, eye dilation, or dryness in the mouth. Emotion must be accorded a place within cognitive affect as an influence on (rather than a direct part of) problem solving that seeks (as distinct from accepts) *satisfying* solutions. It must play a role in the decision of what problem to tackle, what would be an acceptable solution, what might be certain limits on the means to be used, and how much we need a solution. In short, emotion is a contributor to motivation. Emotions become conscious in the very front (orbital/frontal) cortex (e.g., Carter, 2002) – far from its primitive seat. Much problem-solving success depends on awareness. The characteristic patterns of an individual's emotion are part of that individual's personality. Emotion, however, is not the only element in cognitive function that plays this role. All higher centres of the cortex do so too, and the final direction and intensity of evoked motive is an interaction of these parts.

Cognitive affect, then, as its share in problem solving, needs to integrate the influence of an individual's stable predictable patterns of emotion with those of other elements operating in the higher cortex that between them engender (for example) analyses of patterns of past experience, insight, and reason. The stable nature of the pay-off between the elements (e.g., between emotion and reason) is also part of the description of an individual's character. Any notion that, within us, reason is invariably or even frequently in conflict with emotion is suspect; it may be that we only remember conflicting options. Most of the time cognitive affect must accommodate its diversity with unremarked efficiency and accord. In brain structure there are good links between key elements even if the different areas have specialised functions. For instance, a subregion of the amygdala, the central nucleus, is involved in autonomic nervous system responses (like heart rate and conditioned fear response) and is an important link between the forebrain and the autonomic control by the stem brain. It has a link role in a general purpose defence control network (awareness of danger may register as fear, see, e.g., LeDoux, 1998, p. 158). As Fischbach (1994) remarks: 'affect depends on the function of the neurons in the same manner as does conscious thought.' However, emotion is not the most elemental force that makes an impact upon behaviour. 'You are not a brain running a body by switching on hormones. Nor are you a body running a genome running a brain by switching on genes that switch on hormones. You are all of these at once.' Such lines of discussion give rise to problems for many who worry about such concepts as 'genetic determinism' that may seem to dominate the individual, but '. . . it is the body that switches on genes when it needs them, often in response to a more or less cerebral, or even conscious reaction to external events' (Ridley, 1999, p. 152). Behaviour is an outcome of a fantastically complex system of trade-offs of powerful influences, with the cortex at its pinnacle. The whole process, emotion and all, is governed, as Kelly pointed out, by the 'scientific process' (even for animals), whether this is understood by the individual or not. The process is, put simply, setting up a prediction (hypothesis) based on one's 'grasp of reality', acting on it (the experiment tests the hypothesis), and noting the results, which when understood constitute additions to knowledge[31].

All this cognitive activity is aimed at meeting the needs of the individual in terms of tension reduction of needs, both physical and emotional, as well as the acquired needs that can, from time to time, override the more basic, primitive ones. Hence, in the schema, cognitive affect is given the 'departmental' brief of sorting out among its own elements the targets that will meet the individual's needs – the 'I Want' broken into the three elements, as Freud suggested[32], of: I Need; I Like; I Ought. That is, it encompasses the range between the basic physical needs and the higher, learned, acquired needs such as 'self-fulfilment'. In normal functioning, however, the latter is securely based on cognitive function; its problem solving has the ever-present underlying aim of personal survival, even if the elements have become increasingly complex and (like such acquired needs of 'I ought') seemingly remote from the immediate needs of a simpler organism. The schema shows that sensory input is obtained from within the body (the feedback link from covert behaviour to cognitive affect) and, critically for problem solving, from the environment outside. The sensory input system is as primitive as emotion and, perhaps not surprisingly, they are located close together in the more primitive parts of the brain. One could argue that emotion is likely to have its greatest influence on motive, the operation that converts the aims of cognitive affect into action.

In the schema it is assumed that cognitive effect needs to accept direction from cognitive affect. However, once directed, the cognitive effect process is there first to sharpen the problem in preparation for its solution, and then get there. During this process the assumption is that cognitive effect 'fends off' the influence of emotion in its continuing process until the internal evaluation of the potential solution must again require reason to interact with all of affect – checking that what is planned is in accord with what was ordered. The next assumption is that the review process cannot be the same as the initiating process since knowledge has moved on – as Carter noted, no brain can think the same thought twice. Reason cannot be swayed so readily as at the onset; indeed, the suspicion must be that the longer the cognitive process in any segment of thinking, and the more complex the operation, the more reason will dictate the outcome – hence, *Homo sapiens*. In short, the more complex the problem, the lower is the survival value of spontaneity. It seems no accident that the seat of emotion, located in the primitive limbic system, is not only distant from reason in developmental time but is also as distant as possible from it physically. Carter sums up current knowledge of the mapping of the brain: 'The vast majority of the cortex is given over to sensory processing – only the [upper] frontal lobes are dedicated to non-sensual tasks'[33] (Carter, 1998, p. 115).

In the analysis of management initiative it was noted that in complex problem solving, as resolutions progress they set up spin-off problems. It was also noted how even the initiating problems, once perceived, are often inadequately analysed before the problem solver starts looking for a solution. The same corner is cut with the spin-off

31 Neurons process information before passing it on – they are more like little brains than merely switches (e.g., Jonscher, 1999).
32 Freud named those id, ego, and superego.
33 'This brain region is the home of consciousness . . . where ideas are created, plans constructed' (Carter, 1998, p. 180).

problem and, in addition, if the original problem was influenced by emotion during its resolution, spin-off problems must also be influenced. The way in which motive is a trade-off between the influences of reason and emotion will again be played out when the spin-off needs to be managed. However, even this may be an over-simplification, as not all of motive is necessarily conscious, as Freud was the first to note seriously. It is only too likely that if unconscious motivation is powerful, the force it generates is attributable to the more primitive elements of cognitive affect. Freud's attempt to make unconscious motivation accessible to awareness (the higher-order reasoning) is an attempt to turn the customary trade-off of influences into part of deliberate problem solving under better control of the higher cortex. So the schema assumes that the interplay of the diversity within the brain is continuous and, although reason is dominant in mankind, it rests on a foundation of more primitive attributes and systems. The resulting pattern is, nevertheless, consistent, both within itself and in dealing with predictable patterns in the environment[34]. The schema, therefore, assumes that personality is, in part, the description of a person's characteristic motives, making it possible for the self and others to observe continuity and to form insightful prediction – the basis on which collaborative group interaction is possible. Motive is defined as the process by which energy is mobilised, gathered, and directed towards a goal; it is measured in terms of intensity and duration.

For more than a century, there has been scientific study of core aspects of human problem solving. Emphasis has been placed, by writers as far distant in time as Freud, Kelly, and currently Damasio, on the central position that self-awareness plays as a benchmark in understanding reality and as a foundation to reason tempered by emotion. The relationship between them might be depicted by recourse to Archimides' graphic explanation on the power of the lever, for it seems that self-awareness gives the mind a stable platform on which to stand and reason is the lever with which to move the world we understand. Perhaps the most difficult part of this interaction to understand is that suggested by Damasio (1999) of how the 'brain substrate of feeling can become *known* to the organism having that emotion' (p. 8). His book aims at contributing to the elucidation of the neural underpinnings of consciousness in general and consciousness of self at its core – a distinction he advances as critical to the understanding of the problem-solving power of mankind. To have consciousness in general, he argues, the brain needs to be able to create within itself representations (images) of objects and events together with their interrelationships. It also needs to be able to create abstraction of these representations and their interrelationships, thereby creating further abstractions, using every sense modality (sight, sound, taste, etc.) to build up a picture of the world – exactly reminiscent of Kelly's notion of the grasp of reality that shifts the organism from merely reacting to events to anticipating them, which is the necessary foundation of control. Damasio also argues that the understanding of how the brain creates representational images is only the first

---

34 In uncovering, as part of therapy, unconscious motivation and harmful repressed memories that may be related to them, Freud may not have allowed sufficiently for the notion that no one thinks the same thoughts twice. What may be uncovered is likely to be the current content and, therefore, the interpretation of an earlier memory. Trying to reproduce the original element intact may be costly compared to value; in any case nothing should get in the way of the natural problem-solving process which, once set on a helpful track – itself no mean feat – may deal with the problem, including the reinterpretation of relevant events, more naturally and safely.

problem; the second is how 'the brain engenders a sense of self in the act of knowing' (p. 9). It is the concept of self in the context of its environment, with knowledge of its past and the estimate of its future, that is not only at the core of reality for each individual but is also the basis of problem solving.

This chapter argues that the description of self and its characteristic ways of operating (including all the characteristic influences on such behaviour) is personality. If this is so, then personality distinguishes humans from other species and oneself from other humans. This emphasis, that a knowledge of self is essential to having a grasp of reality, offers an understanding of why no one can accommodate so much change as to threaten either one's integrity or that essential grasp of reality. Knowledge of self and reality are both core structures that can be modified but cannot be lost, and this limits the changes any individual can manage.

Cognitive affect and effect

In the schema (Figure 1), it is cognitive effect that plans the behaviour which will try to achieve the desired goal. The given structure of this function has two characteristics: the limits of its planning capacity (potential intelligence; talent) and the preferred style of operation. Both are assumed to have an inherited component. Regarding the potential capacity of the cognitive function, it is still not clear how complete is the dominance of inheritance, since the human brain is so powerful that it is not clear where anyone's limits are. As for preferred style, although all the evidence suggests that the preference does not alter, there is a means, through coping behaviour, for extending the actual range. The reason for the continued cost of coping behaviour is because A-I is not just deep and early set but also has an inherited component; habituation does not diminish the cost of coping – continued practice achieves more effective performance but not less costly coping behaviour[35].

Van der Molen (1994) was the first to argue that adaption-innovation may have an inherited component. Partly on a priori grounds, partly based on his research with animals (on the behaviour of house mice 'leaders'), he suggested that the core elements of adaption-innovation are part of genetic structure and in animals they are exhibited as part of instinctive behaviour. Mice are programmed to submit to grooming by leaders or to groom them on demand. Individuals exhibit small variations in their behaviour which do not appear to be learnt, in 'fitting' within this programming. Van der Molen also draws attention to the work of Cloninger (1986, 1987), who suggests that malfunctions in production of the monoamine neuromodulators dopamine and norepinephrine lead to behaviours that resemble exaggerated innovation and adaption respectively. An excess of the former produced 'novelty-seeking' behaviour and an excess of the latter 'reward dependence' behaviour. It is possible that minute variation in such production can account for the differences in the mice. Recent research in DNA reviewed by Ridley (1999) locates 'risk-taking' (associated with novelty-seeking) on chromosome 11 and specifically with one of its genes, D4DR. This is a recipe for a protein called a dopamine receptor and the differences in the gene are pinpointed to a sequence of 48 'letters' and the number of times they are

---

35 What are inherited are preferred style and the facility for coping behaviour, not how they are used – that has to be learnt.

repeated in the sequence, within each individual. Ridley argues, from his review of research, that dopamine is: 'roughly speaking [the brain's] motivation chemical.' Too little, and the person lacks initiative; too much, and the person is easily bored[36], thus supporting the review by Cloninger. In addition to these inbuilt influences there are those that are almost equally pervasive and compelling but that are learnt in early life, particularly in infancy (e.g., Sullivan, 1953), or somewhat later but which are still highly significant (e.g., Erikson, 1982). Personality structures that have been in place for a long time (including those laid down early and still surviving as potent forces) may well have more influence, over wider domain, than those more recently acquired and of more particular application. The suggestion emerging is that these stable elements of the cognitive effect function are built-in or formed early and are deep-seated. They are made manifest through the problem-solving process, and their predictable nature adds them to the personality profile of the individual.

The relationship assumed between cognitive affect and cognitive effect is that they are independent, although there is constant interaction between them. Motive, as cognitive affect's operating process, does not influence the potential limits of intelligence or the preferred style of operation but does influence the direction in which effort is expended, the amount of effort that is expended, the duration of the effort, and the extent to which importance is attached to the achievement of a current aim. Although the exact position of motive is differently conceived in personality theories such as that put forward by Bandura, nevertheless, there is no disagreement with the contention that 'most human motivation is cognitively driven' (1992, p. 18). He argues that what is vital in selecting the problem to solve and keeping motive operating for its resolution are 'internal standards' assisted by self-reinforcement. In the cognitive function schema, attitudes and beliefs are the means by which such constructs as internal standards can be formed as guiding principles and be located in cognitive affect.

In the schema, cognitive effect contains two elements, style and potential level, which are not the same but which interact. The best way of distinguishing between them is to note that 'how creative am I?' is not synonymous with 'in what way am I creative?' Within cognitive affect few needs are inherited and none are independent elements – most are learnt and form a consistent package. Traits, attitudes, and beliefs also interact and their definitions have elements that overlap; although the facility for acquiring them must be inherited, their content is learnt. However, although the elements in cognitive affect and cognitive effect interact, no correlation is expected between them (knowledge of one does not give information about the other). The same is true of the two elements within cognitive effect – style and potential capacity; they interact but are not related. However, as the contents of cognitive resource are products of the interaction of the other two departments together with the environment, the elements in cognitive resource cannot be entirely independent. One learns those things that are selected within cognitive affect to the degree driven by motive. One learns up to one's potential capacity and within one's preferred style – so resource accumulation is also influenced by cognitive effect. These notions suggest expectation of relationships between measures: A-I does not correlate significantly with measures

---

36 In fact, there are other complicated interactions within aspects of the function of the amygdala, all of which use the same neurotransmitter, norepinephrine, and which relate to characteristics of, among others, being shy and phlegmatic.

of, e.g., attitudes, leadership capacities, anxiety, level of education, or success at work – unless other factors play an intervening role. Such intervention could be whether the environment within which the measure is taken is more or less comfortable to adaptors or innovators.

The role of cognitive resource

A closer relationship is to be expected between both cognitive affect and cognitive effect and cognitive resource, since the last is a by-product of the interaction of the other two. Every organism needs the means of detecting change and responding to it in a way that permits it to survive. These, at a cognitive level, are the functions of cognitive affect and cognitive effect. Organisms that have the physical means to be able to exercise a choice of response need another function: The means to register the outcome of a particular response to a particular stimulus, store it, and later profit from this store of information. This dynamic storing operation is the function of cognitive resource; within it the schema lists knowledge, skill, and its operating element, the learning process. Of the personality theorists, it is particularly Cantor (1990) and Mischel (1990) who emphasise cognitive competencies and skills as the core of personality rather than traits. The competencies and skills, as they see them, involve consideration of the problem setting and the behaviour required to solve the problems. In the most basic form of learning, that of 'trial and error', the organism scouts around until a response is found that meets its need. All these attempts, both failed and successful, are part of the learning process – as negative or positive reinforcement. The higher organisms, having a cerebral cortex, are able to process vast quantities of information and pack it away in meaningful concepts. This is but a preliminary to further processing which produces, as Gagné (1965) suggested, higher-order abstractions, rules and principles, hypotheses and theories – the basis for proactive learning. The process associated with cognitive resource is learning, aided by memory. These processes are, in part, governed by cognitive effect – being limited by potential level and preferred style. They are guided by cognitive affect as to the direction and intensity of their effort. In turn they supply the processed data on which the other functions depend – without cognitive resource the rest of the brain would operate on a permanent *tabula rasa* basis, remembering no past experience. Cognitive resource is the individual's potential made manifest and stored for use. What has been learnt, why it has been learnt, how it is stored, how readily it is retrieved, and how it is used are stable characteristics of the individual and are treated as part of the description of the individual; part of the individual's personality.

Cognitive function and the environment

Acquiring information is the means of acquiring an improved grasp of reality that, in turn, improves the chances of solving problems. The central nervous system, through the widespread network of neurons, has direct contact with and control of every part of the body. It is, however, securely housed in a protective bone case and the penalty for such protection is that this very protection allows no direct contact with the world outside – the effective control of which is its prime reason for being. The sensory receptors, their encoded information, and the elaborate methods of its interpretation supply the system's permanent need for constant reliable information about the environment, on which the success of finding appropriate response is founded. The system engenders various characteristic responses and trade-offs. A-I theory argues, for instance, that faced with the problem of the need for reliable information with the concomitant risk of imperilling one's overall understanding of the world at large, characteristically, adaptors will tend to hold on longer to their current understanding; innovators have more tolerance of ambiguity. In general, both are at equal risk of getting it wrong and paying the price. In neither case can extreme positions be acceptable without difficulties and attendant anxieties becoming a dominating feature of the period of trade-off crises that is occurring. No one can afford to give up their understanding of a significant critical segment of their world in order to accommodate new changes, however pressing they may appear – but we do differ on the cut-off points at which comfort turns to discomfort and discomfort begins to appear as disaster. These stable characteristic differences are part of the description of an individual and, therefore, part of personality.

This means that the individual acquires command of a structure made up of knowledge of external reality, awareness and a knowledge of self that allows sharp, concentrated use of this structure (through consciousness) for the benefit of self. Clearly this structure needs stability in order to be of practical use in the management of the diversity within its scope. Damasio (1999, p. 31) suggests that 'consciousness probably prevailed in evolution because it allowed us to manage life better and that was advantageous'[37]. But this is not all the stability that we need at the core of understanding. Carter (1998) argues that our need to make stable and consistent predictions about critical events has given us 'our urge to rationalise behaviour [which] probably has survival value. The human species got where it is largely by forming complex social constructs – from the hunting party to the political party – and making them work. To work they require that we have confidence in them and to have confidence we need to believe that the actions of these organisations are based on sound, rational judgements' (p. 42). She argues that we also need rational explanations for our own behaviour as part of the need for consistency and stability in, or understanding of, the world we live in. If these explanations are not readily available we tend to make them up, either as a fantasy or a working hypothesis: 'better have a reason for doing things – any reason – than no reason at all' (p. 43). The convergence of view between these biologists and the psychologists explaining the source of attribution theory is close indeed. Further, the contention in A-I theory is that cognitive style is part of the mechanism these authorities assume underlies the stability of the basis of our problem-solving mechanism, which must still allow for flexibility within its operation.

There is another important aspect of the individual's relationship to the environment, especially the social environment, and that is the problems thrown up by the need to collaborate with others. Earlier it was suggested that it is unwise to use the 'shorthand' notion that 'governments do . . .' or 'groups think . . .' Both these abstract terms are names for an association of individuals and it is these individuals who do the doing and undertake the thinking. This may seem an unnecessary distinction but (a) no brain is in direct contact with any other brain; and (b) each individual endeavouring to solve a similar problem to the ones being solved by others in the

---

37 Awareness might be thought of as acting like the super-enlarging segment of a hand-held magnifying lens, or as a spotlight in a large, dark, well-filled factory.

group is faced with the additional problem of learning how to collaborate with them effectively[38]. The schema, therefore, suggests this complication as a functional need, aided by the process of group dynamics. The disadvantages of the 'group-think' and 'group-do' ways of expressing what is happening are numerous.

- The people who are actually carrying out the operation are shielded from view – either unfairly to them (losing credit for their successes) or unfairly to those who are affected their actions (by protecting them from rightful criticism).
- The difficult process of group collaboration is played down in significance. All too often, consultants find that problems of collaboration, the lack of mutual insight, and the poverty of inter-group communication are at least as serious as the assumed intractability of many of the problems the groups were formed to face.
- There is an implicit assumption in 'the group thinks' notion that all the members of it think exactly the same thing – they do not. In every case of a group arriving at a decision, the outcome of group deliberation (at whatever step in the process) is a compromise. How the compromise has been reached, and at what expense to what and to whom, may leave behind concealed problems that are latent sources of difficulty in the near future.

This last point is a reminder of one made earlier, that in order to manage change both widely and well, it is necessary to manage diversity well. There are two kinds of diversity apposite here: diversity of problems and diversity of problem solvers. If the principal problems being faced are not too diverse, a team embodying a narrow range of diversity will manage very well. A problem that lies latent, and perhaps unnoticed, in such a team is that this success is continually dependent on the stability of the current environment; that the range of problems being faced will not radically widen out into a new range of diversity which the members of the current problem-solving team will be less readily equipped to manage efficiently. Some narrow-range diversity teams can last (have lasted) for a very long time; nevertheless, by its nature, on average the diversely narrow team has, if conditions in the environment are held constant, a shorter effective lifespan than a more diverse team – in spite of the fact that the latter is the more difficult to manage. In the schema, the outgoing link between the individual and the environment, as well as the means of affecting it, is behaviour. This is the most readily observable manifestation of personality; the readiest means of making sense of what people do and of inferring the influences at work that keep them stable and predictable. The more stable and characteristic of these patterns of behaviour are also included into the scope of the term personality.

The group dynamic process is suggested as the operating element when collaborating with others. Its characteristic patterns are also included in the definition of personality. Collaboration, through behaviour, is the means to achieve survival, and has two added elements. One is getting the feedback for activities that add to the individual's knowledge of the world and of specific activities providing critical cognitive resource. Another is

---

38 As will be discussed later, when the energy spent dealing with problems of collaboration within the team (dubbed Problem B) begins to exceed the energy spent on the problem for which the team was formed (Problem A) then the team becomes inefficient and may dissolve.

the means of sharing the tasks of survival with others (Problem A) at the cost of learning how to do so effectively (Problem B). The different characteristic patterns of how these activities are achieved, in what characteristic ways, are also part of personality.

In conclusion

In the devising of the cognitive schema represented in Figure 1, there was no intention to take part in the debates on which of the numerous schools of personality theory are more likely to be correct or useful. On the contrary, all the principal schools have merit and it was interesting how much of more than a century's theorising by insightful minds can be included here without serious internal conflict. The schema is essentially based on cognitive theory on the basis that the central nervous system clearly evolved as problem-solving equipment designed to prolong life. If problem solving is the key to life, then the view in this chapter is that the definition of personality is the description of the characteristic ways that we problem solve. These characteristic ways include both the internal processing strategies and the means to understand and apply them, through behaviour, in the environment. Given that all organisms need to survive in an ever-changing universe and do so more successfully by collaboration with friendly others, then the understanding derived from social cognitive theory must apply as well. As an individual acquires mastery of cognitive competencies, those competencies are honed and made useful by learning about the world at large and the workings of the in-group in particular. By being able to discriminate finely over a wide range of stimuli and then by being able to abstract critical common elements from repeated, similar stimuli, the cortex can develop cognitive structures. These range from the vital essential brick of understanding (the 'concept' of the Gestalt school) to grand socially pervasive concept structures, like the paradigms of Kuhn. It has been argued above, and in Kelly and Gagné, that these structures are vital to building up an understanding of reality, from an understanding of self, to an understanding of the universe. In this universe, however, there is no structure that represents pure gain, and only at the end of life is there a structure leading to pure loss. Just as with the given physical structures, the very cognitive structures that are so critical to enabling the organism to survive – or do better than mere survival[39] – are by their nature limiting. Freudian theory was found to be especially helpful with its range of 'demand' structures from the basic, powerful but barely accessible and knowable id, through to the conscious core of minute-to-minute operation and self-understanding, the ego, and on to the higher-order guiding structure of principles, the superego. These are included in the schema under the general title of I Want, as: I Need, I Like, and I Ought. The first is dominated by basic needs and emotions, later added to by those that are acquired or given manifest form by life's experience and learning. The last two represent the notion of potential optional solutions that is the hallmark of the operation of the cortex, i.e., problem solving above the level of simple reaction and more flexible than complex but hard-wired instinct. The focusing process is motive, which is influenced (Freud reminds us) by emotions even when they are not readily accessible to the problem solver.

---

39 Critical elements in physical structure are genes with the biological strategy for survival, but they had: 'found a way to delegate their ambitions, by building bodies capable not just of survival but of intelligent behaviour as well' (Ridley, 1999, p. 27).

So far, it may appear that problem solving is strictly limited to the solution of immediate problems; that the outcomes are mere survival. Certainly this is the base of all that happens. However, there also seem to be drives, the operation of which have the outcome of what appears to be more than mere survival; rather, the need to detect predictable patterns both within the individual and in the individual's environment, to understand these patterns in the sense of using them to acquire a grasp of reality and, with this as a resource, to acquire mastery of the environment. They amount to a drive to develop the use of one's built-in resources and acquired capacities, not just to grow up into adulthood, but to stretch on beyond the immediate requirements of simple survival. This is best expressed in the work of Maslow (1968) and his notion of self-actualisation, which stems from this added need to exploit the potential of the individual.

Individuals tackle their problems in characteristic ways, influenced by the nature and experience of their cognitive function. These differences are essential elements making up their personalities. These characteristic differences are, therefore, part of personality.

STYLE AND PERSONALITY RELATIONSHIPS

The elements of personality, in current theory, are often presented schematically as a step pyramid. At the base of this hierarchy is the most numerous, least stable, and least self-revealing class, that of responses to events. Above this level, in rising order of stability, pervasiveness, and power of influence are habit, trait, and dimensions of personality. A problem with such hierarchy is that the steps seem discrete and much time and effort has been expended in trying to determine, with finality, at what level a particular pattern of behaviour lies and what else lies with it. Additionally, there is uncertainty as to whether an element in question is behaviour or an influence on behaviour and, if it is an influence, whether it is learnt or not. The complexity of observations to be accommodated into the schema is great, especially as all the categories tend to overlap, e.g., inherited elements are built on by learning, and some learnt patterns are virtually resistant to any change while others are so readily modifiable that it is doubtful if they can be classed as personality. Perhaps it would be less confusing and rigid to place all the elements onto a continuum (see Figure 3) from those that may be genetically originated, are most stable and pervasive, and most resistant to any change through to those that are so lightly held, over a narrow range of event and transitory in nature. Dimensions of personality are then firmly anchored in biology at one end and the continuum fades away into almost casual response at the other end; the power of prediction of a person's characteristic reaction to a known given event, from high to low, will accord with the place it has on the continuum.

This figure also implies that the left-hand end of the continuum has fewer elements but that these elements influence the remaining elements further on. It shows a dynamic progression of influence, with those elements having the most influence being those that are earliest formed, deepest seated, most pervasive, and least likely to change (most predictable) over time and changing events, eventually shading, at the other end, into patterns of behaviour that are so limited in scope and so readily discarded as not to contribute significantly to the description of an individual. The 'shading into' notion of a continuum is more accurately expressive of the gradual shift

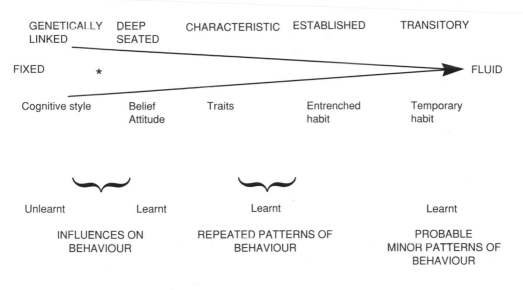

* Direction of influence: the breadth of the shaft depicts the range of influence.

Figure 3 Personality – a continuum of influence

of terms from one to the other than the currently used discrete 'steps', which are akin to describing individuals by placing them in 'personality boxes'. It has been argued earlier that the processes associated with each of the cognitive function's 'elements' are part of brain structure. This includes the problem-solving process in cognitive effect. Within cognitive affect, besides its process, some needs are also part of inherited structure. Within cognitive effect it was argued earlier that both cognitive style preference and potential level (intelligence, talent) have inherited components. This is not so of coping behaviour or any part of cognitive resource (except its process), including any manifest capacity, all of which are learnt. If A-I can be shown to be (a) deep-seated, being not only early set but resistant to modification over time and event; and (b) relating to many traits, giving meaning to their relationships; then it is a dimension, a suggestion first made by Goldsmith (1994). These are matters that will be explored later.

Eysenck (1965, 1967) argues (as did Jung) that dimensions of personality, to be classified as such, need to have a genetic component. Interestingly, a biologist, van der Molen (1994), argues that the adaption-innovation concept is likely to have such a component partly because, even in animals, individuals may vary in their adhesion to group structures and partly also because there are marked descriptive similarities between some behaviours classified as more adaptive–more innovative and abnormal behaviours[40] attributed to a variant output of dopamine neuromodulators. If this is

40 For instance, over-inclusion, associated with schizophrenia, leading the patient to make bizarrely remote associations and to over-generalise and over-abstract (Hawks & Payne, 1972), might be viewed as an innovative characteristic that has lapped outside the normal range of behaviour. Retreat into cripplingly tight ritual structure may be the adaptor counterpart. Dopamine levels are also associated with both normal and abnormal conditions.

so, then the deepest-seated elements of cognitive function (such as introversion–extraversion, neuroticism, and adaption-innovation) are likely to have far-reaching effects on (are modulators of) more specific, learnt behaviour patterns, e.g., habits and traits. If adaptors, for instance, prefer to problem solve within clear structures, much of which they prefer to be consensually agreed, it follows that they are seen as less risk-taking but more methodical than innovators. Earlier it was noted that research of the last decade suggests that risk-taking is genetically linked.

This discussion on which type of personality schema, pyramid or continuum, is more useful does not affect, either positively or negatively, the validity or reliability of the A-I descriptions. These initially depended on observation and are now supported by 'trait' type research.

Risk-taking

The conclusions of these studies are in turn supported by work that suggests a logical interrelationship between the components (traits) which reinforces the statistical relationships found. For instance, it is reasonable to suppose that a person who 'does things better' is also likely to have a preference for precision, reliability, efficiency, discipline, conformity, safety, and soundness; whereas a person who 'does things differently' is just as likely to be characterised by being willing to work with less assisting structure and having to accept that precision, reliability, and safety are not so readily obtained among such ambiguity. The patterns can be predicted by deduction from the theory and its basic assumptions. For instance, A-I theory assumes that people differ in the amount of consensually agreed cognitive structure they prefer to have associated with a problem before being comfortable in seeking its resolution. The more adaptive prefer the added, more agreed structure and so it is expected that:

- their problem identification has good support;
- the information they have concerning the problem is relatively abundant;
- the possible dangers of a course of action are clearer;
- the nature of the solution they seek has a good chance of being accepted by others holding the same cognitive structure; and
- the solution has a good chance of successful implementation.

All this can be contrasted with innovative conditions, where the structure is less abundant and less is known about it – this is because it lies within fewer helping guidelines, some of which are likely to be less well defined. The more adaptive can, therefore, be seen as operating in a cognitively safer environment than the more innovative, or to put it another way: The more innovative live the riskier life. The correlation between KAI and risk-taking can now be confidently expected, in the direction of innovation equalling added risk. Research results are in highly significant statistical support (e.g., Goldsmith, 1984). The descriptions of adaptors and innovators have been a ready source of hypotheses, as can be seen from the studies shown in Table G, Appendix 6. The converse is true; theory can predict, for instance, that some results will not correlate significantly, such as with trait anxiety measures (see below), which are more appropriately located in cognitive affect.

Self-actualisation

More research is needed, not only in unexplored territory but to confirm single studies with intriguing findings and to anchor clear findings more securely to the main theory. This is especially so of measures related to self-awareness and self-evaluation since, as suggested earlier, self-awareness is an element in understanding reality; both are keys to human problem solving. Kirton & Hammond (1980) speculated that there would be a difference in levels of self-actualisation: 'adaptors might be supposed to be more willing to adhere to accepted modes of thought and behaviour that will mould their image of themselves and so are capable of higher self-actualisation; the converse might be true of innovators' – a bold thought that came unstuck. Lipsitt's (1958) measure of self-concept was used; it has two forms, each containing the same list of stimulus adjectives (such as happy, bashful). Respondents respond to Form A in a way 'which best shows how you see yourself' and to Form B: 'how I would like to be'. The results were unexpected – an insignificant correlation. However, it was noticed that the item pairs were not linearly related but U-shaped, with the base located half a standard deviation towards the more innovative. Taking this as a point to divide the group, the more adaptive subset yielded a mean of –.48 and the more innovative one of +.60. The explanation given for these groups differing in their perception of themselves in this way still seems weak, and Beene (1985) later criticised it. Using different measures (Lipsitt, 1958) and dividing the subjects into three groups (more adaptive, middling, more innovative), Beene's results were that the more innovative scored significantly higher on self-actualisation and lower on anxiety. The results that higher innovators may be inclined to hold themselves in more esteem received some support in another study by Goldsmith & Matherly (1987a), who used two measures (Rosenberg Self-Esteem Scale and Crandall's Adjective Check List) with 127 young business students, equally balanced for males and females. The two measures correlated .50 between themselves but only .15 and .21 with KAI. Buttner et al. (1999) concur; they write: 'Adaptive managers, as defined by KAI, were more likely to underrate themselves, while self ratings [on skills] of innovator managers tended to concur with the ratings of others.' These results need confirmation and, if confirmed, the explanation of them must be made clearer. This may lead to useful understanding of the relationship between perceived self-actualisation, perceived self-esteem, and cognitive style. Perhaps the more adaptive feel better protected by the prevailing paradigm and can afford to project themselves more cautiously. Innovators report that they feel less confident when they feel 'enmeshed' into prevailing structure. Perhaps it is the conditions in which the respondents exist that are the key, e.g., adaptors' self-esteem may be higher in familiar settings – for instance, Elder (1989) notes they are less anxious in such settings (see below).

Anxiety

Anxiety is placed in the cognitive function schema in cognitive affect. It should therefore not correlate significantly with cognitive style, which is placed in cognitive effect. However, intervening variables may play a part in this expectation. As is now being suggested, future studies may need to search not just for trait differences between adaptor and innovator but the particular conditions in which they may manifest. More refined hypotheses need to be devised to explore conditions that can be derived from the theory, for example, that adaptors are likely to feel more comfortable (self-actualised and with high self-esteem) when their paradigms are not under threat and innovators more comfortable when not wedged in the core of a well-established paradigm. Such a finding would suggest a possible relationship between the integrity of internal structure (expressed as well-being) and perceived enveloping social structure, and suggest less importance to small general differences across all situations. There are some clues that suggest this line of study is worthwhile. The correlation with the 16 PF anxiety (trait) measure was insignificant (Kirton & de Ciantis, 1986 – see Table G, Appendix 6). Elder (1989), however, had found that although the correlation obtained between KAI and Spielburger's measure of anxiety trait was insignificant, the correlation with his measure of anxiety state was significant, albeit small, at −.23. The measures had been given to the same sample of students under unfamiliar conditions thought to cause marginally more alarm to the more adaptive than to the more innovative. Goldsmith et al. (1986; McNeilly & Goldsmith, 1992) noted that differences between adaptors and innovators on job satisfaction seemed to be related, at least on some variables, to different environmental conditions, whereas there was no significant relationship for job satisfaction in general. Gryskiewicz et al. (1995) confirmed this finding. Wunderlly (1996), found innovators tended to be more optimistic than adaptors.

Many of the studies not only offered confirmation of expected interrelatedness of variables but also did so in a sequence or pattern. Here are two examples. The first is that the work of Rogers' (1959) was thought in part to describe the innovative pole of the A-I measure. As part of the validation study, one of Rogers' observations – that the creative loner would be likely to be extravert rather than introvert – was tested and the results bore out his prediction. The second example is provided by Goldsmith (1984), who noted that no one had tested the assumption that the more innovative may perceive themselves as risk-taking. He noted that no A-I literature had speculated on the relationship with sensation-seeking, yet other work showed the latter to be correlated with risk-taking. His study predicted, and then showed, that the three measures do intercorrelate significantly, to the same magnitudes and in the directions expected. Many of the studies that have been quoted show interrelatedness of traits among themselves as well as with adaption-innovation. It is this clustering that led Goldsmith to the view that KAI was measuring a dimension of personality. Others also explored areas and relationships not given in the earlier description of A-I theory or included in earlier studies. Isaksen, Dorval & Kaufmann (1992, using Paivio's measure, 1971) opened up new territory, finding differences in the preference for scale imagery by innovators compared to a preference for verbal presentation by adaptors.

There has also been work that explores adaption-innovation and the relatively new five-factor model. Gelade (2002, Tables G and H, Appendix 6) in a review of several studies (already separately reported) lines up their findings with assumed relationships to this model. As expected the innovation pole correlates markedly and persistently with conscientiousness and openness to experience; more modestly with extraversion and insignificantly with feeling and neuroticism. Equally useful is the work undertaken exploring relationships with variables that are not related to adaption-innovation (see Table G, Appendix 6), which help to delineate the boundaries of the concept. The hypothesis that has so far been sustained is the following: Measures relating to cognitive affect have insubstantial relationships with those of cognitive effect. The finding that neuroticism had virtually zero correlation is to be expected if it is noted that its alternative title is 'lability of emotion'. In the cognitive function schema, emotion has been located in cognitive affect; it has already been noted that anxiety traits correlate negligibly with KAI. Not only does the Anxiety Factor from Cattell et al. (1970) 16PF (Kirton & de Ciantis, 1986) also correlate negligibly, but so also do 11 other measures in this battery, all for the same reason. One MBTI type (Myers, 1962), Thinking-Feeling, also a measure from within cognitive affect, correlates insubstantially with KAI scores (Gryskiewicz, 1982; Goldsmith, 1986a; Jacobson, 1993; Tefft, 1990; van Rooyen, 1994). A small, significant correlation (.22) was found using a measure of life stress (Holmes & Rahe, 1967) suggesting that innovators see themselves, not perhaps unexpectedly, as generally under more pressure than adaptors. It is true that in discussion, the more adaptive often believe innovators cause themselves stress because of their predilection for crashing into social barriers, but this correlation is so small it needs further confirmation. So do those observations that, in general, innovators may come to less harm in crashing into barriers than adaptors would, should it happen to them.

A politician's view

Basic contentions in this book are that individuals have characteristic styles of problem solving and that the more effective style is dependent on the nature of the problem and what can be accepted as the appropriate solution. Although not couched in exactly these modern-sounding ways, this essential thought is hardly new. If one roughly equates the terms adaption and innovation with 'circumspection' and 'impetuous' (and set the problem within the times in which it was perceived) then that master political theorist of the early 16th century, Niccolo Machiavelli, had a useful contribution to make: '. . . we see that some princes flourish one day and come to grief the next, without appearing to have changed in character or any other way [. . .] I believe that the one who adapts his policy to the times prospers, and likewise that the one whose policy clashes with the demands of the times does not. It can be observed that men use various methods in pursuing their own personal objectives [. . .] One man proceeds with circumspection, another impetuously [. . .] one man goes about things patiently, another does the opposite; and yet everyone, for all the diversity of method, can reach his objective. It can also be observed that with two circumspect men, one will achieve his end, and the other not; and likewise two men succeed equally well with different methods, one of them being circumspect and the other impetuous. This results from nothing else except the extent to which *their methods are or are not suited to the nature of the times*' (Bull, 1981, translation of *The Prince*, p. 151, our italics). Such nature, outlook, laws and customs are, as Polybius (c.150 BC) wrote, related to the mode character of the citizens of their state.

Machiavelli has an explanation of why using a style that is not in accord with the climate (and, therefore, the majority's view of the problem) does not make for easy problem solving. In this translation, Bull uses the term innovator for the agent of change, but the text reads just as appropriately for an adaptor introducing change into an innovative climate. 'The difficulties that [rulers] encounter in acquiring their principalities arise partly because of the new institutions and laws they are forced to introduce in founding the state and making themselves secure. It should be borne in mind that there is nothing more difficult to handle, more doubtful of success, and more dangerous to carry through than initiating changes in a state's constitution. The innovator makes enemies of all those who prospered under the old order, and only lukewarm support is forthcoming from those who would prosper under the new. Their support is lukewarm partly from the fear of their adversaries, who have the existing laws on their side, and partly because men are generally incredulous, never really trusting new things unless they have tested them by experience. In consequence, whenever those who oppose the changes can do so, they attack vigorously, and the defence made by the others is only lukewarm. So both the innovator and his friends come to grief' (p. 51). A similar insight into adaption-innovation clash, from the opening page of a modern novel, is seen in Box 8 below.

Box 8 A novelist's view

'Business meetings are more or less the same all over the world, and have been since the beginning of time. There is the man in charge; the man supposedly in charge; the man wanting to be in charge; their minions, their enemies and those waverers who float gently downstream, hoping things won't get too choppy. And there is always a dispute, which serves the purpose of making half-felt antagonisms real. Sometimes these are of importance and justify the energy expended on them. But not often.

So it was one afternoon in September in a large but utilitarian room in a shambling, run-down set of buildings in that section of Rome loosely known as the Aventino. There were twenty people, all men of between thirty-five and seventy-five years old; fourteen items on the agenda, and two factions, each determined to sweep all before them and rout the forces of (on the one hand) dangerous and puerile innovation and (on the other) hidebound traditionalism irrelevant to the needs of the modern world' (Pears, 1999, p. 1). Used with permission of the author.

The Adorno scales

From the time of the validation study of KAI, predictions were made and tested, as a number of traits seemed to be 'extensions' of the A-I core description. The first of these hypothesised extensions that was tested was the 'Adorno' group of concepts – that is, a group of scales that had been developed by or inspired by Adorno, viz., measures of dogmatism (Rokeach, 1960); intolerance of ambiguity (Budner, 1962; MacDonald's 1970 revision of Rydell & Rosen, 1966), inflexibility (Gough, 1975), and conservatism (Wilson & Patterson, 1968). Adaptors, working within the protection of added structure, are the more likely to remain within those structures and, therefore, define more tightly (and more narrowly) the area of solution search[41]. Working within observable structure, however large or small, they are the more likely to be seen by the more innovative as inflexible, less tolerant of ambiguity, and conservative; within the

---

41 The size of the structure is a level variable, unrelated to style. A high-level, high adaptor can work readily in an area larger than a low-level, high innovator could manage.

Table 3 A-I differences in paradigm consistency[a]

Test	Innovators[b]	Rest
1. Dogmatism (Rokeach, 1960)	0.81	0.97
2. Intolerance of ambiguity (Budner, 1962)	0.63	0.78
3. Intolerance of ambiguity (Macdonald, 1970)	0.68	0.71
4. Inflexibility (Gough, 1956)	0.73	0.81
5. Conservatism (Wilson & Patterson, 1968)	0.83	0.89
6. All measures together	0.83	0.82

Notes

a Differences between the first 5 sets of results are significant; 1, 2, 4, and 5 at $p < .01$ and 3 at $p < .05$, but 6 is insignificant.

b Split at 0.5 *SD*; Innovators $n = 197$; Rest $n = 365$; Total $n = 562$.

structures of which they are the more assured masters (and where they prefer to be), they could be seen as more dogmatic. The results (see Table I, Appendix 6), using nearly 300 subjects from those general population samples, show all these measures to be positively related; adaptors lean in the direction of the titles as given. The internal reliabilities of the five Adorno measures were all high, they intercorrelated highly and when combined into a single super-measure yielded an internal reliability of .83; their relatively uniform relationship to A-I supports the notion for the existence of a dimension of personality.

Consistency

Many people are concerned, when responding to measures, to do so consistently, which is just as well or these measures would lack the required reliability. A hypothesis can be formed that the more adaptive would be more concerned to be consistent than the more innovative. The data derived from the Adorno battery offered a useful means of testing this hypothesis, as it consisted of five measures that were, in general, reliably answered, and were closely interrelated with a probable common underlying cognitive structure. So, if anyone aimed at perfect consistency, on which option would they concentrate – consistency on each measure separately (accepting a little less consistency between all the measures, overall) or overall consistency (accepting a little less on each one)? It was supposed that the former strategy might appeal to the more adaptive and the latter to the more innovative. The results only partly turned out as expected, for on the overall (super-measure) there were no differences between the two groups. The measure-by-measure results showed, on first calculation, only slight differences. However, when the groups were divided not at the general population mean, but again as a previous study had suggested, at the half of a standard deviation mark (higher moderate and high innovators versus the rest), the results were clearer cut (Kirton, 1985; also see Table 3).

There does seem to be a curious, as yet unexplained, significance of a 'turning point' in the scale, somewhere between one half to (under) one whole standard deviation (8–16 points) in the direction of innovation; a division at this point which often yields better predictions than division at the general population mean. It suggests that, below the mean, adaption may progress (in fact, diminish) in stricter linear fashion than innovation does above it; that the slope begins perceptively to deviate

Table 4 A-I reactions to official guidance

Guidance given	Adaptors	Innovators
Required	100%	87%
Recommended	58%	26%
No statement	20%	50%

from linearity at about 10 points or so above the mean. This was independently calculated as the observed magnitude of the just noticeable difference (the magnitude at which people begin to notice that another's style is not the same as theirs). Another example relates to behaviour of individuals in response to openly given structure. Foxall & Bhate (1991; also see Table 4) were interested in the extent to which university course requirements would influence adaptors and innovators differently, with division at the group median, which was again slightly innovative. The sample was drawn from three courses, the first of which required the students to be familiar with specified computer packages; the second recommended it, and the third made no statement.

These differences have evoked interest in the managers to whom they have been shown in training courses. Adaptor managers, indeed whole administrations, tend to perceive the adaptor pattern as 'normal' and that of innovators as 'deviant'. Certainly, it accords more to the 'logic of the situation', but logic is derived from the perceived underlying 'rule' and this, to be a rule that is used in society generally, needs to be consensually agreed, i.e., the essential guidelines for the more adaptive. Innovators, of course, need guidelines, but they do not treat them in the same way – *initial* structure is not necessarily perceived as the means to solve the problem but as the starting point for problem solving. Hence initial structure is more readily negotiable in the interest of seeking a solution rather than being assumed, as a matter of course, to be the best way available. So adaptive leaders are liable to be nonplussed by what, for them, is casual regard (too often, casual disregard) for rule. Conversely, the innovator leaders are as often surprised by being asked for clear guidelines of what is required by more adaptive subordinates, a request that these bosses often mistake as a request for *prescription* to be slavishly followed, or as incompetence. Conversely, the more adaptive administrators can expect only the equally more adaptive subordinates to make the same link that they do between stated guideline and 'appropriate' response. They may not see the need for further explanation and encouragement to innovators to make the same link. This is part of the cost of investment into diversity – if innovators are needed their weaknesses need to be accommodated along with their strengths – just as the converse is true. The investment is worth the price if efficient solutions are found as a result. The pay-off for the community is the availability of enough adaptors and innovators for a variety of style to be engaged on all its many, diverse problems.

In review

All the results, both positive and negative, that deal with style and personality are consistent and interrelated in a pattern that could be expected by the theory. However, many of the correlations, although comfortably above minimum significance levels, are still not accounting for the bulk of the variance. The correlation, for example, between measures of inflexibility and adaption-innovation, although highly significant, accounts for less than a quarter of the variance. We must therefore expect minorities (e.g., politically radical adaptors) that are nonetheless numerous, in absolute terms. Research has yet to give support to the commonly held view in politics that until adaptors join the party it has no chance of getting into power, but will remain talking and scheming and unelectable. Research has also yet to test another common-sense notion, that these less common groups, the 'cognitive minorities', may not be evenly spread in the community, e.g. more academic staff may be both innovative and intro-vert than might be expected by random distribution and that will not be distributed evenly over the departments within their universities. (Conversely, more innovator extraverts than expected by chance, are thought to congregate in marketing depart-ments, especially in those offering new trendy goods in a rapidly changing, highly competitive environment.) These minorities may have their own particular advantages and difficulties; for example, dogmatic innovators may be particularly difficult to cope with, if the matters on which they are unyielding are difficult to predict and/or to integrate in any given system. This is balanced by their likely excellence in persisting with the introduction of a much-needed, highly radical change in the face of sub-stantial indifference or even hostility. As always, it is a fine line between when the same attribute can be seen as positive (I am steadfast, dependable, and reasonable) and when negative (you are stubborn, pig-headed, and disturbing).

It will be seen from the mass of data now available that the A-I dimension is closely associated with a clear cluster of personality traits, in groups with different but related underlying theoretical rationale. However, the relationship between adaption-innovation and any single trait is far from perfect; e.g., the extent of overlap with extraversion, although significant (between .4 and .5 and a probability coefficient of <.001), is around 20%. Allowance must be made not just for the differences between adaptors and innovators, but also for the wide variation among adaptors and among innovators (all arrayed on a continuum) for the exact mix and strengths of the person-ality characteristics held by each individual. It must be remembered that the range between the highest and the most moderate adaptor is wider than the range between the most moderate adaptors and the most moderate innovators. Nevertheless, the stability of the general matrix and the stability of the traits themselves allow people to judge the relative positions on KAI of themselves and others with accuracy (e.g., Kirton & McCarthy, 1985). This may be analogous to a concept of a gene package that identifies members of a family. A group of mild innovators (say) have enough of the total characteristics associated with mild innovativeness and hold most of these characteristics in sufficient strength to be clearly recognisable as mild innovators. An exact and very even pattern of particular traits is not needed for secure identification. This applies in each area of the continuum, remembering always that a continuum has no true internal boundaries, and that any selected group has members on its periphery who have more in common with close neighbours just outside than they may have with those located in the middle of their group[42].

---

42 The weakness of grouping personality scores into 'boxes' when they represent locations on a measure of a continuum is that comparisons between individuals can be misleadingly close or distant.

5 Structure and cognition

PROBLEM SOLVING AND LEARNING THEORY

Behaviourism versus Gestalt

The study of problem solving originates in the field of learning theory, a scholarly domain that has differed markedly from creativity in its methodology. Beginning in the 1890s, it is principally laboratory based. Early work in learning theory began with the principal aim of understanding how and under what conditions learning could occur and identifying the key elements at its core. The famous experiments by the Russian biologist, Ivan Pavlov, broke fundamental ground by pinpointing the stimulus–response (S-R) bond as the key building block, coupled with the conditioning response of reinforced association of two or more elements. In his classic experiments he showed that the sound of a bell could substitute for the presentation of food to elicit a salivation response in his canine subjects. This experiment demonstrated a proposal by William James (1890), that when two elementary brain processes have been active together or in immediate succession, one of them, on recurring, tends 'to propagate its excitement' into the other. This demonstration that a reflex can be conditioned laid the foundations to the serious scientific study of learning, since it showed this process in operation at a very basic, almost mechanistic level. The experimenters interested in these phenomena, under a later general title of Behaviourism, examined the conditions and the mechanisms by which particular stimuli and particular responses became connected.

The Behaviourist School flourished at the turn of the 20th century, its principal concern being to understand the learning process. At base, it was first conceived as a 'trial and error' process and such pioneers as Watson, and later Osgood, developed the notion of basic S-R bonds into S-R chains. A stimulus became bonded with a response when the outcome of the association was favourable, that is, the feedback yielded positive reinforcement; the bond was broken by negative reinforcement. Thorndike (1913) concentrated on working out the ground rules for association in his famous 'law of effect', first published in 1898, isolating such independent variables as recency, repetition, vividness, and contiguity[43] and their effect on reinforcing the learning

---

43 Recency: how long since the pair was perceived; repetition: how often; vividness: how dramatically; contiguity: how closely together (time or space). These terms are, interestingly, still useful in describing how the content of a single neuron competes for the attention of awareness (e.g., Carter, 2002, pp. 122–124).

bond. This gave a greater depth of understanding of why a particular S is associated with a particular R, particularly in his emphasis on the importance of motive, both for the formation and continuance of a bond and for its discontinuance[44]. At that time and up to until comparatively recently it was not understood how different parts of the brain, at different levels from primitive systems to the sophisticated cortex, might be involved at different parts of the process. The notion of recency would seem to involve short-term memory and repetition or habituation (i.e., repetition to habit forming), both of which are primarily likely to involve the striatum[45]. The notion of vividness might relate to the link between emotion and the limbic system, especially the amygdala, as an intermediary role between sensory input and emotion. It may, therefore, assist in 'selective attention', which helps select those to respond to from among incoming stimuli.

Having established some underlying principles, great debate soon emerged as to how so basic a structure as S-R bonding could explain the complexities of the behaviour observed, particularly in the highly complex thinking of humans. The behaviourists were sure that arrays of single S-R bonding was an over-simplification and introduced the notion of the formation of more complex S-R chains or patterns. This higher-order collection of single S-R bonds was thought to form complex patterns of loosely connected associations that lay at the core of complex behaviours. Thus, S-R bonds became patterns of ever-increasing complexity, eventually establishing an overall entity (called a concept) that is more meaningful than its constituent elements. Problem-solving research was evolving from the mechanical 'trial-and-error' behaviourists' view to the more complex notions of insight learning, the core interest of what became known as the Gestalt School. Gestalt thinking usefully concentrated on human learning and had less concern than behaviourists with exploring instinctive behaviour[46]. It was also influenced by the philosophic view of *tabula rasa*: The notion that, for humans at least, the brain starts off as a blank sheet on which experience (learning) writes, a notion that rightly disposes of human instinct but goes too far in ignoring basic built-in mental facilities (see, e.g., Pinker, 2002).

The Gestalt psychologists found great difficulty in accepting the S-R bond as the basic unit of analysis in human learning; trial and error learning seems more appropriate to animals or, perhaps, to humans under very restricted conditions, where past experience does not provide much help. They dismissed even its more sophisticated forms as overly simplistic and of little practical value in understanding complex patterns of behaviour. The problem that they faced was how a 'mix of red, yellow and green becomes the sight of fruits in a bowl? [. . .] Gestalt psychology understood that Galileo's feat was not simply being the first on his block to point a telescope skywards. Somehow he had recognized the meaning of the data that he had collected'

---

44 The critical importance of positive and negative reinforcement in this process is also important in understanding why, despite individuals frequently having to behave in ways not in accord with their preferred style, they do not change their deeply seated preference; they are instead more likely to become stressed.

45 See, e.g., Mishkin et al. (1984); Mishkin & Appenzeller (1987).

46 This German group, lead by Wertheimer, Koffka, and Köhler, flourished in the early 20th century; they had an interest in animal behaviour, vide Köhler's work on *Mentality of Apes*, but their emphasis was on human behaviour. Koffka's *Growth of the Mind* was the main assault on Thorndike's behaviourist position (see, e.g., Hilgard & Bower, 1966, p. 229).

(Bolles, 1999, p. 274)[47]. The thesis that developed from this school was that the human brain builds up complex clusters of associative elements, establishing their interrelationships to form complex patterns of loosely connected concepts[48]. A concept, then, is a cognitive construct (has a meaning boundary) within which a number of elements are associated and the resulting entity defined is relatively stable. The stability ensures that the number of elements and their interrelationships are sufficiently enduring for the meaning, derived from this association, also to be stable. An accumulation of concepts, formed into interrelated structures and having clear definition and stability, is the means by which an understanding of reality can be gained, stored, and used not only to react to stimuli but to anticipate them; accommodating not only the phenomenon of insight but also foresight. Concept formation became established as the basic building block of cognition and its unit of analysis and was used in the fields of intelligence and creativity. Individuals with high intelligence could be described, for instance, as being able to manage more complex or difficult concepts and a larger number of concepts than those who are less intelligent. In idea generation, although innovators and adaptors may produce different quantities as a matter of strategy, they also produce characteristically different new concepts and use them differently.

The Gestalt psychologists studied problem solving through what they termed 'insight learning', drawing upon the theories of perceptual organisation and pattern recognition. They saw the key element of problem solving – a condition arising whenever a path to a desired goal is blocked – as the perceptual reorganisation of the problem resulting in insight (Köhler, 1947). These theories clearly bought creativity and problem solving into the same realm of cognitive function by emphasising the cognitive restructuring of concepts as the core activity. Such reformulation they saw primarily as overcoming mental set or 'functional fixedness' in problem solving, that is, the tendency for problem solvers to become 'fixated' on, say, an object's more usual function. In this case the structure set by past experience limits the search for a solution; sometime usefully, sometimes not.

A number of classic problems, which might require the problem solver to reconceptualise the problem in order to reach a particular solution, were devised to demonstrate this phenomenon. Maier (1931) devised the 'two string and pendulum' problem; Duncker (1945) performed experiments on functional fixedness using his 'candle and holder' problem; Scheerer (1963) devised his well-known nine-dot problem; Luchins and Luchins (1959) put forward their classic water jar problems. The latter is a classic example that can be used to illuminate the field. Subjects are confronted with a series

---

47 An even clearer example of the way that meaning is not just a collection of its associated items is the phenomenon of the cinema, where what is presented is a number of 'stills' that cognitive process translates into the appearance of movement and narrative. Bolles argues against the suggestion – on mathematical grounds – that this is a case where the whole is *greater* than its parts; he suggests instead that the whole may be *different* from its parts (1999, p. 277). However, it is certain that cognitive function can derive more meaning from a perceived pattern than from a collection of events – this book, too, is based on this notion.

48 Pinker (1998) in his review chapter 'Thinking Machines' (pp. 59–148) argues powerfully that the Gestaltists still have the better of this argument. Machines, however formidably powerful, still operate on the behaviourist principle, which works well for calculation but not for extracting understanding from vast arrays of input that life manages very well. There is a critical, if sometimes subtle, difference between actual intelligence and proxy (including artificial) intelligence that suggests the latter application of the term is a misnomer.

of problems all involving a set of three jars of different sizes. The problem is to present in one of them a quantity that is not equal to the size of any of the jars. The size of each jar, in each set of three, also varies from trial to trial (e.g., the trial three set of 18, 43, and 10 requiring a quantity of 5 as the solution, and those in trial four: 9, 42, and 6 requiring a quantity of 21). After a trial run or 2 (with only two jars) the experiment contains 11 trials, divided (unbeknown to the subjects) into two groups. The first group's solutions are all achieved by the formula: Jar B − A − 2C, even though the actual volumes of the jars vary set by set. The second group can be solved two ways: (a) by the current formula and (b) by a simpler (more efficient) variant, e.g., A − C or A + C. Respondents characteristically differ, switching readily, later than others, or not at all.

The concepts being explored in all these experiments underpin many of the more recent and current approaches in the teaching and practice of creativity. For instance, De Bono's (1975) techniques of 'lateral thinking' principally focus on stimulating an innovative style reconceptualisation of the problem-definition stage of the problem-solving process as a precursor to solution search. Cognitive techniques such as brainstorming are discussed in a later chapter in detail; but the issue, in brief, that arises from the Luchin Jar experiment is that these experiments are often presented as level tests, and in some cases they are. Yet, although in the examples above the levels of any of the solutions are all within the capacity of subjects, these experiments are used to 'prove' that innovative style is more creative. But this view is narrowly reached; a fuller set of hypotheses derived from A-I theory would suggest that the more adaptive will be more persistent and more successful, over time and complexity, with a 'given' formula, and generally make better use of the current system than innovators. The more innovative, who are likely to try to carry out alternatives that fail (or to lose interest) when the system still works will exploit this seeming disadvantage when the current system no longer works well. Note, however, this does not mean that high innovators can do without a system; rather they are readier at substituting it, both when necessary and even when not.

The notion of concept

A concept was conceived as a 'package' of information comprised of an ordered arrangement of chains and patterns, forming an integral whole and operating as a basic unit of cognition. An updated view is:

- a concept has a boundary that distinguishes what is its content from what is not;
- within the boundary of the concept there are elements (of relevant knowledge and observation, like the array of S-R bonds) that are stable, in number and ordering, and which give, for the individual holding it, a consistent general meaning;
- if the location of the boundary (and its contact and order) is held by more than one person, then the concept can be shared and communication of ideas (i.e., language) and complex human group collaboration becomes possible;
- concepts can be related together into higher formations (see Gagné's schema, 1965, 1974 and Box 9 overleaf)

Problems may need to be solved not just by individuals working alone, or even individuals working in groups, but by collaboration of many individuals formed in

Box 9 Gagnés' hierarchy of learning

1. Signal Learning: The establishment of a simple connection in which a stimulus takes on the properties of a signal (classical conditioning).
2. Stimulus–Response (S-R) Learning: The establishment of a connection between a stimulus and a response where the response is a voluntary movement and the connection is instrumental in satisfying a need or motive (operant conditioning).

1 and 2 are prerequisites for:
3. Chaining: The connecting of a sequence of two or more previously learned S-R connections.
4. Verbal Association: The learning of chains that are specifically verbal, important for the acquisition and use of language. Enables a number of learned connections involving words to be emitted in a single sequence.

3 and 4 are prerequisites for:
5. Discrimination Learning: Making different responses to similar stimuli. Involves more than simply making isolated S-R connections because it is necessary to deal with the problem of interference between similar items.

5 is a prerequisite for:
6. Concept Learning: Learning to make a common response to stimuli that form a class or category but which differ in their physical characteristics. Requires representing information in memory, classifying events, and discriminating between them on the basis of abstract properties.
7. Rule (Principle) Learning: A rule is a chain of two or more concepts.
8. Problem solving: Involves recombining two or more principles into new ones, making it possible to answer questions and solve problems, especially important to real-life human problem-solving situations.

more than one group, not all necessarily in close proximity or frequent contact. Each hierarchy of collaborating structure involves more attention to the forms of structure needed to achieve this widening of diversity of means to solve a diversity of problems. As a trade-off, some diversity, e.g., variations in meanings of the common structure used, may need to be diminished. The cooperation of groups involves even more forms of structure that need to be agreed. Nevertheless, the paradox continues to work. Although the relatively stable structure of the concept is a vital element in this, the ability of each thinker to change the structure (for self and so also for the group) is equally important – too little structure and there is insufficient common understanding to bring about agreed collective change; too rigid a structure inhibits further needful change.

Box 9 shows Gagné's (1974) relationship between simple and more complex learning. In addition, Gagné shows a theoretical relationship between learning and problem solving. He regards learning as hierarchical, with eight levels of learning. Each level builds on earlier, simpler abilities, which thereby represent prerequisites for later, more complex patterns of learning. At the bottom of the hierarchy are the basic mechanisms of establishing the simple connections of classical conditioning, which lead up to the beginnings of S-R chains. Gagné places *problem solving* at the pinnacle of this hierarchy, representing the highest, most complex form of learning, of which all the others are prerequisites. Thus, within the realm of cognitive function, problem solving and creativity can be linked or overlapped. The potential capacity of the cognitive function is termed intelligence; the characteristic manner of performance is the preferred style. Both of these have their influence in the build-up of cognitive resource (the depository of manifest capacity), through the twin processes of learning and memory. All interact with the environment as understood and interpreted by the cognitive function operation.

Summary

This section has touched on two critical matters. One is the interrelatedness of the elements of the cognitive function: creativity, problem solving, and learning. The other is the paradox of the need for and the limitation of structure, which is ever present in the workings of the cognitive function.

1   Gagné's figure offers a clarification of the link between learning and problem solving. Earlier it was argued that creativity and problem solving are largely indistinguishable as products of the cognitive function. Naming some of the products of cognitive function differently from others may be more useful linguistically than it is to scientific classification; the products still remain closely related to one another through their common generation source, the same brain function.
2   Creativity and problem solving share a key element: concept. It is common to learning theorists and creativity researchers as the core unit of analysis. A concept is envisaged as having a boundary, so that it is possible to know what is included in and what is outside the conceptual notion in mind. It includes a number of definable elements arranged in a stable order. If individuals share the same boundaries, containing the same contents, then meaningful communications become possible.
3   Concepts, the Gestaltists realised, are the bricks of cognitive function. The lesson to be learnt in the field of creativity is the paradox that the structure of a concept, as with any other structure is not only enabling – e.g., no structure = no language – but also implies restriction. The limits are enabling because they helps us focus (concentrate) on a limited range, a trade-off of limit versus directed thrust.

Having explored the term problem solving it is now useful to undertake some exploration of the term decision making. The domain of decision making is far more recent as a notion of study, emerging largely in the management field. Decision making is sometimes viewed as a facet of cognitive functioning, and also as the end stage of the broader process of problem solving, i.e., as pertaining to evaluation.

DECISION MAKING

Of the areas of study explored so far, problem solving and creativity, learning and decision making, the latter only impinged later on scholars. An early writer, Chester

Barnard (1938), had a particular interest in the stimuli that brought about decision making at work, listing:

- authoritative communication from superiors;
- cases referred upwards for decision by subordinates;
- originated as the initiative of the executive concerned.

Taken together with other text, this suggests that he viewed decision making as an activity undertaken mainly by management. This is a much narrower view than that of those who have studied problem solving, but not narrower than those who attribute creativity to an elite. However, he was among those who drew the attention of managers to the need to analyse decision making as a key element in management – an aim shared by this book.

The first problem of defining the term decision making is the scope of the term rather than the scope of the activity. A good deal of discussion on decision making tends to treat it as a problem-solving activity merely involved at the end part of the process, namely occurring at evaluation, or the stage where alternatives are selected for implementation. When decision making is defined this narrowly, it involves a choice between some alternatives; for example, there is a tendency among many to focus upon the final moment in which the person selects a course of action. If there is no choice of, say, a solution to a problem then no decision is needed. This would reduce decision making to a part of the problem-solving process. This is not unreasonable, but concentration upon the final choice is unhelpful, as it tends to obscure the fact that decision making is in reality a process in which the choice of a particular solution is only the final stage of many. Like problem solving, the term for most of us is more useful if it includes the whole process, as for instance does the definition of Delbecq & Mills (1985): problem identification, solution generation, evaluation, and implementation. If the wider definition is accepted, it seems logical, therefore, to include decision making within a single domain that includes creativity and problem solving, as they all involve both the generation and resolution of novelty by which the individual brings about change – i.e., the terms at least overlap or all three may, indeed, be synonymous. The relationship between decision making and problem solving, however, is not a topic on which much research and critical analysis has been undertaken, although a relationship is not denied. It is generally accepted that both can be measured in terms of capacity, hence both are likely to involve intelligence. There is little in the literature that indicates clearly that decision making can also be measured as a style. In theory, if this term is synonymous with, or substantially overlaps with, problem solving and creativity, then it can also be measured in terms of one's characteristic preferred style. Sometimes, by implication, it is.

One distinction often made in the literature is between tactical and strategic decision making. In a number of ways this is also used as a level distinction. Strategy is stated or implied to be at a higher conceptual level than tactics; this is underlined by dividing the term paradigm into subsets to determine whether an operation is related to a subparadigm, a segment of a paradigm, or a superparadigm. The notion has a similarity to an onion, with the outer layers representing the more abstract structures and the inner layers those most immediate. The implication also is that higher management deal more or less exclusively with strategy, and juniors deal with tactics. The further implication is that the higher the strategic level, the looser the enveloping structure and the more likely the environment is assumed to suit innovators. Conversely, tactics are seen as always tightly prescribed and more suitable to the nature of adaptors. But if there are both adaptor and innovator strategists (as well as adaptor and innovator tacticians), what might be the difference in observed characteristic behaviour? The possibility that innovator strategists could ask for particular tactics in a manner too loosely to suit adaptors, or that adaptor strategists might ask for their tactics in a manner too tightly to suit innovators, are not options seriously studied in the literature. However, anyone with senior management and consultancy experience comes across these variations frequently. A-I theory assumes that whichever level is involved, the operator can be operating more or less closely in accord with the prevailing notions on how such problems should be solved (method) and within which guidelines (structure); in short, adaptively or innovatively. It is accepted that strategic decision territory is wider, by definition, than that which is tactical; nevertheless, for instance, a tactic can be devised that appears outside the 'rules' hitherto obtaining, whilst a strategy can be devised that is wholly within the 'rules' that appear to pertain to it. Their different chances of success depend on what is needed for the resolution of each different problem within each of their respective scopes.

In A-I terms, decisions can be ranged along a continuum from those made within tight structures of well-defined rules or policies to those in which either of these structures are much less well defined or have been deliberately broken and reformed as a prelude to solution search. However, as for problem solving, all but the simplest decisions will involve both structured (that is, well-defined) and unstructured (that is, less or ill-defined) elements. Decisions near the structured end of the continuum are characterised by high adaptive efficiency, the great advantage of which is to maintain, improve, and exploit the current paradigm. As with problem solving, decisions at the opposite end of the continuum involve, conversely, less structured situations and structures that are less familiar and generally agreed. They involve less complete knowledge of the nature of the problem's context and, therefore, fewer accepted methods of resolution; they, also, are seen as more risky. They are more likely than adaptive decision making to fail at the onset or, if not capable of becoming more efficient (more adaptive development), may fail later – the fate of many an innovative initiative. If these parallels are accepted, then decision making is another name for problem solving and creativity.

A good observation on decision making, not put into a wide perspective, is that of Cyert & March (1962), who argue that a search for a solution is progressive. They noted that managers begin a search for alternatives by turning to familiar ones that have been previously used and tested. If these alternatives seem unsuitable, the search becomes wider and less familiar possibilities are explored; nonroutine decisions, by definition, often require the latter. There are a number of difficulties with this limited approach. By not taking different problem-solving styles into account, a single cognitive procedure is presumed that progresses from micro to macro in successive stages. However, the words used imply that, *in all cases*, micro equals *minor*, custom dominated, and adaptive. Conversely, macro equals *major*, revolutionary, and innovative. If A-I can be seen to apply, then even when capacity is held constant, style will affect all the problems viewed and tackled whether they are minor or major. Of course, it is also necessary to take account of other critical factors, and these Cyert and Marsh do point out; e.g., in searching for solutions, decision makers face constraints like time and money, which limit their sphere of discretion. These often act as barriers that preclude certain choices, which would otherwise be selected as more desirable. What would be useful is to place these barriers into a wider context of guiding structure and explore how different problem solvers deal, in general, with such structure and how they vary their approaches (and preferences) according to classes of other intervening variables.

If style differences are not explored then only level (capacities, abilities) differentiates managers. The most successful managers must then be expected to have a high level of whatever attributes are needed in any task undertaken – this notion leads to supposing the existence of ideal managers. Simon (1960, 1971) is well aware of the problem and posits that individuals do not have 'objective rationality', i.e., allowing a manager to identify *all* possible alternatives and predict all possible consequences; instead, he or she operates under conditions of 'bounded rationality', viewing situations through their own limited frame of reference. Ideally, objective rationality requires knowledge of events that have not yet occurred, but the future is uncertain and factual knowledge is never complete. The manager must select the solution that appears to offer the most desirable results, assigning probabilities (based on past experience, forecasts, intuition, etc.) to the perceived alternatives and coping with the debate, or even power struggle, involved in others' acceptance of the final choice. In the literature, capacity is often viewed as the only key variable.

The Management Initiative study is useful in adding weight to the argument that problem solving and creativity are explicitly involved in decision making, the process itself showing strong overlaps with models of broader cognitive functioning, such as those of Wallas (1926), Guilford (1967), Tuckman & Jensen (1977), or Delbecq & Mills (1985). The notion that concepts have boundaries enclosing content of ordered meaning and that managers, as any other problem solvers, handle these differently, makes it easier to relate adaption-innovation, up to now often anchored in biology and psychology in this book, to management. However, the term manager is not to be taken as narrowly as Barnard and many others suggest, at least implicitly. The term implies rank and, therefore, a select group; but management is an operation open to everyone at any time (as is problem solving). One's management can be measured as a capacity or as a style, and the extent to which it can be used depends on opportunity. The same may apply to the concepts of leader and leadership. The argument is that only individuals think, but although groups do not, the role of others is critical in providing the facilitating or hindering climate of the individual thinker. As a consequence, individuals have to collaborate to take advantage of the number and diversity of others. In doing so, however, their collaboration must continue to reflect the nature of the individual problem solver who does the thinking. How groups seem to deal with problems, and the structure they use or manipulate to do this, are explored next in relation to the way in which the individual manages. Then it will be easier to establish the relationship between cognitive style and decision making as overlapping concepts within which style plays a significant role.

FROM CONCEPTS TO PARADIGMS

Kuhn's paradigms

To be able to think and to communicate any thought, a structure is required within which to identify, classify, and order stimuli in relation to stored experience relating to this structure, in ways that give these stimuli meaning. The resultant understanding is necessary before we can formulate a course of action that will allow us to cope with these stimuli in such ways as will increase our safety or satisfy our needs. Getting and making sense of the feedback to our actions adds to our ever-growing store of information about this world, which will in turn allow us to carry out further identifying, classifying and ordering with greater probability of success. One of these vastly important structures, for both animals and mankind, is a system of signals or, in its advanced state: language, the basis of collaborative problem solving.

Because this cognitive structure, within which and through which all this occurs, is so important to us it is known by many names. Although they do not have identical meanings, these terms are essentially describing the same phenomenon, although sometimes their use is limited to a specific field. For example, in science, theory holds a central place; in administration, a policy; in law there are rules; in ethics, mores; in debate there is consensus; in biology, classification; in psychology, frames of reference[49]. One term that is more general in application is paradigm, which as it becomes more popular in speech is beginning to lose its wide meaning. This was the term selected by Kuhn (1970) in his seminal work, *The Structure of Scientific Revolutions*. Kuhn's work goes a long way, by implication, in making the case for the distinction between adaptive and innovative styles of problem solving in the realm of scientific thought and practice. The notion of a paradigm is central to his thesis, being both an essential guide to theory construction and associated measures – the stuff of which science is made – and a restriction to progress. This view fits well into A-I theory and not just into problem solving in science.

Kuhn defines a paradigm as a set of beliefs, shared by a science's practitioners, which defines for the science in question what is its proper domain and what is outside it. So, to use concepts familiar to the ancient Greeks, any problem that belongs to the domain of metaphysics is outside the scope of the domain of physics. The nature and ways of the Gods cannot be understood by using scientific method. The paradigm, then, is a very wide, socially defined, guiding structure that assists in determining, generally within a consensus, what particular problems are appropriate for a particular science to tackle. Further, this structure gives guidance on which data are to be included or excluded. For instance, the classic mediaeval problem of 'how many angels can dance on the point of a pin?' is not relevant to the paradigm containing the discipline of physics (pins can be included, angels not). Within the paradigm of science, the method of intuition is quite permissible to aid in defining the question (forming the hypothesis) or speculating on the value of results, but not permissible in any part of proof – the test of the hypothesis. The paradigm also provides guiding limits on the way in which problems are to be perceived and the very kind of solution that is to be sought. Physicians in the ancient world always prescribed a medical nostrum, such as a herbal potion, together with a recommended prayer to be taken with it. They collected their fee for a two-paradigm solution, designed to be on the safe side.

This paradigmatic structure, as Kuhn saw it operating in the world of science, offers limits (and so, focuses) on the ways and means by which a solution can be sought. Those limits include the theoretical notion, methods, and technology deemed

---

49 Among many other synonyms.

appropriate to this seeking. Crucially, also, the science's paradigm provides the criterion of proof or falsification of the solution reached. In today's world that sounds like a whole lot of restriction, which it is – but it does have critical value. The value lies in the fact that the paradigm imposes order on the problem, defining an area of operation within which to work, indicating appropriate methods of work and appropriate aims of such work. Without such order there may be no way to begin – for instance, in the very identification (definition) of the problem. Archimedes faced a rather similar problem in describing the limits of the lever. With the right one he reckoned, in theory, to be able to move the world, all provided he had a place on which to stand! In a way, the paradigm is the place on which (or strictly, within which) we stand and the scientific method is the lever by which we move the world of knowledge to our advantage. Also, Kuhn assumes that the (current) scientific paradigm is there because it is efficient; it was chosen because of its proven success in past problem resolution. Confidence in any paradigm is, therefore, based on previous and exemplary scientific achievements. Being of proven worth, it contains the promise, granted that its principle and practices are observed, of resolving all the 'residual puzzles' that the paradigm has initially defined as appropriate and deserving of solution. Consensus, under the paradigm, professionalises a science's practitioners.

We can take an example of how a paradigm works from the history of astronomy. The prevailing paradigm was once that the Earth was the centre of the universe and that the heavenly bodies went round it in perfect spheres. Alternative and, as it happened, more accurate views were known but not generally seriously accepted at this time. Instead, the accepted paradigm was steadily and ingeniously 'improved'. This consisted of adding 'epicycles' to the 'perfect sphere' concept. These epicycles, themselves perfect spheres, were grafted on to the main orbit, so that the path of a planet (the Greek name for wanderer[50]) could take a deviation, of a similar perfect nature to the core paradigm, and allow the planet to turn up again on the main orbit in accord to observation, 'on schedule'. Increasingly, data still did not fit this paradigm readily and doubts began to grow, until the advent of the telescope yielded a mass of further anomalies; a paradigm collapse occurred.

No paradigm, then, is perfect. One glaring shortcoming is that it is built on past experience and so is designed to accommodate known information. Indeed, a paradigm cannot be designed to accommodate novelty – that is, data which were not known at the moment of its very latest development. Novelty can only be accommodated (and alter the paradigm) when its existence is acknowledged and predictions about it can be confirmed (i.e., current events become assimilated into current knowledge). At best, then, a paradigm can only *offer*, with a degree of confidence related to its past success, the promise that by its use such new data, events, and novelties can be accommodated, explained, and become knowledge. When this happens the paradigm is altered, having now been modified to accommodate the stimuli that had been its challenge. It is therefore the task of the professional, during periods of what Kuhn called 'normal science', to explore, redefine, refine, modify, improve, and develop the paramount paradigm. During this predominantly adaptive time of paradigm extension, all the data that amount to novelty are perceived as 'residual puzzles' to be resolved in terms

---

50 Sages, in ancient times and in many places, had observed that planets did not move round the Earth in perfect circles – as they 'should'.

of the paradigm. In the clearing up of the residual puzzles, Kuhn argues, the practitioner is closest to the professional stereotype, winning acclaim as a professional problem solver, broadcasting results in short technical papers comprehensible mainly to other practitioners. The point to remember is that practitioners know that any paradigm is not perfect, so in accommodating new data they inevitably modify, refine, adjust – use what term you will – the paradigm, which is then, indeed must be, continually changing. However, these are seen as adjustments that *retain and improve* the paradigm during the time that it is paramount, and that is all the modification that the practitioner thinks is needed, not its radical revision or replacement. Such improvement of the paradigm can equate, in A-I theory, with adaptive creativity.

But what happens when a paradigm cannot be brought to accommodate a novelty that is deemed appropriate to it? What must be done when, say, the technical efficiency that develops during periods of normal science exposes facts of nature that pose something more challenging than residual puzzles? There are times in science when clear evidence begins to accumulate suggesting that the explanatory promise of even the paramount paradigm cannot be entirely fulfilled, and confidence in using it to resolve its own residual puzzles is shaken. If these persisting anomalies are central enough, they are eventually seen no longer as residual puzzles but as Kuhn's 'counter instances' requiring revolutionary insights and paradigm replacement or modification: in other words, innovation.

Kuhn viewed such periods as 'science in crisis', when an alternative paradigmatic 'tradition' is needed; one based on radical new exemplary scientific achievement. This new paradigm must be able to cope with these troublesome, intractable novelties as well as take over the successes of its predecessor. To be adopted it must also give fresh confidence, as a problem-solving 'Archimedean lever' for rearranging past limits to enable more effective use of the new data. Once this new variant paradigm is found and accepted ('legitimated'), a new period of normal science begins, thus, Kuhn argues, completing the cycle. We must note that as each loop takes off and ends with periods of normal science, these are no circular tracks but rather spirals progressing science ever onwards. In A-I theory, both periods of science are not so clear-cut; a significant part of a structure can be restructured without, at least at the start, affecting the rest of it to any great extent. Also, both Kuhn's periods are required for continuing progress, just as both adaptors and innovators are needed, over time, to ensure continued successful problem solving. The emphases in this paragraph, that are not Kuhn's but an extension of his work, are that:

- structure needs constantly to be changed, sometimes radically, but to operate cognitively without any structure is not possible;
- having a preference for more or less cognitive structure is an individual attribute – society only reflects the views of its members.

Kuhn extended to cognitive style

Kuhn was interested in the progress of science. A-I is concerned with the problem solver, alone or in a team. Therefore, a problem unresolved by Kuhn needs to be addressed here: When does the individual know when to save the paradigm and when to replace it? In Kuhnian terms, 'it becomes clear' that the present paradigm is failing. But surely that implies that everyone agrees, wholly and at the same time, either that it has failed or what strategy is to follow? Maybe some will still see merit in expending effort (and reputation) to improve the paradigm whilst others are advocating a replacement? Kuhn might well agree, but did not predict who are likely to be found in one camp or the other. A-I continuum theory sets up a means of such prediction.

Those more adaptive will be most at home in the structure of the (Kuhnian) paradigm, creating change within it by redefining, refining, modifying, and improving it to greater levels of operating efficiency. Faced with problems of unresolved novelty, the (high-level) high adaptor will stretch to find ever more clever and ingenious ways to support the paradigm and make it work – the epicycle seems an adaptive approach, whoever took it. The more adaptive are likely to perceive novelty as residual puzzles more readily than as counter instances. Meantime the (high-level) more innovative person is more likely to devise ever more clever and persuasive alternative paradigmatic structures that can be a threat to the very existence of the current one. The more innovative perceive novelty as counter instances rather than as residual problems more readily than the more adaptive do. The advantages of both the adaptor and the innovator are at once apparent. The progress of the human condition is dependent on the able functioning of people located along the whole range of cognitive style.

This suggests that both adaptors and innovators are equally successful with changing paradigms, each in their own way. In relation to any particular problem, at any particular time, more adaption or more innovation will be the more appropriate style (more easily perceived by hindsight) to achieve the more useful long-term solution. So there are advantages to being located anywhere on the continuum, that is, everyone has the advantage – sometimes!

Are there disadvantages? The *faults* of the different styles are only faults when the style seems inappropriate to the problem: The adaptor stays with existing structure (in this case, the paradigm) too long and the innovator will try to abandon it when it has still good mileage available. Of course, these decisions – to improve or to replace a paradigm – can sometimes be a lot easier than at other times. When a consensus forms that a paradigm has 'clearly failed', there may be very few left willing to support it. In the field of social politics the collapse of the taboo culture of Hawaii or the more recent collapse of the communist system in Russia are notable examples. These paradigms seemed to collapse overnight, having for so long seemed unchanging and, indeed, unchallengeable. These collapses cause uncertainty and even fear, just as, when the development of the telescope, by revealing a flood of additional paradigm-challenging observations, finally put paid to the commonly held mediaeval notions of astronomy. Likewise, when a new paradigm has been adopted, such as a new theory of genetics or a new technology like computers, its promise is so powerful and its structures still so lacking in completion that all, from the most adaptive to the most innovative, can be accommodated readily within it, to their (and its) great and immediate benefit. These times may, for all their attendant anxieties and excitement, be the easier occasions for diversity of decision; these times, therefore, seem memorable and clearly different from the longer periods of Kuhn's 'normal science'. It is at times like these that the pace of change seems to pick up, with both innovative and adaptive changes occurring at the core of a paradigm. As adaption manages to create a more stable and efficient core much innovation will move to the peripheries – its more customary place – and the peripheries, moving further from the core (as the core expands and consolidates), will appear to characterise current development less than those matters occurring at the core. Hence, innovative periods in social history, such as the Renaissance, the founding of modern science and such institutions as the Royal Society, and the start of the Industrial Revolution, appear to be times of very rapid change – both adaptive and innovative. The periods in between appear less so, no doubt because the core becomes larger and more stable, adaptive change is less dramatic, the paradigm covers more territory, and any one change is less visible. This may help account for the fact that Kuhn's periods of normal science are thought to be of much greater length than periods of revolution. Yet appearance may be deceptive as it may be more the nature of the changes, how centrally they are placed within the prevailing paradigms, and the importance of a changing paradigm in the perception of key elements of the society that characterise periods, rather than how much is actually changing. The concept that is emerging from this discussion is that although cognitive style applies only to individuals, nevertheless, people loosely attribute this human characteristic to whole times, epochs, institutions, and societies.

The examples given above are notable and shake large numbers of people, even whole continents of people. Just as difficult for the individuals and the small groups of which they are members are those events – redundancy, divorce, or a collapse of faith – that can happen within a lifetime. More often, there are many occasions when we find ourselves in agreement with some colleagues and in disagreement with others on whether we 'should' seek radical or improving solutions. Do we steady or rock the boat, in our hunt for an answer? The tendency, in the usual situation that offers a lack of clear answers, is to choose the kind of solution that is in accord with one's preferred style, tempered by the need to remain 'in fit' with the structure formed by the group – made up of those 'significant others' who form our social environment.

Berger & Luckmann's universes

The work of Kuhn can be seen to apply outside his initial boundary, which was the understanding of the progress of science. Inevitably it has implications for understanding the behaviour of the science's practitioner. A-I has, as its initial domain, the understanding of individual differences of cognitive style. Inevitably, too, it has meaning for the group within which the individual problem solves. Berger & Luckmann (1967), in their sociological study of the meaning of social reality, have also come up with similar understandings on the nature of cognitive structure. In examining the relationships between reality, knowledge, and social structure, they hold the view that reality is a phenomenon which, unlike fantasy, is outside the manipulative reach of personal preference. In other words, reality has existence outside that of the individual. Individuals differ in what they believe, from time to time and in different degrees, but it is *functionally efficient* to have concord on what is reality. The plausibility (the term they use has a parallel with Kuhn's use of 'proof') of any particular reality, that is, the certitude with which it is held, is a function of the social support it enjoys. Belief in the validity of any element of reality continues whilst it remains part of social consensus. This makes reality a social product.

Even closer in accord with Kuhn's views are the ways in which, for Berger & Luckmann, reality is formed. They argue that society 'educates' into its members a 'symbolic universe', which is 'a way of interpreting experience', and is the guide to action and to solving problems. They say that we are educated in the ways of cognitive operation that are legitimised by social consent, itself made manifest by institutional prescript and practice. The distinction between this theoretical position and that occupied by paradigm seems fine indeed. One important difference is the notion of how knowledge of 'norms' or 'symbolic universes' is acquired. The education that society provides 'inculcates' these concepts so that the individual internalises the consensually agreed views of society.

The problem that runs through much of the literature of change is how 'normal change' comes about at all. Certainly Berger & Luckmann's views make it hard for us to envision it happening casually or developmentally. There is one probable explanation: That they ignore most of the changes that occur around us all the time and concentrate solely on those that are both large and radical! Kuhn often seems to be equating revolution (in science) with change, thereby treating the changes that occur in 'normal science' as being of much less significance unless, like the development of the telescope, they end up as being major factors in the subsequent revolution. The field of creativity also seems based on these narrow views of change; unless the event is large, high-level, acclaimed, and innovative it does not rate as change worthy of the name. This inevitably leads to a theory in which only the select few are creative.

This lack of attention to 'normal' change is strongly seen in Berger & Luckmann, for what can disturb so powerful, even ponderous, a process, which leads to whole societies perceiving, legitimising, and being educated into common moulds? Change, to come about, must be more than life sized! Outside influences are allowed to play their part – the Four Horsemen of the Apocalypse might ride through a community that had little part in setting them to charge. But these occurrences are too dramatic and drastic to take as the norm for change. Kuhn's paradigm exchange must necessarily be preceded by changes at the core as well as a good deal more at the edges of a healthy paradigm, and such extensive change must be happening long before the paradigm is generally perceived as having seriously aged. In fact, these changes have brought about the aging. The very terms used by Berger & Luckmann are too extreme to explain the ordinary. Yet what is ordinary also needs to be explained, as continual change is the norm for all the inhabitants of this world. Many of the terms used – the switching of worlds, transformations that appear total, resocialisations that change the very core of subjective reality – are only a little tempered by more modest terms such as 'partial transformations'. There are many other examples of such lofty, overly selective views of change: for Coser (1967) the precursor of (social) change is social conflict; for Merton (1957) structural change (in society) is a response to anomie, which is a form of social pathology or disjunction. Merton distinguishes between cultural and social structures – where the former refers to a set of values governing the behaviour of members of a group and the latter to a set of social relationships within the group. Disjunction is when the culture calls for behaviour that the social structure prevents individuals embedded in it (say, because of social position or in-group belief) from realising. Nothing less than *upheaval* is the result.

What is needed from the literature is a less cataclysmic view of great change that, at the same time, admits the importance of minor change, be it extra- or intra-paradigmatic, occasional or persistent. Suppose we envisage a continuum of change that ranges from no change at all (a concept of total rigidity impossible to envisage in our universe as we know it) to a state of totally random formless change – the physicist's entropy. In this range, life could not exist at *either* extreme or anywhere near them. Although in this universe continual change is the norm, such changes, although constant, are not random, formless, or wholly unexpected, or else life (for any organism) would be impossible. Underlying perceived continuity is also a phenomenon that allows us to learn about the world, to value experience, and to *build on* past knowledge. Somewhere in the middle of the theoretical change continuum is a smaller range within which there is some balance between flexibility and stability. The structure present must be enough to allow us to manage change, allowing knowledge and experience to remain (more or less) relevant. At this edge of even this restricted range of change, where there is too little structure, confusions and uncertainty arise – for an individual, the term alienation might here apply. Where there is more core change than is desirable (which, if seen by an individual as hostile, may lead to a state of anomie), more than will permit more normal, gradual, adjusting changes, then the conditions arise for more drastic change, e.g., revolution as distinct from evolution. However, to apply psychology to these sociological terms, what is too much and what is too little structure for comfort within a given situation (environment) is a matter of individual judgement – which brings us back to the notion of cognitive style.

The theory of change that is being built up treats as separate concepts the degree (extent) of change, the style of change, and the subjective importance of change, however and by whomever it is evaluated. Without taking narrow, elitist, or pejorative stand points, the A-I approach assumes, among many other factors, a range of degree of change from small to great and a range of problem-solving style that shows individual preference for more or less structure around the problem to be solved. Any evaluation of any position on these ranges must be strictly in accord with the problem in hand. In short, we deal with contingencies in which, for instance, a small adaptive change is more valuable than a large innovative one – *if, and only if, it is appropriate to the situation.* This condition of appropriateness applies to all evaluations of cognitive style. We are not, therefore, concentrating on major change, radical change, or any other *specific* kind of change; the aim is to understand and manage *whoever needs whatever change*, at the place and time such need occurs. There is also a need to have better understanding with which to evaluate the success of any change, but this must be done in terms of its appropriateness to the problem, within the constraints of knowledge, resources, time available, and such other factors as are pertaining at the time problem solving (creativity or decision making) occurs.

Summary

Given that all people problem solve and are creative, the A-I (preferred style) continuum locates them in accord to their preference for more or less structure associated with their problem solving. The more adaptive adhere more closely to both the Kuhnian paradigm and the Berger & Luckmann universe and treat them with more respect than do the more innovative. The latter cannot function without structure, be it concept or paradigm, but they can manage with less, and less of what they use needs to be consensually agreed. They differ from adaptors in another way; adaptors will use the paradigm to solve problems (altering it in the process), whereas innovators are more likely to bring about change to the existing prevailing structure in order to solve problems. This is their advantage on offer to their colleagues. The equally clear advantage of the more adaptive is as the protector of the paradigm by redefining, modifying, extending, and improving it. Note how the advantages of both cognitive inclinations, adaptive and innovative, make proactive, not just reactive, change agents in relation to the paradigm. This fits into the A-I assumptions that there is no such thing as 'no change'; that everyone brings about change and is creative, even if no one likes all the opportunities of change currently on offer.

The disadvantages, to look at the other side of the coin, are that the more adaptive are inclined to stay with a worn paradigm too long; the more innovative are too likely to try to ditch and replace a paradigm that still has use and vigour. Knowing for sure which is the 'right' strategy may not be possible, even with hindsight. The meaning of 'success' can be as markedly subjective as the perception of the problem and as the appropriateness of the methods; all of them are, most usually, bounded not only by the cognitive structures of the individual but also by the norms (structure) of the group[51].

THE PARADOX OF STRUCTURE

Despite all that is written here about all people being creative and there being no position on the A-I continuum that is inherently good or inherently pejorative, some people will have doubts! Many of the practitioners in the creativity field are among the more innovative; this is predictable as, being a new field, its boundaries are less determined, which they find attractive. However, their view that this innovative style 'in this day and age' is 'more desirable' is to be resisted strongly. Ages, countries, and groups all go through periods when either adaption or innovation is the trendy mode. When the trend is 'in', the less favoured mode continues to struggle to establish its worth or to appear under the opponents' guise (nowadays, adaptors leave many creativity courses obliged to admit that they are not creative, or that they are now convinced that they are innovative!). The problem is that climates (like formal rules or any other structure), even innovative ones, are coercive; they are structures, and people, however adaptive or innovative, prefer to live in structures that suit them whenever they can. In the earlier days of the last century, adaption 'ruled OK'; but today innovators are having their heyday! Wisdom suggests that the problem and the type of solution needed, not the vogue, determine the style that is required. It is not the vogue but insight that determines if the nature of the problem (or a whole class of problem) has changed and what style is now needed for its resolution.

The use of the term structure[52] is based on a long history of theoretical analyses in psychology. The arguments, arising originally from the weaknesses of the seemingly opposing position of behaviourists and Gestaltists (now given as functionalism versus field), had been polarising discussion on the way in which perceptions formed and yet remained sufficiently stable to be interpreted with confidence whilst also permitting

---

51 The earlier discussion on learning theory will help show how it is that being obliged to behave in ways not in accord to one's preference, however often one has to do so, does not change one's preference. Almost a century ago, Thorndike's (1913) work is clear that mere repetition, without positive comfort as an outcome, is not enough to maintain an S-R bond. Later theorists used the notion of positive versus negative reinforcement; the latter may be a disincentive that has to be overcome. Since this is always at a price, enforced repetition does not make coping behaviour easier (see Stability of style, p. 76).

52 The term structure has been preferred to two other near-synonyms, 'constraint' and 'specification', despite their common use in, e.g., physics, engineering, and business, because these two may be perceived as stressing (if only slightly more) the limiting element at the expense of that of enabling, for those less familiar with their use.

change in a changing world. The first major review was by Allport (1955), who argued that: 'What was needed, it seemed to the writer, was neither the familiar and easy functionalism nor the intangible notion of the "whole", a "configuration", or a "field" – but an overall, explicit concept of a *structure*' (p. xviii). He was only too well aware of the difficulty of using any term that implied a mechanistic type of rigidity – too many theorists were searching for core elements that were unchanging (although changes could occur in their relationships) as opposed to others whose notions probably led directly to chaos and catastrophe theories. Allport seems to be searching for a balance: 'A forced and probably misleading distinction arose between structure or mechanism on the one hand and function on the other. Such a rigid view does not comport with the highly varied and changeable character of life and behaviour. The flow of an ever changing and adapting function does not come out of a machine-like system. But if, on the other hand, structure is more flexibly conceived, there then seemed to be no possibility of the explicit denotation of its elements and their relationship.' He sought a definition that would 'reveal and preserve the "structural format" of behaviour and collective activity' (or, if we understand him well: to give these actions stable meaning to the actor and the observer) and yet have 'a concept of structure that would itself be, as a structure, so mobile, flexible and dynamic that the distinction between structure and function would not be needed. [At the same time,] if such a notion of structure were at all sound, it would have to hold in other levels of nature besides those of behaviour and society' (pp. xviii and xix). Also of value to the discussion here, he further argues: 'This structuring, moreover, is not a human artefact, but a part of the very constitution of the organism, and, as such, is not particularistic, but highly lawful and general. If this were not true, our perceptions could not have the stability and regularity which they obviously possess' (Allport, 1955, p. 630). In A-I theory's use of terminology, the innate capacity to form cognitive structure is assumed to be another of those genetically created processes in the brain that are part of the individual's inheritance.

There is an undoubted need for the individual to have sufficient stability of physical and mental structure[53] to create and maintain an integrity of identity, yet have the means to respond successfully to ever-changing needs and an ever-changing environment. The basic element of cognition, concept, is conceived of as balancing the elements of stability and change: Its content is limited, ordered, and stable yet its boundary is conceived of as sufficiently permeable to novelty to enable change. The definition of concept is embedded in all the other terms that specify the same cognitive structure in various fields. Giorgi, in evaluating Kuhn's contribution, states that: 'We feel that the introduction of the notion of paradigm is a significant advance for understanding science. According to Kuhn, scientific revolutions are changes of worldviews. When

---

53 One of the principal elements in personality (on which cognition is a prime influence) is the concept of 'trait'. For Allport (1937), trait and attitudes are predispositions to respond, i.e., lead to predictable patterns of behaviour: '. . . behind all confusion of terms, behind the disagreement of judges, and apart from errors and failures of empirical observation, there are none the less *bone fide* mental structures in each personality that account for the consistency of behaviour' (p. 289). So, for Allport, both traits and attitudes initiate and guide behaviour; both are the joint outcome of genetic factors and learning. The essential distinction between them is that an attitude is linked to a specific object or class of objects and a trait is not. 'Between them they cover virtually every type of disposition with which the psychology of personality concerns itself' (p. 295).

paradigms change, the world itself changes with them[54]. [. . .] Kuhn states that it is rather as if the professional community had been suddenly transported to another planet where familiar objects are seen in a different light and are joined by unfamiliar ones as well . . . paradigm changes [that] cause scientists to see the world differently' (1962, p. 110, our footnote). Kuhn also argues that the very characteristics he describes 'are built into the perceptual process itself' (Giorgi, 1970, pp. 106–109).

At the start of this section is a collection of terms that relate to structure; that lie between those selected for deeper analysis: concept and paradigm. It is apparent that each branch of study of human activity is concerned with its structures and often has its own term. Among these are those most used by management, such as policy and, one to be explored later, organisational climate. Management, whether of business, government or the military (see Appendix 5) has long been concerned with the efficient exercise of its structure. The study of it, however, is comparatively recent, mostly since the Second World War. Here is an early example from Pugh & Hickson (1968): 'All organisations have to make provision for continuing activities directed to the achievement of given aims. Regularities in activities such as task allocation, supervision and coordination are developed. Such regularities constitute the organisation's structure [. . .] The concept of structure is thus central to modern organisational theory' (pp. 374–375). The authors note that whereas each organisation must have a unique structure, yet if this is explored in any detail, there are general patterns sufficiently common to many organisations for more general, theoretical study that will yield better understanding of organisations. Like many scholars before them, they are concerned with understanding this structure, although the aim of Pugh and his colleagues in this decade is the better measurement of organisational structure.

In examining the notion of structure related to problem solving, two dangers are being advanced. One is that the divisions within the terms related to the notion are not sufficiently flexible: e.g., whether one accepts change or not rather than how many changes one accepts and of what kind; whether one breaks boundaries or not rather than what boundaries one does break under what circumstances. There is an inherent difficulty in associating a dichotomy of strategy with a cognitive process, which is more likely to be a continuum ranging from one extreme to the other. The supposition is that alternative strategies exist because each has advantages or disadvantages, depending on contingent circumstance (such as the nature of the problem; the means of resolution available). A continuum of strategies offers more flexibility for analysis because any point of the range can be assessed against any other. The other danger in using the notion of structure is that the term may not be seen in wide enough context to draw general conclusions. For this reason the overlapping nature of many terms, from concept to paradigm, has been stressed. Given both flexibility and stress, then the inherent cognitive problem in the management of the paradox of structure may become clearer – it is constant (as is problem solving), it is widespread (so that it applies both to Kuhnian observation of scientific progress and, as Allport noted, to individual cognition in animals and people), and it is capable of subtle analysis (any point of a continuum of style can be related to an array of different problems).

One other aspect that needs noting is the attempt to resolve conflicting aspects within the paradox of structure. Here is an example that may help. It lies in a different

---

54 Or rather, we would say, our perception of the world changes.

field and a different epoch to the ones given so far. Aristotle (384–323 BC) noted that there were (in his time) two current political systems: oligarchy, the rule of the few, and democracy, the rule of the many. Each, he noted, has its advantages: The former has tight disciplined structure capable of focusing sharply on specific aims followed by rapid decision making and swift change; the latter operates on wider consensus and is based on wider diversity of talent. Each has their disadvantages: Oligarchy tends to favour the few and drift towards tyranny; democracy finds it difficult to pursue an unpopular but necessary course of action and tends to drift towards quarrelsome in-groups and anarchy – in short, enabling at the price of too much structure or too little enabling as an outcome of too few limits. Solutions are not easily found; the British inched over centuries to their solution of democratically electing an oligarchy with a limited life, requiring renewal every few years. Not that the problem went away altogether. In every country that has adopted the system there are times when electorates lean heavily towards more structured or less structured manifestos. However, the current system does discourage the movement towards political extremes, theoretically allowing every critical social element to have some power to achieve, but to be accountable to and have its powers limited by other institutions that, in turn, exist within similar balances of power. The outcome of the interplay of adaption and innovation in social progress is also seen in the next example.

Music and structure

So far most of the examples given here have been in the fields of science and management; it seems fitting at this point to include a somewhat fuller example from the field of art. The essential difference between music and noise is that music has a patterned structure; to many it is also an advantage if this structure is pleasing. Pythagoras (6th century BC) was the first to perceive a connection between numbers and music; the terms 'harmonic mean' and 'harmonic progression' in his writing are still in use. The flash of innovative insight that greatly influenced his thoughts on the relationship between mathematics and music was hearing blacksmiths at work. He noted that one of a group of smiths, when striking his anvil, was 'out of tune' with the others. By weighing the hammers he began to understand why this might be – the odd hammer out was not in an appropriate location within a mathematical progression of weight relative to the others. The connection between music and patterned structure had now been conceived.

In the West, on the fall of the Roman Empire, the rise of Christianity gave music a central place in culture. Hundreds of sacred chants of the Mass, the psalms, the hymns, and the scriptures were sung to cover every kind of service for every day of the year. Purity and consistency of reproduction were regarded as critical needs (the Dark Ages had seemed alarmingly short of civilised structure) and were largely in the keeping of hundreds of monks spread over Europe and parts of the Middle East and North Africa. The exacting standards demanded depended entirely on individual memory. Achieving this standard was no mean feat, as Goodall (2000) estimates that by the 10th century it may have taken 'over 10 painful years to teach a young boy chorister the chants he would need to know by adulthood for the singing of services in abbeys, cathedrals and churches [. . .] this repertoire amounts to the equivalent of memorising the total output of Beethoven and Wagner put together (roughly 80 hours of continuous music) without the help of music notation' (p. 14). There was an additional problem: 'If one singer knew the tune he was about to sing, how would he coordinate with another singer standing next to him to agree on the melody in the same place at the same time? These conundrums plagued the musical directors of all the abbeys and churches across Europe' (p. 15).

Various attempts were made to codify the system, beginning with the setting up of a 'master choir' by Pope Gregory. The words had long been written down and 'a system developed of writing squiggles and lines above the words . . . rather like acute, grave and circumflex accents [as used today]' (ibid. p. 17). This was not enough direction for the standards wanted. For instance, these neumes (as the squiggles were called): 'give you the shape of the tune you are singing but they do not tell you from where you are starting . . . To make matters worse, hardly any two musical monasteries across Europe used the same dots, squiggles and accent marks' (p. 17).

Nevertheless, progress continued and by the end of the first millennium the neumes of a number of leading musical centres were approaching some kind of agreed pattern. A basic note unit was agreed, that was not too long or too short, called a punctum. For longer notes, two notations were used, one just above the other, called pes (feet). Another way of: 'side-stepping disagreement about the correct interpretation of the neumes was to have one leader, or cantor, who read the signs, and the others would copy slavishly what he did. They followed his intentions by watching his hands' (p. 19). The notion of arranging notes in a series of steps was not new; the Greeks thought of it but the problems faced in the Middle Ages were how many steps there should be, how close together, and whether they could be exactly the same distance apart. It was not until the very start of the 11th century, with Guido d'Arezzo, that these problems were largely resolved; written music of the time, using the classic pattern of groups of lines with notation on or between them, aided by clef notations, can still be readily understood. Goodall argues that just as Darwin did not invent evolution but demonstrated how he believed it worked, 'Guido did not invent the way notes in a modular ladder exerted power over each other, but he came up with a rock-solid guide to these properties which any musician could use as a compass' (p. 25). He also built on the past, having known intimately of neumes and pes as well as the custom of the Greeks before him, of naming notes after letters of the alphabet. His method was called 'sol-fa' comprising Ut, Re, Mi, Fa, Sol, La. His advance was none the less stunning in its impact; the principal change over 10 centuries to his system was the renaming of Ut to Doh and the addition of Te.

One question that arises from this example of human progress: Is this a case of problem solving or is it creativity? Is it adaption or innovation? Certainly the requirement, or one might say the problem as set, was distinctly adaptive, as was the solution. The impact could also be described as highly innovative since there is general agreement that this discovery made possible a development in the composition of music of vastly greater complexity and variety than could otherwise have occurred. 'Guido paved the way for the emergence of a new, distinct species of musician: composers. What is so striking about what happened next, the creation of the conceptual artist – someone who made up new musical ideas in their head, not just by improvising with an instrument – is that the responsibility for the making of new music shifted from performers to thinkers. The Western music that issued forth after Guido's description of notation is characterised by the existence of composing specialists. These dreamers thought up music that could not possibly have been conceived by spontaneous playing; what is more they were able to construct forms and structures for long pieces of music that were way beyond the capabilities of a normal person's short-term memory. Notation paved the way for great feats of musical composition' (Goodall, 2000, p. 36). His other 'monumental contribution to the development of Western music was to [have] come up with a system of notation that allowed his choristers to read . . . music' (pp. 27–28). Adaption and innovation lead into one another in the progress of sustained creativity; neither need be judged more or less creative than the other (e.g., Selby & Treffinger, 1993; Brinkman, 1999).

Feynman describes scientific creativity as imagination in a straitjacket; in Box 10 he is quoted among an array of other thinkers from different fields. Other physicists note how one great scientific discovery lends itself to becoming the foundation of further discovery that would not have been possible without it. The paradox of structure – that it is at the same time enabling and limiting – is also imbedded within the notion that progress is catalytic in nature. As an idea progresses, helped by its structure, it gradually becomes impeded by the structure that has made it efficient. The structure is gradually loosened to permit it restructuring into a form that opens up more opportunities – many of which will fail, but some of which are vital to further significant progress. This process is the tweaking of Feynman's straitjacket to create fresh enablement. But the new structure is experimental, unproven and, as yet, inefficient – a state that is corrected by an improved and tightened structure. This might seem like a loop, or a swing of a pendulum. Over time, however, it can better be seen as an upward spiral – a catalytic progression – each loop never really returning to the same point twice but, building on experience, arriving at a point beyond (further advanced from) where it started. The question is not, therefore, whether creativity is enhanced or hindered by structure – structure is vital all the time. Rather, the progressive changes to the structure and progressively different ways of using the structure are the keys to understanding cognitive progress. In the example of writing music, the original need was indubitably adaptive, but the structure which solved that problem led to both adaptive and innovative outcomes. Sometimes these outcomes clashed, for example in the forming of unanswerable questions such as: Which is more creative music, playing in accord to given notation or improvisation[55]? Many clashes have an unrealistic base as they come from evaluating style as capacity; when these are treated separately the interrelated value of different styles to the achievement of long-term complex progress is more easily seen. Goodall sums up Guido's contribution to music: 'In the 3000 years from Moses to the time of Charlemagne, music basically consisted of a tune and some rhythmic accompaniment. From the arrival of notation, the speed of change and the development of music up to our own century was in comparison dizzyingly fast. I do not think that he [Guido] realised quite what a genie he was letting out of the lamp, giving music a grid to work on and thereby making billions of harmonic combinations possible' (2000, p. 41). All the examples given in this book so far, across management, science, war, and art, suggest that the brain carries out its problem solving in much the same way for any problem in any context and in any age. Heifetz, professional musician and management guru, helps

55 The same question is asked in painting – how much craft should underlie its structure for it to reach the level of art and how much might debar it? See Appendix 3, The Curse of Progress.

Box 10 The paradox of structure in science

Here are extracts from works in science and philosophy; they suggest problem solving is fruitful only when it operates within the extremes of over-tight and over-loose cognitive structure. Their authors thread a careful, practical line but are handicapped by having no psychological theory to guide them. Relate these extracts to the information, above, on the way a brain works, remembering that it is only people who think, and so the progress of science must reflect the nature of the individual brains that create it. The first quotation is from a Nobel Prize physicist:

'Scientific creativity is imagination in a straitjacket' (Feynman, 1965).

EVOLUTION–REVOLUTION
'. . . . evolution depends on a certain balance among its factors. There must be gene mutation, but an excessive rate gives an array of freaks, not evolution; there must be selection, but too severe a process destroys the field of variability, and thus the basis for further advance. Prevalence of local inbreeding within a species has extremely important evolutionary consequences, but too close inbreeding leads merely to extinction. A certain amount of crossbreeding is favourable but not too much. At all levels of organisation life depends on the maintenance of a certain balance among its factors' (Wright, 1977, p. 40).

NOVELTY IN PHYSICS
'Popular wisdom might have you believe that new discoveries in science always centre on radically new ideas. In fact, most often the opposite is true. The old ideas not only survive but almost always remain seminal. While the universe is infinitely diverse in phenomena, it seems to be rather limited in principles. As a result, in physics, there isn't as much premium on new ideas as there is on ideas that work' (Krauss, 1994, p. 57).

EMINENCE IN PHILOSOPHY
'[The] independence of thought on the part of philosophical geniuses adopts a peculiar form. [It] has a closer intellectual affinity with the ideas that preoccupied the previous generation of thinkers. It is as if the most impressive minds are engaged in consolidating, even synthesising the notions that were being tossed around when they were youths; they are in a sense old fashioned, behind the times, yet they, in the process, bring the past into an intellectual culmination. Aristotle did this for Greek philosophy, al-Ghazali for the Muslim faith, Chu His for the Confucian tradition and Thomas Aquinas for the Christian religion' (Simonton, 1976).

A–I THEORY AND STRUCTURE
* Adaptors cannot problem solve in a structure so tight that novelty cannot intrude – in this universe there is no such state as 'no change'.
* Innovators cannot dispense with all structure, as without it they would not be able to think – in this universe structure is ever-present.

us fit guids into our schema 'creating music takes place in relation to structures and audiences. Structural limits provide scaffolding for creativity' (1994, p. 6).

In summary

There are three key points, followed by the summary of the matters relating to them:

- All people (indeed all organisms, within their own species) can be seen as having vast similarity of operation in regard to structure – it is needed in problem solving, which is the key to survival in an ever-changing environment.
- All people have a stable style preference which they vary, at a cost, by coping behaviour.
- Within the range of enabling and limiting aspects of structure, enough individuals need to survive for long enough to ensure the survival of their own species.

To suggest that those with more or less preference for either adaption or innovation are in some way 'better' is absurd; the value of preference is conditional on the problem being solved. This notion of cognitive structure can be placed in contexts that range from biology to sociology, from art to war. Earlier, in the review of the relationship between creativity and problem solving, it was pointed out that a common core element was that of concept. A concept can be described as a package of elements of knowledge, which the behaviourists assumed were arrays of linked S-R (stimulus–response) bonds. These elements lie within a boundary determining the scope of the concept, are arranged in a particular order, and need to be stable to yield meaning. This is the basis of individual learning and problem solving and, to the extent that concepts can be shared, it is also the basis of language and group collaboration. Nevertheless, the paradox of structure operates: The tighter and more stable this concept structure, the more enabling; but also, the tighter this concept structure and the more enduring, the more limiting it is. The individual, as Kelly (1955) made clear, is constantly faced with the trade-off of changing constructs to keep their notion of reality updated and keeping them stable to retain a sufficiently understandable meaningful world. With the possibility of losing track of reality, we could now border on the field of abnormal psychology, itself a subset of cognitive psychology. Turning to examine Kuhn, the core of his theory is the concept of paradigm, which in order to be useful needs to be definable: have boundary, have commonly agreed content, and be stable; in short, paradigm is the notion of concept in a wider context, involving just the same paradox, requiring just the same trade-off. This paradox seems inherent in the nature of problem solving irrespective of who is the problem solver or what, where, and when is the problem to be solved. In every case, individuals are (a) generally bound by this paradox (hence the overwhelming similarity of cognitive operation) and (b) have the same preferred, if narrow, flexibility within which they undertake personal problem solving.

This argument, that all structures are at once limiting and enabling, is an observation not confined to cognitive style. For instance, moving to cognitive affect: Its main process, motive, is subject to the same paradox. No motive means no action – no 'movere' = no movement at all. Yet enabling as a motive obviously is, the more intensity and duration it requires, the less energy can be devoted to other issues that might otherwise generate motive behind them – motive is limiting because energy is not boundlessly available. Attitudes and beliefs are structures within which an understanding of events is obtained so that they may be ordered in priority and preference. Every other cognitive element and process is in this way related, e.g., we concentrate on learning one matter rather than another; the more attention given to one issue, the less can be given elsewhere. It is true that we can concentrate on a large number of issues, especially as these can be done serially and in some order. But in the end we are limited to the extent of the issues we can master or execute. The habituated pattern of choices in which we indulge shows that we are setting up structures so that some matters can be concentrated on successfully but at the expense of others. How much we can do is a matter of level; the extent to which we value a structure's potential to enable or to limit, relates to style.

The notion of the paradox of structure might appear, at first glance, like another trendy thought in management practice: too strict a rule leads to fatal inflexibility and too loose a rule to equally fatal inefficiency. However, this paradox may not only apply to all human thinking but also exist in nature. Holmes (2002), reviewing some recent experiments in biology, suggests that: 'plants and animals may have hit on a way to seize the throttle of evolution, accelerating it where necessary and slowing it down when not.' A 'chaperone' protein (hsp90) seems to have the function of masking an individual's latent mutations under conditions that are currently standard for the species but releasing them when these conditions drastically change. Some of the mutations may find the new conditions congenial and the species (as so modified) survives. We may have no instinct to guide us but best problem-solving practice may still accord with nature's principles.

6 Problems with creativity

ITS DEFINITION

The problem in general

Knowing about effecting change, detecting change in a seemingly stable environment, locating stability while all appears to be change and, above all, detecting predictably repeating patterns within changes that are potentially critical, are vital concerns to us all. It is not surprising that whole areas of study, such as creativity, problem solving, and decision making, are devoted to these concerns. The argument in this book has been that these terms are interlinked, but many treat creativity as different from, or even opposed to, problem solving. A review of these arguments in the context of definitions of creativity may help in deciding which view is held more easily and is more useful.

The term creativity has had a plethora of varying definition attached to it, and this lack of precision has played a significant part in the inconsistent findings generated by much of the research relating to it. Other terms that were once in vogue, such as cognitive complexity and rigidity, were similarly ill defined and some are now largely disregarded as viable areas of investigation[56]. Creativity seems destined for the same fate because it is plagued by poor definition. In much of the literature, its relationship with innovation is uncertain or confused; whether it is a style or a capacity or both is unclear, assuming that this distinction is even mentioned. If it is both a capacity and a style, these two attributes are so conflated that it is not clear which is being referred to at any one time. As a result, the hypotheses of many studies are also unclear and their conclusions are difficult to interpret, especially as it is uncertain which attribute they are supposed to be measuring. The measures used often fail to correlate consistently with logical expectation. Wallach & Kogan (1965) found that a sample of measures of creativity – which, one must assume, all aimed at measuring the same concept – intercorrelated, on average, less than .3, that is, having less than 9% overlap. What cannot be defined cannot be measured. Adaption-Innovation (A-I) theory is clear on two issues. First, creativity, problem solving, and decision making are terms for the cognitively driven operations by which change is brought about by humans. These terms are seen to be at the least

---

56 For instance, Chown's (1959) wittily titled article: 'Rigidity – a flexible concept'.

substantially overlapping, or more likely synonymous. Second, the theory, supported by research, is clear that style does not correlate with either potential or manifest level (e.g., intelligence or capacity).

Creativity, problem solving, and decision making, even if not synonymous terms, can be linked together because each is involved in the generation and resolution of novelty. It may appear at first that creativity seems better related to the generation of novelty and problem solving to its resolution. However, generation and resolution are closely linked: Novelty is generated in order to resolve a novelty, as the process of resolving each problem, and the solution when it emerges is always new. If both these terms involve the generation and resolution of novelty, then the terms are cognitively synonymous. The view that they are at least closely related was advanced by Guilford (1977, p. 161): 'The very definitions of [these] two activities show logical connections. Creative thinking produces novel outcomes, and problem solving involves producing a new response to a new situation, which is a novel outcome. Thus, we can say that problem solving has creative aspects.' This argument for their considerable overlap can be pushed further in that both are products of cognitive function, devised specifically to problem solve, and it does not appear that the brain makes any distinction between them within any of its processes. If this is accepted, then their difference may lie largely in linguistic custom. Certainly the processes are markedly similar, as Guilford again points out (ibid. p. 161): 'Similarities between creative thinking and problem solving are further shown by writers, who have attempted to describe the major steps in either process. [. . .] The American philosopher John Dewey concluded that a complete episode of problem solving includes the following steps, in order: (1) a difficulty is felt; (2) the difficulty is located and defined; (3) possible solutions are suggested; (4) consequences of those solutions are considered; and (5) a solution is accepted.' This is closely similar to the two processes that will be discussed in the next chapter (see *Process*), those of Wallas (1926) and Guilford (1967). Another example of process given earlier was derived from analysing the behaviour of groups of managers in the pursuit of management initiative. This is a problem-solving activity indulged in by individuals acting as a group.

Creativity and problem solving do seem to overlap; in every case where there is creativity, there is also problem solving and decision making. In the course of painting a picture (generally thought of as an exercise in creativity) one needs to decide what to paint, for whom, and to what end; one needs to solve problems of style, perspective, and medium, as well as acquire mastery of the technology involved – as a minimum. Conversely, the resolution of some problems is called creativity – not only the painting of Raphael but also the theories of Einstein, Fleming's discovery of penicillin, or the brainchild of the Wright brothers. So creativity, problem solving, and decision making are closely related, even to the point where it becomes difficult to make a sharp distinction as to whether they are different words for the same thing or inter-related facets of the same cognitive operation underpinning the generation and resolution of novelty, i.e., the operations of cognitively driven change. As for decision making, it is either defined in the same way as problem solving (as a process that has the same sort of sequence and content as the processes described above) or as a part of such process (e.g., deciding on the specific solution to be implemented when that stage is reached). Usually, it is given the wider meaning, for instance, as described by Delbecq & Mills (1985) it is problem identification, solution generation, evaluation, and implementation – pretty close to Dewey's conclusion.

Creativity as defined in the literature

The literature is awash with literally hundreds of definitions of creativity, some overlapping, some confounding, and others simply unclear or unusable; a statement for which Isaksen's (1987) anthology provides ample, if seemingly unwitting, evidence – the authors in the anthology rarely even quote each other, and he provides no initial or concluding overview. Ebert's (1994) summary of creativity definition is that although the term is used as if general agreement exists, in fact there is no consensus. Daniels-McGhee & Davis (1994) are equally unequivocal: '. . . there is no uniform agreement on either a definition of creativity or the makeup of the creative process' (p. 161). Parkhurst's (1999) review article has the clear conclusion that there is no generally agreed definition of creativity. He states, in just one compelling passage, that as early as 1960 there were already: '. . . between 50 and 60 definitions extant in the literature on creativity. Commenting on the situation in 1961, Rhodes said that: "The profusion [of definitions] was enough to give the impression that creativity is a province for pseudo-intellectuals"' (p. 306). Twenty years later, an extensive literature review forced Welsch (1981) to conclude that: 'the literature contains such a variance of definitional statements that the task of defining the concept of creativity is a challenging one' (p. 3); '. . . No more agreement exists today than then' (p. 2). Another useful, recent review, contained in Isaksen (2000, pp. 7–16), clearly shows the complexities and confusion in the field. He lists some of the many attempts to define the term, also starting with Rhodes' observation that the many definitions available were 'not mutually exclusive' – a state of the art that suggests alchemy rather than chemistry. He himself does not stick to one version – and does not seem to notice.

Many attempts have been made to find an agreed definition. Guilford, by 1967, was calling for a sharper definition: 'Creative thinking, at its best, leads to tangible products, such as a story, a poem, a painting, a musical composition, an invention, or a scientific theory. But most creative thinking is of a more common, home-grown variety, without any distinguished product. The activity may not even emerge in a visible product at all. Some of those who define creative thinking demand not only that there be a product but also the product be novel in the population as well as socially useful. From a scientific, psychological point of view, these requirements go too far' (ibid., p. 160). This definition seems to limit creativity more than most, yet this narrowness still does not seem to achieve a sharp enough definition. Indeed, even the term 'novel' needs to be treated with caution when used to distinguish between problem solving and creativity, or between one creative notion and another, if all mean change anyway! Even more doubtful is the tendency of some in the creativity field to distinguish one notion or product as more creative because it is 'more new' – which is surely an illogical term[57]. For Eysenck (1996), creativity is an ability that needs to produce something new: ideas, insights, inventions, or art that are assessed by expert opinion as scientifically, technically, socially or aesthetically valuable. This excludes from creativity anything that is not valuable[58] – a doubtful point taken up further below. Many of the distinctions come about through differences in what is the main focus of the definition, whether it is the entity undertaking the creativity, the process that is used in its operation, the outcome of the process, or the evaluation from the environment

---

57 See also p. 150, para 2.
58 Or deemed valuable at the particular time by the particular evaluator.

in which it all exists. Guilford (e.g., 1975) and Torrance (e.g., 1988) after him were largely content to define creativity in term of its process. However, Parkhurst (1999) rightly states that: 'This is akin to saying that the steps in the scientific method are the same as the definition of science, a statement that few would be likely to accept' (p. 12). To define creativity by calling it a process is not enough. Is a better start to relate it to problem solving?

Vinacke (1952) and Torrance & Torrance (1973) treat the term creativity as virtually the same concept as problem solving but also emphasise presumed differences. In exploring this point, Isaksen selects from the Torrance text the following illustrative extract: '. . . becoming sensitive to problems, gaps in knowledge, missing elements, disharmonies, and so on; identifying the difficulty; searching for solutions; making guesses or formulating hypotheses about the deficiencies; testing and re-testing these hypotheses and possibly modifying and re-testing them; and finally communicating the results' (p. 6). Maltzman (1960) goes further and straightforwardly suggests no fundamental difference; Guilford (1977), however, is a little hesitant: '. . . problem solving and creative thinking are closely related. [. . .] problem solving has creative aspects' (p. 161).

For Newell et al. (1962), the relationship between problem solving and creativity is that of set and subset: 'Creative activity appears . . . simply to be a special class of problem solving activity characterised by novelty, unconventionality, persistence and difficulty of problem formulation' (p. 63). The problem with this is that the subset, as they define it, looks significantly distinct from the rest of the set. In contrast, Russell (1956) is of the clear view that the terms are not the same: 'Creative thinking involves the production of new ideas whereas critical thinking . . . involves reaction to others' ideas or to one's own previous ideas' (p. 306). This is bothersome since it raises the problem that the term 'critical' thinking is distinct from any other kind of thinking, as well as the need to find a definition of 'new' that excludes the products of critical thinking. On the latter issue, the difficulty has already been raised of treating the term 'new' as if it is a continuum when, in strict use of language, something is new or it is not. A-I theory holds strictly to the latter view: It is not 'newness' that varies but its context.

Although those who stress differences between creativity and problem solving have many differences between themselves, Isaksen finds much in common, as he displays in Figure 4, using three bipolar measures. Strangely, while his schema is entitled *Linking Creativity & Problem Solving*, when reading down the columns it actually describes their differences. The argument for the difference is often couched in a way that distinguishes occupations; crudely speaking, occupations within the arts would be creative and those within science would not. A parallel distinction is that innovators are creative and others are not and a third division is that creativity is a higher form of cognition than problem solving. Put together, this suggests that only innovators are creative, are artists, and are superior thinkers, which is quite obviously untrue. One problem this evaluative description raises is that it could imply that any piece of art by any child of whatever talent is creative and any piece of problem solving by any scientist (even at Nobel Prize level) is of a lower creative level. No authority actually writes this but the implication underlies their work and causes problems. MacKinnon (1978) describes Einstein as a creative thinker on the interesting grounds of: '. . . his inability to understand the obvious' (p. 47). Many people might hesitate to ask MacKinnon for a reference. Getzels & Csikszentmihalyi (1976) write that: 'the aim of

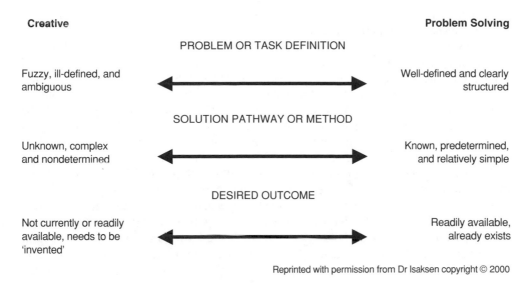

Figure 4 Linking creativity and problem solving

creative activity is not to restore a previous equilibrium but to achieve an emergent one' (p. 243). Yet all progress, in any field, depends on the alternating rupture and consolidation of the existing paradigm, both to make its current operation more useful and to act as a base for its radical modification. The argument against these divisions has already been made that, with other variables held constant, the only distinction is that both adaptors and innovators are creative in different preferred ways and can operate in any field of activity. This avoids generating the kind of anomaly seen in Isaksen's schema; that every toddler's finger daubing paint is creative but not problem solving and that all scientific work is uncreative, relatively simple, and readily achieved. The bias against adaptive creativity abounds in the creativity literature. Mostly, as for example by Kaufmann (1993), it is denied altogether; sometimes it is admitted but treated as inferior to what is deemed (correctly or otherwise) as innovative creativity: 'An organisation can be internally creative, through implementation of cost-saving technologies [etc.] . . . However, the biggest impact derives from external creativity [such as] novel responses to radical market shifts' (Csikszentmihalyi & Sawyer, 1995, p. 243).

The words 'relatively simple' in Figure 4 add level as a key distinguishing difference between creativity and problem solving. Yet level and style are conceptually different from one another (by how much as opposed to in what way), and research supports this distinction. If this distinction is accepted then any definition that ignores it must be made up of a compound of uncorrelated elements. The prime reason for the need for precision and purity of definition is valid and reliable measurement; the need for such a measure is to test hypotheses and, even more, the theory behind them[59]. If such precision is not possible (e.g., the definition of the term being measured contains uncorrelated elements in an unspecified ratio) then the measures produced are suspect. Wallach & Kogan's results are now not a surprise but logically expected, giving

59 Without theory we are back to the speed of progress of the more intelligent animal.

rise to serious fallout. Any assessment of people and any advice to them based on suspect measures is unethical, since such assessment would essentially be based on little more than an untested hunch. In addition, further progress in any direction would be based (if any progress could be securely said to have happened) only on old Greek polemical argument, for which proof could not be sought. This is an intellectual slide back of more than two millennia, and such regression is unacceptable. Unfortunately, even slight knowledge of the creativity literature suggests that the Isaksen schema (published in this century) reflects it with reasonable accuracy and that the standards of measurement and proof in the field of creativity are weak (as Getzels himself has attested, see Getzels & Jackson, 1962).

So, the field makes disappointing progress and a backlash will be inevitable. Staw (1995) expresses an early *cri de cœur*: 'The average person may become intrigued when the glories of successful creativity are hailed by the media. But when confronted with the bald truth that most scientists never come up with any earth-shaking findings, most new businesses end in failure, and most whistle-blowers get demoted or fired, it is not surprising that people generally opt for a safer, more normal life . . . For years I have been among the advocates of creativity . . . Well, I've had enough.' Perhaps the main problem with creativity is its over-drawn definitions that no one can match. The term 'creativity' is embedded in the language and clearly has it uses – in common, nonpedantic parlance to provide a loose subset within problem solving, as Newell et al. (1962) suggest. Since, however, the meaning of creativity is currently so variable it is surely unethical to use it as a professional term in proffering advice, in evaluating the work or person of any unfortunate employee, or as part of a hypothesis[60].

Look at the problems it causes. This part of the argument has deliberately depended on analysis of a single review text, that of Isaksen (2000), because it usefully reflects the literature it reviews: Level and style (unrelated concepts) are conflated into a single concept to be used, inter alia, to test theory and both to measure and to train people. The quotations are from a review chapter that are part of a general argument for support for a compound term: 'creative problem solving,' and the book, the cognitive technique it espouses, and its teaching approach seem dependent on this argument being accepted. A foundation statement reads: 'My colleagues and I currently see CPS [creative problem solving] as a broadly applicable process that provides an organising framework for specific generating and focusing tools or heuristics to help design and develop new and useful outcomes for meaningful and important challenges, concerns and opportunities' (p. 15). This is a bold, ambitious, and challenging prospectus and a hostage to fortune if the client gets the feeling that it has not delivered. 'Organising framework' and 'specific' are key terms carefully included in the presentation to give credence to other terms such as 'tools', 'heuristics', 'meaningful', etc. The pattern and the promise are clear – this offer is clearly stated as being built on a sound, tested structure that can be well defined and agreed on by operator and client. Unfortunately, if this is so, it cannot be creative according to the key schema – the kind of dilemma one frequently encounters in this field. Take, for a second example: 'One of the major components of this operational model is called Understanding the Challenge, which includes a systematic effort to define, construct,

---

60 Just as the term genius is no longer used in research. A physicist may complain the soup is not hot but merely warm or tepid, but the term temperature is only used in research.

or formulate a problem. Although many researchers have focused on problem finding as a process separate from problem solving, such a distinction may be arbitrary . . .' (p. 15). 'The Generating Ideas component . . . has only one stage. This stage (Idea Finding) has two phrases: generating and focusing' (p. 16). All of which suggests, as is supposed in A-I theory, that all thought, whether it be deemed creative or not, needs cognitive structure to exist at all. Defining creativity as a subset of problem solving that is characterised as highest level thinking within lowest amount of cognitive structure requires more explanation than the exercise seems to be worth[61]. Defining innovation as the implementation stage of creativity, as Isaksen and many others in the creativity world tend to do, is no great help either; style, level, and process should not be conflated.

Parkhurst (1999), searching for common ground in the works of at least a dozen of the most notable thinkers in creativity, is sure that two notions emerge. One is the notion of novelty, originality, and uniqueness (note the singular use of the term, 'notion') and the other is the requirement of an outcome: a solution to a problem, a communicable idea, or a product, whether the latter be: 'an invention or a work of art' (p. 17). Note also that he eschews any evaluative additions as to what level or how useful such original product needs to be to qualify as creativity. Such evaluations might be applied to such products but are not a part of their definition. His own attempt, at the end of a work of thought and scholarship, should give us, in our turn, pause for thought: '[Creativity is] the ability or quality displayed when solving hitherto unsolved problems, when developing novel solution to problems others have solved differently, or when developing original and novel (at least to the originator) products' (p. 18). It is clear that this definition still lacks the precision and clarity needed to build a scientifically sound work. It overlaps with the notion of problem solving so greatly that we are surely better off using the problem-solving concept for the purpose of research and assessment – leaving the term creativity for use in general discussion; as an unashamedly subjective accolade awarded by one person about some of the work of another. This is pretty well how the term genius might best be used – as a term of subjective admiration, reserving the term intelligence for more serious purpose.

Problems in measuring creativity

This chapter began with the recurring problem that there is no agreed, clear, precise definition of creativity in the literature. Some descriptions include elements that cannot be combined into a single measure; a problem if one presumes that creativity is a single concept. Ekvall & Parnes (1984) combine originality, usefulness, and elegance into their definition. This problem of terminology is increasing rather than decreasing and laps increasingly into the field of management; it is spreading from culture to

---

61 If creativity is characterised by significant absence of structure, could this ever lead to ordering junior to bed as a punishment and dire warning because he was caught defining every term in an essay title, given by teacher as homework, before starting to write it? An error compounded by then concentrating over a long period of time to finish the essay. Could one imagine saying that the punishment was loving, corrective action justified on the grounds that such extravagant use of cognitive structure would damage potential creativity?

culture. Unfortunately, wherever there is such lack of precision, related measurement cannot be trusted, as Wallach & Kogan (1965) found. The study of creativity cannot become a respected science because the difficulties faced by the researchers, who are needed to advance it, are so formidable. Amabile, at a Creativity conference at the State University of New York at Buffalo in 1984, revealed how she had uncovered in a survey of the literature dozens of definitions of creativity. She also noted that these definitions embraced a wide span of approach to the topic, ranging from the most mechanistic of scientific research designs through to the more esoteric and metaphysical explanations and accounts of the subject. For instance, some people believe that creativity descends like a bolt from heaven in the form of 'divine inspiration'. If this is the case, then clearly creativity is unknowable and cannot be measured, as nothing divine can be fully known, much less measured psychometrically. However, if we assume creativity to be simply a product of human cognitive function, then we may expect to see some daylight, somewhere. She endeavoured to reduce the number of disparate variables that seemed to be built into current definitions of creativity and end up with one she could use. In sifting through this array of definitions for some underlying basic pattern, Amabile found that they almost all had three key elements in common:

- discontinuous thought;
- high level;
- useful.

This leads to a definition less parsimonious that Parkhurt's (1999) – and to even more problems. The first two common criteria identified by Amabile, and still better accepted than Parkhurt's tighter definition, are already describing creativity in terms of one end of each of two independent dimensions, viz., innovative style and high intelligence. The second element is often dichotomised, high level and, therefore creativity are associated with an IQ of (circa) 120 plus (e.g., Getzels & Jackson, 1962; Siminton, 1987). The third element is too woolly for any measure to be structured on it, even if it is as minimally defined (by Amabile) as: 'useful to self plus one'. It is clear, in fact, that no single measure can be constructed of three such disparate elements, especially when present in unknown proportions. This latter statement might be worth examination in more detail since, if accepted, it may dispose of much unfathomable and immeasurable myth, which poor definition and difficulties in interpreting research results has not dispelled. Creativity definition leaves problems for measurement, for prediction, for the exclusivity of creativity, and the possibility of ending in absurd conclusions, as are reviewed below.

Measurement

An array of psychometric instruments has been developed with the aim of measuring creativity. The bulk of these, mostly paper-and-pencil measures, have focused on measuring personality characteristics (e.g., Torrance's Right-Left Brain Hemispheric Preferences, 1974) while others have attempted to measure the creative product (e.g., Consensual Assessment Technique, Amabile, 1983). Not all the measures are clear about what they are measuring; however, whatever the differences, positive significant correlations are generally expected between all the measures purporting to measure the same concept. But when these various measures of creativity were intercorrelated, Wallach & Kogan (1965) found an average correlation of .25 – which might just make statistical significance (statistically likely to be repeated) but yields an average of little more than 6% overlap. Wallach & Kogan believe that this weak correlation is because many of the instruments in the field of creativity are psychometrically poor, while others are technically invalid (i.e., do not measure what others measure). What cannot be defined well cannot be measured accurately; the results just quoted could have been predicted. If Amabile's analysis of current meanings of creativity is correct, then most measures contain uncorrelated variables. As none of these measures are likely to contain the same mix of uncorrelated variables, the mean correlation found by Wallach & Kogan may represent 'test contamination' as much as anything else.

Prediction

Scientific method requires an initial prediction, or the setting up of a hypothesis that can be tested. Randomly casting about for answers when no clear question has first been formulated is no way to forward understanding. A prediction or hypothesis should be derived from theory and amenable to getting a clear-cut, unequivocal state-ment once it is tested. The creativity literature finds this is hard to do when using current definitions. Getzels & Jackson (1962), for instance, in exploring the relation-ship between intelligence and creativity, implicitly set up an unclear hypothesis: There is no relationship between intelligence and creativity, except that a person needs to be intelligent (generally expressed as IQ of 120+) to be creative. This is not a prediction but the tentative finding of their correlated results. Any such derived definition could imply that a few points variation of an IQ score could classify a person as creative or uncreative; once they are classified as creative (or uncreative), intelligence is no longer a predictor of creative level.

This theoretical position as to the relationship between intelligence and creativity may have stemmed from a trendy distaste for creativity being the prerogative of the intelligent – an argument that is understandable, as much (of this same) creativity literature makes the assumption that some (or most) of us are uncreative. Getzels & Jackson carried out a correlational study using an array of IQ and creativity measures. Their sample selection has been criticised for being skewed towards the more intelligent. The study, in any case, yielded a low (but statistically significant) correlation average across studies but a very wide range. Such a pattern of correlated results again suggests some construct definition problems. The average coefficient found was too high to say there is no relationship but not high enough to be of any meaningful (as distinct from statistically significant) value. What magnitude and range suggest is that the measures may be tapping different constructs or different aspects of the same construct. This can be explained once a distinction is made between *level* and *style* of creativity.

This work has been both widely quoted and influential, but it has also been criti-cised. By as early as 1970, Alice Heim, reviewing the field, was reporting that: 'some creativity testing enthusiasts [. . .] claimed, for instance, that there is a substantial minority of individuals (a) who are high on creativity and low on I.Q. (b) Another minority consisting of those high on I.Q. and low on creativity . . .' She attributes the support for these assertions to be founded on the work of Getzels & Jackson on *Creativity and Intelligence* (1962). She points to problems of the acceptance of the prime study they undertook: '. . . the 450 adolescents tested by Getzels & Jackson were all intellectually able, being drawn from a private school of high academic standing, and having a mean I.Q. of 132; that the creativity tests and the I.Q. tests correlate positively and significantly; and that, therefore, in order to attain their (a) and (b) groups, Getzels & Jackson were forced to take children who came in *the top 20 per cent* on one criterion (summated creativity scores, or I.Q.) and in the *bottom 80 per cent* on the other criterion (I.Q. or summated creativity scores). Even so, this yielded only 26 boys and girls for the high creativity-low I.Q. group and 28 boys and girls for the high I.Q.-low creativity group. Those subjects who scored highly on both measures were ignored. Note that high scorers on both counts plus low scorers on both counts constitute 88 per cent of the total group.' This is poor research technique.

Over-exclusivity of creativity

On face value it appears that using the literature definition, too many people and too many ideas are dismissed as uncreative. Using an IQ benchmark of circa 120, by definition only a few per cent of the population have the capacity or potential for creativity; by confining creativity to discontinuous thought and usefulness to others, creativity becomes limited to an exclusive elite comprising perhaps less than 1% of mankind. A-I is not an elitist theory; a quite logical argument can be made that any definition of problem solving (or its subset, creativity) that allows for only a tiny percentage of humans to be adequate problem solvers (or to be creative) must surely be unsustainable. With no instincts (wired-in problem solving) available, it is improbable that mankind could exist in the evolutionary stakes if most of its members had such a serious deficiency. One might also wonder why so many of us have such a large cerebral cortex.

Absurdity

A historical example may help to illustrate the convoluted outcomes of pursuing the creativity literature definition to its logical conclusion. In the early 19th century, a monk, the Abbé Mendel, probably both puzzled and amused his companions by doing the work more normally done by bees; transferring and mixing pollen in his garden himself. A passionate gardener, he noted that local breeders (his area was noted for its cattle and apples) had little idea of the principles underlying their practical attempts to improve stock. Working first on plants, in 8 years of experiment he planted 30,000 peas of different kinds, seeking to discover with mathematical precision the predicted outcome of mixing yellow pea with green pea, wrinkled pea with smooth pea, and so on. This he managed to do but had difficulty in publishing the results, which eventually occurred after some 4 years of persistent submission, in 1870. He died largely unknown as a scientist or scholar and dismissed, by those few who knew him, as eccentric. By the usefulness element of the literature definition, he was certainly not a man of great genius and creativity. In 1900, he was 'discovered' in three different places by three different botanists, who now began to realise his achievement – that he had laid down the fundamental work for the understanding of the whole emerging field of genetics. If one accepts that being creative implies having thought of something acknowledged as useful, then he died 'uncreative'. He had difficulty in publishing his work and it attracted no interest when it was published. It was many decades after his death before he became regarded as of Nobel Prize standard. The definition of creativity needs to separate both a personal style and level (of operation) from notions of success, or we shall have to accept that people can become creative after death.

A-I theory endeavours to address these problems. It posits that humans are supreme problem-solving animals; that everyone generates and resolves novelty; that creativity is part of the same cognitive function as problem solving; that both concepts may be measured; and that people differ in both level (capacity) and style – independently. The relationship between creativity and other variables, like intelligence, depends on the kind of measure of creativity being used: e.g., a level measure or a style measure. There is a distinction between the person, the product, and the evaluation of the product by others.

Given better refinement, it will be possible to make better hypotheses on what is being measured, then to be able to produce more valid as well as reliable measures, and finally, to have a better chance to get readily interpretable results that have been clearly predicted. In short, what is needed is more rigorous scientific method in creativity research. The source of the problems of definition outlined above, together with the related issues of measurement, may lie in the historical approach to different aspects of cognition. Below is a brief review of how the three areas of problem solving, creativity, and decision making came about in terms of their background in empirical research and theoretical understanding. This is followed by a suggested model for unifying these terms through common use of terms such as concept and paradigm explored in relation to cognitive structure, although first other confounding terms, such as invention, are separated out.

CREATIVITY, INNOVATION, AND INVENTION

Some of the earliest studies in cognitive function occurred in the context of understanding the exceptional capabilities associated with genius. Sir Francis Galton (1869) pioneered this field, his key contribution being the finding that genius tends to manifest, more frequently than by chance, in certain families. Galton's contributions are significant also for his rigorous scientific methodology. Originally it was assumed that the genius was somehow different in a qualitative sense to the rest of population at large, and therefore distinct and separate from other men. Such common sayings in English of being 'touched by the hand of God' and 'genius is akin to madness' reflected the prevailing notions. The terms 'creativity' and 'genius' have always been linked, even in earliest times. The meaning of creativity in classical times, but derived from Hebrew, was: 'the making of something (often: life) out of nothing' – a condition that left creativity as the sole prerogative of God (Stein, 1987) – although there was a lesser form of creativity, viz., '. . . [making] or bringing forth new things by making combinations out of those things that already exist. Man, therefore transforms . . . but does not create' (ibid., p. 421). Creativity is not something possessed by 'ordinary' people nor can it be understood by them (Koestler, 1967). The notion of 'genius' was of Latin origin and had the original meaning of begat (the creation of life), but in later classical times was used more generally to refer to the essence of the begatter – as in the favourite use by the Romans: the Genius of Rome (Grant, 1993, p. 165). All these terms were conceived as being out of reach of most of us until Galton's work challenged myth.

Another historical turning point was when Binet, in 1900, was commissioned by the school authorities of Paris to solve the problem of identifying those capable of further education from among the children at school. Binet set out to measure potential problem-solving capacity and his work later developed into the now well-known notion of the Intelligence Quotient, or IQ for short. The work of Galton had brought the concept of genius into the realm of scientific study – indeed, to further such work he invented the statistical technique of correlation. The work of Binet placed genius at one end of a continuum, defined by another statistical notion, the Gaussian or normal curve, as very high IQ. Thus the concept of genius shifted from being seen as qualitatively different to being quantitatively at a higher level on one end of the normally distributed continuum. A new problem has arisen as to where the cut-off point is between high, very high but still normal, and genius. So genius still remains a poorly defined term and is complicated by other factors, e.g., is it, within a person, general or highly focused in a particular area? What other factors, such as motive or persistence, might be involved? As in the case of Mendel, is it also defined by acknowledged success?

The work on IQ was also clouded with problems of fairness. Could a measure be given to people who had less knowledge of the language or of the concepts being used? The issue of what was an appropriate base or culture to permit fair comparison became of great concern in the measurement of IQ. The quest for producing 'culture-free' measures that do not favour or discriminate unfairly between particular groups is still a technical problem with us today. The technical aspects do not directly concern us here.

Very high intelligence is a necessary condition for genius, but is it a sufficient one? Intelligence is a concept of potential, so if the individual under examination had learnt nothing (if that were possible), no manifestation of genius would be apparent nor could it be measured. Hence, those writing about genius usually add other variables into the definition, e.g., Simonton (1984) would add high level of creativity, leadership, and success, which most scholars and practitioners regard as fairly highly related. Once again, problems arise with such composite definitions – could some of these geniuses not be leaders and not be successful? Indeed, some of them are 'discovered' after their death, but to suggest that they become (or are acknowledged to have become, to be precise) geniuses *after* they are dead would suggest that the term is a social accolade.

Genius is either a term for a very intelligent person or a very successful problem solver, and it often seems to be used in both ways. Simonton (1987) follows Getzels & Jackson's lead in suggesting that: 'once a person achieves an I.Q. of around 120, further increments in intelligence represent no corresponding gain in creativity' (p. 72). This suggests that genius might manage on comparatively modest amounts of intelligence, which does challenge its use in the common language. Unfortunately the studies used to support this contention (Simonton quotes Cox, 1926) are among a number that use samples carefully selected to be all of high intellectual level; not surprisingly, the key individual differences are small and of modest significance.

Following Guilford's seminal address to the American Psychological Society in 1950, challenging scholars with the notion that intelligence alone is insufficient to understand fully all human cognitive effect success, research in creativity proliferated. At the time, Guilford was concerned primarily with the level of intelligence – the power of the engine – rather than with style or manner of cognitive function. It was the level aspects of how concepts are handled, manipulated, and stored, and speed of processing, that also interested him. His work on laying out and describing the Structure of Intellect (Guilford, 1967) is quite explicit on this; he labelled one of his three dimensions 'Operations' and described each step within its process as different abilities (see Figure 7). Guilford, the expert in potential cognitive level, had set off on an intensive research initiative in the understanding of creativity. He had opined that intelligence was not enough to explain all of the outcomes of cognitive functions involved in the attainment of human success and turned delgates' attentions to creativity as an additional source of variance. Unfortunately, it was not clear whether such a term was to be conceived as another form of potential level that was, nevertheless, different from intelligence (e.g., talent) or preferred cognitive style. The difficulty was discovered early. For instance, Rhodes (1961) noted the complexity of the current definitions, which were not mutually exclusive but overlapping and intertwining. Torrance (1965) suggested breaking up the field into the elements of person, process, product, and environment, so that each might be defined and studied separately. The problems remain: The definitions used are too inclusive and imprecise for accurate measurement and theory suffers. Rather like genius, creativity can be used as a term of admiration, but serious study had best confine itself to the more precise terms of intelligence and problem solving, treating these other terms as subsets within them.

Innovation and invention

Innovation (following the more short-lived reign of initiative) has come into vogue with an equally vague definition that overlaps with creativity to the point that the two terms are often synonymous, as van Grundy admitted (1987, p. 358) in his extensive review of this literature. He pleaded for a distinction between these terms so as to clarify their use in the literature. His suggested division, of attributing idea generation to creativity and its implementation to innovation, is not useful as it implies that neither term is a complete process; that creativity does not lead to a conclusion and innovation does not involve problem perception. Anyway, the word implementation adequately labels the concept implementation, without need for help from a word that means something else. Koestler (1967) uses the term 'bisociated' rather than innovation, opposing it to the term 'associated'. As with the creativity literature, only one of these terms denotes creativity. Associative thought involves 'routine skills of thinking on a single plane, as it were [whereas] the creative [biosociative] act . . . always operates on more than one plane' (pp. 35–36)[62].

For a few researchers (e.g., Thompson, 1965; Shephard, 1967; Zaltman et al., 1973; Pierce & Delbecq, 1977), definitions of innovation have excluded any mention of creativity or idea generation. For example, organisational innovation has been defined as: 'first or early use of an idea' (Becker & Whisler, 1967, p. 463); 'the adoption of means or ends that are new' (Downs & Mohr, 1976, p. 701); 'the adoption of change that is new' (Knight, 1967, p. 478); 'an idea, practice or object that is perceived as new' (Rogers, 1983, p. 11); and 'adopted changes considered new' (Daft & Becker, 1978, p. 5). Quite how these authorities envisage change that is not new or something new appearing without change being involved is not explained. Even since van Grundy's review, the loose use of terminology in the creativity field has continued. Generally,

---

62 For a detailed comparison of Koestler and Kirton on these issues, see Mudd, 1995.

associations in the field and some business training establishments use the terms synonymously; others, either alternatively or simultaneously, define innovation as the implementation of creativity. However, in a well-known training establishment that used the terms in both of these ways, their library shelves held a publication by a member of staff entitled *Implementing Innovation*. There is a better chance of progress if terms can be defined with one precise meaning and, preferably, in accord with common usage. The use of uncertain of terms associated with measures of people and as the basis of training or counselling them becomes an ethical issue.

Kanter (1983) was not at her clearest in this matter: 'Innovation is the generation, acceptance and implementation of new ideas, processes, products and services'; she thus holds a similar view to those above but adds that innovation 'involves creative use as well as original invention' (pp. 20–21). The implication here is that invention implies implementation, which creativity does not. Again, this implication is not in accord with English language usage. Drucker (1985), among others, searched for a qualifying adjective that would help produce more refined distinctions, like systematic innovation, which 'consists in the purposeful and organised search for changes usually of an economic or social nature' (p. 35). It may be that innovation could be viewed as a purposeful activity, although that might imply that creativity was not – not a very useful distinction, and again not in accord with general usage. A few years later this notion of the practicality of innovation over creativity became more specific: 'a new way of doing things (termed an invention by some authors) that is commercialised' (Porter, 1990, p. 780). Often the link with creativity is made by implication. For Amabile (1995, p. 77), the highest levels of creativity rightly require a high level of knowledge and high motivation (these levels should correlate), but only in 'cognitively flexible people'. One suspects this is means that only high innovation, at high level, and with high motivation, equals creativity.

The most difficult outcome of conflating creativity with innovation is that if both are exclusively defined as breaking structures as a means of solution then adaptive creativity ceases to be. Yet the generation and resolution of novelty that improves paradigms and infills existing intellectual structures is legitimate creativity that can also be significant, large scale, and important. This does not mean to say that adaptive creativity is always at this high level; it can also be trivial and unimportant, just as some innovation can – level and style are uncorrelated. This is a fundamentally different position from supposing that innovation is always at high level and that adaption is barely to be regarded as change at all. This is volte-face from an earlier time when the 'best' way of tackling any problem, whether the project was deemed creative or otherwise, was within approved structures. In addition, there is also a school that views creativity (presumably, if the distinction between style and level was understood, creativity of any kind) as always being unrelated to any other *level* measure. Sternberg (1988) reported that business professors rated wisdom and creativity negatively – in fact at −.24. The correlation is not high but it is negative and more than large enough to require explanation – as a start, one wonders about the wisdom of the professors – but if wisdom is a capacity, then a zero correlation is expected. However, Sternberg (1997, pp. 19, 79, 75) also states that: 'style is a preferred way of thinking. It is not an ability' – or a belief. He states that different environments tend to reward different styles (p. 100); to fit in, people 'differ in their stylistic flexibility' (p. 85); and that style can be taught (p. 90) – but whether it is preferred style or behaviour that is flexible or that can be taught, is not clear.

Difficulties of meaning create difficulties in practice, including the interpretation of research results. Such uncertainties cause problems for managers and consultants making sense of their own observations. Here are just a few observations that reflect the confusion. In Porter's (1990) experience: 'few companies make significant improvements and strategy changes voluntarily; most are forced to' (p. 52). But people are always changing, so what kind of changes are they not making, according to Porter? No doubt a stimulus is always required (and the environment is ever present to provide it), but is this what is meant? Since, later, Porter states that: 'companies achieve competitive advantage through acts of innovation' (p. 74), is it his meaning that 'real' change can only be innovative and is he complaining that the organisations in question are not in a permanent state of 'breakthrough' activity? This reasoning is found widely in the creativity world, but if all adaptive solutions that compete with innovative ones are seen as 'resistance', a good deal of such resistance can be expected and, if the arguments here are accepted, it is beneficial that a goodly proportion of these adaptively creative ideas succeed. As ever, with any published opinion that touches on creativity, one cannot be sure of the exact position. Porter (1998) later writes: 'Much innovation is mundane and incremental, depending more on a cumulation of small insights and advances than on a single major technological breakthrough' (p. 162). This suggests an alternative position: that 'adaption' is part of innovation (or is it 'creativity'?) but only as a second class element. These muddles do need to be resolved.

The notion advanced in this book – that adaptive creativity exists and that it is beneficial – attracts criticisms because the term 'adaptive creativity' is regarded as something of an oxymoron. For instance, Hill & Amabile (1993) sum up this objection by stating that: 'to insist that adaptors are just as creative as innovators, but in a different way, redefines creativity in a way that makes the concept too broad to be meaningful' (p. 414) – not a surprising view from Amabile if the earlier quote from her has been rightly interpreted. Kaufmann (1993) is in full agreement: 'Whereas innovative problem solving logically requires creativity, adaptive problem solving does not' (p. 148). Not many, confronted with the issue, might be willing to confine the notion of creativity to a handful of high-level innovators, within the whole, hugely biologically successful population of *Homo sapiens* (with emphasis on the *sapiens*). However, mirroring Porter, Kaufmann also states that: 'radical newness is not necessary to define the concept of creativity . . . furthermore, it is not desirable, since it [would] exalt the concept to almost divine proportions' (p. 152). If 'radical newness' essentially means 'innovation' and other kinds of 'newness' are also creative, then his position is not at all clear. Confining the attribute of creativity to only some humans does seem unnecessarily elitist, even without appealing to the wide-ranging research that has used KAI and that uniformly points to a contrary conclusion. However, if anyone threatens to place creativity beyond easy reach this must be Kelly (1963): 'A person who always uses tight constructions may be productive – that is, he may turn out a lot of things – but he cannot be creative; he cannot produce anything which has not already been blueprinted. [. . .] But, just as a person who uses tight constructions exclusively cannot be creative, so a person who uses loose constructions exclusively cannot be creative either. He would never get out of the stage of mumbling to himself. He would never get round to setting up a hypothesis for crucial testing. The creative person must have that important capacity to move from loosening to tightening' (p. 529). In A-I terms, for Kelly, creativity demands coping behaviour from every individual or collaborative diverse effort before being worthy of the term. The under-lying thought, however, is not easily dismissed – no one position, no narrow range on a problem-solving/creativity-style continuum can be relied on to achieve sustained notable progress. We must agree with Kelly: Creativity involves both adaption and innovation and high levels of creativity are hard to reach.

A difficulty that faces many in the creativity field is that they believe that only innovation yields anything new; yet a smaller, less influential group believe this term applies to the implementation stage of the creativity process, thereby dragging such terms as invention into this confusion of definition. Neither group seems to consider it worth noting that an opposing term to innovation is renovation; both groups are likely to suppose that renewal is not creative. Yet both innovation and renovation contain in their core the Latin version of the term 'new'. If we avoid the trap of supposing that some things can be 'more new' than others – since things can only be described as new or not new – then the difference between new things has to be found in variables that are not part of the term new, such as where they are perceived in respect to their related structure (inside it, at its edges, or outside it). The casual dismissal of all adaption-orientated mental output and even anything other than high-level innovation as uncreative is riddled with weakness, not least because in operation, as distinct from theory, a range of styles are needed within a single project. Mass production is an attempt to find exception to Heraclitus, for its aim is to have no (unscheduled) flux at all! As an operation it could be perceived as being in the furthest position away from creativity. However, devising mass production, setting it up, and maintaining it, together with the standards of quality and economy and other integral elements that are its hallmark and raison d'être, requires high-level problem solving or creativity that would be dominated by adaption but certainly not exclusively so. Often, to achieve the aims of mass production, innovative elements need to be intro-duced that contribute to its 'stable' nature. Much ingenuity is required to defy Heraclitus and his notion that 'all is flux'.

The notion that some people are creative and some are not is not one that will be held by a psychologist, much less one of the standing of Guilford: 'It is probably only a layman's idea that the creative person is peculiarly gifted with a certain quality that ordinary people do not have. This is a conception that can be dismissed by psycholo-gists, very likely by common consent. The general psychological conviction seems to be that all individuals possess in some degree all abilities, except for the occurrence of pathologies. Creative acts can, therefore, be expected, no matter how feeble or infre-quent, of almost all individuals' (Guilford, 1950, p. 446). This is the position held over problem solving and the concept of intelligence, for all people problem solve and all have some degree of intelligence. Indeed, Torrance & Goff (1989) are close to the position taken in this book, that if creativity is a subset of (if not entirely synonymous with) problem solving, then: 'Some degree of creativity occurs whenever a person solves a problem for which he or she has no previous learned or practical solution' (p. 117). We can add that if one knew the answer to a problem when it was presented then there is, in practice, no problem to solve or any creativity needed – a reflex might be enough.

In innumerable discussions with consultants to management, the problem voiced about confining the term innovation to one of style, of no more or less value than adaption, is that the term has become so popular in its looser meaning that they fear loss of business by advocating a more precise use. There is no doubt there are problems in taking a strictly professional approach unless one is sure of one's ground. One consolation is that, although the term is popular, the concept is not. This may sound a surprising distinction but it is made on sound research foundation. When the first trials of the Adaption-Innovation Inventory were undertaken, the title was given in full on the top of the sheet. Some bias towards innovation was detected and so the title was changed to KAI. The response bias, in general, ceased; once the term vanished the responses to exactly the same items redistributed as a normal curve. During validation and since, several studies have been carried out that included a check on whether the inventory (as KAI) showed social desirability bias; it did not (see Table E in Appendix 6). The times when it will, according to many reports in personal communications, is when 'innovation' appears to be favoured by the administrator (e.g., when using titles or terms like Professor of Innovation; Department of Innovation, creativity and innovation). These reports have yet to be supported by a study specifically designed to check their validity, but other reports indicate that if the presenter changes the biasing title the problem abates or disappears.

The term 'inventor' is sometimes caught up in the confusion of terms that surround that of creativity. It is often associated with innovation yet it too contains conflicting elements. One inventor stereotype is an extravert 'doer' who bubbles over with ideas versus the cold, withdrawn, introverted thinker; another is the brilliantly precise and capable person versus the bumbling genius; a third contrast is the technically polished versus the Heath Robinson contriver; and so on. This lumping together of such disparate elements tends to conceal the underlying dimensions of style and level, personality dimensions, and performance evaluations, just as many of the definitions of creativity do. This confusion can spread into practice, as many consultants discover when asked to help find people who can develop new products, just as they have difficulty in helping to find people who can 'bring about change'. There are no people who cannot bring about any sort of change, at any sort of level, in any field – everyone living can bring about some change. The hunt for such an all-succeeding elite is fruitless, and often they know it. In practice the consultants tend to set aside terms like creativity and get down to the hunt for people they feel have qualities that match the problem and appear to be willing and able to solve it.

Divergence and convergence

'In addition to the disagreement over what constitutes the demonstration of creativity, definition of the term has been hampered by controversy over the extent to which divergent thinking ability equals creative thinking ability and creativity' (Parkhurst, 1999, p. 4). In endeavouring to unravel this confusion, Parkhurst begins by stating the general belief in the creativity literature that 'divergent thinking' is the opposite of 'convergent thinking'. But Guilford devised divergent operation and convergent operation as steps in a process, and such steps, although all contained with the same progression, must be discretely different; that does not mean that they are opposed since opposition (opposing stages) would not fit into a continuous progression – they are different as befits different stages. Neither could it follow that in a continuum of creativity (or any other such concept) some integral elements (in this case, stages) do not contribute to creativity, much less hinder it. It cannot be supposed that in a process common to all people, some people cannot succeed in part of it. A-I theory suggests that the steps in a cognitive process need to have different content and aim to assist its progress, and that they can be undertaken by each operator, using different skills, at different levels (of, e.g., skill), and in different styles, thereby separating out process, level, and style. This distinction is helpful for the problems raised in defining divergence and convergence.

Parkhurst has no more to say on convergence other than it is thinking that requires a single answer. This is not the same as defining it as part of the process, for instance: Following divergence, it satisfies the need to concentrate on finding a solution that might be acceptable, on the way to the implementation stage of problem solving. In his discussion on divergence Parkhurst begins by dividing it, in accord with current practice, into two types. One is the production of a quantity of possible answers, but he rightly queries whether sheer quantity can demonstrate creativity. The second type is the production of novelty – which, he points out, is another area of contention, for: 'It is over the extent to which this type of divergent thinking ability is representative of creative thinking that the disagreement [in the literature] lies' (p. 5). It is easier to assess level as a separate variable than to include any element of it in part of a style or process definition. *Within style*, quantity of response becomes not an ability but a strategic alternative way of operating: either by proliferation, with heavy loss of ideas until a solution is found or, further along the continuum, sufficiency of idea- tion, where one solution from a targeted few needs to be chosen. In the sufficiency mode, ideation can efficiently occur essentially within consensually agreed cognitive structure; in the proliferation mode there needs be less regard for such consensual structure. Whatever the values or locations of level or style exhibited in a process schema such as that of Guilford, they will not alter the position of any stage in the progression of the process or its relationship to creativity (or, more precisely, to problem solving).

In the following chapter, thinking style is distinguished from capacity, process, and technique. To confuse these elements is to block the progress of creativity towards becoming a serious study. As part of this disentanglement of terms, divergence and convergence are placed into context. The creativity literature often supposes that adaptors cannot diverge widely enough to crack problems or search for effective solutions, while innovators cannot converge on and implement a solution. Such pes- simism is absurd when human progress, far from being crippled by such handicaps, is progressing at a rate that is often uncomfortable in its speed, depth, and breadth.

In summary

Serious problems arise when creativity and innovation are treated as synonymous terms. The most important is that level and style also become synonymous. If, in addition, innovation gets some additional distinction of meaning, that of being asso- ciated with implementation, then the meaning of creativity may be confined to idea generation. However, many writers, like Torrance, are ascribing creativity (and innova- tion) to people, process, and product and the last of these, at the very least, must involve implementation. A-I theory offers clearer separation of elements and a better chance to set up sharper hypotheses that might yield more readily interpretable re- sults. Creativity is a subset of problem solving. Innovation is one pole of a continuum of style; style is unrelated to any level measure, including level of success of the outcome. Problem solving is a process that includes the perception of a problem needing resolution through to its implementation. It is continuous in that the solution to any problem is a novelty that, on coming into being, is part of the resource (and part of the stimulation) that permits (and promotes) further problem solving. Everyone can problem solve and be creative. There are differences in preferred style and in level of operation. Every style can be appropriate to some problems and not to others – so all styles can make contributions, more so on some occasion than others, though no one is as comfortable with problems that require a different style for their resolution than the one they prefer. Many different kinds of level (e.g., of knowledge or skills) are required to solve an array of problems faced by a team over time. As with the value of different styles, so the team benefits from having different sorts of level (knowledge, skills, talent) available.

The acknowledgement of the use of a diversity of level and style moves the study of problem solving and creativity away from a search for an elite on whom the rest of us may be thought to depend. An exploration of the nonrelationship between style and level follows, together with the exploration of some other terms that are frequently confounded, to the frequent disadvantage of progress in the field of creativity.

7 Style, level, process, and technique

LEVEL

Adaption-Innovation (A-I) Theory assumes that the elements within cognitive effect are unrelated and, therefore, that cognitive level and cognitive style lie statistically orthogonal to one another. The first published article (Kirton, 1976) on this theory made this an initial assumption but did not offer empirical support. This is exactly the position in two other studies published in the same year, Kogan (1976) and Messick (1976), although the former worried whether in practice the distinction could be sustained. Both are equally clear in theory that level of performance, with its measures ranging from high (or correct) to low (or incorrect), is sharply different from the manner in which problem solving is undertaken, which in turn is dependent on 'the manner [in which] individuals acquire, store, retrieve and transform information' (Kogan, 1976, p. 105). Both Messick (1976, 1984) and Guilford (1980) assume styles to be based on individual preference in the manner of organising and processing information and that there are consistent individual differences. They are less clear on the assumed relationship between style and personality, although both suppose that style develops around underlying personality traits, which implies that it is, or it acts like, a dimension of personality. Guilford, in his 1950 address to the American Psychological Association, made a number of defining statements of which two key ones were: (1) 'Creative abilities determine whether the individual has the power to exhibit creative behaviour in a noteworthy degree' – that is, level; and (2) 'Creative personality is . . . a matter of those patterns of traits that are characteristic of creative people' – that is, personality. Not surprisingly, Guilford, an expert in cognitive level measures, defined creativity as being based on ability and the behaviour associated with it is described as personality (e.g., see his review of relevant definitions, Guilford, 1982). Style is not explicitly mentioned, but Guilford also thought that the IQ concept alone was not enough to account for all creativity. This gradually clarified into creativity being *Way Beyond IQ*, the title of a book published in 1977, in which he suggests that creativity is another ability, different to and not strongly correlated with intelligence.

Kogan, by 1976, is also clear that Guilford: 'explicitly subsumes the creative *abilities* within a theory of intelligence. Unlike the latter, however, creativity (as distinguished from the creative abilities) has been endowed with qualities that extend beyond sheer cognitive skill' (p. 161). Here lies part of the problem of the conflation of level and style – essentially, at the start, one of terminology. If we posit that creativity can be measured in two (independent) ways, by either level or by style, then it is inconsistent to suggest (directly or by implication) that style is 'beyond' skill instead of being just different. Kogan (p. 161) suggests that creativity is of three kinds: styles based on accuracy–inaccuracy; styles based on value (one extreme is superior to the other); and 'purely stylistic' (having no value judgement attached). A-I theory can accommodate this analysis and would classify the first two as level (which might correlate between themselves) and the last as style (which should not correlate with either of the others). Just how difficult it is for a scholar to classify measures without a clear guiding light in the relationship between level and style can be seen in a more recent attempt by Stamp (1986), whose figure is given in Appendix 3.

There is now a considerable body of evidence (see Table 5 and, e.g., Mudd, 1996) from studies using the A-I inventory (KAI) that support, the assumption that cognitive style is uncorrelated with both cognitive (potential) level and manifest capacity. First, there are numerous studies all showing no significant relationship between KAI and educational level and occupational status – and these are level measures. Second, there are 12 studies, using large samples, which tackle this problem by directly testing the hypothesis that cognitive style is unrelated (uncorrelated) with both (potential) cognitive level (e.g., intelligence, talent) and manifest level (e.g., management competency). Of these, six studies (Kirton, 1978a; Gryskiewicz, 1982; Kirton & de Ciantis, 1986; Prato Previde, 1987, unpublished; Taylor, 1993; Flegg, in Kirton, 1994), involving 11 measures and nearly 1700 respondents from the UK, USA, Italy, and New Zealand, explore the relationship with intelligence. The results, all insignificant, range from .12 (the largest positive correlation) to −.14 (the largest negative correlation), with a mode of −.01. There are two US studies (Gryskiewicz, 1982; Goldsmith, 1986b) using three measures of cognitive complexity (widely regarded as a level variable), involving 295 respondents, with (insignificant) results of −.08, −.07, and .17. Finally there are three studies (Kirton, 1978a; Hammerschmidt & Jennings, 1992; Schroder, 1994) using attainment measures, respectively: (1) the English university entrance exam, with 413 NZ late teenagers; (2) a management competency battery, comprised of 11 measures, with 83 US manager respondents; and (3) leadership effectiveness (management skill profile) comprising 12 measures, with 187 US managers. The correlations ranged from −.01 to .22, with a mean of .09. Of these 24 measures, 1 just touches the minimum level of significance. Buttner et al. (1999) found: 'The absence of a relationship between creativity style [KAI] and others' ratings [on skills].' Chan (1996), with a sample of 253 Singapore engineers, found that: 'cognitive style and cognitive misfit were uncorrelated with [level of] job performance.'

Other studies (Selby & Treffinger, 1993; Taylor, 1993) using teenage children yielded similar results, supported by a 14th more intensive study by Brinkman (1994, 1999). From 122 high school students enrolled in the school's two bands, 16 of the highest adaptors and 16 of the highest innovators were asked to partake in a musical composition test. They each tried their skill under two conditions, 'open' with few restrictions except for time of completion and 'closed' using several musical restrictions, e.g., in 3/4 time. Three judges, who knew nothing of KAI, were asked to rate the composition for (level of) 'musicality' and found no differences between the two groups. An interesting thought here is, was this a test of problem solving or creativity? Whatever the answer to this question, the results of the studies above are clear: As expected in A-I theory, level and style are not statistically related.

Scholars commenting on the theoretical separation of style from level, whether potential or manifest, agree that the distinction is useful (see, for a review, Isaksen & Dorval, 1993), but worry, as did Messick (1976), whether they can always be so separate in practice. Isaksen had earlier found this hard to believe (Isaksen & Puccio,

Table 5 Correlations with potential and manifest level measures

Intelligence	Corr.	(N)	Test reference
PH2 General[b]	.12		
CT82 Shapes[b]	−.01		From National Institute
GT90B Verbal[b]	.12	(437)	of Industrial Psychology
GT70B Nonverbal[b]	−.01		(NIIP) Battery
EA2A Arithmetic[b]	.09		Nelson-NFER, 1964–1979
VMD Diagrams[b]	.04		
Otis Higher, Form A[a]	.00	(415)	
Mill Hill Vocabulary[a]	.02		
	−.01	(95)	
Shipley[c]	−.14	(83)	Shipley, 1940; Dennis, 1973
	−.04	(161)	
	−.11	(99)	
Factor B (16PF)[d]	−.06	(83)	Cattel et al., 1970
Cattell Culture Free (3/Form A)[e]	−.01	(198)	Cattel, 1981 (Italian)
AH5[f]	−.03	(106)	NIIP Battery – see above
Level of complexity			
Rep Test[g]	−.08	(106)	Bieri et al., 1966
Role Category Questionnaire[g]	−.07	(94)	Crockett, 1965
Barron-Welch Revised Art Scale[c]	.17	(95)	Barron, 1953
Attainment			
English Exam (compulsory)[a]	−.03	(415)	NZ High School Cert.
Management Competency[h]		(83)	Schroder, 1986
Information Search	−.01		
Concept Formation	.22*		
Conceptual Flexibility	.12		
Interpersonal Search	.09		
Managing Interaction	.08		
Developmental Orientation	−.03		
Impact	.10		
Self-confidence	.13		
Presentation	.10		
Proactive Orientation	.05		
Achievement Orientation	.18	(187)	Bailey, 1990
Leadership Effectiveness[i] LS & I	Insig. *t*-test		Personnel Decisions Inc., 1985
(subset Mgt. Skills Profile)	−.15 to .15	(104)	Personnel Decisions Inc., 1982
Management Skills Profile (11 scales)[j]			

Notes
* Significant $p < .05$.
a Kirton, 1978a.
b Flegg, 1983 (unpublished; reported in Kirton, 1994).
c Gryskiewicz, 1982.
d Kirton & de Ciantis, 1986.
e Prato Previde, 1987 (unpublished).
f J. Taylor, 1993.
g Goldsmith, 1986c.
h Schroder, in Kirton, 1994.
i Hammerschmidt & Jennings, 1992.
j Buttner et al., 1999.
  (See also Chan, 1996, in text.)

1988). The first problem in such studies is clarifying all the terms before interpreting the results derived from the measures, which might themselves be misnamed or have otherwise unclear validity. For instance, Guilford (1977, p. 160), normally so precise in terminology, wrote that: 'intelligence is readiness to solve problems.' The context might suggest that style was implicated (e.g., 'a habitual readiness'). But surely, from Binet onwards the prime aim of the refinement and measurement of intelligence was to gauge the *capacity* of an individual to learn. In any case, readiness is much more suggestive of motive, which in the cognitive function schema lies in cognitive affect; it is a process that focuses, in intensity and over duration, the energy expended on a particular problem solution. There is surely a marked difference between the latent power of a motor and the *readiness* of the driver to motor towards work or a party.

A related sticking point is that if style and level are uncorrelated, then the current fancy of the creativity field for innovation, in whatever circumstance creativity is to be exercised, is undermined. It means that innovation is intrinsically *no better* than adaption. This notion is as difficult to get across today as it was, in earlier decades, to argue that adaption (however then called) was not the best way forward. Trendy views do not readily yield informed hypotheses. The problem of getting acceptance for the notion that the value of innovation, like adaption, is contingent on the problem to be solved rather than on the fancy of the problem solver continues to be uphill work, as we can see from the reactions (already mentioned) of Hill & Amabile (1993) – and Kaufmann (1993) agrees. Their position can be challenged on more than one point. First, there is an a priori objection to the contention that creativity is the attribute of only the few. Second, brain function does not distinguish between problem solving and creativity. Third, every level of problem solving (and creativity) is potentially valuable to a team, as is every variation of style; but the *extent* to which any one is valuable is *contingent* on the needs of each specific situation. A-I theory posits that all people can be deemed to be creative, although not all at the same level or in the same way. This leads to the suggestion that all diversity, not only of style in a group – except hostility to it (even for the 'best', politically correct reasons) – is of potential value to its members, in some circumstances, at some time (see Table 5).

A more detailed objection to this overevaluation of innovation is that it depends on a chain of seemingly logical progression, but the links are not necessarily secure. It runs: innovation proliferates ideas; so more ideas = better = creative. For A-I theory, the initial element is accepted only if associated with the term spontaneous. Innovators proliferate ideas as a strategy (accepting also the greater loss of discarded ideas compared to adaptors, whose strategy is to generate fewer ideas but accept their loss less readily). The A-I theory posits that the more adaptive will produce more if asked (Kirton, 1978a; Casbolt, 1984; Kubes & Spillerova, 1992), just as innovators will produce less if asked – although the asking may also, for them, invoke coping behaviour. The importance of the stimulus – what instruction is given – to these variants in behaviour is typified in one example taken from Kubes (1998). In a brainstorming session, a technique that aids the production of the largest number of ideas by simulating innovation and which is therefore less appropriate for adaptors: 'We worked in small groups, created according to KAI scores, without telling subjects the division criterion. The behavioural differences of the extreme groups were amazing. While adaptors worked out a system of work immediately and the session remained a well-structured meeting, the group of innovators behaved as if engaged in a quarrel. In accordance with A-I theory, there were no significant differences in the number of

Table 6 Intelligence and factor traits

IQ test	SO	E	R	KAI	(N)	STUDY
Otis (High Form A)	−.02	.04	−.01	.00	(413)	Kirton, 1978a[a]
Cattell (Factor B)	−.11	−.05	.00	−.06	(83)	Kirton & de Ciantis, 1986[b]
AH5 (NIIP)	−.06	−.06	.04	−.03	(106)	J. Taylor, 1993[c]

All correlations are not significant. For references relating to the measures see Table 5.
Notes
a New Zealand 17-year-olds, data collected and analysed by Drs Martin and Mulligan.
b British managers.
c British 16–17-year-olds.

ideas generated by the two groups. Both adaptors and innovators can produce a large number of ideas, if they are motivated to do so (e.g., if asked). If they are not asked to act in a particular way, they generate ideas in their preferred ways.' So the number of ideas actually produced by an individual in any circumstance depends on many factors: differences in style, knowledge (i.e., level), and motive are the three most obvious. Isaksen et al. (1998) note that trainers in creativity sessions may vary what responses they are getting by small unwitting changes in instruction. For the rest of the chain of argument that more ideas = better = creative, the weakness of its links is more obvious, in that 'better' cannot be entirely dependent on 'more' (if they are not better, we are better off with less); nor can more or better entirely define creativity (or problem solving).

If the position that creativity is synonymous with innovation is examined experimentally, the numerous studies in A-I literature bearing on this matter make a formidable counter case. In addition there are other studies that can be brought to bear. Payne (1987) argued, on a priori grounds, that creativity is innovation (proliferation at high level), suggesting that the KAI showed this. His argument is that KAI's factor traits SO (sufficiency of originality) and R (rule/group conformity) are measures of style and that E (ranging from adaptive to innovative style of efficiency) is a measure of level. The research shows, however, that neither KAI as a whole including Factor E or Factor E alone correlate significantly with any form of level measure, such as IQ or management competence (see Table 5; Kirton, 1987). Payne does not explain why these results do not undermine his supposition. The results most difficult to explain away are from three studies in Table 6; in each study all three factor traits correlated equally negligibly (and, of course, insignificantly) with three different measures of IQ. There are, of course, arguments and supporting studies on this issue that preceded those relating to A-I. Perhaps the persistence of the level and style dispute lies in the supposition that grew up after the Second World War, that creativity and intelligence were uncorrelated. However, creativity was not defined specifically as either a level or a style variable, so what relationship was expected between creativity and (say) IQ measures was not clear. The influential study by Getzels & Jackson (1962) offered evidence for the notion that the link between these concepts is significant, as long as it is accepted that those who are deemed creative are intelligent. This hypothesis is hard to accept as testable. This work and its findings have been subject to criticism; the objections of a leading British psychologist were cited earlier, in the previous chapter.

Two earlier studies, by Thorndike (1913) and Wallach & Kogan (1965), reviewed the then existing literature and generally concluded that there was no clear separation between creativity and intelligence. In later studies, Kogan generally believed that they

Table 7 Factor analysis of the Torrance matrix

Scales	Reference	Factors[a]	
		I	II
Left Hemisphere Style of Thinking (C) ⎫	Torrance, Reynolds, Ball, & Riegel, 1978	.84	–
Right Hemisphere Style of Thinking (C) ⎭		.76	–
Creative Personality (WKPAY)	Khatena & Torrance, 1976	.72	–
KAI[b]	Kirton, 1976	.66	–
Creative Self Perception (SAM)	Khatena & Torrance, 1976	.57	–
Creative Motivation	Torrance, 1971	.56	.33
Cue Test	Stein, 1975	.42	–
Originality (Rorschach)	Hertz, 1946	.35	–
TTCT Fluency ⎫		–	.87
TTCT Originality	Torrance, 1974	.35	.84
TTCT Flexibility		.33	.69
TTCT Elaboration ⎭		.35	.67
Possible Jobs	Gershon & Guilford, 1963	–	.41
Similes	Schaefer, 1971	–	.36
Movement (Rorschach)	Hertz, 1946	–	.31
(Cumulative Eigenvalue %)		(50.5)	(67.7)

Notes

a Only loadings > .30 entered. Tests not loading .30 on either factor (see text): Integrated Hemisphere ST (heaviest loading on Factor 3); Seeing Problems (Factor 4) – Guilford, 1969; TTCT Creative Strengths Checklist (Factor 5) – reference as above.

b KAI weakened as blind item scored in error – this analysis of data is by kind permission of Professor Torrance (for original data: Torrance & Horng, 1980).

were separate, at least under certain conditions. These conditions were, essentially, related to the perception of the aims of the 'testing sessions', as transmitted to the respondents by the instructions and the test ambience. He and others noted that as the setting and instruction became more nonevaluative and permitted the respondents to be more relaxed, they exhibited more spontaneity and the link with intelligence appeared less (Kogan, 1973). It was also noted that in the less obviously 'testing situations', older subjects exhibited less anxiety and revealed an 'improved performance'. In another statement, Kogan (1971) concluded: 'that a permissive context is not really necessary to bring about a separation of creativity from intelligence, provided that the former is confined to measures of ideational fluency.' He was influenced in this work by his reanalysis of Cropley & Maslany's work using the Wallach–Kogan creativity tasks, in which they had concluded that complete statistical independence of intelligence and creativity could not be established. Kogan's reply was that they had failed to factor their results. When he did so three factors had emerged, one of creativity and two of intelligence. This was just the technical reappraisal Heim was asking for, above, and which Kirton also undertook on Torrance & Horng's (1980) results (Table 7). Despite Kogan's own clear vision and encouraging results to support it in 1971, by 1973 he was still worrying that: 'The issue does not seem to be closed' because a range of correlations continued to be reported. But rarely has the main aim of these studies been directed specifically at resolving this problem, and there have been problems in making direct comparisons. As Kogan (1973) further observed: 'It is worth noting that evaluative and permissive conditions can be contrasted in terms of several attributes – group versus individual administration; unlimited versus restricted amounts of time; test-like versus game-like (or neutral) descriptions of task; typical institutional versus atypical or home setting for completing tasks; authoritative, demanding versus relaxed, supportive examiner. One or more of these contrasts have been employed in every relevant study, but studies have varied in the number and choice of contrasts employed. No doubt this has contributed to the mixed outcomes reported' (p. 98).

Kogan was not alone in finding the clear conclusions that the data revealed hard to accept, for as will be seen below, such confusions and mixed results continue to this day, while the literature generally continues to posit, rather more hopefully than with persuasion, that creativity (level) is independent of intelligence. If the underlying theory, the derived hypotheses, and the planning of the experimental design contain confusion, the results will be confusing. In this instance, we might readily suppose that the more the instructions and setting call, or seem to call, for a level response, the more level will be evoked, and these outcomes will correlate with at least some other level measures such as intelligence. The less level is evoked, the more individuals' styles will predominate and the less their output will correlate with intelligence, or any other level measure.

One problem in settling the debate on whether style measures might correlate with level ones is the validity and reliability of the measures used. Wallach & Kogan (1965) had earlier complained that many of the measures of creativity they had explored were found to be poorly intercorrelated. They opined that the reason was that many of the measures were either psychometrically poor or technically invalid (i.e., measuring something other than creativity). One can but agree, however, this may not be the only reason for a low average correlation between these measures. The contention in this text is that creativity, like problem solving, can be measured independently for style and level. If the test constructors did not work on the assumption that level and style are uncorrelated then the tests in Wallach & Kogan's battery could not only be:

- psychometrically poor, and
- invalid (not measuring creativity),

but also:

- measuring pure (creativity) level,
- measuring pure (creativity) style, or
- measuring an indeterminate mixture of level and style.

This complexity would be hard to unravel without some key. Given the right hypothesis, however, factor analysis is a useful method. Torrance & Horng (1980) administered KAI and a number of measures all purporting to measure creativity to a sample of subjects. The resulting correlation matrix yielded the usual jumble of results that had caused Wallach & Kogan's complaint. Torrance kindly permitted Kirton to factor analyse these data. The expectation was that two principal factors should emerge, one of level and one of style. In addition, a few measures could be expected not to have significant representation in either factor; if so, these might be the ones that are 'technically invalid' (at least as it is defined in the bulk of the material included) or that have poor psychometric properties. It is most likely that these latter measures would each be found dominating their own factor and largely unrelated to any other measure. It can be seen from Table 7 that the two expected factors emerge. Some measures are pure (load significantly on one factor), whereas some are predominantly of one sort but contaminated by the other. The remainder, those that are technically invalid (not measuring whatever the others are measuring) and those that are psychometrically poor, are found, isolated, on later factors. Factor 1 contains both right/left hemispheric preference and KAI with high loadings, and neither makes a significant contribution to the second factor. Therefore this factor has been labelled *style*[63]. In the second factor is the group of measures in the TTCT block, which owe much in their naming and concept to those originally devised by Guilford, who was an expert on level. Such measures were already known to be insignificantly related to KAI (Kirton, 1978a), suggesting that this second separate factor should be labelled *level*. This pioneer study, based on a small N from a single group of university students, has since been followed up by studies specifically designed to test the method used (factor analysis and relatively secure 'markers') and its conclusions. Using better samples and a research design tailor-made for the purpose, the outcomes from two studies (Goldsmith, 1986a; Tefft, 1990) yield even clearer-cut results in support of the hypothesis of level–style unrelatedness.

There are four other published studies, however, containing seemingly anomalous results. Their results are immediately relevant to this discussion as they reveal confusions in their hypotheses which make their results hard to interpret. Kirton & de Ciantis (1986) found a correlation of .25 between KAI and a higher-order factor, derived from Cattell's 16PF, labelled 'creativity'. This correlation is either inconveniently high or inconveniently low, and at first glance looks as if it is one of those anomalies that often disturb the pattern. However, this is not strictly a factor that Cattell derived statistically but a concept made up of elements from the 16PF that seemed to the author to be related to creativity. Its composition resolves the anomaly; it includes both a number of characteristics that fit the adaptor-innovator description and a doubled-weighted factor B score, which is an estimate of intelligence that, unsurprisingly, does not correlate significantly with KAI. So this is a composite measure of creativity including both level and style; its compound make-up is accurately reflected in the correlation with KAI, which is neither high nor low.

From the second anomalous study emerged a similar confusion, found in the Myers Briggs Type Indicator Manual (Myers, 1962) by Carne (Carne & Kirton, 1982). This measure is based on Jung's theory of types, which does not seem to have any relationship to any level concepts. Despite this the manual claimed (pp. 32–34) that two of its types (Sensing-Intuition and Judgement-Perception) are indicators of more or less 'creativity', especially in combination. However, MBTI is styled as a type indicator and the description of the measures is given as 'preference' for (not 'degree' of), so there appears here a conflation of level and style, with style measures attempting to predict level. Further confusion is suggested by the insertion in the explanatory text that potential rather than actual creativity was meant: 'However important a preference for intuition may be, it is certainly not a sufficient condition for creativity' (p. 34). In fact, the results of this study showed that S-N and J-P do have a moderate relationship with KAI (i.e., style scores); these scores rise fractionally if they are

---

63 The significant correlation between KAI and R/L hemispheric preference is supported by Prato Previde & Carli (1987).

combined into SJ-NP. The correlation with MBTI's Extraversion–Introversion scale was weaker and that with the Thinking–Feeling scale (more likely to lie in cognitive affect) weaker still (results supported closely by, e.g., Jacobson, 1993). Gough (1981), however, suggested a summation formula for all four MBTI types: $3 \times SN + JP - EI - .5 \times TF$, as a Creativity Index. For some reason, he suggested that this level–style mix would only work well with male subjects. Tefft (1990), in a study using 615 subjects, found the correlations between MBTI types and KAI scores much as she expected, as did Carne & Kirton (see Table G, Appendix 6); there was no significant correlation with Gough's mix. We can conclude that there is surely no serious suggestion that Jung intended level measures in his theory or that the MBTI is anything else but a measure of preferred styles, or types, as its name states. None of the four dimensions should correlate with level measures, independently or in any combination.

So the results of all four anomalous studies can be challenged, leaving the conclusion of all the other studies intact – level and style measures do not correlate.

In attributing level to quantity, precision is needed to avoid simple errors. One is that more = creativity. Another is that more = better. A third relates to the instructions given in eliciting a response. For instance, if the instructions ask for 'as many ideas as you can find', the more adaptive have sometimes been known to produce more ideas than innovators (reported by Prato Previde in private correspondence). There was no suggestion that the additional ideas that adaptors produce in these circumstances are any better (more useable) than those they might first have produced. As with innovators, quantity of production is likely to lead to quantity of rejection. The value of generating more, as a strategy, is that there are more possibilities of a viable innovative solution being on offer. If that is what is needed to solve the problem then an advantage has been gained – otherwise not.

The same is true of the predilection for working within or across boundaries – as strategies, each can sometimes be useful and at other times not. A general view in creativity is that working in a structure (Feynman's straitjacket?) is not only not creative, it even means having no 'new' ideas. This can lead to more unlikely anomalies. Eddison has frequently been quoted as saying that he never had a new idea in his life – he did very well making the ideas of others work and be profitable. An anonymous article in the *Economist Technology Quarterly* (2001) states a generally agreed view that Dr Carver Mead is one of the most significant and prolific contributors to computer technology. This is particularly so in the development of the capacity of the chip. Yet he, too: 'says he has never had an original idea in his life.' Can this American's statement be false modesty or an indulgence in some masterly British-style understatement – or is there a more likely down-to-earth explanation? A further quotation from this same article may shed some useful light. It quotes Mead as also saying: 'What I have done for most of my life was to give people a framework for thinking about things, which made it easier for them to do what they needed to do.' Perhaps his first comment startles because it is, in fact, very precise. As stated earlier in this book, the original meaning of creativity was producing something out of nothing – therefore the prerogative only of a deity. If, then, all ideas emerge from current structures, creativity (all problem solving) involves the management of cognitive structure – how to use its current limits to get more enablement from it or how to work round its current limits, in each case creating fresh ones that yield the required enablement. However, this might lead to the interpretation: 'there is nothing new

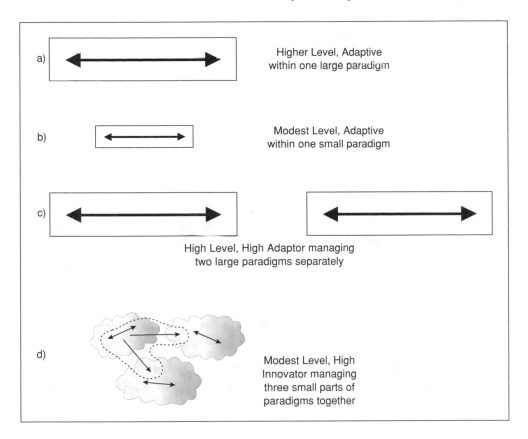

Figure 5 Breadth, level, and style

under the sun', to quote an old saying. Alternatively, all style approaches (anywhere within the whole range of style in the continuum) are within the province of problem solving and, therefore, of creativity.

Rearranging a boundary could leave one, in theory, with exactly the same cognitive space – the same overall creative scope – but breaking boundaries more readily implies added breadth. The creativity literature places much emphasis on breadth of vision, which it usually equates with *greater breadth* and level of creativity. One element used to distinguish the more adaptive from the more innovative is that the latter are liable to shed detail in order to obtain a wider perspective. Is this an indication of level or of style – or can breadth be a factor in both level and style? If so, it mirrors the argument above that quantity in production can be the result of preferred problem-solving strategy, capacity, or other factors (such as motive). The drawings in Figure 5 may help to unravel the principle involved by suggesting how high-capacity adaptors can be 'broader' in viewpoint than lower-capacity innovators, even though for many in the creativity world, innovativeness seems to imply greater breadth in its very definition. Remember, adaption-innovation is defined in terms not of breadth in general but in terms of the structure or paradigm within which *or* across which the problem is being solved. In (a) is a box of great breadth, within which the adaptor depicted is at home from end to end. In (b) we have another adaptor, equally comfortable, but in a smaller box. The differences in box size represent paradigm width within which the problem is embedded. We may further assume that content complexity might also be greater in the larger box. If, then, these two adaptors are each working to the highest level at which they are capable, (a) is of higher capacity (level) than (b). Here style is not a factor as they may have *exactly* the same style.

Next depicted, in (c), is a high-level adaptor managing *two* paradigms. Let us suppose that, if drawn to full schematic size, each is at least as large as the one in (a). This adaptor is probably now stretched, but able to manage the full width of each paradigm. For comfort, this person's characteristic style tends to keep problem solving to one or other box *at any one time*. Such style leads to high *efficiency* within each paradigm, sometimes at the expense of high efficiency across paradigms. Compare this now with (d) a high innovator of much lower capacity than the adaptor in (c). This person has a preference to operate at the edges of a paradigm and sometimes move, or even drift, into another, while probably neither using all of the start paradigm nor all of either of the others. To represent the level variable, each of these paradigms is drawn as a much smaller box than those of the higher-capacity adaptor. Note that the edges of the innovator's 'boxes' are less firm and less complete, even though they are smaller. Innovators define less, and do so less clearly than adaptors. They are less likely to be efficient *within* each paradigm, though they are likely to be more effective than adaptors wherever the structure is looser. Innovators may be more consistent in material that relates to more than one structure (Kirton, 1985).

The similarity between two high level people, one adaptor and one innovator, is that both can manage wide and complex situations. There are no differences in capacity. There are, however, clear differences in style. Irrespective of capacity, an adaptor is more comfortable working within the paradigm; capacity determines the degree of breadth and the level of complexity that can be tackled in comfort. The same is true for innovators: Irrespective of capacity, they work more often to the edges of the structure, in parts of the paradigm least well defined or complete, or even reach across to other paradigms in their idea generation. They are as limited by their capacities as are adaptors, and this determines the levels of problem solving they are able to undertake with success.

Note that because adaption-innovation is not a dichotomy but a continuum, strictly speaking the terms to use are: more adaptive and more innovative.

Conclusion

The KAI was devised as a measure of style and not in any way a measure of level. There is much value in conceiving these two concepts as completely independent of each other. One critical outcome is that *neither adaption or innovation is good nor bad – each is just a part of the style of problem solving or creativity*; another is that *all people, not just high level, high innovators, are creative*.

Defining creativity so that it appears to be the prerogative of a small elite is harmful. At work, this mistake is too frequent at present. There is the danger that high level adaptors are ranked, *in ability*, equal or below modest level innovators (and more so if they are high innovators). There is the danger that elite groups, often called 'change agents', are selected to bulldoze in mainly innovative change (or, occasionally, adaptive change masquerading as innovative change), believing that other members of the organisation are, to a greater or lesser degree, 'resisters to change'. A-I theory posits that everyone is an agent of change, although we can all do with the help of experts. This is similar to the position taken up, years ago, by the quality management field, which is that all the employees should be concerned with quality and the experts are there to help them reach high standards. But stating that all people are agents of change does not imply that anyone accepts all change; people are selective in the changes they are ready to adopt, and one factor in the selection is style, another is level, a third is motive, and there are many other factors that leaders would do well to study as part of the management of change.

PROCESS

When psychology first emerged as a separate study from philosophy, its primary aim was the analysis of mental process. Its primary methodology for this study was introspection. As this methodology become less favoured, the study of process languished. Wallas (1926; Figure 6) offered perhaps the earliest model of process, listing four progressive stages of learning and problem solving: preparation, incubation, illumination, and verification. Perception, the initial cognitive stage, was studied primarily in the Gestalt tradition. In the 1960s, with the advent of the computer, cognitive psychology came more fully into being. It included the study of perception, memory, attention, pattern recognition, problem solving, decision making, and other closely related topics. As the concept of information processing developed, attempts to trace the flow of information through the 'system' became a paramount goal in the new field (Neisser, 1976); in turn, this led to exploring the nature of cognitive process more deeply. Cognitive process makes use of the acquisition, organisation, and use of information and knowledge, marshalling these into a flow that is, usually, for ease of

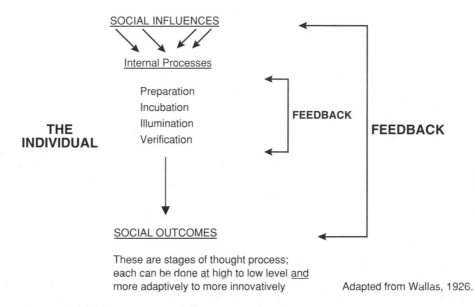

Figure 6 Thinking process – Wallas

understanding, depicted as occurring in stages. Of course, the whole of cognitive function is itself a process, but in the cognitive function schema (Figure 1) concentration is
on the operating element of each of the main departments depicted. In this section the
problem-solving process is explored.

Schemata often represent a sequence of well-defined and distinct stages, from a
beginning to an end, through which the individual passes in a defined order to achieve
a tangible outcome; this creates a 'road map' or idealised schema for modelling and
guiding action. Process is, therefore, presented as a *dynamic schema* that contains a
given number of elements, which represent its content and show its progress from
some onset to some finish. The schemata that purport to reveal a process do so by
stripping observed behaviour of its hesitation, mistakes, confusion, and backtracking
steps already taken, thereby offering a view of the idealised map as a template. The
advantage is that the process is revealed cleanly and simply and is no longer related to
a single event but suggests a general operation that can be revealing and taken as a
guide. The progress concept embodies the assumption that the activation of any given
stage is contingent upon passing through its preceding stage(s). A process may be
envisaged as either 'internal' – within the mind, whether conscious or not, of the
thinker – or 'external' – made manifest in behaviour. The cognitive function schema
suggests group dynamics as the process that operationalises collaborative problem
solving. External process in a group may also be implicit but the process stages can be
uncovered retrospectively by analysis, as was done in the study of management initiative. Knowledge of the process held by members of a group involved in collaborative
problem solving can also help the development of a common methodology and a
guide for action. This book began with one, suggesting the content, in progressive
steps, of management initiative.

These process schemata assume no variations between people and are thought to be
applicable to all minds in any circumstance; the differences between people are the skill
or way they undertake the stages. The advantage of revealing the steps of the process
is that when, in practice, individuals and groups digress from the idealised progression
or are (perhaps unwittingly) working in different parts of it, the schema offers a
guiding framework. One can ask questions such as: 'Where in the process am I? Am I
in the right stage? Do I need to go back a stage?' A process, as distinct from level and
style, is not a precisely measured and *quantifiable* aspect of cognition, but is evaluated
in terms of its 'truthfulness' (not contradicting presumed known information about its
operation) and its usefulness in any given situation. In the schema of cognitive function, each main element – cognitive affect, cognitive effect, and cognitive resource – is
allocated an operating process through which it makes its influence. Cognitive affect
identifies the problem that the individual wants to resolve and the operating process is
motivation. This choice of the problem to be solved, from among whatever else is on
offer, has been reached through reason and emotion and with the help of cognitive
resource. Motivation is the process that marshals and focuses energy, measurable in
terms of the duration and the intensity that it is deemed necessary to expend in the
attainment of each goal. Since the individual can only pursue a limited number of
goals simultaneously, motive is prioritised effort. This provides another cognitive
structure with the same paradox met earlier, for motivation is a structure and each
motive is both enabling and limiting. In the cognitive function schema, cognitive
resource has two related processes, learning and memory. When individuals combine
into groups, collaboration occurs through the process of group dynamics.

Cognitive effect (I plan) has the thinking (or problem-solving) process applying to both its elements, style and level. In the literature, most problem-solving schemata start with something like 'perception of the problem', end with 'implementation', and have one or more steps suggested in between to mark the main elements of the progression from one to the other. In the representation of the problem-solving process advanced by Wallas, there are two theoretical boundaries. The inner one relates to the individual's internal process and the outer one includes the stimulation received from the environment and the feedback of output back into the environment. The wider schema shows that the initial stimulus that sets the process in motion comes from the environment. When the individual has reached a full or an interim conclusion that has been internally verified, the output is passed back out to the environment. A social, as distinct from a personal, verification can now take place.

Mapping style and level onto process

Cognitive level, style, and process are separate concepts but they interact in problem solving. A-I theory supposes that level and style can be 'mapped on' to process to make the whole complex more revealing. The assumption is that the thinker undertakes each stage of a process at either a high or low level and in either a more adaptive or more innovative style. (Note: Both are continuous.) It remains to set a hypothesis as to which level or style a person will use and at what level. As to level, the hypothesis is that it is initially set in accord with motive. The higher the motive, the sooner this problem-solving task will be started, the higher the level of operation accorded to it, and the longer the duration over which the chosen level of intensity of effort might be maintained to achieve its end. In short, a person will use the level that seems appropriate, *up to (limited by) the maximum of that person's potential or actualised capacity.* The thinker will try to be consistent in the chosen level of operation throughout the stages of the process, unless error, misjudgement, or outside circumstances intervene.

The thinker will be likely to use preferred style, unless the thinker's own perception of the problem indicates that this is inappropriate (that preferred style is not achieving the required results) or perception emanating from an outside source (such as group climate) indicates this. When that occurs, the individual needs to indulge in coping behaviour, which is itself 'switched on' and kept in being by the relevant motive. This argument keeps the notions of process, level, and style separate, sharply defined but available for collective use in analyses of the thinking function of individuals or groups.

The cognitive process is a theoretical structure which is assumed to be common to everyone. It describes, in theory, how the brain (all brains) work. The very method by which it is revealed is aimed at uncovering a common pattern. But does everyone, in practice, effect change just as it appears in these schemata? No, that is not what any schema assumes; no one could be expected to operate as perfectly as an idealised 'map' or template. In practice, the first insight we may get, even as late as halfway through the process, is that as yet we know too little of the problem and need to return to an earlier stage to attend to this deficiency. If we start a cognitive process at a high level, does this mean we go on at that same high level? No, during the process, a set of factors unique to this event (even external events, like changed time schedules) may affect the operation of the process. The same argument goes for the consistency of style in which the process operates; if no other factors are involved, we are liable to start in our preferred style and stay with it. One last question: How final is the final

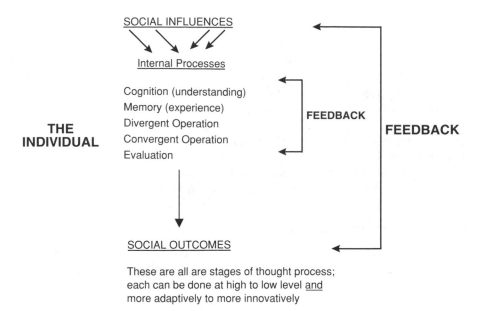

Figure 7 Thinking process. (Adapted from Guilford, 1950.)

stage of a cognitive process? It is not final at all, for it represents an addition of knowledge and that becomes a new position; each 'final' position is a base from which new problems can be tackled. Knowledge advances catalytically; cognitive process leads to the next process in the endless development of thought that can only end, for the thinker, in the cessation of being.

The literature is not always clear on the meaning used for cognitive process. The creativity literature frequently seems to conflate style, level, and process. Because of these confusions, Guilford's model (Figure 7) has been included to aid this discussion. It is common practice to extract from Guilford's tridimensional model of the structure of intellect just one dimension, that of operations, and from this dimension extract only two of the total of five stages: divergent operation and convergent operation; an early example is Hudson, 1966. These two stages in the process are then treated as styles as well as, or usually instead of, stages in a process. To confound the picture completely, the divergent operation is seen as inherently superior to the convergent style, in the sense of being 'more truly creative', thereby also scrambling in the level concept. For instance, Kolb's Experiential Learning Theory (Kolb, 1974) has woven into it the same conflation of three independent concepts: process, level, and style. First, it is a process made up of four stages arranged (second) as two bipolar dimensions depicted as lying orthogonally to each other. Third, the resulting quadrants are labelled as types (with level implication). All of this is supported by a single measure, which is more than any one measure can bear. Since the theory emerged, the replication of the data underlying it has been difficult. The bipolar measures do not replicate; there is uncertainty as to which pairs make up which dimensions and which then reflects on their validity; the level of their reliabilities are not always acceptable. However, in a study (de Ciantis & Kirton, 1996) that used Honey & Mumford's (1992) items, a rigorous item analysis was carried out. As a result, several items were discarded (insufficiently related to rest of measure) and some assigned to different stages (better related to them), but the result confirmed the original Kolb theory. Two bipolar measures emerged that were readily interpretable in Kolb's terms and had high internal reliabilities. The process (the sequence of the four stages) was not treated as part of the statistical analysis – it does not need to be; as a process it is enough to show it to be true and useful, which it certainly seems to be. So, by having a clearer notion of the separateness of concepts (in this case process and type) it was possible to concentrate on the reliability of the bipolar measures and be left with a useful process – as Kolb intended.

Summary

A cognitive process is defined here as an operation that progresses from a presumed start to a presumed finish. Such schemata are necessarily simplified to allow the principles of their operation to be considered, stripped of the clutter of less than perfect operation and peripheral detail that happens in real life. It gives a useful theoretical overview of the developing operation, theoretical step by theoretical step; showing the hypothetical stages, their order, and often their relationship. The presumed stages are essentially arbitrary, since a process is a flow and the stages are a mere convenience to easier understanding and for corrective action. Nevertheless, if these stages are well thought out, they will represent a single continuity that will be interrupted by personal, internal, or environmental factors.

A particular concern in A-I theorising is in defining cognitive process to ensure that there is a clear distinction between process and both cognitive style and cognitive capacity. This allows better evaluation of the schema's value. This is not tested statistically, but decided by the extent that recourse to it increases the understanding of the user; given that its whole and its parts do not contradict other known information, the test is: Is it useful and is it true? The relationship expected between process and both capacity and style is that there is none, because they are different in kind. Process answers the question: 'Where am I?' or, for a group: 'What stage have we reached?' Style asks the question: 'In what manner am I operating?' Capacity asks: 'At what level am I operating?' All three concepts may be needed to understand any cognitive output. Each stage of a process is essential to its successful progress; each stage can be undertaken at a particular level and in a particular style.

TECHNIQUE

Technique falls within the cognitive function element of cognitive resource. It needs to be distinguished from cognitive (potential) level (as distinct from manifest level, which is also part of cognitive resource), from cognitive style, and from process, which is the template of the way cognition operates. Technique is different from the concepts in cognitive effect, as it comprises a wholly learnt set of skills. Some techniques are more readily learned than others because their operation is closer to one's preferred cognitive style; we concentrate on learning some techniques rather than others to meet the needs identified within cognitive effect.

Cognitive technique can be defined as the learnt ways that allow us to use our potential mental resources to better advantage. Some techniques are intended to enhance level (capacity). For instance, if idea generation is blocked we may be advised to stop working on the task for a while and go off and do some gardening (a change is as good as a rest, as grandmother used to say). The aim of this temporary change of tack is to reduce fatigue or anxiety that may be impeding best use of capacity – it does not get the job done, but may help to do so later. Another more sophisticated capacity-enhancing technique is the use of mnemonics – aids to memory retention and recall. There are available many lists of useful points that can be used for acquiring insight into processes, with suggestions on how to use them. Kanter (1983), for instance, has identified 10 general reasons why people are likely to resist a particular change. One of them, 'loss of control', directly relates to Kelly's teaching that people cannot accept proposals of change that seem to threaten their self-integrity and grasp of the environment. Kanter's suggestions for helping to overcome this problem are to offer to team members a wider variety of operational options and greater individual involvement in the decision process.

Some techniques are intended to simulate cognitive style. One such technique is brainstorming. From an agreed start point, it is aimed to help practitioners funnel out in a deductive process to widen their problem definition, their information search, and their cognitive operating area. This widened area is expected to offer them added alternative perspectives of the problem and to assemble a wider array of possible solutions to be considered. The advantage is that solutions may emerge that the current system has not yet reached. The opposite, the inductive process of funnelling in, assumes that an adequate breadth of problem has already been attained, more or less from the start, and the relevant variables within have been identified and assembled. The problem now is to sift through them intensively to reach the solution that lies somewhere within this system – that is, within the cognitive boundary as selected and delineated. This involves redefining and tightening the key terms and boundaries of the problem and undertaking exhaustive analysis and solution search within them. This process often works best by successively eliminating alternatives until both the core of the problem and its solution are revealed.

So, some of these techniques aim to help improve level performance, thereby increasing effectiveness directly. Others, relating to manner of performance, simulate methods of innovation or adaption. They indirectly increase effectiveness by selecting and enhancing an appropriate style for the specific occasion. They make no changes to a person's potential capacity or preferred style, but do add to the person's knowledge, and skills (cognitive resource). An example of level technique is when trying to identify an object in movement. In poor light, we should look off to one side so as to stimulate the rods at the outer edges of the retina. These are contrast sensitive to light and dark and so are more effective in poor light compared to the centrally located cones, which are more effective in good light and for colour discrimination. In addition, the rods are wider spaced than the cones and are more effective in detecting movement. This sideways-glancing technique makes for better use of the eye in conditions that are not optimal for its design. Knowing the technique has not improved eyesight or the design of the eye; it has improved effectiveness in certain conditions. In this example, even though performance is improved – we can distinguish something in a different light condition to normal – our eye and eyesight remain unaltered. This is the definition of technique: It makes better use of what is available, without any alteration of the basic attribute, in specific conditions.

Technique generation and application mean that the problem solver needs to know (a) enough about the nature of the problem and what is blocking the path to the solution and (b) enough about the techniques available to select the one that might be of assistance. When in doubt, the naïve problem solver falls back on persevering with the natural preferred style or just gives up. The wilier thinker experiments with known techniques. First, the problem solver may try one that suits (but enhances) preferred style or a known, tested trick to circumvent a mental block. If these do not work then there is a shift to less tried ways that are simulations of a less preferred style. The simulation of a nonpreferred style, though valuable if well selected, involves a form of 'coping' behaviour; the added cost balanced against the pay-off. However, unfortunately, techniques tend to be taught as if each one is the complete answer to every problem in every circumstance. Clearly switching jobs, even taking time off to do some restful gardening, may be valuable as a technique on a particular occasion, but not necessarily as a way of life. Using brainstorming (simulated innovation) when the answer needed is adaptive, or using sharper, clearer methodology within the existing paradigm (adaption) when a paradigm-cracking solution is sought, are both misuses of technique. Another error that is often made is to assume that the teaching of a technique leads to a 'better' problem solver (a more creative person) when it should be seen as leading to being more effective in a particular situation. Unfortunately, most current teaching of techniques reveals little about two important issues in their use: (1) how to recognise when they are needed (and when not), which entails knowing the basis on which to select the appropriate technique for the particular problem; and (2) that techniques need to be practised if they are to continue to be used successfully.

Curiously, there are two distinct sets of literature devoted to different kinds of cognitive style technique: one is the creativity literature and the other is generally described as quality management. In general, the practitioner of one set of techniques does not seem to use the techniques of the other set. As much of the creativity literature values innovation above adaption, it is not surprising that techniques aimed at enhancing innovation are preferred – irrespective of the nature of the problem to be solved. In the quality management field, especially in the production, safety, and allied departments, adaption-enhancement techniques are usually preferred. Again, the assumption is that most problems in this field are solved by this method (e.g., accidents are only caused by innovators). There can be doubts about these narrow views. From the quality management field a new one, generally described as re-engineering, has emerged and it is useful to distinguish between these two. Quality management generally accepts (in theory) the current paradigm, including the main goal and the rationale concerning its choice and scope. Its evoked adaptive creativity concentrates its novelty generation on improving the process by which the group's ends are achieved. Its outcome is increased efficiency and while changes to the process are intended, changes to the paradigm are welcomed readily as an *outcome* of improvement. Re-engineering also generally accepts the prevailing paradigm (e.g., management grand strategy) but is liable to attempt wider problem definition and solution search in order to seek, as an outcome of solving problems, a more radical change of the process. As such it has both adaptive and innovative creativity elements built into different parts of its operation.

A-I theory assumes that different people have a tendency to prefer one method or another and to congregate in environments that they perceive are more likely to contain problem clusters that more readily yield to one method or another. Whatever their style, people do well within their preferred environment and method of effecting change as long as the environment itself does not change or is so complex that all types of problems abound. When the environment is stable, the majority group making up the climate will want to aid their problem solving with techniques that are in accord with their style. When the environment is not stable, they find that their preferred style *and their preferred techniques* are less appropriate, although they are likely to stay with both. Here is how developing structure becomes limiting. Many jobs are perceived, rightly, as being as dominated by adaptive or innovative style problems. People tend to be attracted to the jobs that suit their style. A climate develops that gives precedence, prestige, and command to the dominating in-group. Skills and style not in the mainstream can be regarded as not useful, or useful to those dealing with the less common problems, which may be deemed as less important. Unfortunately for those in the group's mainstream, some of the less common problems may be more important than is realised – failure in these areas may be fatal. Another danger is that these variant problems turn up rarely, and when they do the group fails to alter soon enough or to have the skills and style in the right places to deal with them successfully. Finally, new problems can emerge either because of changes to the environment or because the very success of the group changes the environment. When these things happen, a narrow range of skill and style can be disastrous. Then there is the next class of problem: the weakness, in any given situation, of the preferred style itself.

So far in this section the advantages of different methods have been stressed, but each also has its disadvantages, which have been discussed before. Adaption encourages staying with the paradigm too long; innovation encourages leaving it too soon. There are no prescriptions available to be sure, in any particular circumstance, how the term 'too' should be defined. Each thinker's style will certainly play a role in its definition. When the adaptive funnelling-in fails, the only hope is to return to start and widen the area of search – which can threaten to be an innovative exercise. When the innovative approach has filled a large wall with slips each containing a bright new idea, somehow what is required to be done needs to be extracted from this array. This need can threaten to evoke an adaptive exercise. Rarely will one style, or one range within one style, be adequate for long in complex problem solving. We must ruefully conclude that problem solving is not easy.

One caution must be made in attempting to equate deductive and inductive reasoning with problem-solving techniques. In philosophy, both systems develop within tight rules throughout their respective logical sequences. In induction, once a syllogism has the major and minor premises selected, the validity of the conclusion is in the correctness of the system, even if the conclusion is untrue because a premise is unsound. When the deductive method is used in, say, brainstorming, the tightness of the method at all stages of the process is deliberately loosened in order to achieve the innovative effect desired – finding a solution that aims to break structure; tests for validity and truth come later. The end result again may or may not be true, but it may also be invalid because the progress was not logical in philosophic terms – innovative idea generation has a higher casualty rate than the adaptive mode! Adaption and innovation can use both deduction and induction, but it seems that the systems are at their most effective when adaptors use induction and innovators use deduction, as long as the style and method are appropriate for the task. We might suppose that deductive search used innovatively is in constant danger of dissipating energy into far-fetched and impractical solutions when it is a ready practical solution that is required. Inductive search, used adaptively, is in constant danger of proceeding from such a narrow

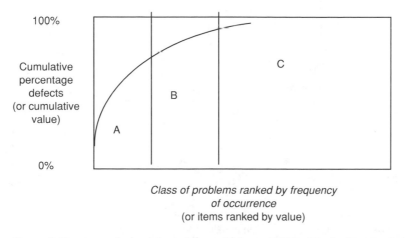

Figure 8 Pareto analysis. Adapted from Bicheno (1998). Used with permission.

array of input that it may not find the radical solution needed to resolve the particular problem on hand.

Techniques are learnt for the purpose of facilitating problem solving by making better use of the attributes one has. Their use can be enhanced by tools that have been designed for this purpose, some of which can be of the simplest design. For instance, let us suppose that we wished to arrange the array of perceived problems that might be currently facing us so that we can tackle them in some order of priority. We may chose to apply the Pareto Principle (see Figure 8[64]), which states that, within a particular situation, 80% of all the problems that occur within a system can be attributed to only 20% of all the types of problem that occur within the system. The tool used in this technique is the Pareto Analysis. Each member of a team uses it to list the types of problems that are causing concern and ranks them in terms of priority; these are then submitted to the group and are turned into a single agreed list against which the cumulative number of troubling incidents are plotted. The aim is to identify which problems are assigned top priority. A more sophisticated 'tool' is the Ishikawa (Fishbone) Diagram (see Figure 9), in which the most pressing problem (when identified) is shown as the backbone of the skeleton of a fish, with time represented by its length, progressing from left to right. Other key problems are represented as ribs in places that represent the order in which they need attention. Alternatively, using a 'static' version, the contributory problems can be grouped around the spine by class, e.g., problems relating primarily to people, machinery, materials, etc. Note that, in both these examples, the basic technique is first to accumulate the array of variables derived from known incidents and then to order them.

However, there is a tendency to call techniques 'tools', as in saying that, e.g., brainstorming is a tool. In a way they are, but if this terminology is used then the distinction between the method and some artefact that has been designed to assist its use has been lost. That may be unhelpful because, as Isaksen et al. (1998) suggest,

---

64 Adapted from Bicheno (1998), who provides an excellent review, in note form, of 'quality management' techniques. The 'tools' that aid a group in using a technique may be limited to sheets of paper.

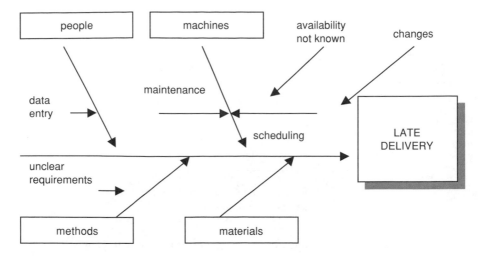

Figure 9 Fishbone diagram. Adapted from Bicheno (1998). Used with permission.

people use tools in different ways from the original intention of those who devised them, even when using the same technique. When that happens it is easier to see user variation if one can separately examine users' perception of the technique and their actual use of the tool designed as its aid. Sometimes the tools derived from techniques are also described as processes. Again, to make best use of all the terms the distinctions between them need to be understood and respected. Process can be confined to the operation associated with the use of both method and tool in the course of solving the problem. In this way the Kepner Tregoe system (Kepner & Tregoe, 1981) could be described (certainly in its original form) as a tool based on adaptive style (essentially of induction or funnelling in) that aims to find a cause, and then the solution, of a problem. It systemises the search from a set position (the initial array of data within the definition of the problem). It guides the process and so simulates best adaptive practice. It is often used over a lengthy period by a number of people on complex, knotty problems. As a tool, then, it uses a subprocess that mostly simulates adaption in particular classes of problem (i.e., in production).

Summary

Training and practice in the use of techniques are just part of a person's continuing education and not the correction of a flaw in brain function.

Teaching one technique for all occasions is like providing a craftsman with a single tool. A kit is required, together with the training to know which to use and when. Cognitive techniques fall into two main classes; those that enhance (release additional potential) capacity and those that simulate style. They operate effectively both for individuals working alone or in a team. The skilled problem solver needs to know how to select, from a range of techniques, the one deemed most appropriate to the problem in hand. Knowing which to select (or realising early that a technique which has been selected is inappropriate) is a skill in itself.

Many techniques have had tools developed to assist in their execution. There is a tendency, encouraged by trainers of specific techniques, for people to select one technique and its tool to apply to all problems. It is likely to be a technique that accords with their preferred style. However, a toolkit of different techniques is needed to resolve a diversity of problems. The problem-solving craftsman (that is, all of us) needs to keep in practice with the most generally useful of these tools and to keep improving them as theory advances or as experience suggests.

Many techniques can be used by collaboration in groups; some have been specially designed for this. Such collaboration needs to be practised so that each individual can play a positive part, allowing for the differences in their knowledge of the task, their style, and their knowledge of the technique and its tool. A member of a group, not necessarily the formal leader, should be encouraged to take the lead in guiding the group through the procedure of a collaborative technique session so as to make maximum use of such expertise. This is no different from the procedure any experienced, successful group would follow when faced with managing any other kind of specialism and that specialism's acknowledged, resident expert. The separation of the cognitive elements, technique, level, style and process helps to:

- make the need for an array of techniques, and the need for information on the limitations of each one, more easily understood;
- make the teaching of a wider range of techniques more acceptable – a person's need to learn a technique implies no automatic assumption of initial inferiority;
- encourage practitioners to apply their techniques with better discrimination to particular aims and occasions;
- show practitioners that even if the technique being taught is close to one's own style, they still need training on its use, especially when in collaboration with others.

There can be dangers in confusing, even confounding, style, level, and process with technique, which is easily done as some techniques also present themselves as dynamic progressive systems. These are techniques of greater complexity than, say, brainstorming, which nevertheless can be presented as having a procedure and rules. A tool, like the eponymous Kepner Tregoe (1981), helps the users to work tightly through a series of progressive steps, e.g., to identify the problem, sort out a solution, and move towards its implementation. This progression clearly suggests a subprocess. However, it is usually thought of as a tool aiding a technique. If one wanted to simulate an innovative style one would need to find another that seems more appropriate, located in a different part of the A-I range. Such a technique is likely to be found within a cluster inspired by Osborn's work. Level stimulation is based on quantity idea-generating ploys (e.g., Alternative Uses) and will be found on another continuum, in which style plays no role unless it interferes.

This chapter has argued that process (such as the problem-solving process in cognitive effect) is not the same as style or level. However, each of its stages is influenced by preferred style, potential level, and learning of all kinds, including that of cognitive techniques and the use of the tools associated with them. Of course, the initiation and continuation of a process are influenced by many other variables, the chief of which is motive. Each variable within this array plays its critical role. Such variables as attitudes and beliefs, knowledge and opportunity, scope and climate, self-esteem and confidence will bear on the complexity that is behaviour. Unravelling, understanding, and measuring these variables aid the management of diversity and change.

8 Link with the management literature

PROBLEM SOLVING AND SOCIAL STRUCTURE

Management initiative

The notions leading to Adaption-Innovation (A-I) Theory did not commence with an analysis of the literature. They initially began with observations that many people seemed to regard the problem solving of others that was different from their own as cause for amusement or irritation. Many people seemed to regard differences in others as inferior ways of doing things, especially when differences of culture or subculture were involved (e.g., differences of nationality, occupation, class, sex, or age). Returning briefly to the research project, Management Initiative, it strongly suggested that this sort of misattribution was commonplace and that those critical, irritating differences seemed to be related to deep-seated traits. These observations, greatly reinforced since then, began to take shape as an informed hypothesis. The critical findings found that are relevant here were that:

- all the managers were interested in, and appeared to welcome, change;
- it was harder to get acceptance for proposed changes that were perceived as 'radical';
- the definition of 'radical' was whatever challenged the existing ways of operating (or of thinking about the problem to be solved), e.g., innovation among higher adaptors and adaption among higher innovators;
- what was deemed radical in one department or company was commonplace in another, and vice versa; and
- people varied as to how easily each could accept a particular change; they all found some changes easier and some harder to accept – they varied according to the kind of change rather than by these managers' personal general capacity.

These findings were hardly new and had hitherto been regarded as a level issue: Clever people could manage radical ideas better than less clever people and some people were creative and some (or even most) were not. However, the new finding was that there were no general 'resistors to change'; all people accepted some changes and all found others hard to accept. Some of these differences were relatively easy to understand because they related to well-known level issues, such as the technical knowledge needed, the scale of the proposed operation, or the effect on personal status. But, however, the reactions to many changes seemed to relate to a person's style of problem solving.

In this chapter many of the concepts already dealt with are reviewed against the literature to which they most relate, or which inspired them. Much of the literature deals with one specific area; these are often different and do not appear to relate to one another. This review will show that they can be related, often with small modification – and those, usually, to issues not relevant to their core. In this review, it is hoped that problems left unresolved by one theory can be diminished by the findings generated by another. It is hoped that drawing together these strands from different literature will give them more useful meaning within a more general context.

The Management Initiative study left some problems unresolved. It seemed to be showing that there were those who proved eminently capable of initiating changes which improved the current system, but who were viewed by some colleagues as persistently failing 'to see possibilities outside the accepted pattern' (Kirton, 1961, p. 1). Others were marked as capable of generating ideas for more radical change, but often failed in getting their notions implemented. Often they failed to get the ideas accepted, in no small part because of the damage they threatened to make to the existing (adaptive or innovative) climate and culture. The development of these observations led to the formulation of the present notion of an adaptor–innovator cognitive style continuum. The theory posits that there are differences in a person's general readiness to initiate and accept change, not only in terms of capacity but depending on whether the stimulus for it emerged from predictable or unexpected lines of thought (e.g., Kirton, 1994). It was only later that this new informed hypothesis emerged and became the main thrust of exploration:

- that people differ in their style of problem solving; and
- that the differences are often misinterpreted as differing capacity.

The task now began of turning these observations and hypotheses into measurement. As this developed, appropriate literature was explored to see whether it provided some support for the existence of trait or, as was becoming clearer, a cognitive style.

Problem-solving structure in sociology

As these characteristic style differences were being worked out in detail, it became apparent that some of them had already been, in part, described in the literature, but not related to each other. Further, when they appeared, they did so as unipolar (level) rather than bipolar (style) concepts. As already observed, the research of others became relevant as the A-I concept was explored. Because adaptors and innovators either (respectively) support or threaten existing paradigms in their creative problem solving, Kuhn's (1970) analyses of scientific progress could now be seen to yield relevant, if implicit, knowledge of individuals' problem-solving behaviour. The classic study by Berger & Luckmann (1967) was also now seen to describe the way people related to their enveloping (cultural) structure. First, paradigms and symbolic universes are clearly analogous as cognitive frames of reference. Each is a basic conception of what is and how things are done. Each is a guide on what to take into consideration and what to ignore. Each is a context in terms of which experience within it can be satisfactorily interpreted and which problems can be readily resolved. Each gives a feeling of confidence that one is on the right track; each offers a shared version of reality among a defined (significant to self) community.

Second, both works agree that the simple knowledge that there are believable alternatives to current practice and belief can disturb the peace. The fact that competing scientists do not see things in the same way can be troubling because it challenges certitude when and where certitude is needed. Both paradigms and symbolic universes are to be followed because they select, from among alternative versions on current offer, accepted ways in which experience can best be understood and then use those versions that have promise of future success. Such promises are credible because they have been built up on wisdom derived from their past usefulness. Finally, symbolic universes and paradigms have further resemblance in their common fate. As symbolic universes may be switched, so paradigms may be exchanged. This may happen when they can no longer accommodate new experience (a) the validity and relevance of which cannot be denied, but (b) the explanations as to why it cannot be denied have become increasingly inadequate. Such transformations require, for both theories, something like a conversion experience – a sense of revelation. Otherwise, their originators state, they may change in a second way – by increment, patchwork, or accommodation. So both innovative and adaptive change can be detected in each theoretical framework. In fact, what distinguishes Berger & Luckmann's analysis most sharply from that of Kuhn is the former's scope, their concern for: 'everything that passes for "knowledge" in a society' (p. 15), while the latter is confined to the progress of knowledge in the sciences.

Structure and observed behaviour

Analysts in management are also concerned with these large influences on performance in institutions and on the people who work in them. For example, the aim of institutions has long been seen as the efficient accomplishment of known and defined tasks, in set and approved ways. Drucker (1969) posits that bureaucrats and managers have been sought who, when confronted by problems, adapt rather than innovate, being chosen for: 'the ability to do better rather than the courage to do differently' (p. 50). Drucker does not elaborate this notion either theoretically or as a measure, but over-generalises by suggesting that most managers are bureaucrats and that all bureaucrats must be, in the term used here, adaptively inclined. He says little about the needs of the particular job, concentrating more on a general presumed failing of the operators, and he seems to have a preference for those with courage rather than those with ability. Surely both are useful. His full text suggests that his preference is for those who tend to break structure rather those who solve problems within it. It is agreed that those who are liable to break more structure, the innovators, take more risks and so seem to have (or, at any rate, require) more courage – or from another point of view seem to be more foolhardy – but they are surely not less able. Adaptors also feel the need to take risks from time to time. They are related to the management of arrays of detail within the system – their reputation depends on them reaching a high standard of (adaptive) efficiency. Their milieu is less tolerant of failure.

As links with the literature were revealed, the breadth of the A-I theory immediately became apparent, for these studies lie in the fields of sociology and social psychology, whereas A-I theory essentially lies within the discipline of psychology. Within psychology, a relevant major theoretical work, that of construct theory, expounded by Kelly (1955), also lends support to the A-I notion of the different ways that individual problem solvers react to cognitive structure. This theory shows the same concern that structure is a means of understanding reality, acting as a foundation for the understanding of new experience. Yet its integrity can also be threatened by new information that cannot readily be accommodated. As we have seen, the individual builds up a grasp of reality, an understanding of the world, through the repeated abstraction of concepts – as Gagné (1974) suggests – into rules and principles, culminating in the highest form of learning, that of problem solving. All of these hierarchically tiered structural elements, as suggested above, are the psychologist's 'frames of reference'; cognitive structures that enable thinking to occur. Kelly argues persuasively that constructs are the necessary elements on which understanding of reality is founded. They need to be sufficiently flexible to incorporate fresh experience and to make full use of increasing experience. But an individual could not risk critical constructs being overwhelmed by new information, in case the current grasp of reality was altogether lost. Better to have an imperfect vision than none at all. The notion of 'concept' and that of paradigm here converge, and A-I theory uses both within a more general term, that of structure. These notions are turned into a theoretical statement by advancing the postulate that the more innovative are more impatient of the limits of (perceived) structure and the more adaptive are more grateful for its enabling aspects. However, all of them need structure (including, as Kelly notes, such stable images of 'self' and 'other') to be able to interpret reality consistently and to solve problems by predicting events and outcomes. Paradigms exist to help solve problems; in helping to solve problems, they are themselves modified. At times the paradigm has to be challenged directly and modified deliberately and extensively in order to solve the problem, rather than, while still believing in it, modifying it to accommodate a successful solution. People differ in their comfort with this variation of strategy. This is (preferred) cognitive style, which can also be described as a dimension of personality.

Studies in bureaucrat behaviour

As the first set of data in the validation process was subjected to exploration by factor analysis, the results indicated that the work was linking with other major studies. The authors of three of these studies – Rogers, Weber, and Merton – were chosen to name the emerging A-I factors (SO, E, R). This was not because there was complete agreement with them – far from it. It was that these studies could be seen as part of the foundations of a theory of problem solving of greater vista than any of us had at first envisaged. A view needed to be taken on the nature of the domain within which the work was being undertaken. It was now conceptualised as problem solving and, within this field, the preferred style that individuals naturally used for it. So A-I theory needed to accommodate the stretch from Weber's Bureaucrat to Rogers' Creative Loner and to unite these concepts into one domain; indeed, within a single concept – problem solving. This was assisted by the assumption in A-I theorising that style was unrelated to level or capacity and that the concept of style is bipolar. This transforms the other pole of Roger's Loner from being an uncreative person to one with a different style of creativity. The opposite pole of Weber's Bureaucrat is a different sort of problem solver, one more concerned with initiating changes to structure than with the efficient operation of the existing system.

A wider view of style, uncluttered by level, permitted support for the disagreement with Rogers that only a few people were creative, whilst finding room for Merton (managers) and Weber (bureaucrats) in creativity. In fact, if creativity is a subset of problem solving one can, with the help of Kuhn, readily make the case that vast endeavours in science, whether 'normal' or 'revolutionary', could also be described as *both* creative and problem solving. So might the manager's endeavours be described when running a business and coping, as all life has to do, within a constantly changing and challenging environment.

A-I theory can accommodate the work of these authorities from occupational/ organisational psychology as well as the work of Rogers, in that it strongly suggests that because the more adaptive are more at home within cognitive systems, they are also likely to fit more readily into bureaucratic structures. This is now a derived hypothesis and one that can be tested by showing that the means of established stable groups will vary predictably, contingent on the dominant nature (among a variety of the required needs) of their jobs. The descriptions, in behavioural terms, of the needs that are generated by bureaucracy (e.g., Parsons, 1951; Merton, 1957; Weber, 1970) should relate to each other within the theory in a consistent and reliable way. They can each be seen to be one pole of a dimension and they should appear, in readily interpretable form and with reliable coefficients, in a factor analysis derived from a measure containing such descriptive items. For instance, for Weber the aims of the bureaucratic structure are precision, reliability, and efficiency. Merton observes that: 'the bureaucratic structure exerts a constant pressure on officials to be methodical, prudent, disciplined . . . [and to attain] an unusual degree of conformity' (p. 198). These qualities, as attributes of the adaptor, describe 'the bureaucratic personality' as an 'organisation man' (Whyte, 1957) suited to work within institutions. As Weber and Merton made clear, this person seems best fitted to work within set structures, works in impersonalised relationships, reduces conflict, minimises risk, and manages to solve problems by proceeding at a disciplined pace, in a predictable direction. Bakke (1965, p. 43) wrote that a bureaucratic aim is to provide a 'roster of familiar strategies for solving recurring problems.' The corresponding adaptive weakness is the tendency to be too entrenched within these same systems, failing to see that newly presenting problems are not being solved by this roster. So the adaptor may be led to 'pathologically inappropriate responses' (according to Veblen, 1928; see also Warnotte, 1937; Parsons, 1951). Merton (1957), for instance, believes that bureaucrats have uncorrectable flaws, in that he holds that bureaucratic structures *typically* become unchanging and inflexible to the point of inefficiency – the very reverse of intent – because the personnel within them become insensitive to changing demand and to the needs of the people whom they were employed to serve, as both Veblen and Warnotte agree. However, others hold an equally bleak view for the opposite reason, that bureaucracies are often flexible and adaptable, even to the point of staff in government departments acting illegally (e.g., in unfair discrimination) to serve some clients' needs (Blau, 1963; Cohen, 1965, 1970).

Many authors at the time of the first stages of A-I development, and most authors now, however, seldom dwell on the advantages of the bureaucrat and the bureaucracy; that, for instance, all large organisations, whose clients require them to act predictably and efficiently whilst being accountable to them, require a strong structure of rules and agreed procedures for their operation. Changes need to be readily defensible, often in detail, from a variety of critics. To meet these needs changes often have to be undertaken in a disciplined fashion at a manageable pace, in ways that prudently attenuate risk, essentially leaving most structures intact in any one operation. The foundations of these thoughts were set early in management literature. F. W. Taylor

(1911) offers three components of scientific management: centralisation, stratification, and specialisation. These seemed to those following to be guards against undue risk, rather than required conditions. Among the risks to be avoided are upsets (as distinct from evolutions) of: 'the clear-cut division of integrated activities that are regarded as duties inherent in the office' (Weber from Merton, 1957, p. 196) and of: 'the systems of prescribed relations between the various offices' (p. 195). In Bakke's (1965) view, social organisation can be said to: 'live [by preserving] its unique wholeness in the face of internal and external problems and change [achieved, in part, by setting up a]: roster of *familiar strategies* for solving recurring problems' (p. 43).

In short, within bureaucratic institutions change is thought desirable, by those within it and those they serve, to be in expected ways and directions (Bakke, 1965). It is not possible to have unalloyed advantage from any system. Bureaucracy tends to the fault of progressing towards too rigid a structure. This view became entrenched by the 1980s. Kanter (1983) thinks that it is doubtful if: 'large organisations can accommodate, let alone take advantage of, individuals with an entrepreneurial spirit, especially where there has been a tradition of subordinating individuals to the routines and rules of the bureaucratic system' (p. 23). This is the old cry: The 'powerful they' in the overdominant 'organisation' are anti-creative – but, if true, how in today's world does so much creativity flourish? Kanter is one authority who heralded the view that bureaucratic (adaptive) change is not change at all: 'change threatens to disturb the neat array of segments [in the organisation] and so is limited' (p. 29). Hage (1980) agrees, as he considers that those who have status and power, the traditional enemies of 'creative' people without enough of either, veto change because of the fear of loss of position and failure of operation. Vicere (1992) has dubbed these folk, with these characteristics, as aristocrats – presiding over the terminal stages of their organisations. All overlook their exaggerated position: Many of these organisations have become powerful and survive for years – if they are so inefficient, how do they manage this? In addition, they also overlook another matter, that innovative change tends to lead to a different fault, in this case increased risk, uncertainty, and imprecision (Bright, 1964); that because it makes for less conformity to rules, social norms, and accepted work patterns it can appear to be disconcertingly unpredictable; and that it can even lead to deviation from accepted notions of good reason (Charpie, 1960). Innovative change and bureaucratic practice do not make easy bedfellows; the precepts of the latter work against the adoption of the former and, for this reason, considerable innovation (except during times of crisis) rarely occurs widely in a bureaucratic setting. When innovation is attempted, especially simultaneously in several parts of the organisation, it can cause uncertainty within its ranks and the appearance of confused operation. So when such change has to happen quickly, it appears like a time of revolution and the resulting confusions and uncertainties attendant on the initiation of all large-scale innovative change usually cause a chorus of further complaint from within and without. Consider the fall of such organisations as Enron and Marconi.

The literature is generally agreed that a person who does well in bureaucratic institutions is one who can go about his business reducing conflict (Weber, 1948; Parsons, 1951; Merton, 1957) and minimising risks by favouring changes that are supported by a maximum of experience and widespread acceptance (Kirton, 1961). But there will be occasions when changes in an organisation will be too slow – too far behind the changing demands that come from the outside – or of the wrong kind when they are made by officials who, trying to adapt to current pressure, pay insufficient regard to the original goals of the institution (Merton, 1957). Then changes may need to be innovative, with all the attendant risks of instability and friction. But selection, training, and promotion may have left few personnel able to recognise this need, and among those who do, fewer still in a position to effect the appropriate changes easily. In such circumstances the institution will be governed by inappropriate norms (Cruzzort, 1969) that are entrenched, and time may now be short to carry through the better, well-considered innovative changes. Both adaption-orientated personnel and the system will reinforce each other's inappropriateness. Adaptions introduced to forestall more radical surgery will not prevent many observers from judging the institution as essentially unchanging, inflexible, and ossifying. Nor is this the end of the complications when it is remembered that adaptor initiators (fearing resistance) often 'sell' adaptions as not really being changes at all, while wily innovators (fearing even more resistance) may dress up innovation as adaption.

However, the protagonists of these different modes of problem solving have been observed to have a tendency not to combine, but rather to expose each other's weaknesses (Whyte, 1957). So, a possible value of A-I theory is that the better understanding thereby engendered will lead to higher mutual respect, which in turn will bring about more fruitful collaboration and less personalised conflict, which Weber (1970) suggests are other accepted aims of institutions. A practical demonstration of how this may happen and to what effect is shown in Hammerschmidt (1996) – when A-I theory was explained, fewer problems in collaboration occurred. Among the lessons learnt in this study was that, in life outside management courses, teams rarely have the luxury of working on problems or with people exclusively suited to their cognitive style mode. The need to be able to manage heterogeneous groups without undue friction is, perhaps, the most important of the constant challenges that teams who have heavy problem-solving commitment face. The key problem of any such group is: How to get close to the efficiency of a homogeneous team on any critical single-style task, whilst commanding the advantages of the more broadly diverse heterogeneous team. A-I theory and KAI are increasingly being used as foundations to courses on the management of diversity. It is an argument in A-I theory that in order to manage change both widely and well it is at the same time necessary to manage diversity well. A prime diversity that needs managing well is cognitive style, which is built into or deeply held by each individual's problem-solving facility. Not to be able to manage this diversity magnifies other differences and makes them appear impossible to accommodate into normal change. Yet most people are engaged most of their time with what, for them, is normal change.

ON DEFINING NORMAL CHANGE

Friedrichs (1970) suggested that we explain acts and events as we have perceived and characterised them. Such characterisations (within both the social and the physical sciences) are founded on Kuhn-type paradigmatic traditions. Sociology has a strong tradition in viewing social change as veering between the nonexistent and the catastrophic. Nisbet (1972) argues that within classical functionalist writings little emphasis was placed on the role of the individual as a thoughtful originator of social change. Instead, he argues, this literature views the individual as a (not altogether reliable) reflector (he uses the term 'replicator') of social practices that have become standard through past usage and been 'educated into him'. If the individual is not viewed as a problem solver, the emphasis in the analysis of social change is not on the intended solutions of individuals confronted by problems but on the unintended by-products of the actions of individual role-players. These by-products may summate to generate dysfunctions – forms of social pathology – that will be felt differently as pressures for change at different locations in the social matrix (Merton, 1957). This line of thinking suggests that changes are not directly traceable to the decisions of individuals but rather from the changing properties of social structures. These changes are thus seen as both cause and effect; indeed, Blau & Schoenherr (1971) stated in reply to Homans (1964), that it was: 'time we push men finally out, to place the proper emphasis on the study of social structure in sociology' (p. 357). This must surely be nonsense, for by this reasoning individuals are powerless to bring about, or even influence, much of the change that impinges on them. Furthermore, it then becomes necessary to explain change by such concepts as government, economic powers, large institutions, the working class, or the aristocracy, all of which can be seen as social structures and which operate as bureaucracies. The essential weakness of this argument is that large groups (made up of smaller groups, in turn made up of individuals) are assumed to have capacities to think and act as if individuals, whilst these same capacities are denied to the very individuals of whom they are composed. Surely, it is only the individuals who think, not the institutions. One could hardly put the argument for the unchallengeable position of the individual as the thinker better than the early 18th century poet, Pope, does: 'the proper study of mankind is man.'

Within the view that individuals have little or no influence on social change, novelty in social contexts seldom has a cheerful origin; such change is viewed instead as the product of socially corrosive conditions. In Merton's (1957) elaboration of Durkheim's ironical notion that deviance is itself socially generated, structural change is a response to anomie – a form of social pathology. Parsons (1951) claims to see his own typology of motivations for change reflected in Merton's and shares a similar view of the origins of change. In Coser's 1967 analysis, the precursor of change is endemic social conflict. Such macro-level analyses seek to reveal a pattern only between social facts and not between their originators. This patterning is not attributable to the conscious problem solving of individuals but appears to have design features, purposes, and intentions that are anthropomorphically ascribed to social objects (such as institutions), which logically cannot possess them (Allport, 1924; Moore, 1969; Ryan, 1970). Even when some sociology literature gets close to examining people, it is liable to do so, especially when searching for a source to blame for the lack of change (of the sort favoured by the author, of course) such as Veblen's (1928), by referring to the: 'vested interest of the status group'.

Half a century on, the blame attribution is along the same lines. Perrow (1970) observes that any pressure to change (particularly that emanating from outside the organisation) only reinforces the need to identify more deeply with the current rules and the status quo, even when this may not be in the interest of the organisation. It is hard to find in this literature any hint that those opposed to *this* change (or, often with more accuracy, *my proposed* change) should not be perceived as, *therefore and inevitably*, against all change. If the views between two groups are mutual, a collaboration block may form based on blinkered views complaining about others' blinkered views. The language used in the literature may long have become a contributory factor. For instance, Legge (1978), in an otherwise careful argument about different changes required in the progress of professionalism in personnel managers, suggests this distinction: 'whereas the conformist innovator goes along with the existing organisational ends and adjusts his means to achieve them, rather than making his activities conform to the dominant values about what constitutes organisational success, the *deviant* innovator attempts to change the means/ends relationship by gaining acceptance for a different set of criteria for the evaluation of organisational success and his contribution to it' (p. 85). This is not an argument that will easily be got across with clarity and without difficulty – the terms conformist and deviant may well be the first stumbling block[65]. Quine and Ullian (1970) have suggested that what we need are sharper psychological concepts, which might show how the study of individual differences in the perceptions of problems and in the capacities and styles of solving them might lead to different kinds of solution to the problems; it might help direct the study of role management (Goode, 1960; Gouldner, 1960) which, in turn, might assist the study of social change. Adaption-innovation tries to inject precision, without treating all opponents of any particular view pejoratively; accepting their legitimacy, without necessarily agreeing with them (on any particular issue).

In making these links with the earlier literature, it was necessary to ensure that the A-I concept did not spread its definition until it became ill defined and unmeasurable. Experience in consultancy and teaching suggests that managers often confound extensive change with innovation. 'Breakthrough' – a favoured term and apt only when describing change that has pierced the cocoon of a major enveloping structure – is often indiscriminately applied to any large-scale change, regardless of its kind. In another field, Dahrendorf (1959), writing on analyses of political change, rightly complains that: 'the term "revolution" is often used indiscriminately for both particularly radical and particularly sudden changes' (p. 234). Ironically, Dahrendorf commits the error he was concerned to correct. Carefully specifying that by revolutionary change he means sudden (not radical) change, he goes on to write that Marx: 'tended to believe that the only way in which social conflicts could produce structural changes was by revolutionary [that is, sudden] upheavals' (p. 125). However, he also notes that in the Industrial Revolution – a process that Dahrendorf describes as radical but slow – Marx saw structural changes on the grandest scale emerging: 'slow-paced through the interplay of social tensions.' This is really confusing; surely it can be put more precisely and more simply: Changes may touch few, many, or all; they may appear to race or dawdle and, also quite independently, changes may differ in kind. The notion that innovation may swiftly slice through current thinking to arrive at a dazzling new truth and that adaption always lumbers along may only sometimes be true. The converse is also sometimes true; some innovation takes years to develop and much adaption, aided by existing cognitive structure (current consensually agreed knowledge and collective experience), can get to a polished solution very quickly. Currently, even into this new millennium, management is going through a phase in which any change that can be thought of any consequence needs to be radical (a breakthrough) leading to large and even spectacular outcomes; any other kind of change seems hardly worth the bother of acknowledgement. Unfortunately, this trend overplays

---

65 Here again is the danger of broadening out terms like innovation until they are meaningless but, nevertheless, cause great confusion, resentment (of those who feel excluded), and stress. It might not be very difficult to contend that the current, trendy 'creativity and innovation' set do more harm than good.

innovation and underplays adaption, just as, in decades past, the case was reversed. Some balance is occasionally restored when, by redefining terms, some large-scale, thoroughgoing reforms within a paradigm are wrongly dubbed as innovative.

Sociology can take a grimmer view of large-scale change, mostly in the form of revolution as an antidote to stagnation, as seen in many of the writers quoted above, including the main reviewers of this territory, Parsons (1951) and Merton (1957), as well as others such as Hage (1980) and Ekvall (1983 – in his climate measure contrasting innovation to stagnation). Consider how almost virtual denial of normal change is highlighted in Merton's analysis of one type of social change. Distinguishing between cultural and social structures – where the former refers to a set of values governing the behaviour of members of a group and the latter to a set of social relationships within the group – Merton argued that a disjunction between these structures may occur in which people cannot achieve the ends that they are educated to pursue along the social routes that they are obliged to follow. In such situations, where the culture calls for behaviour that the social structure precludes, normlessness (anomie) arises. Merton (1957, p. 139) calls the different kinds of responses made by people to such means – end disjunctions 'adaptations', and he distinguishes five types, viz., conformity, innovation, ritualism, retreatism, and rebellion; the last three have a distinctly pathological flavour. Merton's point is that the mode of adaptation one is likely to adopt when faced with the socially pathological condition of anomie will be a function of one's place in the social structure (e.g., status and role), not one's personality. If differences in such behaviour are solely linked to status, then the different response styles that individuals occupying the same social positions exhibit must be treated as variants, perhaps no more than mere products of random social error. Yet if people can be found who, *irrespective of their status*, characteristically conform rather than innovate, or who ritualise rather than retreat (using Merton's terms), then his analysis is (at best) incomplete.

A balanced view

A-I theory suggests that we take the *sapiens* in *Homo sapiens* seriously and treat one complex product of cognition, the sociocultural system, as an organised set of solutions to the problems of social living. In such a system individuals are socialised to organise both their experience and behaviour in ways that incorporate these solutions. Yet the set of solutions that constitutes the sociocultural system is, like any other paradigm, a structure that has been devised by past experience and still reflects it. It cannot have been designed to accommodate novelty before it is experienced, since novelty cannot be predicted (or it would not be novelty). As problem solvers, individuals working in groups will evaluate novelty as either residual problems or counter-instances and, responding adaptively or innovatively, accommodate anomalies into existing structures or greatly altered structures. The aim is to master novelty and turn the solution into profit. We call such cognitive practices 'normal change'. However, as structural – functionalist writers (like Merton and Parsons) have stressed, the process of normal change in some social practices may have consequences for the set as a whole. Both independent adaptions and innovations may gather and sum to generate a folly, and the system of solutions as an organised set may contain major contradictions and dysfunctions. Such conditions of social pathology will promote a search for adaptive or innovative solutions that will restore coherence to the set. The resulting social change may occur gradually and steadily, and be seen as adaptive, but may summate into change that only in retrospect can be seen as large-scale and radically innovative in nature. The same result could have occurred rapidly and been seen, at the time, as radically innovative. Dahrendorf surely has a point, for speed of change is one defining element that distinguishes evolution from revolution. However, speed of change must be perceived relatively, primarily against the scale of events and secondarily in relation both to the insight and the style of the viewer. But revolution, irrespective of speed, does have a more overriding element; that of perceived discontinuity – a perception exacerbated by its speed. However fast the change is unfolding, if its direction and purpose can be contained within a known prevailing paradigm, then it is at least 'paradigm comfortable'. Conversely, if an unfolding change cannot be perceived within known structures that give it clear meaning (that is, with promise of control) then the unfolding events have 'paradigm deficit'. However, surely only a small percentage of the change brought about by individuals is pathological or catastrophic in nature, even though from time to time the pace and nature of particular changes can be disturbing to some and exciting to others.

The argument of this section is that to be aware of a weakness is helpful, but criticism may go too far as when writers find flaws, which cannot be corrected by those who make them, but do not see the balancing advantages or overlook corresponding flaws elsewhere. The criticism of bureaucrats and bureaucracies that does not also mention their advantages, or even the disadvantages of not having them at all, is a case in point. By way of balance it is suggested by van der Molen (1994) that the rise and fall of groups might be related to whether the more adaptive or the more innovative predominate in relation to whether the circumstances are appropriate to the group's prevailing style. That is, overly innovative organisations fail for lack of efficient adaption and overly adaptive organisations fail for lack of innovative flexibility in the face of unexpected change[66]. These notions have been further explored by Vicere (1992), on the rise and fall of organisations, and by observation by Kubes (1994), on the fall of the Communist empire.

Because the more innovative are liable to break patterns of accepted modes of thought and action, some of the literature on 'creative man' is also pertinent. It is enough here to repeat that the literature on creativity has concentrated on describing innovators. The reviewers of this area, Rogers (1959), Taylor (1964), and Shouksmith (1970) agree that the 'persistently creative':

- have little awe of traditional thought or consensus;
- display a high need for social recognition – they want their novelties to be judged as good; and
- toy with ideas compulsively.

These three points seem to fit the innovatively creative better than the adaptively creative. However, the position may be overstated. The adaptor is not just to be seen as being in awe of consensus but can readily find that a particular structure is useful

---

66 For the more adaptive, unexpected events emanate largely from outside their immediate system. The more innovative often fail to predict threatening events from within their structures; threats more readily perceived by adaptors. Collaboration may yield wider insight.

and should not be discarded lightly. The second point is common to problem solvers in groups – the difference is in the way that recognition is sought. The more adaptive try not to depart from consensus, moving with it or encouraging the changes as plans unfold. The more innovative set out to achieve consensual approval as a need for getting ideas accepted. The last point is related to other literature; Wallach & Kogan (1965) distinguish associative from combinatory play. The former can be associated with innovation and its practitioners appear to enjoy the production of ideas for their own sake. The latter is more adaptive; elements judged relevant to one another are brought into novel rearrangement, with the aim of solving problems being more evident throughout.

THE SEARCH FOR IDEAL LEADERS AND IDEAL SOLUTIONS

Most of the literature quoted immediately above was perceived relevant at the time A-I was formulated, placing its development into the perspective of the time. The current literature has, interestingly, many of the same concerns, strengths, and weaknesses. One major concern is with the speed of change and the perversity of the world at large (but not, of course the authors) in not being willing or able to keep pace – with the large organisation still singled out as the prime laggard. Much of this literature seems written by those who are both more able and more innovative, have had bruising but successful careers in large organisations, and who have then moved out to earn more success as highly critical consultants. They seem to work on the notion that yesterday's idea must be wrong, overlooking the possibility that the current, more trendy idea is almost certainly shallow (the more it is of recent origin, the less it has had time to be thought through) and even more likely to be wrong (tomorrow is the graveyard of more innovative than adaptive ideas). Finding the balance of ideas that work, that are relevant now and will still be so tomorrow, is as hard to get today as it has always been. In *The Fifth Discipline* (Senge, 1990) on the jacket (and p. 4) there appears the challenging quotation from an issue of *Fortune* magazine: 'Forget your old, tired ideas about leadership. . . .' However 'tired' is defined and measured, ideas of this ilk must surely be suspect. Is this implication, that ineffective (irrelevant, unworkable) ideas are always those that are old, a true one? To lose all our 'old' ideas is to lose all cognitive structure, knowledge, and experience – and to be as helpless as a newborn babe. Fortunately, Senge's book is packed with useful information acquired over a lifetime of experience. His reference list is predominantly from literature of the 1980s, with the '70s and '60s well represented, together with a sprinkling from the '50s. He is rightly prepared to search back even further for useful thoughts such as those of Ford in 1926, Khalil Gibran in 1923, and even Bernard Shaw in 1903, as well as one passage that 'borrows from many spiritual traditions, from developmental Christianity to Zen . . .' (p. 399). It is, then, not old ideas that are the problem but those which, in the perception of the thinker, are in need of modification. The objection is not a matter of pedantic linguistic precision, but a plea for a more sophisticated argument for change than that 'new is better'.

Most people have experience of the difficulty of raising sensitive issues in groups and then helping to manage the resultant exchanges into mutually useful conclusions. During the Management Initiative study, it was observed that managers rarely explored past failures or, even less, past successes. Some of the difficulties are obvious, such as lack of time and fear of splitting groups and undermining cohesion. For many of the managers, 'debate' equalled 'argument', which in turn equalled 'conflict'. Yet some literature accepts conflict (stress, turbulence) as inevitable and even useful – although this seems to advocate the seeking of success through the means of last resort as a standard procedure. What most teams lack is an understanding of different means of achieving nonconfrontational idea exchange and some practice in how and when to use them. Senge (1990), concerned with the precision of words, explores one term relating to the reaching of agreement: 'To the Greeks, *dia-logos* meant a free-flowing of meaning through a group, allowing the group to discover insights not attainable individually. Interestingly, the practice of dialogue has been preserved in many "primitive" cultures, such as that of the American Indian, but has been almost completely lost to modern society' (p. 10). The second statement is a gross exaggeration, but the first sentence is valuable for reminding us of the use of different kinds of idea exchange and possibilities of progressing knowledge. Useful insight can be found from a comparison with this word and 'discussion', which Senge defines in the same paragraph as a more robust procedure, more a 'heaving of ideas back and forth'. His discussion is a reminder that both these methods of idea exchange are useful, especially in specific contexts – and that the skills of using them are too little appreciated. The advantage of dialogue is as Senge gives it; the corresponding disadvantage is that it is not likely to lead to a single conclusion that can unite a disparate group behind a single, united course of action. Discussion achieves this better, and so is used more often at work, despite its disadvantage of the risk of becoming confrontational. Indeed, to diamond cut a little finer, experience in organisations leads one to the gloomy conclusion that managers often do not use dialogue when it might be useful. They are often in too much of a hurry to get to a conclusion.

The main bar here is that some areas of discussion are 'dangerous' politically, especially those that are in the realm of 'political correctness'. Some arguments may be left unexplored simply because they are 'unfashionable'. 'Tired' as the idea may sound, mediaeval monks had long ago come across and tackled this problem – they devised a variety of discussion called debate. In this technique, every aspect of an issue was parcelled out and dissected. To make sure that every aspect was covered, however unfashionable its defence, the Devil himself was represented by an advocate. No harm befell the advocate, for not only were they selected for the task as part of a role (as any modern lawyer), but they might hope to be picked in another debate for the opposing side and shine by winning both. Perhaps we should teach skills in dialogue, discussion, and debate more widely, as was once done in every university, taking care also to teach the advantages and disadvantages of each of the techniques within this cognitive toolbox. Perhaps we need to pay more attention to learning to recognise the circumstances when one or other technique should be used and train our groups to use each technique as appropriate. It might be noted, for instance, that some adaptive ideas fail, unexpectedly to many, because they seemed so plausible when presented that they were inadequately explored. Just as dangerous are those notions that fit so well within current 'politically correct' structures that, even when most of those present have private misgivings, no Devil's advocate spontaneously emerges – to the disadvantage of all. Innovative proposals that might otherwise properly receive close, critical attention in searching debate fail to get this needful scrutiny and discussion if they are seen as challenging intimidating structure; they are just dismissed. If dialogue, debate, and discussion could all be used in appropriate circumstances, more disagreement may be aired but with less conflict. Conflict may sometimes yield a small net advantage but, like war, it should be resorted to when all else has failed.

The literature of the last half of the 20th century has certain aspects in common. It concentrates on problems of how to manage, which do not seem to have altered greatly over the years. For most of the literature, the aim is to find the ideal solution, advanced by the ideal problem solver, that fits most problems being faced. This is instead of a pragmatic search for the best way to deal with each set of problems, accepting that each set, if not each problem, may require different approaches, knowledge, techniques, and leadership (although not necessarily a change of leaders). This literature, on the whole, does not measure or analyse its results and refer them back in order to amend the underlying theory. Some modern studies do measure; in the field of leadership a turning point for the acceptance of a science-based approach started in 1947 at Ohio State University and, in 1950, at the University of Michigan, both of whom introduced the then latest methods of psychometric measurement and analysis to the understanding of the subject. The general conclusion was that two elements had been detected. The Ohio school called them Consideration and Initiating Structure, and they were conceived as independent bipolar factors, although in each case there is clearly a 'preferred' pole and, therefore, an 'ideal' to be extracted. The Michigan school's elements were dubbed Employee Centred and Production Centred, and they were conceived as a single unipolar continuum with the more preferred pole being less obvious. Studies from Harvard University in 1958 showed something similar, using the terms Socio-emotional and Task Centred, which were envisaged as separate types. In every case the aim seemed to be to reveal and measure ideal leadership traits that operate optimally, irrespective of the problem and its setting.

This was made more explicit in the work and measure of Blake & Mouton (1964, 1984); in their four-cell management style grid, of which just one cell is stated to contain the 'ideal style'. The clash between an intellectual assumption that 'good' leadership can be diverse and an almost emotional need for a single ideal has continued for a long time. The Michigan and Ohio studies, together with the contingency theory of Fiedler (1967), lead to Blanchard's (1985) situational leadership approach, which would seem to have arrived at an acceptance of leadership as a diversity of roles. However, a more recent development places situational leadership as 'one of several "transactional" approaches' (Cacioppe, 1997). This author neatly sums up the transactional leader as one who 'understands and helps the followers reach their goals and at the same time achieves the goals of the organisation,' which may sound the ideal some want to find. In fact there is a generally agreed 'hierarchy' of leadership terms, in rough order of their appearance in the literature, beginning (at the 'lower' state) with the search for appropriate traits, followed by situational leadership, transactional leadership, and finally, transformational leadership. The transformational leader is depicted as a lofty fellow who, again quoting Cacioppe, 'has a worthwhile and challenging vision that is communicated, motivates and inspires the followers [and] considers the individual.' So, leadership notions moved from the search for the ideal (traits) towards a more varied role (situational) and back again towards the ideal, leaving the management of diversity with the aid of diverse problem solvers by a diversity of leaders somewhat on the sideline.

Heifetz (1994), concentrating more directly on the leader as problem solver, starts more cautiously in his book: *Leadership Without Easy Answers*. He first frees the definition of leadership by easing it away from being viewed exclusively as related to massive authority and influence and by defining it instead as an activity or, one might suppose, as a social role. Indeed, he may go too far by suggesting that his definition excludes authority and even its influence as an essential part of the definition of leadership, although he appears to be mainly concerned with widening the role so that: 'A President and a clerk can both lead' (p. 20). This breadth to the role of leadership is not new but is worth restating. The military have known for centuries that success in war and battle depends not only on the aptness of the political direction and the brilliance of the commanders but also the competence and leadership down the ranks of an army to its numerous corporals. Heifetz also suggests that leadership can operate without authority and influence, citing as evidence numerous leaders whose distinction was that they challenged authority, for instance, Gandhi and Martin Luther King. But surely these men were effective because they did acquire authority and wielded great influence, to such an extent that they successfully challenged a prevailing authority. Indeed, so powerful did they become that they altered critical aspects of the prevailing authority they challenged; their authority and influence, inside their increasingly powerful following, played a vital role in their success. The term 'informal leadership' has long been used in industrial psychology but not to imply no structure; neither should the term be used to imply that it is always better, more effective, or more socially useful than other structures, for these evaluations depend on other factors.

There is further difficulty when Heifitz's elaboration of his definition of leadership becomes yet more exclusive. First, there is a distinction within leadership between technical and adaptive aspects versus leadership and authority, of which the: 'first points to different modes of action required to deal with routine problems in contrast with those that demand innovation and learning' (p. 8). This supposes that there can be an entire class of problems that can be solved without any learning and without the help of innovation – which is a completely incredible statement that might only be true for behaviour governed by instinct. The adaptive aspects are defined as consisting: 'of the learning required to address conflicts in the values people hold, or to diminish the gap between the values people stand for and the reality they face' (p. 22). Not the clearest of operational definitions, but the example he gives of Hitler's failures in this regard helps us to understand it.

- 'He played to people's basest needs and fears. If he inspired people toward the common good of Germany, it was the good of a truncated and exclusive society feeding off others.'
- 'Although dramatically mobilising his society, both socially and economically, he did so primarily in the direction of avoiding tough realities. By providing illusions of grandeur, internal scapegoats [e.g., the Jews, the Gypsies, the Communists], and external enemies, Hitler misdiagnosed Germany's ills and brought his nation to disaster.'
- 'Conceptions of leadership that do not value reality testing encourage people to realize their vision, however faulty their vision. Thus Hitler's error was diagnostic as well as moral.'

Heifietz's conclusion to this evaluation of Hitler's doings states that: 'By the criterion of adaptive work used here, we would also say that Hitler failed to exercise leadership' (p. 24). This is a view that must find few followers; there is no doubt the man exercised considerable leadership, along with such fellows as Genghis Khan and Josif Stalin; the debate, surely, is how the world could have arranged to manage without their leadership.

Heifietz does not criticise Hitler's management in the way many historians do. Under his leadership, Germany did not release as much military potential as did his main enemies. He was notorious in the management of his own entourage, giving important tasks to more than one person at the same time and leaving them to compete against each other for his approval. This method was efficient only in preserving his autocratic power. Such analysis suggests that the terms leader and manager overlap (leaving out the notion that some jobs are regarded as of 'management status' and not that the incumbent is a leader or a manager). Leadership is often used to mean helping the group in the selection of the problem, the assignment of value to its importance, and the mobilisation of the group's energy to solve it, at a cost in time and effort appropriate to its priority – the task carried out within every individual by cognitive affect. Management is more in the realm of cognitive effect – planning how to get the job done efficiently by the group. But, in practice, single individuals often undertake both tasks, although many may be noted more for one element than the other. A critical feature in A-I theory is that the elements that make up a study of problem-solving style need not only to be inclusive (all people are creative) but, in addition, each of them has individual definition and measurement. This means that a distinction has been made between style, level, other cognitive functions, and the success of any initiative. The danger of not making such distinctions can be seen in much of the literature reviewed here. Some are too narrow, e.g., Rogers' concept of the Creative Loner implies that too many people are not creative; Hiefetz's definition of leadership, like many of those of creativity, includes elements of social need and success. In some definitions, Hitler and Stalin might be found to be lacking in both creativity and leadership. One might wonder, then, why their century made such heavy weather of living with them. The current literature struggles with the same topics and is tempted by the same distractions of earlier years.

In his book reviewing past and current notions of leadership, Northouse (1997) offers a definition that attempts to embrace every kind: 'Leadership is a process whereby an individual influences a group of individuals to achieve a common goal' (p. 3). This leads him away from the trait definition of leadership, which he subjects to sharp criticism. Much of the literature he reviews looks for the 'natural leader' and lists such desirable qualities as height, intelligence, and extraversion. His general conclusion of these numerous studies, carried out over 50 years, are that they are inconclusive; too many exceptions for each trait abound – for instance, in the military field, such outstanding leaders as Caesar, Nelson, and Napoleon were all on the short side. More useful than a search for a definitive set of characteristics of leadership is the matching of specific qualities to specific problems in specific contexts. Nor can the relationship between qualities be made too simply. The more adaptive leaders and the more innovative leaders can both be either democratic or autocratic. The adaptive leader can use 'influence', however that is defined, to *persuade* the group to solve problems by the use of rule and other consensually agreed structure or to *demand* that the members do. The innovative leader can cozen the group into breaking the rule or force them to do so. The same variations apply to other styles, which feature in the literature as: formal or informal; assigned or emergent; directive or supportive. Which of these combinations of characteristics will prevail depends on many factors, not least the particular aim and the circumstances in which it is to be achieved. It is not surprising, therefore, that this search for ideals persistently fails; Atwater & Yammarino (1993) write: 'Given the importance of individual traits for the understanding leader behavior and effectiveness, why has research in this area diminished drastically since the 1960s? In part, the reason stems from the inconsistent results'; which was as true then as it is now.

The breadth of leadership mirrors the breadth of problem solving

Much of today's literature still does not try to measure but develops notions built on undoubted experience and a fund of case history. Regrettably, this lacks the discipline of examining the argument with a method that is independent of the writer's personal evaluations. This seems to lead to definitions that leave out half the population, and does not link elements together that are clearly functionally and operationally related (like creativity and problem solving) but links elements that are uncorrelated (like innovation and success). We can be led to rewriting history, in which a powerful but evil influence can be written off as uncreative and lacking leadership in defiance of all evidence to the contrary. Heifetz (1994), for instance, is himself aware of these dangers, since his first criterion of a 'prescriptive concept of leadership' is that the term must 'sufficiently resemble current cultural assumptions.' His second criterion is that the definition should be practical. But the third and fourth criteria undermine the precision of the others, for he lays down the notion that leadership should 'point toward[s] socially useful activities [and] should offer a broad definition of social usefulness' (all from p. 19). If these definitions were to be taken seriously all sorts of difficulties would arise, as they do when the same elements are included in the term creativity (discussed in an earlier chapter). Heifetz mentions, as great leaders, the founding fathers of the United States – Jefferson, Washington, Adams, Madison, Hamilton, Monroe, Benjamin Franklin. First, they were leaders against an established authority and underline how such an alternative authority and influence can be acquired. But second, following his guidance we could, with tongue slightly in cheek, challenge their right to leadership status. They and their adversaries King George III, his prime minister, Lord North, and the Tory administration (but not the Whigs under Fox) squandered too much time, treasure, and lives on a solution that might have been more socially useful if it had resulted in the resolution of the difficulties within a single, powerful, mostly peaceful, freedom-loving, democratic Commonwealth. They could all be demoted for failing to look ahead at the social value of such a political entity and for failing to foresee how it could have intimidated War Lords of the succeeding centuries such as Napoleon, Kaiser Wilhelm, Hitler, and Stalin (the latter of whom slew more people than all the rest put together). While awaiting the emergence of these future enemies they could have turned their combined wisdom and authority to dealing with a pressing problem or two in their current times, like the slave trade. If only we had an assured supply of such leaders we would not need to spend time trying to understand leadership but just relax and feel suitably grateful for having it – but as it is, we had best continue our study, searching for appropriate rather than ideal leadership.

One distinction that is sometimes made, more in practice than in the literature, is to separate management from leadership; crudely put, the distinction made is that one does and the other inspires. The upshot are articles like those of Church & Waclawski (1998) – using KAI, with little knowledge of the theory or the breadth of its literature

– which search for distinction between transformational versus transactional leadership characteristics and success. The result is circular: Adaptors exhibit adaptive behaviour (and can be seen to do so) whilst innovators exhibit more innovation, equally visibly. The value of making these terms and style into dichotomies is limited; the problems faced by both managers and leaders overlap but differ widely in any particular situation, and so must the ways and means of solving them. For instance, few problems faced by senior managers are simple, so they rarely require for their resolution only a few resources of a similar nature. An array of problem solvers, having between them an array of styles and other characteristics, attributes, and resources are frequently required to solve a single, large, difficult problem. Yet the same team with the same leadership must manage it all, preferably successfully and usually in limited time.

These studies are, however, useful if they cease looking for ideals and concentrate on matching key variables relating to people with particular classes of problem, in particular situations. This is a necessary foundation to tackling the task: making best use of the available information on these variables in practice. How do the protagonists, the problem-solving leaders, knowing more about themselves and significant others and with deeper insight into the nature of certain crucial problems, seek out and apply the advantages available in the problem-solving group and mask its disadvantages? The answer to the question seems to be more like what is required of successful leadership. A-I theory posits that not only can innovators lead and adaptors manage (however the terms lead and manage, are defined), but also innovators can manage and adaptors lead – they just do so differently. Success in either sphere depends on many factors but, essentially, it helps if what is available to solve the problem matches what is needed to solve it.

All the activities of mankind and all the institutions and artefacts, deriving as they do from the same brains, must mirror them in some way. Even the tools that the brain devises are extensions or specialised refinements of the body that need to be used by the brain for its convenience and are designed accordingly. The notion of leadership is no different and its functions originate in the individual's brain and then are made manifest, through behaviour, in the environment. The perception of a need to lead or to be led emerges from the operations of cognitive affect. Leaders and followers must carry out the following, for and within the group (a function that, within the brain, is the specialism of cognitive affect): select the problem to be resolved (the Problem A that requires leadership) and resolve the spin-off Problem B on how to manage each other (to achieve Problem A). These tasks and the understanding of the kind of solution that will satisfy (limited by certain boundaries) are assisted by cognitive resource – with all the available accumulated knowledge and skills of a lifetime, however long or short. This latter information is shared with the operations of cognitive effect – which prepares the actual plan, influenced by style and limited by potential level, that will need to be implemented – through behaviour. The roles of leader – autocratic, democratic, charismatic, and others – will be played out in the environment through the social dynamic process, as will other related roles such as those depicted by Sternberg (1997, e.g., Monarchic, Hierarchic in the context of their function, or e.g., Legislative, Executive in their operation). Feedback from here returns to cognitive affect, further processed and stored in cognitive resource, to continue the catalytic progress of increasing command of problems with success.

Within the group, mirroring the working of individual problem solvers, there needs to emerge a shared understanding of the environment; a shared motive, taking into account all kinds of needs, including those associated with emotion, so that the group can identify with a suggested solution when it, in turn, emerges. What helps this process is the relevance of the role of leadership to the problem requiring to be solved, the environment within which it must be solved, and the brains that are doing the solving. Hence there is room for both the charismatic and the cooler reason-dominated leadership approaches, even with the same problem being tackled by the same group at the same time. It is the shifting balance of these factors, as the problem unravels and progresses, that leadership must manage along with all the other factors that are present – just as the successful individual brain must manage its internal array – as a continuous process. Problem-solving leadership, then, inevitably has management functions that are in many ways mirrors of the interaction of cognitive affect with cognitive effect and cognitive resource; leaders need to preside over the tasks of refining the problem, marshalling the knowledge pertaining to it, searching for methods and solutions, and initiating implementation. Note how this supposes that leaders are expected to preside over these activities, not carry them all out themselves; they not expected to carry out all tasks, have all the knowledge, or even make all the decisions – cognitive affect is depicted as only one department of the brain. Perhaps this suggested link between the operation of the individual's cortex and the way the group needs to collaborate (and be led) may be of help to the understanding of the operations of both.

Leadership, management, and innovation

The present trend that promotes 'innovation' as the panacea for all ills may be weakening. Fortunately, there are always those who look for practical, pragmatic solutions. Valéry, writing in the *Economist* (1999), shows healthy scepticism: 'Innovation has become the industrial religion of the late 20th century. Business sees it as the key to increasing profits and market share. Governments automatically reach for it when trying to fix the economy. Around the world, the rhetoric of innovation has replaced the post-war language of welfare economics. It is the new theology . . . but what precisely constitutes innovation is hard to say, let alone measure. It is usually thought of as the creation of a better product, or process. But it could just as easily be the substitution of a cheaper material in an existing product, or a better way of marketing, distributing or supporting a product or service.' Clearly, Valéry has difficulty with so catch-all a term and sets about limiting it. 'One way to describe innovation is to explain what it is not. The husband and wife who open a sandwich bar opposite a new office block may be gambling their life savings, but they are not innovating. The Japanese electronics firm that launches a niftier video camera is merely [sic!] cramming its distribution channels in a bid to push competitors' goods off the shelves. The drug firm that makes a generic version of a blockbuster ulcer pill is simply [sic!] cashing in on the expiry of a rival's patents. All these are business ventures, not innovation . . . Innovations . . . break the mould . . .' This sharpening of terms is admirable, except for a tendency to imply that what might not be innovative is simple, less lofty, and less significant – the standard conflation of level and style. Perhaps, even despite the scepticism, some of the least helpful kinds of research still do catch the eye. He quotes 'one American study' which found that 17 successful innovations (however defined) made in the 1970s averaged 56% return compared with 16% average for all American business over the past 30 years. Given leave to be that selective, one could prove anything. Given that a tenet of A-I is that innovation has, by its nature, more failure than adaption, how would the figures look if 34 unsuccessful innovations were added to the calculation? The problem lies not just in limiting the term innovation to matters that are innovative (instead of just attractive), but in setting up a contrasting term to achieve a concept that is bipolar and nonpejorative – something that is equally worthy but different, as is suggested here by the use of adaption. Valéry quotes from Drucker's *Innovation and Entrepreneurship* (1985) his list of seven sources of 'innovation':

- The unexpected success that is gratefully received but rarely dissected to see why it occurred[67].
- The incongruity between what actually happens and what was supposed to happen.
- The inadequacy in an underlying process that is taken for granted.
- The changes in industry or market structure that catch everyone by surprise[68].
- The demographic changes caused by wars, medical improvements and even superstition.
- The changes in perception, mood and fashion brought on by the ups and downs of the economy.
- The changes in awareness caused by new knowledge.

Neither Drucker nor Valéry raise the issue as to whether or not anything on this list is exclusively innovative. Some may lean more in that direction than towards adaption, but some go the other way. All, it might be argued, can be carried out in various styles, just as they can be carried out at different levels. Valéry writes: 'The irony is that officials, academics and even entrepreneurs pay far more attention to the riskiest form of innovation (trying to exploit some science-based discovery) than to the easiest and quickest type of innovation with which to turn a profit (capitalising on some unexpected success). This may have much to do with the glamour of research and development – not to mention the large sums of public money that governments make available, directly through grants as well as, indirectly, through tax credits, for companies to do R&D. Also, there is good evidence to show that if a new product or service comes to market as a result of some proprietary breakthrough in the company's own laboratories, it usually yields high returns; just think of DuPont's pay-off from Nylon or SmithKline's from Tagamet, one of the most successful prescription drugs in history. But such big breakthroughs usually happen only once or twice in a company's lifetime[69].' In short, to use our terminology, there is a need to value both adaption and innovation at high and low levels since all contribute, each in their own way to our survival. This is the notion to which Valéry seems to be heading: 'innovation has more to do with the pragmatic search for opportunity than with romantic ideas about serendipity, or lonely pioneers pursuing their vision against all the odds.'

---

67 As noted in Management Initiative.
68 However, there are always some who foresee the precipitating event.
69 To say nothing of the costs of all the innovative ventures, initiated and pursued at the same time, that failed. Rosie Murray-West, in the *Daily Telegraph*, comments on vast losses in R&D ventures incurred by the top pharmaceutical companies: 'Companies have been seduced by novelty' – yet many success are 'me-toos' rather than radical concepts (6 January 2001).

Surely, beside a tightening of terminology (to ensure clarity), it is a diversity of approach that is needed.

AN EXAMPLE IN DEPTH MAY HELP

In reviewing the literature that was initially linked to the emerging notion of A-I, it first seemed necessary to determine whether the notion was both a cognitive style and a dimension of personality, and to play down the distinction between problem solving and creativity that is the centrepiece of nearly all literature in creativity. This meant widening the field so that contributions came from several disciplines and fields of study, from biology to sociology. This breadth underlined the second necessity: that of separating terms, used differently in the same and in different fields, and so frequently conflated or just confused. These separations helped in leading away from 'ideal' creative people as well as from 'ideal' leaders and some well-held myths about organisations, such as the notion that institutions kill initiative – a belief that continues today, with the word innovation substituted for initiative. As has already been suggested, there are two major problems with this belief. One is that the 20th century, more than any other has seen the rise of more huge institutions, whilst more progress in every field has been made during its existence than in any other.

The second major problem is this: It seems improbable that mankind collectively sets about the creation of structures that constricts *all* mankind, on *all* matters, *all* the time. This really sounds like special pleading that might be more clearly rendered as: 'my creative ideas are being rejected by the stodgy, bone-headed uncreative people, like you.' This is no different from the special pleading that sounds like: 'my sound sensible ideas are rejected by the shallow, irrelevant, easily distracted, butterfly-brained people, like you.' In short, it refers to the difficulty of selling ideas to those who are not like the proposer. This special pleading might more profitably be seen in the context that all ideas, tools, and structures (disciplines or institutions) set up by mankind are reflections of individual brains. As such they are designed to solve problems perceived by individuals and the solutions that have so far emerged will not be perfect or suit everyone but are (one hopes) the best so far available. If the problems that set up the structures continue to be important then the solutions will continue to be improved; but at any time, every implemented solution (which is a structure) will be both enabling and limiting, as is the nature (and paradox) of structure. For any structure, in any particular situation, at any one time, the individual perceiver will be more conscious of the aspects that enable or the ones that limit – being grateful or resentful accordingly. Because every structure must be a reflection of the brains that produced it, then it is better to view each structure value in that light: No structure can accommodate all equally comfortably since every structure is less diverse than the problem solvers who might need it and less diverse than the problems that need to be solved.

Cognitive style is a significant variable that needs to be understood and used at individual and group levels. It needs to be better understood that each location on the continuum has its advantages, which should be used by the group as one more resource, as well as its management and leadership, that is available to all individuals in the same group. Yet it must be conceded that every style is valuable in general but not necessarily in any particular situation or time, as is true for any other attribute or resource. What particular style is an advantage or a disadvantage is constantly changing – all evaluation needs to be in the context of the time and circumstance in which it occurs. Tolerance and understanding are needed to ensure better collaboration between the diversity of problem solvers. There is thus a need to learn better how to 'sell' our ideas of change, just as there is a need to learn better how to evaluate the changes proposed by others that are not in our preferred style.

If problem solving is an unending catalytic process, then each solution found, besides being immediately useful, could also be seen as merely a novelty that adds to the cognitive structure, which is in turn used to solve more problems. We often treat problem solving as if the aim is to identify a problem, solve it, and then suppose that is the end of the matter. This is convenient, since it seems to offer an identifiable start and a distinct finish – at which point we can turn attention elsewhere. However, it is easy in the human milieu to find a problem (or a problem complex) that has required thus far in its resolution, a very long period of time and a large number of problem solvers as the task progresses; and even then, seen in this perspective, it is clearly but a step in an endless search for knowledge and survival. Studying one of the long sequences, even in brief, is an instructive exercise that readily reveals a theme that we are pursuing: How no one person (however much regarded as a genius), no one style, no one set of capacities, no one institution, even over its lifespan, can hope to make massive life-changing progress. This puts paid to any notion that some simple ideal resource, in a relatively short span of time, can achieve an advance that can be seen as a final definitive solution a century afterwards. In studying the variables that lead to problem-solving success these limitations need to be taken into account – and the notion that anyone can find an ideal resource or strategy needs to be set aside as utterly improbable.

Below is a simple history of a major advance in human theorising and practical endeavour, which has been of immense value to mankind. It is not essential reading to the progress of this exploration of problem solving, but its length and detail, despite the fact it is but an outline of events, is useful in setting the wider scene of problem solving as opposed to solving problems. This example is about progress in science, and fits well with the reference to and contribution of Kuhn. For those with less interest in science there was a similar example, given earlier in the chapter on creativity, taken from the history of art about the writing of music. For those with a catholic taste, a comparison of these two examples may help set the preoccupations and biases in the past and current literature into perspective. The example from music showed an advance made over a short time that has had an impact over the 1000 years of progress since. In this example, the advance occurs over many hundreds of years, and covers a wide spectrum of level ranging from lofty philosophy to greedy fraud, from the correct path to discouraging error, from pure theoretical science to practical technical experiment, and from speculation that sought new boundaries to experiment within tight structures. Its progress was not made only by brilliant flashes in the pan or by painstaking grinding at some minute element within the core, but by both – and every other variation in between. It involves a wide range of other cognitive functions and characteristics, not only conflicts in styles of problems solving but also learning and motive, reason and emotion, and persistence and integrity, as well as the confusion of fact and fancy. Within this story all the elements of problem solving so far discussed, including style differences as just one variable, should be detected. One thing that is hard to detect is which person, which thought, which method – even when, in hindsight, they can be seen as being in error – was a pure gain to the system and which was a pure hindrance. When even error is at times useful, the search for the ideal is unrewarding. Another element is easier to detect: That progress is catalytic; however able the thinker, unless some earlier advance had been made (the development of scientific experiment, the use of a chemical or electrical current to separate materials into constituent parts), progress was hopelessly stalled.

The case of the periodic table

Early in their development, humans appreciated the need to understand in order to be able to predict – as a prelude to taking more deliberate, conscious control over their own destiny. In addition to sheer brainpower, some special facilities are needed for the achievement of such ambition; one is the ability to appreciate the difference between even closely similar things, events, and people, i.e., discrimination. Such fine judgement yields a plethora of significant input that, unless managed, would threaten to clutter thought, overwhelm memory, and impede learning and understanding. There is a concomitant need for a highly developed facility for both accurate and flexible classification in order to provide sound and meaningful simplification of this potentially stifling quantity of input. The resulting fewer, simpler patterns make possible a shift to a higher strategic grasp of reality. The elements that are needed to achieve such advances all need to be present.

Greeks, in classical times, went through a period of outstanding creativity. Among their achievements, they were the pioneers of systematic classification, making important progress in sorting out and describing, in written texts remarkably available to other scholars, the main divisions such as those between matters physical and metaphysical. They explored the very intellectual means by which they arrived at conclusions, such as inductive versus deductive reasoning. They tried to reduce the vast array of things by subsuming all of them within the smallest number of inclusive groups of basic substances or 'elements'. Empedocles of Akragas (circa 430 BC) set the number at four: earth, air, water, and fire. Aristotle, about a century later, added 'aether', of which he supposed the heavens to be made. The Greeks made no more accepted additions, nor could they demonstrate that they had them all or even that those they had proposed were valid; they lacked the proofs that only science was to provide[70]. But they were not done yet, for they had started another line of argument: Whether matter was continuous or discrete, that is, whether matter could be forever divided into smaller and smaller particles or whether a point would be reached at which the particles finally became indivisible, forming the bases from which all else is built. Using hindsight, it is easy to identify the foremost thinkers in this field as Leucippus of Miletus and his better known pupil, Democritus of Abdera (circa 450 BC), protagonists of the 'indivisible particle' notion, which the latter called atoms (atoma means 'nondivisible' or literally 'uncutables'). Democritus went further, pushing a combination of intuition and logic to hardly surpassable intellectual heights, by

---

70 The Chinese also groped towards the same notion of basic elements or 'powers'. They also suggested air, earth, and fire, adding wood and metal. While the original thinking was on track, of 10 guesses, involving 7 different 'elements', all were wrong and, worse, there was not then any certain means of knowing they were wrong. There was a long, hard road ahead.

putting forward the notion that all the different substances that are perceived are made up of different atoms and that one substance can be converted into another by rearranging them. In the light of the notion of the paradox of structure and competing styles of problem solving, it is fascinating how they achieved both the major demolition of current paradigms and the setting up of intellectual structures that were tighter – disposing of loose boundaries that were, however, the consensually agreed knowledge of the time and replacing them with classifications and definitions that were both different and efficient so as to lay the foundations of new disciplines of learning. What they lacked, however, was proof – the need for it and how to get it was beyond their knowledge.

Brilliantly clever innovative guessing as this turns out to have been, it failed to carry the bulk of scholarly opinion in its age; both those formidable intellects, Plato and Aristotle, did not accept its reasoning. It is hard to fault them; they did not have the knowledge base available today to help their assessment – they could hardly be classed as 'resisters to change'. As today, new developments on the edges of paradigms that seem to be working well are hard to accept. They do not seem to offer much gain in exchange for the disturbance they threaten. Even if these idea generators had had the notion of scientific experiment to help test their speculations, such results may not have been enough, as happened later in this example of problem solving.

Yet not all the early Greeks dismissed Democritus (there always seems to be someone who perceives the offers embedded in impending precipitating events, when others cannot). His ideas were adopted by Epicurus of Samos (circa 300 BC) and were taught in his school of philosophy. A later important Epicurean, the Roman philosopher Lucertius, included the 'atomic theory' in his book *On the Nature of Things* (circa 60 BC). This book was later one of the first to be printed, atomic theory having become a topic of great interest in mediaeval times because of the rise of scholarly interest in the paradigm-cracking pursuit of alchemy. The alchemists tried to add to the approved number of elements. Their increasing meticulous experiments added to the number and use of mineral acids: nitric acid, hydrochloric acid, and sulphuric acid, when earlier only the far less potent acetic acid had been known. Their wild speculations, although quite unsuccessful, had nevertheless produced structures and methods on which not only they but others could build. By the 17th century, chemistry, based on experiment, had made strides in replacing alchemy; for instance, by 1661 the British chemist, Boyle, could offer the modern definition of an element: A substance that can be combined with others to form compounds, but which cannot, itself, be broken down. It would not be long before all but mercury, of the original list of elements, had been removed and the formerly elusive gold was found to be an element – and therefore not made up from other mixtures! Their methods had become so good, that their original aim was proved to be impossible[71].

The approach to the problem now changes tack; continued speculation, within tight theory, aided by increasingly refined experiment joined to tackle achievable objectives. By the late 18th century, the Frenchman Lavoisier had published a list of no less than

---

71 Alchemy lasted a long time down its blind alley and one wonders how much it helped to found chemistry and how much it delayed its development. Alchemists were desperately concerned with experiment but also with secrecy; their ranks included great intellects (such as Isaac Newton, no less) but many more charlatans, with little real knowledge but able, by sprinkling simple text with attractive trendy words, to make a living from those who knew less. Some might be with us today as innovation consultants.

33 elements. It is true there was also some more pruning by the use of better techniques; for instance a Briton, Davy, using electric current for this purpose for the first time, found that the erstwhile elements lime and magnesia both contained oxygen. He did not, however, actually reduce the number of elements by these experiments, since the residues after oxygen was removed yielded calcium and magnesium respectively, and these were recognised as new elements instead.

The new problem emerging was multiplicity without an underlying simple pattern; just where the Greeks had started – but at a higher level! At the turn of the 18th century, the Italian, Avogadro, put up a hypothesis that equal volumes of gas contained equal numbers of particles, which suggested that if these particles were compounds or, more precisely, molecules, then their elements might have different weights. This raised the possibility of the classification of elements according to weight. Despite the magnitude of the challenge, given the level of technology available at the time, by 1828 the Swedish chemist, Berzelius, had published a table of atomic weights, setting up as a universal standard either hydrogen, with an arbitrary value of 1, or oxygen, with an arbitrary value of 100 (note the degree of learned speculation). In 1850 the Belgian chemist, Stas, suggested the current alternative of oxygen at 16 and hydrogen at 1. Despite the increasing rigour of the science, histories write of these methods as shaky, and it was not until the Italian, Cannizzaro, presented colleagues with better methods of measurement that a consensus for support from among scientists was obtained. By 1862, the French geologist Chancourtois was able to arrange an array of atomic weights in a table, on one axis in order of magnitude, on the other axis in groups of similar properties – the now familiar periodic table. In 1864 the Briton, Newlands, did the same without knowing of Chancourtois' work, since neither could get their papers published! Both eventually got credit for their work, but it was the Russian chemist, Mendeleev, in 1869, who got the highest recognition, for the fullest explanation and exposition. This included two critical matters, both of which looked especially awkward for the acceptance of the whole scheme. The first was that if placed according to weight, the element called tellerium should follow iodine in upward order of magnitude. If that were done, then the down axis of grouping would be wrong – for it to be 'correct', their order needed to be reversed. Daringly, this is what Mendeleev did. Even more boldly, when Mendeleev found that only by leaving blank spaces on the regular table was it possible to accommodate both axes in accord to simple symmetry, he did that, too. This allowed him to predict that not only were there three elements missing but also to make accurate predictions as to their nature. He deserved the luck that followed; all three (gallium, scandium, and germanium) were discovered soon afterwards, each with the precise characteristics he had predicted.

The last step that needs to be mentioned is that means were found to measure the wavelengths of these elements. A Briton, Moseley, not only did so in 1914 but also noted that they progressed in such a minutely and regularly ordered way that the table's current pattern could be further precisely confirmed, and that all the remaining, missing elements could be predicted. By the mid-20th century this phase was over as the last of these stable, missing elements was 'named'.

The example's lessons

This story of endeavour stretched over two-and-a-half millennia; it involved countless people, known and unknown – some of great integrity and others outright crooks.

Some broke boundaries to great effect, while others worked tightly within the boundaries that were being formed; most of them must have accepted most of the boundaries while making a contribution by modifying one of them. One can easily suspect that the whole A-I range is present in this tale, but which bit is attributable to which particular style score defies plausible guess. But in all of this, are we studying problem solving or creativity – and does it matter? It may not. The value of science and the scientific method is that it has systematised the need to find simple, stable order in apparent wide, unrelated disorder. The periodic table makes a useful example. From a seemingly innumerable array of 'things' about us, this search first found an amazingly small number of 'elements' – the irreducible number of irreducible substances – and then arrayed them in a table that shows the pattern of their interrelationships. All this was supported by a test using another method. As Archimedes might be induced to agree, without this foundation on which to stand and unaided by the lever of scientific method, from intuitive hunch through, stepwise, to reasoned proof, we could not have moved our world so far to our advantage.

The point to be made from this example is that problem solving is not simple: No one style or one kind of savant, philosopher, professional, technician, or lucky DIY bumbler is enough for such advances to be made. Neither the 'old way' of revering the 'book' and proceeding by intensive exploration of a current paradigm, nor the wholesale damnation of every current paradigm, is a single guaranteed method for progress. Nor can mankind rely upon genius alone to drive the rest of us along. Pinker (1998) reminds us that: 'when nature presents us with objects that perfectly fill a rectangular bank of pigeonholes, it is telling us that the objects must be built out of smaller components, which correspond to the rows and the columns. That is how the periodic table of the elements led to the understanding of the structure of the atom. For similar reasons we can conclude that the warp and weft of our thinkable thoughts are the concepts composing them. Thoughts are assembled out of concepts; they are not stored whole' (p. 120). The story of the discovery of the periodic table is of the interplay of adaption and innovation, creativity and problem solving, arrays of capacities, foolishness, and errors, as well as much perseverance from many people. Perhaps it is this sort of disparate amalgam that makes up the nearest thing we can get to an ideal – but for the fact that, for a century now, we have known that the atom is not indivisible.

9   The management of diversity

DIVERSITY OF PROBLEMS AND PEOPLE

The main underlying issue of this chapter is the diversity of problems that need to be successfully resolved by *Homo sapiens* if the species is to survive. This, in part, is because every individual, as any other organism, has never-ending requirements and lives in an ever-changing environment. For the human species, however, there is another part of the strategic problem of survival, for the basic requirements are now associated with ever-developing expectations of satisfaction. In addition, our ever-changing environment is continually being extended by the exploitation of ever-wider territorial domains, each presenting a fresh array of different conditions. All this needs to be managed, aided only by the originally endowed physical equipment, such as the brain and its receptors, but unaided by instinct, which would provide complex, unlearned, and instant solutions to a limited number of critical challenges.

The physical body itself was the first problem in the management of massive diversity that had to be solved before mankind appeared on Earth. The body is made up of some 100 trillion cells, comprising a multitude of variation in specialised function. It is governed by a management team of 100 billion neurons; these, in turn, have a multitude of tasks and each has a powerful computer (Jonscher, 1999) with direct contact with some 10,000 other neurons. The system, as Ridley (1999) wittily puts it, has the underlying support of a book of basic organisation recipes, the 24 chromosomes, containing in total 60,000 to 80,000 stories (genes), which each contain innumerable paragraphs (exons), which each contain a countless number of words (codons). Fortunately, this diversity is largely dealt with automatically (i.e., like every boardroom, we are not aware of the detail), leaving one product of the massive cortex, the conscious mind, to manage the vast complexity in the world about it with the primary aim of survival. This is not the end to the notion that as individuals we bring order to random chaos or even find pattern in chaos (Carter, 2002, p. 123) all for our benefit. Life constantly throws up random genetic mutations; some 100 each generation in *Homo sapiens*, which does not seem to be a large number – especially as most have no long-term effect – but any one of them might be disastrous. Although biologists are certain that the production of mutations is random, the selection of them (in the process of natural selection) is the very opposite of random (see Dawkins, 1987, and his notion of the selfish gene). Order, leading to increased efficiency, is imposed on selection from a randomly generated pool of options. So successful has been our management of every level of diversity that from a beginning of a relative handful of ancestors we now number 6 billion individuals – causing no small number of additions to our problems.

Biological survival, or for that matter sociological progress, depends on successful change. The basic elements in successful change are:

- the opportunity for change (living in an iron-bearing geographical location is a prerequisite for initiating the iron age);
- the perception of the need for change (but my bronze weapons are superb);
- the perception that a particular available opportunity is the means to the solution (recognising the potential of iron ore);
- the perceived benefit of the exploitation of the opportunity against its perceived cost (my bronze weapons are what gives me my status).

To explore the first of these – the presence of opportunity – in the field of biology leads immediately to the requirement of diversity (as source of potential opportunity) and then to its management. The body is a fine example for demonstrating the relationship between diversity, opportunity, and continual (often successful) change. At genome level, the vast bulk of its diversity is not useful to the body and neither is it hostile. It is carried at little cost and may be useful in that any change in structure that is required by new threats to survival may make use of any of this diversity that fits. The adult body also accommodates some 2 lb/1 kg of bacteria on the same basis – a few potentially hostile, a few friendly, and the rest neutral but a pool of potential resource[72]. The lesson is that neutral diversity, as long as it is only modestly expensive to keep, is well worth tolerating by the host as a potential pool of diversity from which change can emerge when the need arises. This is widely known and has long been understood. Fisher (1930) proposed that: 'the maximum rate of increase in evolutionary adaptation must be proportional to the amount of genetic variation for adaptability present in the population. . . . [That is,] the more variation there is, the more evolution can take place' (p. 261). 'Selection, whether natural or artificial [i.e., selective breeding] is much more likely to proceed rapidly when a population is full of genetic variation' (Wills, 1998, p. 72). One difficulty with applying continued evolution to the progress of mankind is that it may be perceived as increasingly inapplicable, given the present low birth rates and equally low death rates of those below the age of puberty. However, as Wills points out, evolution selects: 'not only for new genetic variants that [arise] by mutation but also for new combinations of old genes that are produced by the genetic shuffling, known as recombination, that takes place each generation' (p. 5). Nevertheless, according to Wills, there is still scope for the traditional paths of natural selection; one obvious selective element is the number of women who choose not to have children or who are unable to do so. In addition, allele combination might well be continuing apace as an outcome in today's world of wide intermarriage of disparate groups hitherto relatively isolated from each other, thereby widening the readily available pool of genetic diversity. Wills suggests that: '. . . the prevalence of

---

72 As Jones (2000) explains, on the understanding of such vast surplus: 'the central difficulty is one of scale. A few tens of thousands of functional genes fit into three thousand million DNA letters. As most genes use only the information coded into several thousand bases there seems to be far more DNA than is needed. Mapping shows that just one part in twenty represents part of a gene. Our genome has an extraordinary and quite unexpected structure' (pp. 71–72). Yet in that surplus diversity is the key to success in constantly developing to survive, e.g., in combating hostile micro-organisms that are themselves in constant development.

out breeding in the natural world [especially in species, like chimpanzees, that live in small groups] has led many evolutionists to suspect that genetic variation must, in itself, be valuable' (p. 178). The work of Petite (1960) gives support to such a suggested process of natural diversity. She found that male fruit flies with characteristics that were rare in the population were more successful at mating with females than if they possessed the more common characteristics. This 'rare male effect' is just one of the frequency-dependent phenomena that operate in the natural world. Another example of this phenomenon is that a 'rare' tree or animal can multiply in a favourable environment because of the equal rarity of hostile pathogens or predators. This advantage eventually disappears as numbers of the rarity increase until it eventually, by its success, becomes common. Clearly, nature points to the conclusion that genetic diversity is a critical pool of opportunity for change that is vital to the survival of species.

An individual's management of diversity begins within the brain. It is intriguing to note the extent to which the human body has accumulated such diversity. Recent work in biology suggests that the degree to which mankind is right-handed is related to increased specialisation within each half of the brain – particularly the left hemisphere. Few other organisms have such specialisation; even among chimpanzees only half of them were found to be right-handed (Hopkins, 1999), a quarter left-handed, and nearly a quarter ambidextrous. As part of this crucial cerebral specialisation, mankind has developed the potential for language; the main language areas have also developed in the left hemisphere of the brain, in both the temporal and frontal lobes. 'Once language had taken hold, it rapidly annexed large parts of the left hemisphere ... and appropriated most of the locality previously given to spatial skills. . . . This was the beginning of the hemisphere specialisation that now makes the human brain uniquely asymmetrical in function' (Carter, 1998, p. 139). Another specialisation that dominated our species' earliest years, during the hunter-gatherer period led to a marked learnt specialisation of male–female tasks (hunting and defence versus gathering and nurturing). The development of this specialisation, also beyond that of any other organism, led to an understanding (because it is learnt) of the advantages of other specialisations, which may have laid the foundations of our present complex society. This is unlike other species, such as ants, that have social specialisation which is limited and instinctive. For us, social specialisation is just one more kind of diversity that needs not only to be learnt but also managed well. As early as the 5th century BC, the plays of Sophocles explored the dash between 'maleforce and female will' and differences between the sexes still fascinates.

We need to learn an understanding of some critical others and of ourself – enough to make frequent successful predictions. As we have made our world more complex and have become more dependent on collaboration with other problem solvers, this learning has become one of the most important knowledge structures we need to master. It requires, for instance, an understanding of another complexity; that of 'we' as distinct from 'they'. The ability to discriminate is used to sort out every form of distinction (anomaly of pattern – a basic biological facility, e.g., Carter, 2000, p. 150) and is used progressively as a means of understanding and managing as a lone individual and then as a member of a group. This development opens up a vast addition to the diversity management that faces individuals. The distinction between 'we' and 'they' is that the former are categorised as same, safe, and therefore useful, whereas the latter seem to be less similar and possibly less safe; perhaps, then, not useful, even hostile. Among higher-order organisms that have developed instinct to give useful immediate strategic guidance in such problems, this distinction and its management is largely determined; in mankind collaboration with others is another problem to resolve.

To review this last section in a day-to-day practical context, it is suggested that problem solving aims to make what is significant but unfamiliar into what is familiar and predictable, as a basis for its successful management. Two individuals, an individual and a group, or two groups (whether they be equal in number and power or a majority and a minority) will all be (or be made up of) individuals with brains that function in the same way, with the same facility for discrimination (detecting anomaly), and with the same requirement of problem solving that turns what is dissimilar and unsafe into what is similar and safe. Able to discriminate but with no instinct to guide them, individuals have two problems when collaborating: to solve the problem requiring their collaboration (Problem A) and the management of each other (Problem B); successful groups spend much more energy on Problem A than Problem B. It is a fundamental issue in understanding the management of diversity that groups face the paradox that diversity (diverse structure) is both enabling and limiting. An individual alone has insufficient range of resource to solve many of the problems to be faced. Conversely, when in a group, the individual may acquire, yet manage badly, too much diversity, allowing Problem B to take up resources required for the efficient resolution of Problem A – the very reason for the formation of the group (any group: human or other). A-I theory must imply that adaptors and innovators manage Problem B differently, just as they manage Problem A differently. Adaptors are thought notorious by the more innovative for insisting on the resolution of Problem B before they are comfortable in solving the main task. If this does not happen readily, they are liable to exert more and more pressure for conformity in an increasingly wide area of operations. Equally notoriously for the more adaptive, innovators are liable to threaten to fracture the team with personally held diverse perceptions of the problem and searches for solutions. They also seem to risk abandoning the team in the hope of finding an unlikely solution around which they might then try to re-energise the team – however much its members may doubt its potential for success. All these issues on style have to be faced, in addition to those other issues that throw up variations of Problems B, such as power politics or the insistence that a particular skill (e.g., language) not possessed by most of the team can solve all its problems.

Managing what we learn

Humans tend to oversimplify problems that need resolution, as has been noted in the study of Management Initiative, and get caught out from time to time when the problem is in fact more complicated than was first perceived. This oversimplification process can lead people to ignore diversities that seem merely to complicate matters or to try to dispose of them in the simplest way by imposing a convenient uniformity (e.g., insisting that others be more like us). When diversities persist, then they may become a significant addition to the main problem. This often generates tension and hostility: What is dissimilar persists in remaining dissimilar and, therefore, may increasingly be perceived as unsafe or threatening. This developing negative appreciation may lead to different groups feeling that they are the target of adverse discrimination and attempting to hold their own by the use of hostility (punishment), each imposing their notion of 'sameness' onto the others. If this point of standoff is reached, it is hard for the members of different groups to perceive diversity as a potential additional problem-solving resource. This suggests that there is a need to understand better the trade-off between the obvious economy of effort that comes with dealing with limited diversity (e.g., people like us) and the immediate or potential value of accommodating wider diversity. The example of how the body makes the balance is instructive. Any diversity that signals hostility to the host in any way is attacked, to become destroyed, neutralised, or converted to a state of mutual use. Any diversity that is useful is used and any that is neutral (neither hostile nor unduly expensive) is tolerated. The resulting pool of nonhostile diversity is a guard against changing conditions that might require different resources to manage them successfully. One marked spin-off of mankind's internal diversity is the specialisation of brain function; the same is true of human society.

Interestingly, the same problem of juggling resources between Problem A and Problem B occurs generally in nature. One vital reason why species exist is because individuals can reproduce their DNA accurately and produce viable young. In such complex creatures as mankind, much effort is expended to ensure that the copying is accurate enough. Mark Ridley (2000) explains that: 'life deals [with such] error by preventing it from happening, by correcting and concealing it and by purging it. The use of polymerase enzymes and DNA, for instance, helps to prevent errors from happening to begin with. Another set of enzymes corrects most of the errors that nevertheless arise. Proof reading and repair enzymes correct errors in the code; developmental troubleshooting enzymes correct the expression of faulty codes without correcting the code itself. Finally, sexual reproduction may have evolved to shuffle the errors that slip through all these defences, such that they can be purged efficiently, in multiple form. Mate choice in favour of error-free members of the opposite sex also increases the efficiency of the purge' (p. 257). This is a great deal of effort and resource set aside to maintain the integrity of a complex system: The alternative, in biological terms, is mounting error until mutational meltdown, as such an end is called. Despite this effort, the system must retain its flexibility in a changing environment. In such complex entities as humans, it is interesting to speculate at what point our Problem A, of managing the environment, is overtaken by the drain of resources to solve Problem B, maintaining the system itself. What nature manages blindly, humans need to do by learning, through experience and transmitted knowledge, to achieve large efficient organisations. The underlying principles seem to be the same. So, a prime task of the problem-solving leader is to assist the group to manage motive, as well as manage diversity and opportunity (helping the group to perceive opportunity, share it, and exploit it) – all as part of managing change.

Mastering the art of successful collaboration involves having shared structures that bear directly on the common problem, including the language for communication. Signs and signals are readily available to other species, and some of these systems are rich and expressive, but language, with its added syntax, vast vocabulary, and infinite capacity for subtle and refined expression is available only to humans, at the heavy price of constant intense learning. It is not surprising that we have the longest period of pre-adulthood, being unable to operate alone for so many years without depending on any other human at any sophisticated level. Collaboration is effective when it involves enough common ground to allow it to happen and enough diversity to match the diversity of the common problem. For the whole to be greater than the sum of its parts requires more than one favourable factor. Bolles (1999, p. 105), in his anthology of great scientific writing, remarks on the capacity of Leonardo in the context of his times: 'Leonardo's meditations show a fine scientific imagination striving in an unscientific age . . . [but] Leonardo was unable to push his observations toward proof. His notebooks indicate that a scientific imagination is a human characteristic that might appear in any age, but without the organised companionship of like-minded people, science does not advance.' Silver (1998) in his *The Ascent of Science* chooses a quotation from Kuhn to make the same point: 'Those who carry out scientific research are the recipients of a culture developed by previous generations' (p. 103).

It can be argued, then, that the greatest source of diversity now available to the human community in its problem-solving activity comes from the learned specialisation of individuals, as long as they have sufficient common grounds and means. Heard (1939) argued that: 'It would appear that man has, physically speaking, specialised in unspecialisation and by this means has won himself a new span of evolutionary life and development . . . but that change has henceforth to be with increasing speed and increasingly psychological [from the epigraph].' This has led to high levels and wide varieties of learnt specialisation based on small variations of specific capacities, interest, opportunity, and, of course, style. It can be argued that man, free from instinctively driven collaborative diversity, is, as a consequence, able to deploy what might be termed 'deliberate collaborative diversity' in which adaption-innovation plays a useful part. Wills (1998) points out that simpler societies may require less diversity. For instance, he thinks it likely that the earlier hunter-gatherer groups may have needed all their men to be strong (stone club wielders, say) and it mattered little if they were clumsy. When small, carefully made flint arrowheads were needed, men capable of more delicate precision would then be needed, even at the expense of some brute strength.

Wills continues by stressing that although no genes have been found that contribute to so specific an attribute as, say, musical talent or mathematical ability, small basic inbuilt variations, built on uniquely by each individual, lead to significant variations of potential difference. Humans, therefore, have acquired specialist roles, not by instinct or by splitting into subspecies, but by learning both the specialism and how to deploy it, to advantage, within a group. Such exploitation needs group acceptance and mutually perceived opportunity. So: 'if our environment reveals previously hidden genetic variation in our genetic pool, the effect of natural selection can be greater. The progressive unveiling of this variation, which is taking place as each succeeding human generation faces a more complex environment, can have unexpected results' (ibid., p. 228). Differences in adaption-innovation are just such 'revealed' variation that can be increasingly useful in a complex environment. Such variation helps to solve problems requiring different kinds of approach and solution – variation that needs even further exploitation by mankind. Wills points out that as the conquest of diseases gathers even greater pace, 'genetic variation related to them are becoming less important to survival. Intellectual challenges from our environment, not disease-based challenges, will become more important in future' (p. 234). He believes we shall rise to the challenge: 'Research on animals suggests that as a result of environmental enrichment, their brains become better at dealing with the unexpected' (p. 248). This is likely to be true for all higher animals but especially so for humans.

Within the management of diversity, all organisms need to work on a principle of economy of energy – all activities are undertaken for a purpose, whether conscious or not. So dealing with familiarity and similarity is easier – more reassuring – than diversity. Instinct, that mechanism for supreme economy of problem-solving process, imposes similarity of action and response in relation to prescribed stimulus; in nature, it seems, the guiding social principle is the successful management of *similarity* in order to achieve collective aims. Mankind, in dispensing with instinct, has more options in accommodating and making use of differences to achieve a common aim (Problem A), which is shared with others. Since sharing costs effort (Problem B), the balance of cost against gain needs to come out on the right side of the effort balance sheet. This can be seen just as clearly in less emotive settings than conflicting group behaviour. Pinker (1998), analysing the similarities of operational principle as well as differences between brain function and computer operation, points out that information processors should only be given limited access to diverse information '. . . because information has costs as well as benefits. One cost is space . . . a limitation that is all too clear to microcomputer owners deciding whether to invest in more RAM [. . .] A second cost is time . . . having to take a hundred years to solve a problem is, practically speaking, the same as not solving it at all. [. . .] A third cost is resources, information processing requires energy.' The ideal, he states is that: 'only information relevant to the problem at hand should be allowed in.' But the ideal, like every other ideal, is unattainable and we are left with the reminder, in deciding how much diversity to carry about against future need, that, like any other information-processing operation, '. . . information processing can be part of the problem rather than part of the solution' (pp. 137 & 138). So this is the paradox of diversity (structure) management: Both too little and too much can be disadvantageous, and the calculation may vary depending on whether it is viewed in the short or the long run. Hence, although members of a group may be tempted to accept some additional diversity, caution is also appropriate and this caution, and its reason, must be taken into account in the conscious management of diversity. Appeal to mutual enlightened self-interest, rather than to an abstract principle that is not well understood but sounds unsettling, may be more rewarding for getting some specific diversity to be accepted.

ADAPTION-INNOVATION AS A PROBLEM OF DIVERSITY

To collaborate with others in problem solving, an individual requires some understanding of self and of others and a means to communicate. How good, then, are individuals in being able to discriminate how similar to or different from others they are, in terms of such a concept as adaption-innovation? Some early work with the KAI items provided interesting information. These useful data were collected from a number of respondents who were included in the pilots used in the construction of the A-I measure. At the onset of the inventory's development a list of statements describing aspects of adaptiveness and innovativeness was constructed. Twenty senior managers were then interviewed to find out if the typology was consistent with their experience. They thought it to be so, and they were then asked to suggest additions to the list of statements. A second sample of 20 managers was collected and each was asked to divide the augmented list of statements, each placed on a separate card, into two groups; one group to contain those statements that the sorter considered as favourable characteristics and the other group to contain those that were considered as unfavourable. The next instruction given was the key one. It was to sort one of the two piles of cards, favourable or unfavourable, into the smallest number of piles, such that any single pile could represent a single person without internal contradiction. When this had been done for both the favourable and unfavourable piles, the sorter was then invited to reduce the piles further by combining a group of favourable with a group of unfavourable cards to make a balanced picture of an individual, containing both favourable and unfavourable comments. The two groups of managers, the first using the interview method and the second using card sorting, tended very largely to agree that all descriptions could be grouped into two sets, one representing 'adaptors' and the other 'innovators,' as they were later dubbed. Both sets contained more favoured and less favoured items, to form a 'balanced' whole description of a person. The extent of individual agreement among the latter (card-sorting) group was such that on average only 2.2 cards out of the 24 presented were not in accord with the expected model. This was a high level of insight, which suggests that the future results of the measure would be readily absorbed and that people would be able to use them to mutual benefit in collaboration. Research shows that this has happened.

Greater interindividual disagreement occurred, however, among these respondent managers when they were asked if they thought that any of the items were pejorative if applied to them. It was most interestingly to note, during these interviews, that individuals did not find any items pejorative in the pile (adaptive or innovative) with which they personally identified, but all found some in the other pile! In short, items perceived as applying to self were rarely classed as pejorative; these were more likely to be among those that described other people *not like self*. Thus, early in the study the first evidence emerged that those who would later be found distant from each other on the KAI continuum might have difficulty in collaborating – which was the observation that started the whole study! However, one element of this finding has come as a surprise of many course presenters using KAI: People can readily live with seemingly unattractive elements that pertain to themselves. For instance, innovators tend to accept being seen as, at times, disruptive or abrasive, whilst adaptors can accept being seen, at times, as precise to the point of pedantry, but neither wanted to be associated (even at times) with what they see as the unattractive elements of others not like them.

In general, once informed about A-I, a wide range of respondents were able to make reasonably accurate estimates of others, in relation to themselves – the necessary basis for being able to use the information in practice. Studies have shown that people on a training course, who did not know each other beforehand, can, after a day or so of interaction, rank order each other with some accuracy – rank order correlations averaged circa .4. However, when the team members have known each other well they achieved correlations of circa .8[73] – four times more accurate. They were also able, in discussion, to flesh out the descriptions of the more adaptive and the more innovative reasonably accurately, that is, only occasionally mixing in level or other unrelated descriptors (for review, see Kirton & McCarthy, 1985; also Rickards & Gaston, 1995; Masten et al., 1988). These results have been repeated by Clapp & de Ciantis (1989) using members of one department of an industrial organisation. This study varied the method of estimating other people's scores. Instead of rank ordering their colleagues, Clapp persuaded people to fill in as many KAIs as there were people in each of the small teams in the sample – one for the individual and one for each other person, as perceived by the scorer. The results confirmed the capacity of people to judge each other well, with correlations better than .8. Each person's KAI

---

73 As .4 represents 16% overlap between self-estimate and other-estimate, and .8 represents 64%, then the difference is not just twice as accurate but four times as accurate.

score could then be compared with the average of their combined scores derived from the others in the team. This change of method allowed the combined estimated scores to be subjected to an internal reliability test, which averaged .9. Using KAIs as estimates of others, Selby (1992; Selby & Treffinger, 1993) also noted that parents and teachers were able to rate (the same) children accurately; encouragingly, parents (with their own children) managed this somewhat better than the teachers!

Not all the added descriptions of adaptors and innovators offered by participants in those early intensive interviews seemed to fit the theory. These 'failed' additions were treated as a separate group for study because they were distinctively:

- made about adaptors by innovators or vice versa;
- pejorative;
- denied (as a characteristic) by those so described.

The most numerous and strongly put views, some exaggerated and some wrong, were the subject of exploration parallel to the routine validation study. Adaptors often perceived innovators as:

- neurotic: a term that remained poorly defined;
- extravert: used to mean exhibiting irritating periods of ebullience without cause and being insensitive to others;
- extrapunitive: liable, when frustrated in 'selling' their unique viewpoint, to direct hostility outward; and
- inner-directed: rigidly adhering to reference elements not held by others.

Innovators often perceived adaptors just as pejoratively:

- stodgy: dogmatic, inflexible and conservative;
- timid: having a marked distaste for venturing into cognitive uncertainty; and
- compliant: having a predilection for agreeing with their bosses (innovators over-looked the term consensus – which is not the same as 'boss').

One conclusion of the early exploration is not unfamiliar. People often tend to find others who are not like them inferior, as differences tend to be perceived as variables of level. This is a key problem in the management of diversity. The perceptions of some of the key differences, favourable or unfavourable, were, however, worth exploring, since at least some might be correlates of A-I.

One group of measures were found to have insignificant correlations: Neuroticism (using EPI, Eysenck & Eysenck, 1964); Inner-Other Directedness Scale (Riesman, 1950, as devised by Kassarjian, 1962); and Hostility and Direction Hostility (HDHQ, Caine et al., 1967, which is divided into measures of Intropunitiveness and Extrapunitiveness). Some of these results have been listed in the section on Style and personality relationships (pp. 100–109). Those for the Adorno group of related measures showed that the more adaptive were inclined to be more conservative, dogmatic, inflexible, and intolerant of ambiguity than the more innovative; they were also inclined to be more introvert. These measures unfortunately have what are generally agreed as negative titles. The link with adaption is just a greater preference for structure; taken to extremes the titles are apt, but inapplicable to the bulk of adaptors. This is the more easily seen when the terms more adaptive and more innovative are used, since to describe a person who is moderately innovative as being always, even inherently, dogmatic compared to a high innovator is clearly questionable. Also the correlation, between .4 and .5, although moderately high, leaves room for many a dogmatic innovator. What was instructive was how easily these A-I differences could be conceived pejoratively among senior team-leading personnel. Some of the terms that some respondents suggested, like neuroticism, were found to be uncorrelated with A-I. Other pejorative terms abounded in general conversation, especially when the teams were deliberately chosen to have similar KAI scores and invited to describe others not like them. Several innovator groups complained that adaptors got on because they always agreed with bosses. This was put to the test (Kirton, 1977) by administering KAI and Chapman & Campbell's (1957) Superior–Subordinate Scale to 93 managers from several British companies. At .11, the correlation was insignificant. The A-I theory is specific: The structures that people need are not necessarily what some other person thinks appropriate. Particularly for the higher adaptors, the need is to find an appropriate paradigm, which, by definition, is a consensually agreed pervasive construct. It was fascinating to listen to high ranking innovators complain about this presumed fault of adaptors, being prone to licking their superiors' boots, when only a little later, in the same discussion, they held forth on the difficulty of getting 'uncooperative' adaptor subordinates to follow them! Adaptors complained that innovators caused stress to those about them but innovators made the same complaint of adaptors. The correlation between KAI scores and a measure of Live Stress (using Social Readjustment Rating Scale, Holmes & Rahe, 1967) involving 202 respondents in a randomly selected subsample of a general population sample was, at .22, barely significant. It is possible that the slight tilt of the mean towards innovation may be that the more adaptive feel that they get more support from most climates that they work in than do the more innovative.

Not that all the misinterpretations went in the same direction. Adaptors misread innovators just as readily. First they complained that innovators broke rules in order to irritate, then that they broke rules because they were casual and careless, and finally (most often all of these in the same discussion) because they failed to calculate risks sensibly. They tended to overlook another possibility; that innovators often unwittingly break rules. What adaptors tend to demand is 'targeted breakthrough', which seemed to mean innovation carefully controlled for direction and depth, that is, their version of 'calculated' risk. If this is the kind of 'innovation' they practice, it is indistinguishable from adaption – but the confusion of terminology leaves them uncertain what it is that they want or how to communicate it precisely. In a training course run by a major British bank, each course was divided into three groups; the higher innovators, the higher adaptors, and a mixed middle group of moderate scorers. In a leadership discussion exercise they were asked (before being given individual KAI score feedback) what kind of leaders they thought would be most useful to their bank in the future. On A-I issues the reporting back sessions sometimes came close to war. The innovators, mistaking innovation for a level measure, argued that only innovators had the 'vision to lead any large-scale long-term operation.' Adaptors, infuriated, responded that innovation was useful 'in small, controllable doses' or the whole enterprise would descend into chaos. The middling group looked pained and reported that the cross they had to bear was having 'extremists to left and right of them – very distracting!' Furthermore, the differences actually led to reported difficulties, including stress, in individuals in teams. Each group eventually tended to agree that banks which had failed did so because of an excess of the attributes of the other groups.

One study specifically examined the effects of adaptor-innovator collaboration. Hammerschmidt (1996) used KAI to form teams to solve problems on a training course. The exercise required problem solving by teams of eight, divided into two subteams of four: The first subteam needed to solve a problem and then communicate to the other subteam what the problem was without showing them the original material (a problem of precise communication). The first 500 managers to play this management game were allotted to teams and subteams randomly, or at any rate not on variables relevant to A-I. Frequently, teams failed to solve their problems in the time allotted because one or other of the subteam's members disagreed so vehemently among themselves that time ran out. The experiment was then tried on a second set of 500 managers. This time the subteams were all homogeneously similar in A-I terms, although *all* other variables were either mixed or randomly allotted. The result was that in this second set, *no subteam failed for reasons of internal disagreement.* Having people like oneself in a team may limit problem-solving scope but it does lead to more harmony for less effort. This brings up the problem of the management of diversity as a survival matter: How much diversity can we accommodate when diversity may lead to loss of efficiency in the shorter term but the nature of the current problems may change significantly over time? This is not an easy balance to get right.

Making use of style diversity

From the earliest use of KAI it was clear that people well apart on the scale might perceive at least some of each other's behaviour pejoratively. Lists of such pejorative evaluations began to be used as a teaching technique. In some training courses, in which serious subjects were treated more as money-spinning entertainment, the technique backfired. Numerous ex-course members rang known KAI experts as they sought guidance on their 'faults' and complaining about the way they had been 'exposed' in training groups. It appeared that the adverse comments were not seen as a joke and any teaching point was missed. One consultant, Dr Charlie Prather (USA), wrote in to say that his method of teaching this issue was to encourage mixed groups to throw pejorative terms about freely, writing up contributions on flip charts. Then he asked them what would be the effect on cohesion in any team in which some its members believed that these descriptions were a true evaluation of what the others thought of them! The course members were then invited to alter every pejorative term into one that, by using a synonym of the original term, kept the essence of original description but now presented it as a useful attribute. (Along the lines: I am economical, you are mean; I am generous, you are profligate.) The members went home with the double list – an aide memoir in problem-solving leadership.

One aspect of A-I wrangles that is repeatedly observed is that when teams fall out on what are essentially issues of style, pejorative terms flow freely. This should not be unexpected, but in addition, the disagreements rapidly became bitter and became attached to other, hitherto unrelated, personal differences that veered towards personal distrust and dislike. Some teams fractured and some became unworkable (e.g., Lindsay, 1985; Kubes & Spillerova, 1992), while others that coped with the differences thrived. The main difference was that in those that thrived the participants spent time and effort in understanding one another, patching up differences, and frequently complementing each other – a practice wittily likened to ape grooming. The more cohesive groups reported, with pardonable pride, high success in tasks as a result of their effort to understand each other and high satisfaction in so doing. They were convinced that mutual respect (especially of the very differences that were causing the effort) was the key to their success (e.g., Rickards & Moger, 1994). The team Lindsay was asked to help fell to bits at its next crisis point. The view derived from such experience is that if a internal dispute, although based initially only on style differences, is allowed to develop, so many additional causes for continued war arise that mistrust (and even active personal dislike) make the disorders within the team incurable. Kubes & Spillerova (1992), however, report what might happen, even after the start of inter-team hostilities, if mutual enlightenment can occur in time – see the case study in Box 11. In some of the reported cases, especially that of Hammerschmidt (1996), friction within homogeneous subgroups was rarely a matter of concern – the later problem, of reforming the group back into a single but diverse team with a single conclusion to implement, was another matter. What has now been noted in practice is that if the teams know about this style collaboration problem (as part of understanding A-I theory) *before* they split into subgroups, then the members of the groups will *plan* to try to take these differences into good account. Forewarned is forearmed!

A lesson learned from both Lindsay's and Kubes's experience, as well as from those many consultants who made use of their experience in their own work, was that differences in cognitive style can cause at least two tricky problems: (a) the original difficulties can become personal issues and (b) other differences between the protagonists may well become involved. These new 'causes for war' may cause more difficulty than the original problems. Groups can be reminded that this phenomenon has often occurred when countries go to war. The war may start with an ultimatum requiring the recipient to desist from some action (Imperial Germany attacking Belgium, Nazi Germany attacking Poland, Iraq sending troops into Kuwait), but once the war begins the issues between the warring parties multiply rapidly. The method used by consultants using A-I theory is to try to set aside the added issues, to avoid casting blame on any issue, and to instruct both parties on A-I theory without directly referring to the problems that have arisen until those present begin to see that there is a connection between the theory and their problems. At some appropriate stage, the key message is got across that diversity is more difficult to manage than homogeneity but is worthwhile

---

Box 11   Kubes' case study

Kubes was in a company on a consultancy assignment when he was asked, because of his psychology background, for some advice on 'a difficult young woman' in the enquirer's team. It transpired that she had recently joined the team (recruited from elsewhere) and was creating friction with another member of the team with whom she needed to collaborate as part of her job. This other team member disliked the way she did her work, reported on it, and her general manner of operating. In her turn, she found him difficult but the rest of the team clearly sided with him. They all felt that her background (the degree and experience she had) was different from the rest of the team and that could also be a factor. Neither of the pair wished to talk to one another and the woman began to give her reports to the boss and the colleague preferred to pick them up from the boss's office. Messages about the reports were beginning to be passed through the boss, who increasing felt like 'a telephone exchange'. The matter was reaching crisis point – with possible dismissal in the air. Kubes began by finding out some key facts. He asked the boss: (1) When asking for an added member of staff did he (or the team) specify whether they wanted a man or a woman? Answer: No. (2) Kubes then asked if they had specified any particular age range. Answer: No. (3) When asking for a new member of staff, did they specify a particular degree and experience? Answer: Yes, the ones she had. (4) When she first began, was she seen as difficult? Answer: No. KAI scores suggested a clue to the problem – the team (all older men) were found also to be moderate adaptors, except the boss, who approximated the male mean. The woman was a high innovator.

Armed with a clue, Kubes used Lindsay's tactics. He began by giving the team information on A-I theory, and went on explaining until they began to see the 'style gap' in the team for themselves. Then came the scores and more discussion. Kubes steered the discussion onto the management of diversity, which is always needed in a team as it is so potentially useful. The wider the diversity, the more potential at the team's disposal; the wider the diversity, the more difficult is its successful management. Later he discussed tactics with the boss. They agreed to suggest to the team members not directly involved to keep clear for the time being to see if some arrangement could be worked out. Tension dropped as a result of the intervention, so this seemed a possibility, at least for the immediate future. Then Kubes got the boss to agree that playing the role of 'bridger' was not below a leader's dignity. They arranged for these two clashing colleagues to meet him each week in his office as a threesome and to receive and discuss the report and any action that was needed to implement the contents. Coping behaviour was now the norm – the boss's presence helped to maintain it and the temperature dropped some more. A way of operating had been found in which adjustments to operations and behaviour could be explored on neutral territory. As the system worked so the matter stabilised and at that point Kubes lost contact. Not a perfect but a workable solution.

SUMMARY: The lessons learnt were that differences of style are often seen as differences of level, then of stupidity or/and of hostility; from there the problem might escalate further. The sequence can run something like this:

If I am successful and you are not like me, you are probably inferior.
If you disagree and persist in being different, you are probably hostile as well.
If you are hostile, then every difference between us is a source of friction, for which you are responsible.

to all parties if it can be done successfully. When that is seen, the added issues may well fall away (as long as intervention has come in time) and a spirit of challenge to succeed often replaces one of frustration, irritation, and fear of failure.

There is a marked tendency for people in general to believe that if something has been found to be useful, an endless amount of it is always endlessly desirable. Innovation is the latest craze, replacing the earlier notion that the only sure way to proceed is adaptively. This 'blank cheque' assumption always has its dangers; in relation to the needs of specific problems being tackled, too much or too little structure is decidedly unhelpful. For example: A highly adaptive problem, requiring a highly adaptive solution, can be managed more quickly and efficiently by a small team of high adaptors. This argument translates to other diversities; a purely accounting problem, requiring a purely accounting solution, may well be best managed by a small team of accountants. However, many problems are not so narrowly based, and even those that are may, over time, generate fresh problems, often as a result of a team's very success in tackling the original one. These new situations are very likely to require a wider range of cognitive style, knowledge, and skills. At this point the previous ideally selected team is at a disadvantage. Much consultancy with past successful teams confirms their reluctance to realise that their once ideal composition is currently less than ideal – especially because that very past success makes current possible weakness hard to credit. A team requires an amount of diversity that can deal with the current problem, and either it needs additional diversity to manage the follow-up or it needs to place a 'shelf life' upon itself at which time (or stage of progress) it will require reform. The first solution adds diversity to the group that is not immediately required and which, if aggressively exercised, may cause a perceived loss of efficiency and irritability among its members. The second solution requires a hitherto successful team to consider its own reform by seeking to import more diversity, *before it runs into difficulty*, to order to manage a class of problems that it has itself helped to throw up. This requires a good deal of insight, which in turn needs to influence planning in good time (foresight). Fortunately, a general inability of managers to select homogeneous problem-solving teams with accuracy often accidentally leaves teams better balanced than they intended. This helps them meet unexpected classes of problems by having available unexpected amounts of diversity. This is a useful bonus, as long as the team members have not managed to ignore the diversity or drive it underground for so long that they fail to notice its value when the time comes. If unplanned, no team can rely on the fortuitous presence of this bonus or of being able to use it well even if it does happen to be available.

The argument is that a diversity of style, although more costly to manage, has potential value in the management of a diversity of problems that, over time, could face any group. This notion need not be confined to diversity of cognitive style, but any other diversity that is available to any team; this notion has been advanced by Ashby (1956) using the term requisite variety, which he applied to the physical, natural, and social sciences. Numerous publications have followed, in one of which Miller (1990) argues that organisations having requisite variety can more easily sense and adjust to the changing environment. The definition of variety is wide, in Miller's case covering abilities, skills, and products. Van der Molen (1994), in discussing the life cycle of company products and the rise and fall of organisations, and Vicere (1992), on the life cycle of organisations, reached similar conclusions, with the added notion that different parts of the cycles are dominated (always precariously, not always for the better) by different cognitive styles and that this can be predicted from theory. The highest failure rate in organisations (products, ideas, empires – any grouping or product of mankind) is at their start, when they are likely to be innovator-dominated and short of structure, planning, and managed resources; or at their advanced maturity, when they are likely to be dominated by adaption and too preoccupied with the efficiency of the current system to be sufficiently sensitive to a changing environment.

DEVELOPMENT OF COMPLEXITY

Complexity in nature

On a continuum of life that ranges from the most simple to the most complex, mankind must surely lie at the extreme of complexity. If the scale was designed to measure behaviour along the same range, mankind would be hanging over the edge. Earlier, it was noted that mankind faces a diversity of problems, many of them the added outcome of spectacular success and overweening expectations, and to solve these requires a wide diversity of resources and all the available diversity of problem solvers. Darwin was puzzled by the very existence of complexity in life, being unable to account satisfactorily for the pressures that impelled its development or the means by which it occurred. Modern experiments in biology show that simple molecular chains, representing RNA, that exist in ideal experimental conditions become smaller and less 'complex'; this 'stripping' of such demanding surplus permits them to reproduce faster, giving the trimmer chains an evolutionary advantage. In fact, the development of complex life is dependent on the development of mechanisms (like the availability of repair enzymes and the sex-related double helix genetic structure) that allow the organism to reproduce with smaller 'copying' error; the added complexity gives more resource in survival (see Mark Ridley, 2000, pp. 10 & 11). Organisms ranging from the level of virus up to that of eukaryotes (the most numerous of life forms) are very simple in construction. It seems that the variations that exist among each species generally exploit the opportunities on offer to organisms of their level of complexity, rather than tend to become more complex. However, Ridley argues persuasively that there may be particular pressures on some varieties that are at the ends of this narrow range of complexity. Those at the simplest end of the range have nowhere else to go but become more complex; they are more likely not to change in complexity at all. Their problem is that the next, nearest, more complex niches are already occupied. Those at the other, most complex end also have limited opportunity, as the niches for organisms slightly less complex are full, too. It may only be on these already complex organisms that there is pressure to evolve into even more complex forms. Here, Ridley (2000) draws an interesting analogy with the human business opportunity – explaining his point by using the same sort of parallels that we have been using, but in reverse! 'The species that are already near the top of the range are likely to be the ones that do the pioneering because evolution usually proceeds in small steps: we, or some other great ape, are more likely than a worm or a jellyfish to give rise to a more complex species than us. [. . .] No doubt capitalists do sometimes get carried away by business opportunities that appear to be completely new, particularly if they use new technology. In reality, it may be easier to make a living, or a profit, by exploiting existing opportunities better than competitors rather than seeking out unoccupied space. At least you know that a niche for a business does exist within the range of established businesses; the question is whether you can compete. On the other hand, you know that beyond the range you will not have to worry about competitors; the question is whether a business niche even exists' (p. 51). This is a neat summing up of frequent differences of view between the more adaptive and the more innovative managers – from a biologist's perspective. Basic principles have wide application; they are worth studying widely.

Diversity aids the management of complexity

Continued life requires organisms to reproduce successful offspring – that is, like themselves, the progenitors who have lived long enough to reproduce. The problem is to replicate RNA or, with more difficulty, DNA that is error free. However, not all errors made in the copying of DNA sequences are harmful. 'We can divide mistakes into three classes: advantageous mistakes, which makes things better; neutral mistakes, which make no difference; and harmful mistakes, which make things worse. The first two kinds of mistakes underlie all evolutionary change' (Ridley, 2000, p. 61). This parallels the argument above about the need for tolerance of the same two (of three) kinds of diversity. However, research with the simplest of living RNA sequences has shown, at least in theory, that such organisms benefited, in ideal conditions, by stripping out surplus genetic baggage, sequences that could be dropped without impairing the organism and which aided reproducing more efficiently. Carrying extra baggage, even if potentially useful and neutral in nature, can be a disadvantage. Yet the biologist is also clear that survival often requires the exploitation of a neutral pool of potentially useful opportunity for change. The nature of the balance that needs to be struck, then, depends largely on two factors: the complexity of the organism and the corresponding complexity of the environmental problems faced. The more complex each is, the more complex their interaction, and the greater the advantage of carrying potential answers to problems not yet met, much less solved. The problem, emerging from complex situations such as those created by mankind, needs a constant adjustment of the view between such cost and such potential advantage. Often, balances are achieved by a series of over-corrections, first in one direction and then in the other. This can be seen being acted out in long-lived companies that tend to oscillate between bouts of optimistic amassing and managing new complexities and diversities whilst in a confident, expansive mode and bouts of nitty-gritty cost paring, everywhere and at almost any long-term cost, when the contrary mode prevails.

These swings (dubbed the pendulum of change in A-I theory) are frequently led by those of different cognitive style, who over-play their respective style strategies by overestimating the nature and possible duration of the environmental changes that appear to suit their natural mode of problem solving. The lesson learnt, from both biology and business, is that the cost of carrying neutral diversity is dependent on the complexity of the operator and the complexity and instability of the environment. In the case of mankind, the advantage of carrying this neutral diversity appears compelling – however, in practice there may still be disagreement on just how much is useful compared to the cost, over a particular time and set of circumstances. Adaptors and innovators often come to slightly, but nevertheless significantly, different viewpoints from the same evidence. Mankind seems to be the only living creature able to understand the problem; able not only to assess whether a specific diversity is neutral or hostile, but also to weigh the advantage or disadvantage of accommodating surplus neutral diversity. But then humans are the only individuals able to learn, each as the owner of noticeable diversity, how to present their unique brand as an attractive opportunity to others rather than as costly baggage or plain threat. In our ever increasingly complex world, this learning is a priority.

Leadership in mergers

Mark Ridley[74] suggests that, in nature, the most significant step towards the development of complex life was the merger between a large and a small one-celled organism that created the eukaryotes. The combination may have proved more efficient than either alone, as it appears that each possessed complementary skills. This new cell now possessed two management teams of DNA and it is instructive to consider how the merger worked out, especially as: 'in modern eukaryotic life forms, such as ourselves, the descendants of the engulfed cell still exist in the form of our mitochondria.' The value of the merger becomes clearer: 'mitochondria are a major competitive advantage for eukaryotic cells, because they are twenty times as efficient at producing energy as are [the engulfing] bacterial cells.' This is the kind of fact that engages the interest of every boardroom member of a company considering the likely pay-off of a proposed merger.

The whole subsequent merger process is still not fully understood, but one set of DNA became the larger and dominant (nuclear) set, probably made up in part of elements from the smaller (organelle) set[75]. On reproduction, the two have developed different systems of merger; the DNA in the nuclear element organises a sexual merger. In the organelle, the male contribution is eliminated. Here are two ways of sorting out this Problem B and achieving the harmony required to concentrate on Problem A. No doubt, in evolutionary time the matter of elimination was settled at first, by battle and total massacre, as still happens in algae and some boardrooms. However, this method of achieving early harmony is expensive – e.g., cooperation between the sexes to maximise their individual contribution is more efficient. This dictum has not led, in this instance, to the nuclear-type solution but to a more fascinating, if still wasteful, solution that Ridley calls the 'origin of gender'. The gender distinction is that the female gamete (egg) has become an organelle-excluder – biological-speak for a retainer of DNA-loaded mitochondria – and the male gamete an organelle-ejector, which means that it ejects the DNA in its own mitochondria even before the merger, to facilitate the process. However, this is a workable solution as it brings harmony. The continuing disharmonious state is not a viable alternative, as: 'complex life could not exist if large chunks of the DNA were given over to subversion and counter-subversion. Life would become like East Germany before the fall of the Berlin Wall, with one police informer per 6.5 citizens' (Ridley, 2000, p. 177).

---

74 Ridley, 2000, Chapter 6: Darwin mergers and acquisitions, pp. 134–166; a useful and readable exposition of these problems.

75 The difference in size became prodigious: in mankind, the nuclear element contains some 60,000 or more genes and the mitochondria barely 40 – a disparity that, in a modern business setting, would leave the junior partner little scope to determine the development of the merger.

It seems that nature has long tried out different systems of merger management. Modern management does this also. Usually there is a stronger partner within the pair and the weaker management is almost always expected to fit the dominant culture. The problem in business management is resolved by cognition, so which general system of merger is used may depend on what is the dominating principle behind the merger. If it is absorption of assets, which does not include interest in the acquisition of the added diversity on offer from the newly acquired management team, then the mitochondria 'only-one-set-left' approach may be used. This assumes that the diversity represented by one of the sets of management is not an asset, not only on acquisition but also in the foreseeable future. Alternatively, the (taken-over) management that created and nurtured the assets, which were so desirable that a merger was sought, is welcomed by the taking-over management as an added resource. This makes for a more difficult merger but the added difficulty is acceptable for the longer-term gain. The problem for management is to work out what they want and not drift into the alternative approach, e.g., first seeking diversity and then eliminating it. As a third alternative, Ridley points out, management has an additional resource not readily available in cell management – that of head hunting. Rather than going without a merger (and avoiding the problem of seeking efficient integration), or seeking the advantages of added diversity by absorbing an entire subculture, management can select the particular sort of diversity needed and recruit just that element[76]. The danger is the same with a merger; first of looking for a missing specific diversity but, then, on acquiring it trying to get it to respond in the 'approved company way' – thereby cancelling out some of the diversity just bought in high cost of cash and effort. The eukaryotic cells are not the only organisms with merger problems.

MANAGEMENT OF DIVERSITY NEEDS TO BE TAUGHT

The universe abounds with constant diversity; to be successful (indeed, to survive), all individuals need to manage much diversity well and, in the case of mankind, other than that diversity of which we are made, the management of all diversity needs to be learnt. Because the knowledge is needed for the management of change, the management of diversity, therefore, needs to be taught. The foregoing argument has stressed that, in nature, diversity is largely 'neutral' and represents a pool of latent possibility for good as much as for evil. Relatively small amounts of the general diversity impinge on us as being useful and less of it as hostile. Managing diversity involves turning as much of the diversity around us as possible into advantage for ourselves. Since much of this diversity is best managed by groups, then the aim is to turn much of the collective diversity into mutual advantage, treating the diversity of the group as a potential advantage, like the rest of the otherwise 'neutral' potential pool available. One part of the pool of diversity we need to manage is other problem solvers.

The first requirement in the teaching of the management of diversity is that diversity needs to be acknowledged. It is not a recent trend that differences are ignored or even denied when they can be and attacked when they cannot; it is just that some of the

---

76 Actually, nature may also do this by selecting some DNA letter sequences from the lesser partner, but such occurrence, in evolutionary time, must have happened rarely and then only by chance.

examples may be new. Modern examples include the views that there are no differences between men and women, between doctors and shamen, or between any worker and any other worker – all must be and must think alike. One term that has almost become a part of commonly used language is 'organisation man' (Whyte, 1957). In fact, the evidence in cognitive style shows that small differences are readily noticeable and often require effort to be accepted and integrated into one group. Curiously, those who are most vehement in the pursuit of the elimination of differences also find the term 'stereotype' offensive – nearly as much as they do the term 'discriminate[77]'. Yet all central nervous systems must be able to discriminate – perceive anomaly – or they could not problem solve. All higher-order brains need to be able to form abstractions from a collection of events or else each event would require to be understood 'from scratch' – experience would not be valuable. It is not ever these abilities that are at fault but rather how they may be used, for what purpose, by which person, and in relation to whom. The evidence for small differences in cognitive style being noticeable and requiring effort to manage them is solid. In organisations, individuals whose KAI scores are far from the group mean may:

- be temporary members, such as new entrants being moved from department to department for induction training – they often try to prolong stays in 'fitting units' and shorten the stay in others;.
- have found or created a niche that suits them, developed a particular role within the group acceptable to its other key members, or become part of a small but powerful elite;
- be exercising coping behaviour – where the rewards for doing so keep up motivation;
- be unhappy.

If differences between people are not ignored or denied, then the next step is to determine if they are useful. Differences, for the most part, add to the array of options in problem solving. Because of them some people can do readily, and at less cost, things that cost others more effort. On these grounds most differences are either immediately or potentially useful. It could be argued that two classes of difference cause problems that make them unwelcome. One is a difference that is not immediately required by the group but which the owner insists on exercising (the input of innovative ideas in the closing stages of the implementation of an adaptive solution is an obvious distraction). The other is a difference that is aggressively deployed for the prime benefit of the displayer (and supporters) regardless of whether it is perceived within the group as a distraction, a disadvantage, or even whether it threatens the group's survival as an

---

77 A stereotype is a metal mould for holding old style printer's type. It also became used to mean a classification rather rigidly applied to a group of people, sometimes pejoratively. As a simple basic description of salient characteristics of a group of people, its value is in providing enough knowledge of a group so that an encounter with a (an unknown) member of it will indicate a way to start up a friendly contact. Stereotypical polite behaviour, like a standard greeting, is aimed at having this effect. Stereotyping, when applied aggressively, treats *known* persons contemptuously as types, not individuals; the content of the stereotype is then highly likely to be pejorative. Unfortunately, many people who react emotionally against others who they claim stereotype them, themselves often stereotype their perceived opponents, compounding the ill effects.

ultimate consequence. The examples already given above illustrate these issues[78]; it is noted that, in much current custom, the term discrimination is not used to describe a cognitive function in general but to describe some forms of inter- or intra-group hostility. The weakness of this approach is that little understanding of any situation is generated and learning to accommodate diversity successfully is replaced with further division by the hostility of yet another group or subgroup. If, on the other hand, the term 'discrimination' is used as a neutral description of a facility available to brain function, it is easier to isolate presumed faults from other useful uses. The correction of the faults should not follow the same pattern as the faults themselves (replacing one unacceptable form of discrimination with another unacceptable form). Getting acceptance for a diversity should follow the pattern normally used by the brain for this task – demonstrating, at the least, that the diversity in question is not threatening, and at best that it is actually mutually useful to all the parties concerned. As was said earlier, the need for membership of in-groups is acquired early by the very nature of our need for selective others in infancy. We build on this need by widening our tolerance for diversity. As we mature we learn more of the diversity of problems that we face and the usefulness of a diversity of problems solvers and problem-solving methods to obtain the breadth and level of success to which we aim. Education and insight rather than hostility is the way to widen tolerance. Further examples of the impact of style difference follow.

Gul (1986) surveyed the students of accountancy classes on their preferences for aspects of the curriculum. The more adaptive among them preferred accounting, auditing, and, above all, taxation. The more innovative preferred general subjects and extra subjects. Each year at the end of course review, the group, dominated by the more adaptive, voted to ask authority to drop general subjects and extra subjects from the curriculum altogether because they were not felt to be useful. Many of the innovators of this sample would not be likely to use accounting directly in future jobs[79], but some would be likely to gravitate towards finance, a subgroup in accounting that had a high innovative mean, quite different from the rest of the accounting profession (see, e.g., Kirton, 1980). In the studies above it was observed that new entrants into a group whose established members had a mean unlike theirs are likely to have a selective turnover that results in the new group's mean shifting year by year towards that of the established group they have joined. This almost certainly reflects the difficulty that the management of this difference engenders in both subgroups, and results in some members of the less powerful group leaving the job. The members of these groups often lack the knowledge that might make the effort of all its members acceptable in accommodating a broader range of cognitive differences. On the other hand, the established group are not necessarily wrong – some jobs are better suited, in general, to those with particular styles, outlooks, and skills; there can be times when the added breadth demands more cost than gain. The calculation is a difficult one and the solution lies in cool choices that are open to discussion and that take likely future needs into account rather than just those that are readily perceived at present. If adding to the range of variance seems the right choice, then care must be taken to

---

78 Management Initiative study, chapter 1, p. 13.
79 Foxall's studies on the distribution of KAI scores in occupational groups, quoted above, have shown that innovators are more likely to change profession – not just their job – than adaptors.

ensure that the need for the change is widely understood and that different newcomers are welcomed – with the emphasis on why they should be. At the same time, the newcomers must be given the same kind of understanding of the role expected of them and given advice on how to present their advantages to others – those different others – in the establishment.

Closing gaps is the job of both sides (everyone, in fact) aided by leadership; a prime task of a problem-solving leader is to help resolve Problem B, not promote it. This is not an easy task, for the leader has as many preferred structures as anyone else and irritation caused by the exhibition of the preferences of others soon shows – even in the greatest minds. Francis Bacon (1620) made this observation: 'The human understanding is of its own nature prone to suppose the existence of more order and regularity in the world than it finds.' He went on to suggest that where regularity is missing people make it up, but being wrong does not seem to be the main fault – being persistently wrong is worse. 'The human understanding, when it has once adopted an opinion (either as being the received opinion or as being agreeable to itself) draws all things else to support and agree with it.' This is bad enough; there is more: 'and though there be a greater number and weight of instances to be found on the other side, yet these it either neglects and despises, or else by some distinction sets aside and rejects; in order that by this great and pernicious predetermination the authority of its former conclusions may remain inviolate' (from Bolles, 1999, p. 89). Clearly, people have been worrying for a long time about how other people manage structure, which structure they can manage, and how they can be moved to a more accommodating structure – defined by me rather than by you.

At a time when the staff of the Occupational Research Centre were still trying to understand the implications of their observations on the problems of cognitive style differences in groups, a person they dubbed as 'the bright tie statistician' was encountered. The team was about to undertake some research in a research department of a local government organisation, beginning by interviewing key staff and collecting some data (like KAI scores). It was noted that some of this department's research staff admitted that whereas they enjoyed planning research and collecting data, they disliked being involved in detailed statistical analysis and writing up. It was noted that the members of this subset were among the more innovative of a generally innovative department. As they got to know more about A-I theory they volunteered that they were lucky in having a statistical advisor who was also innovative – they got on with him and 'shared problems' rather than found themselves being pinned down and lectured in terms they did not understand. The man they were referring to, however, turned out to have an adaptive score – mildly so in general population terms but representing quite a gap for his colleagues among this subset. Another curiosity is that whereas all the other people were freely discussing their KAI scores this man did not, except that he vaguely seemed to confirm their wrong assessment of him. He was interviewed alone and was soon gurgling with laughter. It turned out that when he was offered the job he was warned by 'the administration' – which he now recognised as adaptive – that this team were 'friendly but difficult to manage'. They had the reputation for bending rules and cutting corners as well as having a cavalier approach to detail and schedules. The interviewers had noted, however, and even remarked on it at the interview, that the applicant had a bright tie and had arrived in a racy-looking sports car, so they thought that he would get on with this group. The statistician then admitted to the ORC team that he had been introduced at university to sports cars by a close friend and, although he reckoned that he drove with care, noted that he had acquired a reputation as a dashing fellow. Indeed, he thought that it had all helped to collect a pretty (and more innovative) girl, who was now his wife! This wife had, however, worried about his choice of ties. She got into the habit of choosing them for him. Finally equipped for life in the faster lanes among innovators, he acquired, in his first job, some useful experience in dealing with people he now knew as innovators (like some of his university friends and his wife) and discovered, as a result of initially being shy, that if he offered advice largely by asking the right questions he did better than if he disagreed. He said he had spent much time in this first job learning how to put the questions so they sounded interesting – even challenging – but not threatening. As a sensible and careful adaptor, he even wrote down several likely specimen openings to responses he could give to the very often standard questions. All these assets were deployed on the new job. Now thoroughly mistaken for a modest and clever innovator with a useful knowledge of statistics, he was doing well; he just wondered what might happen when they learnt his KAI score. What the Occupational Research Centre team learned were the first lessons in using A-I theory as a means of managing diversity.

Cognitive style difference is one of many differences that create problems in teams. Perhaps because it is a difference that originates in the very problem-solving equipment itself, it can be pervasive and focus round it other differences that affect group cohesion. The main problem is that cognitive differences are not clearly understood and style is mostly viewed as level and 'correctable' unless the 'deviant' person is also stupid or hostile (or both). To an elite subset, 'deviant' can include the majority.

Cognitive style subsets within a group are all convinced that they have the 'best' method of solving most problems. In friendly well-managed teams there is considerable tolerance – these teams are also deemed successful (often, even when they are going through a 'bad patch'). It is their success that helps them manage well, be friendly, and be tolerant, for success makes all the team members feel secure and willing to experiment with variation (be tolerant).

When troubles arise repeatedly, tolerance might wear thin. There is now no longer the feeling that the risk of failure permits experiment in unlikely ways – 'unlikely ways' are defined 'by me as ways that are far from being like mine' but almost never stated in such blunt form. A feeling grows that the team is losing command of time – danger is increasing and the time to solve the problems shortening, thus enhancing the sense of risk. The 'best' ways are those that have succeeded before; innovative for teams with an innovative orientation but adaptive for those with an adaptive orientation. Advice from outside that advocates a change of style in solving problems is likely to be ignored or resented. Team members favouring them, particularly if it is appreciated that this is their natural (deviant) line of approach, are often perceived as traitors.

When groups clash in hostility, the skills in the management of diversity may no longer be regarded as useful. Time for that may come, maybe, when the danger passes. Once style difference has caused problems, almost any other difference within the group can be perceived as deviant, adding to the initial problem. However, if the style problem can be resolved, tolerance might return (as long as hostilities have not reached some critical level). So, the spiral of developing intolerance can be reversed; indeed, a better understanding of the value to the group of a range of style differences often helps the acceptance of other quite unrelated differences. This seems to be because, once diversity in such a critical area as problem solving for the team's survival is found useful, it is a lot easier to perceive other diversities as potentially useful rather than as divisive. There is little more central to a one's image of self than characteristic aspects of one's problem solving. Maurice Dubras, in private communication, offered an example of how insight acquired while managing one diversity can help in dealing with others. At the time a senior manager in Canada's Atomic Energy Authority, he was detached to assist a United Nations project in the late 1980s. It had been noted how the members of such projects tended to fragment along national and cultural lines – often exacerbated by language problems – causing problems in collaboration. A clear case of Problem B taking too much of the resources required for Problem A. He was able to collect KAI scores from the members of this group, promising to give feedback later when work permitted. After a lunch break, now knowing their scores, he resumed the main task of planning the project, with a difference. Instead of letting them choose their place around the table (mostly congregating into national groups), he had each person's place marked and said he had a plan that might help. Taken by surprise, they conformed. They did not know it but they were now arranged in a continuum from the highest adaptor at one end of a horseshoe table pattern to the highest innovator at the other end. Then they were formed into adjacent subsets (first four, next four, and so on) representing closely homogeneous style sets that were culturally mixed. The whole group was given a problem to tackle, then set to work some ideas first among themselves, then to report their finding to the whole group – a technique they expected. Despite the fact that the subsets were not only culturally mixed but some had language problems to overcome, their members were surprised to find that they got along very well with their problem solving. The next task was to attempt to resolve the inevitable differences that had emerged between subsets. The problem now became one of convincing other subsets that they were taking an appropriate and fruitful line. The aim, Dubras told them, was to get convergence first with groups close to them, then widen until there was general agreement. They soon realised that the subsets close to their own were the easiest with whom to seek convergence and those further away were those with the largest gaps to close. During a second session it began to dawn on them that their arrangement in the seating was a factor. At this point Dubras broke off the hunt for Problem A solutions and turned to giving the feedback on their style score – much to the group's amusement. Dubras reported that the incident helped start the process of breaking up the original pattern of forming sets, at least some of the time – as people realised that they had 'cognitive allies' elsewhere in the overall group. Discussion of the management of diversity generally became a more common element in their further work together.

As was discussed earlier, emotion is a factor in all problem solving; in the cognitive function schema of the management of the mind it is located in cognitive affect. When diversity is perceived as an irritant or a threat, emotion may lock in this assessment and prevent a ready reassessment in cool logical terms. Reversing negative discrimination is likely to involve emotion, which may need to be taken into account (on both sides) before logical reappraisal begins. One way is to show that there is potential mutual profit in tolerance and to give time for the point to sink in.

It seems important that the leaders of the search for understanding, in teaching about these dividing issues, should not themselves be seen as protagonists of one partisan group. They must not be, or be seen to be, dedicated people with burning zeal, full of righteousness and armed with wide authority to punish some deviant subset who have hitherto ruled and (in their view) should do so no more. Regrettably, those with axes to grind have a tendency to use them, with yet more division being the result. True cohesion is readily lost, and even if opposition is driven underground and the remaining individuals coexist, they can barely be called a team – certainly not one that is likely to use all its members effectively. They could even cease to be a team in all but name.

The aim of intervention is to try to find value in all the diversity, not replace the dominance of one variant with another, however popular the new views have become. A trend can be observed to develop by the liberal number of its fashionable terms that are sprinkled over new policy documents. When such documents contain the term, say, 'innovation' a dozen times on the first page, adaptiveness and all its adherents, however able, are in for trouble, as, eventually, is the organisation, from an excess of innovation. When the documents stress the need for tight control, the ruthless elimination of waste, and a return to basics, this is often a signal that it is the turn of innovation to be in trouble. All too many companies have, over time, failed either for lack of, or an excess of, innovation (whatever its current name). Usually, an exodus of yesterday's folk, with the help of suitable consultants who breathe the new trend, follows the introduction of the newly stated policy. The alternative is for the suffering population to develop the meaning of the crusading term until it becomes so wide as to be meaningless, bland, and relatively safe. Unfortunately much hardship is caused while the trend lasts and at the end of it a meaningless term has been acquired.

A review

A number of lessons have been learned from the studies of differences in cognitive style for those considering training aimed at achieving an increased tolerance for some diversity. In general:

- All life is diverse, as are its problems. Managing diversity is the key to managing change; managing change is the key to life.
- The human body itself is composed of a diverse assembly of cells, with an immense array of specialisms numbered by the trillion; the management of this empire is itself staggeringly vast and complex in its diverse specialisms numbered by the billion. Fortunately, it can be left to manage itself until something goes wrong or we try to squeeze that something extra out of its current level of performance.
- The body's defences are vigilant and active in destroying, neutralising, or converting to use all diversities that arise within it or intrude from without.
- Human group dynamics reflect the methods used by the individual; as humans have no instinct, these have to be learnt.
- Individuals collaborate in groups to enhance individual problem solving.
- The first serious problem we face in managing diversity is how to manage mother, and after that everyone else needed as a resource in surviving. Mankind is not made up of sub-breeds or types within which there is little individual variation to manage. Much of the diversity available to humans is made up of small differences between the ways individuals problem solve, and we must make the best of this rich but narrow range of diversity
- As with our own bodies (including, critically, our brains), all diversity within a group is potentially useful to its members expect that which is manifestly hostile.

- Each individual needs to survive and, therefore, has a self-interest in being in the group, but the diversity it represents needs to show that it is useful, or at least not harmful.
- If the diversity is neutral, then its presence should be seen as yielding more reward than cost. To worry about diversity that is neutral or to spurn one that has a net advantage are the prime ways of mismanaging diversity. Tolerance of neutral diversity is a long-term strategy of survival; acceptance of the cost of managing diversity is a price of survival.
- Emotion is attached to most appraisals of diversities in people – reversals of appraisals are best approached by reviewing the benefit of diversity to the group. Righteousness tends to be divisive.
- The human body and brain abound with specialised areas, which must all work together in smooth collaborative efficiency for the person to survive.
- Gross diversity between human groups does not exist – mankind does not divide up into breeds. Mankind's only major biologically based invariable division is that between the sexes, which led to the early specialisation of some tasks among hunter-gatherers.
- From biology to sociology, from the complex organism to the complex group, survival depends on limiting the scope of individual action and developing specialists.
- Learnt specialisation is a characteristic of mankind.
- The management of diversity is (mostly) set in the context of group problem solving:
  a   whenever a person asks for another's help and gets it, each person now has two problems;
  b   Problem A, the original (main) problem over which the group has formed, and
  c   Problem B, the added (subsidiary) problem – that of managing each other effectively.
- Successful groups expend considerably more effort on Problem A than Problem B.
- Homogeneous teams (those with minimal diversity) are easier to recruit, are easier to manage, and are more efficient in a limited area. Their weakness is the possibility of their main problem changing radically. They work best in relatively stable environments, bringing about change at a safe measured pace.
- Heterogeneous teams (those with wide diversity) are more difficult to recruit, more difficult to manage, and are more efficient over a wide range of problems. Their weakness is that more effort needs to be expended on Problem B (possibly at high cost). They work best in more turbulent environments, coping with more rapid, radical change, on more than one main front.
- The aim of every group is to use its available diversity of problem solvers to solve a diversity of problems effectively.
- Among the key inbuilt diversities, which are useful but need management, are A-I differences in cognitive style.

In detail:

- Accommodating diversity costs extra effort; it is reasonable to examine cost against gain.

- Teaching tolerance of diversity is not the same thing as teaching that a new diversity should replace an existing one.
- In such teaching the use of any loose terminology, which can be misrepresented or misused, is counter-productive (e.g., instinct, when applied to man; innovation, when it means anything new; discrimination, when it only means negative discrimination; modern, when it means my view as opposed to yours).
- Most people can readily appreciate that there is a wide diversity of problems to solve. Having available a diversity of approach and a diversity of people that can readily manage them for the common good is useful. It remains for them to be convinced that a particular diversity is not threatening but potentially helpful.
- Attacking people for not accepting some particular diversity mostly leads to backlash.
- Newcomers to a team should be trained to show that they are willing to accommodate to the existing members (that they represent more mutual gain than cost); existing members should be trained to look for useful diversity (leading to more mutual gain than cost).
- To get anything worthwhile done, one needs a clear view backed by strong motive. Clear views and strong motives are structures that are limiting as well as enabling.

Suggested action:

- Suggest that the cognitive process requires the problem solver to: discriminate differences, formulate patterns within the differences, acquire insight from the patterns, develop foresight, and then use such prediction to exercise control. Control involves managing diversity as a springboard to managing change, within the limits that the integrity of the problem solver (the identity of the group) is not imperilled by the quantity or the nature of either the diversity or the changes that need to be accommodated. (The time scale of change needs to be managed well.)
- Note that management of diversity is a requisite for the management of change; it needs to be taught and practised.
- Adaption-Innovation is a diversity that needs to be managed.
- Get a group to undertake a diversity audit. Then challenge the members to see how much of the diversity can be immediately used and what might be useful later; agree only to be intolerant of anything that is manifestly hostile to the group.
- Get the group to consider that the first requirement in managing diversity is to accept its existence. Accepting diversity means acknowledging that although no person or group should be unfairly exploited, no person can expect to perform uniformly well at all times in all circumstances.
- Each person in a group has to balance efficiently an appropriate degree of independence (identity) with a willing interdependence (exploiting diversities) to make useful contributions to the team and acquire the benefits of being in it.
- Get the group to undertake a diversity failure audit. Estimate the costs of the failure to accommodate diversity, defined as unwillingness to accept different roles and responsibilities that might capitalise on differences of styles, skills, attributes, temperaments, and background experience that may leave the surviving elements short of diversities. If this happens the variety of tasks that need to be

done may not diminish but some potential help has – those left still need to do these tasks without this help.

- Examine the loss to humanity if all diversity is lost. For every migrant made to become, or who aims to become, exactly like the hosts (or the converse); for every woman to aspire to every job done by any man and to do it in the same way (or the converse); both these may mean much loss of diversity to the community. Such loss of diversity is wasteful.
- With increasing size and complexity of communities, more options open up with more need for specialists. Such proliferation requires a higher level of managing diversity by each individual in every group, for both the individual's and the common benefit.
- Explore the relationship between the management of diversity and the management of change.
- Explore the role of A-I in the management of diversity.

A concluding note:

If, isolated within a skull, we are each a minority of one, then the advice of Philip Stanhope, Earl of Chester, to his son in a letter, 16 October 1747 is very relevant: 'do as you would be done by'.

This can be a tenent for every team member.

10 Managing cognitive gap

AGENTS OF CHANGE

If all individuals solve problems and are creative so that they might survive, then they are all agents of change. As, indeed, are all living creatures. If people differ in how well they problem solve and in what way, then they differ in the extent that they are agents of change in any specific situation and how effective their current intervention is. If all people are not only able to change but willing to do so, this does not mean that anyone is willing to accept any and every change on offer. No one is that uncritical. Everyone is willing to take up those opportunities for change that are acceptable, and most are clever enough to avoid most changes that are not, much of the time. All people are selective in the changes they accept and reject. No style of change can in safety be pursued without restraint; unlimited use of a narrow range of style leads to positions that go beyond the optimum. The magnitude of change that is needed or can be tolerated is also limited; too little and the grasp of (changing) reality is jeopardised and the chances of survival shortened; too much and one's sense of self is endangered. The differences between adaptors and innovators on this issue are ones of degree within specific contexts – there are no absolute positions that can be held. The changes that are acceptable are those that, on balance, benefit the changer. The balance is not always easy to calculate either in the short or the long term, but one's problem-solving equipment has been designed constantly to try to achieve this appropriate balance.

There are many factors that govern what is or is not an acceptable change. One variable that is always taken into account is the 'fit' between proposed change and one's cognitive style. For instance, adaptors are more likely to find proposed changes acceptable if they are within a seemingly consensually agreed paradigm; innovators are more comfortable with looser structure. Put positively, innovators are more comfortable with innovative notions and environments, adaptors with adaptive ones. Put negatively, adaptive solutions, novel ideas, or new products may be dismissed by the more innovative as mere 'fine tuning' and 'hardly creative'; innovative solutions may be viewed warily by the more adaptive as being unduly risky, peripheral, or even plain silly. It is hard to please everyone in a group with wide skills and diverse viewpoints; Problem B often threatens to overtake Problem A as the prime concern of a struggling group. It takes much learning and experience to achieve close collaboration with others notably different from oneself.

The terms adaptive and innovative are comparative – almost everyone, in any group, is more adaptive than some of its members and more innovative than the rest. The KAI score locates respondents on a continuum, but to be of use to a person it needs to be

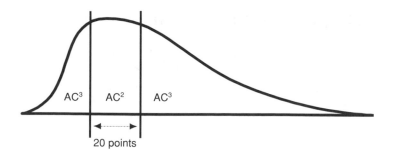

Note: 20 points is (close to) 1 *SD*. The consensus group lies 0.5 *SD* on either side of the mean.

Figure 10 Agents of change

related to some benchmark. It can, of course, be related to the mean of a general population. However, no one works with, plays with, or sets up home with an entire population. We relate closely to only a few individuals at a time and in person with not all that many in total. These are an individual's 'significant others' – and the difference between an individual and any one of these other individuals is a less abstract, more meaningful comparison than between an individual and a general mean. A combination of research and experience (Kirton & McCarthy, 1985; Clapp & de Ciantis, 1989; Kirton & de Ciantis, 1994; Hammerschmidt, 1996) suggest that a 10-point KAI difference between two people is, to use a venerable term in psychology, the 'just noticeable difference'. At 20 points difference, difficulties in mutual understanding and collaboration begin to become apparent; after that the difficulties seem to rise steeply rather than linearly. Earlier, research was reviewed to show that it is to be generally expected that small, homogeneous work groups have means that are skewed away from the general population means. The direction of the skew is usually readily predictable from an understanding of the bulk of the problems they need to solve. The means of cost accountants, marketing executives, and production managers are significantly different from each other. This skew is predictable and stable, as long as the group has been established for some time and is successful, as the table of occupational means shows. It is now possible to link the findings of score differences to these distributions.

If every individual problem solves then everyone is an agent of change (AC) – so let every individual, simply by existing as a biological entity, be dubbed, in notation form, an AC[1] (see Figure 10). But every individual can be a member of more than one group. In this social context, every person can *also* be described as an AC[2], whenever his or her KAI scores are located inside the majority or consensus subset of the group. The dividing line is set, based on research and practice, at 20 points wide, 10 points on either side of the mean of the group. If their scores locate them at or outside this (20-point) subset they can each be described (whether they are adaptors or innovators) as an AC[3]. So, simply by moving from one group to another, a person can shift from being an AC[2] to an AC[3] or vice versa[80], though additionally

---

80 Alternatively, of course, a person can change social role in problem-solving terms, by remaining in a changing group; as people move in and out the mean shifts and so does the individual's position in relation to it.

remaining, as an unchanging individual, always an AC^1. So, every AC^1 (as a biological entity) becomes, additionally, either an AC^2 or an AC^3 (as a social entity), whenever they are in a group of three or more, located as in Figure 10.

As the width of the AC^2 group is set at just over one standard deviation wide around this theoretical group's mean (note that one standard deviation of the general population is about 18 and the standard error of measurement about 6), the AC^2 group comprises approximately 40% of the whole group. Given the standard shape of the curve, this is the largest number that can be expected in any subgroup occupying the same range within the whole group. This subgroup, then, has a number of characteristic features. Its members lie within a range that involves the least difference between the members' cognitive style. This is, therefore, the largest subset for which there is the least need for coping behaviour. This range represents the largest 'problem-solving comfort zone' available, so it could also be said to represent the largest consensus subgroup. This consensus subset often contains at least some, if not most, of the group's leaders. The reason for this is exactly the same as the reason why the group is predictably skewed in the direction: It reflects the skewed distribution of its collective problem-solving concern. This group has two sources of influence; its size and the presence of its leaders. The value to the whole group of the consensus subgroup is obvious. They represent the largest well-knit group, being within a 'comfort zone' in which the minimum coping behaviour is required. They are in best 'organisation fit', both in relation to the group (as individuals) and to the bulk of the group's problems (as problem solvers). They are likely to perceive the same precipitating events that emanate from the core of the group's concerns and readily collaborate to deal with them with the minimum of dissent or uncertainty.

By contrast, those dubbed AC^3s are in a less naturally comfortable position, unless they have settled into a protected niche within the organisation. Their value to the whole group (as with many other kinds of diversity) is the widened potential they offer for problem solving outside the mode of the consensus group. Their cognitive differences allow them to specialise in those tasks they naturally prefer and which the consensus group does not. The AC^3s value seems obvious and, in theory, it seems a certainty that prominent, able AC^3s must be in hot demand. However, this is not the case, for all too often they are not well regarded, their worth is downgraded, and they are poorly integrated in the group. The experience of KAI users suggests that one reason could be that jobs people do not naturally do well are often avoided and treated as inferior or, at best, necessary evils that are done by lesser folk: Who would want to do a job like that? In short, by downgrading jobs that are not readily done well and not (therefore) liked, it seems there is also a marked tendency to downgrade their practitioners. The converse process seems to hold good. If the value of the task or process can be enhanced in the group's perception, then the value of, and tolerance for, an able practitioner of it also rises. As all this seems to be obvious, why does not every group appreciate – indeed hunt for – appropriate AC^3s to be sure to have the necessary diversity available within the ranks? The answers lie in the cost of diversity, the comfort derived from a homogenous in-group, and the power exerted by different forms of social climate contrasted with the contrary need to survive in a complex changing environment. The probability of getting this balance ideally right, not just for a single problem or space of time, but over all problems faced by the group over long periods, is all too often hard to get.

The size and close cohesion of the AC^2 subgroup suggests that it has the force of a consensus group at the core of a social climate. This could be called a cognitive climate – the structure by which the group shares a view of the problem and the solution that is likely both to satisfy and to be deemed feasible. It has long been understood that the group within which an individual interacts over a long period exerts a moderating influence not only on behaviour but also on the influences on that behaviour (e.g., attitudes and beliefs), that is, on a person's understanding of reality. If climate is a shared interpretation of the social environment, it must have a marked influence on every individual. Those closest to the individual, those with whom there is the most interaction, exert the largest amount of influence – hence, mother is the first and most critical element. As the influencing group widens, the more likely it is that different parts of the social environment it represents may exert influence in different ways. The extent of the influence will depend on a number of factors: the key people in any group; the size of the group; the extent to which its interests and outlooks are acceptable; and the extent to which its members can provide rewards and punishment when interacting with them. These might be summed up as significance, identity, and power, the influence of all three being moderated by the distance of the source from the individual and the extent to which the interaction of the parts are in accord.

In brief

All people are agents of change (AC^1) simply by being alive. Taking a work group as an example: If the group is long-standing and successful, it can be assumed that its members are in it for similar reasons (Problem A), solving similar problems for the common good. For each of its members, this group is likely to contain others who for them are 'significant others'; because of common interest, the group offers shared identity and its success spells power for each of its members. That, however, does not mean that for every individual all the elements are equal and the same as for others; variation is everywhere, even in the most close-knit groups (Problem B). To name one variation, all the individuals in a group will additionally be either an AC^2 or an AC^3, depending on their relative position to the mean of the group on the KAI continuum. This variation, like every other, has the potential to be useful or divisive. The AC^2 subset is a group within a group, though its edges may well be less sharp than those between the whole group of which it is a member and other (whole) groups. The AC^2 subset is the largest in-group within its group; its identity is formed by common views on problems and the cognitive style strategy used to solve them. As the largest group with 'cognitive cohesion', it has power. It forms a problem-solving 'comfort zone' or consensus group of shared strategy. It is also likely to contain the majority of the group's leaders; their presence adds yet more power to this subset, giving rise to an influence formula: The power of number (N) times the power of status (S) equals cognitive climate, or, in notation form:

$$N^p \times S^p = C^c$$

This notion of climates of change is to be explored next.

CLIMATES OF CHANGE

Organisational climate

Climate is a concept that covers a succession of enveloping, interrelated layers of concepts, each with a distinguishing name. The term, at the outer layer and in its broadest meaning, is usually called 'culture'. Payne & Pugh, in their useful schema (1976; Figure 11), set 'organisational climate' into a wider context, referred to as the 'wider economic and cultural environment' and to an inner layer, referred to as the 'individual's immediate environment'. This implies that each individual perceives a unique personal environment whilst contributing to and being influenced by the whole system. For Payne & Pugh the economic-cum-cultural concept is composed of the economic, political, and (wider) social macrosystems. These in turn envelope succeeding layers of concept clusters of which organisational climate is one; others are organisational context, organisational structure, the immediate work group[81], and the individual. The schema does not clearly relate these layers but the clear assumption is that they all interact. The economic system, to take one example of influence, may directly stimulate the development of a technology; just as, in turn, technology, as an element in organisational context, may strongly influence the type of authority system chosen (Woodward, 1965).

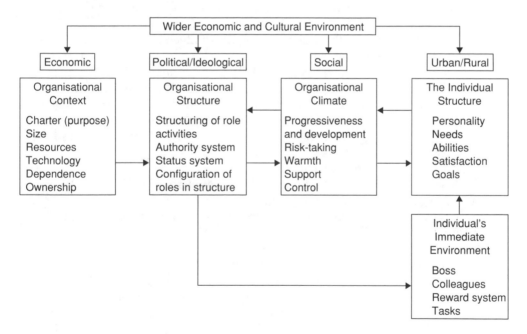

Figure 11 Payne & Pugh's climate schema. Reprinted by permission of Professor Roy Payne.

81 Other groups that would appear at this level would be the family, but many of these terms overlap –
  e.g., over many millennia the family group and the work group were nearly synonymous concepts.

The social system, to take a second example, influences individuals' contributions to the group's belief system, one element of which could be the notion of 'progressiveness', which in turn could encourage those individuals, especially those who are leaders, also to experiment with alternative forms of authority systems (Burns & Stalker, 1961). All the while, political concepts in Payne & Pugh's wider society may incline individuals to value one authority system over another. Each of these variables, then, can interact directly with another, act indirectly through others, or be itself an intervening variable. All the systems in Payne & Pugh's model are man-made and individuals must, therefore, be the critical elements within them. No explanatory theory should underestimate the power of these systems to affect individuals, or the intractable nature of some variables. If it is accepted that the individual is the all-pervasive influence, then the range of individuals' characteristic cognitive styles is a primary source of influence on all the factors in this model. Once the systems exist, the individual alone may have little impact on the large, more stable elements, as it is also true that the organisation sets limits and influences people's behaviour. The extent of influence any individual has is as a function of several variables:

- the nature of the climate (the more the climate is dominated by operations that are being carried out by the individual, the more the individual has influence);
- the number of others involved (the more there are, the less impact any individual has);
- the distance from the core of the consensus group (the closer the more influence);
- the salience or power of the individual (e.g., through leadership).

The climate within which the individual has least influence is culture. For culture, the consensus is conceived as large and the core as remote and formed over long periods of time, while its content is generally that of the meaning of the elements it contains. This seems more *descriptive* (and explanatory of internal relationships of notions held) and less *prescriptive* on any particular individual, unlike the climate of a work group. In his general review of the literature, Denison (1996) argues that, in comparison to the above definition of culture, climate is usually conceived as being:

- smaller in the extent of its territory;
- closer set to the individual (although there are numerous layers within layers, as, say, in huge international companies); and
- more concerned with particular operations that have direct, immediate, interactive effect on individuals.

These smaller groups, individually and more so collectively, are able to affect climate in their turn in their interaction with the wider, more remote groups – it is they who interpret it within and to themselves. In turn, through the medium of more immediate, intimate, small group climate, culture and the wider climates need to be interpreted by the individual. These close groups act as the immediate structure within which the individual operates, 'policing' the wider climate and culture structures through the feedback they dispense, exerting both social reward (for conforming) and punishment (when transgressing).

Transmission of information and interpretation of the meanings attached can be by wholly impersonal means, but books and policy papers cannot enforce rules;

only people can. Denison (1996) notes that one group of theorists argue that only some people create the climate even if all are affected by it, while other authors accept that all, to a greater or lesser extent, influence their own climate. Denison argues that the followers of the Lewinian field theory suppose that within a climate there are some who are its 'agents' and many who are its 'subjects', and explains that: 'the agents of an organisational system, such as management, are often assumed, but seldom studied directly. They create the climate that others work in. The subjects of that system, most often employees, workers, or subordinates, are the primary objects of study. They work within the climate, but they do not create it.' Presumably, one set of 'they' do not have much, if any, influence within the climate, the other set of 'they' do, a view that is readily shared in sociology and politics when describing the helplessness of individuals compared to 'inevitable' trends of 'progress' and the action of elites and governments. Perhaps the best way of reconciling these two views is that they may fall on a continuum of operation, one spot being a more exact representation than another in a particular place and time. There may be underlying pressures which ensure that the wider consensus cannot be ignored for long with impunity. 'In contrast to the proponents of the Lewinian logic who [. . .] tend to assume that individuals are either subjects or agents of a social system, users of the symbolic interaction perspective (Mead, 1934) and the social construction perspective (Berger & Luckmann, 1967) underlying the organisational culture literature assume that the individual cannot be analytically separated from the environment and that the members of social systems are best regarded as being agents and subjects simultaneously. Thus, rather confusingly, social context is regarded as both the medium and the outcome of social interaction. Furthermore, this literature often defines the primary topic of interest as the recursive dynamics between the individual and the system (Giddens, 1979; Riley, 1983; Lave & Wenger, 1990) rather than the impact of the system on its members' (Denison, 1996). This last paragraph is not, admittedly, easy reading, but the message is clear enough: do all who partake of a climate influence it or not?

A-I theory has taken the position of Lewin (1951) that person, environment, and behaviour can be separated analytically, the better to understand their interaction. However, person is redefined as personality that influences behaviour, with environment as a vital, principal source of feedback. What is rejected is that within a climate some members are agents and some subjects. The view on this point is closer to that taken by Berger & Luckmann (and this book): Everyone is both an agent and a subject, although not necessarily equally, all the time, on every issue. Earlier, during the discussion on the need for personal cognitive construct, the sources were seen to lie in the very nature of the problem-solving brain and its formation of concepts. In the social field there was recourse to the work of Kuhn (1970) and his notion of paradigms. The paradigm represents a social type of structure that was treated as a subculture because Kuhn used it as a structure applicable to the way professional scientists perceive the ideal way of collaborating, which creates a 'cognitive climate' for the individual. This sets Kuhn's notion within the wider theory of Berger & Luckmann without internal contradiction.

It is clear that a whole range of factors needs to be considered to understand climate, including the influence of people's cognitive style and its aggregation into cognitive climate. There are three matters of specific interest in this section relating to the influence of the individual in specific circumstances:

- the individual whose contribution is seen as immediately needed (exerting power: a particular individual in a matching situation);
- either as part of the consensus group (an AC^2 exerting power: individual × number) or not (an AC^3 as a lone individual: individual × N of subset);
- or as a leader (exerting power: individual × status).

Aspects of personality have long been, at least implicitly, associated in the literature with both cognitive style and organisational climate. More explicitly, in a review of organisational behaviour, Schneider (1985, p. 589) noted: 'a development in leadership and management has been a renewed focus on traits as correlates of effectiveness. The newer efforts focus on cognitive complexity or cognitive style . . . defined as the way people process and evaluate information.' Although this is rather a narrow view of cognitive style, it fits well into the wider view of A-I theory. The interest in cognitive style was generated in the early studies on climate because of a widespread supposition that one of its main effects is that people may be more satisfied and effective if they are working in conditions that are compatible with their cognitive personality style (Goodenough, 1985). One key area of compatibility for Goodenough is between the problem-solving style and the job characteristics produced by the technology of the work processes being performed. Technology has been defined as the array of techniques employed by an organisation and its subunits to transform inputs into outputs (Perrow, 1967; Hunt, 1970). It has been related to variables at both the organisational (Woodward, 1965; Hickson et al., 1969; Mohr, 1971) and individual (Trist & Bamforth, 1951; Cooper & Foster, 1971) levels of analysis. These sociotechnical theorists have argued that technology affects individual behaviour. This link was, however, thought best seen through function differences (e.g., production or marketing) or differences in organisational structure. The rationale for suggesting different functional specialisations is because they use different technologies in achieving work goals, which in turn are reflected in differences of job characteristics. For example, Forbes (1975) analysed various functional specialisations and placed them on a continuum representative of the degree to which technology related to varying degrees of uncertainty. Having done so, the use of formal rules and authority was demonstrated to decrease from finance/accounting, through production, engineering, marketing, and sales, to personnel and training, thus providing support for the validity of the hypothesis that job characteristics represent crucial variables in linking technology with individual behaviour. A-I mean scores derived from samples of people in different jobs are also expected to vary predictably (Tables J & K, Appendix 6) – the old hypothesis is now tested by measurement.

Perrow (1967) and Pierce (1984) were interested in the way that the perceived aspects of technology (routine versus nonroutine) result in organisational structures such as those described by Burns & Stalker (1961) as 'mechanistic' or 'organic'. Other research has generally focused on changes to or from batch, mass, or process technologies and the effects of such changes on job characteristics (Woodward, 1965; Billings et al., 1977). Woodward found that in batch production technologies decision making was more likely to be directive, but in continuous processing technologies there was greater participation. These studies suggest that there is a link between technology and job characteristics, just as other studies found great consistency in KAI mean scores from different job samples, in different studies, irrespective of national culture (Tullett, 1997). However, job function as an intervening concept has received less direct attention than it deserves (see Slocum & Sims, 1980), and more needs to be known. On the other hand, the closely related relationship between job characteristics and individual behaviour has been more extensively researched.

Much of the earlier work investigating job characteristics focused on such variables as task variety (Cooper & Foster, 1971) as a determinant of employee motivation, satisfaction, and performance (Hackman & Lawler, 1971; Brief & Aldag, 1975). Motivation has often been studied in the context of the development of the job characteristics model of task design (Hackman & Oldham, 1975, 1976; Roberts & Glick, 1981; Kiggundu, 1983). Other useful explorations involving organisational process and performance behaviour were initiated by Lawler et al. (1973) and, for job satisfaction, Schneider & Snyder (1975). Later work, such as that of Hannaway (1985), found initiating and search behaviour to be influenced by the degree of task certainty. These studies offer substantial support to the notion that relationships exist between the variables of technology, organisational process, function, job characteristics, and individual behaviour. Such relationships, in turn, lend support to a growing view that these variables conglomerate into what is generally described, in the literature, as organisational climate, confidently assumed to impinge directly upon individual behaviour. The variables comprising the climate variable need to be understood and interpreted by each individual as a basis for appropriate behaviour to ensure the desired feedback. This is a short step from setting out to demonstrate that a group-derived consensus on the interpretations of all the above variables could result from each individual in the group helping to create a collective interpretation of what amounts to organisational climate. As noted above, Goodenough (1985) introduced cognitive style as a core concept into this notion of a general social environment; a step foreshadowed by work that envisaged cognitive style as a critical intervening variable in work performance (Robey & Taggart, 1981; Robertson, 1985). In A-I theory it is individuals who set climate because institutions do not think and so cannot impinge on anyone. It must be individuals, influencing their immediate groups, who set up and legitimise social structures such as organisational climate. In this everyone has a share.

The central argument of this section is that part of the formation of culture and organisational climate (or any social guiding structure) stems from a consensus group sharing a very similar cognitive style. The argument is that the patterns are set as each person problem solves and each then contributes to common knowledge and experience, outlooks, and evaluation of outcomes, etc., contributing to a consensus view of shared reality. Underlining this common view of reality are all the common processes relating to problem solving, one of which is cognitive style – the characteristic way individuals interpret the conglomerate of variables just described, which over time, within a successful and cohesive group, becomes a cognitive climate. This consensus affects all problem solving within the group, but especially those elements that are critical to the group's continued survival and success. In turn, these views will affect some of the behaviour associated with the operation or 'management' of the group and its problems. For example, it operates by a tendency to emphasise certain job characteristics to which the individual's preferred style is most attuned, and by delegating others, to which the individual's style is less attuned, to other people. It is assumed that the viewpoint of the 'consensus group' plays a key role in the interpretation of the job characteristics, viz.:

- the degree and direction of change within the company;
- the type of precipitating event to which most attention is paid (those emanating from 'within' the system a opposed to those emanating from 'without'); and
- the extent of tolerance of alternative viewpoints within the group.

Since if it is the individual, interacting and generally collaborating with others, who is the prime initial source of all climate, all other structures that envelope climate, such as culture, are a reflection of the individual members and their cognitive processes[82].

COGNITIVE CLIMATE

Throughout this book, a contention is that if it is only individuals who think, all human constructs are reflections of the individual problem-solving process. If cognitive style is an element in an individual's problem-solving process, it will play the same role in the same way within a group. A group forms and stays intact because it is of problem-solving use to the individuals in it – not necessarily equally or for exactly the same reasons, but by having a sufficient identity of common aims. This is true when the rewards for staying exceed those for leaving or the punishment for leaving is not worth risking. Additionally, small groups tend to have specialised aims and, over long periods, find that the principal problems they need to solve can be resolved more readily by either a more adaptive or a more innovative style, creating a generally shared recognition of a 'desired' cognitive climate. Within this climate, diversity is tolerated either because the individuals possessing it can accommodate (cope) often enough to satisfy the others in the group or because the diversity is found to be of advantage to all parties. It has been argued that, over time, the composition of groups will alter; the mean of the style of the group will reflect the mean of the style of the largest number and the style required to solve the problems that are perceived as being of greatest importance to the group. In this sense, climate is a structure that both facilitates problem solving and limits the options readily available; in this regard it applies to the understanding of groups just as to the individual. There should be evidence that climate is a structure useful to the survival of the group, and this is shown by the stability of the mean over time and event. There should also be evidence that the limits imposed by any structure give rise in individuals to feelings of pressure for conformity, and this should be evident in the degree of coping behaviour needed and its predictably variable cost to different individuals in the group. Both sets of supporting evidence are reviewed below.

It has already been shown that occupational groups tend to have skewed KAI distributions and that the direction of their mean displacements is expected according to whether the demands of the job, in the researcher's view, are more suited to an adaptive or innovative style. This pattern is also noted in samples from different

---

82 The distinction in the literature between culture and climate is not clear or consistent. One suggestion is that culture might be described as the structure that gives understanding to why the various elements in the social process are thought, by individuals, to work in relation to each other in the way they do. This is a macro understanding of the whole operation, whereas the lesser pervasive climates give operational detail within this grander structure, as well as more prescriptive pressure on individuals.

countries using KAIs in different languages. These predictable variations can be contrasted to the general population samples, also drawn from various countries, using KAIs in various languages; general populations deal with so wide an array of problems that narrow specialisation in problem solving is a luxury that its members cannot afford. The same goes for large groups, which cover a wide range of differing specialisms, as both Kirton (1980) and Foxall (1986b) noted; see also Table L analysing engineering groups. Table K shows five sets of data for 'managers in general' and four sets of data for 'teachers in general', for which the means hover around that of the general population. In addition, they contain two studies of nurses and two of samples of 'work groups', all made up wholly of women, with means that reflect closely the female general population mean[83].

Groups such as bankers, accountants and those involved in production, who are largely required to work in a system within which the answers to problems can be found, tend to be more adaptive (Kirton, 1980; Thomson, 1980; Kirton & Pender, 1982; Hayward & Everett, 1983; Gul, 1986; Foxall, 1986a; Holland, 1987; Gryskiewicz et al., 1987). Where high levels of safety are involved, adaptive means are also expected; the same is true of general medical practitioners (Salisbury et al., 1998). Conversely, the group mean tends to be innovative where employees are required to work in an environment that embodies more than one system (e.g., some quality control units can consist of both monitoring and negotiating) or to act as an interface between systems (e.g., personnel in finance must operate within the company paradigm and relevant outside financial institutions' paradigms). Research has shown employees in R&D, planning, personnel and marketing to be on the innovative side of the general population mean (Keller & Holland, 1978a; Kirton, 1980; Thomson, 1980; Kirton & Pender, 1982; Lowe & Taylor, 1986; Foxall, 1986a; Gryskiewicz et al., 1987).

The evidence for the stability of cognitive style has already been presented. It seems largely unaffected by age, culture, job, or training. Cognitive climate is made up of a large homogeneous group clustered round the mean of a group, usually reinforced by containing a disproportionate amount of the group's leaders. The question arises: Will this mean change and, if so, how? One factor that seems ruled out, theoretically and empirically, is that all or many of the existing members will, under the pressure of changing circumstances, change their personal preferred mode. There are two other ways on offer. The first is coping behaviour on the part of many for an extended period; this is certainly possible, as every reader must have experienced at some time. To maintain high levels of coping behaviour needs insight into the need to do so backed by the vision of high rewards (or the fear of high penalties). But if the requirement on many individuals for change increases and is sustained over the long term, the cost may be perceived as too high: Selective turnover and replacement is the second way out. As some leave, cashing whatever gains they can, who will take their place? Will it be those like them or those more attuned to the now perceived required climate? The latter is the norm and a number of studies support this conclusion. Clues on how the cognitive climate facilitates change in group composition turned up early in work on A-I theory; selective recruitment (including self-selection) and turnover

---

83 A number of studies show that even skewed groups may be composed of distinctly different subsets (e.g., Gul, 1986; Foxall, 1986b; Gryskiewicz et al., 1987).

that accounted for both stability of group means and climate profile and the changes to it, when circumstances disturbed the pattern of current events.

In an early study, Kirton (1980) noted that adaptors and innovators perceived the same climate as more and less turbulent, respectively. It was at once assumed that this could be a factor in influencing behaviour, such as increasing one's effort to appear conforming or leaving, or, alternatively, putting pressure on others to conform or leave. Kirton & Pender (1982) analysed 15 independent studies involving nearly 2400 subjects, from the USA, UK, and Singapore. The first conclusion was that mean KAI scores are more innovative for occupational groups that deal with more numerous and less rigid paradigms, and more adaptive for the opposite type. The second finding looked at the mean scores of managers on courses, comparing those of managers who had made a personal decision to come with those who had been sent. The volunteers were more innovative on those courses considered to deal with general subjects. The notion emerges that people responded to climates differently. This was first studied by Everett (1982; Hayward & Everett, 1983) who, as reported earlier, got permission to set up a money-making unit in a local government authority. This was a novelty and, not surprisingly, when he administered the KAI to his new employees he found that the mean of these new recruits was innovative. However, the staff of the department within which it was operating, all of whom had been in post for, on average, 5 years or more, yielded an adaptive mean. When the new unit showed a record of persistent success, to the surprise of many of the department's other managers, the authority decided to accept it as a permanent addition to the department and to accept its staff as permanent employees. In exchange, the authority insisted that they now conformed to the usual rules and regulations. This demand changed the climate of the group; the new employees were expecting change but, rather than cope, a third left over a relatively short time (see Table 4).

Holland et al. (1991) reported results from a pharmaceutical company that add further general support both to the change of personnel coming about from pressures exerted by climate and to changes of climate coming about from selective changes of personnel. They found that recruitment policy can, on occasion, produce a new entrant group mean that is different from that obtained from the current establishment. In this case it was more innovative and this occurred because the establishment were 'aided' in their recruitment process by a personnel department. Evidence here and from other studies showed that personnel department staff tend to have innovative means of about a half standard deviation from the mean (circa 105). So the recruiting group were selecting those in their image and not in the image of the employing group. Unfortunately, the losses among these new staff showed a disproportionate number of innovators leaving. In the same company there were a small number of departments that had won a political battle and were allowed to refuse the help of personnel department recruitment advisors, on the grounds that their work was 'too technical to be understood by laymen'. The people recruited into these departments had means almost identical to the established group and their losses were fewer and showed no skew. This work also confirms common belief that people tend to recruit (admire, get on with) people like them. The further clear implication is that if a 'diversity' – in this case a noticeably different problem-solving style – is inserted into a group, selective (including self-selective) turnover will progressively reduce the amount of diversity unless it is seen to be valued by those making up the cognitive climate.

Table 8 Interactive fit of person and climate

Climate	Person	
	Adaptor	*Innovator*
Adaptive	Easier	Harder
Innovative	Hard	Easy

The study by Thomson (1985), reported earlier, sheds light on possible reasons why the 'cognitive deviant', the unhappy AC[3], may want to leave the organisation. Her sample of Singaporean (ethnic Chinese, English-speaking) executives working in Western multinational companies showed that those who reported themselves as not-fitting also reported that they were planning to leave the organisation. The measure of 'non-fit' was based on questions that asked them if they thought their colleagues empathised with their problems at work. Although innovators are more likely to change jobs than adaptors and innovators are much more likely to change function (i.e., move from accounts to marketing) than adaptors (as Foxall had reported), it was adaptors who reported themselves as more ready to leave if they felt in 'non-fit'. (The notion of adaption being in non-fit is an oxymoron.) This study confirms the relationship between climate fit and discomfort – people who feel that they are not in climate fit may also be liable to feel that their problems are not understood and will want to leave the climate. Their loss will diminish the diversity of the group – if this loss is not desired, the cognitive gap that exists needs to be tackled by the group. Flegg (private communication, 1989) reported, in a consultancy-research programme involving over 600 apprentices in a training department of a multinational company, that results showed that the best predictor of whether individuals would eventually pass was their score on the R (rule/group conformity) factor score of KAI. The more adaptive were more likely to succeed in this adaptive environment. Consultants, in discussing this work, confirm that in their experience adaptors operate more comfortably in adaptive climates and innovators in innovative climates. From these discussions Table 8 has been speculatively constructed.

The smallest groups

The smallest group is just two people. The evidence accumulating from research and practice suggests that the climate in such small groups has much the same effects on individuals as that in larger ones. There is the same need for 2 people as for 10,000 to be able to find a common aim as a basis for collaboration – their Problem A. Given this, they may well acquire the insight and develop the incentive to solve their inevitable spin-off Problems B. Insight is critical, as the differences between them need to be seen as mutually useful and not irritations that can be temporarily overlooked. Practitioners in marriage guidance, using KAI as a means of explaining unchangeable differences that may be useful if well managed, are adamant that it is not lust that keeps a pair together as much as mutual respect and growing interdependence on each others 'strengths' and 'weaknesses' in different situations. There have been many instances in history of the ways pairs operate, in this regard. The great musical combination of Gilbert and Sullivan, in Victorian times, became famous both for their success and for the mounting difficulty of getting on with each other. Despite the fame and wealth that was the result of their collaboration, their respect for each other declined, which seems to have been the key to the friction between them.

Other disparate pairs have also had spectacular success, at least for a while, such as the First World War German generals, Hindenburg and Ludendorff. They were different in a number of ways: Hindenburg came from Prussian nobility and was an exemplar of its paradigm; Ludendorff was not noble, Prussian, or anyone's exemplar. The pair faced a problem of needing to slow down the advancing Russians in East Prussia to give their high command a chance of winning the war in the West against Britain and France, before turning eastwards in overwhelming force. Ludendorff, as chief of staff, devised a daring plan of using the railway system to transfer the bulk of their troops facing the Russian army on their left wing, adding most of them to the troops facing their right wing, and then winning a crushing victory before the Russians detected the plan. This required the one Russian wing to be held by a mere screen of German troops until such time as victory allowed the screen to be massively reinforced in their turn. Such a plan was not entirely new; millennia earlier the Romans used the precise tactic in the last battle against Hannibal in Italy, with great success. The difference was that 20th-century armies were very much larger and needed masses of heavy equipment and stores. The only slender means of movement was the relatively new railway system, hitherto used by the military merely for support and supply. Because Hindenburg supported the plan wholeheartedly, resistance to it did not seriously materialise, and this innovative venture was planned and executed with brilliant adaptive efficiency by the General Staff. When the war ended, however, so did the partnership, with Hindenburg becoming President of Germany and with Ludendorff disappearing into out-group obscurity. An example of another pair of famous generals, who actually fought each other, is that of Napoleon and Wellington. Napoleon was famous (or notorious) for making significant changes to any system that seriously interested him, including war, government finance, politics, and law; he changed structures in order to solve his problems (e.g., Cronin, 1994, pp. 195–209; Barnett, 1997). As Glover (1968) points out, very different was: 'the key to Wellington's success. The organisation of [his] army was chaotic, the men recruited from "the scum of the earth", the officers of infantry and cavalry were untrained and the generals inadequate. These factors were immutable. Any field commander who devoted his energies to trying to bring the whole anachronistic agglomeration into some supposedly logical framework would have been defeated by the politicians, the civil servants, public opinion and, for the most part, his professional colleagues long before he could have brought his troops within range of the enemy . . . [Wellington] was not an innovator. In tactics, for example, he devised nothing new. He took what was best from the various schools of tactical thought current in his day and welded it into a combination which proved unbeatable' (p. 227). Wellington changed, by improving, every system that concerned him. In war they were mainly training, discipline, tactics, and supply[84]. He played a considerable part in his country being on the winning side. He made the same kind of improvements in government as minister and prime minister.

---

84 He also grumbled like an adaptor: 'Nobody in the British army ever reads a regulation or an order as if it were to be a guide to his conduct, or in any other manner than as an amusing novel' (Glover, ibid. p. 231).

Another disparate pair, this time of American astronomers at the beginning of the previous century, were Lowell and Slipher, the man he appointed, and who subsequently became his successor, at the Lowell Observatory. Gribben (1998) writes that: 'Lowell's achievements were real and many.' They included the prediction that a new planet (later named Pluto) existed and where it might be found. However, he also was carried away with the notion that life existed on Mars: 'reporting not only canals but oases and clear signs of vegetation to an eager world [. . .] Slipher was in many ways the antithesis of Lowell. Where Lowell was a flamboyant extrovert eager to jump to conclusions, Slipher was quiet and methodical, painstaking, and never willing to announce his discoveries until he had dotted his *is* and crossed his *ts*. The difference in their characters was so marked that it has been suggested that Lowell, aware of his own strengths and weaknesses, deliberately picked Slipher to join the team at the Lowell Observatory to provide the necessary ballast to Lowell's own impulsiveness' (from p. 74). Among Slipher's contributions, Gribben lists his outstanding work on the measurement of the Doppler shift in the light from the Andromeda Nebula, which assisted the development of the theory of the existence of background radiation throughout the universe. He also initiated the research that found the planet Pluto, the culmination to Lowell's own achievements, after the latter's death. These examples show how some pairs can combine successfully by contributing their personal style to the partnership. Alone they are more limited or unsuccessful, although the strains of collaboration can be great.

Conclusion

A foundation on which this chapter rests is that the cognitive style of individuals is stable and can only be varied, at a price, by coping behaviour. This stability has been generally accepted in the earlier literature, e.g., Messick (1976) and Goldstein & Blackman (1981), and is well supported in A-I work. Additionally, this strongly held underlying preferred style is not altered, even by direct training, as Kagan & Kogan (1970) noted; a finding also well supported in A-I literature, e.g., by Watts (1985), Goldsmith & Kerr (1991), and Murdock et al. (1993). Another foundation assumption is that although KAI scores are expected (and have been found) to distribute normally in the general population (or similar large, widely drawn samples), more homogeneous groups whose members deal with a narrower range of shared problems will be skewed in a readily predictable direction. However, even from the first study it was also noted that the range of scores of quite small groups remained wide, whichever the direction of the skew. The assumption that all people are creative was followed by the assumption that everyone is an agent of change (AC[1]). When collaborating with others, the agent of change notation divides into membership of an AC[2] subgroup or an AC[3] subgroup. Such membership is socially determined: whether or not the person in question is part of the group whose style is in close accord with the style of the principal problems that face the group. In many cases the group was formed with the express intention of solving a particular class of problem and, if its members succeed and the group continues to exist, the present skew in the group's mean style will continue largely unaltered. It will continue to do so as long as the nature of the main problem does not change. However, another assumption made is that all the people within a group (however large the group) contribute to its climate, although they do not necessarily do so equally, at all times, in all circumstances. Therefore, membership of a group makes each individual both an agent in setting or fine-tuning the climate and a subject of it. So, the humblest subject of the most demanding tyrant backed by the most ferocious Praetorian Guard contributes to climate – though not much, admittedly. However, every tyrant knows that the oppressed masses need to be constantly watched, as indeed does every member of the Praetorian Guard. The expenditure of cognitive and physical effort of this group on Problem B is a significant element in such prevailing climate – so the least powerful do contribute significantly, if there are enough of them. The system survives while the supporting paradigm does (Problem A) and the rewards for conforming (Problem B) continue to exceed the cost of the penalties for desertion or revolt.

The breadth of the range of the AC^2 role seems to be set at barely over half a standard deviation from the mean of the group. Beyond this range research showed that more work pressure is reported. AC^2s, then, represent a consensus group and, therefore, an essential core of climate, which consists of about 40% of the membership. Looked at another way, in most skewed groups the amount of style diversity available exceeds, in the gross number of individuals, the consensus group by some 50% (40% against 60%). This leads to two obvious questions that need some sort of answer: How does the skew remain stable and how does the diversity get there and survive over long periods with only minor adjustment? There seem to be three ways that AC^3 subgroups can be composed:

- (positive) those who, whether selected deliberately or by accident, have found or created a niche that suits them, in which they offer a particular role and expertise that is acceptable to the group;
- (neutral) temporary members, who may have been recruited in error and who will rectify this by leaving; there are also those who are in transit, e.g., undergoing training in a succession of departments – they may well play down their diversity;
- (negative) those who are in a state of virtual high and permanent coping behaviour in order to remain, at varying degrees of discomfort, in the group (i.e., the perceived rewards for staying or the penalties for leaving are currently being perceived as higher than cost).

It is assumed that group cognitive style consensus (or cognitive climate) is part of the wider organisational climate, itself a part of a wider, general culture. Another part in the assumption is that cognitive climate impinges on individuals, as do other elements of organisational climate. Individuals feel a pressure to conform to the climate guideline structure, or to show that any variation is at worst harmless (and the butt of amiable jokes, which acceptably underline the difference without hurt) or, at best, is positively useful to those typifying the climate.

Research confirms that groups of similar homogeneity (i.e., groups with similar problem-solving needs) will have predictably similar (expected) mean scores on KAI. This occurs because of selective recruitment or selective turnover unless new diversity is found welcome. Finally, cognitive gap needs to be closed one way or another, but this is not always done wisely:

- by denial: the gap between the way the problem needs to be solved and the way the person (or persons) prefers it to be done is ignored;

- inefficiently: continuing to struggle (using persistent coping behaviour) because the diversity is being seen as more threatening than useful;
- by avoidance: the problem can be downgraded in importance or there can be an attempt to shift locality or target, so as not to confront it;
- by specialisation: limiting activities to what can be done readily and well (e.g., subcontracting or selling an ill-fitting element).
- by added diversity: acquiring a more diversified team and accepting the added cost of diversity against an even higher return.

How these issues are managed is a major topic in itself.

LEADERS AND BRIDGERS

In the discussion on agents of change, it was argued that in successful established groups, a significant portion of the leadership are likely to be found in the consensus (AC^2) subgroup. The reason for this expectation is that the skew of the group as a whole has occurred in response to the nature of the bulk of the problems the group faces, especially those that are most critical to group survival. Leadership is where the bulk of the shot and shell are landing, so its task (irrespective of the type of leadership – democratic, autocratic, charismatic – or in whatever combination or blend, at whatever time or sequence) is likely, in established successful groups, to reflect the main problem-solving needs of its group. So, between them, the AC^2 group and the leaders in amongst its members make up the cognitive climate. Bringing about change is easier for an AC^2 than for an AC^3, by being able to operate within the majority-core of the group, especially if the bulk of the leadership is also AC^2. This state can be defined as 'organisational fit'. On the other hand, for groups that are large enough, there is a need for a minority of the leadership to belong to the AC^3 grouping to ensure a constant leading presence in other critical areas so as to deal with a varied, complex, and challenging environment. The leadership needs to be a diverse sub-group[85] whose members need to collaborate, both respecting and making best use of their internal differences, just as in the wider group that they lead. Many consultants earn a living helping groups who fail in these respects.

All group activities, including those of leadership, are founded on the way an individual thinks. How does one 'lead' oneself? As suggested in the cognitive function schema (Figure 1), cognitive affect is the 'department' that is constantly in the process of sorting out a vast array of input and deciding what is to be acted on and with what degree of priority. What is known about the problem to be solved and the means of achieving this end (with recourse to cognitive resource)? What is the strategic aim of the resolution and what are the limits to be placed on its achievement? What detailed instruction is needed to initiate action in cognitive effect – planning the steps of resolution? What feedback is expected from the environment? Even with just this selection of subproblems to solve as part of the package, the process sounds just what management is all about. Leadership behaviour is the public outcome of the principal function of cognitive affect made conscious and collaborative.

85 Hence the pointless search for the ideal leader, as was discussed above.

The biological and psychological value of any group is that, because of its existence, its members solve more problems, more readily, than they can as individuals. Therefore, one of the crucial functions of leadership is to create an effective team in which every member is used to best effect. Raising the group's level of acceptance of useful diversity is one of the first steps in the process of achieving group cohesion founded on mutual respect. Such a group can cope with large amounts of internal disagreement and dissent in the pursuit of concurrence for a group's own ultimate good, which becomes a divisive threat only when it turns to conflict. At moments when it can afford the time to explore and disagree, it would be wise to do so. In times of crises there is less tolerance for either of these necessary pursuits; the devil's advocate is liable to be burnt at the stake. This is a problem for managers who pride themselves as survivors of constant crises as their method of management; the team's members need to have a good appreciation when to follow the looser or the tighter path, for the mutual good of its members. A-I theory may have a particular use here, for when expounded to a group it may increase each member's insight into the value of cognitive (and, by implication, other) diversity. Insight might then lead to tolerance of such useful diversity. Increased tolerance has a good chance of improving collaboration within the group, which in its turn could lead to greater success. That need not be the end; it could be the beginning of a spiral of increased cohesion and effective working. Interestingly, experience in the field suggests that a group whose integration is founded on mutual respect can tolerate quite strongly argued differences of opinion within it without undermining its integrity. Less cohesive groups avoid such confrontation as being potentially too damaging, either by ignoring AC³s or by ignoring all or part of the problem – or even both. To repeat a point made earlier; when people collaborate to solve a problem, they immediately acquire two: Problem A, the reason for the formation of the group, and Problem B, how best to manage each other to achieve the solution of Problem A. The more effective the resolution of Problem B, the more surely Problem A can be solved effectively as well.

> **One part of the definition of a good leader is:**
>
> - **the ability to make good use of a member**
> - **very different both from the leader and from the group mode**
> - **for the benefit of the whole group.**

One of the themes of this book is that all human social activities are a reflection of the individual human's brain. The way it is constructed and the innate way that it operates leads it to acquire a sense of self and of reality, which in turn provides the structure of understanding into which feedback from its problem solving will increase its grasp of reality. The team must mirror this – acquiring an identity of common purpose and a shared understanding of its environment and the problems that emerge from it. In the problem-solving schema, therefore, cognitive affect is the 'department' that evaluates the competing pressures of a great array (in number and diversity) of incoming stimuli and determines what to respond to, for what purpose; just as leadership has these tasks in the community. In mirroring the function of cognitive affect, it has to get the group to take into account both emotion and reason; the influences of attitudes, beliefs, and other cognitive guidelines, whilst making use of whatever resource is available. The aim of a possible solution to the problem selected must take account of the possible response from the environment. Leadership has to arrive at a collectively agreed course of action, behind which is the appropriate motive (reflecting the expected intensity and persistence of required effort) and then to transmit and delegate these prioritised orders to the planning function for implementation. Like the brain's activities, the leadership's tasks are never done; it has then to await feedback from the resulting behaviour so that subsequent learning and fine-tuning can occur. Leadership needs to do what the individual brain does by construction, but overtly, collaboratively with others, and by learning. The individual, for instance, has had to learn how to anticipate unhelpful feedback by attending to warnings of precipitating events that are not within the natural style (using coping behaviour). The leader also needs to learn to attend to and evaluate warnings of precipitating events that are causing alarm to 'dissimilar' others. This poses difficult questions: Can one rely on these warnings from others being truly dangerous and so act on them despite one's own bias? To what extent are these warnings, which are coming from others as biased as oneself but in another direction, just as likely to be wrong as right? There are no simple answers, only the certainty that if problems are difficult when posed they are surely insoluble if unseen or left unaddressed. The members of a group have to solve these kinds of problem collaboratively, just as they have to do as individuals, only more openly, more laboriously, and more slowly – but hopefully better than any of the group's members could do alone. Still remaining with the scenario of the leader being an AC^2, it is now useful to explore another group resource in maintaining cohesion; the role of bridger, who might also be a leader or a prime support to leadership.

One of the most difficult strategies that a leader needs to learn is that there is more pay-off in delegating to a person not like themself – to ensure the widest use of diversity and so that this diversity can have the most freedom to exploit its own (different) attributes unhampered by close, critical control. But all of us find that it is easier to trust those like us, especially if the successful execution of this task is vital to our well-being. But then, neither successful leadership nor successful delegation is easy to learn or execute – especially under personal pressure.

Bridgers

To concentrate first on bridging *within* a team: Bridging is reaching out to people in the team and helping them to be part of it so that they may contribute even if their contribution is outside mainstream, as for any AC^3. Those who are not leaders can play this bridging role, although the leaders carry the main responsibility for this role to be done well within the team. Bridgers, like good leaders, play a significant role in group cohesion and thus to the diminution of Problem B, permitting added focus on Problem A. Companies sometimes use skilled people as roving 'bridgers'. Having an expert about is always useful, but bridging should be regarded as a task, like quality control, which is a concern for anyone in the team who can help, rather than only as a specialised function. The expert's role can then be to reinforce those who are willing to bridge – a policy which makes sure that everyone in the team is concerned with its members working well together. Experience shows that most people can help; for instance, many women are particularly interested in relationships between people; bridging skills can be added to this interest. Older men and women with wide experience have a fund of knowledge that can often be deployed in characteristically different ways, each being valuable in different situations. The skill of leaders is to identify, encourage, and arrange added training for the different potential talents and interests of different people in the group for mutual benefit. In short, the job of leaders is to make the best use of the diversity available to them.

There are two forms of 'cognitive gap' that need to be bridged. They are:

*   the distance between one's preferred style and the behaviour that appears to be needed in some situation;
*   the distance in a social interaction, between the preferred styles of: (a) two people, (b) a person and a group, or (c) two groups.

The magnitude of the gaps that are noticeable, that need some careful attention, or that are a constant challenge may not be very different in either of these conditions. Earlier it was noted that 10 KAI points difference between two people is a difference that is just noticeable to them and to others who know them well. Research also shows that a gap of about 20 points requires effort by the user to ensure close accord between them. One or both individuals of a pair 20 points or more apart, are going to need increasing amounts of coping behaviour, at least from time to time, to continue to form a smoothly operating team.

In this diagram, the gap between the isolated person on the right and the others in the group could cause problems, even though all five could locate on the same side of the mid-point of the scale (all can be adaptors or innovators[86]). It is the size of the gap that matters. When the gap is one of 30 or more points, evidence accumulates that the effort required for successful coping behaviour rises (increasingly steeply; possibly even exponentially) with the increasing size of the gap. It is additionally more difficult when the gap lies between two people of whom one is the boss, or when the rewards and penalties for success or failure are notably high.

Cognitive gaps need to be managed successfully. They are system problems that need to be resolved while (or even before) solving other problems relating directly to survival. As with any other problem, the first requirement is to recognise it, which comes with insight through learning. Knowledge of A-I theory has been found useful to engender insight not just into a specific event but also into this class of problem generally. As wider insight dawns, then the relationship with another with whom there has been persistent friction, patched up on an event-by-event basis, can be better understood in a more abstract (less threatening) general perspective. The difference here is that not only can the differences between the protagonists be better understood, they can be seen as inevitable, since they are based on deeply entrenched preferred style that, if well managed, can be more useful than irritating. The other

---

86 The continuum can run from adaption to innovation or vice versa. This diagram applies also to other forms of diversity (e.g., one person in a group with a different skill or culture).

person need not necessarily be viewed as awkward or hostile – merely different. There should now be perceived a mutual problem that is difficult and that needs resolution, but is not so intractable and is worth resolving. Training and education have no effect at all on one's preferred style, but coping behaviour, insight, and such other matters can be the themes of learning sessions to good effect. No studies have been specifically devised to explore these suppositions in detail. However, information from practitioners using KAI suggests that although added effort is always required to find ways to bridge the cognitive gaps in cognitive style, knowing about them gives increased motive to achieve this and clearer understanding of the gains to be made when it has been achieved. In addition, many ploys and stratagems (including the use of techniques) can be devised and used to assist with coping with this problem.

The dangerous way of dealing with cognitive gaps is by ignoring them. There are many ways to assist the closing or avoiding of cognitive gaps, such as changing jobs, changing the job, delegating, reorganising roles in a team, and other such commonplace ploys. One more way is to be a bridger or to find someone who is willing to be a bridger, whose skills can be improved by training. Bridging is a social role for which it is useful:

- to have an intermediate KAI score between those to be bridged (consultants, especially those working alone, often find themselves cast as bridgers but without the good fortune of having an intermediate score);
- to be willing to undertake the role (many people do not at all like being 'piggy-in-the-middle');
- to be skilled, or else there is a danger of making matters worse.

It might seem that those people located around the mid-point of the KAI scale would make, or might even be, the natural bridgers of society. Unfortunately, this is not necessarily so, since a person located here may be neither willing to take up the role nor skilled enough to be effective, even if willing. They may not have a score that lies between those who need a bridger and so may find the task additionally difficult. (Having a score in the middle of the KAI range is not so useful when trying to bridge between, for instance, a mild and a high innovator.) In fact, even with a score close to the mid-point of the general population, one could be the highest adaptor in one group and the highest innovator in another. Each time one moves from one group to another one also moves one's position in relation to the 'middle', depending on who else is in the group. The same is true if one does not move from the group but someone else does. The exact relationship between self and a group may frequently change and have a noticeable effect on the role of the individual's contribution to change within a group. A large change is a change of role from that of AC^2 to that of AC^3 or vice versa because of changes in group membership. Of course, one does not need to have an intermediate KAI score between those who need a bridger, but if this is not the case then greater effort and skill are needed to simulate this position. To sum up so far:

- *Bridging is not a score but a social role.* It helps, but it is not essential, if the would-be bridger is located somewhere between those needing to be bridged, or 'coping behaviour' is required.
- *When a gap needs to be narrowed it is more effective, over a long time, if all members of a widely diverse team indulge in some coping behaviour.* Because

bridging is a social role, one necessary element is that the person concerned is willing to undertake that role. In teams with poor morale, many do their best to avoid getting 'caught in the middle'.

* *Every social role needs skill to do it well.* So bridgers, too, need skill and good motive to risk intervention. Most people have been in the position of a potential mediator where, despite deploying the best skill available, the protagonists across the gap seem only to agree on one matter: They didn't like the intervention – and as a result, they may not like the mediator, either! No wonder many, especially those who are without high motivation and good skills, prefer to stay on the sidelines.

There are many elements in the skills that make a willing bridger successful, like being seen as acceptable (sympathetic) to both parties, not imposing a solution but allowing them to find one suitable to them, having the kind of knowledge that is respected by both parties, and so on. Having the judgement to know when and how to intervene is the hallmark of the professional, but not everyone is a professional. In an organisation it is useful if everyone tries to help others tolerate and manage diversity. The *concern* of bridgers may be a most useful element of this segment of the climate. It is useful if a person with more skill than others in a group is available, who can be used openly to assist its cohesion but not by taking all the responsibility of group cohesion, even if that person is the boss. Of course, the problem-solving leader must always take more of the responsibility than anyone else, but they cannot be best suited for every role in every particular situation; they cannot be expected to be the resident expert on every problem that faces the group. The job of a problem-solving leader is to lead the group to finding the appropriate problem to solve, find the best solution currently available, and tackle implementation in the best way needed by the solution. The leader also needs to set the scene so that the group can readily direct its efforts and deploy its diverse skills, persistently and consistently, so as to complete the task for the benefit of the group. The prime skill needed by a problem-solving leader is be able to lead, which is the specialism of the job; anything else may be useful, or may add needed credibility, but what the group needs the leader for is to lead it well. So the leadership's knowledge and methods of operation must first reflect the needs of the problem so as to aid the group achieve its common aspirations. That includes managing the group so that it can cope with the necessary diversity of problems needed to be solved, including those generated within itself (integrating the team's own diversities) as its members problem solve. Managing the bridging function is one of these tasks that the leader must see resolved, even if he or she is not the prime operator in the process.

Bridging in teams

So far, the bridger and the bridging role have been examined as a personal role, but this is essentially a team role, in which the bridger and the bridged are part of a larger group whose members may well benefit significantly, if indirectly, from any success of the bridging activity. To return to the skewed distribution of KAI scores typical of small groups, the group centred around its mean (one half standard deviation on either side) has been variously described as the AC^2 group and the consensus group, while the space its members occupy is referred to as the comfort zone (Kelly's 'range of convenience'). Together with any leaders that reside in its ranks, the whole group makes up the core that determines the nature of the group's climate. In a group with poor leaders (irrespective of whatever other benefits they may provide for the team and for which they may have been primarily promoted) there is a marked tendency (a) for only those in the 'climate group' to be in close touch with the leadership and (b) even within the climate group, for an inner subset, a power elite, to form. This inner AC^2 in-group is made up of those whom the leader can trust and get along with easily. They are those who 'understand' the leader almost intuitively, are most in tune with their view of the principal problems to be solved, the order of priorities mentally listed in the same order, the precipitating events to be prepared for, the kind of solutions that are 'known to work'. Communications within this subgroup are good with comparatively little effort; in short, they are in organisational and cognitive fit with each other and those in the leadership. The danger to the group is that to have reached this position they have almost certainly had a run of success and are confidently looking forward to more. They may be unaware that there are inherent faults in every machine and, because theirs may not yet have proved dangerous, so the thought of failure is not uppermost in any of their minds. They have AC^3 colleagues, who undoubtedly perceive the present and future somewhat differently, but in the poorly led team their opinions are not sought or given much weight when presented. This all applies to both the more adaptive and the more innovatively oriented teams.

The poor problem-solving leader finds it enough to manage those in fit and expect those in diversity to conform enough to maintain the team's overall comfort level; here diversity is mismanaged at worst by default; that is, ignored. When circumstances change and the wider diversity of human attributes is needed to solve a new and wider diversity of problems, this may be less available in practice than in theory. One reason may be that a subgroup, which has been habitually overlooked as a general source of advice and expertise, may simply be overlooked again when it is needed. The reason seems to be that once a subgroup has been perceived as 'not fitting' it is hard, in a crisis, to think of any of its members as useful or to be trusted when the stakes have noticeably risen. Even more difficult is that there may have been a persistent policy of informing all the team's members on a general policy on a 'need to know' basis. It may follow that subgroups who are not in fit need to know less than those who are in in-groups. When the nonfit subgroup's opinion is sought, they will be expected to know less because they are not of in-group status and they *will* know less because they have not been informed. Here is a prophesy fulfilled to baleful effect. It can be compounded; not only may they know less but, because they do not feel well regarded, they may care less, except for their own immediate fate.

One way of closing cognitive gaps between groups is by the judicial use of those best placed to bridge and who are skilled in the role. In Figure 12, one ideal position for an AC^3 potential bridger is indicated by the X, about one standard deviation from the mean. The suitable person with a score on or around this point is in easy touch with at least one edge of the consensus group and not uncomfortably far from the mean of the whole group – the core of the consensus group. From this vantage point a person could offer distinctive diversity whilst being 'within easy reach' of half the core group so that their alternative views are likely, most times, to get a hearing. This person needs careful selection and thorough training (in the social skills needed to be a bridger) and to be trusted with all the information that may hitherto have been available only to selected members of the in-group. This person should have standing

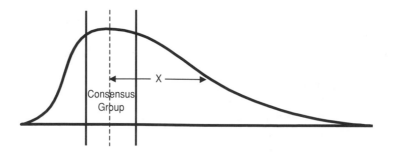

X is a likely spot for a bridger, close to the mean of the consensus group
but outside AC^2 boundary

Figure 12 A likely bridger

among those in the relevant out-group and skills to which the in-group must learn to
attend – or frequently admire. This person and the in-group members need to know
how to help by having these alternative ideas and activities well executed and well
integrated with the main activities in order for the in-group itself to prosper. The
tactics are to show that the task this person does is vitally needed and that those in the
in-group are not as well suited to do it as this selected out-group person. As the view
of the job changes upwards in esteem, so does the view of the person who does it well.
A person of appropriate skill, with the visible appropriate trust of the management,
kept fully up to date, and an acceptable member of the appropriate prestigious groups,
will ensure integration not only of the person but also of the needed diversity. This
person will then be responsible for creating the bridges with their own subgroup
(raising it in the esteem of the consensus group). As an additional bonus, the bridger
may be able to help close the cognitive gap between the consensus group and those
of more extreme diversity (the further out AC^3) within the whole group. The value of
such people is so obvious that all this should hardly need saying – and in many places
it does not. Yet the truth is, that in a great many cases this does need saying, and it is
difficult to get real acceptance, as distinct from mere acquiescence. This is especially
true when a crisis has blown up and fear makes in-groups close their ranks and reduce
their tolerance of diversity.

There are also the problems of groups where the leader is in the AC^3 group. This
can happen, for instance, in an successful entrepreneurial company where the innovator founder has need to expand and consolidate, using increasing adaption. Survival
depends on the leader managing this problem, particularly by remembering that the
qualities exhibited by him or her in foundation are now not the ones most needed to
survive. An assistant manager-cum-bridger is one frequently found solution.

Consultancy and teaching on business and management courses repeatedly shows
that managers are likely to see the roles they fill well as critical roles in the company.
The feeling of being in a vital in-group, from which one derives one's standing and
security, is liable to give that role undue importance, often by playing down the value
of other roles. Some of the catchphrases that pass for grand strategy are something
like this (in their more simplified form): 'This firm is market driven'; 'We lead by
product design'; 'Accounting is the bottom line – it's here we have gained the advantage' and so on. The fact that there may be much truth in each assessment, for most

of the key problems and profits may indeed lie in the 'lead' area, should not conceal the probability that problems which can destroy the whole organisation can also lie elsewhere. A team that is at once diverse and integrated is better suited to forestall these hidden dangers. As has been said, one main reason why key people in various out-groups, like AC^3 subgroups, are not given an appropriate place in high councils is not only because they do not fit but also that the tasks they represent are not seen to be as important as those undertaken by the members of the in-group. One way to promote the better use of diversity is not by making politically correct remarks about diversity, which often irritate without curing basic problems, but by ensuring that the group knows of the survival value of attending to a diversity of problems – their problems.

This is the first step in welcoming a diversity of problem solvers and putting the diversity to the common good. The reason why such behaviour is not readily seen is that coping behaviour is expensive, so the problem and the diversity needed to solve it have to be defined together and all the costs involved in its resolution, or failure of resolution, examined. Another reason is that many teams are run primarily for the interests of a minority, the AC^2 group, for instance, or for a rank elite. These are forms of leadership but they are often unstable – requiring much policing of the junior ranks of the 'outsiders', which is a multiplication of Problem B. The military have learnt (and often had to relearn) that in the midst of a battle, commanders who cannot rely on their troops' close identity with their aims are those who risk defeat. The Duke of Wellington was a hard man and a brilliant, if autocratic, commander, but was well liked by his men. The reason was only in part that he often won the battle and was known to do all he could to keep down the number of casualties, but it was mostly because he was concerned for all his men, all the time. From his correspondence one sees clearly his concern: 'I know of no [point] more important than closely to attend to the comfort of the soldier: let him be well clothed, sheltered and fed. How should he fight poor fellow if he has, beside risking his life, to struggle with unnecessary hardships?' (quoted from Glover, 1968, p. 231). The phraseology may sound dated but the sentiments are as fresh and true today as at any time in the past.

It is an interesting fact that no one has undertaken any study of bridging in the A-I literature. One possible reason is that it sounds obvious and so is not a rewarding line of study in which much can be learnt. Yet the opposite seems closer to the truth, the more the concept is explored. If the theory sounds obvious the practice may, on closer examination, seem old hat too. If the bridger's repertoire of subroles, such as counsellor, mediator, or negotiator, is examined, it can be seen that they are all well known and the subject of many a training course. Once the concept is understood in the context given here – once there is a conscious willingness to accept diversity in general as a resource – then the skills that are needed to undertake a bridging role are well known and little modification to courses is needed. These courses need to be able to:

- give every member of any team help in distinguishing the diversity that is needed from that which is latently hostile;
- help in neutralising hostile diversity or find protection from it;
- note and accommodate at low cost diversity not of immediate use as a potential resource;
- explore the notion of the appropriate price for the accommodation of the diversity that is needed;

- explore how to present one's own diversity in a manner that makes it readily tolerable and, on occasion, desirable to a group;
- explore the ways of managing cognitive gap so that the amount of energy required is no more than is required by the magnitude of the gap;
- identify and manage compounding emotive factors that arise from a fear of, or from sheer irritation with, what is less comfortingly familiar by appreciating the current or potential values of diversities.

COPING BEHAVIOUR

A definition

One's preferred style of problem solving seems to be deep-seated; research confirms that it is determined early in life (if not inherited) and is highly resistant to change. Problems cannot always be solved in one's own preferred style; however, style is not behaviour but an influence on it, so when necessary, everyone is able to tackle their current problems in what is for them a nonpreferred way by using coping behaviour. In general, coping behaviour operates in difficult circumstances, e.g., 'tax or exceed [one's] existing response patterns' (Burke & Weir, 1980) – a matter of capacity. In the strict context of cognitive style it is defined as behaving (problem solving) outside one's preferred style by the minimum amount for the least time (see Figures 13a and 13b).

All behaviour costs effort, but working in a style away from one's preferred style is additionally expensive. Coping varies along two axes – intensity and duration – and the added expense involved rises as each or both of these rise; research, practice, and introspection strongly suggest that the rise is not linear throughout but becomes increasingly steep. The point or points at which the steepness becomes marked is not yet well determined, but this may be because these points are related at least as much to the person as to the event. All individuals indulge in coping behaviour because of the narrowness of the range of style within which they feel fully at ease, compared with the wide range of style needed to manage the usual array of diverse problems the individual needs to solve. Adaptors are obliged to move away from familiar, consensually agreed structures into territory with more of those kinds of risk they are usually careful and skilful to avoid. Of course they can use techniques, which can be taught; but there is a big difference for an adaptor indulging in, say, a brainstorming exercise on a course away from the job in an approving setting and in one carrying out the same exercise in an environment that might be less understanding. Innovators, too, have their difficulties using newly acquired adaptive-simulating techniques in an innovatively inclined group. As converts, they must constantly remind themselves to master rules and operate adaptively, creatively, and effectively within consensually agreed restraints within a not so appreciative environment.

If operating cognitively outside one's preferred style can be expensive, what keeps us at it? The answer is motive, which generates the additional energy and discounts the additional discomfort until either the task is complete, or it becomes possible to pursue it within limits closer to one's preferred style. Should the cost of continuing coping become perceived as higher than one is prepared to pay, then motive switches off and coping (behaviour) ceases. Actual behaviour, then, is a blend of behaving in one's preferred style and coping behaviour.

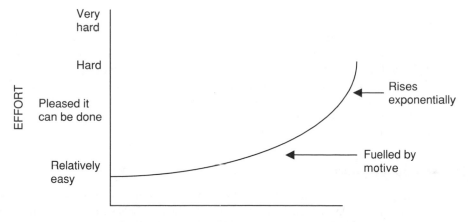

Figure 13a   Coping behaviour – schema

Definition:	– is behaving (problem solving) – outside one's preferred style by – the minimum amount for – the least time.
Function:	– link between preferred and actual behaviour (behaviour is a blend of: – behaviour in one's preferred style and – coping behaviour).
Operation:	– is fuelled by motive; – is psychologically costly: – when motive switches off, – there is a return to preferred style.

Figure 13b   Coping behaviour – definition

One question that frequently arises in teaching A-I theory is: If a person is in a situation that requires much coping behaviour, does coping become easier for that person? Theory suggests this is not so; and information from practitioners supports this. The first reason is that preferred style is highly resistant to change; the evidence for the persistence of KAI scores has been given earlier. Therefore, every time a person needs to operate in a style different from the one preferred, then coping behaviour, with the same added effort, occurs. But the question of whether coping behaviour becomes easier is not answered by the supposition that it continues to be needed. There are three further variables to take into account. One is that if the motive for coping behaviour is high (and the perceived rewards are also high), the individual may make light of the added effort – although from time to time there may be sharp reaction and doubt. The second variable is that the person may develop a number of skills for reducing the task, such as offloading parts of it or finding techniques that help. Grandmothers are wont to tell us that if we do not like doing a job, we should do it early (so that one thinks about it for the least time), do it well (so that it takes the least time), and feel good about having done it both early and well. The third variable is best explained whilst studying Figure 13. The amount of effort required for coping is related to how much is required and for how long. Since effort is always needed for any task, small amounts of coping behaviour may barely be noticed. Large amounts, over long periods, and in circumstances that have implications likely to raise anxiety are all too readily available to consciousness.

Link with the literature

Here is the bare bones of the description of coping behaviour, as yet unrelated to hard evidence, that can be elaborated from its literature. Steed (1998), in his useful review article, elaborates the key issues well. Historically, coping was conceived of as a defence mechanism within psychoanalytic theory, a: 'tradition that is continued in the work of Haan (1977) and Vaillant (1977) [which] led to [it] being conceptualised as a style or trait . . . that operates over the life span.' The principal counter-opinion he singles out is that of Lazarus and his colleagues (e.g. Lazarus & Folkman, 1984; Folkman & Lazarus, 1985), who point out that the style approach does not adequately deal with the complexity and variability of actual coping efforts or the nature of the specific contexts that evoke (or provoke) coping in the first place. Folkman (1984) defined coping as the 'constantly changing cognitive and behavioural efforts to manage specific external and/or internal demands that are appraised as taxing or exceeding the resources of the person' (p. 141). This definition points to coping as process-oriented rather trait-oriented, a distinction that is critical for understanding and measuring the concept. In the first place, the trait-oriented approach would lead us to expect a highly consistent pattern of behaviour to measure and interpret, but not necessarily in a process influenced by situation. This gives rise to problems that are not easily resolved. In the case of style, overall consistency could come about because of a tendency either to appraise events consistently or to behave towards such events consistently (Newton, 1989). On the other hand, if the emphasis is on the range of coping responses to evoking events, McCrae (1984) has explored no less than 27 different coping strategies and, in addition, the many coping tactics that these strategies may have spawned. The interesting theoretical development pursued in McCrae's study is that these strategies are not all equally consistent, although he suggests that they may fall into two groups; those that are related to disposition (i.e., style) and those that are more related to specific situations. This approach neatly backs both horses, for the findings suggest that those strategies most related to disposition are more consistent (better predicted) than those more related to specific event. As this combined approach seems to account for the data from research better than either one separately, it is currently the strongest supported (e.g., Edwards & Trimble, 1992; Frydenberg & Lewis, 1994; Terry, 1994).

Coping in A-I theory

Clearly the definition that developed from work with A-I has no quarrel with the one proposed by Lazarus. Coping is defined as a process, switched on by motive, which offers the individual, at a price, added range of resource when problem solving. Style is not the only cognitive element that needs to be related to the concept of coping; any form of level is also related. So one can expect discomfort as one feels obliged to extend oneself over time (i.e., have the motive) to solve a problem that is on the edges (or even at the onset, beyond the edges) of one's levels of knowledge, skill, or whatever capacity or level attribute seems needed. The data available from the use of KAI are clear in suggesting that although there is massive evidence that A-I is stable, the coping behaviour associated with it may be less so. For instance, specific coping behaviour can be directly predicted from a person's style, status, or particular skills. That said, there is one prediction that can be made – it can be readily and safely assumed that of the diversity of problems that a person faces, not all will be solvable within that individual's preferred style range, however much a person might try by choosing spouse, friends, associates, and environments, to say nothing of the problems arising from them, to suit preferred style – some, at some times, will not fit. For A-I coping, the range of grand strategy is limited, for the strategies that avoid the problem, pass the buck, indulge in prayer, or any other negative strategy that McCrae (1984) lists, are in the end reduced to one: Some coping behaviour is often needed. Where consistency of prediction is variable is in the *extent* to which motive may drive a person either to undertake more coping behaviour or the degree to which a person will take pains to lead a life of minimum stress, even at the expense of achievement. The *tactics* used in coping behaviour need not be that consistent, as McCrae emphasises, since there is variation in how much people learn to manage better every time a class of event repeats. Steed (1998) is clear that there are formidable difficulties in reducing the whole domain of coping behaviours to a few dimensions, even if they are those that are more readily predictable. There may be only two main divisions under which all the variations of response can be grouped. One is manipulative adjustment, comprising such responses as changing one's aims, changing the situation within which the problem arises, and getting others to undertake those tasks least fitting to one's style. The other group involve personal adjustment and relearning procedure and methods, often with the help of learned techniques such as (innovative style) brainstorming or one of the more adaptive options, which helps confine the problem solver to a given system within which the solution is likely to be found. Clearly, however, there is consensus in the literature that more work needs to be done to understand this notion better.

Figure 13a was developed as a result of using KAI; its origin began with using the example of the 'bright tie statistician' as part of teaching about the management of diversity. It was noticed that small amounts of coping (in extent or duration) caused almost no bother, and were certainly reported rarely, especially by those who were confident and unharassed. This experience accorded with Steed's section on the variable effect of coping on the individual. Noting the problems of getting accurate information from scales designed to measure coping, he points to inconsistencies in individual response. He quotes the findings of Frese (1986), who concludes that only those coping strategies that are problematic are consciously represented and noted in a questionnaire. 'Ordinarily we use automatic, over-learned coping strategies. Only when the normal, easy-to-use, automatic coping strategies do not work do we think of them consciously' (p. 210).

Although the notion of coping behaviour in relation to that of A-I was well understood by the early 1980s, no measurement was attempted until later (the concept by Clapp, 1991; see also Clapp & de Ciantis, 1989; the measurement of the effort involved by McCarthy, 1993). The members of a department of a large multinational, who yielded a KAI mean that was slightly more innovative than other departments, took part in a study organised by Clapp. Small subteams (containing up to two dozen personnel) were invited to respond to the KAI as it applied to themselves and then to fill in one for each other member of their subteam, indicating how the respondent perceived that person. The results showed that participants responded on the KAI that related to themselves with high internal consistency (.8). They also perceived each other consistently; in each team the KAI item-by-item responses of 'self by all others' were pooled – the combined estimates of others (of each 'self') were found to have an even higher internal reliability (.9). The correlation between self-score and the means obtained from the average of others' estimates of self exceeded .8. All these people knew each other well. However, there was found to be a mean difference between the self and others scores of nearly half a standard deviation, skewed in the direction of adaption. This result was attributed to small amounts of constant coping behaviour that must have been accepted by colleagues as standard behaviour, which helped bridge the cognitive gap between the members of this department and other units in the same organisation. This was an important finding, as it offered evidence that some coping behaviour can be detected by colleagues and could be treated as 'trying hard' whereas other coping behaviour was not seen as such and the cost to that person of 'trying hard' was overlooked. This finding is in accord with the managers' own perceptions but more work is needed on this 'informed' hypothesis.

Undertaking her research at the same time as Clapp, McCarthy (1988) reported that her sample of women managers had each been asked to fill in two inventories, one for themselves and one for 'a typical colleague'. She found that the larger the gap between the two scores, the more the women reported work stress, as measured by Davidson's (1982; Davidson & Cooper, 1983) Work Pressure Questionnaire. The point at which the work pressure scores began to rise markedly was when the difference between the two scores was one standard deviation towards innovation. Thomson (1985) specifically aimed to explore the relationship between person fit in work (using a simple measure devised by her) and KAI score. Her results were that an individual's score on fit correlated with expressed desire to stay or leave the job, a finding that is hardly surprising. Then this finding was related to the individual's KAI score. The first of these further findings was that, again not unexpectedly, innovators are more likely to state that they were considering leaving the organisation. This accords well with data from a study by Foxall (1986), which show that while many young MBAs are likely to change jobs at the start of their careers, innovators were significantly more likely to change the type of job (e.g., moving from production to sales) than adaptors. Thomson's second finding was revealed when she divided her sample into four groups, two styles (adaption versus innovation) by two degrees of fit (fit versus not fit). The pattern of results obtained is in logical accord with derived A-I theory. Adaptors in fit were the group most likely to state they intended to stay in the job; they were followed by the innovators in fit. Next in the progression, the innovators who perceived themselves as not fitting indicated that they were more likely to leave. The group most strongly indicating an intention to leave were the adaptors who felt they did not fit. This group, nicely in accord with theory, was the smallest of the groups – 'adaptor not in fit' is a contradiction of terms, and it is no wonder that these adaptors felt most under pressure. If coping behaviour is required to make good any cognitive gap and coping behaviour is costly, then higher rewards are needed if one is to remain in a situation that calls for a good deal of coping behaviour over long periods. Adaptors may feel this strain more than innovators because a perceived need for constant large amounts of coping may suggest that they are in an inappropriate environment. Innovators can readily feel trapped in an adaptive stronghold and do suffer frustration, insecurity, and stress; however, they may be more ready to blame the environment (structure) and feel less stressed in doing so (Kirton & McCarthy, 1988).

More work is needed in this area, not only using total KAI scores but also the factor scores; this may prove of immediate help in counselling. Chilton (2001) suggests in his study on person–environment fit that innovators, required by conditions to moderate their idea generation (factor SO), feel less strain than adaptors do when working in the corresponding contrary environment. It is adaptors who were found to show more strain when asked to use innovator methods (factor E) and manage in looser structure (Rule/Group factor). Undoubtedly other elements, in each specific situation, complicate this pattern; this work may yet yield much useful insight in theory and practice.

Summary

In both style and level coping, cognitive techniques might be learned and used. This is one of a wider range of coping strategies. There are those who concentrate on the process definition aim of tapping individual variations in behaviour (e.g., striving or denying the problem). In addition, though less explored, are the lists of suggested strategies, based not on theory but on experience; e.g., one can cope by shifting one's job to one more 'satisfying' or refocusing the job to an area 'that is critical for this group'. It is easy to think of other typically stated ploys. Then there are the strategies that make the best use of others – leadership, it is widely argued, is not a role in which the person endeavours to do every task required by group and situation better than anyone else in the group. Everyone rightly regards this as poor leadership. More effective problem-solving leadership is making use of the diversity available within the group and deploying this diversity in order to achieve an aim that all the members, rallied and inspired by their leader, want to reach. This opens up the trait and even the specific problem 'coping approaches' into wider territory. If the best way of tackling a complex job over long periods of time is to include in one's team a wide range of diversity, the leader needs high coping behaviour but that of others in the team may be reduced. An aim of leadership is trying to understand the value of every member; learning to tolerate diverse behaviour even when it grates (especially when tired and anxious) in order to use it well; managing tensions between others who have less insight in order to get higher cohesion; disarming those who, even with the best of intentions, set about others in the name of cohesion to stir up resentment; not to introduce hostility under the guise of good intentions; and a host of other problems. The pay-off has to be right for this great effort; good leadership is not lightly achieved and deserves reward. One element in problem-solving leadership is that of managing stresses caused by coping behaviour; one guide could be:

Good leadership:

- exacts the minimum coping behaviour from each team member – in normal times;
- is offered the maximum coping behaviour from each team member – in crisis.

COPING, STRESS, AND DISORDER

The evidence supports a common-sense view that coping behaviour costs more effort than solving problems in one's own preferred style. Much of the evidence is implied and relates to climate as much as to coping, so most of the references given here have already been mentioned above. For instance, the story of the statistician and his use of colourful ties as a means of closing the visible cognitive gap between him and his more innovative colleagues shows how the concepts intertwine. He acquired insight into his problem and used a device that minimised the effects of gap, although he still had to expend effort to do this, which suggests that effort is always needed but that success justifies it. A review of the A-I studies that imply the cost of coping behaviour yields a respectable haul. Already mentioned is that of Hayward & Everett (1983), in which the markedly innovative team of the new enterprise, once they had been seen as succeeding, were rewarded by being accepted as permanent staff. This brought them the usual advantages which, when appropriate, were backdated. However, this meant closer conformity to the established practice, which reflected the adaptive mean of the long-established group. It can be confidently assumed that those who would require the most coping behaviour in accepting the reward would have been the most innovative in the group that was to be integrated. It could be expected, then, that among those who may have left would be those who found the change 'expensive' – disproportionately greater among the higher innovators, and this is what Hayward & Everett show (see Table 4). The study can be used to set up all the theoretical elements involved in coping behaviour:

- style preference does not change;
- behaviour can change, at a price;
- style preferences within a group can aggregate up into cognitive climate, which exerts a conforming pressure, as does any other kind of climate;
- if the price of coping rises to discomfort levels, either the reward must be high or the individual moves out of reach;
- the individual's choice pattern might be predicted statistically, in that the higher the assumed coping cost, the more rewards are needed by some and the faster the others will leave;
- some who stay (or cannot readily move) but find getting the reward overly expensive will pay a visible price such as illness or need for counselling;
- the bigger the cognitive gap to be closed, the greater the effort required to change;
- when individuals fall out primarily over a cognitive gap issue, other differences that were not until then regarded as important will become involved, making the dispute more difficult to resolve.

It remains to review the rest of the studies that have most bearing on this concept and to note how many of these theoretically derived hypotheses are likely to have validity.

McCarthy (1988, 1993) showed that when her women respondents were asked to project onto a KAI how they thought a 'typical colleague' would answer it, the results ranged between being close to their own KAI score or very distant from it. These women were also asked to respond to another measure, contained in the same package but not seemingly related; a work pressure questionnaire. The larger the gap between self-score and typical colleague score, the larger the score on work pressure, suggesting that the cognitive gap is expensive; the rise was a little more than linear. Also, the same person filled all three measures, so it is the *perceived* gap that may be more important than the actual gap. This point arose when the author was undertaking some consultancy in a company. An older, senior woman director needed to collaborate frequently with a recently appointed, younger, less senior male director. They came from different management backgrounds: personnel and accounting. She felt that their collaboration was not as 'meshed' as she would like and hoped the author could offer some advice to help them 'close the gap' (her terms). The woman admitted and the man confirmed that she seemed to be seeing a larger gap than him, although she suspected that he felt the need to play down differences. To deal with what turned out to be the key issue, they were each given a KAI to fill in for themselves and then another to fill in as each perceived the other. She turned out to be quite a high innovator and he turned out to be decidedly adaptive; using the second KAI scores, she saw him close to where he scored but slightly more adaptive, whereas he saw her as mildly adaptive. Using his estimate of her, she seemed to be coping by a prodigious 30 points or so; he was coping, if at all, slightly *more* adaptively than he rated himself – the wrong 'direction' to close the gap. She was feeling the strain of the real and perceived gap; he felt little strain, as the gap he perceived was a lot less than it actually was. With these data available, they promptly got down to finding a mutually useful solution.

Lindsay's (1985) trio, reported earlier, were not just uncomfortable with each other, they had come to open conflict – indeed, the 'deviant' (the junior) was eventually fired (or resigned, whoever story one chooses to believe). With the boss scoring 90 and the deputy boss (who did the firing) at 82, the mean gap between them and the subordinate, at 118, was another instance in the 30-point class. This time it proved unbridgeable. Conflict is rarely a matter of a single issue: In this case the unit was under great work pressure and the boss become ill as a result. When the boss went off sick it left the other two under more pressure, and whatever accord was left blew up over some matter or another – neither was sure exactly what. Mullany (1989) reported, in a study in South Africa, that when consultant systems analysts were the targets of complaints by their customers, the most prominent correlation resulted from a gap in KAI scores between consultant and client. It is a fine researcher who can manage to get collaboration and reliable scores in such situations! Kubes & Spillerova (1992) reported a clash between a newly appointed young woman and an older man in a long-established team. The man, the boss, and the other men in the team were doubtful of the value of this 'young woman'. However, the issues of age and sex were never raised when she was appointed, nor was any aspect of her behaviour at the time. Kubes suspected that the clashes had developed out of different ways of work. Style differences were revealed by KAI scores that showed a 40-point gap (78 and 128) between the protagonists, with the rest of the team being much closer to the adaptive score of the established man. Kubes was able to find a way of containing the impending battle (getting to the crises early helps with this, as Lindsay had found). Instead of letting them continue to report to each other directly, the bulk of the exchanges were (for a time) done together with the boss, who had been made more insightful as to the likely prime cause and the value of bridging skills. Gradually the pair learnt more about each other and what was needed for them to collaborate more effectively. The boss's presence helped damp down clash and win time for the learning to take effect.

Of course, not all large gaps need such intervention as a matter of rule. Rickards & Moger (1994) report on a partnership with an 80-point difference – and it was highly successful. This is not to say that cost was not involved, but that close collabor-ation worked long enough for the rewards that can be squeezed out of wide diversity to be all too clear to both. As the old adage has it, nothing succeeds so well as success – they found that the gap paid off and the price, although sometimes high, was willingly paid. Here the main long-term ingredient that keeps the partnership oiled and working smoothly is mutual respect, based on something like: 'my colleague can do readily what we need on this matter, a matter that I would find impossible to do well, easily and consistently.' Clapp & de Ciantis' work (1989) was also among the early studies that seemed to be measuring cognitive gap and showing that wide differences could be tolerated in stable teams with high morale. Clapp has taken the multiple KAI technique further than anyone else so far by handing out to each respondent as many KAIs as there were people in the team. As reported above, the reliability of self-score collected was high, as was that of the combined scores made by respondents on others – a useful foundation for the credibility of the results. The results obtained from self were compared with the average obtained from those made by others on self. As had been found before (see review: Kirton & McCarthy, 1988), the accuracy of these judgements of self by others (who are well known to each other), using rank order correlation, is better than .8. In this study, accuracy in rank ordering was high and actual scores close, but there seemed at first glance to be a persistent error of about half a standard deviation towards seeing colleagues as more adaptive than they perceived themselves to be. This seemed to be measuring that amount of coping behaviour that was accepted by the observer as 'real self'. One assumes that much special coping behaviour can be detected as such by knowledge-able observers – but a residue might be 'bought' as true. Clapp reasoned that if this discrepancy of scores reflected a response to the climate, then it should follow that for those whose actual scores fell within the 'core climate range', the mean of the discrepancies between self-score and that of the observers would be close to zero; those whose scores fell on the innovative side of this score (in this case, the majority) would be perceived as more adaptive than they reported (coping in the adaptive direction) and those on the adaptive side would be perceived, on average, as more innovative. The results fitted this pattern with precision. Only one variant among these data needed further thought – the 'core climate range' was not that of the unit but of the whole department, the former being slightly more innovative than the latter. It seems that, intuitively, individuals know the pattern that they are expected to use as a conformity guideline and 'cope' in the appropriate direction. As the team was successful it had good internal relationships and low turnover – the price of coping was acceptable.

It appears that some teams analysed in the literature managed internal diversity well and others badly. This raises the problem of how success can be helped to occur so that it brings further cohesion as a foundation for further success. Work is only at the start of this problem in the A-I domain. There are some clues emerging, however. Thomson (1985) showed in her study that those in fit are less likely to want to leave their jobs than those who are not. The interesting element here is the combination of two variables, the difference in style and the feeling that significant others (those comprising the immediate, intimate climate) 'understand my problems', part of Thomson's definition of 'fit'. This early study helped put the different outcomes reported by, e.g., Lindsay (1985) and Rickards & Moger (1994) into perspective: Preferred style is essentially neutral – theoretically it can be used, ignored, or be the cause of friction. What matters is in what manner it is perceived and managed. This is something to which training should be able to make a substantial contribution. Unfortunately, much diversity training is more aggressively driven than insightfully conceived; indeed, one can think of occasions when it appears that the operators are less tolerant on some key issues than their course members. This kind of teaching needs tolerance at the teaching level. One example, already mentioned, of how to start is given by Hammerschmidt (1996), who used an exercise in his courses that required one subteam of four to construct a shape from several pieces – the hollow square. The difficult bit was to communicate the whole exercise to another subteam, who had limited information of what had been done, sufficiently clearly to allow them to also to produce a hollow square within a set time. Nearly 500 managers had been through the exercise before KAI was used to select the subteams; the experience and data from this group acted as a control base. Then the KAI was used on just over 500 more managers so that each subgroup (of four within each full team of eight) had relatively homogeneous scores (less than 12 points) but the pairs of subteams could be either less than 20 or more than 20 points apart (so making some full teams containing a relatively adaptive and a relatively innovative subteam). It was assumed that the tasks of the two subteams favoured either adaption or innovation; one, called 'planners', had to find a structure and communicate that structure to the other group – adaptors might be more readily effective at this. The other group, the 'implementers', had to work with minimal clues to get enough structure to get the job done, a task thought to favour innovators. A first finding, which seemed secondary at the time but is crucial for this discussion, is that in the (KAI-unselected) control group many teams failed to solve the problem in time because one or other of their subteams fell out among themselves on how to go about the task. In the (KAI-selected) experimental group *no such outcomes were recorded*, as all subteams were of homogeneous style. The other results were spectacular enough: The control group averaged 52% success rate. For the experimental group that used 'worst scenario', with the more innovative as planners and the more adaptive as implementers, the success rate dropped significantly to 42%. Groups selected to be in the 'best scenario' condition produced a success rate of 85%.

Spectacular as this is, in real life such narrow tight control or team recruitment is not practical or even desirable except in quite specific (mostly short-term) circumstances. However, this kind of exercise is very useful, first as a test of theory and second, and much more importantly, to underline to managers how the management of diversity offers long-term pay-off. Since this kind of selection is not feasible in practice in most cases, the next task of trainers is to set up exercises that gradually 'mix' teams, so introducing increasing diversity and helping managers learn:

- to appreciate diversity;
- how to teach this to others;
- how to manage it themselves – with the help of everyone in the team.

> **Stress, including that generated by excessive coping behaviour:**
>
> - **is expensive even when well related to achievement and reward;**
> - **is counterproductive in the long run, when poorly related to achievement and reward.**

The sequence of the process that leads to coping behaviour is that first a need must be there to generate motive, which switches coping behaviour on and keeps it switched on until the need is met. The need is perceived through insight that the preferred style is not applicable in this event, at this time, with this group. That would be a reactive response; better still is the anticipatory response, when insight is replaced by foresight.

One other way that coping behaviour comes about is if the person is obliged to indulge in it by another (or others) – obliged to indulge because they have not the insight that would have led them to do so on their own initiative. One possibility is that having initially been obliged to cope, as a result, the person acquires the insight. At that point the coping behaviour becomes driven by personal motive. The other possibility is that insight is not acquired (I do so only because you say so), so that other must continue to supply that motive. In this circumstance supervision needs to be constant, because delegation is not possible. A function of problem-solving leadership is to provide the knowledge and inspiration that provides colleagues with the insight to do what is appropriate and to encourage self-motive to provide the energy to cope, when needed. The added pay-off is the opportunity for delegation.

Further applications

Rickards & Puccio (1992) note that on course exercises and projects, advantage can be taken of reliable predictions of differences between the more adaptive and the more innovative members. They ran a number of exercises to demonstrate this and then followed up the lessons with practical learning on how to manage diversity. Course members noted, for instance, that groups selected for homogeneity of KAI score got on because of the lesser need for coping. These observations were used as a base for the learning they were to follow. The authors then noted that in later-created, mixed-style teams, by now well alerted to the problems that arise from cognitive diversity, the members were concerned to find, make public, and make use of the differences among them. In short, they first accepted diversity then made use of it. Puccio et al. (1993; Puccio et al., 1995) have explored a variant of cognitive gap that involves a three-way difference between the style preference of the individual solving a problem (carrying out a task), the style the individual thinks might best solve the problem, and the style required by the boss. Some reviews are now emerging that deal with the basic assumptions used in practice, e.g., Rickards (1990) and Talbot (1997). The search is also widening to personal problem solving that needs help in one form or another.

Chilton (2001) notes the differences between adaptors and innovators in managing change that may or may not accord with their preference in dealing with the paradigm – e.g., the added pressures to adaptors when working in climates of paradigm shift. Kozan (1996, 1997) found that the more adaptive predominate among those long-term unemployed who need special counselling, especially those who had responsible positions before being made redundant. They found it difficult to cope with the change in the 'structure conditions currently prevailing in Slovakia'. The fall of communism in Eastern Europe has represented a collapse of paradigm[87] and it is the more adaptive who are the masters and upholders of the paradigm. For them a collapse is hard enough to manage, but when they lose position and self-respect as well it can become a major personal crisis. It is not only the more adaptive who suffer when a paradigm collapses. Most will feel initially lost when the largest, previously highly successful paradigms collapse. In addition, some paradigms are innovatively orientated and their collapse bothers innovators. In the company that is innovatively orientated, it is the more adaptive staff who are at a disadvantage and the more innovative staff who feel most at home; this time, it is the innovators who are often prepared to defend that position in the same put-down ways that those who are more adaptive tend to use when they are on top. So when an innovative climate runs into difficulty, as will be seen later, and the pendulum of change swings against the more innovative, the same stress and distress appears among the consensus group that was. No one welcomes all change!

One general observation is that the rejection of an idea or a solution by a person close in cognitive style to the originator seems to be more easily accepted than when the objector is located far away on KAI. Indeed, as McCarthy's work (above) has shown, people who perceive their typical colleagues as far from them in KAI scores report more work pressure. Part of the problem is having one's notions challenged in ways that those closer in score are unlikely to use – alternative acceptable presentations can be taught. Managing this problem is all part of the coping pattern. The fundamental difference, perhaps, between challenge of ideas from those close to one in style as distinct from those far away is that the former may not appear so readily as criticism of the proposer as well as what is being proposed: 'You cannot challenge my whole approach if yours is much the same as mine. Either, then, you must be dealing with a minor matter, or, because you come from the same background, you see something to which we *both* have to respond' (at cost to both, relatively equally).

Some problems relating to cognitive gap and coping can be even more serious than mounting stress; for instance (Marcus, 1992; Kirton, 1995; Clapp, 1995; Pounds & Bailey, 2002, and unpublished correspondence), adaptors and innovators might have accidents for different reasons. The current belief in the accident prevention milieu, which tends to be dominated by adaptors, is that innovators have all the accidents; when adaptors have accidents it is not their fault. However, there is growing evidence that whilst innovators have accidents because they bend or disregard safety rules, adaptors can be caught applying a rule despite evidence that it may have become inappropriate. One example is of a Korean airliner, on a course from the USA to Japan, which mistakenly flew over Soviet Russia. An error had occurred in punching in navigational data at the start of the flight and this had led the aircraft fatally off

---

87 See also Pendulum of change, in Chapter 11.

course. Unfortunately, modern navigational equipment is thought to be infallible and contraindicators were ignored. Invariable acceptance of an agreed structure can be dangerous. This difference of performance related to style suggests that although safety courses may not need to be greatly changed in principle, some parts need to be stressed to different extents for those with different styles.

Saggin (unpublished correspondence) has noted, in a large pilot study of over 100 women patients with eating disorders, that their KAI scores reflect the nature of their problem. She observed that anorexics, having acquired a wrong image of their bodies (which does not seem to have anything to do with style), ruthlessly pursued a dietary objective. The ruthless style of operation suggests adaption. Conversely, those with binge eating as their problem were not thought to have any difficulty with body image, but a difficulty in staying within a prescribed therapy, a structure within which they themselves wanted to remain – and could not. This suggested an innovative problem. The results have been spectacular, with the two groups lying on the A-I continuum exactly where expected. The person from each group whose score was closest to the nearest person from the other group was nearly a whole standard deviation away. A third group suffered from bulimia. This group swings from indulgence to fierce adherence to counter-correction. These patients yielded middling scores; this group overlapped the other two, but none had scores reaching the mean of either the other two groups. This shows a remarkably distinct pattern of results. Of course, style does not 'cause' the problems; but if one has eating problems it seems that their nature is likely to accord to one's style. The studies on accidents and eating disorders are closely linked to each other and with that on problems at work with style implications. The link is that all the participants face problems and these problems are characteristically attacked, admittedly with very different levels of success. Style is not the only variable involved, but it is one that often seems significant. The lessons for managers, teachers, and therapists alike are that no one prescriptive corrective approach is likely to work across the whole range of the A-I problem-solving style continuum – current trends of thinking notwithstanding. The ideal solution is no more to be sought than the ideal teacher or manager, the ideal patient or pupil, or even, to try grim wit, the ideal accident. Diverse problems need diverse treatments to be used by diverse problem solvers.

A number of hypotheses are still to be tested. One is based on the observation that pupils and students of diverse cognitive styles are studying in different courses, in different institutions, taught by different teachers and tutors and tested in different ways – an array of structures of authority, each with a characteristic style. The possibility of mismatch of style between the student and any one of these structures is greater than the possibility of style match. Yet in education, as in any other management problem-solving situation, there is a constant search for the ideal approach to problem solving (teaching and learning) in the field as a whole. As has happened in society as a whole, there is a swing between seeing the ideal approach as tighter or looser structure, irrespective of the nature of the elements. There can be no perfect overall match in so diverse a problem array. The search should be on how a variety of approaches can be accommodated to solve the diverse array of elements. If agreement could be made on what the aim of the courses should be, then members of a team can concentrate on exploring how different approaches can be used to enhance the chances of different problem solvers solving different elements of the problem, so reaching the agreed overall goal. Sometimes, this diversity of approach seems to be followed except for the fact that it is, nowadays, nearly always advocated by the more innovative and therefore interpreted innovatively (Kirton et al., 1991, touches on this problem); conversely, adaptors continue to search for more precise targets – and so the war may break out again. From observation, the most successful teachers search for ways to present material so that it makes the best impact on particular students. When one method does not seem to work with some students, they find another – even if it is not one they prefer. The best teachers may find it hard to explain their success because they have no clear theory and measures to back up intuition – could each success only be related to some individuals? In fact, these good teachers seem intuitively to supply more of what their problem solvers need: To the more adaptive, closer structure as guidelines on their way to the target, balanced by encouragement to 'look round the problem'; to the more innovative, they give guidance in making the best use of guidelines. Neither approach will kill creativity, different as their creativity may be, while student confidence is built on growing knowledge.

Another study that is in its early stages is on delinquency. Delinquents are often seen as a single class of problem, like patients with eating disorders or students. There are some sharply contrasting stereotypes as to how delinquents become delinquent, which may be useful in indicating different subsets. One is that the youngster comes from an area that abounds with crime: 'so what would you expect?' The other is of the youngster who, as they say: 'comes from the finest background, yet has kicked over the traces'. The types may be different and require different approaches. The first type is to be better fitted into a more rewarding background that will allow them to come to terms with society at large. The other is rebelling against their immediate background – it may be more their rebellion than their (general) background that is the problem. One might involve taking an adaptor away from past structures to ones that are unfamiliar – a difficult task. The other is to return those, who are probably the more innovative, into structures that have not proved comfortable – another difficult task, but one that is essentially different.

KAI has been used in marriage guidance counselling sessions as part of getting two people to understand their different approaches. They also need to accept that their preferences will not change but that constant misinterpretation and the need for coping behaviour is increasingly tiring. The same rationale and methods are used as in getting teams at work to collaborate – the differences, if they can be accepted, may be rewarding. This same cognitive gap difficulty could be important in mother–child relationships and among every other one within the family. Once more, the lack of instincts in humans deprives parents and children from having a number of simple inbuilt, unlearned rules to manage each other. The child has no information source except the family, which occasionally causes it problems. A mother's knowledge of child rearing is derived from her own mother, the peer group, and the latest trendy notions on child rearing. This array of often conflicting advice needs to be sorted out by a brain that has its different experience and style preference. Not surprisingly there can be problems! So far, the pay-off is that, on balance, we still manage better than any other species.

A more difficult area for hypothesis formation is that of dyslexia and its possible link to the innovation pole of the A-I continuum. The reasoning is that dyslexics may have problems with instability of cognitive structure involving the process stage of sensory input. A small pilot study found a modest correlation in this direction, but even if further supported it is not yet clear whether the relationship is because dyslexia is an unfortunate exaggerated form of innovation or whether the problem is simply a system fault that simulates innovation. This is a similar problem to that of unravelling the possible genetic connection with A-I, suggested earlier. Another hypothesis that was advanced in the early 1980s was that extreme forms of A-I could be described as abnormal behaviour: The link thought most promising to test was that of innovation and over-inclusion, an element in schizophrenia. Over-inclusion manifests as the intrusion, into a line of thinking, of information that could be described a bizarrely irrelevant, causing problems for the patient's contact with reality. Unfortunately, the study was abandoned after an extensive search for a reliable measure of over-inclusion failed before funds ran out.

More speculation has occurred on a possible link with attention deficit problems. Clearly, to start with there are problems of definition. Are some of the symptoms the result of poor parental teaching of social structure? If hyperactivity is always implicated, can hyperactivity be associated more with innovation than adaption? Is there a link with style at all? In a review of the current thinking on the specific effect of gene malfunction and problem behaviour, Wills (1998) takes the view that the link is neither perfect nor precise. In referring to ADHD[88], he argues that: 'probably the defective gene is able to affect the level of hyperactivity, but it hardly produces the behaviour' (p. 224). He continues that the work on related thyroid activity: 'does not constitute the discovery of a specific "gene for hyperactivity". Rather it tells us that a specific defect in the mechanism of binding the thyroid hormone to cells may exaggerate behaviours' (p. 224). Stressing the underlying complexity of interrelated defect on such behaviour, he also implicates the neurotransmitter dopamine and a similar compound serotonin, both of which have been found to be correlated to a whole web of behaviours. If, as expected by some, A-I (and cognitive style in general) has an underlying genetic foundation then it seems likely that defects in this system will be found to give rise to what seems to be exaggerated characteristic adaptive or innovative behaviour.

One line of reasoning that emerges is that the first element that needed tackling in all these cases is whether the behaviour that is thought linked to adaptive or innovative style is learnt or not. If it is not, then there is a possibility that only adaptors are likely to have some of the disorders whilst innovators are likely to have other ones – learning simply exaggerates an established inclination in problem solving. If the fault is built into the individual's general physiological structure then anyone with this defect will have this form of disorder, concealing whatever would otherwise be the inclination of this person if the fault had not been present. At present we are at the edges of our understanding of these kinds of failed problem solving.

Summary

No person can be at home with all levels of capacity and any style. To work at the edges of one's capacity (beyond one's comfort range) requires coping behaviour. To extend one's range of preferred style, coping behaviour is also available. There are many forms of it but most seem to fall into two categories. There are manipulative adjustments, which includes changing aims, changing the situation from which the

---

88 Attention deficit hyperactivity disorder.

problem arises, and getting others to undertake the least 'fitting' of the tasks involved. The second is personal adjustment, which includes learning new information and methods that will extend the reach, such as cognitive techniques mentioned above. A review of the main points made about style and coping include:

*   all people are more comfortable operating within their own level limits (capacity, knowledge, know-how, familiar scope) – coping to reach beyond these is expensive;
*   all people are more comfortable problem solving within their own style range – each range has its advantages and its disadvantages in relation to the style nature of the problem and its perceived desired solution;
*   coping behaviour also bridges behaviour that is preferred and behaviour that is deemed desirable in a particular situation; what is preferred is set and what may be needed is variable;
*   one's style is not learned but its application is; coping behaviour needs to be learned;
*   when coping behaviour is no longer needed one returns to preferred style;
*   high coping behaviour demand is expensive in terms of stress;
*   gross failure to cope may be because of a system or leadership fault.

11 The management of change

ALTERNATIVE CLIMATES

General population samples from various nations, languages, and cultures yield normally distributed KAI scores. So, also, do groups made up of members with wide interests, activities, and arrays of main problems; they have titles that are generic rather than specific, such as managers or teachers. However, most smaller, more homogeneous groups, e.g., R&D managers, production staff, or science teachers, and especially even smaller groups, e.g., a section in production (e.g., safety) almost always have skewed distributions. These differences are readily predictable and are well supported in the literature.

The differing means of these more specialised groups should reflect the needs of their prime job, as understood by the groups' members, through successful experience over time. So they are also readily predictable by those with an understanding of the measure and the job. It is no surprise to such experienced people to find that accounting departments are close to 80 in mean, while R&D departments averaged 102 and both marketing and personnel lie in the narrow range 105–108, all compared to several general population sample means of circa 95; a difference of only 5 points between groups is noticeable. Research and a good deal of experience have shown that although the means of groups vary, the ranges within the groups are relatively stable and wide (examples of all the above departments have been found to have ranges of between 50–125 for the more adaptive and 65–145 for the more innovative). Often, if a group is big enough a range of over 50 points can be expected.

These data are coupled with further information that the greater the cognitive gap the harder it is to achieve accord across such diversity, especially gaps that rise to 30 points or more. The paradox of cognitive diversity is that the narrower a group's range (the climate), the more immediately comfortable it is for its members. Yet the narrower the diversity, the greater is the danger that the group will fatally fail to solve, over time in a changing environment, some of its critical problems from the array it faces. This mirrors the lessons learnt from biological success; the smaller the gene diversity and behavioural flexibility available, the narrower the ecological niche within which the organism fits neatly and the greater vulnerability of a species to a changing environment. When these issues were discussed previously and placed into the context of a structure, the notion was advanced of everyone being an agent of change (AC^1) simply by being alive. In addition, they play out, when in company, the role of either AC^2 or AC^3, depending on their relationship to other members. That is, each person is either part of the numerous central 'in-group' that forms a core of the group's climate, or part of an 'out-group' subset that has a different perspective on the nature of the group's collaborative problem solving. Finally, the simplest scenario was explored, when the bulk of the leadership is associated with the central consensus group so reinforcing the climate that is generated. Now, however, alternative climates need to be explored. These can underlie clashes between groups and subgroups, deriving initially from differences in cognitive style and then from more complex differences than those so far explored. There can be significant mean (and distribution) differences between:

- groups doing seemingly the same job (like groups in the same company but in different locations);
- groups with the same or similar titles but doing different jobs (different types of lawyer or accountant);
- a group's present (cognitive) climate, which the members feel is the right one to achieve their goals, facing a proposed change wanted by significant, powerful others;
- those in the consensus subgroup and its leadership, expressed as the power of number versus the power of status, which this time adds up to potential conflict in climate, viz. N^p versus S^p = Conflict.

It is not expected even in theory that two people can have the same perceptions of the same event. It is not surprising that different people and different groups of people can be readily perceived to take different views of the same job – a diversity that can be seen both as an advantage and as a nuisance by different collaborators at different times. It is unlikely that the team members will disagree on every issue. Most cultural and climate-guided responses to similar, familiar stimuli may be so taken for granted by each member that the possibility of disagreement may not occur to anyone: To take an exaggerated example to make the point, people often consider which clothes to wear to work but not whether to wear any or not. When such examples are given it becomes clearer that most of a social structure is taken for granted and that this is a necessary condition for society to function effectively. Often the issues that cause problems are seemingly minor, and what often trips up managers and consultants is when everyone seems to agree on what is wanted but some are subtly reordering the key elements of the job in hand in importance, placing different emphases on different elements. This may be done for many reasons; one of them is the influence of differences in style. As the gap widens and the edges of the gap harden, there may be a reduction rather than an increase in willingness for coping behaviour. These variant elements pull collaboration apart; the differences help to set up alternative climates that focus rivalry. Such a foundation for potential persistent clashes needs to be resolved before any of the parties may be ready for further close collaboration. Those familiar with the workings of military services and units are sometimes cynical enough to believe that even participation in a full-scale war is barely enough to distract some protagonists from in-service and intra-unit struggles for supremacy. The same diversion of resources into internal disputes is true in many other organisations.

Thomson (1985) found that although her large Singapore samples of ethnic Chinese, English-speaking managers in the Civil Service and local industry had means that were indistinguishable from large, comparable samples in other countries, the means of those in multinational industries were significantly more innovative. The presumed reason for this difference is that the latter had crossed a cultural barrier, even though they had done so while remaining in their own country. The more innovative mean for their multinational expatriate colleagues was accounted for, in the opinion of many senior cynical managers, by the fact that Singapore was far enough away from European and American head offices to satisfy a disproportionate number of their companies' higher innovators. If both explanations hold, in these organisations style means may be predictably similar for different subgroups for different reasons. In addition, if units undertaking the same tasks and function are in different locations, the staff inevitably face different environments within which they need to accommodate. They will be more conscious of these differences than the staff at head office. Some of these differences of view lie in the selective reordering of priorities of events, rules, elements of the job, and any other issues that are selected by different groups as being in some way in need of critical variations of operation. Head offices that have an overriding aim, not necessarily shared equally with any daughter unit, of standardisation of operation, will periodically be strongly tempted to spend effort to 'rationalise' operations, often in the teeth of as much objection as the daughter units dare show. Differences in the 'nature' of the staff, such as different knowledge, mean age, experience, etc., will widen the gap, which may now be exacerbated by group mean differences in style and all that that implies. It only needs to add such factors as suspicion from head office that their colleagues 'cannot' keep to proper structure and that they are in out-stations because they are not best suited to be in headquarters. This is matched by similar pejorative view of headquarters by the outlanders and the scene is set, in organisations that are poorly led, for a good deal of friction. So style differences may support, if not always initiate, a complex array of differences and a see-saw of repression and tolerance from powers above and beyond. The leadership of all the out-groups concerned will be placed in the dilemma of lining up with either their immediate climate or that of a more distant power group. They may find that they are forced into a compromise that leaves them not quite fitting anywhere.

There are two circumstances that are the more common exceptions to the rule that the leadership is primarily located in the consensus group, that is, it may not even be an AC^2. The first is when an innovative, entrepreneurial unit has come to an adaptive stage in its development, when it must both expand and consolidate its procedures or perish. In this event the additions that the founder needs to recruit and establish are very likely also to be more, sometime much more, adaptive. The second is when the environment of an established unit changes in style significantly and the unit is being made to respond, either by a powerful subset from within the existing members of the group or, more often, by coercion from a power outside the group.

In private correspondence, Rosenfeld and Dubras, then senior managers in Kodak and the Atomic Energy of Canada, respectively, reported that the means of members in entrepreneurial units were significantly more innovative than the mean for their managers in general (circa 97). Indeed, roughly speaking, high innovators (using a cut-off point of one standard deviation or more) made up nearly half the group. In the first case, a subgroup was distinguished among R&D personnel because they contributed ideas to a specially set up unit that aimed to facilitate employees' ideas that were deemed useful to the company but which did not directly relate to their immediate job. The KAI mean score of the Kodak sample's members who did not contribute to these schemes was identical with R&D means collected elsewhere, 102; this select group returned a mean of 113. Further analysis showed that if this contributing subgroup were further subdivided into a group that contributed one or two ideas and another containing those contributing three or more, then the respective means were 108 compared to 124. Dubras had called for volunteers from an R&D group (estimated mean, from the scores of a sample, was 101) to give of their spare time to an idea-generating project that would aim at suggesting and exploring possible viable notions for future company operations. The volunteer group also yielded a mean of 113. In contrast, the 34 students of Goldsmith & Kerr (1991) attending a course for intending entrepreneurs returned an innovative class mean of 102 (these patterns are persistently recurrent). They selected another class of 24 students (with a slightly higher proportion of men) as a control group and it yielded a mean of 98 (the general population male mean). The point being made about these examples is that there are always variant subgroups about. They form and reform, but their outlooks are different from the mainstream. This is their advantage and the source of potential clash. Even in seemingly homogeneous groups, alternative subsets with matching subclimates exist – and need to be accommodated if they are to be of use.

Tandon (1987) and Buttner & Gryskiewicz (1993) not only confirmed that their samples of entrepreneurs yielded means in close accord with the earlier pilot work but both also noted (a) the expected high casualty rate among entrepreneurs in general and (b) that the high innovators accounted for significantly more of the failures. Entrepreneurs were expected to yield a higher innovative mean score as it is generally considered that entrepreneurial businesses involve higher risks than other businesses and innovators are known as higher risk-takers. What was less obvious was that, even in innovative environments, it is the high innovators who are more prone to fail – by the nature of innovation. Innovation seems, then, to be a positive factor in setting up an entrepreneurial business and a negative factor for surviving in it. It appears from such little work that has been done so far, that high innovator entrepreneurs enter riskier ventures (even by entrepreneurial standards) than do the more adaptive, allowing less margins for error and mischance and having undertaken less detailed planning on administrative and procedural issues. The running of their businesses may be too loose for safety. The venture capital organisation associated with Tandon's work, like any other financial loan business, had staff members who were well aware of this entrenched innovator fault and tried to allow for it. However, if strict adaptor rules were to be applied the venture business may cease to operate at a viable level – high adaptor assessors might not lend money to any innovator! In addition this would not solve the problem of the, admittedly fewer, failures among those more adaptive (which, because of the way Tandon divided the sample, included mild innovators). These tended to fail because, although they had planned the exercise more carefully and more fully, there were often factors (like rapidly changing conditions and fashions) that they had not been allowed for sufficiently. Unlike the high innovators, who more readily changed tack swiftly – indeed, sometimes when it was not necessary – this group hung onto their master plan too long and slowly perished. The venture capital assessors, who were responsible for monitoring progress, were empowered to take over a failing business and appoint a possible saviour. Tandon found that when they did this it seemed that they had intuitively selected a high innovator as the successor for a more adaptive failed entrepreneur and a more adaptive successor for a failed high innovator.

An interesting hypothesis that emerged from these findings was that if the high innovator succeeded it was often because of help from more adaptive staff (just as the converse can be true, for the opposite kind of reasons). It seemed that one critical factor for both expansion and survival was that the innovators learnt how to manage a more adaptive group, both by being able to give appropriate leadership and by being able to delegate vital tasks to those not like them. Here, then, is a case where the boss is not an agent of change within the consensus group (AC^2) and is unlikely to become one. The problem now is how to prevent competition between alternative climates becoming the prime occupation of the members of the group – the inefficient promotion of Problem B over the more vital Problem A. Being an AC^3 underlines to a leader that most of the other people are different within what needs to be a closely collaborating team. Unfortunately, most leaders see their task as making decisions in the light of the prevailing paradigm as they interpret it so that the team can implement them. The problem-solving leadership task might be better defined as the setting of conditions that allow the team's members consistently to make better use of their diversity, effectively making decisions and accomplishing tasks in the light of the prevailing paradigm as all agree it should be interpreted – not an easy task. However, this view inevitably tilts the paradigm interpretation towards the nature of the bulk of the problems being tackled – the very same interpretation of paradigm that guided the selection of the staff and the reason why they are the AC^2s when the leadership is not. If the leader has had the insight to select the staff that makes them the AC^2s and the leader an AC^3, the next insight needed is to make sure they (the AC^2 staff) can do the job for which they have been selected – if necessary despite that AC^3 leader! The onus is on the *problem-solving leader* not to set up competing alternative climates – the one that the leader prefers against the one that is needed and that the staff members have been *specifically selected to prefer*. This line of reasoning assumes that a prime job of a problem-solving leader is the management of people; being also the resident expert in some of its problem areas is an additional advantage that should not detract from the leadership task. Even if, in some situations, the job expertise is crucial to the success of the group, the two tasks must still be treated separately so that a variety of personnel can be used to good effect. Otherwise the diverse staff so necessary for continued success will instead be greatly distracted by its leadership's narrowly conceived notion of organisation fit, dominated by a single expertise (level), style, or both.

These notions learnt from the study of entrepreneurs are more widely applicable. They apply to every person (or group of persons) in a place in which they may be deemed culturally 'unexpected'. For instance, the woman taking up a post that women have not done before in a particular setting, the recent immigrant, the new entrant with particular different skills, knowledge, or ways of operating are all people who have crossed a cultural boundary. They are not always more innovative but are often treated, warily, as different. They often find themselves under more pressure by being seen at the edges of 'organisational fit'. Unpublished examples from the consultancy activities of the Occupational Research Centre have been given added support; Clapp & de Ciantis' (1989) study yielded additional information that is pertinent here. The members of a number of groups gave KAI scores both for themselves and as each one perceived others in the group. The largest subgroup in this sample contained an equal number of men and women: 11 to 12. This group contained the unusually large ratio of 6 out of the 23 who were rated by colleagues a whole standard deviation or more away from where they rated themselves. This group seemed to be reflecting 'climate' pressure. Of these six, five were women; this might imply that women were under greater pressure to fit a prevailing climate. Further analysis showed that on dividing the 12 women into the 6 more innovative and the 6 more adaptive, all the 5 women who seemed to be indulging in high coping behaviour were in the more innovative subgroup. The question arose: If this tiny pilot can be relied upon, what is the more critical variable that might account for these data – being female, or being innovative? Other consultancy results offered a clue.

At the high tide of white South African dominance, the Occupational Research Centre was asked for advice, by white staff in a South African University, on a project to train young blacks in small business management. The aim was to help them to set up small entrepreneurial businesses in the hope that this would increase the number of more affluent blacks. It was also hoped that increasing wealth would raise prestige and diminish discrimination, as was thought to be happening in the United States. It was noted that women were well represented – so a useful comparison could be made between them and the men on KAI scores. The expectation based on other studies was that this group would have an innovative mean, because of the aim of the course and because they were drawn from elements in the society that had little or no expectation of attending a university for any kind of course. In fact the women had exactly the same mean as all the Western general population samples available at that time – that is, slightly more adaptive than might have been expected for this study. The men, however, returned a mean that was more adaptive than the male populations means elsewhere, indeed more adaptive than the general population female mean. The first thought was that the project leaders had discriminated, wittingly or unwittingly, at least against innovative men. It turned out that the university authorities had had a share in the selection of students and the suspicion was that some 'lively' males had failed to get a place. Of course, any regime concerned with the possibilities of revolt would be likely to be more wary of males than females and of anyone liable to find given structure a challenge. The studies were beginning to point to the general conclusion that style could be an underlying variable that was not at first perceived, so that other variables were thought to be the prime factors.

A third consultancy assignment came about when a major British bank asked the Occupational Research Centre to investigate for them whether they were, in their recruitment practice: 'carrying out non-discrimination successfully, to the letter and in the spirit of current law.' As expected, the team found little on which to comment – it is the companies that do not call for such an investigation that may need it. One anomaly was uncovered, however. Although not part of the original brief, KAIs were collected from the 'high flyer' (fast track) programme. Among them, the young, highly educated males had a high innovative mean of 109, compared with the mean of other bank trainees drawn from this and other banks in the USA and UK, of 98, and also the means of bank managers in general (from several banks from the UK and USA), of 91 (Holland, 1987). In fact, it is closer to a mean of 114 obtained from a similar sample of fast trackers from the British Civil Service. The women's mean of 93, however, was close to that of the women's general population mean of 91. There were no anomalies with other variables in the sample in this study – e.g., for members of ethnic minority groups the same expected difference between male and female means was found. Before these data were disclosed a number of the principal staff concerned with this selection project were asked some questions: 'that would help clarify policy as background for the report.' The first question was how long the high flyer recruitment programme had been going. The answer was: 'many years for men, recently for women.' The next question was: what was the average loss rate among the men? The reply was that is was between 10 and 15% over a span of some years for each year intake – and this was regarded as not unreasonable and quite acceptable: 'given the difficulty of making such hard choices on such little track record.' Then came the key question: 'is this the loss you will now expect for the women?' There was an immediate sharp reaction – in fact they were hoping for virtually no loss. The scheme had only recently started and they were keen to be able to report that it was going as near perfectly as could be. So here was the underlying shift of emphasis; the selectors were anxious to reduce female loss, but it appeared to be an unwritten 'political' decision aimed at avoiding a criticism of bias! The selectors were concerned to select candidates who, they hoped, would last the first few years of induction, that is, those who appeared the more likely to 'fit', the less likely to do the unexpected, challenge the system, or do anything that could cause them to leave (or be asked to leave). These bank selectors, knowing nothing of A-I theory, had intuitively arrived at the same conclusions as financial assessors in the studies of Tandon and Buttner & Gryskiewicz – among entrepreneurs, once having set up the business, it is disproportionately the more adaptive who are the more likely to survive. The study by Thomson (1985) offers a further clue. She noted that although innovators were more likely to report that they were preparing to leave the organisation they were in, the small subgroup of adaptors who felt that their 'problems were not appreciated by their colleagues' were significantly more unsettled than other subgroups. Choosing the more adaptive personnel so as to reduce turnover would require more attention to their feeling of fit. The personnel managers in the bank had made provision for this attention, having intuitively arrived at a politically safe solution.

Summary

From the theory and studies and experience related to it, it is clear that one principal hallmark of good leadership is the ability, constantly and consistently exercised, to create what might be called a 'wider consensus' group. Ideally that means everyone in the group, in full and direct contact, being able to contribute directly to the common aims of the whole group, cutting across 'cognitive climate'. Where the group is too large, too diverse, too specialised, or too distant to act easily as a single unit, then special provision is needed to ensure that the AC^3 subgroups are integrated on all key issues and have the means to communicate readily with all other subgroups as needed. One such provision is to ensure that the notion of bridger is understood and accepted. There is no easy way to widen the narrower consensus group. However, this knowledge can be incorporated into policy which explains that the effort to accommodate diversity pays off in the long run. Even being seen to be concerned helps – it engenders both appreciation and self-help.

In the earlier discussion on the management of diversity it was suggested that groups might periodically take a diversity audit for the range that is available within its ranks. This information can then be used to train members of subsets how to present their diversities so that they can be better understood and more useful to others. If the group fails to find an immediate use for a particular diversity it should still be noted for possible future use, in other words, treated as a potential resource. Discussion should be on the best way to ensure that such diversity is not used negatively whilst awaiting positive application. Minorities need to be aware that accommodation to their diversity, especially one that is unfamiliar, costs others additional effort. The aim is for their diversity to be accepted and used while the cost is perceived as low and the reward as high.

The second lesson is that all members of a minority subgroup are to remember these lessons whenever they find themselves in the majority group – when a minority irritates, it is worth remembering that, in the final analysis, we are all minorities of one. One good start is to remember the number of occasions that each found themselves as part of a minority – and how each managed. Their task is to find the means by which the diversity range within the group is known, used, or 'stockpiled' as a future resource. It is not in the majority interest that the use of the diversity of others should cost those in the minority a higher price than the rewards they gained by being used. Dialogues on means of achieving *best fit at least price* should be the key theme. The key to understanding and appreciating this problem of accommodating diversity is that every person does their own thinking and is unique[89]. Every person when collaborating has two problems: the problem for which the group is formed and how to manage collaborators. To be effective Problem A needs to remain the main problem and Problem B the minor; AC^2s and AC^3s need to collaborate and to do so need to understand the separate contribution of each to the other. Getting these balances right so as to be effective for the common good, over event and over time, is the responsibility of every member of every set, as well, of course, as the problem-solving leader.

THE PROGRESSION OF CHANGE

Clapp (1991; Clapp & de Ciantis, 1989) was involved in a major cost-cutting exercise in an international oil company. Previously such exercises had been undertaken by setting up a management working group and, once this group had planned the operation, to set about its implementation. Clapp had noted that this procedure customarily ignored the bulk of the employees' useful detailed knowledge of the working of all parts of the company and failed to win their enthusiastic support. At best it obtained their acquiescence. This time, the whole workforce of this major division of the company received a letter from the managing director asking them for their assistance in the exercise, aimed at cutting an optimistic 40% off the budget. Achieving a change by cutting costs by a few percentage points is one that can usually be accommodated within the existing climate for most people. On this small scale it is likely that only a few people will be seriously affected by getting a less satisfactory job or by the loss of it. Such modest outcome of adjustment may well be seen as beneficial to the group as a whole and eventually to most of the existing staff. Managers, however, frequently believe that more of the same good policy is a purely quantitative difference. But scaling up a plan by 5 or even 10 times means aiming at a target that is liable to produce qualitative difference – a change of climate. This may, on balance, be no bad outcome, except that it is better that significant change is planned rather than that it happens; adverse spin-offs from the main, intended effects can then be anticipated

---

89 This is no new notion; Allport (1937), when defining traits, wrote: 'In the strict sense of the definition of traits only the individual trait is a true trait [. . .] because traits are always in individuals and not in the community at large' (p. 299).

and mitigated. In this case, the staff took up the offer to take part and contributed significantly to the achievement of impressive reductions to the budget. In the process, some people were 'regrouped' and others received 'generous severance pay' – the process was not painless but these outcomes were, for the most part, anticipated and procedures were in place to mitigate adverse effects by sympathetic handling or by generous compensation to those opting for voluntary redundancy. However, the ripple effects of the exercise continued for quite some time and it may have appeared to some of the more adaptive personnel that rapid, widespread change was to become a 'way of life'. In fact, it is more likely that events outside the company would continue to exert steady pressure to change but that the upheavals within would also steady. This might well have been anticipated by the senior management but was not communicated to others. As a result, at a time when Clapp and his team were beginning to consolidate after the main effects of the changes were working through, they found that three of the key adaptor staff, some of those most able to help in the follow-up phase, had found other jobs. Because the change of climate looked permanent, pressure had built up on the very staff needed for the next phase; their going would mean a further shift of climate – thereby fulfilling their prophecy.

This highlighted the relationship between phases of major change within a company, generally as a result of outside factors, and the consequent changes in the climate being perceived, wrongly, as permanent. Each change was perceived as being advantageous to some and disadvantageous to others for a number of reasons, including whether the nature (style) of the change was or was not in accord with the style of the different individuals concerned. This change of role, from that of an agent of change in the consensus group (AC^2) to an agent of change outside it (AC^3), has been reported to lead to staff turnover, in turn further affecting climate, usually accelerating changes in the new direction. These developments mirror those in biology. Species adapt (using the term as do biologists: becoming more fitted to survive) and become modified as they do so. Some adapt to such an extent that they transform into other species; others reach a dead end and, failing to adapt, become extinct. This also describes the progression of human ideas, organisations, and the artefacts that they produce.

Van der Molen (1994), in an exploration of this progression in A-I terms, observes that a number of social animals have characteristics closely similar to A-I in man. The behaviour of these social organisms is tightly controlled by reflex and instinct but in higher-order animals there is still enough learned individual variation for it to be observable and measurable. He notes that among the basic requirements of social behaviour are at least two sets that can be in conflict, which need to be resolved by a viable balance. Each individual, being a social animal, has: 'drives for social contact and interaction [which] are, by definition, an important part of its behaviour-genetic endowment [. . .] it also has a set of, perhaps, even more basic drives to ensure the fulfilment of a range of non-social needs, e.g., water, food, cover, etc.' But the amount of resources available to meet them: 'is often limited, thus causing competition and social conflict. . . . Most of the time this dilemma boils down to the question of whether or not to submit to the initiative of other individuals at the cost of fulfilling personal urges and desires' (p. 138). Animals have personal, observable, characteristic behavioural differences and it is appropriate to refer to these as personality characteristics that do not just distinguish a species from any other but distinguish the individual. Van der Molen argues that the dilemma of balancing personal and social needs is associated with: 'a range of personality characteristics [which] have to be strongly intercorrelated, e.g., self-will, thing-orientation, individualism and innovative creativity on the one pole and compliance, person-orientation, sociability, conformity and creative adaptiveness on the other. Individuals differ from one another as far as the balance between these polarities are concerned [and] this variation between individuals must have genetic components' (p. 140). As with humans, the common characteristics of leaders and those of most followers provide a group norm that distinguishes it from other groups – what has been referred to above as 'climate'. Biologists can readily manipulate which individual is leader in some groups, such as mice, thereby being able to create groups with characteristically different leadership. Van der Molen noted that the 'adaptive-led' groups are more concerned with stricter compliant social behaviour, more control, less exploratory behaviour, and patrolling and enforcement of wide territorial boundaries, compared to 'innovator-led' groups. Adaptive-led groups may even end up with a territory too narrow to feed an expanding set whilst innovator-led groups may fragment and scatter; just as companies can veer between policies of consolidation or expansion. In addition, these tendencies can be reinforced by additions to the group of new members who are acceptable to its leadership (and find it acceptable), whilst others in the group who are less fitting are often driven out. The conclusion from these observations is that all social institutions have a life cycle and that: 'the selection rate determines the speed of ossification [or, presumably, the fragmentation] and the life expectancy of a social structure is, therefore, roughly inversely proportional to the internal selection pressure' (p. 142). Van der Molen continues by stating that all this applies to human ideas, artefacts, and institutions that have life cycles on an even larger and more complex scale but are founded on similar underlying factors, as exemplified by A-I theory, which he has linked to the workings of catastrophe theory. He suggests a common progression, from birth to death, made up of the steps:

Foundation → Consolidation → Internal selection pressure → Increasing ossification and a reduction of flexibility of the social structure → Eventual attempts to compensate these effects by means of striving for both growth and power → Catastrophic collapse by sudden environmental changes or competition.

Bleakly, for van der Molen the biologist, a sticky end is only a matter of time.

Vicere (1992) was also concerned with the rise and fall of institutions – those of companies. He argued that companies that began with small foundations were very likely to have been set up by an innovator or a small highly innovative group. If such a foundation is to both survive and grow, increasing amounts of adaptiveness are needed, through selected added staff or regular outside advice. Gradually a balance of adaption-innovation would be reached that was ideally suited to the new competitive conditions that the company faced. This added adaptiveness provides the efficient management of the complexity of increased size, the need for more economic operation, tighter production processes, delivery schedules, etc. The development of adaptiveness is liable to progress until it takes over and van der Molen's nightmare scenario of ossification unto death duly unfolds. Vicere labelled the steps of his schema from a start dominated by the highly innovative prophet, followed by crusader/barbarian, explorer, builder/administrator, bureaucrat, and, in the final fatal stage, the highly adaptive aristocrat. He seems to have overlooked the possibility that some prophets had an adaptive message and also that all crusader and barbarian armies were led by their aristocrats – his terminology threatens to undermine his schema. However, his light grasp of the historical fine issues apart, his progression and van der Molen's have much in common. Both have one weakness, among much shrewd observation; they are both inclined to see growth and salvation as outcomes solely of innovation and death the outcome of inevitable, excessive adaption. In fact, A-I theory suggests a process that is more even-handed. Government and other institutional data on the fate of small, recently founded entrepreneurial enterprises show that although they may be flexible they also tend to lack experience, resources, efficient maintenance procedures, and other useful structures, and are highly vulnerable. As in nature, units need to grow fast to reach a viable size and stability so that they have a likely future. But, in general, it would seem that human institutions, again mirroring nature, are at their most vulnerable as infants and as old folk – constant rejuvenation seems to be the route to longevity, if not immortality. The problem is, what does this mean in practice? The most likely answer, from the studies in A-I, is the constant adjusting of style, among other key variables (e.g., different levels of knowledge and skills are also obviously implicated) to maintain a balance suited to the changing array of problems that face the problem-solving group. That may not mean any inevitable move from a high-innovation stage (if it can survive) to a high-adaptive stage, but a shift to more or less innovation or adaption to suit (or anticipate) changing conditions. For problem-solving leadership, this implies that any condition, from highly innovative orientation through to highly adaptive orientation and all stops in between, is fatal if it is out of step for long with the current needs. If this match is not made, the faults of excess adaption or of innovation will become more apparent than their virtues.

What is emerging is the notion of a progression from a small, vulnerable but thrusting, highly flexible, innovative onset to a deliberate, staid, adaptive decline in which the declining, ageing system is inevitably replaced by the rising, youthful success. The two researchers quoted both place less emphasis on the mortality rate of the innovative start and heavy emphasis on the adaptive end. This balance reflects the bias in the creativity literature, which also believes that innovative new ideas must be 'better' – more creative – than any (new) development of an old idea, for the latter is doomed. Much management literature retails stories of innovative attempts to save adaptor systems from premature death. In real life, there are as many stories of adaptor attempts to stave off wildly dangerous innovator flights of fancy. A-I theory suggests that what one is likely to believe most readily may be the scenario most fitting to one's style.

Style clashes are so common that some literature makes a virtue of them, believing that conflict (stress, turbulence) is a *necessary* requirement to success. It seems more productive to treat conflict as the undesired alternative to debate, which is the more valuable when free from personal hostility. Ekvall et al. (1983), for example, list conflict as a standard element of organisational climate. Unless a difficult and complex situation is explored well, the chances of getting to a satisfactory resolution are sharply diminished. To make sure that such future possible dangers are uncovered and are well represented in management deliberations, it may be necessary to appoint a devil's advocate – as Senge (1990) reminded us, just as mediaeval schoolmen did. This way the less popular and less comfortable aspects of an issue can be fully and formally aired, even in the teeth of the prevailing contrary inclination, as part of normal debate and not raised only by the brave or the foolhardy. In the language of this book, the value of AC^3 input is so potentially valuable that it must be formally included rather than rely on exceptional people or exceptional circumstance to give it voice. The context is not that every view is as valuable as any other[90], but that a range of views must be routinely examined as a matter of long-term collective safety. This is needed even when the current paradigm (whether adaptively or innovatively inclined) has, hitherto, proved a reliable guideline to success. It needs to become common knowledge that both the alternatives of tightening or loosening current structure are viable even if one is *currently* preferred as the better line to pursue. In short, by deliberately building in the examination of alternative principles as a matter of course, they can be examined routinely (including even the most innovative options) and debated rather than be casually dismissed or be the subject of destructive conflict.

THE PENDULUM OF CHANGE

Most people have had the experience, at some time, of being part of a major change. Invariably, to a greater or lesser extent, cognitive style is a feature among the variables. It might be useful to set up a hypothetical example and examine its progress. The lessons learnt may help highlight not only the principles but also the practical ways of managing such principles in practice. Let us suppose that a senior management group, such as a boardroom, has become dissatisfied with the performance of a group. The members of the senior critical group and the operating group will try to diagnose what is the core of the problem and then see that the perceived faults are corrected. Among the wide range of problems that might be prime factors is that of cognitive style; even if not seemingly the main cause, such differences are often implicated. These differences within and between groups on the perception of the problem are liable to prevent the people concerned from reaching a mutually satisfying solution.

Let us suppose that the scene opens with top management asking the group to change, addressing certain general issues. There are two classes of general disagreement on the current mode of operation that particularly concern this chapter (see again, for the dramatic backdrop, the opening page of the novel by Pears, Box 8, p. 106). They might be summed up as either:

- the ruling group is more innovative than the operating group and wants a more innovative input into operations;
- the ruling group is more adaptive than the operating group and wants a more adaptive input into operations.

Whichever way round the difference is, the two groups disagree on fundamental style matters, emerging as such issues as the nature of the climate that leads to best results, the nature of the problem, and the nature of the most desired outcome. Not

---

90 The problem, for instance, with politically correct views is that they are often deemed more equal than others, as Orwell might have said.

infrequently, in the more intractable cases, consultants are brought in, often with an aim of backing-up management's hunch as to what (and who) is wrong so that the management's view can be further legitimised in preparation for any drastic action that may have been planned to follow. It is not always a case of competent top management castigating an incompetent lower group. Quite often, behind the instances or general issues, lie differences in the view of what the job is, how it is to be done, the interpretation of the current and future environment, what constitutes success, and other such matters in which cognitive style differences of problem-solving view may be heavily involved. At any rate, that may be the position at the start. However, if (to take one of the above examples) the operating group responds not by doing differently but by doing, in their view, even better, exasperation may begin to appear in the more innovative ruling group[91]. The ruling group (whatever its A-I orientation) may not now see such contrary proposals as a reasoned approach to what seems to be an agreed problem but as an inability to perceive the value of the 'obviously required' view, as expressed by those with, in their view, more vision, more experience, and more ability. The latter estimate often has truth in it but this is less often the case when the new proposals require high coping behaviour. In addition, the ruling group and the operating group often overlook that the former are a better position to have considered strategy and the latter know more of the details of operation: Both need to take each other's strengths into account before decision making.

Not infrequently, after a period of rising disagreement and frustration, top management takes the direct action of changing the group leader. The strategic part of the brief is often in cognitive terms that match the pair of principles listed above, either:

- 'go stir them up, widen horizons, loosen structures, look for radical change, etc.'; or
- 'go put down the riot, find out what goes on, get out them to do something we want, pull in their horns, rationalise, bring order, system and proper structure.'

The boss of the group under fire (for whichever reason) is seen as having an inappropriate style to what is now needed; a new boss is picked for having the appropriate style. Managers or work people don't usually think in quite these terms; more likely it is phrased in general terms, as listed above. The issues are also seen as limited to specific problems or the shortcoming of specific people; rarely are the principles examined in depth, in a detached way, and in the long term. The intuitive feeling is that the present problems may be demanding an approach that the current staff cannot manage (being incapable of 'real' change or 'realistic' change) and so they may need to be replaced. It is not uncommon that newly appointed managers, backed by consultants selected by them, believe that the original staff have been lucky so far because yesterday's problems, which have been successfully solved, were easier than today's problems, which have yet to be resolved. This luck may have concealed the present team's underlying lack of competence and current problems may only be resolved by those who are 'in tune' with the problem-solving style needed today. The evaluation of different style affects the view not only of the problem but also of the evaluation of those who disagree. A clash is set between a ruling group, holding a new

---

91 Or, conversely, the innovative group responding to demands to tighten structure infuriate the more adaptive ruling group by trying to sell it three more new way-out, unproven ideas.

view possibly because new elements have been introduced into it, and the established operating one.

It is usual, in established teams, to find the boss (and much of the power structure) inside the consensus group. In the change now about to be forced on the established group, its AC^2 leadership is the first in the firing line; indeed, the start is usually its 'reshaping' or some such ominous term. The new appointee as leader of the operating group has been chosen as a person who can be relied upon to carry out the style of change that is now required; the brief is to make this change quickly. Almost certainly (especially if the new appointee is experienced and has negotiated the 'right' terms for the task) the ruling group has given the newly appointed chief a mandate backed by the wide powers of authority to change. Because the old leadership did not change in the desired direction it is assumed to be made up of 'resisters to change' (mistaking *this* change for *any* change). There are other reasons for the new boss to undertake reforms speedily. First, there is the mandate, with tight time triggers built into the mandate and progress noted by watchful eyes. Second, at the onset of appointment, the new leader is not associated with any act in the past with which the ruling group might disagree; but the longer reforms take, the more this freedom from past association is eroded. The old leadership must move on, out, or down and the new strategy must be brought in, free from possible objections powerful enough to slow down the process. Among the old leadership, any who have the opportunity to move (which undoubtedly means the best of them) will do so; others of like mind and opportunity may well follow, depending on current conditions in the labour market. As these are people associated with 'failure', this loss does not seem to matter even though they clearly represent skill and experience once seen as highly valuable. Some of the people leaving will be replaced, even though part of this exercise could be downsizing. These are very likely to be people who will be located on the A-I continuum in the old AC^3 area, near where the new boss is located or slightly further out – not, that is, anywhere near the 'old set' unless there is a very special reason, say of rare technical knowledge. Given the losses on the one side and the replacements on the other, the shape of A-I distribution will start to alter. The change seems to be becoming 'permanent'.

The process can be summed as:

- it can be expected that the old consensus group and the new boss with the new mandate do not agree on key issues and strategic outlook (e.g., cognitive style);
- the new boss has been wise enough to come with a mandate to change people as well as policy, so key people from the old set will be asked or encouraged to leave;
- others who go will be overwhelmingly from the out-of-favour consensus group.

This has two effects – push and pull – it will reduce resistance to the new changes and will leave vacancies for new people who are picked because they fit the new ideal. This aids the new boss who is in a hurry:

- to meet the expectations of those who made the appointment;
- to strike before resistance can form and become effective;
- to be able to off-load every error or otherwise undesirable feature onto the past and onto those who have been demoted, have left, or are earmarked for departure;
- to assist the process by choosing replacements who are in fit with the new pattern, agree with the new boss and are even more devoted to the new form of 'progress'.

So far, this is well understood by the large percentage of working people who have experienced just such a process. However, there are snags to this process, dubbed here as the pendulum of change, largely because some elements are often seriously misplayed. To what extent, in these common exercises, is it usual for the initiators, among all the factors they do consider with care, to consider how far a particular change should be allowed to go? The fallacy has been stated before: One cannot have too much of a good thing too soon; good things deserve blank checks. This notion can be seen with clarity in a diagram of a pendulum. Suppose that the diagram shows a pendulum stuck high up on the right side. This represents a fairly extreme mode of adaption or innovation (for the explanation it does not matter which it is). This is the perception of the ruling group – an operating mode far over to a side that is not what is wanted. The aim is to kick-start it into moving to a more appropriate position (to a different style mode balance) and it seems, at least at first, that this is so desirable an end that it can hardly be envisaged to have a limit in the foreseeable future. Discussions with many managers suggest that in many situations, it seems that the need to predict when to halt the progression, in what is currently regarded as an appropriate direction, is not considered at the outset. Any such suggestion might be viewed as a dragging of feet; as special pleading by 'resisters of change'. It seems that if any direction of change is thought good, the possibility of reaching a position in which it might become a disadvantage does not often appear on agendas. So the process described above acquires a momentum, fuelled by its own internal process, and the initiators may easily lose fine control.

The pendulum analogy helps highlight the problem. As it starts, those who see some of it disadvantages will have their protests silenced. As they move on or lose power, those who were close to them, probably favourable in the initial stages to the new changes proposed, now find themselves wondering how far this process will go, since they are now the folk to see best its potential *disadvantages*. In the current aggressive climate for the new change (whichever it might be: more adaptive or more innovative) raising a voice of caution may still not be safe. Aided by additional new staff in favour, the momentum increases and then increases again. How long will it be before the natural course of events swings the pendulum way past the mean point and up towards the opposite side? What happens when it gets to a point well up onto that other side? A-I theory predicts that the pendulum has a tendency, in changes that involve marked changes of style backed and opposed by powerful in-groups, to swing well over, then the new group will settle (changes in personnel diminish) and the new style will consolidate and entrench among the new consensus. The distance from the mean may be as far to the left as once it was to the right. The new group will have few of the earlier perceived disadvantages of the old, just as planned, but also few of its perceived advantages. A-I theory is clear that no position on its measure has any inherent advantage or disadvantage; it has only advantages and disadvantages relative to the current problem. Suppose that the swing has gone too far for the best resolution of these current problems. Suppose that the current problems were somewhat misjudged, or that in the meantime they have changed. Suppose that the ruling group have begun to appraise the latest changes to the organisation's environment and, perhaps aided by further changes within itself, see the needs differently – from having, say, too little innovation available in this operating group it now appears that the disadvantages of having too much have become apparent – or vice versa. In all these cases, the need is for the pendulum to swing back a bit. But how far is a 'bit'? What is to be done now?

There is now a second factor to consider. When the new guard took over, many of the most senior, experienced staff that represented the 'old' style ceased, shall we say, to be available. Even though they may well have been replaced with younger, more fitting, but less experienced staff, the result was that this progression, in direction, speed, and losses of key personnel, still seemed to be on the right track. However, if after a period of time the pendulum may be required to swing back – because the new policy's weaknesses are seen to be outweighing the strengths that brought it into being – now the old approach, under another name, again begins to look tempting. That less experienced group, specially recruited to bring in the new change that is now itself outdated, has by this time just acquired the knowledge and skills it lacked when appointed. Its members are now, in their turn, those threatened. The once new boss, further battle-hardened, may have already moved on, possibly taking the pick of those who were most successful at hammering-in the change that is now established. The scene is set for a new loss of experienced but dated staff in exchange for new, less experienced staff, now seen as compatible with the latest (older!) change. Truly, then, this represents no true management of change but the presiding over a pendulum of change. Of course, not all the original staff will have left, nor will all the once-new group – there are always those who survive, some of whom may primarily be distinguished for this ability. If repeated trends sweep the organisation, each time carrying off the protagonists of the 'wrong' side, those that stay will hardly be the boldest or most desirable in the market place; they will be most interested in nothing other than making sure they irritate no one. A team composed of cowed staff, of low morale and with a prime interest in doing little that might mark them out, is not the best kind to ensure that the enterprise survives.

This example, drawn from much experience, shows that as the pendulum gets under way, staff changes occur that give the swing added momentum and the appearance that the change is permanent. As the advantages of the new regime become taken for granted its disadvantages become more apparent – hence the pendulum. One conclusion from the Management Initiative study was that there were always people in the larger groups (certainly from about a dozen upwards) who were able to foresee precipitating events that others overlooked. It was not always the same people, so it was not always a capacity-linked problem but often one related to style; different people perceived different events. Adaptors and innovators were sensitive to different potential threats; for innovators, they were those that came from outside the system and for adaptors, those that might arise from within it. These companies were also subject to occasional pendulum effects that discriminated either against the more adaptive or the more innovative. But the pendulum never seemed to make clean sweeps – there were always some left of the former in-group or those who had not yet become part of any in-group. If these are not just residual second-class citizens but part of a carefully selected group, then they form the necessary balance for the present and also the nucleus of the next swing. In well-led groups these swings are less costly in personal relations, less pronounced, and overall seem more consistently efficient. It seems there is often a fine line between the near-panic demand for large immediate shifts that cause unnecessary costs, and moving far enough and fast enough to stave off a serious threat. Probably the most consistent critical variable in settled groups is recognising the danger, in sufficient time, and so avoiding making overfast overcorrection of a currently less attractive option. The danger is in supposing that the current pattern needs eliminating and replacing with the new, when a safer option is to restructure the power balance between adaption-innovation to meet a developing need, wherever in the organisation it can be predicted. This accepts that the new needs will, in due course, also change; this must be catered for with knowledge and experience.

The pendulum of change may not only apply to operations involving cognitive style as a major element; it may also apply to capacity (how effective the problem solving). One example of a problem that has dogged nations is that of inflation. A roaring economy, stoked, for political reasons, by low interest rates and over-high expectations, leads inevitably to roaring inflation, which once under way is hard to check. Yet even the corrections – raised interest rates and higher taxation – have their own inflationary dangers. Clearly, economies need handling with care and radical therapies need to be applied in appropriate quantity in good time. This took a long time to learn over this past century, with almost every country experiencing a sequence of 'boom and bust' economy, compounding the problem by holding conflicting theories and politically biased views on what is a 'good' balance for competing groups in society. For the most part, the underlying principles of control were (a) the degree to which economic structure needed to be tightened or loosened to achieve the desired end for (b) which element of society (who might benefit first or most and why). On a smaller scale, innumerable companies have faced the problem of expansion, which it seemed could be wholly paid for by this same expansion, versus panic contraction, paid for by all, in the hope of better times tomorrow for those who survive. The pendulum of change proceeds rather like the progress of learner drivers, who tend to overcorrect, speeding and braking or veering to left and right, both too late and for too long. They lack the experience to know what they want with precision and to anticipate and allow for the lag that is built into their (and the machine's – the system's) reactions. In addition, when groups (as distinct from individuals acting alone or in a single small group) are involved the lags are greater, as there are more subdecisions to be made on the way to collective action.

As will be discussed in the next section, The spiral of change, there are never fewer than two classes of problem facing the members of any group: the main problem, for which it was formed, and, in addition, the problem of managing themselves – i.e., managing the diversity of problem solvers collaborating to solve a diversity of problems. This makes two problems, yet there is a third that can readily apply, remembering one of the key findings in the Management Initiative study: There is a marked tendency for problem solvers to study the probable solution more intently than the problem itself – concentrating on a quick arrival to what 'I want' rather than what the problem needs for its resolution. The Management Initiative study discovered that this is exacerbated when dealing with spin-off problems thrown up by the implementation of solutions – which can be treated even more lightly. There are times when we appear to be more expert on the nature of cars than we are on the nature of drivers – more attention may be needed not just to the nature of the problem but to the nature (style, skills, tendencies, needs) of the available problem solvers. However, there are also notable successes to record. Governments in a number of countries have now tended to set inflation targets (thereby providing automatic upper and lower limits to guiding structure) and set up committees of experts with agreed delegated means of control to steer the economy close to those targets. Such developments tend to separate problem (identification) from solution (selection and implementation) on the grounds that governments are better at the former than the latter, just as senior management needs to delegate its control of most detailed operations. Such thoughts lead back to the notion of the Paradox of Structure, which might now be refined as:

> **Managing structure, by adjustment and readjustment, so as to set just sufficient limits that will achieve maximum enabling.**

Summary

It has been suggested that all organisms, their notions, and their artefacts have a beginning and an end following what seems to be a natural progression: a small, flexible, but vulnerable start; a reaching of vigorous prime with all-round ability to manage; and a gradual decline in the ability to respond to new challenges, balanced for a while by acquired skills and cunning. However, success can also be measured by how long the process takes and how successful those are who are associated with its longevity, in other words: How much has it delivered while it lasted? Many factors are involved and no one factor, no one style, answers all problems, although one factor, one style, may need to take the lead in one setting or another, from time to time. So there is a need to identify the competent, experienced people who, although currently at a disadvantage (and seemingly out of favour) in the current environment that is unfolding, are desperately going to be needed:

- to slow down the pendulum in due, reasoned course;
- to help consolidate it at an agreed desired level, for a time;
- to be aware that it is wildly unlikely that any long-term complex problem can be solved by pure adaption or pure innovation, or any other single variable.

Collaboration by those who collectively command diversity is likely to be the more successful approach. It is true that not all of an old guard will stay or be needed. But once it is clear that some will be needed as, even by a team's very success, the nature of the problem alters, then it is planning rather than chance that should be the feature of their selection. Members of a team are almost always assessed on current performance. There is then the tendency to concentrate in the short term. So it is the problem-solving leadership that needs most to concentrate on what will be needed when the current phase has transformed the conditions and what will be needed in the next phase. Although leadership takes prime responsibility because it is in the best position to view the process as a whole, it is a better team that shares in the insights of the leadership and assists by, for instance, anticipating new precipitating events.

The notion of a pendulum of change, set off by protagonists reflecting extremes of a particular critical variable like thinking style, does not only apply to business management but to groups in general – business is only one place where humans solve problems. Kubes, a Slovak scholar and management consultant in the (then) Czechoslovak Academy, soon after coming across the A-I theory, was fascinated to note how it applied to his country's current fortunes and vicissitudes. He had made his first visit to the West from Slovakia (then Czechoslovakia) to attend an A-I international conference in 1987. Not long afterwards the Iron Curtain began to fall apart. He notes, as part of a personal view in the introduction to *Adaptors and Innovators* (Kubes, 1994):

'On the political scene of the former Czechoslovakia, we have experienced several massive swings, from adaptive to innovative and vice versa, of the pendulum of change that Kirton discusses. After a long period of ossification, the innovators (dissidents) took the lead and caused the revolutionary change of the political paradigm. Perhaps the most dramatic consquence of the shifts observed is the split of former Czechoslovakia into two independent states. Within the last four years (1990–3) we can observe several "returns" of the pendulum as the new political leaders introduce more adaptive (hopefully effective) changes. Such a trend is viewed with hope by the population, but also with fear of the possible return of the past. Meanwhile innovators (former leaders) now constitute the political (conservative!) opposition' (pp. xxxiii–xxxiv). Since then, the pendulum has swung again – and again!

THE SPIRAL OF CHANGE

Style is one of the cognitive structures that aid in acquiring understanding and control of the environment. Unless this structure is stable, meaning cannot be obtained or maintained. However, the structure cannot be so stable that new inputs cannot be accommodated, for then the grasp of (changing) reality will be lost. This is the nub of the paradox of structure; it involves a constant problem of balancing cognitive structure so that the limits imposed, which allow it to be enabling currently, will not prevent it from enabling in the future.

Successful resolution of the paradox of structure is by no means easy, yet it is a key to understanding the management of change. The first thought on any matter leaves a memory that influences the second thought on what only seems to be the same matter. If each thought builds on other thoughts and in turn is the foundation of thoughts to follow, returning to a thought on some matter is never analogous to making a cognitive circle but a cognitive spiral – the original thought has progressed. This notion of spiralling progress is implied in the problem-solving process as typified, for instance, by Wallas or Guilford. The schemata they produced were idealised templates of how the process works in theory, that is, stripped of all the errors, iterations, and confusions that may occur in practice. Each step in the process generates novelty; every solution is added novelty (or there would have been no problem). But novelties are not only generated, they also need to be accommodated, since they have necessarily altered the existing pattern. The constant generation and resolution of novelty aimed at an improved grasp of reality permits higher and higher forms of problem solving in a constantly demanding environment. As the cognitive function schema shows (Figure 1), every operation adds to cognitive resource (knowledge, experience, learning, and insight), leading to an ever-steeper spiral of achievement. The more an individual knows and uses knowledge, the more knowledge is added to the store; the more opportunities are recognised to put the knowledge to better, more appropriate use; the broader is likely to be the horizon, in a seemingly endless cycle. This helps to increase not just the efficiency of operation but the speed with which more can be learnt. To give a twist to an old adage – that the more one has, the more one can get – in problem solving the more one tries the more one is in a position to succeed and the faster one can do so. One step in progress acts as a catalyst for the next, so the process of progress is not then just a cycle but a spiral that mounts in power catalytically.

The catalytic acquisition of learning is not confined to mankind but is in its very nature. Whiten & Boesch (2001) had observed over many years that a group of chimpanzees in the wild, isolated from other groups by geographical features, had learnt to break nuts by using two stones; one as a hammer and the other as an anvil. The knowledge spread through the group by imitation so that most, but not all, in the group now use the new equipment to access a new source of food. A subset of these operators had also learnt to steady the anvil-stone when on uneven ground by inserting a steadying stone under it in the appropriate place. This additional skill was added to the first; it would not be available to any other group that had not learnt the first skill. Those making the first advance now increased their advantage, using the first advance to lead to the next. Bocsch has dubbed this catalytic progress as the 'ratchet effect'.

The catalytic progress in knowledge was explored in a triadic movement, called the dialectic, proposed by the early 19th-century philosopher Hegel, for whom the cardinal principle of life is change[92]. He argues that 'whole' reality (as the known state of knowledge) is the part of the movement called the thesis. However, reality may have in it no element that is self-contradictory (technically, the knowledge of reality needs to be perfect), so any apparent contradiction is the antithesis. But the antithesis is not perfect because it does not accommodate the thesis, therefore a syntheses is necessary – which, when achieved, becomes the new thesis. This process is endless because of our imperfect knowledge of reality. The sway between the appropriateness of adaption or innovation to any complex situation, as perceived by the leading problem solvers, fits this notion well; except that A-I is a continuum, not a dichotomy, and the synthesis achieved to solve any complex problem may be less of a compromise between competing views but more a patchwork of elements, each having a style appropriate to a specific element rather than to the whole process.

The schemata of Wallas and Guilford are essentially to be read as depicting the process within the individual, although it is obvious that they can be applied to groups. The fact that groups do not think gives rise to the notion of Problem B. Applying Wallas' and Guilford's schemata to groups touches on both notions – each person in a team gets through the stages in relation to the others involved. Both these schemata include a feedback loop, set by the thinker at the earlier stage of identifying the problem, which checks whether the solution selected meets the requirements. There is a second feedback loop, also implying a Problem B, when more than one group is involved. If the stimulus for the onset of the process came from outside the problem solver (or the group of collaborating problem solvers), then once the *internal* loop has been found satisfactory and overt behaviour alters the original stimulus source, the second *external* feedback loop comes into operation – reporting to another group (or the boss).

There are other schemata relating to problem solving (sometimes used to depict creativity) that are more obviously derived from the study of problem solving in groups, although, conversely, they can also be applied to individuals. The schema devised from the study of Management Initiative is one of these. A particularly well-known example is that of Tuckman (1965; Tuckman & Jensen, 1977), which is

---

92 For a useful review of this element of Hegel's thinking that fits well with the argument made here, see Lord Bertrand Russell, 1946, pp. 758–760.

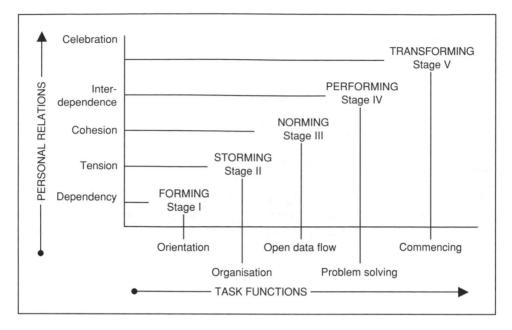

Figure 14 A model for group development. Copyright © Tuckman & Jensen (1977).

specifically intended as a model for group development (see Figure 14). Here, progress towards the resolution of a problem cluster (more usually described in a management context as a project) is set within two sets of variables, one axis relating to the people concerned and the other to other aspects of the task or project. The variables progress in the traditional steps of schemata on both axes. This schema offers insight and learning to groups whose problem may have become the process itself – getting on with each other more effectively by knowing where they are in the process and remaining in step during its resolution. It gives a glimpse of how much is being learnt on both axes or where a subproblem lies in relation to the whole, as does the fishbone schema (p. 174). As we collaborate with others better, we learn more of how to manage in a group and as a group within a wider group. As we learn more about the complexities of the problem – and its resolution – we learn more about problems and groups.

Learning piles up on learning and experience. As Newton wrote, in 1676, in a letter to Robert Hooke: 'If I have seen farther, it is because I have been standing on the shoulders of giants.' But, in truth, all our progress depends on our able use of the knowledge and experience of countless others – few of whom are giants – and of the structure this provides towards knowing what to improve, on what to differ and in which direction and manner to add our own contribution.

The problem as a moving target

There is a marked tendency, when teams are set up, for the initiators to spend time and care in assembling the best possible combination of people in style, talent, knowledge, and motive appropriate to the problem needing solution. The most skilful team builders do not begrudge spending the extra effort to ensure they have the right, clear brief and then to look for the matching personnel to launch the team, in the most propitious setting they can contrive. In practice, the composition of the team is then likely to remain unaltered by management *until the team fails.* This procedure can be described best by that classic organisational term, management by exception or, in colloquial American: 'If it ain't broke, don't fix it.' This is reactive management – but a system equivalent to preventative scheduled maintenance is more appropriate for those projects that are too important for a breakdown to be risked. The argument here is that teams, by their very success, often create new conditions and that these new conditions can give rise to needs that the current team is not best equipped to solve. A team selected to devise a product in the research department may not be the best one to mass-produce it in the production department. In other words: Progressive success in tackling a complex problem may so alter its nature that the current team can become progressively less suited to its further resolution[93].

Let us take, for example, a team that has been formed to solve problems that are barely understood – a team whose brief is, essentially, to find the problem. Let us label this way-out research unit R_0. Units of this kind are usually both very small (two or three people) and highly innovative[94]. As the ideas form on the nature of the problem so the mental process shifts to the stage of refining the alternative perceptions of the problem, which in turn leads to a reduction in the number of alternatives deemed likely. Increased effort now needs to be focused on the more likely ones. This progression in the development of the solution to the problem can be represented by a progressive shift from R_0 to R_1 to R_3 and so on, each stage representing added structure – clearer aims, more detail, and more data. As this process develops, various possible solutions emerge in their early form. Management may well show particular interest in some ideas – adding to the structure (suggested added specification), adjusting budgets, setting targets, and looking at early encouraging reports. Unfortunately, if the initiators of this process are two very high innovators they are liable to generate more ideas in the R_0 mode as well as trying to meet the needs of the latest R_4 stage; but this is not the time (as some managers have put it) to continue to shower ideas about like confetti at a wedding. In addition they are not at their most convincing when managing budgets and presenting reports to the more adaptive colleagues who are likely to be requiring them – after all, most of their colleagues are likely to be more adaptive than this group. Management may now respond impatiently, with firmer demands for specific progress on selected ideas that were reported to them earlier. A feeling that the team is disappointing may then start to emerge. If progress, as defined by such management, is not soon forthcoming, a sense that the team is not fulfilling its promise may set in, leading to action that could eventually reform the team and restructure the way things are being done. They may feel the team has, at least in part, failed. In order to make some key points

93 Companies also form product project teams with members of other departments represented: e.g., sales, costing, etc. Other representatives may be vital for the setting of targets but they cannot easily be *integrated* into a research team at its earlier stages, as these staff may not be able to manage them. They may best function, through a manager intermediary, as periodic target monitors.
94 The innovators find some lack of structure more challenging than daunting. Teams given tighter structure may need more adaption available within them.

clearly, this example presents a rather simple scenario and progression of events, but in more subtle and sophisticated ways events such as these happen often enough. The team, of course, has a different view about its progress and can acquire a marked sense of grievance.

If this segment of the process is seen more widely, this sequence of progress does not stop at this early stage. The original team, or a reformed successor, will run into fresh but similar situations as it progresses from R_3 and R_4 on into developmental stages: D_1 to D_2 to D_3 and onwards. If the project should involve a production department in its final stage, then D_4 leads to PE (production engineering) on its way to production and final implementation, having picked up other inputs such as views from marketing, finance, and costing on the way. At this point in this illustration it is hard to envisage, in the setting of a large manufacturing company, the same two high innovators arguing both with those running the sales campaign and with those involved with costing, at the same time as actually producing a prototype. They may not be at home in the increasing adaptive environment with, in addition, a whole range of different technical and administrative skills to master. In a way, this is what often happens among tiny entrepreneurial enterprises, which have a notoriously poor survival rate. What is obvious is that as the project succeeds the team needs to be cognitively rebalanced (in style and skill) to continue successfully to its next logical stage. By, say, the R_3 stage a less innovative, more adaptive input ratio is required, even if the whole is still innovatively orientated. This rebalancing progresses until, at mass production stage, a predominantly innovative input is hardly needed and adaptive problem solving is in much greater demand. Where, then, would the original initiators be? Hopefully back at the earlier reaches of the R(esearch) mode, doing something they are better at, rather than solving problems that creatively keep a whole paradigm structure purring along at high adaptor efficiency. This tale does not imply that adaption and innovation are either–or concepts; adaption is required at the earliest stage and innovation continues to be needed at the latest stage – the balance simply needs adjustment; there is never the complete triumph of one mode over another.

The fact that people may be temperamentally better suited for one part or step of an organisational process rather than another is well known; practice does not always take this into account and massive coping behaviour is then called into play. The information that this example suggests is that teams should be formed with a target statement and a shelf life stamped on them. Teams can be rewarded for transforming the stage of the problem rather than punished for struggling in a later stage. If all parties know and accept the changing needs of progression, then the team will look forward to its reform as a mark of success. Of course, some people will want to stay on after a team has been reformed, possibly more than once. This is a matter for negotiation and is by no means harmful to person, group, or company as long as everyone knows certain outcomes and their consequences. High innovator R&D initiators who want to stay with their baby can do so under agreed conditions, e.g. take a management role after suitable training or shift to a more suitable role such as, say, continuing as consultants to the team whilst their main work lies elsewhere. There are many solutions that could be worked through and be viable and successful; but solutions that ignore the problems of preferred cognitive style related to the progressively changing job are less likely to work well – just as would be the case if changing skill requirements were ignored.

THE MAKING OF RESISTERS TO CHANGE

In the study of Management Initiative, the term resister to change was often used by proposers of change wherever instant acceptance of the proposal was not obtained. The charge was commonly made when idea proposers had been, in their view, excessively held up by significant others in obtaining agreement for it from authority. The reaction to getting the agreement at last, backed by the felt need to make up for lost time, often had a marked effect on the proposers in getting acceptance of change from those hitherto uninvolved but whose backing was now vital. For them, now, the cry was: We don't want it perfect, we want it Wednesday. These newly involved people, mostly more junior and less experienced than those concerned with deciding whether to give agreement to change, were now expected to absorb the proposal, understand it, whole-heartedly agree with it, and see their place and role in helping to achieve it, all in a fraction of the time their seniors had taken. Any failure to do so might be labelled resistance to change.

One must note that the term is resistance to change – not to *this* change or *my* change. This is not to be dismissed as a subtle difference. There are no organisms that are resistant to *all* change – all are selective as to what change to accept and what not. We are all resisters to some change – any we deem that, on balance, is not to our advantage. So why is the term resister to change so popular? Possibly because it throws the entire blame of the rejection (or even delay in acceptance) of a proposal for change on to those to whom it is proposed. If the term used was 'resistance to my change,' then the blame might need to be shared: 'you may be slow taking up this proposal but I may not have presented it well.' The stereotyping form offers more protection to the proposer-implementer.

Nevertheless, some sympathy needs to be expended in the direction of the determined proposer. Most agree that the tempo of marked change has picked up speed. There seems now, even more than in the recent past, a danger in pausing to reflect instead of indulging in more rapid change. It must always have been the case that those who saw the need for change, especially when associated with an impending precipitating event only they seemed to be able to appreciate, must be naturally impatient of delay in accepting the existence of the problem. Delayed at the early stages, they then need to move fast along a line that has, over the period of the delay – they think – 'become surely more obvious to all sensible people.' Therefore the frustration, which has built up in moving those with power to legitimise needed action, may overflow onto those who threaten further delay for almost any reason. The added problem is that current notions may legitimise this impatience and sanction crude methods of overcoming of it. The complementary term to 'resistor to change', in popular currency, is 'change agent'. The dangerous element here is that it seems to imply that most of us are not change agents. The two terms together set a scene that seems to have accord with the notion in the creativity literature that there are a small percentage of us (like the authors) who welcome and initiate change and the bulk of us who have to be towed along the path of progress. Accepting a more complex position is more useful: We differ in experience, in style, and in perceiving opportunities for change. It is the existence of this diversity of problem solvers that is a prime resource in solving the diversity of problems that we face. To use such terms as resister to change and change agent suggests otherwise and so may be dangerously divisive; they strongly imply that an elite can solve our problems as long as we trust and follow them, whether or not we agree with them.

If the term resister to change is seen more simply as resister to this change then there is much relevant literature on the barriers to understanding a proposal for change. Although lack of high intelligence is an obvious possibility, high intelligence may also give the ability to uncover, in some proposals, more good reasons to resist a change. Specific lack of information and knowledge is a more likely cause; these are not always related to intelligence but to selective learning. However, much of this imbalance of knowledge can be remedied by time, as long as proposers are willing to spend such time and think they have that amount of time available. They may, truly, be able to make a good case for the shortage of time, but if the group that is needed to effect the change, and live with its consequences, is not won over, much more time might eventually be wasted.

This dilemma can be exacerbated by the view taken of the best means to solve problems. One line of action open to proposers is to oversimplify the problem and the means to achieve the solution – as a way of getting acceptance for their plans. One of these simplifications is to suggest that a single skill or method will solve much of this problem and most of the other key problems faced by the group. In industry this oversimplification can take the form that there are no problems facing the company that cannot be solved, or contained by, for example, sound financial arrangement – 'a cash flow balance is the answer to most important problems round here.' Others believe that the work of the production department, the marketing department, or R&D is their key to success. One difficulty this raises is that there may be many who do not accept the oversimplification – or they may prefer a different one. They may be cautious of challenging the myth openly because it may well be backed by a powerful group, such as those in the AC^2 role in the team. It is this group that is almost certain to possess the particular knowledge, skill, and range of style that is deemed most appropriate to solve the team's problems. Overevaluation of this narrow array must lead to underevaluation of whatever characterises those in the team's AC^3 roles – who are now to be seen, at best, to play only a minor part in any change of consequence to the team. This exacerbates all the problems of the management of the outlying roles: If they play a minor role they need not be fully consulted, and if they are not fully part of the current process they need not be fully informed. People not informed or consulted can often exhibit a naïve view of what is going on, which may only show how right one was not to ask their opinion – the prophecy loop is complete. If these people then show hesitation in accepting the proposals being advanced by the elite 'change agents' then, as 'resisters to change', they must be coerced. Meanwhile, their loss as sensors of those precipitating events that are characteristically missed by the in-group could, in time, be fatal. The elite perceives itself as an enabling structure – and rightly so – but it has its corresponding limits. These limits are noted more readily by those in the out-group than by those in the in-group – and vice versa. This interchange needs to be pursued with less turbulence and have smoother joints.

The use of terms that distinguish between problem solvers pejoratively adds to team division. If an AC^2 in-group believes that innovation, breakthrough, turbulence, thinking-out-of-the-box, radical reform, blue-sky-vision, and much else of the same ilk are the answer to every 'real' problem, then every adaptor feels at a discount, devalued, and side-roaded, with no 'serious' part to play. Either they lose interest in the endeavour and play no helpful part or, resentful, they would be happy to see it derailed. The same, in reverse, is true for innovators in an adaptor climate. If an innovator cannot navigate and contribute within the detailed heartlands of the current paradigm, they must be second-class material, goes the more dangerous adaptive thinking. The one-horse view of problems (and solutions) denies that there is a diversity of problems; there is only a multitude of problems. If there is no diversity of problems there is no need for a diversity of problem solvers – except for some lesser characters carrying out some minor tasks who can be taken for granted. To go further, when innovation, say, over-dominates, then the problem may be posed as wholly innovative, requiring an innovative solution, devised by innovators; and so on. From the first, most high adaptors will be wary. To them this may be another wild innovative venture they will need to live through. As the pace and slanted rhetoric pick up tempo, the milder adaptors may feel left out. If, now, dedicated change agents of high innovative style are appointed: 'to bring about significant change and total rethinking in the shortest time,' by now doubts and uncertainty may extend even to the mild innovators. The nature of the normal curve distribution suggests that by this time most people are on the wrong side of the change proposed. If, among the remainder, there are also some doubts, as few as 10% of the group may be preparing to tow the remainder behind the project. The 10% may have set up a prophecy: that change agents are few and the rest of us are, to a greater or lesser extent, resisters of change. They may have overlooked the possibility that these resisters may have been made by the system (their system, in fact). We need to remember that we all have our biases – our individual contributions that enable us to make changes are also limiting. Books and tutors also must take no sides – there is no ideal style. Because of the danger that this book might over-emphasise style in problem solving, the cognitive function schema was devised. Its aim is to ensure that cognitive style rests in a definable and limited place – being, in truth, a critical variable among others, but one that may also not be overlooked without danger and difficulty.

Summary

A common, if often implicit, view in the current creativity field is that there are few of us who are creative, hampered by the rest. This view supports the divisive thought that only a single line of change or one kind of changer (usually, nowadays, an innovator) will solve every current problem. These notions engender disbelief and resentment among those who feel treated as unworthy change agents, so promoting resisters to change. The final outcome seems to have helped create new schools of thought which suppose that high tension, turbulence, and even conflict are necessary and desirable states in the management of change[95]. In A-I theory these are states of last resort – like defensive wars; the management of change may require much more teaching, informing, and attention to cohesion than the elitist view credits, even at the expense of other treasured variables, like immediate solutions and the reputations of key problem solvers. This is not to say that time is unimportant and status necessarily makes a negative contribution; far from it. It means that all the key variables need taking into account, including all those that use the bulk of the problem-solving

---

95 That they may be useful on some occasions is a far cry from believing that they are often so. This divisive view may, however, be useful as an excuse for poor leaders.

diversity available towards the achievement of an agreed aim. It means that the management of change is not the same thing as the coercion to change. It means that within the management of change, time must be managed not only in the short term but in the long term also. It means that a large diverse group of problem solvers, working in partnership, may, over time, out-achieve groups led by a small subset of more homogeneous thinkers – an elite distracted by having to drive their many doubters along with them. So the divisive terms to watch, besides those already suggested above, are: best practices (meaning those in vogue), ideal leaders (meaning me), ideal solutions (meaning mine), ideal methods (those favoured by the elite), and so on, all applied not to a single problem in a particular situation and time but idealised terms that are applicable across the board. What is needed are guidelines that are less prescriptive:

- practical solutions, those that are solved in ways appropriate to each problem,
- with as many of the team actively contributing as are needed,
- bringing to bear their distinctive contributions within reasonable time,
- with the minimum of turbulence as a close examination of the problem and respectful attention to diverse views can permit.

Devices like that of devil's advocate and other such problem-solving techniques should be explored and practised. This is not only for their direct contribution to problem resolution but also because they assist in the understanding and the using of diverse skills and viewpoints whilst holding the team intact. It is explored disagreement that can be helpful, even stimulating, but it is less effective in a tense setting of intra-group conflict. The management of diversity as well as the management of change should be the task of all, aided by leaders and experts. If the change agent's role is that of teacher, not of thug, then it ceases to be a divisive element.

Having tackled the more personal problems of team diversity, now one can look at the last part of the cognitive function schema, the relationship between problem solver and the opportunities offered by the environment. Cognitive style and manifest level need to match with perceived opportunity, and if there are no personal threatening factors, then appropriate levels of motive may be generated to exploit the opportunity. This cannot always be done.

THE ENVIRONMENT AS OPPORTUNITY FOR CHANGE

The cognitive function schema lists climate, culture, scope, and opportunity as key variables related to the element of environment. All of these variables relate to interaction with other people and some also relate to nonhuman factors. One long-standing and fascinating problem relating to the variable performance of teams is the extent to which the differences are embedded in the nature of the members or in the circumstances in which they operate. Current opinion often leans away from intra-human differences, yet the information that people differ in capacity is too well attested for the whole problem to be off-loaded only onto the chance of finding the right environment. However, one difficulty in making an assessment in this area is the tendency for too many differences to be classed as those of level even if they are more likely to be ones of style, motive, or opportunity. A general assumption within in-groups is that they are for the most part better to be in than not (otherwise why stay?) and represent the norm standard for their members. Any obvious disadvantage from which the group suffers (like being regarded as the bottom of some else's pile) is often attributed to bad luck or unfairness, or may even be thought untrue. It can be amusing, if also disheartening, to note the confidence of some innovator groups (often those sporting titles including 'creativity & innovation') who brim with confidence that they have the 'right' approach as self-styled 'change agents'. They are so convinced of their position as people unfettered by boundaries (theories, policies, or whatever is clogging the system) that they deeply believe that the (more adaptive) out-groups they are inclined to despise are not creative. In fairness, this is only a reaction to an earlier dominance of adaptors who often prefer interaction with innovators in small doses – and so the pendulum goes. But for any individual, diversity cannot only be challenging but also unsettling, even frightening. A natural tendency is to be wary of diversity; in nature, black crows drive out albino crows – instinct is not amenable to reason. It is not surprising that when groups form their members try to assess each other in terms of friendliness and set an assessment of their strangeness against an assessment of their capacity. If this is done consciously, it might be verbalised as: How useful might they be, yet how dangerous might they also turn out to be?

This is an important calculation. From time immemorial, groups have met and clashed and one of them has got the worst of the meeting – and this applies not just to mankind but also to every living organism. Occasionally symbiotic alliances form, but these too are at the expense of others (us against them). There have always been views that take a one-sided evaluation of this natural process, attaching blame and guilt to one special group that will act a general scapegoat. The difference between such views in the past and those of today is which side is to take the blame. In fact, successful survival of any species means that it does better than others, altering the environment as it does so. Sometimes this is to its distinct advantage, like eliminating competitors, sometimes it over-reaches itself, and as the subsequent outcome of, for instance, vastly increased numbers can alter the environment to its own disadvantage. When they fail and fade away, then other species expand to fill the gap – the rise and fall of species is mirrored in human behaviour by the rise and fall of companies and empires. Trying to get the victors to feel guilty about the means of their success is a wholly human and relatively very recent phenomenon. This may not, on balance, be too unreasonable since mankind has become so formidable that even the victors may become undone by their own activities – more than has happened to any other organism in the past. However, the assessments that all groups make about each other need to become more sophisticated and realistic before too much drastic action is based on them. One lesson that needs absorbing is that *Homo sapiens* is dangerously competitive – not some but all are capable of barbarous acts (see also: Introduction, Appendix 5). We need to remember that, in Africa, *Homo habilis* coexisted with and eventually replaced the gracile *Australopithecenes*, to be replaced in turn by *Homo erectus*. We believe that Neanderthals replaced Cro-Magnons just as, later, *Homo sapiens* coexisted with and eventually replaced whatever *Homo* had by then survived. No group of *Homo sapiens* has yet been proved peaceful for long, and diversity programmes aimed at better coexistence need to look to the future rather than try to rectify the past; the justification of such programmes must not aim at old-fashioned revenge but human survival, preferably in a little more comfort and with a little less stress. The message is that mankind needs to solve the diversity of problems emerging from an increasingly man-made environment by the better mutual use and exploitation of a diversity of problem solvers: differing in mental process, such as of culture and capacity; in perceived need, interest, knowledge and skill, as well as in opportunity. Among the critical diversities in problem solving that need to be managed well is cognitive style.

It can be instructive and less personally threatening to extract and examine some examples of human change from history. Diamond (1997) has reviewed, in substantial and compelling detail, the arguments that have raged about whether the differences between human groups in technological knowledge and its applications were an outcome of the differences in the potential capacity between those who were more advanced and those who were backward, or whether the differences could be attributed to the conditions in which they lived. For those interested in collective problem solving there is much to be gained from getting to know more about this intriguing problem. In the last 500 years, roving Europeans and other technologically advanced groups have come across people who still roamed as stone-age hunter-gatherers, a state that had begun to change in the Fertile Crescent (in the Middle East) some 10,000 years before. These discovered folk were dismissed as backward savages, probably incapable of ever closing the gap between themselves and those who had stumbled on them. The powerful newcomers were well prepared to brush them aside in the pursuit of their own interests. This has happened throughout time by every other successful species and variant within species. The human newcomers had also, inadvertently, brought with them diseases, which caused them problems but which struck down the indigenous people. The indigenous people's losses from disease were substantially greater (often over 90% of the original population) than the casualties inflicted in one-sided wars[96]. It is true that they returned the complement, passing on a few diseases of their own – but the new folk had better resources, were more numerous, and came, on balance, to less harm. From the point of view of a study in problem solving, how does it happen that some people can get so far ahead of another? Is there anything useful, to the benefit of all mankind, that can be learnt from teasing out some of the variables? Possibly the two main contending hypotheses hinge round in-born differences between people as a result of heredity (that can only be changed by breeding) and differences in opportunity (that can be changed by fresh opportunity and learning). It is best to deal with each in turn. If one begins by assuming, in the large scale, that opportunity is the key – how reasonable is this assumption?

Mankind has been around on Earth a comparatively short biological time, perhaps as little as 100,000 years, although the period of visibly significant advance began about half that time ago. From a very early stage, as best as the scant records show, man was a hunter-gatherer and tool-maker (as distinct from other animal tool users), with a skeletal form and a brain that has possibly changed very little, if at all. The generally agreed view is that North East Africa may have been the place where man originated

---

96 The deadliest diseases were those that the recipients had never met before; these were mainly derived from keeping domesticated animals. For instance, from just two of the principal domesticated animals came: from cattle, tuberculosis, measles (via rinderpest) and smallpox (via cow pox); from pigs, flu and pertussis (whooping cough). Of course the locals had some diseases lying in wait for the invaders. However, the latter got by far the best of this exchange. The principal means by which the diseases developed are noted by Wills (1998): 'An ecological disturbance, such as the introduction of agriculture to central Africa, can lead to the temporary success of a poorly adapted pathogen. The pathogen can survive even if it causes a severe disease in its human hosts, because the hosts are now so numerous. As a result of our efforts to change the world, we (and our domesticated animals and plants) have suffered dreadfully from diseases' (p. 89).

and the Fertile Crescent seems to be the place where the earliest significant advances (in gathering, hunting, tool-making, the use of fire, etc.) really got under way. Progress, at least by today's standards, was by minute steps – one can readily believe that of those who lived to see grandchildren reach maturity, few could have detected much noticeable progress. Clearly, however, progress there was and gradually the tools and weapons become appreciably more effective. As far as can be assessed, the whole population of *Homo sapiens* was of the same skill, the same brain size, probably the same intelligence, at the same state of advancement, most likely with the same skin colour, and lacking any significant characteristic behaviour variation that could pass as culture. Any differences in these variables may have had to develop later. Then a change occurred that seems to have quickened the pace – generally considered to be about 40,000 years ago – which suggested that high success was leading to increased population density and diffusion. An early casualty of this expansion was Neanderthal man – who vanished at about this time (after 60,000 years of cohabitation with *H. sapiens*). So did a number of the larger (and, most probably) tasty and nutritious mammals. Mankind's serious impact on the environment had begun. Quite what was the prime human advantage aiding this change is a mystery, although many experts guess that it may have been started by a significant development of a resource such as language that will have left no early trace for the archaeologist. Current thought is that a nearly common language existed at this time and researchers into language development suppose that the remains of this common language are still detectable. Although few in number, there are enough words (relating to such fundamental concepts as body parts) that can be found remaining in languages all over the world to support this theory. Development of tools was proceeding but as yet no great differences between groups had emerged – the Aborigine, on arrival in Australia tens of thousands of years ago, had tools at least as advanced as has been found anywhere else. Yet serious differences between people had begun to emerge by 8000 BC, among groups in the Fertile Crescent as they began to settle as food producers. The key question that Diamond's work addresses is: Why the Fertile Crescent? This is only a comparatively small area, from the eastern seaboard of the Mediterranean to just beyond the riverbanks of the Tigris and Euphrates. One startling answer is opportunity, which, once exploited, began an autocatalytic spiral of progress that started to leave other groups far behind. There were several different reasons for this that became interrelated.

The first was the availability of food that could be farmed. Blumler (1992) suggests that of some 200,000 species of plants available worldwide, only 56 have been identified as falling into a class that could have transformed mankind into a food producer. They include such staples as wheat, millet, rice, corn, and beans. Of this handful, no less than 32 grew naturally at that time in Europe and West Asia, the bulk being within the Fertile Crescent.

The second reason was that the Fertile Crescent was relatively accessible to a vast area, from Britain to Japan. This area had few serious barriers dividing up the lands and a relatively similar (east–west, moderate) climate; exchange of ideas, animals, technology and, at first above all, plants were possible. Of the 56 vital crops, only 1 was located as far away as England with 6 in East Asia – all 7 not so totally cut off that, over the millennia contacts and exchanges of crops and ideas could not be made. By contrast, America possessed 11 of the crops that create farmers. But this land and the crops in it were more equally divided into three areas, North, Middle and South, between which communications were poor and, because of the different (north–south) latitudes involved, crops could not readily be exchanged. Sub-Saharan Africa, cut off from the Fertile Crescent (including borderland Egypt), had only four of these crops and Australasia did not have any. This imbalance has been exacerbated by hunter skill. Roberts et al. (2001) remind us that, for instance, the disappearance of almost all the large animals in Australia occurred over a relatively short period of between 10,000 and 15,000 years, using what was, for the period, good mainstream weapon technology – the period being the early Stone Age some 40,000 years ago. Stone-age immigrants with high hunter technology devastated North American animal life, destroying many species before the latter could cope and the new arrivals had learnt to domesticate them. Easier east–west communication in Eurasia meant that new ideas and artefacts moved along the vaster, richer progress pathway, which was not so easily done elsewhere. Hill (1996), in his study of the early progress of engineering (from the earliest known dam in the 3rd millennium BC, in Egypt, to the achievements at the end of mediaeval times), shows how ideas moved along this pathway with increasing speed. Water raising machines, such as the *shaduf* (to use the Arabic term), which were used particularly for irrigation, were depicted in Akkadian reliefs in 2500 BC and first appeared in Egyptian reliefs in 2000 BC. By the 12th century AD, development reached a peak with huge water wheels, some with a diameter of 20 meters, being constructed in Islamic lands; but this variant had first been designed in India by the 2nd century BC, had reached the nearby Hellenistic world a century later and China by the 2nd century AD. There was no such (relatively) easy pathway between, say, West African cultural centres and Egypt, between the Aztecs and the Incas, or between Burma or China and Australia. The long-term advantage to mankind, of the concentration of opportunity in the Fertile Crescent as an accessible unit to most of Europe, North Africa, and Asia, was vast.

The third advantage of this fortunate area was also highly significant in that: 'the wild ancestors of many of the Fertile Crescent crops were already abundant and highly productive, occurring in large stands whose value must have been obvious to hunter-gatherers. Experimental studies in which botanists have collected seeds from such natural stands [. . .] show that annual harvests of up to a ton of seeds per hectare can be obtained, yielding 50 kilocalories of food energy for only one kilocalorie of work expended. By collecting huge quantities of wild cereals in a short time when seeds were ripe and storing them for use as food through the rest of the year, some hunter-gathering peoples of the Fertile Crescent had already settled down in permanent villages even before they had begun to cultivate plants' (Diamond, 1997, p. 136).

The fourth advantage was the distribution of the larger mammals that are most useful to mankind and most readily domesticated. Diamond lists the five most important as sheep, goats, cows, and pigs, all found in the Fertile Crescent, and the horse, found in South Russia and Mongolia, between which contact was made even in the Stone Age. The other areas of the world were, by comparison, not so lucky. The early domestication of this group of animals lead to new resources or improved the supply of those already known, providing: 'milk, milk products, fertilizer, land transport, military assault vehicles, plough traction and wool' (p. 158).

The Crescent had one more advantage; the fifth natural bounty was a supply of metal ore – including the vital ones of copper, tin, and iron. The catalytic pace of progress picked up from millennia to millennia: from plant producing in 8500 BC, the domestication of the larger mammals by 8000 BC, the discovery of pottery by 7000 BC, the setting up of chiefdoms by 5500 BC (villages had come into existence in 9000 BC), the wide spread of copper and/or bronze by 4000 BC, the setting up of states by

3700 BC, the invention of writing by 3200 BC, and the widespread use of iron by 900 BC. Meantime the tanning of leather, the invention of weaving looms, the use of dyes, and much else were fitted in as the rate of progress gathered pace. By comparison, the Far East, relatively accessible to the Crescent, reached the same state on the first four on this list a mere 1000 years later, contributing, in turn, other items to this cultural progress pathway, such as the horse and silk. Opportunity plays a key role in successful human problem solving. It is true that opportunity is not always taken, but it is the lack of it that is the greater factor in progress.

The last question that arises from this general example of human problem solving in the context of different environments is: Can the environment account for the bulk of the differences between how much and how well groups progress? The answer must be qualified: First, a great deal does depend on environmental factors, but they cannot account for all the discrepancies. But, second, when new ideas reached groups from contacts (those that had them), not all the groups responded in the same way – the response ranged from some who responded positively and briskly to some who did not respond at all. This pattern does at least clear away one notion that whole vast populations reacted in the same way and that, therefore, some of these vast populations were inherently superior to others; more accurately, some became more advanced than others mainly because of environmental advantages. That said, why did some of those, like some Maori tribes, promptly take up the musket and terrorise ancient enemies who did not? Why did the Japanese, in general, take to Western technology soon after coming across it? In contrast, why were the Chinese slower, then gave some of it up – surely not because they mislaid some of their intelligence for a few centuries? Differences in intelligence, even using measures mainly validated on white populations in the beginning of the last century, do not lead to conclusions that neighbouring Maori tribes had, by breeding, acquired different levels of intelligence or that the Chinese and Japanese found a way of lowering their mean IQ after millennia of cultural dominance. The main clues must lie elsewhere.

One thread that runs through this historical example is that people are selective in the kind of ideas they pursue or adopt; the main argument being that no person ever rejects them all and no person ever accepts them all or at the same time. This pattern applies to groups as well, for the same reasons. Individuals pursue the ideas and artefacts that appear to be of use to them compared to the perceived cost of acquisition. This is true even at the point of accepting new information about the environment, as Kelly has pointed out. If the new data threaten to disturb the current paradigmatic structure, the individual's very grasp of current reality or their understanding of self, both vital structures in the pursuit of problem solving, it is the data and notions that are rejected. Of course, it has long been known that some ideas are more difficult for their originators to get adopted. In this book, the argument is that those ideas which are innovative and therefore challenge the prevailing structure are riskier and less easily to assess – and so less easy to access. Those asked to accept them must first change their view of the current paradigm; only then can they truly assess the specific change on offer. This is a double task that inevitably takes more time. Gribben (1998), in the context of advances in astronomy, points out that: 'Science doesn't always progress in an orderly fashion. A discovery made today may have to wait for years, or decades, for its significance to be appreciated and slotted into place, while another observation, made tomorrow, may be of obvious and immediate importance' (p. 71). This phenomenon has puzzled any number of managers, just as it puzzled the researcher in the study of Management Initiative at the beginning of this book. The difficulty of managing the paradox of structure was just not fully appreciated. It was even less appreciated that not only would adaptors have difficulties in an innovative environment but that innovators would have much the same problem in an adaptive environment; not because, in this case, the paradigm was different, but rather that adaptor and innovator progress depended on treating it differently.

A hunter-gather group that felt it understood its world and was comfortable with it might not even have considered changing such a satisfactory life for one that had too few perceived advantages and too many disadvantages. If they lived in a perceived settled environment, adaption may have been the prevailing mode – even if, as expected, A-I was normally distributed. In the early days of European settlement in the USA, three groups of land users – the farmer, the cattle herder, and the shepherd – felt mutual contempt for each other, only exceeded by their shared agreed contempt for the city dweller. A whole way of life that is currently giving satisfaction to those in it is more important to them than possible gains that might damage it. It is the more so when a whole package of the elements that make up the way of life are closely interrelated so that a change will affect them all. In such circumstances the wildest innovators might hesitate to disturb the pattern. Many Red Indian tribes found no difficulty adopting the horse and becoming noted, dashing cavalrymen as well as users of packhorses. Nor was it a serious problem for most tribes to adopt the gun. But it was a major problem for most of them to give up a nomadic lifestyle, even when the rewards for such style were clearly declining. A number of Maori tribes adopted the musket and promptly subdued traditional enemies who had not done so, in a series of battles called the 'musket wars'. By the time the Europeans arrived the Maori had slaughtered all the earlier invaders of New Zealand, the Moriori. However, there remained a group who, like most such survivors, lived safely at an unfashionable address; the small, cold Chatham Island. They were discovered by a whaler, which reported their presence to a Maori tribe. This tribe raised an army and in a brief, single, disastrous raid slew and ate the majority of the Moriori men. Although they took many of the women as wives, the Moriori, 1600 strong at the time of the raid in 1835, numbered less than 300 full-blooded members in a count in 1848 (Buck, 1950, p. 15). Although armed with muskets, the Maoris generally slew the prisoners in the traditional way: by blows with beautifully polished, stone meres. The possession of the muskets had left their original lifestyle largely intact, from the retention of meres down to ritual cannibalism[97]; just as, even today in 'advanced' societies, some people using computers believe in witchcraft or that the world was created in 4000 BC.

---

97 'While it was politically correct during the 1970s to presume that savages were peaceful and noble, the discovery of what appear to be burned, split and butchered human bones at many places in both the Old and New Worlds has changed the assumptions. [. . .] Such unspeakable practices [as cannibalism] might have played a much larger role in our past than we have thitherto dared to admit.' But he continues, hopefully, that in his view: 'we have, on the whole and for better or worse, intellectualised our world. Our efforts have made the world a tamer place and have modified our behaviours accordingly. Over time, in such a diverse but less dangerous world, selection for survival may have had effects on us that are similar to the selection for docility that has taken place in [our domesticated animals]. Hunlike behaviour is less advantageous that it once was. Perhaps we, too, have been tamed' (Wills, 1998, p. 173). Cannibalism has occurred throughout mankind's history in every continent; it occurred among others hominids, such as *Homo erectus* and Neanderthals (White, 2001). The grim thought is that we all have barbarian ancestors; the pleasing thought is that, unhampered by instinct, all barbarians become civilised, given time.

There must be caution in supposing that advances found by some groups as good are uniformly so and cannot be lost. Diamond (1997), in his anthropological historical review, notes that on many occasions groups 'lost' knowledge when circumstances rendered the knowledge of less value or the circumstances stopped them using it (e.g., local resources did not yield the materials needed). Others failed to acquire what may seem to us was vitally needed. One outstanding, well-documented example was that of the Norse in Greenland. They represented an advance guard of the new Euro-Asian technology and tried to establish themselves in lands new to them. On this occasion their number was few, the support from 'home' was weak, and their advantage in unfamiliar conditions was slight. Like most advanced invaders they probably saw little benefit in learning or copying the techniques of those they were displacing – this time the Eskimo. But over a few centuries the weather changed and the slim advantage of the Norse way of life in these conditions vanished – they needed Eskimo skills to survive, particularly in catching fish. These they had not learned and duly perished, whilst the Eskimo are still there.

It appears, then, following Kelly (1955), that ideas and artefacts that do not disturb the core of a lifestyle, or which actually enhance it, are readily acceptable while others are not. The Maori tribes most liable to take up the musket were those who had not been overwhelmed at once by the new invaders (had time to reflect) and were the most militant. The Japanese adoption of Western artefacts began as a result of a realisation that the new weapons could be added to their existing armoury (the samurai sword continued to be an object of veneration for hundreds of years to come[98]) whereas the Chinese did not place military prowess so closely at the core of the nation's identity. It must be remembered, however, that the Japanese did not take up the new ideas, which they eventually commanded so well, without having serious second thoughts. They first came across those guns and other artefacts in the middle of the 16th century but gave them up – as culturally unacceptable – by the end of it. As Keegan (1994) noted: 'an available improvement in the technical means of waging war was outlawed in the interests of preserving the existing social structure' (p. 23). It was not until two-and-a-half centuries later, when Commander Perry turned up in the mid-19th century, bristling with cannon and briskly stated demands, that the Japanese settled for disruptive progress, at short notice. Only half a century after this and they were re-equipped and ready for their neighbours again, starting with the Chinese and Russians – the latter they defeated, in 1905, helped by a more modern fleet than that of the Russians. The West, within its borders, has its own stories to tell, as most teachers, consultants, and managers can attest. The Luddites marched to destroy the new looms that undermined their miserable existence of weaving on their home, foot-powered looms, in a vain effort to halt progress in this direction. The British navy, at the height of its powers at the turn of the 20th century, deliberately produced a new type of battleship (the Dreadnought) making, at a stroke, every other battleship including theirs, obsolete – a most courageous move. Yet, amazingly, at about the same period the very same British navy high command was dangerously antagonistic to developing the submarine or even seriously considering an answer to it, because this craft did not represent a

---

98 Just as the Maori adopted the musket and kept the mere, officers in modern armies still use swords on ceremonial occasions – some elements of past social structure are still useful in protecting current identity and status.

gentlemanly method of war, and the outcome of the Great War hung in the balance. This is a curious view to the outsider, which echoes that of the French knight faced with the English longbow and the Japanese samurai faced with the weaponry possessed by those they regarded as barbarian Westerners. In each case the adoption of some (but never all) appropriate new tactics and weapons would have been perceived as undermining the standing (and *amour propre*) of these elite groups. The armies in Europe, bar the British, all entered the Second World War dependent on the horse. In 1939, Polish lancers actually charged German tanks. Diamond argues that some northern groups of Australian Aboriginals came across and must have spurned the use of the bow. In living memory, in the technologically dominant West, no company that was famed for producing Swiss movement watches switched to producing innovatively variant digital ones – most went out of business, although a few went upmarket with increased standards and more highly jewelled versions. In every case, a dominant factor is that the solution, be it the adoption of new weapons, a new method of fighting, or a new product opportunity, did not accord in style with the problem-solving group's collective image of itself. Hence, the opportunity was instead perceived as a threat to its integrity. Consultants today, in innovation-mad environments, fail to allow the time for whole established groups to adjust and accommodate to changes in paradigm – believing them to be only changes in technology. A better understanding of this problem might well give them more sympathy and more success with less backlash.

It must always be remembered that turning down an opportunity, even if this is subsequently seen as unwise, does not mean that any of the people concerned were against all change – far from it. The problem is not whether or not to change, but which change opportunity is to be accepted as an appropriate challenge and which is not to be accepted – decisions that are made for what appear at the time to be the best of reasons. No group has had, or should consider it now has, a monopoly of foresight and wisdom in the management of its change. In all fairness, the advantages of innovative devices are not always readily apparent from the performance of their early examples. To take an example relating to the deadly bow and well-tried trebuchet: 'Guns were not at first used for battering [castle] walls, lacking the necessary power, but were anti-personnel, as at Crésy [in 1346], where Froissart describes the cannons that they (the English) had in the battle "in order to frighten the Genoese." Villani makes a similar comment of the same battle, remarking that the guns were "for the purpose of frightening the horses" largely from the noise they made' (Bradbury, 1998, p. 288).

Even if some proffered notion was seen to have more merit, the problem of accepting change opportunity balanced with keeping individual and group identity is universal. Intelligence and other level variables are often not the main key to understanding how differences in idea development and adoption occur in very large diverse groups, only perhaps accounting for significant differences among small groups. Many factors play a part; style differences may play a larger part than has thitherto been suspected. The relationship between style and change is not simple. Large-scale change requires, over time and in complex problem solving, a range of style appropriately applied. Innovators, with their lesser attachment to consensually agreed structure, may be better placed to take up ideas that challenge strongly held cultural barriers. Yet these are not all innovators, but only a few of the high innovators, for whom most of the rest of mankind are relatively adaptive. Their task at 'selling' their changes is not easy. When they begin to do so they are often not the people who can take these ideas and prototype artefacts into general, effective use. Others with different styles and skills are better placed to consolidate and develop these notions. The interweave of variables that involve style is made up of the mode style of the power group (reflecting the success of past problem solving), the nature of the new problem, and the extent of the perceived threat that either the problem (if acknowledged) or its likely solution (if accepted) poses to the perceived identity (and continuity) of the group. As these variables unfold so, at the same time, the variables relating to level, skills, and knowledge, to say nothing of opportunity and motive, need to contribute if there is to be a final successful change.

In the examples above it is easy for critics to see the wrong decisions and the missed opportunities of others. Denigrating others' decision making from the viewpoint of hindsight is done more easily if the examination is shallow and not set in the context of the time in which it was made. To take another example: At the turn of the 19th century, Napoleon was at the height of his military power and only had Britain left to be thoroughly beaten by his army. He foresaw no problem in beating the British army; the problem was getting his own army across the English Channel in the teeth of a navy strong enough, at the time, to destroy all other European navies combined. As Parkinson (1994, pp. 94–96) notes, there were three possibilities. The first was to distract the British navy to some other place for long enough to make the crossing in safety – this was the plan adopted and it failed. Another was to find a way to cross in a dead calm – unfortunately if the British fleet was becalmed for lack of wind, so would be the French fleet and those of its allies. The last possibility was to find a weapon against which the British had little defence. Interestingly, the solutions to both the latter problems were to hand – as prototypes. At this time, Frenchmen were experimenting with steam-driven paddle boats, which would have been no match for British warships able to move, but which could have steamed past them if the wind would not blow for long enough. These devices were not seen as viable at the time, and effort was not expended to see if they could be improved enough to carry out the task of towing barges across the open sea in flat calm. For the last possibility there appeared in Paris, in 1800, an American artist-turned-engineer – a metamorphosis that was undertaken in Britain! Fulton had a plan to produce a 'torpedo', which the French authorities examined and finally turned down after a not sufficiently successful performance. Fulton then turned up again in Britain, where the naval authorities gave his idea a thorough test, which, they considered, it failed. Fulton next moved to the USA, where he was again given an opportunity to produce a device for test, but died before he could do so and the idea was dropped. Interest there was; faith there was not. The question is whether the French would have been justified in continuing an uncertain experiment. Perhaps they were right; there was insufficient time and knowledge to make such vessels that were reliable in sufficient numbers. Perhaps they were wrong; further resources on a sufficient scale may just have succeeded – even now, a prediction would be hard to make that would convince most experts. By the nature of adaption-innovation, it is easy to miss a viable innovative idea because it lacks sufficient known structure to allow us to make secure evaluation. It is also easy to miss a carefully worked out adaptive potential failure because it seems so well supported by its known structure. In some cases, too, the decision faced is not so much whether to accept an innovative notion or not but *when* to accept it. Most inventions require development time to meet the minimum requirements for practical use. These changes take time and very necessary adaptive input to ensure success. Also, when evaluating past decision making one needs to do it in the light of information and beliefs around at the time – and learn more how the limits of the current structures were still enabling. Would we then make better guesses than those at the time did?

Opportunity for change in time perspective

In the process of development, changes occur that damage the original structure: This is inevitable. If all is change then even action that attempts to preserve the current paradigm alters it. All organisms, in succeeding, do so at the expense of others. Mankind succeeds at others' expense in a variety of ways: eliminating them (like mammoths[99]), raiding and despoiling them, subjugating them (as all empires have done), enslaving them (slavery was a widespread practice throughout the world, over various long periods of time, well into the 20th century), driving them into unfashionable places (Chatham Island, 'native' reservations, or the place across the tracks), and even ritually eating them (cannibalism has occurred at some time in every continent)[100]. This natural tendency of deliberate or merely casual aggression is, in mankind's new-found wisdom, up for careful examination, less, perhaps, because there is a deep feeling that the old ways are now seen as unethical; more, perhaps, because they are seen to work less well[101]. This is just one more example of our solving problems that threaten survival. The constant concern of choosing which new idea to adopt and develop and which to resist continues, as it always will.

Summary

From time immemorial, successful groups have looked down on others, believing them to be inherently inferior. The Ancient Greeks coined the word 'barbarian' to mean anyone who did not speak Greek – the foreigners sounded funny, as if they were always saying *Bar Bar*. In recent times, the growth of psychometric measures offered the means to measure variables like intelligence and so to obtain norms for whole populations. Here was a chance to equate the progress of some groups with superior attributes. There were weaknesses with the procedure, however. In the first place the tests were validated during construction mainly on the group deemed superior, leaving

---

99 Alroy (2001) describes a computer model that correctly predicted the extinction or survival of 32 of 41 large prey species in a study of overkill by human hunters. Simulations indicate that a human density of 1 in 20 square miles: 'almost invariably leads to mass extinctions'.

100 Also human sacrifice to placate the Gods: from Carthage (to hypocritical Roman horror), Mycenaean Greece (Agamemnon's slaughter of his daughter, Iphigenia), with Abraham's son having a near miss (as reported in the Old Testament). Then, to continue round the world, there was sacrifice for the comfort or entertainment of the dead in India (suttee: wives burnt on their husband's pyre until latter-day British rule), to the hundreds of slaves, captives, friends, and relatives to serve the Chinese monarchs of the 3rd century BC Qin dynasty in the hereafter. And still on a vast scale, but in more recent times, back to the Aztecs and Incas, and so girdling the Earth. We need to learn more about how we think, not to attribute blame but so that we may manage the future better than we did the past.

101 Where the past continues to satisfy it is still desired. There is at present concern at losing the tiger, which is no longer any danger but of great interest to mankind. However, no one has complained that the last organisms capable of producing smallpox are now contained in a few bottles under close guard. No one complains that this is cruel and that they should be let out, now and again, although some have queried whether it's worth risking the danger of keeping any at all. Such fellows as the malarial mosquito and the tsetse fly, among others, had best take care; their doom may be nigh. Assisted survival is still for those who please.

others at a disadvantage. Second, the gaps found not only did not always favour whites (those of Far-Eastern descent often did marginally better), but no gap obtained with reasonable measures ever turned out to be large enough to account for the gap in technological advance. Small groups, within single populations, may be found to have variations, but there is no good evidence that large sections of us have any such mean differences; no evidence at all that there are subspecies within *Homo sapiens*. The same biology, the same brain, and the same variations among key variables bind us all. Diamond points out that the people who first reached Australia, at the time when the whole of mankind was in the paleolithic age, were technically among its leaders. They had advanced tools and weapons for their age; had: 'developed some of the earliest known stone tools with ground edges, the earliest hafted stone . . . axe heads . . . and by far the earliest watercraft in the world. Some of the oldest known painting on rock surfaces . . .' (1997 p. 297). Failures of earlier hypotheses to be sustained and the accumulating new data suggest that we need to know more of the true reasons for success and failure in problem solving by groups, both large and small. In the Australians' case, opportunities of climate, communications, as well as plant and animal life suitable for domestication were not available in anything like the quantities on offer in the Fertile Crescent.

However, opportunity alone is insufficient to account for gaps between groups, whether in the past or the present, or whether between ethnic groups or within a local team. We are all bound by the same limits; for progress, we need both the opportunity and the perception to exploit it successfully in good time or time to recover from taking the wrong decisions. We need time, as Kelly (1955) observed, for change to come at a pace that does not destroy or impair the individual's personal identity and the collective feeling of a group's identity, such that it weakens understanding of the environment and the events occurring in it. The position is no different for all life, at all time, in every place – just a matter of degree, except that mankind wants more control and therefore needs more understanding. Mistakes throughout time have left those who succeeded, more usually than not, to impose themselves on those who did not. The ways in which they did, less some of the grisly bits, sound like a modern management training manual. It is the way all progress has occurred and, in its basic outcomes if not always its cruelty, the way it continues to do so.

It has been argued that society is a reflection of the individual, who is its basic element. To bring about change, the individual, like societies, needs to find an opportunity and then be willing to accept and act on it. This initially depends on the recognition, acceptance, and management of diversity – of which opportunity is an outcome. The acceptance of diversity and the subsequent management of change can only occur if the perceived advantages outweigh the perceived disadvantages – and a key disadvantage is the threat to the integrity of self, at an individual level, or of the society at the group level. To concentrate again on societies, all successful ones have expanded at the expense of other life, including other societies. This has been seen as the natural course of events, until perhaps now, when the expansion of successful groups can be seen to have possible long-term effects that may be as harmful to the successful as to those less so. In the past, all over the world, groups that have been successful have shown contempt for the losers – the ancient Greeks were not the only ones to think of foreigners as barbarians. Where the defeated group contributed little to the victors they were driven off, eliminated, or absorbed. Westerners as well as the Aztecs, the Incas, and the Chinese, in their expansion to the South East during the long Zhou dynasty (1100 to 221 BC), absorbed many people. During the Zhou dynasty, for instance, several local native languages vanished and were replaced by a form of Chinese. Occasionally conquerors respected groups that fought valiantly: The British respected the Gurkha, the Zulu, and the Maori, as long as they were no longer a threat within the Empire. When they remained a threat, then both groups could end up being both wary and contemptuous of the other. The Chinese faced the Mongols on their northern border, just as Rome faced the Goths, Vandals, and Slavs. The civilised power, even when it lost, was always contemptuous of the 'barbarians' but tried to imitate their military success (their soldiers often imitated barbarian cruelty); the barbarians in their turn were uncertain how far to ape the conquered civilisation, disliking the contempt but fearing that they might become 'decadent'. Mergers can create problems, as has already been noted. History shows groups desperately trying to pick up another's advantages whilst retaining their integrity and identity; problems not solved in merely a few generations. It is interesting to speculate what the ancient British (mainly but not wholly Celtic) people, left by the Romans and invaded by streams of barbarians (Angles, Saxons, Jutes plus Vikings, Danes, and eventually Normans), would have thought if told that this disparate amalgam of Celts and Teutons would again eventually be proud to call themselves British (and conquer others in that name) – more than a millennium after the mutual massacres. The management of diversity can require learning many hard lessons and, in the process, can generate a pile of added challenging problems.

THE PROBLEM-SOLVING LEADER

A prime aim of this book is to get a better understanding of thinking style, which of all the elements of cognition is, today, probably the one least understood. This is not just an academic exercise, for, once understood more clearly, it helps further understanding of problem solving – that process on which all human progress has and does depend. The book concentrates on four key elements: perception of opportunity, generating the motive to exploit the opportunities selected, and using whatever appropriate diversities of style and capacity are available to do so.

The book then turns to the larger problem of which style is but a part and problem solving but the means of resolution. There are today a great many large complex problems that need resolution, most of them created by ourselves – our hugely successful human species. We are increasing demanding that these problems be cracked quickly and, from the start, highly efficiently. Given such conditions, few such problems can be solved by individuals working alone or by dominating their teams – no single person has a sufficient range of the required depth and diversity. Teams are needed to solve problems, deploying all the diversities available to achieve their common aims without allowing these same diversities to divide and delay them. The prime task of the modern problem-solving leader is to aid the team to manage their members' diversities so that they achieve the perceived commonly desired change.

This book has presented argument and evidence to show that differences in cognitive style play an important part in problem solving and creativity. It is an early-set, deep-seated, stable characteristic that may have an inherited component. It contains many descriptive elements but essentially they are all interrelated to the way in which the individual relates to guiding structure. One of the core differences is that the more adaptive use structure to help them solve problems and accept changes to the guiding structure as *an outcome of* implementing the solution selected. Such changes are seen as having improved the initial structure. The more innovative are liable to change the structure *in order to* help them solve the problem. Both strategies can be useful, depending less on the preference of the problem solver and more on the nature of the problem and the solution sought. These differences are not related to capacity but to style – when the preferred method does not work, coping behaviour is needed. However, many see these style differences as ones of level and this causes friction and frustration in teams that need to collaborate to get different tasks done. The current creativity literature is inclined to attribute creativity only to innovation; but before this trend, Kelly went so far as to suggest that neither adaption nor innovation alone could achieve creativity. A-I theory suggests that we are all creative (problem solving) to a greater or lesser extent and in different ways; it does, however, support Kelly in assuming that one level or one narrow range of style is not enough for significant sustained intellectual progress. To achieve the effective collaboration of diverse teams attempting to solve diverse problems requires knowledge and skills that need to be learnt – including how to manage ourselves and others, and how to close gaps between us and between the problem solver and the problem. All this must be done by patient, persistent learning, unaided by instinct.

Cognitive style is one of many elements that influences problem solving. From examining the general way in which the brain solves problems, one aim of this book is to show the differences between various key elements – some of which are often confused with others, yet show that although separate they all interact to achieve desired problem solving. Capacities, both potential and manifest, interact but are not correlated with style. The level of the capacity is not the same as the manner in which it is deployed. Knowing how much motive is being generated to complete a task does not reveal the way the problem's enveloping structure is being treated. But interactions between these cognitive elements occur – e.g., if coping behaviour is needed to vary one operating style away from the preferred mode, then motive is needed to initiate and maintain this coping behaviour until the task is completed. How much one can learn is a matter of level: How one learns is related to style; what is learnt is related to attitudes and beliefs; motive is how long one persists and at what intensity. Making sharp distinctions between these has been useful in helping to distinguish which variable is contributing what effect in the overall pursuit of solutions. Some distinctions may only seem of academic interest, until it becomes apparent that confusions of the meanings of these terms can lead to errors in managing change and diversity. One such problem is that of treating innovation as a capacity instead of a style[102]. The disadvantage here is that this labels too many people as not creative – when all are – and does not tend to make the best use of everyone who can and is willing to contribute to problem solution within teams. Trying to solve complex arrays of problems over long periods of time by over-emphasising the merits of one particular capacity, body of knowledge, or cognitive style is not only naïve but also damaging.

---

102 Or even worse, as a stage in problem solving. Perhaps the most crippling intellectual approach is to use all three 'definitions' in a conflated mess of misunderstanding.

Those who have other views, based on a different diversity of views, skills, and styles will feel excluded and resentful – turning them from willing change effectors into resisters of change. Much of the book has explored concerns of such waste of talent and goodwill.

To help place these terms in clearer relationship to each other a schema has been developed. This shows the different 'departments' of brain function and helps show why some terms are distinct from others yet are all part of the same system. It may help show why there are fewer variables that are capacities than seems generally believed. In the last chapter, the relationship of problem solving to opportunity was explored. Taking up or missing opportunities was shown to be a general characteristic of which level is just one component. When examining wide development involving many people over long periods of time, level variables, although critical, play a smaller part than is commonly believed. The need for stability of structure – leading to a continued understanding of self and of the world at large, is an issue that involves all the cognitive processes and functions.

The suggestion has been made that four elements cover much of the territory concerned with bringing about change: style, level, motive, and opportunity, backed by stored but accessible experience. The more logical order of listing is different. What is first needed is for the opportunity for change to be available and for it to be perceived and accepted. For this to occur, current structure, in the particular circumstance, needs to be perceived as more enabling than limiting. If the challenge that is presented is accepted, then motive will be generated to take it up – within a person when working alone or in each person in the group. No two motives can be identical, but there needs to be enough in common to ensure concentration on Problem A and a willingness to treat as secondary every emerging Problem B. Next, the person (or the group) needs to have available the appropriate skills and other resources to be able to pursue and complete the task. Finally, the individual (or the group) must be able to deploy the appropriate cognitive styles throughout the operation to get it completed efficiently. It can be hard to get together, in appropriate measure, this combination of desirable variables. To date, problem-solving mankind has learnt to rely on experts to guide the group in such complex matters. Such expertise is invaluable – but, increasingly, more among each group of us need to know more of this knowledge for ourselves, if the complex operations being undertaken are to be completed efficiently. We may need to use experts more often to help us think but not to suppose that they think for us.

And so we come to groups and leadership, which is exercised by some within the group but should be aided by every other problem solver in it. The problem-solving leadership task is to help identify the common Problem A and help resolve with economy the group's revealed Problems B. It needs to marshal the group's diversity, balance its emotional and physical needs with what reason suggests are its beneficial aims, then help generate the motive to achieve what are its perceived needs. In doing so, this leadership must help the group maintain its identity and yet be flexible enough to meet an ever-changing environment; it must help set (and be ready to reset) its focus and limits in order to concentrate on enabling success.

Societies' paradigms are built up like the thoughts of the people that make them up. For groups to survive, their members need to cope with paradoxes of structure, manage diversity, and manage change over both the short and the long term. In the process, the members need to manage themselves and other groups in order to achieve their own ends and problems. We often talk as if groups think – they do not – but this shorthand error merely underlines the fact that collective behaviour is but a reflection of the individual processes that make it up. To write, for the moment, collectively, the group needs to discriminate collectively, just as each individual does as part of cognitive affect, to note diversity as a prelude for choosing which change opportunity to take up and how to deal with it. Collectively there must be an evaluation of reality, distinguishing reasoned fact from emotive requirement; backing judgement with emotion so that motive has not only appropriate direction but also the required amounts of intensity and duration. The group must calculate the cost as well as the gain, not only for the direct outcome of a planned action but also for the ripple effects; anticipating, in time, dangerous precipitating events. For this the store of knowledge and skills needs constant updating. Pushing against the limits of capacity is one constant struggle. So is changing the predominant operating style, so that the current choice is appropriate to the problem – a task even more difficult to achieve between the members of a group than for an individual. The difference is that the individual may overlook the need to indulge in coping behaviour but, once the need is seen, needs to convince no other brain. The same goes for the management of any diversity. The formation of groups creates more structure as, at the same time, it offers more perceived opportunities and solutions to problems. The cost of group formation is that this added structure is harder to restructure when it needs to be and so is slower to respond the larger it is. Yet large groups are needed for the accomplishment of great achievements that no individual alone can do, hence the effort to interact efficiently within large groups is another vital element in human problem solving. The diversity of style within the group is both its advantage and also its added cost.

The cognitive process requires the problem solver to discriminate differences, formulate patterns within the differences, acquire insight from the patterns, develop foresight, and then use such prediction to exercise control. Control involves managing diversity as a springboard to managing change, within the limits that the integrity of the problem solver is not imperilled by the quantity or nature of the changes that need to be accommodated. However, one last look at the paradox of structure reveals that the management of change itself helps keep the integrity of the system (the problem solver or the identity of the group), although emphasis on a strict maintenance of this integrity can so reduce the necessary flexibility of structure as to destroy the very system being protected.

If mankind fails to continue to solve the vital problems that it faces, there is any amount of other life ready to take over its biological niche. The chance of error is high; any rash changes we make, any vital progress we eschew, any unwarranted limits we impose on ourselves, any indulgences such as careless waste of resources we indulge in, may be the fatal flaws from which we do not recover. Mankind, therefore, needs to get even better at understanding problem solving, with its concomitant problems associated with the management of diversity, since the stakes for failure and success are raised higher than they have ever been. One lesson that is being learnt is that (other than simple differences in capacity) people can be expected to have good reasons, as they perceive them, for accepting any particular change or not and that all people have similar problems of what to choose, what not, and when. The need is to find better ways of making (and communicating) these judgements, especially when the decision is related to those ideas and artefacts that seem to be needed but which threaten to cut across some deep grain and pose some serious challenge to integrity.

That goes for all of us, across such divisions as adaptors through to innovators and every other kind of diversity, for each has its limits as well as its advantages. We return to the paradox of structure: Every diversity is a structure; every structure contains the potential, at one and the same time, for being both enabling and limiting, of being potentially advantageous or fatal. Mankind is the only living being that has such mastery of its own fate, especially having become free of instinct, a development that has left us highly flexible if also highly vulnerable. Since our species evolved, we did not need to *breed* ourselves into a new niche but in fact *thought* our way into every conceivable niche available, however unlikely many of them are, given our limiting inherited structure.

So, one way and another, this means that the problems we face increase in difficulty, at an increasing rate, and the outcomes may be even more successful or even more disastrous. We will need to study problem solving as a discipline as never before. In the past, such study could safely be left to a comparative handful of experts with some tested conclusions, mixed with some more doubtful trendy notions, trickling down eventually into common knowledge and use. This is rather like the way quality control, in the field of industrial production, was viewed before new thinking placed the prime responsibility on every person in the company and used experts to help them; a policy that is quite different from leaving a handful of people to see that quality standards are being met. In like manner, there is now a need for more of us to know more about how the individual's mind works, how (in general) it solves problems, including that of collaborating with others, managing each other's style and level, emotion and reason, motives and ethics – whilst still leaving room for competition and progress. With so much power at mankind's disposal, in a closely integrated world, with natural resources increasingly under strain, the problem of how we all continue to succeed is too critical a matter to be left safely to the few. This truth has already been found in the field of politics; now it needs to be found in the understanding of ourselves.

For a long time now we have vainly searched for ideal leaders who can, with the help of their teams, be guaranteed to solve specific arrays of problems. But we have long known that such leaders cannot hope to solve any such increasingly complex arrays by relying on knowing enough personally to arrive at all the answers. It is the whole team that needs to solve the problems with the help of capable, knowledgeable leaders. Just as engineers need to master the underlying basic physics, so, today, problem-solving leaders must accept that while they cannot hope to have all the knowledge required to solve any specific set of problems, they need to know more of the theory and practice of problem solving and about their key resource – the problem solver. They need to manage minds as much as matter, by knowing better how to assist and inspire the different members of a team to collaborate effectively in deploying of the whole team's available diversity of style and skill and in exploiting the available diversity of opportunity. The problem-solving leader needs more basic understanding in achieving these aims, so as to help the team better to achieve common motives towards reaching commonly desired ends. This is not new, except perhaps for a change of emphasis. Mintzberg (1973, 1979), for instance, very thoroughly analysed the key roles of the manager at work a generation ago. Using his terms, there is still the need for being a figurehead, with the practical role of the group's spokesman. Needed also is his notion of the leadership role, which knits the group together, helping to provide an appropriate climate, by monitoring and disseminating information, as well as by linking each group to other groups. It is more the role of entrepreneur that needs rethinking. In this third role, we need less of the exercise of personal authority to initiate changes (including deciding what they should be) and on deciding how to 'handle disturbance', however unexpected. These tasks are more those of the group as a whole, powerfully aided by the leader's first two roles. This re-emphasis is more likely to play down the particular job-related skills and the basic preferred style of the problem-solving leader and instead allow better use of more of the whole array of attributes that are available to the group, as is required in complex problem solving.

Complex problem solving is now the norm, brought about by our very success in solving our earlier problems. As said earlier, the stages of our development, named after our principal artefacts of the time: stone, bronze, iron and whatever next, are passing in ever more rapid succession. Perhaps it is time to think of another progression that emphasises less the material of key artefacts and more the nature of problem solving achievement, such as: Opportunity revealed, opportunity sought and opportunity made. In our exploitation of opportunity – the theme of this last chapter – our progress was first dominated by opportunity revealed. Finding a use for antler and flint were significant advances. This stage might be thought dominated by the brilliant observer – the flash of insight, the thoughtful pondering of possible relationships of seemingly chance events; the brilliant thinker who may not even have the knowledge in depth about the events or materials considered. This stage is followed by opportunity sought. It is not enough to be able to use a flint flake but to make one and if the most convenient flint is not about – to look for one – even mine for it. Probably this stage always requires more deliberate, focused and team orientated problem solving, involving more collective knowledge and skill to achieve success. This stage also requires the traditional, skilful and efficient leader. Finally, in our latest millennia is opportunity made, the pinnacle of problem solving achievement we are beginning to undertake almost as a matter of course. Once we exhausted the potential of the Periodic Table we began to make the materials we needed even if they are not found in nature.

Of course, opportunity revealed is still a prime force – we still use flint to ignite our modern lighters. Sir Alexander Fleming noted that whatever was destroying his preparations was a destructive force that could be put to use. In doing so, he opened the gate of opportunity sought to high technical teams in this field as a consequence of his discovery. A further change occurs in the final stage of problem solving, opportunity made. More highly complex team problem solving is needed, with widely diverse skills and a new kind of leader – such as has been suggested above. A team may sometimes even need to pass through all the stages – beginning at opportunity revealed, then through opportunity sought and finally into opportunity made – ringing the changes on what is required from person and team. Such changes need to be managed by the team, whilst holding its diversity together in the interest of the common aim. This book ends by suggesting that this is done more surely with the help of leaders who know more than in the past about the problem solving process and problem solvers.

Appendix 1
Management Initiative case studies

These cases illustrate the stages of the management initiative process as first perceived. Later study helped reveal the style element among the key factors.

EXPANSION INC – ANALYSIS OF THE PROBLEM

Expansion Inc was suffering from a shortage of good managers and supervisors, and from lack of promising potential among those in junior positions; most people, both those in the company and those who had dealings with it, saw the management generally as 'thin' and 'green'. The few good and experienced managers were rushed off their feet with day-to-day matters and crisis limitation exercises. Most meetings concentrated on short-term problems and their immediate likely solutions. Although it was agreed that a long-term problem existed, there was no drive to get anything done about it. What was needed was some person, or group, to lobby for the state of management to be taken as a collective problem and for some ideas for its solution to be put forward.

Eventually, the subject of training across the company arose at board level and came up again at other formal and ad hoc meetings that were being held to discuss organisational problems. This appreciation of the value of training was reinforced when the managing director complained of waste in the factory, especially of expensive materials, and of the operatives' apparent apathy and lack of interest in their work. This time, this observation was formally minuted in the record. During the discussions that had led up to this minute, the majority of the managers had taken the view that the primary need was for them to train their own workers. This notion was discussed in a follow-up senior management meeting, which produced a brief outline plan to this effect. The core of the problem – whether the managers were competent to undertake such employee training – was touched upon, but was not followed up or mentioned in the text.

The managing director, late on in the board meeting to which the outline was presented, stated he was not opposed to the idea of training as such, but he did not like the plan that had been presented. On the one hand, he thought it would over-stress the importance of the personnel department and might lead to an unnecessary training officer being added to their ranks. On the other hand, he was not convinced it was the right solution to the problem. He put forward two objections; that the managers had more than enough work already without undertaking training schemes; and that he was not at all sure that they were capable of training their staff. The notion was referred back to the proposers.

Consequently, the matter was briefly discussed again at the next meeting, when the managing director's intervention was: 'If you are going to start doing any training, start on yourselves.' This provoked a good deal of discussion at the management meeting, which began to take the matter a lot more seriously: What, exactly, was the problem? This time, their summary analysis showed that they thought two things were required. One was that the management themselves should acquire the sort of basic knowledge that is a standard part of many management courses. Second, since they were mostly new to the company, they needed some sort of follow-up and on-the-job training to relate this new 'academic' knowledge to specific company requirements. The first solution, it would appear, was produced without analysis in anything like precise terms, so that the solution, or rather the series of barely related mini-solutions, did not appear to cater for the whole problem. It only catered for that part which consisted of acquiring new knowledge, by sending certain individuals on courses for training and persuading them to join professional associations. Even this part-solution was not based on a comprehensive and continuous plan. The managers were sent to courses sporadically; there was no basis for selection. The persuasion to join professional associations consisted almost entirely of publicising the policy that the individuals' fees would be paid for by the company. Since the problem was not fully understood and no clear-cut plan put forward to meet it, it is not surprising that the isolated schemes and ideas, offered as solutions, provoked little enthusiasm.

Some months of this kind of activity led to a 'position report' to a boardroom meeting, which showed little progress and less cohesion. The sponsors of the plan were invited to appraise it again. It was several months after the managing director had originally told them that they should train themselves before trying to train others that the whole management were presented with the final scheme. This now laid down the general aim and generated specific aims relating to departments and individuals on management training that the company approved in principle. Then followed an outline plan, which showed the probable lines of development of the scheme through-out at least the key areas of the company that were suffering most from 'green' leadership at all levels. This time the management, from top to bottom, accepted it with little or no flurry. Just 2 weeks after this, the more detailed and comprehensive plan began to operate. The first group of managers embarked on an 8-week course of talks and discussion that had been assembled from the admittedly good earlier staff work but which had initially lacked an acceptable core plan. This first group was followed a week later by the second group. Later this scheme was referred to as: 'an institutionalised clearing-house for the exchange of experience and information', and was generally agreed to be a success. It was not by any means the final solution, rather it showed that the problem was grasped and, as was remarked: 'something was being done about it'. From this beginning the plan unfolded with more assurance and direction into a series of developing solutions that aimed to transform the operating quality of the management within 2 years.

ICE CREAM CO – ANALYSIS OF THE SOLUTION

An ice-cream-making company became concerned that its sales force was expanding yearly, yet although it was over-stretched in summer, it was under-used in winter. The board debated the problem and two solutions stood out: to make ice cream more popular to customers in winter or to find a winter product they could sell.

The first solution seemed, at first, the best but most daunting and longer term. Plans were set in motion to consider how best this could be done. Then an opportunity arose when a person known to one of the board approached him with a formula for a particularly nice-tasting tomato soup and some new ideas on how to produce it economically. The board leapt at the timely suggestion that this might be the alternative winter product solution, which looked the easier of the two to find and implement. The small management team picked to explore the notion (actually told to get it to work) went into the aspects of production and, equally fortunately, found a small manufacturing unit for sale that could easily handle the production function needed and in the ways the team wanted. They then explored the market potential of this gift product and found that sales of tomato soup had been slowly and gradually rising over the last few years. They rapidly decided to go ahead with this plan, since here, they were sure, was one very likely way of solving their main sales force problem.

Planning seemed to go both quickly and near-painlessly. Production and most aspects of the launch kept to schedule. The main problem was that their marketing plans lacked punch and were late. They had not paid sufficient attention to the fact that although their marketing department was rated as excellent, no one in it had the relevant experience for this project and they had treated the early problems encountered slowly and casually. Spin-off problems generated by this master plan would surely be easily solved, when they could find the time to do this. These matters did straighten out and a somewhat delayed launch got under way, although not quite as crisply as they were used to with similar exercises in their own field.

Very early feedback from their representatives in the field, whom they had thoroughly trained and enthused in the new product, were encouraging but not spectacular. They now realised that they had opened many new outlets and no one had done enough homework on this problem, which they had not foreseen through an overconfidence in their ability to handle any sort of retailer. The real shocks came later, as repeat orders fell away sharply instead of rising steadily as was predicted by the advantages they knew that their new product enjoyed. They discovered that the manufacturers of other tinned foods were now reacting aggressively. This was simply not expected in their plan; they had not taken too much note of exactly who their new rivals were or what might be their reaction, much less what was to be done about it. The rivals were all manufacturers who could offer a range of tinned food, and their counter-attack consisted primarily of threatening retailers with cutting off supplies of the whole range they had on offer, leaving them with only one brand of tomato soup in the product field. The retailers could not withstand this thrust and were not making repeat orders, even whilst agreeing that the new product was beginning to catch on with their customers.

The aggression of the new rivals was sharpened by another unpredicted factor. The ice-cream company had, as noted above, prudently and with justification, called for a market survey for the new product. They had asked for the current position on the sale of tomato soups. But:

- they had not used a survey company that was knowledgeable in the food retail field;
- they had overlooked asking for a breakdown by kind of packaging;
- the selection of the survey company had meant they did not have any compensating good advice.

The true position, which they later found was temporary and lasted only for another 2 years or so, was that packet soups were in fashion, and overall the current sale of tinned soups was gradually falling, and not rising as they had supposed. The subsequent aggression (and alarm) of the new competitors was all the more vigorous because they were under pressure themselves in this field and found the sudden incursion of an established company of some size and standing in a related field very disturbing. The newly revealed rivals' reaction was another spin-off problem this management had created in their narrow-vision pursuit of a much fancied solution aimed at solving their own, different, problem.

In the pursuit of solving one problem, they had set up a few more. Some problems, mostly related to production and other internal issues, were being sorted out mainly because their general management expertise could allow them to recover from these fairly easily, although it spoilt their reputation, at least in their own eyes, as smooth and experienced operators. Some of the other problems, particularly in marketing, were, however, close to causing a near-disaster by the critical nature of the difficulties encountered and the consequent unexpected heavy losses. Eventually they sold the new production unit at a good price (to one of the irate new competitors!) and concentrated on promoting ice-cream sales the year round. At the meeting that showed they had dug themselves out, the top management team made a note that the next time they diversified they would pay more attention to problems arising as well as problems existing.

SOLATRON LTD – AGREEMENT TO CHANGE

This case study was collected at the time when electronics was still in its earliest pioneering stage. Equipment was sold that was new and exciting but unreliable and hard to repair, supported by unreadable manuals. Often even the tasks the equipment was to be used for was not clear, but having it was fun – an innovator's purchase.

Solatron had at least one product that was different. Its single-beam oscilloscope was accurate, reliable, easy to repair, and economical in price, and adequate stock, to meet all likely orders, was on hand. It was easy to use and was backed up by a comprehensive and readable manual. It sold well and was a bread-and-butter item as far as revenue was concerned – no mean matter in a smallish company heavily engaged in developing new products that their potential customers had not even heard about, and so, were certainly not waiting for. Meantime, the current single-beam oscilloscope was, somewhat loftily, getting to be regarded – by R&D particularly – as a boring little exercise.

Marketing had for a while been getting information from the representatives that the customers were keen to get a Solatron-made double-beam version. Production, as always, were loath to disturb a well-run production line, unless the new product could be seen as a volume winner. For once, R&D were disinclined to take up Marketing's needs; there were many commitments on hand – most of which were more exciting; only one rival company had such a product, which they had well protected with a tight patent; this company was in the USA, and did not seem to be an immediate threat. A casual enquiry suggested that buying into the American patent could prove expensive; breaking it could be time consuming. A boardroom battle broke out.

The Marketing director brought extra facts to buttress his case: A survey by his representatives of the principal customers showed that 80% were interested in the new product and would buy, if the product was as technically good and as favourably priced as the single-beam version. R&D countered with a technical report from their staff that the existing single-beam model could meet 80% of the current customers' needs – and, therefore, it would be unethical to try to sell their best customers something they did not need! Needless to say, Marketing was not impressed with this argument; Production left them to it, hoping the problem would go away. The battle warmed up, taking up so much time of each boardroom meeting that finally the managing director stated that he wanted a 'moratorium' and the issue was off the agenda for 6 months, after which time it could be raised again.

A few weeks later, an electronics trade exhibition was held and the director of R&D and his most senior manager went to it. To their considerable concern, on a table in the reception area was a bird's nest model (no case, all the workings on display) of a British-made double-beam oscilloscope being prepared for production. Their only delight was that it had broken down and its company's technicians were sweating to get it going again, which they did periodically throughout the day, monitored by Solatron.

On their way home by train, the Solatron pair emptied from their cases all the exhibition papers that they had collected and tore out all the sheets which had one side blank, and settled down to outline a draft design of a double beam oscilloscope. Two weeks later they asked for an emergency meeting of the board, at which they submitted plans, specifications, and estimates. They were asking for resources twice as large as previous estimates (suggested conservatively by Marketing and turned down by them) and had cut the originally expected lead times (originally suggested by themselves) by half. Curiously, no one at all raised the matter of the moratorium or any of the earlier, sometimes heated, discussions. Neither was any of this mentioned, in interviews, to the researcher or noted in the minutes. Neither were any of the previous objections mentioned or noted anywhere in any subsequent minutes or memoranda, all of which were made available to these researchers. It was as if total amnesia had struck the lot of them. In record time, the directors happily and proudly assured the researcher, Solatron had marketed a volume match-winner to the standards set by the single beam, which it soon replaced.

This case history is in contrast to precipitation events that were not bombshells. All the companies studied produced forward plans or contingency plans, which had precipitating events fully anticipated and built in as triggers to set them into operation. This one blew up in their faces and alarmed all of the key players no little amount – which probably accounts for the collective amnesia. It was too full of foreboding and menace even for anyone to crow about having been an early advocate.

These differences between the anticipated precipitating events and those that appeared, at least to some, as bombshells are now easily explained, if the idea that is being debated can be seen in the context of its distance from the core of the prevailing paradigm. The further out it is, the more likely the establishment will overlook it (not relevant, easily dealt with by improving the present approaches, horror-mongering) and the nonestablishment find it hard to get a hearing. If the establishment is adaptor inclined then this group, together with many of those who are innovator inclined, will fail to perceive precipitating events that are approaching from outside the organisation's usual field of operations. If the establishment is innovator inclined this group's members are, equally, poorer – without constant training and prodding by the more adaptive among them – at picking up and addressing the dangerous precipitating events that appear from within the system in good time. These are the ones that are best addressed by adaptors, and which innovator establishments eschew: downsizing, cost-cutting, waste-cutting, tightening methodologies, and other such exercises. These exercises are related to those kinds of detail often left to adaptors; in such innovator-inclined companies they may be seen as helpful but lesser matters or, more dangerously, even as irrelevant solutions to the particular current problem, which requires 'vision' for its resolution.

VENTURE CO – ACCEPTANCE OF CHANGE

The problems

In this example difficulties occurred early in the management initiative process and multiplied as it proceeded through the succeeding steps, as the study in management initiative suggests may be expected to happen. The history of this change began when the managing director made a review of the industry of which his company was a part. From this review he thought that the greatest future potential would lie in fields that his company did not now work in; therefore, he concluded, the company should enter these fields. His perception of the problem was not wholly accepted by the bulk of the board or the immediate group outside it. They felt there were more immediate problems that needed attention. For the managing director's colleagues the problem might be a time- and resource-consuming project; for him it was now how to achieve solution – that is, to find the most suitable way of entering these fields. A second problem was also in his mind at that time: He wanted to find a product that would be ordered well ahead of delivery and would thus provide the cushion of an advance order-book and make it easier for the company to keep production on an even keel through a depression. This would add to the security of the firm in the eyes of the bankers and brokers and thus make it easier to borrow the money always needed to develop new markets and products.

The managing director suggested that the company should employ someone to make a thorough survey of the most likely expanding fields in the industry, to assess what would be the future requirements, what the firms already in the field were doing, and what were the chinks in their armour. When no one made any real effort to find such a person, he himself found a suitable man, who was duly appointed to do the survey and who eventually threw up a number of 'interesting ideas'.

Opposition to agreement to change

Opposition to the project came mainly from the research division, who objected that these ideas were too big for the company and too ambitious for its resources at that time. Others attributed this opposition to resentment at new ideas imposed on them from outside, since the research division personnel felt that development of new ideas was their responsibility. Also they were closely orientated towards that field of the industry in which the company now worked, and the man who had just been appointed to carry out the survey was working in a new field (as the managing director intended). This man himself added fuel to the opposition's fire by the way he conducted the survey. He took nearly 2 years over it, and did not appear to the research staff to be doing any work at all. Moreover, he managed to spend a great deal of money in expenses; money that came from the limited development funds for which all research workers fought like thirsty travellers in a desert. Added to this he was alleged to have a difficult personality and was disliked by most people.

Eventually the survey was finished and the report completed. Decisions now had to be made on, first, whether to go into this field at all; if this was agreed, then which of the products suggested by the survey to develop; and whom to employ to take charge of the project.

When the matter came before the board of directors, the head of the research division opposed any extension and he was strongly supported by another director, who feared that going into the new field would have a diversionary effect on the company's present efforts. Argument on these matters went on for a long time. The company secretary took a neutral stance for most of these discussions. At some point it was conceded unwillingly that the company should enter the new field and a limited budget was allowed for doing so. The decision to start a long-term project was re-corded as policy in the annual report of the year. But the argument as to which of the suggested projects to back continued, with the principal two opposing directors using it as a last stand against going into the new field at all. There was also no agreement on who should take charge of the new project.

This Gordian knot of argument seemed impossible to unravel, so the managing director decided that it would have to be cut. He proposed to set up a subsidiary to deal with projects in the new field. This would also serve the very important purpose of announcing this new development to the world, thus helping to attract capital for the company's expansion in general and this project in particular. Outside money for this project would be more than usually necessary because of the limited budget allowed to it by the parent company. This proposal was carried out.

Limited agreement leads to low acceptance of change

Agreement to allow a project in the new field to get started had been obtained, a limited budget had been granted, and a new subsidiary had been set up, which, the opposing directors were assured, would not impinge on them by adding to their current problems in any way. But complete isolation was not possible and future development was hampered because there was no general acceptance. The opposition had not accepted that 'this was the right time to go into these new fields' and had only unwillingly agreed that this experiment should be undertaken now.

Two main possible lines of development had come out of the survey, each involving a major project, as well as some less ambitious projects, which had been favoured by the research division. Argument over which of these to choose came to an end now the new subsidiary had been set up and the opposition reluctantly acquiesced in its choice of project.

Delegation is affected, then implementation

In spite of the hostility that existed towards the new man who carried out the survey, no other person was available to be put in charge of the project. It was not long, however, before he considered that his position in the firm was unsatisfactory for a number of reasons, and left. Before leaving the firm he had brought in a junior engineer to assist him. Another senior engineer, who had previously been a consultant to the company, was now given the job of directing of the project. There were a number of disadvantages to this appointment. In the first place, neither senior nor junior knew much about this type of market, since it was in a field new to them and to the company. In the second place, neither of them, because they were new to the company and had no past successes to support them, had at that time the prestige to balance an underlying lack of general acceptance. A further disadvantage was that the senior preferred to act as a consultant to a number of projects rather than as the whole-time leader of any one of them.

Several technical problems inherent in the new project took the interest of the senior and for a time he was immersed in them, but later, as he was consulted on other projects that presented technical difficulties in one place or another, his time became more and more absorbed outside this particular development and he was able to give it less and less of the leadership required. His assistant, who had always been wholly absorbed in the project, came to feel his prestige to be entirely linked with it and to feel responsible for its success. There was a period in which he was, in fact if not in name, project engineer in charge by default.

In addition to the disadvantages of not having acceptance, the new project was a very technical and difficult one to implement and there would have been many difficulties to overcome, however excellent the conditions under which the team worked. The disadvantages of not having general acceptance exaggerated these difficulties. In theory, as the new subsidiary was a separate company, the project was free to develop on its own and there should have been no more difficulties over it with the divisions whose heads had opposed it. But in practice, the new subsidiary was dependent upon others, particularly on the research division, for many common services. Because their priority rated low with 'outsiders' the subsidiary did not do well when competing with other projects for these services, to such an extent that they began to feel themselves treated like poor relations. This was evidenced in many small ways: For instance, there were complaints that they were given the worst accommodation.

The greatest problem of the new unit was how to get the additional money that was needed for development. All projects in this company competed for development funds. The new subsidiary began with a disadvantage in the battle for money because it was concerned with a long-term development and, at that time, it was always particularly difficult to get priority treatment for such projects. Others could point out that any funds spent on the more popular short-term developments would bring a much quicker and more certain return; also, no new long-term project could have the resources of the company allocated to it on a top-priority basis for the whole of its course of development. There had to be times when it might take top priority and others when its priority would be relatively low. Because, however, the team knew that it lacked acceptance, they were perhaps inclined to be more than usually touchy and suspicious about its priority. For these circumstances it was easy for a feeling to develop that even those senior managers who had at first supported the project were inclined to treat it as a Cinderella. The frustration produced by this situation, a situation compounded of part fact and part feeling, did not make for efficient implementation.

After 18 months, the new subsidiary produced a pilot machine. This astonished many people and thus had its effects. For instance, it showed in the most concrete fashion that there was a future in the original idea for entering this field.

Consequently, the project now began to be generally accepted as the beginning of a new company policy; but this spectacular advance brought with it troubles of its own. The key to them was that great optimism now prevailed and most managers assumed that all the major problems were now more or less solved. Because of this, help in sufficient quantity or of the right kind was not always forthcoming. Work was stopped while orders were sought and the team was added to, but some of the new arrivals were salesmen, not technicians. The original team, particularly the project engineer, was not nearly so hopeful that all the problems had been solved. But, partly because the project engineer was not yet experienced in putting up a good case, and partly, perhaps, because he was by temperament, less optimistic, he was suspected by others to be making too much of his case and was repeatedly overruled. As it turned out, he was right, but not always for the reasons he had given. At this stage, the experienced engineers of the research division could have been invaluable, but because they had not accepted the project in the early stages and had taken no interest in it, it was now too late for them to pick up the threads and be able to offer constructive advice. So, many problems attributable to inexperience occurred because acceptance had come too late. Not only could these engineers of the research divisions have lent their experience, but they could also have lent their prestige. No one on the team had, as yet, a status sufficiently high or secure to make a stand on controversial opinions.

Because it was felt that the team members had now become rather touchy, it was difficult to provide help by bringing in skilled engineers to speed up the work. In the first place, it was difficult to find an engineer of sufficient knowledge and standing to appoint as head of the team above the others, whom they would readily accept. Bringing in anyone, in any position, of roughly the same calibre and of roughly the same salary range as, for instance, the project engineer also seemed a tricky operation, and it was not at first attempted.

Not long after the pilot had been completed, an order was booked for the machine and a delivery date set. This was reached and passed but the machine was still not finished. Now it became a case of all hands to the pump, or the company as a whole would lose face. The machine was given top priority, more high-level technical reinforcements were drafted in, and services were offered on a generous scale. To the members of the original team this may all have appeared to show that they had at last 'got through' to the directors concerning the difficulties under which they were working. This was only partly true, however, since resources available at that time happened to make this decision a practical possibility. Even so, whatever conditions had prevailed at that time, because of the failure to meet the delivery date and because the project had now been generally accepted, it is quite clear that sacrifices would willingly have been made at this stage. Success, however, started a healing process and gradually, as the orders began to be met and heartening feedback of the customers' approval was received, the atmosphere lightened.

Interestingly, many of the customers for the new venture were old ones being won over to a new field themselves. The reports of their acceptance of the product were fed back early to the very directors who had originally rejected the project. Much reappraisal was needed and was undertaken by all parties, and the research concluded with a feeling of success but with a general air of wariness held by the project team. Much of this seemed destined to disperse, as all the directors openly admitted that they had not always been right and that the team had succeeded in conditions of some adversity. They were also generous in their promotion of the leader and two of his key staff. Another important factor is that the project team never lost the confidence of the managing director, who was himself being reappraised by his colleagues. In a sense he shared some of their risk and travail within the company.

In this case, we see that problems at an early stage of the management initiative process cascade down through the later stages, despite increasing signs of success.

PRECIPITATING EVENTS

Change is often brought about when an event occurs that brings home, forcibly and dramatically, the need for change to a person or a group of people. This event can be described as a precipitating event. In the first example in this Appendix (Analysis of the problem), the precipitating event occurred when the managing director, one of the few older and experienced managers, noted the deficiencies of knowledge and experience of the whole workforce from the senior managers down. First the problem was underrated and not tackled, then a planning team came up with a scheme to train everyone below them – not an unusual decision in organisations of any kind. As the problems emerged of what to teach, by whom, and to whom, it became dramatically clear that the problem had not been fully appreciated. It was the seniors who first needed basic training, for only then would they be able to ensure that the appropriate training, in the appropriate way, could be planned for others. In this case the precipitating event brought about the change because its occurrence undermined confidence in the belief that what they currently did not know did not immediately matter.

In the example of the underemployed sales force (Analysis of the solution) no such dramatic event occurred; the precipitating event was when the company was asked by another firm to act as agent for their new product. To increase the range of products sold had been agreed as a matter of general policy but it required a specific proposal from outside to bring about action. This proposal was the thought-out solution of another company to a different problem. To the company studied, it was a solution to a problem that had been thought out but it seemed so fitting that this solution was inadequately researched. Adaption-Innovation Theory suggests that solutions which emerge with general consent from within a paradigm may engender over-confidence, and they may not be subjected to enough critical examination. This is a form of 'political correctness' that, as usual, makes it seem improper – to say nothing of being impolitic – to be critical of anything that is closely associated with consensus.

The Solatron example (Agreement to change) is one of those events that are long remembered by the participants, who later see the funny side and dine out on the story. After long and dramatic dispute, the event that precipitated change swept all opposition into near oblivion and the whole group into headlong pursuit of a now wholly agreed goal. In the politics of war, examples that come to mind were, for the British, the evacuation of Dunkirk, and for the Americans the attack on Pearl Harbour or, more recently, the atrocity of the 11th of September 2001. Any discussion of what the country ought to be doing was promptly limited to counter-aggression. In examples of this kind the group can be so swept up in the pursuit of the now-agreed target that other priorities are sharply lowered in importance. However, change in these circumstances is often widespread, deep, and quickly brought about as most minds and comparatively large amounts of other resources are poured in one direction. In this case study example, the precipitating event resolved the problem of whether to change or not to change – the disadvantages of each course of action was clear-cut and mutually exclusive. It is not unusual in a manufacturing company that the sales department advocates the introduction of a new project for such reasons as completing the range by offering something new and better (and fresh revenue). The production department, however, is liable to brood over increased costs, opposing the new product on the grounds that it already has to produce too many different types and the runs on each are shortening. Other departments may take one side or another on similar management principles. In this case a threat in the shape of a rival and its new, directly challenging product provided the precipitating event, concentrating minds along one option.

The last example relates to getting the implementing team to cohere behind the enterprise (Acceptance of change). This is achieved if the leaders see the need to win them over and they see the need to be won over. Failure to spend the initial time in getting adequate agreement for change (which often involves explaining fully what is going on, so that this later process is possible in the first place) is not time well saved. Usually, skimping this part of the process loses much time and effort at a later date trying to repair the fences.

Analysis of the examples of these kinds of dramatic precipitating events in the study of management initiative suggested that the companies were more at the mercy of events than they need have been. Problems that had every chance of recurring again and again were frequently allowed to reach crisis proportions before they were thought about, and then they were treated almost as if they had never occurred before. Only occasionally did the companies deliberately plan to anticipate the kind of examples studied, all of which were likely to recur. Yet here, in this observation, is concealed (to the observer or researcher) the standard danger that can befall the advisor and consultant of seeing all the flaws and summing up by assuming that all managers (except the advisor and consultant) are short-sighted and stupid (in current parlance, lacking innovation). Other evidence was also accruing that in almost every case at least some (admittedly usually the minority) were well aware of the impending possibility of the approach of the precipitating event, but their warnings, not always clearly put or supported with good argument, were ignored or treated with grave suspicion. This observation is well known: Some people, although rarely the person one talks too – much less oneself – are assumed to be short-sighted and stupid. It was only after the original study was published that clearer patterns emerged: The persons who perceived the future and those who missed the cues were not always cast in the same role. Some of the most perceptive in one issue were those that were taken by surprise by the precipitating event in another example, in the same company and at roughly the same time. Seeing one danger but missing another is a general fault of us all. Which danger is foreseen and which not often depends on the relationship between the nature of the problem and the nature of the problem solver. This, when it finally became clear enough to enunciate, became one of the elements that led to the study of adaption-innovation.

As reviewed earlier, the psychologists studying the learning process at the turn of the 19th century postulated that every response needs a stimulus to set it off, and the S-R bonding that followed leads to learning which, depending on the outcome of the response, is positive or negative. A precipitating event has the same function and this is, therefore, a term that is synonymous with stimulus (the 'S' in S-R). If this is so, then it can be argued that most stimuli do not have the 'bombshell' effect of some of the examples above that form the subset called precipitating events. It can be argued that most precipitating events are predictable to many and are therefore acted upon quietly, efficiently, and in good time, and that this is more usual than are stimuli that present as bombshells. As argued above, precipitating events that are predicted and catered for before they happen are called by various names: In business, for instance, this is commonly called forward planning or contingency planning. It might follow that no one can be expert at predicting every class of possible predicting event. Some are missed for technical reasons, such as lack of basic knowledge or experience (because they are very difficult or complex, or because they involve knowledge not possessed to the necessary degree). Some are missed because attention is currently being directed to other, seemingly (maybe actually) more pressing problems that are crying out for immediate resolution. Some are missed, in A-I theory, because they require, for ready awareness, a style different from that of the problem solver. The more adaptive are more readily aware of precipitating events that can emerge from within the paradigm as they are better masters of it; the more innovative are more likely to detect probable precipitating events that may approach from the outer reaches of the paradigm. Each have the converse weakness; each, therefore, need the presence of the other, especially with the longer-term problems and in complex rapidly changing environments[1].

A small number of companies are openly conscious of the problem of detecting events to which they need to respond early, and a smaller number deliberately set up procedures for tackling them. Usually these consist of letting it be generally known that the problem is recognised and this, it is felt, encourages staff at all levels to find ways of contributing their notions in this area. Nevertheless, cognitive style influences their plans. In some cases the system is as wide and general in exposition (and execution) as one would expect from an innovative climate; others try a tighter approach, such as formally noting the proper procedure for raising thoughts in this area. The notions themselves are influenced by the style of problem solver. Miles & Snow[2], in private correspondence (1985), noted that their classification of companies into those they called 'prospector' had a board that yielded an innovator mean and those called 'defender' had an adaptive mean[3]. In the former, the proposals were designed to anticipate threatening events that could arise from outside the company or their customary field. This led to experimenting with ideas aimed at 'doing something different' from what they currently did (e.g., radically different new products were proposed). Conversely, defender companies tended to survey rivals' new products to see if any might be considered threatening; if they were, they prided themselves on being able to move in and catch up with an alternative 'that was better', using superior organisational skills. Similar differences had been noted in the Management Initiative study, in that some companies' more radical notions for new products were stockpiled, thereby avoiding the Solatron bouts of sustained argument, until it was clearer that a problem needed to be solved. For instance, this kind of defence was perceived as: 'the research department has a standing instruction to search for new possible items of production

---

1 The term 'rapidly changing environments' does not necessarily mean innovative environments.

2 Miles & Snow (1978) contains their theory of defender and prospector company differences.

3 They concluded, from a small intensively studied sample, that the difference between defender and prospector companies depended on the orientation of the CEO, with the other board members inclining in the same direction. However, the differences between jobs remained as expected; for instance, in each group the marketing director was more innovative than the production director.

which it might test and submit to a special committee when it is satisfied that the product is to its liking. The committee may approve the choice and no action at that point need be taken. At regular periods a committee decides whether, after examining the market situation and sales figures for all current products the introduction of a new product . . . [from those already considered] . . . would be warranted and the kind that would most fit the situation' (Kirton, 1961, p. 23). In another company there was a stated policy: '. . . to rely upon the efficiency of the company in answering a challenge rather than making one. But the difference in the efficiency of the implementation of the changes studied was marked, depending on whether the precipitating event came as a surprise or not. When it did not, snags in implementation rarely occurred, but when it came as a surprise, time and thought had to be expended on preparing the way towards implementation from scratch, under the strain of a crisis, and therefore snags were more likely' (p. 23).

Despite the wide variety of stimuli to major action that can now be attributed to cognitive style and the climate it engenders, the distinction between cases of precipitating event and forward planning was always clear. Although each precipitating event caught the majority by surprise (that is part of the definition used in the study of such events in group initiative), it was always perceived by someone or even by a minority. Those who saw and those who did not see, and what they saw or missed, depended more on style or shortage of a specific capacity (such as a type of knowledge or experience) than on general capacity.

Because the group (as an entity) were caught by surprise and because, by their nature, precipitating events required immediate action, they were always associated with the skimping of part (usually, parts) of the initiative process, almost certainly beginning with inadequate thought on the nature of the problem and the side-effects of a fancied solution. Once the event was perceived as dangerous, a hasty decision was required to get to implementation: 'We don't want it perfect, we want it Wednesday,' as one manager succinctly put it. The efficiency of the process was then liable to be under strain. When strain in implementation developed, this was met by more effort by more people, often without adequate planning in innovative environments, or by more and more anxious planning meetings in the more adaptive climates. Problem-solving leadership needs to know more about the management of precipitating events.

Appendix 2
Examples of instinct

Hilgard & Bower (1966), in their chapter on the nature of learning theories, admit frankly that the term 'instinct' and others associated with it have in the past caused difficulty. They still do today. 'The older catalogues of innate behaviour usually included among unlearned activities the reflexes (such as pupillary constriction to light), tropisms (such as a moth's dashing into a flame) and instincts (such as bird nesting). [. . .] The concept of instinct has been the most controversial of these terms, partly because of a vagueness of connotation, partly because of a tendency to use the word as explanatory, hence as a cloak for ignorance. After a period of some years in which it was virtually taboo, the respectability of instinct was briefly revived by a group of European naturalists known as ethologists (e.g., Tinbergen, 1951; Thorpe, 1956) only to lead to so much controversy that its advocates have again abandoned it in favour of species-specific behaviour (Hinde & Tinbergen, 1958)' (p. 3). It seemed a pity to let the users of loose terminology put us off employing a perfectly useful concept. The use of instinct in this book uses the standard elements of the definition tightly. The aim was to separate those elements that are simply 'activity according to structure', and that account for reflexes and tropisms, drives, and reactions, from both of the more complex methods of problem solving: instinct and learning. The division may not be so wholly clear at the edges of these divisions, i.e., for conditioned reflexes – behaviours that have been learned but now operate as reflexes. However, these 'touching' edges are possible to distinguish and can be accommodated into a general schema. These divisions and their near-overlapping contiguity implies that all activity and behaviour might be located on a continuum: from that which is most simple and structurally determined to that of higher-order learning. All terms meet at the edges or even overlap somewhat, whilst the distinctions are still valid and having them is more useful than not having them.

Instinctive behaviour (see Boxes 5a and 5b) is distinguished from learned behaviour mainly because it is not learned; it has the whole problem-solving process from recognition of the problem to implementation wired into it, without the individual organism having learned any of it. The (nonhuman) individual also carries out instinct in ways indistinguishable from other individuals in the same species and, once the trigger to set it off has occurred, the individual has no option but to carry out the process. Again, it is accepted that instinct and learned behaviour meet and interact; nature has not evolved for the benefit of the observer, conforming to such neat patterns as will make it easy to understand. In bird nesting, although instinct lays down so rigid a pattern that birds will produce nests that are immediately recognisable by an expert as belonging to their species, nevertheless some elements are affected by learning, such as the safer

Figure A Potential predator image

place (as distinct from: a safe place) to choose from among several options, all of which would fit within instinct imperatives. There are still problems, for the layman, in being sure where the dividing lines are, and in greater refinement this is true for the expert, as Hilgard & Bower observed at the time of the revival of these studies. In Box 5b, it is noted that Pinker suggests language as deriving from instinct, although it may be no more than a refinement of definition separating his view from that expressed in this book. In his later work the narrowness of disagreement can also be seen: 'The innate endowment for language is in fact an innate mechanism for *learning* language' (Pinker, 2002, p. 60, his italics). This is the exact position of this book – the difference is between the *facility* and the *product of the facility*. The former is inherited (but is not an instinct) and the latter is learned. Below are examples of instinct that help show just how different it is from learning and how useful it is to retain this distinction despite some difficulty (as with any other theory and its definitions).

The first example shows instinct relating to protection from predators. In this experiment, chicks are hatched in incubators and tested the following day so that they are just orientated to being out of the egg and feeding. They will have seen no adult birds. Lights are arranged so that the outline of a bird, shown above, is presented stationary and above them. They take no notice of it. Then it is presented as a moving image; moving at a slow but steady rate (as if the figure is flying on a steady course high above them). First, the moving presentation of the image proceeds with the long part of the body first (travelling to the bottom of the page and beyond), so that the image appears to have a long neck and a short tail. The chicks take no notice. The image is presented going in the opposite orientation, so that now it appears to have a short neck and long tail. The chicks stop chirruping, stop eating, stop moving, and squat down and stay there (difficult to see) until the image (potential danger) is safely past. Instinctively (not taught) the chick uses the adult response to danger. The difference between the presentations is that the stationary image does not appear to register as an image of a bird, which, when aloft, is always in motion – anyway, a stationary bird can be no immediate danger. The second image, which appears to have a long neck, seems to be that of a swan, goose, or similar bird that is of no danger to chicks. The short neck and long tail are clear representations of a number of similar birds of prey that are all a danger to chicks. The chicks are programmed (without individual exception) by instinct to recognise the danger (problem) and to carry out the appropriate responses (solution), without learning. This is by recognition of shape alone, without the addition of any sudden or erratic movement, or any kind of loud noise that startles and alerts all animals (and humans) into wariness, for these might indicate a threat that does not set off instinct but programmed reaction. Tinbergen (e.g., 1951), Lorenz (e.g., 1952), and others pioneered many of these experiments at about the same time, including ones in which instinctive patterns were distorted by replacing one precipitating stimulus with another. Lorenz showed that ducklings' instinctive relationship to their mother could be distorted so that the ducklings imprinted (the process by which this instinct becomes operative) onto Lorenz himself, in the absence of any adult duck.

The second example relates to behaviour in bees from Rothenbuhler (see a series of studies beginning in 1964). The experiments included varieties of bees that might be described as 'hygienic' and 'nonhygienic', which had different patterns of behaviour relating to their 'housekeeping' within the hive. When brood died within the cell, the 'hygienic' variety unstopped the cell and removed the remains, ejecting them from the hive; the other variety did not. Experiments then crossbred the variants (queens are only impregnated once and, having been artificially impregnated, thereafter only produce offspring of the same strain). As a result of the crossbreeding, workers were shown, in strict conformity to the laws of inheritance, to behave in new ways. One new variant unstopped the cell but did not remove the dead brood. Another variant initially appeared to be typically 'unhygienic'. However, if the experimenters unstopped the cell, the brood was then removed, unlike the true unhygienic variety, which would not remove the brood even if experimenters unstopped the cell.

These additional examples show that mankind has no such instincts and to suppose that we have is simply misleading. We have no 'programmed' (totally stereotyped and unlearned) complex behaviour like this, that is rigidly and precisely determined, for all members of our species (see, again, Boxes 5a and 5b). Leaving the exact locations of the fine edges between activity 'by construction', by instinct, and by learning to the expert, mankind is unique in having no instinct at all and, other than some basic activities that are part of the inherited structure, must rely entirely on learning for all problem solving. We need to make the best use of the brain we have – and never to suppose, hopefully or resignedly, that any of our problems (as distinct from reactions) can be solved 'instinctively'.

Appendix 3
The curse of progress

'Those who believe that much of art in the late 20th century is in a sad state of decline have many possible sources for blame. One is the drastic fall of standards in English art schools, the result of the removal of drawing and painting techniques from the mainstream curriculum. Another is the involvement of the media, with its destructive influences on real talent; a media which prefers a quick shock to traditional skills. A further source is the influence of state patronage, Arts Council and local museums, which inevitably look for the new rather than quality' (Halsby, 1999, p. 9).

Halsby is making the same points as have been made in the exposition of A-I theory. Techniques and skill are 'structures', located in the cognitive function schema in cognitive resource, that have been built up over time and from which principles can be extracted and taught. Not to teach them is to leave each new learner to reinvent the wheel, and in this way progress is actually retarded. The danger that Halsby sees in ignoring this structure is that there can be less effective enabling; however, those he castigates can see more clearly this same structure as limiting. A-I theory suggests we must make the best compromise in managing this paradox of structure. Halsby agues that in art it is necessary to study the past in order to acquire the principles learnt from the past. He deplores the current position, as he sees it, that: 'the past is not held in respect; rather the reverse. An artist who looks back to, or even dares to copy work from the past is scorned. The constant cry is for originality and the new.' He argues, from his point of view as a modern successful artist, the same principle as is argued in this book – the distinction between level and style should be kept, but so too should the distinction between style and evaluations of worthiness. But his argument is not unbalanced; he is aware that that the counter-argument of the limitation of structure needs to be addressed. Leaving aside the exercises of copying existing works that are set so that learners may the better understand them and learn from such study, he also has this to say: 'All artists are children of their times. Italian historian Alberto Croce said: "All history is contemporary history," and this is equally true of art. No one can mistake a Victorian gothic church for a medieval gothic church, for example. Artists, whether they like it or not, are conditioned by their period. It is not necessary, therefore, to worry about progress and originality, because if you have something to say, your work will be both personal and of its time.' In short, all is change, so change will happen anyway – what needs to be addressed, A-I theory suggests, is the problem on hand, and it is better to address it well than badly; to achieve this, the best use of cognitive resource needs to be made and all cognitive resource has to be learnt.

Those concerned deeply with art, in all its forms, have been in debate for centuries as to what is good art and what is bad – indeed, what is art and what is not. Often the debate rages round whether 'ideal' art is 'tight' or 'loose', free or disciplined, spontaneous or carefully executed. Once again, style is treated as level, leading to denigration of those (and their works) who do not agree. In this field, too, trends tend to swing from one style to the other, with notions of taste and distaste following in the pendulum's wake, as discussed in the chapter on the Management of Change (p. 281). See also, in the main text, the story of the release of innovation by the adaptive invention of Guido d'Arezzo (p. 118) as well as the study of the distinction between capacity and style in music by Brinkman (p. 142).

Appendix 4

Stamp's level vs. style schema

Holistic

1. Problem finder (M & G)
   Moderate or extreme diverger (H)
   Diverger (K)
   Intuitive-receptive (MK & K)
   Flexible (D & M)

   Integrators (M & G)   2.
   Extreme diverger & converger (H)
   Assimilators (K)
   Intuitive-receptive (MK & K)
   Integrative (D & M)
   Type I (MI)
   Conceptual theorist (M & K)

Simple ———————————————————————————— **Complex**

4. Technician (M & G)
   Extreme converger (H)
   Accommodator (K)
   Systematic receptive (MK & K)
   Decisive (D & M)
   Type III (M)
   Company-worker & monitor (M & K)

   Problem solver (M & G)   3.
   Moderate converger (H)
   Converger (K)
   Systematic receptive (MK & K)
   Hierarchic (D & M)
   Type 11 (M)
   Analytic Scientist (M & K)

Analytic

Notes
H = Hudson, 1966; M = Mitroff, 1974; M & K = Mitroff & Kilmann, 1981; D & M = Driver & Mock, 1975; MK & K = McKenny & Keen, 1974; M & G = Morse & Gordon, 1974; K = Kolb & Fry, 1975.

Figure B Stamp's level vs. style schema

Stamp (1986) uses a pair of orthogonally related axes, simple–complex versus holistic–analytic, in her attempt to differentiate between style and level concepts and their measures. She locates seven studies in the design, not at the extremes of the axes but in the quadrants in between. Full orthogonality is not easy to attempt and, as a start, Stamp notes that one study (Mitroff's) uses only three categories (holistic–simple is missing); another (Mitroff & Kilmann) has two falling into the quadrants holistic–complex vs. analytic–complex, the former being in practice, if not in theory, what most theorists concentrate on. Illustrative of the present confusion, Hudson's study is made to stretch into each quadrant by splitting the convergent–divergent dimension, which in much of his theory clearly relates to style alone. Note how divergers and convergers are scattered about the quadrants in ways that are difficult to define precisely. This kind of conflation is replicated in other works that are more difficult to include into Stamp's schema. Two of the Myers-Briggs Type Indicators (Myers, 1962) supposedly *unrelated* dimensions, sensing–intuition and judgement–perception, clearly appear to relate to style and show fairly high correlations with KAI (Carne & Kirton, 1982; Gryskiewicz, 1982; van Rooyen, 1994). Yet the Myers-Briggs manual clearly states that respondents high on *both* measures are *highly creative*; a term that equally clearly relates to level. Just to make matters a little more complicated, we can also read that: 'However important a preference for intuition may be, it is certainly not a sufficient condition for creativity' (p. 34).

Appendix 5

Cognitive style in war

INTRODUCTION

In Appendix 1 are examples, drawn from the Management Initiative study, of managers endeavouring and for the most part succeeding to solve their problems at work. In Appendix 2 are some examples of the way other organisms solve their problems using instinct. In Appendix 4 problems in art are explored by a professional. In this Appendix are four examples of battles that have been strongly influenced, successfully and unsuccessfully, by underlying cognitive style. The lessons to be drawn from these appendices are that whenever human problem solving occurs, the equipment and its inbuilt methods are the same. All these examples are just problem solving, relating to someone's work and well-being, and influencing many others. The other lesson is that although each one of us has a preferred style, which should not overall be assumed as better or worse than another, this does not mean to say that its application cannot be more or less appropriate in a particular circumstance. The method of problem solving applied should not be related to the individual's preference but to the need of the problem. That sounds obvious until one remembers that the mind which has the preferred bias is the only one available to the individual who is making the assessment of the problem and deciding how to undertake it.

It is useful to have a number of examples from various fields of problem solving since this draws attention to the nature of the brain and its general operation: engaged over the centuries with a wide variety of tasks; aided and handicapped by the same strengths, methods, and biases as the reader. The disparateness of the examples, in type of task and benefit of resolution achieved, in the context within which the problem emerged, in the time (year, decade, century, or millennium) lead away from the detail of any one. Concern for such detail might mask the main point, giving reign to subjective judgements as to how the reader would have solved a management problem (if the reader is a manager) or how the reader would have won the battle (if the reader is a general). Instead, the aim is to consider, through a very wide range of problem solving, how the same problem-solving brain operates in all these fields.

The examples given are not modern, partly to show that time is not a prime factor except in the detail of content, and partly to obtain a detached view. In the main text, a passing comparison is made between Generals Wellington and Napoleon. Glover (1968), for instance, is explicit, in his view of Wellington, that he was an 'improver' of the current system. Barnett (1997) devotes his whole book to the personality of Napoleon, who was undoubtedly innovative, among other characteristics that are highly relevant to an understanding of his rise and fall. His speed and dash in unexpected directions, that opponents initially found so disconcerting, were at the expense of adequate supply, thorough reconnaissance, and communication of precise orders to *all* the subordinates needing them. On at least three memorable occasions, slapdash planning led to the overlooking of the significance of a key fortress: at Mantua during the early Italian campaign, at Acre during the Egyptian adventure, and at Bard in the later Italian war with Austria. Despite these incidents being years apart there was no change in style. Meantime, his enemies either had his measure, if not his resources, early – like Wellington – or learnt to cope. By 1814 and in 1815 his opponents had mastered a collective, collaborative, adaptive response that brought him down. Barnett's analysis gives a notable example, in military history, of the weakness on relying on a single approach for too long. This book offers many other examples in other fields. The four military examples in this Appendix each cover a shorter time span, for the purpose of bringing out the main point, that both adaption and innovation have their strengths and weaknesses in different situations. The knack is knowing, in good time, which to use, on whom, and when. Works such as those of Barnett provide the scholar with a grand follow-up exercise. In more modern times there a numerous other examples to be found: the use of tanks as an innovative response to trench warfare in the First World War and its sequel and rejoinder by German blitzkrieg at the start of the Second World War; the adaptive defence of Bastogne by the Americans in the Second World War and their meticulous assaults on Japanese islands; the sound professional defence of Leningrad or of the Gloucester regiment on its critical patch in Korea; and the business-like but innovative oblique approach in the relief of Kuwait.

One question that may arise is how humans ever got round to including such activity as warfare in their problem-solving repertoire. One of today's foremost military historians, Keegan (1994), devotes early sections of his book to this question: Why do men fight? For a start the limbic system is again implicated, as aggression is one of the emotions available to humans. That suggests an inherited component, and chromosome research has uncovered that although only some men inherit an XYY pattern instead of an XY, this group throws up a disproportionate number of violent criminals. But this gene influence is not an instinct, yet Keegan's review shows that many authorities do not entirely dismiss instinct as being involved. The argument earlier in this book also applies to this area of behaviour: Humans are free of such biological imperative and it is not readily predictable as to whether any person or group will, in response to a particular stimulus, indulge in flight, fight, or just freeze. Should a group fight there is no telling how they will do so and with what restraints – as Keegan's review shows very well. Our earlier stated notion holds: We have no instinct but do have a range of emotions (like aggression) and physical facilities – how, where, and under what circumstances we employ them is all learned behaviour. The best prediction that can be made for any person or group as to how they will solve this kind of perceived problem is by knowing the person within the context of the relevant culture – that is, the guiding structure – just as with any other problem-solving situation. For instance, Pinker (2002, p. 57) reviews recent studies showing that all cultures are liable to aggression but the incidence of resulting death can vary by a factor of 50 between extremes. There are differences also even within cultures in the treatment of prisoners and noncombatants.

It has long been an aim of military planners to field 'combined forces' with the appropriate arms, training and leadership that carries the punch of the large 'steady heavies' with the added advantages of numerous, smaller 'light mobile' units. Well led, such forces may perceive and take up successfully a wider array of opportunities currently on offer. The efficient, resourceful management of 'mixed' forces of all kinds is as much a hallmark of high problem-solving leadership among the military as in any other management field. How to mix groups of diverse style and skill, ethos and outlook, and exploit their different advantages whilst maintaining overall morale (i.e., motive) is the key problem. There is constant need to ensure that the advantages of each group are not diminished when collaborating by the disadvantages inherent in another (see, e.g., Jones, 1987, particularly pp. 81 and 197).

In relating these examples of problem solving in the military sphere to those elsewhere, see: the conclusions in the section on Management Initiative, part of the Introduction and the subsection on The environment as opportunity for change in the last chapter, The management of change. Many books have been consulted to draw up these vignettes. The ones to which the text is most indebted are by Labland & Thompson (2000), MacDonald (1984), Morris (1985), Perret (1998), Thomas (1979), Warner (1949, translator of Xenophon), and Warry (1980). For ease of reference, most quotations have been taken from a single selected source in each example.

ADAPTIVE SUCCESS

The Persian expedition, 401 BC

Cyrus, the Persian, in order to sustain a revolt against his king, recruited a Greek mercenary force. Cyrus was killed in a battle and his Persian force disintegrated, so the Greek contingent now had to retreat from the middle Tigris across Media and Armenia to the Eastern Black Sea port of Trapezus. Here, from Greek colony to Greek colony, they might march along the coast to the Hellespont (Dardanelles) to cross back into Thrace and Greece. The whole Persian army was in pursuit. The Greek force was made up principally of hoplites, heavy infantry, well armed, well trained, and formed into formidable blocks that in their day could overbear any other kind of formation. At home they were citizens with military training; now they were being turned into an even stricter-trained professional army. Although they also had an adequate force of equally professional light infantry, including slingers and archers, they had virtually no cavalry. The Persians heavily outnumbered them, having especially large forces of good cavalry including horse archers. The Persians had already had cause to be particularly wary of the Greek hoplites who, when arrayed in unbroken oblong (eight deep) or hollow square formations, were a formidable force. The Persian tactics were to harry the Greek retreat whilst waiting for favourable terrain that made the Greek phalanx less effective. Under such conditions, with hunger, mounting casualties, and sheer frustration caused by Persian harrying with cavalry and light troops, victory would be complete. Greek discipline was the key to their survival against such odds, and it held them together while they solved their problems.

Among the Greek leaders was Xenophon, a general and a historian. Here he writes, describing the Greeks reaching hilly country, less useful to cavalry but also difficult for the phalanx: 'On the day after that they continued their march over the plain, with Tissaphernes following them and shooting at them from a distance. On this march the

Greeks came to the conclusion that the square was a bad formation to adopt when the enemy were in the rear. When the two flanks of the square are compressed, because of the road becoming narrower, or in going through a pass in the mountains or in crossing a bridge, what is bound to happen is that the hoplites get pushed out of position and make heavy going of it, crowded together as they are, and confused; and the result is that, when they are in this disordered state, one can make no use of them. Then, when the flanks diverge again, those who were previously pushed out of position are bound to get dispersed, and the space between the two flanks is not filled up, and, when this happens to the men they get dispirited with the enemy at their heels. So whenever they had to make any sort of crossing, over a bridge or anything else, each man struggled to be the first across, and that gave the enemy an excellent chance of attacking them.

The generals took note of this situation, and formed six companies of a hundred men each. They appointed captains for the companies and other commanders for each fifty men and for each twenty-five men. Whenever the two flanks were pushed in on each other on the march, these six companies waited behind, so as not to cause any disorder in the flanks: afterwards they came up again on the left and right of the flanks. And when the sides of the square opened out, they would fill up the centre, marching into the opening, if it was a small one by companies with six men in front, or if it was larger with twelve men in front, or if it was very large indeed with twenty-five men in front, so that the centre of the square was always full. When they had to make any crossing, by a bridge or otherwise, they preserved their order, the captains leading their companies across in turn. They were also ready for action if there was any demand for it in any part of the main body.

In this formation, they went forward for four days. In the course of the fifth day's march they noticed a kind of palace with a number of villages in its neighbourhood, and saw that the road to the place went across high ground which formed the foothills of the mountain beneath which the village was. The Greeks were pleased to see the hills, as was natural enough, considering that their enemy's force was of cavalry; but when they had marched on and, after ascending the first hill, had just gone down into the valley to ascend the next, the natives made an attack on them. Whipped on to it under the lash, they hurled their javelins and sling-stones and arrows from their high ground down on to the ground below, inflicting a number of wounds. They got the upper hand of the Greek light troops and kept them penned up inside the square of hoplites, so that for that day both the slingers and the archers, being mixed up with the general crowd, were of no use at all. When the Greeks tried to escape from their difficulties by driving the enemy back, they, being hoplites, found it hard going to get to the top of the hill, while the enemy darted away from them quickly. Again, when they made their way back to the rest of the army, they suffered just as before, and the same thing happened on the second hill. They therefore decided not to allow the soldiers to move from the third hill until they had led up into the mountain a force of peltasts (that is, light infantry) from the right flank of the square. When these peltasts got on to higher ground than the enemy who were coming after, the enemy gave up attacking the troops on their descent, since they were frightened of being cut off and having enemies on both sides of them. They marched in this way for the rest of the day, some by the road over the hills and others keeping pace with them along the mountain, until they came to the villages. They then appointed eight doctors, as there were a number of wounded' (from Warner, 1949, pp. 119–121).

Analysis

No doubt there were some useful flashes of innovation to crack this or that part of the problem, but the core of success rested on the precisely disciplined plan, the steady troops, their manoeuvre, and their weapon-skill, both of which were well practised. In this example, even in successive different positions of difficulty, the Greek formation offered little opportunity to their enemies' huge, highly mobile force for opening it up. Had this happened, the Greeks would soon have been scattered and slaughtered.

ADAPTIVE FAILURE

Isandhlwana, 1879

At the opening of the Zulu War, a British infantry force with regiments of the Natal Native Contingent marched on the Zulu capital, the Royal Kraal, at Ulandi. The commander, Lt Gen Lord Chelmsford, an experienced careful soldier, expected that the Zulu impi would be launched against his force before he could get there.

'Chelmsford had issued a profusion of field regulations before the campaign started, covering in considerable detail every phase of camp and march discipline. The very first of these orders dealt with laagering the camps, specifying how the wagons were to be used if entrenchments were not dug, and making clear his intention of turning every halting place into a defensible position. It was clear from the context, however, that the oxen were his main concern, and that large bodies of troops might fight in the open. No campsite of the General Column had been fortified as yet, however, and a few of the officers, especially the colonials, were beginning to comment. [. . .] They well knew the size, discipline and bravery of the Zulu army. Chelmsford was no fool, and he was well aware that he was running a calculated risk. The size of his columns and the ponderous nature of the oxen transport had slowed him to a crawl; he had not the means for a campaign of more than two or three months, and he had to get on to Ulandi. Turning every halting place into a Zulu-proof bastion would have immobilised him, and the column still had eighty miles to cover before it reached the royal kraal. His risk was justified only as long as his scouting arrangements afforded him adequate notice of an impending attack; he had placed his faith in the infantry and he could not afford to be surprised' (Morris, 1985, p. 30).

At Isandhlwana: 'at his first camp, he ringed this one with a circle of infantry posts flung out a mile and more, beyond the stony koppie, beyond the big donga and almost up to the conical koppie, and far up the spur to the lip of the Nqutu plateau. The circle contracted at night, but it still ringed Isandlwana and the stony koppie, and a strong detached picket of the NNC remained on the spur to guard the approach from the plateau. The camp awoke long before dawn and fell in on the parade areas in front of the tents, standing to arms until the sun rose and the day's work began. The quarter-masters stood by the wagons with the regimental reserve of ammunition and mustered the drummer boys, one to a company, who were waiting to carry haversacks filled with the ten-round paper packets to the ranks' (p. 334).

At dawn, Chelmsford sent out many scouting parties well backed by British infantry. That evening one of the NNC mounted groups located a force of more than 2000 Zulus. Chelmsford concentrated and moved up more than half his force for battle the next day. He was now some miles from the camp, expecting to meet the main Zulu force soon. By morning the Zulus facing him had largely retreated, but on that same morning the main camp was attacked.

'[Isandhlwana] was the best camp site for miles about. There was wood in the valleys behind and water in the donga ahead, and if the ground was stony, the surface rubble was small enough to scrape aside, so that the tents could be pitched on bare and level ground. The view of the approaches was as good as could be expected in a hill country, and there was no cover for an attacking force within a mile and a half of the camp. An impi charging the camp would be visible for 25 or 20 minutes in every direction save one before it could close, and a picket posted at the head of the spur where it joined the plateau would cover the single blind approach. The defensive position was strong; the troops could form in a solid phalanx on the open ground in front of the tentage or even behind the regimental transport and the horse lines and, with the precipitous slopes of Isandhlwana protecting their rear, could beat off any attack mounted on the front or the flanks of the camp' (p. 333).

A scout from one of the morning's patrols reached a slope 4 miles from the head of the spur. It turned out to be the edge of a ravine. Looking over, he stared in astonishment for: 'closely packed and sitting in utter silence, covering the floor of the ravine and perched on the steeply rising sides, stretched as far as the eye could see in both directions were over 20,000 Zulu warriors. The main impi had at last been located. [. . .] There was a long moment of electric tension as [the] trooper peered over the lip of the ravine, and the effect on the thousands of Zulus was as profound as it was on the solitary horseman . . . no single warrior needed instructions . . . the entire force lumbered to its feet and the nearest [regiment] started to clamber out of the ravines [as] the horseman, shouting the alarm, turned and fled towards his [troop]' (pp. 163 & 364). It was over 20 minutes before the impi, stretching for a mile from wing to wing, arrived on the plain in front of the camp; time enough for the infantry and dismounted native horse to take up position. The one flaw so far was that some men did not have time to take up more than 40 out of the 70 rounds issued, the rest having been stored in kit bags that were out of reach.

The British force began a cool, deliberate fire and the Zulu charge was losing impetus; in the meantime runners were dispatched for further ammunition as supplies soon ran low. 'The company officers were quite aware of this situation, although it hardly worried them. The battalion quartermasters were stationed by the wagons with the regimental reserve – thirty additional rounds for every man – [as well as the main reserve of] another 480,000 rounds. Long before the pouches were empty they had sent their messengers, drummer boys and bandsmen, back to the wagons to bring fresh packets up to the firing line. The tension was considerably higher around the two battalion ammunition wagons than it was on the line. Quartermaster James Pullen was in the 1st Battalion wagon in the regimental transport behind the 1st Battalion camp, and the 1st Battalion camp was at the extreme right of the tent area in front of the stony koppie, south of the track and more than 1000 yards from any of the five 1st Battalion companies in the firing line. Cavaye's "A" Company, in fact, at the right of the line across the north of the camp, was more than 1800 yards away. Quartermaster Edward Bloomfield was behind the 2nd Battalion camp in the centre of the tent area; he was only responsible for Pope's "G" Company, and "G" Company was 1,100 yards away. [The ammunition was packed in heavy wooden boxes] . . . and the lid of each crate was held down by two copper bands, each fastened with nine large screws.

Pullen and Bloomfield had screwdrivers and they undoubtedly started to loosen the screws on at least one of the crates early in the fight, so as to be ready as soon as a request came from the firing line. Six screws had to be removed to raise a lid, and the screws were frequently rusted into the wood and hard to start. Neither man would have been likely to open more than one box at a time; they were careful, methodical soldiers, who by the light of the times had been promoted to a rank considerably higher than their social origins justified. Cartridges were more than ammunition to them, since each and every one would have to be accounted for as expended after the fight. Even the boxes were accountable.

The requests started to come in, and the two quartermasters began to dole out the packets, eyeing the drummer boys fiercely to make sure they were at the right wagon. Bloomfield was besieged by runners from the line to the north of the camp, who naturally stopped at his wagon because it was the closer, but he sent them all on to Pullen, another 500 yards to the south, because the companies to the north of the camp all belonged to the 1st Battalion. Durnford [commanding the NNC] had sent a few mounted natives back for ammunition almost as soon as he had reached the donga, but their pantomimed requests were refused by both quartermasters. Let the Natal Native Horse draw ammunition from its own regimental reserve; Durnford had surely brought it with him. Since the natives had no idea where the wagons, [which had been] escorted into the camp after the troops had fallen in, might be, they finally returned to Durnford empty-handed. Durnford then sent [his second-in-command, but he] had no more luck than his natives had had.

Lieutenant Smith-Dorrien, [of the Transport Service] acutely aware of the situation on the firing line, collected a few camp casuals, grooms and batmen, hunted out the wagon with the field reserve for the 1st Battalion and set out to open several of the crates. There were no extra screwdrivers, and it was slow work. Chelmsford had requisitioned spare ones for this very purpose, but the order was lost somewhere in Natal. The men hacked at the copper bands with axes or thrust bayonets under them and attempted to snap them or prize them up over the screwheads. Smith-Dorrien finally worried one of the boxes open and began to thrust handfuls of the precious packets into the helmets and haversacks that were eagerly held up to him. Bloomfield, working in the regimental reserve wagon nearby, looked up and saw him. He was horrified. "For heaven's sake don't take that, man," he yelled, "for it belongs to our battalion!" Smith-Dorrien snarled back, "Hang it all, you don't a want a requisition now, do you?" and continued to dole out the packets. A trickle [of ammunition was getting] to the companies, but it was not enough. More and more men were coming back in desperation, searching the wagons until they found the familiar crates and pounding the boxes apart with stones when they found them. The fire in the line began to slacken' (pp. 374–375). Once down to boot, butt, and bayonet the British were no match for the huge battle-hardened Zulu force, many armed with rifles and the rest well trained in the use of shields and stabbing assegais. All the British infantry were killed in their lines; only those native horse who could get back to their mounts escaped, together with half the artillery men who had to leave their two field pieces behind.

From an original force of 950 British and 850 Natal horse, 55 British and 300 horse survived.

Analysis

Superb training and courage allowed the British force to form in short order and stay until nearly all were killed in their lines. Rigid training required men to go to the right quartermaster, with the right authority for ammunition, the boxes of which, until too late, were being opened, one at a time with a single screwdriver. As the men died, nearly half a million rounds of ammunition remained to be issued; about enough to wipe out the Zulu nation. But in peacetime practice, breaking open ammunition boxes was just not done; the Treasury expected them to be used again. On balance, super-adaption cost the day; Zulu numbers, bravery, and discipline were not to be denied the opportunity that such over-adherence to structure offered them.

No solution to any problem is likely to be perfect, whether in military life or any other. Solutions accepted and implemented are so often a compromise between conflicting variables. For Chelmsford, crudely, one choice was between setting up Zulu-proof defences with hours of warning and the need to get on before supply problems crippled his advance. His arrangements seem prudent and professional. The shortfall of ready ammunition for some of the men was a minor flaw that may only have meant they were overwhelmed a short time sooner than their comrades and fewer Zulus remained unharmed.

The key is that tight professional structures and procedures, so necessary to ensure a disciplined force and, for instance, one that operates economically for the benefit of the service, must be applied much of the time – and most of a soldier's service is in peacetime. However, there are also occasions, for however brief a period of time, when a more innovative approach to structure is essential – someone must first bend rule structure in order to solve the immediate problem. Training during peacetime must anticipate this practical problem. It needs to accommodate innovation in looking ahead at problems such as new weapons, possible new emergencies involving different people, customs, and aims operating in different environmental conditions than are being currently accommodated into current training. All armies do this – at different times, and with varying success.

This example illustrates that an excess of adaption, like an excess of innovation, can be fatal in a context which, at that time, needs at least some of the opposite mode of cognitive style. In the military at war, errors can be more completely disastrous than in civilian life. The leadership plays an important role, such as (in this particular case) inserting some flexibility into a rigid adaptive system. This flexible leadership was exhibited a few hours later by the same British army at Rorke's Drift, when 139 men (including 35 sick men emptied out of hospital beds) defended a house and a cattle kraal aided by a hastily constructed low wall of biscuit boxes and mealie sacks, driving off the fresh reserve force of between 3000 and 4000 warriors of that same victorious Zulu army. This tiny highly disciplined force, dexterously managed, lost 17 men but inflicted 600 deaths on the Zulu force (see, e.g., Labland & Thompson, 2000). The differences in these two British forces compare with Prince Rupert's irresistibly dashing cavalry attacks on Parliamentary armies in the English Civil War (in the mid-17th century), which, nevertheless, failed to win key battles when faced by cavalry commanded by Cromwell, whose force showed a more successful blend of both dash and discipline.

INNOVATIVE SUCCESS

The Battle of Matinea, 363 BC

Since 405 BC, the Spartans had been the dominant military and, therefore, political city-state in (classical) Greece. Their power depended on a feared army, at the core of which was the Spartan citizen force of hoplites. This army was large (by Greek standards), well armed, and in almost constant training; it was a very professional, highly disciplined army of high morale. But other city-states were not far behind in quality if not reputation, such as their allies (who they dominated) the Mantineans and their principal enemies, the Thebans, with their own élite corps – the Sacred Band.

The hoplites fought (at this time) in a standard file depth of 12 ranks, their long (10 foot) spears creating a 'hedgehog' effect. The problem was that this formidable array could also be unwieldy, needing a flat unencumbered space to advance over lest it lost formation. Armies were made up of elements from different places and of varying quality. It was accepted practice that the best troops (or in the case of equality – the home team) took the place of honour and greatest danger, on the extreme *right* of the line; that is the 'open' or weapon side, with the least reliable or least skilful on the left, the safer 'shield' side. This convention often meant that each side rolled over their enemies' left flank. So the issues that settled the victory were how long the weak left could hold out, the skill by which the winning right could regroup after overcoming the troops facing it, whether the centre could at least hold its ground, and how much steady courage was exhibited by the enemies' right. Meantime, the job of the light troops and the cavalry was to protect the flanks of their own phalanx from harassment while its hoplites concentrated on the main task of winning the battle.

Nine years before, Epaminondas, Thebes' leading citizen, politician, and general (strategos), had crushed a Spartan-led force by packing, no less than 50 ranks deep, his picked Theban contingent on his *left*, facing the Spartan right. He used a screen of light forces to mask his novel array, giving even less time for the Spartans to appreciate what was he was doing. He had also echeloned back all his other allied contingents to his right in 'refused' formation. While the Spartans were working out this novelty, the Theban phalanx rolled into and over the Spartan contingent while the rest of both armies had a grandstand view of their defeat. The Spartan general and 500 of his elite hoplites were killed, the rest scattered; their allies, appalled, made off without being engaged. To make matters worse for the Spartan military reputation, Epaminondas had been outnumbered at the start: 9000 to 12,000.

At Mantinea, Epaminondas managed to repeat his trick. He ended his approach march in the afternoon by grounding arms in a formation oblique to the Spartans. To start a battle the armies would need to be in opposing parallel lines. The Spartans, therefore, expected him just to stand to while camp was made and then retire for the night. Having relaxed the Spartan command, Epaminondas again used his Theban light troops and cavalry to harass the Spartans and help mask their view of his developing array and its next moves. The picked Theban hoplites, formerly the lead troops in column, formed on the *left* of the army, again facing the Spartan element – and again 50 deep. These moves were facilitated by the original oblique angle at which they had halted. Their Theban allies, following on, now deployed on the more vulnerable right of their line. Although ordered to advance, they had again been echeloned in refused formation, facing the equally echeloned weaker forces of their enemy. The battle was to be between the elite forces of each side. As the dust of the cavalry and light Theban troops, at the critical moment, moved leftwards, the Theban array was uncovered. Surprise was complete. The Mantineans broke, taking the Spartans and all else with them before most of either army was engaged. This second defeat ended Spartan dominance forever.

Analysis

The innovation of the packed *left* wing, with its picked troops, was used again. This second time the Spartans met Epaminondas' tactic, the start of the manoeuvre was concealed by the unexpected advance in order of column march and the development of the plan was again masked by the use of the light troops and cavalry. Innovation creates surprise, which adaption, previously secure in its familiar structure, needs time to counter. Time was, once again, not on offer. However, adaption also played its part for Epaminondas, since it was also he who, taking over the already well-armed, practised, and disciplined Sacred Band, expanded it and trained it even harder. So, for adaptive virtue the armies were equal, with only reputation favouring the Spartans; added Theban innovation tipped the scales decisively.

INNOVATIVE FAILURE

Little Big Horn, 1876

'Custer was afraid of nothing, a quality that led to his being noted five times for gallantry [. . .] in the Civil War. [. . .] He was often in the midst of trouble as he was in the thick of fighting, for, although a stern disciplinarian to his men, he had a contradictory streak of insubordination towards his superiors, his career being dotted with controversies and courts-martial' (Thomas, 1979, p. 78).

'Custer delighted in eccentric dress. [For example] as a major-general in the United States army, he wore a black velvet uniform designed by himself. [. . .] The Indians knew him as Long Hair for his other affectation. [. . . In the Civil War], his brigade paid for their leader's dash with heavy casualties [In 1866, he] led a punitive expedition against the Cheyenne and Arapahos tribes [. . .] and [with] 700 troops of 7 Cavalry found an Indian camp on the Washita River. Without making proper reconnaissance, Custer split his command into four columns and attacked. [. . .] Seeing some Indians escaping, Major Elliot and 19 men spurred after them. A scout reported continuous firing from further down the valley, but again without investigating, Custer retired with his regiment almost intact. Another column found the luckless Elliot and his troopers lying mutilated less than two miles from the village that Custer had devastated' (MacDonald, 1984, pp. 108 & 106).

Custer was subordinate to General Terry, who in turn was one of a three-pronged attack. Custer was to advance 100 miles to Rosebud, then turn west to Little Big Horn River; there to link with a second prong under Col Gibbon. Custer began operations by refusing four extra troops, from 2 Cavalry, and two Gattling guns. Custer covered the first 100 miles between noon 22 June to nightfall 24 June. Instead of resting, he set off on a night march toward Little Big Horn, exhausting the 7

Cavalry still further. Bivouacking in the early morning of 25 June, Custer issued orders aimed at linking with Gibbon and then continuing the advance the next day. By breakfast, however, reports started to come in: 'that the biggest [Sioux and Cheyenne] encampment his scouts had ever seen was only 15 miles to the north-west [...] that the Indians seemed to be preparing to move [...] that there were more Indians ... than the 7th had cartridges.' He believed that he was facing 1500 braves; in fact, there were 3500: 'as he would have discovered had he undertaken proper reconnaissance' (p. 108). Furthermore, 700 of those braves were armed with Winchesters. Despite the tiredness of his men and horses, as well as still not having linked with Gibbon, Custer saddled up.

He then divided his command. First, by detaching Benteen with three troops and McDougall with one troop; then, 9 miles later he ordered Reno, with three more troops, to cross the river (for the third time) and charge the Indian village. This done, he went on with just the remaining five troops. Reno was beaten back and pinned down. When on the battlefield, Custer sent a final but unclear message to his divided command – although by now the possibility of reinforcement was highly unlikely. He failed to get to the best defensive site on the field, either because the order was given late or because the horses were tired, or both. For the battle itself, his force did not have an adequate supply of ammunition and the men, on his orders, were not wearing sabres. Custer and his 225 men were wiped out; 40 Indians died.

Analysis

Cognitive style is always just a single variable that cannot explain everything. Custer, besides being clearly a high innovator – and so a higher risk taker – was also arrogant, dogmatic, and thirsty for fame and had risen to command so quickly that he may have missed some basic military training.

Arrogance may have led to the underestimating of the enemy's number, armament, and leadership, but it also, in general, encouraged the innovative inclination to ignore basic military rules and approved procedures, viz.:

- refused reinforcements;
- wore out both men and horses needlessly;
- did not reconnoitre;
- did not concentrate (with Gibbon);
- did not remain concentrated in the face of the enemy; having only 5 out of 12 troops in the main thrust;
- did not correctly assess, perhaps did not even consider, the tactical skills of the enemy, e.g., of Crazy Horse;
- did not, in the final hour, send a timely, clear message for support, which was a forlorn hope, anyway, given that the rest of his force was divided;
- did not (or could not with tired horses) shift ground to the hill top quickly enough;
- did not have available sufficient ammunition and had ordered sabres to be left behind.

'After the battle, the press and the public hailed Custer as a hero; posterity has judged otherwise' (MacDonald, 1984).

Appendix 6
KAI tables

Table A General population samples

	(N)	*Mean*	*(SD)*	*Internal reliability*	*Range*
UK	(562)	94.99	(17.9)	.88	45–145
Italy	(835)	94.07	(17.7)	.87	46–146
USA	(214)	94.98	(15.9)	.86	44–147
France Belgium Canada	(264)	94.16	(19.3)	.89	43–147
Netherlands Flanders	(516)	95.6	(17.3)	.87	48–142
Slovakia Czech	(353)	95.1	(15.6)	.84	51–149
Weighted mean of means	(2744)	94.76	(circa 17.0)		43–149

Table B Internal reliability

Sample	Internal reliability coefficient	N	Country	Author
General population[a]	Cronbach alpha = .88	562	UK	Kirton (1976)
	Cronbach alpha = .87	835	Italy	Prato Previde (1984)
	K-R20 = .86	214	USA	Goldsmith (1985)
	Cronbach alpha = .84	353	Slovak/Cz.	Kubes (in Kirton & Kubes, 1992)
	Cronbach alpha = .89	265	France[b]	(also: Tullet & Kirton, 1995)
	Cronbach alpha = .87	449	Netherlands[c]	(also: Tullett & Kirton, 1995)
Food shoppers[d]	Cronbach alpha = .82	151	UK	Foxall & Bhate (1991)
Prof & Mgt[e]	Cronbach alpha = .88	150	UK	Foxall & Bhate (1991)
Managers	K-R20 = .88	256	USA	Keller & Holland (1978a)

Table B (cont'd)

Sample	Internal reliability coefficient	N	Country	Author
	Cronbach alpha = .89	203	UK	De Ciantis (1987)
	Cronbach alpha = .91	142[f]	UK	McCarthy (1993)
	Cronbach alpha = .90	221	USA	Keller (1986)
	Cronbach alpha = .89	99	UK	Holland et al. (1991)
	Cronbach alpha = .89	133	UK	Tullett (1996)
	Cronbach alpha = .88	430	UK, US, USA	Foxall & Hackett (1992)
Manager trainees	Cronbach alpha = .81	201	Eire	Hammond (unpublished)
Work group	Cronbach alpha = .89	153	UK	Clapp (1991)
	Cronbach alpha = .87	108	UK	Puccio et al. (1995)
	Cronbach alpha = .87	86	Canada	Hill (1992)
Nurses: Ward	Cronbach alpha = .86	77	USA	Ligman (1991)
Instructors	Cronbach alpha = .88	613	USA	Pettigrew (1989b)
Chief Execs	Cronbach alpha = .88	147	USA	Adams (1988)
Teachers: Sec	Cronbach alpha = .86	182	UK	Kirton et al. (1991)
Prim	Cronbach alpha = .85	80	USA	Jorde (1984)
University 1	Cronbach alpha = .85	123	USA	Ettlie & O'Keefe (1982)
students[g] 2	Cronbach alpha = .84	106	USA	Goldsmith (1984)
2	Cronbach alpha = .86	98	USA	Goldsmith (1986a)
2	Cronbach alpha = .83	138	USA	Goldsmith & Matherly (1986a)
2	Cronbach alpha = .87	123	USA	Goldsmith & Matherly (1986b)
2	Cronbach alpha = .87	114	USA	Hill (1991)
2	Cronbach alpha = .79	103	Eire	Hammond (unpublished)

Notes

a For fuller data on General Population samples see Table A.
b Includes Belgian and Canadian subsamples.
c Includes Flemish subsample.
d Market survey of women food buyers.
e Market survey of adult male home computer users.
f All women: Other management samples were predominantly men.
g 1 = graduates and undergraduates; 2 = undergraduates; for teenage students (13–18 years) see Table C.

Table C Internal reliabilities for teenagers

Academic year	Cronbach alph	
	Experienced administrators	Inexperienced administrators
Sixth forms/grades 11 & 12	.86 ($n = 412$)[a]	.80 ($n = 74$)[b]
		.79 ($n = 367$)[e]
Fifth form/grade 10	.83 ($n = 77$)[e]	.67 ($n = 192$)[e]
Fourth form/grade 9	.74 ($n = 83$)[e, f]	.62 ($n = 154$)[e]
Third form/grade 8	.78 ($n = 85$)[c, g]	.67 ($n = 72$)[b]
		.34 ($n = 87$)[e]
Fifth–sixth forms/grades 10–12		.76 ($n = 375$)[d]
		.76 ($n = 533$)[e]

Notes
a Martin (in Kirton, 1978a), NZ.
b Taylor (1993), UK.
c Selby (1992), US.
d Hammond (unpublished correspondence, 1986), Eire.
e UK study, reported here, using 14-year-old UK pupils estimated to be less bright than average.
f UK pupils were 2 months away from entering fifth form.
g US pupils estimated to be brighter than average.

Table D Test–retest

Sample	Time interval	Test–retest coefficient	N	Country	Author
Students[a]	7 months	.82	64	New Zealand	Martin (in Kirton, 1978a)
Managers	5–7 months	.84	106	USA	Gryskiewicz et al. (1987)
Managers	5 months	.86	55	Italy	Prato Previde (unpublished)
Work group	43 months	.82	69	UK	Clapp (1993)
		(1) Mean (2)			
Students[b]	4 months	91.2 91.1	121	South Africa	Pottas (unpublished)
Students[c]	14 weeks	97.4 98.3	105	USA	Murdock et al. (1993)[d]

Notes
a 17–18 years old (for reliabilities for younger teenagers, see Table B).
b Undergraduates.
c Undergraduates (creativity course; women).
d Total scores; differences for factors also insignificant.

Table E Social desirability

Test	r coefficient	N	Author
EPI – Lie Scale[a]	−.15	286	Kirton (see also Table G)
EPI – Lie Scale[a]	.12	47	Goldsmith & Matherly (1986a)
Marlowe-Crowne	.03	138	Goldsmith & Matherly (1986a)
Social Desirability Scale[b]	.11	121	Goldsmith & Matherly (1987)
YN-2 Yeasaying Scale[c]	.13 ⎫	89	Goldsmith et al. (1986)
K Scale of MMPI[d]	.15 ⎭		
Edwards Social			
Desirability Scale[e]	.22*	104	Elder & Johnson (1989)

* $p = .05$; all others n.s.
Notes
a Eysenck & Eysenck, 1964.
b Crowne & Marlowe, 1964.
c Wells, 1961.
d Defensiveness Scale (conscious presentation): Dahlstrom et al., 1972.
e (unconscious presentation): Edwards, 1957.

Table F Sex differences

	Country	Male		Female	
		Mean	(N)	Mean	(N)
General population samples	UK	98	(290)	91	(242)
	Italy[a]	96	(450)	92	(385)
	USA[b]	98	(60)	93	(147)
	French	99	(130)	89	(134)
	Dutch	99	(233)	92	(199)
	Slovak/Czech[c]	99	(166)	92	(187)
Managers in general	UK	98	(559)	102[d]	(94)
in R&D	UK	100	(71)	104[e]	(22)
Admin & Professionals					
in Advertising/Design	UK	107	(75)	95[f]	(81)
Teachers	UK	95	(117)	93[g]	(65)
Clerical staff	Italy	91	(84)	86	(73)
Work group, nonmanager	Canada	–	–	92[h]	(71)

Means have been rounded. *SD*s are omitted as not all have been published. Weighted means of all general population samples: males, mean = 98, $N = 1329$; females, mean = 92, $N = 1294$.
Notes
a Italy: Prato Previde, 1984.
b USA: Goldsmith, 1984.
c Slovak/Czech: Kirton & Kubes, Slovak Manual, 1992.
d Women personnel managers, McCarthy, 1993.
e Women engineers, McCarthy, 1993.
f Gelade, 1995.
g Teachers, Kirton et al., 1991.
h Hill, 1992.

Table G Personality correlates

Name of measure	Correlation	Reference
Sensing-Intuition	.44[a]; .54[b]; .56[b]; .56[b]; .40[b]; .55[b]	Myers-Briggs Type Indicator (Myers, 1962)[g]
(Sensing)	−.62[c]	
(Intuition)	.55[c]	
Judgement-Perception	.53[a]; .53[b]; .48[b]; .48[b]; .40[b]	
Dogmatism	−.27[e]; −.25[e]; −.19[g]	Dogmatism Scale (Rokeach, 1960); (Troldahl & Powell, 1965)
Conservatism	−.49[e]; −.37	A New Measure of Conservatism (Wilson & Patterson, 1968)
Intolerance of ambiguity	−.38[e]; −.30[e]	Intol. of Amb. (Budner, 1962)
	−.47[e]; .45[e]	″ ″ (MacDonald, 1970)
	−.44[d]	″ ″ (Rydell & Rosen, 1966)
Need for clarity	−.36[d]	Need for Clarity Scale (Ivancevich & Donnelly, 1974)
Flexibility	.43[b]; .49[b]; .33[b]; .34[b] .40[e]; .46[e]	California Psychological Inventory (Gough, 1956 & 1975)
Field dependence/ independence	−.36[k] (male only)	Embedded Figures Test – EFT (Witkin et al., 1971)
Extraversion (I-E)	.45[e]; .46[e]	Eysenck Personality Inventory (Eysenck & Eysenck, 1964)
	.33[b]; .35[b]; −.23[l]	Myers-Briggs Type Indicator (Myers, 1962)
Introversion (E-I)	−.34[b]; −.34[b]; −.25[b]; −.30[b]	Strong Campbell Inventory (Campbell, 1974)
Extrapunitiveness	.29[m]	Extrapunitiveness Scale (Caine et al., 1967)
Humble/Assertive	.42[f]	
Conservative/Experimenting	.60[f]	Sixteen Personality Factor Questionnaire (Cattell et al., 1970)
Controlled/Undisciplined	.35[f]	
Conscientious/Expedient	.44[f]	
Subduedness/Independent	.55[f]	
Tender emotionality/Alert	.26[f]	
Astute/Forthright	.22[b]	
Capacity for status	.39[b] .36[b]	California Psychological Inventory (Gough, 1956 & 1975)
Life stress	.22[m]	Social Readjustment Rating Scale (Holmes & Rahe, 1967)
Imagery-Verbal preference	see text	Individual Differences Questionnaire (Paivio, 1971)
Control-Impulse	.56[b]; .43[b]; .49[b]; .49[b]	Tellegan's Research Scale (Tellegan, 1982)
Need for structure	−.42[b]; −.56[b]; −.54[b]; −.45[b]	Wesley Total (Wesley, 1953)

Table G (*cont'd*)

Name of measure	Correlation	Reference
Risk taking Sensation seeking	.48[g]; .64[c]	Jackson Personality Inventory (Jackson, 1976)
	.47[g]; .67[c]	Arousal Tendency Seeking Instrument (Mehrabian & Russell, 1974)
	.59[c]	General Sensation Seeking Scale (Zuckerman, 1974)
Social presence (self-confidence)	.37[b]; .26[b]; .38[b]	California Psychological Inventory (Gough, 1956 & 1975)
Self-esteem	.27[d]	Self-Esteem Scale (Rosenberg, 1965)
Readiness to change	.38[h]	Readiness to Change Scale (Hardin, 1967)
	.30[h]	Change Index (Hage & Dewar, 1973)
	.31[i,o]; .59[i,o]	Innovativeness Scale (Hurt, Joseph, & Cook, 1977)
	.28[i,p]; .59[i,p]	Jackson Personality Inventory (Innovation – Jackson, 1976)
Structuring orientation (revised Bureaucratic- Executive scale)	−.30[j]	Management Position Analysis Test (Reddin, 1983)
Active reflective learning style (revised Kolb scale)	.61[j]	Learning Style Questionnaire (Honey & Mumford, 1982: revised 1992)
Openness to experience Conscientiousness	.44[q] } −.35[g] }	NEO Costa & McCrae (1992)

Notes
a   Carne & Kirton, 1982.
b   Gryskiewicz, 1982.
c   Goldsmith, 1986c.
d   Keller & Holland, 1978a.
e   Kirton, 1976 (two samples).
f   Kirton & de Ciantis, 1986.
g   See also van Rooyen, 1994.
h   Goldsmith, 1984.
i   Ettlie & O'Keefe, 1982.
j   Goldsmith, 1986a.
k   De Ciantis, 1987.
l   Kirton, 1978b.
m   Tefft, 1990.
n   Reported in KAI manual, 1999.
o   When controlled for Seeking Sensation, reduced to: .00; .16.
p   When controlled for Seeking Sensation, reduced to: .19; .27.
q   Gelade, 2002.

Table H Nonsignificant personality correlates

Name of measure	Correlation	Reference
Shy/Adventurous	.14[a]	
Practical/Imaginative	.19[a]	
Group dependent/Self-sufficient	.02[a]	
Reserved/Outgoing	−.08[a]	
Easily upset/Stable	−.01[a]	Sixteen Personality Factor
Sober/Happy-go-lucky	.06[a]	Questionnaire – 16PF
Tough/Tender	−.02[a]	(Cattell et al., 1970)
Trusting/Suspicious	.11[a]	
Self-assured/Apprehensive	−.11[a]	
Relaxed/Tense	−.05[a]	
Low/High anxiety	−.09[a]	
Introversion/Extraversion	.16[a]	
Locus of control	−.14[b]; −.16[b]; .06[b]; n.s.[c]	Locus of Control Scale (Rotter, 1966)
Field dependence/ Independence	−.20[d] (female only)	Embedded Figures Test – EFT (Witkin et al., 1971)
	.03[e]; .16[e]; .04[e]; .03[e]	Hidden Figures (Witkin & Goodenough, 1977)
Visual complexity/Simplicity	.17[e]	Barron-Welsh Art Scale (Barron, 1953)
Thinking/Feeling	.09[e]; .02[e]; −.10[e]; .02[e]; −.03[f]; −.11[g]	Myers-Briggs Type Indicator (Myers, 1962)
Goal orientation	.09[h]	Learning Style Questionnaire Revised Pragmatist Scale (Honey & Mumford, 1982)
Controlling orientation	.03[h]	Management Position Analysis Test: Revised Missionary-Autocrat Scale (Reddin, 1983)
Intropunitiveness	n.s.[i]	Intropunitiveness Scale (Caine et al., 1967)
Inner-Other directedness	n.s.[i]	Inner-Other Scale (Kassarjian, 1962)
Neuroticism	n.s.[i]	Eysenck Personality Inventory (Eysenck & Eysenck, 1964)
Anxiety (trait)	−.15[j]	State-Trait Anxiety Inventory (Spielburger et al., 1983)
Leadership practice: Challenging; Inspiring; Enabling; Modelling; Encouraging	.15; .14; −.10; .06; .08[k]	The Leadership Practices Inventory (Kouzes & Posner, 1988)
Extraversion	.25[l]	NEO
Agreeableness	−.16[l]	Costa & McCrae (1992)
Neuroticism	−.25[l]	

n.s. = nonsignificant.

Notes

a Kirton & de Ciantis, 1986.
b Keller & Holland, 1978a.
c Shillcox, unpublished.
d Kirton, 1978b.
e Gryskiewicz, 1982.
f Carne & Kirton, 1982.
g Tefft, 1990.
h de Ciantis, 1987.
i Kirton, 1976.
j Elder, 1989.
k Wunderley, 1996.
l Gelade, 2002.

Table I Intercorrelations between 'Adorno' measures

Dogmatism (Rokeach)	X								
Intolerance of ambiguity (Budner)	.56	X							
Intolerance of ambiguity (MacDonald)[a]	.48	.56	X						
Inflexibility (Gough)[a]	.52	.51	.60	X					
Conservatism (Wilson & Patterson)	.44	.36	.59	.59	X				
KAI[b]	−.25	−.30	−.45	−.46	.37	X			
EPI (Eysenck):									
Extraversion			−.23	−.33	−.23	.46	X		
Neuroticism	.26							X	
Lie Scale				.21	.24				X

Main sample subset B: $N = 286$; only correlations >.20 are entered.
Notes
a Reverse scored, so low score = as named for all measures (relating positively with adaption).
b KAI was also correlated with Impulsiveness (a 6-item subscale of Extraversion): .25; with Extraversion less the Impulsive subscale: .40.

Table J Occupational means

Occupational group	Country	N	Mean	SD	Author
Apprentices	UK	624	83.6	9.8	Flegg (in Kirton, 1994)
Bankers	US/UK/ Italy	217	91.3	[14][c]	Gryskiewicz et al., 1987; Holland, 1987; Prato Previde, 1984
Clerical staff					
Secretaries and clerical (female)	UK/Italy	205	89.2[a]	[16.4][c]	McCarthy, 1988; Prato Previde, 1984
Engineers					
See Table K					
Managers					
In general	Singapore	75	95.0	12.6	Thomson, 1980
In general	Singapore	695	96.3	11.3	Thomson, 1985
In general	UK	79	96.9	16.4	Kirton, 1980
In general	UK	88	97.1	16.9	Kirton, 1980
In general	Italy	207	99.3	17.4	Prato Previde, 1984
R&D (all personnel)	UK	93	98.5	14.9	Lowe & Taylor, 1986
R&D (professionals)	UK	192	102.2	14.2	Davies (in Kirton & Pender, 1982)
R&D (professionals)	USA	256	100.9[b]	?	Keller & Holland, 1978
Members: Committees for community-based adult education	USA	208	101.9	15.8	Cutright & Martorana, 1989
Personnel Management trainees	UK	79	103.0	17.1	McCarthy, 1988
Bank	US/UK	127	97.6	[16.4][c]	Holland, 1987
Civil Service 'high flyer'	UK	86	114.0	?	Iliffe (unpublished)
Entrepreneurs Founder/owners	US	134	113.6	[15][c]	Buttner & Gryskiewicz, 1993; Gallagher, 1999
Work groups					
Mainly women	UK	153	88.8	16.1	Clapp, 1991
Nonmanager, women	Canada	71	91.9	12.5	R. F. Hill, 1992
Admin & professionals in advertising & design	UK	156	100.6	18.7	Gelade, 1995

Table J (*cont'd*)

Occupational group	Country	N	Mean	SD	Author
Teachers					
In general	USA	430	95.0	12.8	Pulvino, 1979
In general	USA	202	97.0	14.0	Dershimer, 1980
In general	USA	80	101.4	14.4	Jorde, 1984
In general	UK	182	94.5	18.2	Kirton et al., 1991
Medical					
Nurses	USA	77	92.2	14.9	Ligman, 1991
Nurses	USA	60	92.3	12.0	Pettigrew & King, 1993
Nurse administrators	USA	613	107.5	15.9	Pettigrew, 1989a
Nurse, Chief admin.	USA	147	108.9	12.6	Adams, 1988
General practitioners	UK	180	91.9	16.1	Salisbury et al., 1998

Notes
a Combined data: difference between the two samples' means = 1.4.
b Combined data: difference between the two samples' means = 0.8.
c Estimated.

Table K Engineer samples compared

	Mean	SD	N	Reference
Maintenance & production	91.7	16	31	Kirton, 1980
	87.0	17	19	Janssen Pharmaceutica, 1989[a]
	93.2	17	29	Travenol, 1990[b]
Instructors of engineer apprentices	86.5	11	72	Flegg in Kirton & Pender, 1982
Weighted mean	**88.9**		**151**	
Engineers (unspecified)	97.6	14	20	Kirton, 1980
	97.6	14	20	British Airways, 1989[c]
	98.5	15	93	Lowe & Taylor, 1986
	100.0	17	17	Gryskiewicz et al., 1986
Weighted mean	**98.5**		**138**	
R&D; design	100.9	14	256	Keller & Holland, 1978
	109.3	16	63	Love, 1986
	102.2	14	192	Davis in Kirton & Pender, 1982
Weighted mean	**102.4**		**511**	
Mean of means (unweighted)	**96.8**	**–**	**(800)**	
Other special groups				
Apprentices (16–18 years old)	83.6	10	624	ICI, 1981[d]
Engineers (unspecified) (all female)	102.5	16	46	McCarthy, 1993

For main tables, males greatly predominate – hence the overall mean is close to the general population male mean of circa 98.
See: Acknowledgements (for use of unpublished data).
Notes
a Dr L. Peeters.
b Mr Jeremy Woods.
c Dr Linda Philamore.
d Mr David Flegg.

Table L Comparisons of five occupational groups

Occupation group	Country	Mean	SD	N	Differences between means[c]
Project managers	Belgium[a] (Tullett & Kirton, 1995)	107.9	11.8	53	0.3 ($t = 0.16$, n.s.)
	UK (Tullett, 1996)	108.2	13.7	203	
R&D managers	UK (Davies, in Kirton, 1997)	102.2	–	192	1.3 ($t = 1$ 11, n.s.)
	USA (Keller & Holland, 1978)	100.9	14.3	256	
Bank managers	Italy[b] (Prato Previde, 1984)	92.6	12.3	38	Range 0.2–1.6
	UK (Holland, 1987)	91.2	17.3	51	Range $t = 0.07$–0.63, n.s.
	USA (Gryskiewicz et al., 1986)	91.0	17.3	128	
Managers in general	Belgium[a]	96.5	17.2	92	Range 0.2–3.0
	Italy[b] (Prato Previde, 1984)	99.3	17.4	207	Range $t = 0.11$–1.29, n.s.
	Singapore (Thomson, 1985)	96.3	11.3	695	except Italy-Singapore, where
	UK[c] (Kirton, 1994)	97.0	15.6	167	$t = 2.34$, $p < .02$
Teachers	UK (Kirton et al., 1991)	94.5	18.1	182	1.1 ($t = 0.74$, n.s.)
	USA (calculated from data reviewed in Kirton, 1994)	95.6	–	751	

Table published by permission of Dr Tullett (Tullett, 1997; see Table A for general population data).
Notes
a Dutch version of KAI.
b Italian version of KAI.
c All two-tailed tests; not significant: >.15.

References

Adams, Carolyn, E. (1988). *The relationship between creativity style and leader behavior in directors of nurses*. PhD Thesis, University of San Francisco.

Adams, Carolyn, E. (1993). The impact of problem solving styles of nursing executives and executive officers on tenure. *The Journal of Nursing Administration*, December, *23*(12), 38–43.

Adams, Carolyn, E. (1994). The impact of problem solving styles on NE–CEO pairs on nurse executive effectiveness. *The Journal of Nursing Administration*, November, *24*(11), 17–22.

Alcock, J. (1993). *Animal behavior*. Sunderland, MA: Sinauer Associates.

Allport, F. H. (1924). The group fallacy in relation to social science. *Journal of Abnormal Social Psychology*, *19*, 60–73.

Allport, F. H. (1955). *Theories of perception and the concept of structure*. New York: John Wiley.

Allport, G. W. (1937). *Personality: A psychological interpretation*. New York: Holt.

Alroy, J. (2001). A multi-species overkill simulation of the end-pleistocene mega-faunal mass extinction. *Science*, 1893–1896.

Amabile, Teresa, M. (1983). The social psychology of creativity: A consensual assessment technique. *Journal of Personality and Social Psychology*, *45*, 357–376.

Amabile, Teresa, M. (1995). Discovering the unknowable, managing the unmanageable. In C. M. Ford & D. A. Giola (Eds.), *Creative action in organizations: The ivory tower visions and real world voices*. Thousand Oaks, CA: Sage Publications.

Ashby, W. R. (1956). *Introduction to cybernetics*. New York: John Wiley.

Atwater, L. E., & Yammarino, F. J. (1993). Personal attributes as predictors of superior and subordinate perceptions of military academy leadership. *Human Relations*, *46*(5), 645–668.

Bailey, R. S. (1990). *Leadership style indicator*. Greensboro, NC: Center for Creative Leadership.

Bakke, E. W. (1965). Concept of the social organisation. In M. Haire (Ed.), *Modern organisation theory*. New York: John Wiley.

Bandura, A. (1992). Self-efficacy mechanism in psychobiologic functioning. In R. Schwarzer (Ed.), *Self-efficacy: Through control of action*. Washington, DC: Hemisphere.

Barnard, C. (1938). *The functions of the executive*. Cambridge, MA: Harvard University Press.

Barnett, C. (1997). *Bonaparte*. UK: Wordsworth Editions.

Barron, F. (1953). Complexity–simplicity as a personality dimension. *Journal of Abnormal and Social Psychology*, *48*, 163–172.

Becker, S. W., & Whistler, T. L. (1967). The innovative organisation: A selective view of current theory and research. *Journal of Business*, *40*, 462–469.

Beene, J. M. (1985). *Self-actualisation and anxiety*. From Symposium: The Role of Anxiety in Self-Actualisation, presented at the 31st Annual Convention of the South Western Psychological Association, April 18–20.

Berger, P. L., & Luckmann, T. (1967). *The social construction of reality*. Harmondsworth, UK: The Penguin Press.

Bicheno, J. (1998). *The Quality 60: A guide for service and manufacturing*. UK: PICSIE Books.

Bieri, J., Atkins, A. L., Briar, S., Seaman, R. L., Miller, H., & Tripodi, T. (1966). *Clinical and social judgements: The discrimination of behavioural information.* New York: Wiley.

Billings, R. S., Klimoski, R. J., & Breaugh, J. A. (1977). The impact of a change of technology on job characteristics: A quasi-experiment. *Administrative Quarterly*, *22*, 318–339.

Blake, R. R., & Mouton, J. S. (1964). *The managerial grid.* Houston, TX: Gulf Publishing.

Blake, R. R., & Mouton, J. S. (1984). *The new managerial grid III.* New York: Gulf Publishing.

Blanchard, K. H. (1985). *SL II: A situational approach to managing people.* Escondido, CA: Blanchard Training & Development.

Blau, P. M. (1963). *The dynamics of bureaucracy.* Chicago: University of Chicago Press.

Blau, P. M., & Schoenherr, R. A. (1971). *The structure of organizations.* New York: Basic Books.

Blissett, Sonia, E., & McGrath, R. E. (1996). The relationship between creativity and interpersonal problem solving skills in adults. *Journal of Creative Behavior*, *30*(3), 173–182.

Blumler, M. (1992). Independent inventionism and recent genetic evidence on plant domestication. *Economic Botany*, *46*, 98–111.

Bobic, M., Davis, E., & Cunningham, R. (1999). The Kirton Adaption-Innovation Inventory. *Review of Public Personnel Administration*, Spring, xix–2, 18–31.

Bolles, E. B. (1999). *Galileo's commandment: An anthology of great science writing.* UK: Little, Brown & Company.

Bradbury, J. (1998). *The medieval siege.* Bury St Edmunds, UK: St Edmundsbury Press.

Brief, A. P., & Aldag, R. J. (1975). Employee reactions to job characteristics: A constructive replication. *Journal of Applied Psychology*, *60*, 182–186.

Bright, J. R. (1964). *Research, development and technological innovation.* Homewood, IL: Irwen.

Brinkman, D. J. (1994). *The effect of problem finding and creativity style on the musical compositions of high school students.* PhD Thesis, University of Nebraska-Lincoln.

Brinkman, D. J. (1999). Problem finding, creativity style and the musical composition of high school students. *Journal of Creative Behavior*, *33*(1), 62–68.

Buck, Sir Peter (1950). *The coming of the Maori.* Wellington, NZ: Whitcombe & Tombs. (Note: Sir Peter's given Maori name was: Te Rangi Hiroa.)

Budner, S. (1962). Intolerance of ambiguity as a personality variable. *Journal of Personality*, *30*, 29–50.

Bull, G. (1981). *Machiavelli: The Prince* (rev. ed.). Harmondsworth, UK: Penguin Classics.

Burke, R. J., & Weir, T. (1980). Coping with the stress of managerial occupations. In C. L. Cooper & R. Payne (Eds.), *Current concerns in organisational stress.* London: John Wiley.

Burns, T., & Stalker, G. M. (1961). *The management of innovation.* London: Tavistock.

Butler, D., & Stokes, D. (1969). *Political change in Britain.* New York: St Martin's Press.

Buttner, E. Holly, & Gryskiewicz, N. (1993). Entrepreneurs' problem-solving styles: An empirical study using the Kirton Adaption-Innovation Theory. *Journal of Small Business Management*, *31*(1), 22–31.

Buttner, E. Holly, Gryskiewicz, N., & Hidore, Suzanne (1999). The relationship between styles of creativity and management skills assessment. *British Journal of Management*, *10*, 228–238.

Cacioppe, R. (1997). Leadership moment by moment! *Leadership & Organization Development Journal*, *18*(7), 335–345.

Caine, T. M., Foulds, G. A., & Hope, K. (1967). *Manual of the Hostility and Direction of Hostility Questionnaire (HDHQ).* London: University of London Press.

Campbell, D. P. (1974). *Introversion Extraversion Scale.* Stanford University, CA: Strong Campbell Interest Inventory.

Cantor, N. (1990). From thought to behaviour: 'Having' and 'doing' in the study of personality and cognition. *American Psychologist*, *45*, 735–750.

Carne, J. C., & Kirton, M. J. (1982). Styles of creativity: Test score correlations between the Kirton Adaption-Innovation Inventory and the Myers-Briggs Type Indicator. *Psychological Reports*, *50*, 31–36.

Carter, Rita (1998). *Mapping the mind*. London: Weidenfeld & Nicolson.

Carter, Rita (2002). *Consciousness*. London: Wiedenfield & Nicolson.

Casbolt, Diane (1984). *The effects of idea generation technique, problem type and creative thinking style on individual problem solving performance*. PhD Thesis, University of Ohio.

Cattell, R. B. (1981). *Misurare l'intelliganza con i Test Culture Fair*. Florence: Organizazzione Speciali.

Cattell, R. B., Eber, H. W., & Tatsouha, M. M. (1970). *Handbook for the Sixteen Personality Factor Questionnaire 16PF*. Champaign, IL: IPAT.

Chan, D. (1996). Cognitive misfit of problem solving style at work: A facet of the person–organization fit. *Organizational Behavior and Human Decision Processes, 68*(3), 194–207.

Chapman, L. J., & Campbell, D. T. (1957). An attempt to predict the performance of three-man teams from attitude measures. *Journal of Social Psychology, 46*, 277–286.

Charpie, R. A. (1960). Quoted in Schoen, D. R. *Managing technological innovation*. Harvard Business Review, May–June (original reference not now available).

Chilton, M. A. (2001). *Person–environment fit and paradigm shifts: A model of behavioral results using object-oriented technology*. PhD Thesis, University of Arkansas.

Church, A. H., & Waclawski, J. (1998). The relationship between individual personality orientation and executive leadership behaviour. *Journal of Occupational and Organizational Psychology, 71*, 99–125.

Chown, Sylvia (1959). Rigidity – a flexible concept. *Psychological Bulletin, 56*, 195–223.

Clapp, R. G. (1991). *The fate of ideas that aim to stimulate change in a large organisation*. PhD Thesis, University of Hertfordshire.

Clapp, R. G. (1993). The stability of cognitive style in adults: A longitudinal study of the KAI. *Psychological Reports, 73*, 1235–1245.

Clapp, R. G. (1995). Individual style and its effect on safe working behaviour. *Rail Bulletin*, June, 46–47.

Clapp, R. G., & De Ciantis, S. M. (1989). Adaption-Innovation in large organizations: Does cognitive style characterize actual behavior of employees at work? An exploratory study. *Psychological Reports, 65*, 503–513.

Cloninger, C. R. (1986). A unified biosocial theory of personality and its role in the development of anxiety states. *Psychiatric Development, 3*, 167–226.

Cloninger, C. R. (1987). A systematic method for clinical description and classification of personality variants. *Archives of General Psychiatry, 44*, 573–588.

Cohen, H. (1965). *The demonics of bureaucracy*. Iowa: Iowa State University Press.

Cohen, H. (1970). Bureaucratic flexibility. *British Journal of Sociology, 4*, 390–399.

Cooper, R., & Foster, M. (1971). Sociotechnical systems. *American Psychologist, 26*, 467–474.

Coser, L. (1967). *The functions of social conflict*. London: Routledge & Kegan Paul.

Costa, P. T. & McCrae, R. R. (1993). *Revised NEO Personality Inventory and NEO Five-Factor Inventory. Professional manual*. Odessa, FL: Psychological Assessment Resources.

Cox, Catherine (1926). *The early mental traits of three hundred geniuses*. Stanford, CA: Stanford University Press.

Crockett, W. H. (1965). Cognitive complexity and impression formation. In D. A. Maher (Ed.), *Progress in experimental personality research, Vol. 2*. New York: Academic Press.

Cronin, V. (1994). *Napoleon*. London: Harper Collins.

Crowne, D., & Marlowe, D. (1964). *The approval motive*. New York: Wiley.

Cruzzort, R. P. (1969). *Humanity and modern sociological thought*. London: Holt Rinehart & Winston.

Csikszentmihalyi, M., & Sawyer, K. (1995). Shifting the focus from individual to organizational creativity. In C. M. Ford & D. A. Gioia (Eds.), *Creative action in organizations: The ivory tower visions and real world voices*. Thousand Oaks, CA: Sage Publications Inc.

Cutright, Pamela, S., & Martorana, S. V. (1989). Composing advisory committees for community-based adult education. *Community College Review, 17*(2), 34–40.

Cyert, R. M., & March, J. G. (1962). *A behavioural theory of the firm*. New York: Prentice Hall.

Daft, R. L., & Becker, S. W. (1978). *Innovation in organisations*. New York: Elsevier North-Holland.

Dahlstrom, W. G., Welsh, G. S., & Dahlstrom, L. E. (1972). *An MMPI handbook – Research applications*. Minneapolis, MN: University of Minnesota Press.

Dahrendorf, R. (1959). *Class and class conflict in an industrial society*. London: Holt Rinehart & Winston.

Damasio, A. (1999). *The feeling of what happens: Body, emotion and the making of consciousness*. London: William Heinemann.

Daniels-McGhee, F., & Davis, G. A. (1994). The imagery–creativity connection. *Journal of Creative Behaviour, 28*, 151–153.

Davidson, M. (1982). *Occupational stress in female managers*. PhD Thesis, Department of Management Sciences, UMIST.

Davidson, M., & Cooper, C. (1983). *Stress and the woman manager*. Oxford: Martin Robertson.

Davis, G. (1982). In Kirton & Pender, The Adaption-Innovation continuum: Occupational type and course selection. *Psychological Reports, 51*, 883–886.

Dawkins, R. (1987). *The selfish gene*. London: Oxford University Press.

Dawkins, R. (1995). *River out of Eden*. London: Weidenfeld & Nicolson.

De Bono, E. (1975). *Lateral thinking*. Harmondsworth, UK: Penguin.

De Ciantis, S. (1987). *The relationship of cognitive style to managerial behaviour and the learning of skills in 3-D managerial effectiveness training*. PhD Thesis, University of Hertfordshire.

De Ciantis, S. M., & Kirton, M. J. (1996). A psychometric re-examination of Kolb's experiential learning cycle construct: A separation of level, style and process. *Journal of Educational and Psychological Measurement, 56*(5), 809–820.

Delbecq, A. L., & Mills, P. K. (1985). Managerial practices that enhance innovation. *Organisational Dynamics, 14*, 24–34.

Denison, D. R. (1996). What is the difference between organizational culture and organizational climate? A native's point of view on a decade of paradigm wars. *Academy of Management Review, 21*(1), 619–654.

Dennis, D. M. (1973). Predicting full-scale WAIS IQs with the Shipley. *Journal of Clinical Psychology, 29*, 366–368.

Dennis, D., & Dershimer, Elizabeth, L. (1986). *Psychology*. New York: Harper.

Dershimer, Elizabeth, L. (1980). *Study to identify the characteristics of teachers willing to implement computer based instruction using microcomputers in the classroom*. EdD Thesis, Memphis State University.

Dewey, J. (1886). *Psychology*. New York: Harper.

Diamond, J. (1997). *Guns, germs and steel*. London: Vintage, Random House.

Downs, G. R. Jr, & Mohr, L. B. (1976). Toward a theory of innovation. *Administration and Society, 10*, 379–408.

Driver, M. J., & Mock, T. J. (1975). Human information processing, decision style theory and accounting information systems. *The Accounting Review, July*, 490–509.

Drucker, P. F. (1969). Management's new role. *Harvard Business Review, 47*, 49–54.

Drucker, P. F. (1985). *Innovation and entrepreneurship – practice and principles*. London: Heinemann.

Duncker, C. P. (1945). On problem solving. *Psychological Monographs, 58*, No. 270, 248–402.

Ebert, E. S. III (1994). The cognitive spiral: Cognitive thinking and cognitive processing. *Journal of Creative Behaviour, 28*, 275–290.

Economist Technology Quarterly. (2001). 22 September, 41–42.

Edwards, A. L. (1957). *The social desirability variable in personality assessment and research*. New York: Dryden.

Edwards, J. M., & Trimble, K. (1992). Anxiety, coping and academic performance. *Anxiety, Stress and Coping, 5*, 337–350.

Ekvall, G. (1983). *Climate, structure and innovativeness of organizations: A theoretical framework and an experiment.* Stockholm, Sweden: The Swedish Council for Management and Organizational Behavior.

Ekvall, G., Arvonen, J., & Waldenstrom-Lindbald, I. (1983). *Creative organisational climate.* Stockholm, Sweden: The Swedish Council for Management and Organizational Behavior.

Ekvall, G., & Parnes, S. (1984). *Creative problem-solving methods in product development: A second experiment. Report 2.* Stockholm, Sweden: The Swedish Council for Management and World Life Issues.

Elder, R. L. (1989). Relationships between adaption-innovation, experienced control and state-trait anxiety. *Psychological Reports, 65,* 47–54.

Elder, R. L., & Johnson, D. C. (1989). Varying relationships between adaption-innovation and social desirability. *Psychological Reports, 65,* 1151–1154.

Erikson, E. H. (1982). *The life cycle completed: A review.* New York: Norton.

Ettlie, J. E., & O'Keefe, R. D. (1982). Innovative attitudes, values and intentions in organizations. *Journal of Management Studies, 19,* 163–182.

Everett, C. J. (1982). *The role of the entrepreneur in local government.* MSc Thesis, North East London Polytechnic.

Eysenck, H. J. (1965). *Fact and fiction in psychology.* Harmondsworth, UK: Penguin Books.

Eysenck, H. J. (1967). *The biological basis of personality.* London: Springer.

Eysenck, H. J. (1970). *The structure of human personality* (3rd ed.). London: Methuen.

Eysenck, H. J. (1996). The measurement of creativity. In M. A. Boden (Ed.), *Dimensions of creativity.* Cambridge, MA: MIT Press.

Eysenck, H. J., & Eysenck, Sybil, B. G. (1964). *Manual of the Eysenck Personality Inventory.* London: University of London Press.

Festinger, L. (1957). *A theory of cognitive dissonance.* Evanston, IL: Row Peterson.

Feynman, R. (1965). *The character of physical law.* Cambridge, MA: MIT Press.

Fiedler, F. E. (1967). *A contingency model of leadership effectiveness.* New York: McGraw-Hill.

Fischbach, G. D. (1994). *Mind and brain: A Scientific American special report.* New York: Scientific American Inc.

Fisher, R. (1930). *The genetical theory of natural selection.* New York: Harper & Brothers.

Fisher, S. G., Macrosson, W. D. K., & Walker, C. A. (1995). FIRO-B: The power of love and the love of power. *Psychological Reports, 76,* 195–206.

Folkman, S. (1984). Personal control and stress and coping processes: A theoretical analysis. *Journal of Personality and Social Psychology, 46,* 839–852.

Folkman, S., & Lazarus, R. S. (1985). If it changes it must be a process: Study of emotion and coping during three stages of a college examination. *Journal of Personality and Social Psychology, 48,* 150–170.

Forbes, J. B. (1975). The relationship between management styles and functional specialization. *Group and Organizational Studies, 10,* 95–111.

Foxall, G. R. (1986a). Managers in transition: An empirical test of Kirton's Adaption-Innovation Theory and its implication of mid-career MBA. *Technovation, 4,* 219–232.

Foxall, G. R. (1986b). Managerial orientations of adaptors and innovators. *Journal of Managerial Psychology, 1,* 24–27.

Foxall, G. R. (1994). Consumer initiators: Both adaptors and innovators. *British Journal of Management, 5*(2), 3–12.

Foxall, G. R., & Bhate, Seema (1991). Cognitive style, personal involvement and situation as determinants of computer use. *Technovation, 11*(3), 183–189.

Foxall, G. R., & Hackett, P. M. W. (1992). Cognitive style and extent of computer use in organizations: Relevance of sufficiency of originality, efficiency and rule-conformity. *Perceptual and Motor Skills, 74,* 491–497.

Foxall, G. R., & Payne, A. F. (1989). Adaption and innovators in organizations: A cross-cultural study of the cognitive styles of managerial functions and sub-function. *Journal of Human Relations, 40*(7), 639–650.

Foxall, G. R., Payne, A. F., Taylor, J. W., & Bruce, G. D. (1990). Marketing and nonmarketing managers. *Marketing Intelligence and Planning, 8*(1), 21–26.

Foxall, G. R., Payne, A. F., & Walters, D. D. (1992). Adaptive-innovative cognitive styles of Australian managers. *The Australian Psychologist, 27*(2), 118–122.

Frese, M. (1986). Coping as a moderator and mediator between stress at work and psychosomatic complaints. In M. H. Appley & R. Trumball (Eds.), *Dynamics of stress*. New York: Plenum Press.

Friedrichs, R. W. (1970). *A sociology of sociology*. New York: Free Press.

Frydenberg, E., & Lewis, R. (1994). Coping with different concerns: Consistency and variation in coping strategies used by adolescents. *Australian Psychologist, 29*, 45–48.

Furnham, A. (1990). Faking personality questionnaires: Fabricating different profiles for different purposes. *Current Psychology: Research and Reviews*, Spring, *9*(1), 46–55.

Gagné, R. M. (1965). *The conditions of learning*. New York: Holt Rinehart & Winston.

Gagné, R. M. (1974). Problem solving and thinking. *Annual Review of Psychology, 10*. Palo Alto, CA: Annual Reviews.

Gallagher, B. (1999). *New ideas and new friends: Exploring the relationship between entrepreneurial innovation and networking*. Undergraduate Thesis, The College of Wooster, USA.

Galton, Sir Francis (1869). *Hereditary genius: An enquiry into its laws and consequences*. London: Macmillan.

Gelade, G. (1995). Creative style and divergent production. *Journal of Creative Behavior, 29*(1), 36–53.

Gelade, G. A. (2002). Creative style, personality and artistic endeavor. *Genetic, Social and General Psychology Monographs, 128*(3), 213–234.

Gershon, A., & Guilford, J. P. (1963). *Possible jobs: Scoring guide*. Orange, CA: Sheridan Psychological Services.

Getzels, J. W., & Csikszentmihalyi, M. (1976). *The creative vision: A longitudinal study of problem finding in art*. New York: Wiley & Sons.

Getzels, J. W., & Jackson, P. W. (1962). *Creativity and intelligence: Explorations with gifted students*. New York: Wiley.

Giddens, A. (1979). *Central problems in social theory: Action, structure and contradiction in social analysis*. Berkeley, CA: University of California Press.

Giorgi, A. (1970). *Psychology as a human science*. New York: Harper & Row.

Glover, M. (1968). *Wellington as military commander. Classic military history*. London: Penguin Books.

Goldsmith, R. E. (1984). Personality characteristics associated with adaption-innovation. *Journal of Psychology, 117*, 159–165.

Goldsmith, R. E. (1985). Personality and adaptive-innovative problem-solving. *Journal of Social Behaviour and Personality, 117*, 159–165.

Goldsmith, R. E. (1986a). Convergent validity of four innovativeness scales. *Educational and Psychological Measurement, 46*, 81–87.

Goldsmith, R. E. (1986b). Adaption-innovation and cognitive complexity. *Journal of Psychology, 119*, 461–467.

Goldsmith, R. E. (1986c). Personality and uninformed response error. *Journal of Social Psychology, 126*, 37–45.

Goldsmith, R. E. (1994). Creative style and personality theory. In M. J. Kirton (Ed.), *Adaptors and innovators: Styles of creativity and problem solving*. London: Routledge.

Goldsmith, R. E., & Kerr, J. R. (1991). Entrepreneurship and Adaption-Innovation Theory. *Technovation, 11*(6), 373–382.

Goldsmith, R. E., & Matherly, T. A. (1986a). The Kirton Adaption-Innovation inventory, faking and social desirability. A replication and extension. *Psychological Reports, 58*, 269–270.

Goldsmith, R. E., & Matherly, T. A. (1986b). Seeking simple solutions: Assimilators and explorers, adaptors and innovators. *Journal of Psychology, 120*, 149–155.

Goldsmith, R. E., & Matherly, T. A. (1987a). Adaption-innovation and creativity. A replication and extension. *British Journal of Social Psychology, 26*, 79–82.

Goldsmith, R. E., & Matherly, T. A. (1987b). Adaption innovation and self-esteem. *Journal of Social Psychology, 127*, 351–352.

Goldsmith, R. E., Matherly, T. A., & Wheatley, W. J. (1986). Yeasaying and the Kirton Adaption Innovation Inventory. *Educational and Psychological Measurement, 46*, 433–436.

Goldstein, K. M., & Blackman, S. (1981). Cognitive styles in personality. In F. Fransella (Ed.), *Theory measurement and research*. London: Methuen.

Goodall, H. (2000). *Big bangs: The story of five discoveries that changed musical history*. London: Chatto & Windus.

Goode, W. J. (1960). A theory of role strain. *American Sociological Review, 25*(4), 483–496.

Goodenough, D. R. (1985). Styles of cognitive-personality functioning. In H. J. Bernardin & D. A. Bownas (Eds.), *Personality assessment in organizations*. New York: Praeger.

Gough, H. G. (1956). *California Psychological Inventory*. Palo Alto, CA: Consultant Psychological Press.

Gough, H. G. (1975). *California Psychological Inventory*. Palo Alto, CA: Consulting Psychologists' Press.

Gough, H. G. (1981). *Studies of the Myers-Briggs Type Indicator in a personality assessment research institute*. Paper presented at the Fourth National Conference on the Myers-Briggs Type Indicator, Stanford University, CA.

Gouldner, A. W. (1960). The norms of reciprocity: A preliminary statement. *American Sociological Review, 25*(2), 161–178.

Grant, M. (1993). *The climax of Rome*. London: Weidenfield.

Gribben, J. (1998). *In search of the Big Bang* (new ed.). London: Penguin Books.

Gryskiewicz, Nur, Taylor, S., & Fleenor, J. (1995). Job satisfaction and creativity style: An unexpected empirical finding. *Creativity and Innovation Management, 4*, 258–261.

Gryskiewicz, S. S. (1982). *The Kirton Adaption-Innovation Inventory in creative leadership development*. Invited paper for the Occupational Psychology Conference of the British Psychological Society, Sussex University.

Gryskiewicz, S. S., Hills, D. W., Holt, K., & Hills, K. (1986). *Understanding managerial creativity: The Kirton Adaption-Innovation Inventory and other assessment measures*. Greensboro, NC: Center for Creative Leadership.

Guilford, J. P. (1950). Creativity. *American Psychologist, 5*, 444–454.

Guilford, J. P. (1967). *The nature of human intelligence*. New York: McGraw-Hill.

Guilford, J. P. (1969). *Seeing problems: Manual for administration and interpretation*. Orange, CA: Sheridan Psychological Services.

Guilford, J. P. (1975). Varieties of creative giftedness, their measure and development. *The Gifted Child Quarterly, 19*, 107–121.

Guilford, J. P. (1977). *The way beyond IQ*. New York: Creative Education Foundation with Brearly Ltd.

Guilford, J. P. (1980). Cognitive styles: What are they? *Educational and Psychological Measurement, 40*, 715–735.

Guilford, J. P. (1982). Cognitive psychology's ambiguities: Some suggested remedies. *Psychological Review, 89*, 48–59.

Gul, F. A. (1986). Differences between adaptors and innovators attending accountancy courses on their preferences in work and curricula. *Journal of Accounting Education, 4*, 203–209.

Haan, N. (1977). *Coping and defending: Processes of self-environment organisation*. New York: Academic Press.

Hackman, J. R., & Lawler, E. E. III (1971). Employee reactions to job characteristics. *Journal of Accounting Education, 4*, 203–209.

Hackman, J. R., & Oldham, G. R. (1975). Developments of the Job Diagnostic Survey. *Journal of Applied Psychology, 60*, 159–170.

Hackman, J. R., & Oldham, G. R. (1976). Motivation through the design of work: Test of a theory. *Organizational and Human Performance*, *16*, 250–279.

Hage, J. (1980). *Theories of organisations*. New York: Wiley.

Hage, J., & Dewar, R. (1973). Elite values versus organizational structure predicting innovation. *Administrative Science Quarterly*, *18*, 279–290.

Halsby, J. (1999). The curse of progress. *The Artist*, *5*, 114.

Hammerschmidt, P. (1996). The Kirton Adaption-Innovation Inventory and group problem solving success rates. *Journal of Creative Behaviour*, *30*, 61–75.

Hammerschmidt, P. K., & Jennings, A. C. (1992). The impact of personality characteristics on leadership effectiveness ratings. In K. E. Clark, M. E. Clark, & D. P. Campbell (Eds.), *Impact of leadership* (pp. 469–475). Greensboro, NC: Center for Creative Leadership.

Hannaway, J. (1985). Managerial behaviour, uncertainty and hierarchy: A prelude to a synthesis. *Human Relations*, *38*, 1085–1100.

Hardin, E. (1967). Job satisfaction and desire for change. *Journal of Applied Psychology*, *51*, 20–27.

Hawks, D. V., & Payne, R. W. (1972). Overinclusive thinking and concept identification in psychiatric patients and normals. *British Journal of Medical Psychology*, *45*, 57–69.

Hayward, G., & Everett, C. (1983). Adaptors and innovators: Data from the Kirton Adaption-Innovation Inventory in a local authority setting. *Journal of Occupational Psychology*, *56*, 339–342.

Heard, G. (1939). *Pain, sex and time: A new outlook on evolution and the future of man*. Oxford: Clarendon Press.

Heider, F. (1958). *The psychology of interpersonal relations*. New York: Wiley.

Heifetz, R. A. (1994). *Leadership without easy answers*. Belknap: Harvard University Press.

Heim, Alice (1970). *Intelligence and personality: Their assessment and relationship*. Harmondsworth, UK: Penguin.

Hertz, M. R. (1946). *Frequency tables to be used in scoring responses to the Rorschach Ink Blot Test* (3rd ed.). Cleveland, OH: Western Reserve University.

Hess, E. H. (1964). Imprinting in birds. *Science*, *146*, 1128–1139.

Hickson, D. J., Pugh, D. S., & Pheysey, D. C. (1969). Operations technology and organization structure: An empirical reappraisal. *Administrative Science Quarterly*, *14*, 378–397.

Hill, D. (1996). *A history of engineering in classical and medieval times*. London & New York: Routledge.

Hill, K. G. (1991). *An ecological approach to creativity and motivation: Trait and environmental influences in the college classroom*. PhD Thesis, Brandeis University.

Hill, K. G., & Amabile, Teresa (1993). A social psychological perspective on creativity: Intrinsic motivation and creativity in the classroom and workplace. In S. G. Isaksen, M. C. Murdock, R. L. Firestien, & D. J. Treffinger (Eds.), *Understanding and recognizing creativity: The emergence of a discipline*. New York: Ablex.

Hill, R. F. (1992). *The impact of problem solving styles on problem solving behaviour, interpersonal relations, and job satisfaction in small workgroups*. MSc Thesis, University of Calgary.

Hilgard, E. R., & Bower, G. H. (1966). *Theories of learning*. New York: Meredith Publishing Company, Appleton-Century-Crofts.

Hinde, R. A., & Tinbergen, N. (1958). The comparative study of species-specific behaviour. In A. Roe & G. G. Simpson (Eds.), *Behaviour and evolution*. New Haven, CT: Yale University Press.

Holland, P. A. (1987). Adaptors and innovators: Application of the Kirton Adaption-Innovation Inventory to bank employees. *Psychological Reports*, *60*, 263–270.

Holland, P. A., Bowskill, I., & Bailey, A. (1991). Adaptors and innovators: Selection vs. induction, *Psychological Reports*, *68*, 1283–1290.

Holmes, B. (2002). Ready, steady, evolve. *New Scientist, September*, 28–31.

Holmes, T. H., & Rahe, A. K. (1967). The Social Readjustment Rating Scale. *Journal of Psychosomatic Research, 11*, 213–218.

Homans, G. (1964). Bringing men back in. *American Sociological Review, 29*(5), 809–819.

Honey, P., & Mumford, A. (1982). *The manual of learning styles.* Berkshire, UK: Peter Honey.

Honey, P., & Mumford, A. (1992). *Manual for the Learning Styles Questionnaire.* Berkshire, UK: Peter Honey.

Hopkins, W. (1999). Heritability of hand-preference in chimpanzees: Evidence from a partial interspecies cross-fostering study. *Journal of Comparative Psychology, 113*, 1–7.

Hudson, L. (1966). *Imaginations: A psychological study of the English schoolboy.* London: Methuen.

Hunt, R. G. (1970). Technology and organization. *Academy of Management Journal, 13*, 235–252.

Hurt, H. T., Joseph, K., & Cook, C. D. (1977). Scales for the measure of innovativeness. *Human Communication Research, 4*, 58–65.

Isaksen, S. G. (1987). *Frontiers of creativity research: Beyond the basics.* New York: Brearly.

Isaksen, S. G. (2000). The Center for Studies in Creativity: A quarter century of progress. In M. K. Rainer (Ed.), *International perspectives in creativity research.* New Delhi, India: National Council of Educational Research and Training.

Isaksen, S. G., & Dorval, B. (1993). Toward an improved understanding of creativity within people: The level-style distinction. In S. G. Isaksen, M. C. Murdock, R. L. Firestien, & D. J. Treffinger (Eds.), *Understanding and recognizing creativity: The emergence of a discipline.* New York: Ablex.

Isaksen, S. G., Dorval, B., & Kaufmann, G. (1992). Mode of symbolic representation and cognitive style. *Imagination, Cognition and Personality, 11*, 271–277.

Isaksen, S. G., Dorval, K. B., & Treffinger, D. J. (1998). *Toolbox for creative problem solving: Basic tools and resources.* Buffalo, NY: The Creative Problem Solving Group.

Isaksen, S. G., Dorval, K. B., & Treffinger, D. J. (2000). *Creative approaches to problem solving* (2nd ed.). Dubuque, IA: Kendall/Hunt Publishing Company.

Isaksen, S. G., & Puccio, G. J. (1988). Adaption-Innovation and the Torrance Tests of Creativity Thinking: The level–style issue revisited. *Psychological Reports, 63*, 659–670.

Ivancevich, J. M., & Donnelly, J. H. (1974). A study of role clarity and need for clarity for three occupational groups. *Academy of Management Journal, 17*, 28–36.

Jackson, D. N. (1976). *Jackson Personality Inventory Manual.* Goshen, NY: Research Psychologists' Press.

Jacobson, Carolyn, M. (1993). Cognitive styles of creativity: Relations of scores on the Kirton Adaption-Innovation Inventory and the Myers-Briggs Type Indicator among managers in USA. *Psychological Reports, 72*, 1131–1138.

James, W. (1890). *The principles of psychology, Volume I.* New York: Holt Reinhardt & Winston.

Jones, A. (1987.) *The art of war in the western world.* Oxford: Oxford University Press.

Jones, S. (1999). *Almost like a whale: The Origin of Species updated.* London: Transworld Publishers.

Jones, S. (2000). *The language of the genes* (rev. ed.). London: Flamingo.

Jonscher, C. (1999). *Wired life: Who are we in the digital age.* London: Bantam Books.

Jorde, P. (1984). *Change and innovation in early childhood education; the relationship between selected personal characteristics of administrators and willingness to adopt computer technology.* PhD Thesis, Stanford University.

Kagan, J., & Kogan, N. (1970). Individual variation in cognitive processes. In P. H. Mussen (Ed.), *Carmichael's manual of child psychology, Vol. 1.* New York: Wiley.

Kanter, R. M. (1983). *The change masters: Innovation for productivity in the American corporation.* New York: Simon & Schuster.

Kassarjian, W. M. (1962). A study of Reisman's theory of social character. *Sociometry, 25*, 213–230.

Kaufmann, G. (1993). The logical structure of creativity concepts: A conceptual argument for creativity as a coherent discipline. In S. G. Isaksen, M. C. Murdock, R. L. Firestien, & D. J. Treffinger (Eds.), *Understanding and recognizing creativity: The emergence of a discipline*. New York: Ablex.

Keegan, J. (1994). *A history of warfare*. New York: Vintage Books.

Keller, R. T. (1986). Predictors of the performance of project groups performance in R&D organisations. *Academy of Management Journal, 29*, 715–726.

Keller, R. T., & Holland, W. E. (1978a). A cross-validation study of the Kirton Adaption-Innovation Inventory in three research and development organizations. *Applied Psychological Measurement, 2*, 563–570.

Keller, R. T., & Holland, W. E. (1978b). Individual characteristics of innovativeness and communication in research and development organizations. *Journal of Applied Psychology, 63*, 759–762.

Kelly, G. A. (1955). *The psychology of personal constructs*. New York: Norton.

Kelly, G. A. (1963). *Theory of personality, Vol. 1*. New York: Norton.

Kelly, G. A. (1967). Attribution theory in social psychology. In D. Levine (Ed.), *Nebraska Symposium on Motivation*. Lincoln, NE: University of Nebraska Press.

Kepner, C. H., & Tregoe, B. B. (1981). *The new rational manager*. Princeton, NJ: Princeton Research Press.

Khatena, J., & Torrance, E. P. (1976). *Manual for Khatena-Torrance Creative Perception Inventory*. Chicago: Steolting.

Khurana, R. (2002). The curse of the superstar. *Harvard Business Review*, September, 60–67.

Kiggundu, M. N. (1983). Task interdependence and job design: Test of a theory. *Organizational Behaviour and Human Performance, 31*, 145–172.

Kirton, M. J. (1961). *Management initiative*. London: Acton Society Trust.

Kirton, M. J. (1976). Adaptors and innovators: A description and measure. *Journal of Applied Psychology, 61*, 622–629.

Kirton, M. J. (1977). Adaptors and innovators and superior–subordinate identification. *Psychological Reports, 41*, 289–290.

Kirton, M. J. (1978a). Have adaptors and innovators equal levels of creativity? *Psychological Reports, 42*, 695–698.

Kirton, M. J. (1978b). Field dependence and adaption-innovation theories. *Perceptual and Motor Skills, 47*, 1239–1245.

Kirton, M. J. (1978c). Adaptors and innovators in culture clash. *Current Anthropology, 19*, 611–612.

Kirton, M. J. (1980). Adaptors and innovators in organizations. *Human Relations, 3*, 213–224.

Kirton, M. J. (1985). Adaptors, innovators, and paradigm consistency. *Psychological Reports, 57*, 487–490.

Kirton, M. J. (1987). Reply to Payne's article: 'Individual differences and performance amongst R&D personnel'. *R&D Management, 17*, 163–166.

Kirton, M. J. (1991). Faking personality questionnaires: A response to Furnham. *Current Psychology: Research and Reviews, 10*(4), 315–317.

Kirton, M. J. (1994). *Adaptors and innovators: Styles of creativity and problem solving*. London: Routledge/International Thomson Press.

Kirton, M. J. (1995). A new look at problem solvers. *Network*, Winter, 27–28.

Kirton, M. J., Bailey, A. J., & Glendinning, J. W. (1991). Adaptors and innovators: Preference for educational procedures. *Journal of Psychology, 125*(4), 445–455.

Kirton, M. J., & De Ciantis, S. M. (1986). Cognitive style and personality: The Kirton Adaption-Innovation and Cattell's Sixteen Personality Factor inventories. *Personality and Individual Differences, 7*, 141–146.

Kirton, M. J., & De Ciantis, S. M. (1994). Cognitive style in organizational climate. In M. J. Kirton (Ed.), *Adaptors and innovators: Styles of creativity and problem solving.* London: Routledge/International Thomson Press.

Kirton, M. J., & Hammond, S. (1980). Levels of self-actualisation of adaptors and innovators. *Psychological Reports, 46,* 1321–1322.

Kirton, M. J. & Kubes, M. (1992). KAI Manual-Slovak Language Supplement. Bratislava: Maxman. (Translated by M. Kubes).

Kirton, M. J., & McCarthy, Rosalyn (1985). Personal and group estimates of the Kirton Inventory scores. *Psychological Reports, 57,* 1067–1070.

Kirton, M. J., & McCarthy, Rosalyn (1988). Cognitive climate and organizations. *Journal of Occupational Psychology, 61,* 175–184.

Kirton, M. J., & Pender, S. R. (1982). The adaption-innovation continuum: Occupational type and course selection. *Psychological Reports, 51,* 883–886.

Knight, K. (1967). A descriptive model of the intra-firm innovation process. *Journal of Business, 40,* 478–496.

Koestler, A. (1967). *The act of creation.* New York: Dell Publishing.

Kogan, N. (1971). The clarification of Cropley & Maslany's analysis of the Wallach-Kogan Creativity Tests. *British Journal of Psychology, 62*(1), 113–117.

Kogan, N. (1973). Creative and cognitive style: A life-span perspective. In P. B. Bales & K. W. Schale (Eds.), *Life-span development psychology: Personality and socialization.* New York: Academic Press.

Kogan, N. (1976). Sex differences in creativity and cognitive styles. In S. Messick (Ed.), *Individuality in learning.* San Francisco: Jossey-Bass.

Köhler, W. (1947). *Gestalt psychology.* New York: Liveright.

Kolb, D. A. (1974). On management and the learning process. In D. A. Kolb, I. M. Rubin, & J. M. McIntyre (Eds.), *Organisational psychology: A book of readings* (2nd ed.). Englewood Cliffs, NJ: Prentice Hall.

Kolb, D. A., & Fry, R. (1975). Towards an applied theory of experimental learning. In C. L. Cooper (Ed.), *The theories of group processes.* New York: John Wiley.

Kouzes, J. M., & Posner, B. Z. (1988). *The Leadership Practices Inventory.* San Diego, CA: Pfeiffer.

Kozan, A. (1996). Psychosocoalne maladjustovani unchadzaci o zamestnanie. *Efeta, 6*(4), 4–6.

Kozan, A. (1997). Psychozocialne dosledsky dlhodobejhr mezamestnarnosti. *Praca a Socialna Politika, V,* 16–19.

Krauss, L. (1994). *Fear of physics; a guide for the perplexed.* London: Jonathan Cape.

Kubes, M. (1992). Cognitive style and interpersonal behaviour: The KAI and Schultz's Firo-B Inventories. *Journal of Human Behaviour, 29*(2), 33–38.

Kubes, M. (1994). Introduction. In M. J. Kirton (Ed.), *Adaptors and innovators: Styles of creativity and problem solving.* London: Routledge/International Thomson Business Press.

Kubes, M. (1998). Adaptors and innovators in Slovakia: Cognitive style and social culture. European *Journal of Personality, 12,* 187–198.

Kubes, M., & Spillerova, Dagmar (1992). Dynamics of innovation: Understanding and influencing communication behaviours. *Creativity and Innovation Management, 1*(1), 33–40.

Kuhn, T. S. (1970). *The structure of scientific revolutions* (2nd ed.). Chicago: University of Chicago Press.

Labland, J., & Thompson, P. (2000). *The illustrated guide to the Anglo-Zulu war.* Pietermaritzburg, South Africa: University of Natal Press.

Lave, J., & Wenger, S. (1990). *Situated learning.* Cambridge: Cambridge University Press.

Lawler, E. E., Hall, D. T., & Oldham, G. R. (1973). Organisational climate: Relationship to organisation structure, process and performance. *Organisational Behaviour and Human Performance, 10,* 118–127.

Lazarus, R. S. (1991). *Emotion and adaptation.* New York: Oxford University Press.

Lazarus, R. S., & Folkman, S. (1984). *Stress, appraisal and coping.* New York: Springer of Chicago Press.

LeDoux, J. (1998). *The emotional brain.* London: Weidenfeld & Nicolson.

Legge, K. (1978). *Power, innovation and problem solving in personnel managers.* London: McGraw-Hill.

Lewin, K. (1936). *Principles of topological psychology.* New York: McGraw-Hill.

Lewin, K. (1951). *Field theory in social science.* New York: Harper & Row.

Ligman, Nancy (1991). *Creative problem solving styles and intention to leave work groups in medical/surgical nurses.* MS Thesis, Washington State University.

Lindsay, P. (1985). Counselling to resolve a clash of cognitive styles. *Technovation, 3,* 57–67.

Lipsitt, L. P. (1958). A self-concept scale for children and its relationship to the children's form on the Manifest Anxiety Scale. *Child Development, 29,* 463–469.

Lorenz, K. Z. (1952). *King Solomon's ring.* New York: Cromwell.

Love, Judith, A. (1986). *Design engineering success in a high technology environment: Its prediction and rewards.* PhD Thesis, University of California, Berkeley.

Lowe, E. A., & Taylor, W. G. K. (1986). The management of research in the life sciences: The characteristics of researchers. *R&D Management, 16,* 45–61.

Luchins, A. S., & Luchins, Edith H. (1959). *Rigidity of behaviour.* Eugene, OR: University of Oregon Books.

MacDonald, A. P., Jr (1970). Revised Scale for Ambiguity Tolerance. *Psychological Reports, 26,* 791–798.

MacDonald, J. (1984). *Great battlefields of the World.* London: Marshall Editions.

MacKinnon, D. W. (1944). The structure of personality. In McV. J. Hunt (Ed.), *Personality and the behaviour disorders, Vol. 1.* New York: Ronald Press.

MacKinnon, D. W. (1978). *In search of human effectiveness: Identifying and developing creativity.* Buffalo, NY: Brearly.

MacNeilage, P. F., & Davis, Barbara, L. (2000). On the origin of internal structure of word forms. *Science, 288*(5465), 527–531.

Maier, N. R. F. (1931). Reasoning and learning. *Psychological Review, 38,* 332–346.

Maier, N. R. F., Maltzman, I., & Marcus, A. (1988). Self-estimates of adaptors and innovators on the Kirton Adaption-Innovation Inventory. *Psychological Reports, 63.*

Maltzman, I. (1960). On the training of originality. *Psychological Review, 67,* 229–242.

Marcus, A. (1992). Adaption-innovation cognitive style and coping. *Studia Psychologica (Slovakia), 34*(1), 85.

Maslow, A. H. (1968). *Toward a psychology of being.* New York: Viking.

Masten, W. G., Caldwell-Colbert, A. T., & Morse, D. T. (1988). Self-estimates of adaptors and innovators on the Kirton Adaption-Innovation Inventory. *Psychological Reports, 63,* 587–590.

McCarthy, Rosalyn (1988). *An investigation of role conflict and coping behaviour in women managers.* MSc Thesis, University of Hertfordshire.

McCarthy, Rosalyn (1993). *The relationship of individual characteristics of women managers to the pressures experienced at work and choice of coping strategy.* PhD Thesis, University of Hertfordshire.

McCrae, R. R. (1984). Situational determinants of coping responses: Loss, threat and challenge. *Journal of Personality and Social Psychology, 46,* 919–928.

McDougall, W. (1908). *Dynamic psychology.* New York: Columbia University Press.

McKenna, F. P. (1983). Field dependence and personality: A re-examination. *Social Behaviour and Personality, 11,* 51–55.

McKenny, J. L., & Keen, P. G. W. (1974). How managers' minds work. *Harvard Business Review,* May/June, 79–90.

McNeilly, K. M., & Goldsmith, R. E. (1992). The moderating effect of sales managers' approach to problem solving on the salesperson satisfaction/intention to leave relationship. *Journal of Social Behaviour and Personality, 7*(1), 139–150.

Mead, G. (1934). *Mind, self and society.* Chicago: University of Chicago Press.

Mehrabian, A., & Russell, J. A. (1974). *An approach to environmental psychology.* Cambridge, MA: MIT Press.

Merton, R. K. (1957). *Social theory and social structure.* Glencoe, UK: Free Press.

Messick, S. (1976). *Individuality in learning: Implications of cognitive styles and creativity for human development.* San Fransisco: Jossey-Bass.

Messick, S. (1984). The nature of cognitive styles: Problems and promise in educational practice. *Educational Psychologist, 19,* 59–74.

Meyer, A., Brooks, G., & Goes, J. (1990). Environmental jolts and industrial revolutions: Organisational responses to discontinuous change. *Strategic Management Journal, 11,* 93–110.

Miles, R. E., & Snow, C. C. (1978). *Organisational strategy, structure and process.* New York: McGraw-Hill.

Miller, D. (1990). *The Icarus paradox.* New York: Harper Business.

Mintzberg, H. (1973). *The nature of managerial work.* New York: Harper & Row.

Mintzberg, H. (1979). *The structuring of organization.* New York: Prentice Hall.

Mischel, W. (1990). Personality dispositions revisited and revised: A view after three decades. In L. A. Pervin (Ed.), *Handbook of personality: Theory and research.* New York: Guilford Press.

Mishkin, M., & Appenzeller, T. (1987). The anatomy of memory: A Scientific American special report. *Scientific American,* 1–12.

Mishkin, M., Malamut, Barbara, & Bachevalier, Joycelyne (1984). *Neurobiology of learning and memory.* New York: Guilford Press.

Mitroff, I. I. (1974). *The subjective side of science: An inquiry in the psychology of the Apollo moon scientists.* US: Elsevier.

Mitroff, I. I., & Kilmann, R. H. (1981). A four-fold way of knowing: The varieties of social science experience. *Theory and Society, 2,* 227–248.

Mohr, L. B. (1971). Organizational technology and organizational structure. *Administrative Science Quarterly, 16,* 444–457.

Moore, W. E. (1969). Social structure and behaviour. In G. Lindzey & E. Aronson (Eds.), *The handbook of social psychology, Vol. IV.* London: Addison-Wesley.

Morris, D. R. (1985). *The washing of the spears.* London: Abacus.

Morse, E. V., & Gordon, G. (1974). Cognitive Skills: A determinant of scientists' local-cosmopolitan orientation. *Academy of Management Journal,* 709–723.

Mottram, V. H. (1952). *The physical basis of personality.* Harmondsworth, UK: Penguin.

Mudd, S. A. (1990). The place of innovativeness in models of the adoption process: An integrative review. *Technovation, 15*(3), 165–175.

Mudd, S. A. (1995). Suggestive parallels between Kirton's A-I Theory of Creative Style and Koestler's Bisociative Theory of the Creative Act. *Journal of Creative Behavior, 29*(4), 240–254.

Mudd, S. A. (1996). Kirton's A-I Theory: Evidence bearing on the style/level and factor composition issues. *British Journal of Psychology, 87,* 241–254.

Mullany, M. J. (1989). *An analysis of the relationships between the differences in analyst-user, cognitive styles & user resistance to information systems.* MCom Thesis, University of Cape Town, South Africa.

Murdock, Mary, Isaksen, S. G., & Lauer, K. J. (1993). Creativity training and the stability and internal consistency of the Kirton Adaption-Innovation Inventory. *Psychological Reports, 72,* 1123–1130.

Myers, Isobel, B. (1962). *The Myers-Briggs Type Indicator.* Palo Alto, CA: Consulting Psychologists Press.

Nadler, D. A. (1988). Organisational frame bending: Types of change in the complex organisation. In R. Kilmann & T. Colvin (Eds.), *Corporate transformation*. San Francisco: Jossey-Bass.

National Institute of Industrial Psychology Test Battery, 1964–1979 (1979). Windsor, UK: Nelson-NFER.

Neisser, U. (1976). *Cognition and reality*. San Francisco, CA: Freeman.

Newcome, T. M. (1961). *The acquaintance process*. New York: Holt.

Newell, A., Shaw, J. C., & Simon, H. A. (1962). The process of creative thinking. In H. E. Gruber, G. Terrell, & M. Wertheimer (Eds.), *Contemporary approaches to creative thinking* (pp. 63–119). New York: Atherton.

Newton, T. J. (1989). Occupational stress and coping with stress: A critique. *Human Relations, 42*, 441–461.

Nisbet, R. (1972). Has futurology a future? *Encounter*, November, *37*(5), 19–28.

Northouse, P. G. (1997). *Leadership theory and practice*. Thousand Oaks, CA: Sage Publications.

Nyström, H. (1979). *Creativity and innovation*. Chichester, UK: John Wiley & Sons.

Osborn, A. (1963). *Applied imagination* (3rd ed.). New York: Scrinbner's.

Paivio, A. (1971). *Imagery and verbal process*. New York: Holt Rinehart & Winston.

Palmer, Judith (1991). Scientists and information: II. Personal factors in information behaviour. *Journal of Documentation, 47*(3), 245–275.

Parkhurst, H. B. (1999). Confusion, lack of consensus and the definition of creativity as a construct. *Journal of Creative Behaviour, 33*(1), 1–21.

Parkinson, C. Northcote (1994). *The classic age of naval history 1793–1815*. UK: Sutton Publishing.

Parsons, T. (1951). *The social system*. Glencoe, UK: Free Press.

Payne, R. L. (1987). Individual differences and performance amongst R & D personnel: Some implications for management development. *R&D Management, 17*, 153–161.

Payne, R. L., & Pugh, D. S. (1976). Organisational climate and organisational structure. In M. D. Dunnette (Ed.), *Handbook of industrial and organisational psychology* (2nd ed.). New York: Wiley.

Pears, I. (1999). *Death and restoration*. London: Harper Collins Publishers.

Perret, B. (1998). *Last stand: Famous battles against the odds*. London: Cassell Military Classics.

Perrow, C. (1967). A framework for the comparative analysis of organizations. *American Sociological Review, 32*, 194–208.

Perrow, C. (1970). *Organisational analysis: A sociological view*. Belmont, CA: Wandsworth.

Pershyn, G. S. (1992). *An investigation into the graphic depictions of natural creative problem solving process*. MSc Thesis, New York State University at Buffalo.

Personnel Decisions Inc. (1982). *Management Skill Profile manual*. Minneapolis, MN: Author.

Personnel Decisions Inc. (1985). *Management Skills Profile/MSP: Definitions and development priorities*. Minneapolis, MN: Author.

Petite, Claudine (1958). Le determinism génétique et psycho-physiologique da la competition sexuelle chez drosophila elangaster. *Bulletin Biologique, 92*, 248–329.

Pettigrew, Amy (1989a). *Characteristics of creativity, productivity, cognitive style and perceptions of climate for innovation: An examination of graduate nursing education faculty*. PhD Thesis, Indiana University.

Pettigrew, Amy, C. (1989b). Creativity in graduate nursing faculty: A descriptive study and construct validation of Kirton's adaption-innovation theory. In *Proceedings of the International Conference on Psychological Problems of Creative Scientific Work*. Bratislava, The Computing Centre of the Slovak Academy of Sciences.

Pettigrew, Amy, C., & King, Margaret, O. (1993). A comparison between scores on Kirton's Inventory for nursing students and a general student population. *Psychological Reports, 73*, 339–345.

Pierce, J. L. (1984). Job design and technology: A socio-technical perspective. *Journal of Occupational Behaviour, 5*, 147–154.

Pierce, J. L., & Delbecq, A. L. (1977). Organisational structure, individual attitudes and innovation. *Academy of Management Journal*, *2*, 27–37.

Pinker, S. (1998). *How the mind works*. London: The Penguin Press.

Pinker, S. (2002). *The blank slate*. London: Penguin Books.

Porter, M. E. (1990). *The competitive advantage of nations*. London: Macmillan.

Porter, M. E. (1998). *On competition*. Boston: Harvard Business School Press.

Pounds, Julia, & Bailey, L. L. (2001). Cognition and learning: Performance of adaptors and innovators in a novel dynamic task. *Journal of Applied Cognitive Psychology*, *15*(5), 1–17.

Prato Previde, G. (1984). Adattatori ed innovatori: I risultati della standardizzazione Italiana del KAI. *Ricerche di Psicologia*, *4*, 81–134.

Prato Previde, G. (1991). Italian adaptors and innovators: Is cognitive style underlying culture? *Personality and Individual Differences*, *12*(1), 1–10.

Prato Previde, G., & Carli, M. (1987). Adaption-innovation typology and right–left hemispheric preferences. *Journal of Personality and Individual Differences*, *8*, 681–686.

Prince, M. (1924). *The dissociation of a personality*. London: Longmans.

Puccio, G. J., Talbot, R. J., & Joniak, A. J. (1993). Person–environment fit: Using commensurate scales to predict student stress. *British Journal of Educational Psychology*, *63*, 457–468.

Puccio, G. J., Joniak, A. J., & Talbot, R. J. (1995). Person–environment fit: Examining the use of commensurate scales. *Psychological Reports*, *76*, 931–938.

Pugh, D. S., & Hickson, D. J. (1968). The comparative study of organisations. In D. Pym (Ed.), *Industrial society: Social sciences in management* (2nd ed.). London: Pelican Books.

Pulvino, Carol, A. F. (1979). *Relationship of principal leadership behaviour to teacher motivation and innovation*. PhD Thesis, University of Wisconsin, Madison.

Quine, W. V., & Ullian, J. S. (1970). *The web of belief*. New York: Random House.

Ray, J. J. (1970). The development and validation of a balanced dogmatism scale. *Australian Journal of Psychology*, *22*, 253–260.

Reber, A. S. (1993). *Implicit learning and tacit knowledge: An essay on the cognitive unconscious*. Oxford: Oxford University Press.

Reddin, W. J. (1983). *Management effectiveness and style individual or situation*. PhD Thesis, University of New Brunswick.

Rhodes, M. (1961). An analysis of creativity. *Phi Delta Kappa*, *42*, 305–310.

Rickards, T. (1990). The KAI as a survey-feedback instrument (Review). *Journal of European Industrial Training*, *14*(6), 3–7.

Rickards, T., & Gaston, K. (1995). A re-examination of personal and group estimates of the Kirton Adaption-Innovation scores. *Psychological Reports*, *77*, 491–498.

Rickards, T., & Moger, Susan (1994). Felix and Oscar revisited: An exploration of the dynamics of a real-life odd couple work relationship. *Journal of Applied Behavioural Science*, *30*(1), 108–131.

Rickards, T., & Puccio, G. (1992). Problem finding, idea finding and implementation: An exploratory model for investigating small-group problem-solving. In P. Barron & C. Cooper (Eds.), *Managing organisations*. London: Routledge.

Ridley, Mark (2000). *Mendel's demon: Gene justice and the complexity of life*. London: Weidenfeld & Nicolson.

Ridley, Matt (1999). *Genome: The autobiography of a species in 23 chapters*. London: Fourth Estate.

Riesman, D. (1950). *The lonely crowd: A study of the changing American character*. New Haven, CT: Yale University Press.

Riley, P. (1983). A structurationist account of political cultures. *Administrative Science Quarterly*, *28*, 414–437.

Roback, A. A. (1927). *The psychology of character*. London: Kegan Paul.

Roberts, K. H., & Glick, W. (1981). The job characteristics approach to task design: A critical review. *Journal of Applied Psychology*, *66*, 193–217.

Roberts, R. G., Flannery, T. F., Ayliffe, L. K., Yoshida, H., Olley, J. M., Prideau, G. J., Laslett, G. M., Baynes, A., Smith, M. A., Jones, R., & Smith, B. L. (2001). New ages for the last Australian megafauna: Continent-wide extinction about 46,000 years ago. *Science*, 1888–1892.

Robertson, I. T. (1985). Human and information-processing strategies and style. *Behaviour and Information Technology*, *4*, 19–29.

Robertson, T. S. (1971). Innovative behavior and communication. New York: Holt Rinehart & Winston.

Robey, D., & Taggart, W. (1981). Measuring managers' minds: The assessment of style in human information processing. *Academy of Management Journal*, *6*, 375–383.

Rogers, C. R. (1959). Towards a theory of creativity. In H. H. Anderson (Ed.), *Creativity and its cultivation*. New York: Harper.

Rogers, E. M. (1983). *Diffusion of innovators* (3rd ed.). New York: Free Press.

Rokeach, M. (1960). *The open and closed mind*. New York: Basic Books.

Rosenberg, M. J. (1965). *Society and the adolescent self-image*. Princeton, NJ: Princeton University Press.

Rosenberg, M. J., Hovland, C. I., McGuire, W. J., Abelson, R. P., & Brehm, J. W. (1960). *Attitude organization and change: An analysis of consistency among attitude components*. Fale: University Press.

Rothenbuhler, W. C. (1964). Behaviour genetics of nest cleaning in honey bees. I & II. *Animal Behaviour*, *12*, 578–588.

Rotter, J. B. (1966). Generalised expectancies for internal versus external control of reinforcement. *Psychological Monographs*, *80*, (whole No. 609).

Russell, Lord Bertrand (1946). *The history of Western philosophy*. London: George Allan & Unwin.

Russell, D. (1956). *Children's thinking*. New York: Ginn.

Ryan, A. (1970). *The philosophy of the social sciences*. London: Macmillan.

Rydell, S. T., & Rosen, E. (1966). Measurement and some correlates of need cognition. *Psychological Reports*, *90*, 139–165.

Salisbury, C., Bosanquet, N., Wilkinson, Emma, Bosanquet, Anna, & Hasler, J. (1998). The implementation of evidence-based medicine in general practice prescribing. *British Journal of General Practice*, *48*, 1849–1852.

Schaefer, C. E. (1971). *Similies Test Manual*. Goshen, New York: Research Psychologist Press.

Scheerer, M. (1963). Problem solving. *Scientific American*, *208*, 118–128.

Schneider, B. (1985). Organisational behavior. *Annual Review of Psychology*, 36, 573–611.

Schneider, B., & Snyder, R. A. (1975). Some relationships between job satisfaction and organisational climate. *Journal of Applied Psychology*, *60*, 318–27.

Schon, D. A. (1967). *The technology of change*. New York: Delacorte Press.

Schroder, H. M. (1986). *The development of managerial competencies*. Tampa, FL: The Center for Organizational Effectiveness, University of South Florida.

Schroder, H. M. (1994). Managerial competence and style. In M. J. Kirton (Ed.), *Adaptors and innovators: Styles of creativity and problem solving*. London: Routledge.

Schultz, W. C. (1958). *A three dimensional theory of interpersonal behavior*. New York: Holt Rinehart & Winston.

Selby, E. C. (1992). *The Kirton Adaption-Innovation Inventory as a tool for assessing problem solving styles in eighth grade students*. PhD Thesis, Walden University.

Selby, E. C., & Treffinger, D. (1993). Styles of adaptive and innovative creativity among 8th graders. *Learning Styles Network*, *14*(3), 4–5.

Senge, P. M. (1990). *The fifth discipline: The art and practice of the learning organization*. New York: Doubleday.

Shephard, H. A. (1967). Innovation-resisting and innovation-producing organisations. *Journal of Business*, *40*, 470–477.

Shipley, W. C. (1940). A self-administering scale for measuring intellectual deterioration. *Journal of Psychology, 9*, 371–377.

Shouksmith, G. (1970). *Intelligence, creativity and cognitive style*. London: Batsford.

Silver, B. L. (1998). *The ascent of science*. Oxford: Oxford University Press.

Simon, H. A. (1960). *The new science management decision*. Englewood Cliffs, NJ: Prentice Hall.

Simon, H. A. (1971). Human problem solving: The state of the theory in 1970. *American Psychologist, 26*, 145–159.

Simonton, D. K. (1976). Philosophical eminence, beliefs and Zeitgeist: An individual-generational analysis. *Journal of Personality and Social Psychology, 34*, 805–816.

Simonton, D. K. (1984). *Genius, creativity and leadership*. Cambridge, MA: Harvard University Press.

Simonton, D. K. (1987). Genius: The lessons of historiometry. In S. G. Isaksen (Ed.), *Frontiers of creativity research: Beyond the basics*. New York: Brearly.

Skinner, N. F. (1989). Behavioural implications of adaption-innovation: Management effectiveness as a function of sex differences in adaption-innovation. *Social Behavior and Personality, 17*(1), 51–56.

Slocum, J. W., & Sims, H. P. (1980). A typology for integrating technology, organization, and job design. *Human Relations, 33*, 193–212.

Smith, M. B. (1973). Attitude change. In N. Warren & M. Jahoda (Eds.), *Attitudes*. Harmondsworth, UK: Penguin Books.

Spielburger, C. D., Gorsuch, R. L., Lushene, R., Vagg, P. R., & Jacobs, G. A. (1983). *Manual for the State-Trait Anxiety Inventory: STAI (form Y)*. Palo Alto, CA: Consulting Psychology Press.

Stamp, Gillian (1986). Management styles. *Leadership and Organisational Development Journal, 7*(3), 27–33.

Staw, B. M. (1995). Why no one really wants creativity. In C. M. Ford & D. A. Gioia (Eds.), *Creative action in organizations: The ivory tower visions and real world voices*. Thousand Oaks, CA: Sage Publications.

Steed, L. G. (1998). A critique of coping scales. *Australian Psychologist, 33*(3), 193–202.

Stein, M. I. (1975). *Manual: Physiognomic Cue Test*. New York: Behavioral Publications.

Stein, M. I. (1987). Creativity research at the crossroads. In S. G. Isaksen (Ed.), *Frontiers of creativity research: Beyond the basics*. New York: Brearly.

Sternberg, R. J. (1988). *The triarchic mind: A new theory of human intelligence*. New York: Viking.

Sternberg, R. J. (1997). *Thinking styles*. Cambridge: Cambridge University Press.

Sullivan, H. S. (1953). *The interpersonal theory of psychiatry*. New York: Norton.

Sully, J. (1884). *Outlines of psychology*. New York: Appleton.

Talbot, R. J. (1997). Taking style on board (or how to get used to the idea of creative adaptors and uncreative innovators). *Creativity and Innovation Management, 6*(3), 177–184.

Tandon, R. (1987). *Study of the initial success for early investors in entrepreneurial new ventures*. PhD Thesis, University of Minnesota.

Tattersall, I. (2000). Once we were not alone. *Scientific American*, January, 38–44.

Taylor, C. W. (1964). *Creativity: Progress and potential*. London: McGraw Hill.

Taylor, F. W. (1911). *The principles of scientific management*. New York: Harper & Row.

Taylor, Jennifer (1993). *The relationship between intelligence and cognitive style in schoolchildren, with particular reference to its implications for gifted children*. MPhil Thesis, University of Hertfordshire.

Taylor, Jennifer (1994). The stability of schoolchildren's cognitive style – a longitudinal study of the Kirton Adaption-Innovation Inventory. *Psychological Reports, 74*, 1008–1010.

Tefft, Margaret (1990). *A factor analysis of TTCT, MBTI and KAI: The creative level/style issue re-examined*. MS Thesis, The State University of New York at Buffalo.

Tellegan, A. (1970). Tellegan's Research Scale. In S. S. Gryskiewicz (1980), *A study of creative problem solving techniques in group settings.* PhD Thesis, Birkbeck College, University of London.

Terry, D. J. (1994). Determinants of coping: The role of stable and situational factors. *Journal of Personality and Social Psychology, 66,* 895–910.

Thomas, I. (1979). The Battle of Little Big Horn. In M. Seth-Smith (Ed.), *The horse in war.* London: New English Library.

Thompson, V. A. (1965). Bureaucracy and innovation. *Administrative Science Quarterly, 5,* 1–20.

Thomson, Dolores (1980). Adaptors and innovators: A replication study on managers in Singapore and Malaysia. *Psychological Reports, 47,* 383–387.

Thomson, Dolores (1985). *A study of Singaporean executives: Their attitudes, dispositions and work values.* PhD Thesis, Henley Management College/Brunel University.

Thorndike, E. L. (1913). *The psychology of learning. II: Educational psychology.* New York: Teachers College.

Thorpe, W. H. (1956). *Learning and instinct in animals.* London: Methuen.

Tinbergen, N. (1951). *The study of instinct.* London: Oxford University Press.

Torrance, E. P. (1965). *Rewarding creative behaviour: Experiments in classroom activity.* Englewood Cliffs, NJ: Prentice Hall.

Torrance, E. P. (1971). *Technical norms manual for the Creative Motivation Scale.* Athens, GA: Georgia Studies of Creative Behavior, University of Georgia.

Torrance, E. P. (1974). *Norms technical manual: Torrance Tests of Creative Thinking.* Bensenville, IL: Scholastic Testing Service.

Torrance, E. P. (1988). The nature of creativity as manifest in its testing. In R. J. Sternberg (Ed.), *The nature of creativity.* Cambridge: Cambridge University Press.

Torrance, E. P., & Goff, K. (1989). A quiet revolution. *Journal of Creative Behaviour, 32,* 136–145.

Torrance, E. P., & Horng, R. Y. (1980). Creativity, style of learning and thinking characteristics of adaptors and innovators. *The Creative Child Adult Quarterly, V,* 80–85.

Torrance, E. P., Reynolds, C. R., Ball, O. E., & Riegel, T. R. (1978). *Revised norms – Technical manual for your style of learning and thinking.* Athens, GA: Georgia Studies of Creative Behavior, University of Georgia.

Torrance, E. P., & Torrance, P. (1973). *Is creativity teachable?* Bloomington, IN: Phi Delta Kappa.

Trist, E. L., & Bamforth, K. W. (1951). Some social and psychological consequences of the Longwall method of coal-getting. *Human Relations, 4,* 1–38.

Troldahl, V., & Powell, F. (1965). A short form dogmatism scale for use in field studies. *Social Forces, 44,* 211–214.

Tuckman, B. W. (1965). Developmental sequence in small groups. *Psychological Bulletin, 63,* 384–399.

Tuckman, B. W., & Jensen, M. A. (1977). Stages of small group development revisited. *Group and Organizational Studies, 2,* 419–427.

Tullett, A. D. (1996). The thinking style of the managers of multiple projects: Implications for problem solving and decision making when managing change. *The International Journal of Project Management, 14,* 281–287.

Tullett, A. D. (1997). Cognitive style: Not culture's consequence. *European Psychologist, 2,* 258–267.

Tullett, A. D., & Davies, G. B. (1997). Cognitive style and affect: A comparison of the Kirton Adaption-Innovation and Schultz's Fundamental Interpersonal Relations Orientation-Behaviour Inventories KAI and FIRO-B. *Personality and Individual Differences, 23,* 479–485.

Tullett, A. D., & Kirton, M. J. (1995). Further evidence for the independence of adaptive-innovative (A-I) cognitive style from national culture. *Personal and Individual Differences*, *19*(3), 393–396.

Vaillant, G. E. (1977). *Adaptation to life*. Boston: Little & Brown.

Valéry, N. (1999). Innovation in industry. *Economist*, February, 5–28.

Van der Molen, P. P. (1994). Adaption-innovation and changes in social structure: On the anatomy of catastrophe. In M. J. Kirton (Ed.), *Adaptors and innovators: Styles of creativity and problem solving*. London: International Thomson Press.

Van Grundy, A. (1987). Organisational creativity and innovation. In S. G. Isaksen (Ed.), *Frontiers of creativity research: Beyond the basics*. New York: Brearly.

Van Rooyen, Jopie (1994). *Creativity: An important managerial requirement: A South African perspective*. Proceedings (pp. 49–59). The Myers-Briggs Type Indicator and Leadership: International Research Conference, National Leadership Institute, University of Maryland, January.

Veblen, T. (1928). *The theory of the leisure class*. New York: Vanguard Press.

Vicere, A. A. (1992). The strategic leadership imperative for executive development. *Human Resource Planning*, *15*(1), 15–31.

Vinacke, W. E. (1952). *The psychology of thinking*. New York: McGraw-Hill.

Wallach, M. A., & Kogan, N. (1965). A new look at the creativity–intelligence distinction. *Journal of Personality*, *33*, 348–369.

Wallas, G. (1926). *The art of thought*. New York: Franklin Watts.

Warner, R. (1949). *Xenophon: The Persian expedition*. London: Penguin Books.

Warry, J. (1980). *Warfare in the classical world*. London: Salamander.

Watson, J. B. (1930). *Behaviourism*. London: Kegan Paul.

Watts, W. (1985). *Relationship between specific skills and managerial performance*. MPhil Thesis, North East London Polytechnic.

Weber, M. (1970). *From Max Weber: Essays in sociology* (H. H. Gerth & C. W. Mills, Eds. & Trans.) London: International Thomson Press & Kegan Paul.

Wells, W. D. (1961). The influence of yeasaying response style. *Journal of Advertising Research*, *1*, 1–12.

Welsch, P. K. (1981). The nurturance of creative behavior in educational environments: A comprehensive curriculum approach. *Dissertation Abstracts International*, *41*(09) 3870A. University Microfilms No. 81-06456.

Wes, P. D., & Bargmann, C. I. (2001). *C. elegans* odour discrimination requires asymmetric diversity in olfactory neurons. *Nature*, *410*(April), 698–701.

Wesley, E. L. (1953). Preservative behaviour in a concept-formation task. *Journal of Abnormal and Social Psychology*, *8*, 129–134.

White, T. D. (2001). Once we were cannibals. *Scientific American*, August, 49–55.

Whiten, A., & Boesch, C. (2001). The cultures of chimpanzees. *Scientific American*, January, 49–55.

Whyte, W. H. (1957). *The organisation man*. London: Jonathan Cape.

Wills, C. (1998). *Children of Prometheus: The accelerating pace of human evolution*. USA: Perseus Books.

Wilson, G. D., & Patterson, J. R. (1968). A new measure of conservatism. *British Journal of Social and Clinical Psychology*, *7*, 274–279.

Witkin, H. A., Dyk, R. B., Faterson, H. F., Goodenough, D. R., & Harp, S. A. (1962). *Psychological definition*. New York: Wiley.

Witkin, H. A., Dyk, R. B., Oltman, P. K., Raskin, E., & Harp, S. A. (1971). *The manual of Embedded Figures Test*. Palo Alto, CA: Consulting Psychologists Press.

Witkin, H. A., & Goodenough, D. R. (1977). *Field dependence revisited* (ETS RB-77-l6). Princeton, NJ: Educational Testing Service.

Woodward, Joan (1965). *Industrial organisation: Theory and practice*. London: Oxford University Press.

Woodworth, R. S. (1918). *Dynamic Psychology*. New York: Columbia University Press.

Wright, S. (1977). From Darwinism to the modern synthesis. In M. Ridley (Ed.), *Evolution*. London: Oxford University Press.

Wunderly, Linda (1996). *The relationship among optimism, pessimism, vision and effective leadership practice*. MA Thesis, University of Cincinnati.

Zaltman, G., Duncan, R., & Holbeck, J. (1973). *Innovation in organisations*. New York: Wiley.

Zuckerman, M. (1974). The sensation seeking motive. In B. A. Maher (Ed.), *Progress in experimental personality research*. New York: Academic Press.

Name index

Tests and measures index

Subject index

For behaviour problems, e.g., bulimia, dyslexia, *see*: abnormal behaviour
For examples relating to battles, e.g., Matinea, Little Big Horn, *see*: war
For examples relating to weapons, e.g., musket, dreadnought, *see*: weapons.
For examples involving any disease, e.g., small pox, whooping cough, *see*: disease
For references to peoples and nationalities, e.g., Maori, Norse, *see*: people
Other examples are listed as spelt, e.g., epicycles, shaduf (water wheel)
Terms that may not be recognised as such have originator added, e.g., disjunctions in Merton,
and rare male effect in Petite